Lecture Notes in Computer Sc

Commenced Publication in 1973
Founding and Former Series Editors:
Gerhard Goos, Juris Hartmanis, and Jan van Leeuwen

Gabor Karsai   Eelco Visser (Eds.)

Generative Programming and Component Engineering

Third International Conference, GPCE 2004
Vancouver, Canada, October 24-28, 2004
Proceedings

Volume Editors

Gabor Karsai
Vanderbilt University
Institute for Software Integrated Systems (ISIS)
Nashville, TN 37235, USA
E-mail: gabor.karsai@vanderbilt.edu

Eelco Visser
Universiteit Utrecht
Institute of Information and Computing Sciences
P.O. Box 80089, 3508 TB Utrecht, The Netherlands
E-mail: visser@acm.org

Library of Congress Control Number: 2004113646

CR Subject Classification (1998): D.2, D.1, D.3, K.6

ISSN 0302-9743
ISBN 3-540-23580-9 Springer Berlin Heidelberg New York

Springer is a part of Springer Science+Business Media

springeronline.com

© Springer-Verlag Berlin Heidelberg 2004
Printed in Germany

Typesetting: Camera-ready by author, data conversion by Olgun Computergrafik
Printed on acid-free paper   SPIN: 11338000   06/3142   5 4 3 2 1 0

Preface

Generative and component approaches have the potential to revolutionize software development in a similar way as automation and components revolutionized manufacturing. Generative Programming (developing programs that synthesize other programs), Component Engineering (raising the level of modularization and analysis in application design), and Domain-Specific Languages (elevating program specifications to compact domain-specific notations that are easier to write and maintain) are key technologies for automating program development.

GPCE arose as a joint conference, merging the prior conference on Generative and Component-Based Software Engineering (GCSE) and the Workshop on Semantics, Applications, and Implementation of Program Generation (SAIG). The goal of GPCE is to provide a meeting place for researchers and practitioners interested in cutting edge approaches to software development. We aim to foster further cross-fertilization between the software engineering research community on the one hand, and the programming languages community on the other, in addition to supporting the original research goals of both the GCSE and the SAIG communities.

This volume contains the proceedings of the *Third International Conference on Generative Programming and Component Engineering*, held in Vancouver, Canada from October 24 to 28, 2004, where it was co-located with OOPSLA 2004 and ISSM 2004.

Responding to the call for papers 89 abstracts were submitted, 75 of which materialized as full paper submissions. The papers were reviewed by program committee members and their co-reviewers who together produced a total of 250 reviews, between 3 and 5 per paper. Reviews were often thorough and sometimes actually included the views of multiple co-reviewers. Consensus about the papers to be accepted was reached during the online program committee meeting held in the second week of May 2004. The meeting consisted of a discussion by email of each of the papers by the entire PC so that members could get an overall impression of the quality of the submitted papers, beyond the ones they reviewed themselves. The committee selected 25 of the 75 papers for presentation at the conference and publication in the proceedings. Of the accepted papers, two are co-athored by PC members (from a total of six PC submissions). We tried hard to ensure fairness and held PC submissions to a high standard. Paper submission and reviewing were supported by the open source version of the CyberChair conference system installed at the webserver of the Institute of Information and Computing Sciences of Utrecht University, The Netherlands.

In addition to the technical paper presentations the conferences featured two invited speakers, a panel, four tutorials, five workshops, and six demonstrations.

Invited Speakers. The keynote talk by Jack Greenfield examined the *software factory* approach to rapidly develop domain-specific languages and tools to automate the production of applications in specific domains, combining innovations in adaptive assembly, software product lines, and model driven development.

The invited talk by Peter Mosses gave an overview of the state of the art in *modular language description*, i.e. the specification of the semantics of programming language features in separate modules such that new languages can be defined by module composition.

Panel. A panel chaired by Gabor Karsai and further consisting of Don Batory, Krzysztof Czarnecki, Jeff Gray, Douglas Schmidt, and Walid Taha examined the current state of the field of generative programming, addressing issues such as its relevance for information technology practice, incorporating generative approaches in education, evaluation and comparison of generative technologies, and research challenges.

Tutorials. The four GPCE tutorials gave introductions to important areas of the generative programming field:

- *Adaptive object-model architecture: Dynamically adapting to changing requirements* by Joe Yoder
- *Multi-stage programming in MetaOCaml* by Walid Taha and Cristiano Calcagno
- *Generative software development* by Krzysztof Czarnecki and Jack Greenfield
- *Program transformation systems: Theory and practice for software generation, maintenance, and reengineering* by Ira Baxter and Hongjun Zheng

Workshops. Prior to GPCE 2004 six workshops were held, providing an opportunity for attendees to exchange views in subareas of generative programming.

With the introduction of software product line approaches into the practice, variants and variability add a new dimension of complexity to the software development process. The combinatorial explosion of possible variants in systems with a high degree of variability requires improved and changed concepts for specifying, modeling, and implementing these systems to assure quality and functionality. In the **OOPSLA/GPCE Workshop on Managing Variabilities Consistently in Design and Code** participants discussed and identified efficient ways for dealing with highly variable software systems on design and code level by evaluating existing approaches and new ideas from the research community and industrial practice.

The **Software Transformation Systems Workshop** was designed to investigate the use of software transformation tools to support generative programming by looking at various generative techniques and suggesting how these may be supported by various general purpose transformation tools, leading to a more general understanding of common principles for supporting generative methods.

MetaOCaml is a multi-stage extension of the widely used functional programming language OCaml. It provides a generic core for expressing macros, staging, and partial evaluation. The **First MetaOCaml Workshop** provided a forum for discussing experience with using MetaOCaml as well as possible future developments for the language.

The **6th GPCE Young Researchers Workshop** provided a platform for young international researchers to present their work and receive feedback from experienced panelists.

The **OOPSLA/GPCE Workshop on Best Practices for Model-Driven Software Development** brought together practitioners, researchers, academics, and students to discuss the best practices for the development of model-driven software, and to discuss the state of the art of tool support for MDSD, including emerging Open Source tool products for model-driven development of software systems.

Demonstrations. The following demonstrations were held in parallel to the technical paper program:

- *Implementation of DSLs using staged interpreters in MetaOCaml* by Kedar Swadi from Rice University
- *MetaEdit+: Domain-specific modeling for full code generation demonstrated* by Juha-Pekka Tolvanen from MetaCase
- *Towards domain-driven development: the SmartTools software factory* by Didier Parigot from INRIA Sophia-Antipolis
- *Xirc: Cross-artifact information retrieval* by Michael Eichberg, and Thorsten Schaefer from Darmstadt University of Technology
- *C-SAW and GenAWeave: A two-level aspect weaving toolsuite* by Jeff Gray, Jing Zhang, and Suman Roychoudhury, from the University of Alabama at Birmingham and Ira Baxter from Semantic Designs
- *The concern manipulation environment* by Peri Tarr, Matthew Chapman, William Chung, and Andy Clement, from the IBM Thomas J. Watson Research Center and IBM Hursley Park.
- *Program transformations for re-engineering C++ components* by Ira Baxter, Larry Akers, Semantic Designs, and Michael Mehlich from Semantic Designs.

The program of this year's conference is proof that the GPCE community is a vibrant, lively group that produces significant new contributions.

August 2004

Gabor Karsai
Eelco Visser

Organization

GPCE 2004 was organized by the Assocation for Computing Machinery (ACM), the OGI School of Science & Engineering at OHSU (USA), Utrecht University (The Netherlands), Vanderbilt University (USA), Intel (USA), University of Alabama at Birmingham (USA), and the University of Waterloo (Canada). The event was sponsored by ACM SIGPLAN, ACM SIGSOFT, and Microsoft and co-located with OOPSLA 2004 and ISSM 2004 in Vancouver, Canada.

General Chair

Tim Sheard, OGI School of Science & Engineering at OHSU, Portland, Oregon, USA

Program Chairs

Gabor Karsai, Vanderbilt University, USA
Eelco Visser, Utrecht University, The Netherlands

Program Committee

Uwe Aßmann (Linköpings Universitet, Sweden)
Don Batory (University of Texas, USA)
Jan Bosch (Universiteit Groningen, The Netherlands)
Jean Bezivin (Université de Nantes, France)
Jim Cordy (Queen's University, Canada)
Krzysztof Czarnecki (University of Waterloo, Canada)
Mathew Flatt (University of Utah, USA)
Robert Glück (Københavns Universitet, Denmark)
George Heineman (Worcester Polytechnic Institute, USA)
Michael Leuschel (University of Southampton, UK)
Karl Lieberherr (Northeastern University, USA)
Simon Peyton Jones (Microsoft Research, UK)
Douglas R. Smith (Kestrel Institute, USA)
Gabriele Taentzer (Technische Universität Berlin, Germany)
Todd Veldhuizen (Indiana University, USA)
Kris de Volder (University of British Columbia, Canada)
Dave Wile (Teknowledge Corporation, USA)
Alexander Wolf (University of Colorado at Boulder, USA)

Workshop Chair

Zino Benaissa, Intel, USA

Tutorial Chair

Jeff Gray, University of Alabama at Birmingham, USA

Demonstrations Committee

Simon Helsen (chair), University of Waterloo, Canada
William Cook, University of Texas at Austin, USA
Frédéric Jouault, Université de Nantes, France

Co-reviewers

Nils Andersen	Yvonne Howard	Jeffrey Palm
Anya H. Bagge	Anton Jansen	Emir Pasalic
Ivor Bosloper	Michel Jaring	Andrew Pitts
Martin Bravenboer	Dean Jin	Stephane Lo Presti
Niels H. Christensen	Merijn de Jonge	Armin Rigo
Alessandro Coglio	Frederic Jouault	Matthew Rutherford
S. Deelstra	Kazuhiko Kakehi	Kevin A. Schneider
Juergen Dingel	Karl Trygve Kalleberg	Jörg Schneider
Eelco Dolstra	Markus Klein	Ulrik Pagh Schultz
Alexander Egyed	Andrei Klimov	Johanneke Siljee
Dan Elphick	Jia Liu	M. Sinnema
Lindsay Errington	Roberto Lopez-Herrejon	Therapon Skotiniotis
Natalya Filatkina	David Lorenz	Mike Sperber
Murdoch Gabbay	Andrew Malton	Walid Taha
Hugh Glaser	Katharina Mehner	Edward Turner
Andy Gravell	Anne-Francoise Le Meur	Mauricio Varea
Jurriaan Hage	Torben Mogensen	Andrzej Wasowski
Jan Heering	Dirk Muthig	Andreas Winter
Andre van der Hoek	Karina Olmos	Pengcheng Wu
Kathrin Hoffmann	Scott Owens	

Steering Committee

Don Batory (University of Texas)
Eugenio Moggi (Università di Genova)
Greg Morrisett (Cornell)
Janos Sztipanovits (Vanderbilt University School of Engineering)
Krzysztof Czarnecki (University of Waterloo)
Walid Taha (Rice University)
Bogdan Franczyk (Universität Leipzig)
Ulrich Eisenecker (Fachhochschule Kaiserslautern)

Previous Events

GPCE emerged as the unification of the SAIG workshop series and the GCSE conference series.

GPCE 2003, Erfurt, Germany
GPCE 2002, Pittsburgh, Pensylvania, USA
GCSE 2001, Erfurt, Germany   SAIG 2001, Firenze, Italy
GCSE 2000, Erfurt, Germany   SAIG 2000, Montréal, Canada
GCSE 1999, Erfurt, Germany

See also the permanent website of the conference series `http://www.gpce.org`

Sponsors

ACM SIGPLAN and ACM SIGSOFT

Table of Contents

Invited Speakers

Author Index

Generating AspectJ Programs
with Meta-AspectJ

David Zook, Shan Shan Huang, and Yannis Smaragdakis

College of Computing, Georgia Institute of Technology
Atlanta, GA 30332, USA
{dzook,ssh,yannis}@cc.gatech.edu

Abstract. Meta-AspectJ (MAJ) is a language tool for generating AspectJ programs using code templates. MAJ itself is an extension of Java, so users can interleave arbitrary Java code with AspectJ code templates. MAJ is a structured meta-programming tool: a well-typed generator implies a syntactically correct generated program. MAJ promotes a methodology that combines aspect-oriented and generative programming. Potential applications range from implementing domain-specific languages with AspectJ as a back-end to enhancing AspectJ with more powerful general-purpose constructs. In addition to its practical value, MAJ offers valuable insights to meta-programming tool designers. It is a mature meta-programming tool for AspectJ (and, by extension, Java): a lot of emphasis has been placed on context-sensitive parsing and error-reporting. As a result, MAJ minimizes the number of meta-programming (quote/unquote) operators and uses type inference to reduce the need to remember type names for syntactic entities.

1   Introduction

Meta-programming is the act of writing programs that generate other programs. Powerful meta-programming is essential for approaches to automating software development. In this paper we present Meta-AspectJ (MAJ): a meta-programming language tool extending Java with support for generating AspectJ [9] programs. MAJ offers a convenient syntax, while explicitly representing the syntactic structure of the generated program during the generation process. This allows MAJ to guarantee that a well-typed generator will result in a syntactically correct generated program. This is the hallmark property of *structured* meta-programming tools, as opposed to lexical or text-based tools. Structured meta-programming is desirable because it means that a generator can be released with some confidence that it will create reasonable programs regardless of its inputs.

Why should anyone generate AspectJ programs, however? We believe that combining generative techniques with aspect-oriented programming results in significant advantages compared to using either approach alone. MAJ can be used for two general kinds of tasks: to implement generators using AspectJ and to implement general-purpose aspect languages using generation. Specifically,

G. Karsai and E. Visser (Eds.): GPCE 2004, LNCS 3286, pp. 1–18, 2004.

MAJ can be used to implement domain-specific languages (i.e., to implement a generator) by translating domain-specific abstractions into AspectJ code. MAJ can also be used to implement general-purpose extensions of AspectJ (e.g., extensions that would recognize different kinds of joinpoints). Thus, MAJ enables the use of AspectJ as an aspect-oriented "assembly language" [13] to simplify what would otherwise be tedious tasks of recognizing patterns in an existing program and rewriting them. A representative of this approach is our prior work on GOTECH [18]: a system that adds distributed capabilities to an existing program by generating AspectJ code using text templates.

The value and novelty of Meta-AspectJ can be described in two axes: its application value (i.e., the big-picture value for potential users) and its technical contributions (i.e., smaller reusable lessons for other researchers working on meta-programming tools). In terms of application value, MAJ is a useful meta-programming tool, not just for AspectJ but also for Java in general. Specifically:

- For generating either AspectJ or plain Java code, MAJ is safer than any text-based approach because the syntax of the generated code is represented explicitly in a typed structure.
- Compared to plain Java programs that output text, generators written in MAJ are simpler because MAJ allows writing complex code templates using quote/unquote operators.
- MAJ is the only tool for structured generation of AspectJ programs that we are aware of. Thus, to combine the benefits of generative programming and AspectJ, one needs to either use MAJ, or to use a text-based approach.

In terms of technical value, MAJ offers several improvements over prior meta-programming tools for Java. These translate to ease of use for the MAJ user, while the MAJ language design offers insights for meta-programming researchers:

- MAJ shows how to minimize the number of different quote/unquote operators compared to past tools, due to the MAJ mechanism for inferring the syntactic type (e.g., expression, declaration, statement, etc.) of a fragment of generated code. This property requires context-sensitive parsing of quoted code: the type of an unquoted variable dictates how quoted code should be parsed. As a result, the MAJ implementation is quite sophisticated and not just a naive precompiler. An additional benefit of this approach is that MAJ emits its own error messages, independently from the Java compiler that is used in its back-end.
- When storing fragments of generated code in variables, the user does not need to specify the types of these variables (e.g., whether they are statements, expressions, etc.). Instead, a special `infer` type can be used.

The above points are important because they isolate the user from low-level representation issues and allow meta-programming at the template level.

We next present an introduction to the MAJ language design (Section 2), discuss examples and applications (Section 3), describe in more depth the individual interesting technical points of MAJ (Section 4), and discuss related and future work (Section 5).

2 Meta-AspectJ Introduction

2.1 Background: AspectJ

Aspect-oriented programming (AOP) is a methodology that advocates decomposing software by aspects of functionality. These aspects can be "cross-cutting": they span multiple functional units (functions, classes, modules, etc.) of the software application. Tool support for aspect-oriented programming consists of machinery for specifying such cross-cutting aspects separately from the main application code and subsequently composing them with that code.

AspectJ [9] is a general purpose, aspect-oriented extension of Java. AspectJ allows the user to define aspects as well as ways that these aspects should be merged ("weaved") with the rest of the application code. The power of AspectJ comes from the variety of changes it allows to existing Java code. With AspectJ, the user can add superclasses and interfaces to existing classes and can interpose arbitrary code to method executions, field references, exception throwing, and more. Complex enabling predicates can be used to determine whether code should be interposed at a certain point. Such predicates can include, for instance, information on the identity of the caller and callee, whether a call to a method is made while a call to a certain different method is on the stack, etc. For a simple example of the syntax of AspectJ, consider the code below:

```
aspect CaptureUpdateCallsToA {
  static int num_updates = 0;

  pointcut updates(A a): target(a) && call(public * update*(..));

  after(A a): updates(a) {          // advice
    num_updates++;                  // update was just performed
  }
}
```

The above code defines an aspect that just counts the number of calls to methods whose name begins with "update" on objects of type A. The "pointcut" definition specifies where the aspect code will tie together with the main application code. The exact code ("advice") will execute after each call to an "update" method.

2.2 MAJ Basics

MAJ offers two variants of code-template operators for creating AspectJ code fragments: `[...]` ("quote") and `#[EXPR]` or just `#IDENTIFIER` ("unquote"). (The ellipses, `EXPR` and `IDENTIFIER` are meta-variables matching any syntax, expressions and identifiers, respectively.) The quote operator creates representations of AspectJ code fragments. Parts of these representations can be variable and are designated by the unquote operator (instances of unquote can only occur

inside a quoted code fragment). For example, the value of the MAJ expression
'[call(* *(..))] is a data structure that represents the abstract syntax tree
for the fragment of AspectJ code call(* *(..)). Similarly, the MAJ expression
'[!within(#className)] is a quoted pattern with an unquoted part. Its value
depends on the value of the variable className. If, for instance, className
holds the identifier "SomeClass", the value of '[!within(#className)] is the
abstract syntax tree for the expression !within(SomeClass).

MAJ also introduces a new keyword infer that can be used in place of a
type name when a new variable is being declared and initialized to a quoted
expression. For example, we can write:

```
infer pct1 = '[call(* *(..))];
```

This declares a variable pct1 that can be used just like any other program
variable. For instance, we can unquote it:

```
infer adv1 = '[void around() : #pct1 { }];
```

This creates the abstract syntax tree for a piece of AspectJ code defining (empty)
advice for a pointcut. Section 2.3 describes in more detail the type inference
process.

The unquote operator can also be used with an array of expressions. We
call this variant of the operator "unquote-splice". The unquote-splice operator
is used for adding arguments in a quoted context that expects a variable number
of arguments (i.e., an argument list, a list of methods, or a block of statements).
For example, if variable argTypes holds an array of type names, then we can
generate code for a pointcut describing all methods taking arguments of these
types as:

```
infer pct2 = '[call(* *(#[argTypes])];
```

That is, if argTypes has 3 elements and argTypes[0] is int, argTypes[1] is
String, and argTypes[2] is Object, then the value of pct2 will be the abstract
syntax tree for the AspectJ code fragment call(* *(int, String, Object)).

Of course, since AspectJ is an extension of Java, any regular Java program
fragment can be generated using MAJ. Furthermore, the values of primitive Java
types (ints, floats, doubles, etc.) and their arrays can be used as constants
in the generated program. The unquote operator automatically promotes such
values to the appropriate abstract syntax tree representations. For example,
consider the code fragment:

```
void foo(int n) {
  infer expr1 = '[ #n * #n ];
  infer expr2 = '[ #[n*n] ];
  ...
}
```

If n holds the value 4, then the value of expr1 is '[4 * 4] and the value of
expr2 is '[16]. Similarly, if nums is an array of Java ints with value {1,2,3}
then the code fragment

```
infer arrdcl = '[ int[] arr = #nums; ];
```

will set `arrdcl` to the value '[int [] arr = {1,2,3};].

We can now see a full MAJ method that generates a trivial but complete AspectJ file:

```
void generateTrivialLogging(String classNm) {
  infer aspectCode =
    '[   package MyPackage;
         aspect #[classNm + "Aspect"] {
           before : call(* #classNm.*(..))
           { System.out.println("Method called"); }
         }
    ];
  System.out.println(aspectCode.unparse());
}
```

The generated aspect causes a message to be printed before every call of a method in a class. The name of the affected class is a parameter passed to the MAJ routine. This code also shows the **unparse** method that our abstract syntax types support for creating a text representation of their code. The abstract syntax types of the MAJ back-end[1] also support other methods for manipulating abstract syntax trees. One such method, **addMember**, is used fairly commonly: **addMember** is supported by syntactic entities that can have an arbitrary number of members (e.g., classes, interfaces, aspects, or argument lists). Although the high-level MAJ operators (quote, unquote, unquote-splice) form a complete set for generating syntax trees, it is sometimes more convenient to manipulate trees directly using the **addMember** method.

2.3   Types and Inference

We saw earlier an example of the MAJ keyword **infer**:

```
infer adv1 = '[void around(): #pct1 {} ];
```

The inferred type of variable `adv1` will be `AdviceDec`. (for "advice declaration"), which is one of the types for AspectJ abstract syntax tree nodes that MAJ defines. Such types can be used explicitly both in variable definitions and in the quote/unquote operators. For instance, the fully qualified version of the `adv1` example would be:

```
AdviceDec adv1 = '(AdviceDec)[void around(): #(Pcd)pct1 {} ];
```

The full set of permitted type qualifiers contains the following names: IDENT, Identifier, NamePattern, Modifiers, Import, Pcd, TypeD, VarDec, JavaExpr,

---
[1] We currently use modified versions of the AspectJ compiler classes for the MAJ back-end, but may choose to replicate these classes in a separate MAJ package in the future.

Stmt, MethodDec, ConstructorDec, ClassDec, ClassMember, InterfaceDec, DeclareDec, AdviceDec, CompilationUnit, PointcutDec, Pcd, AspectDec, FormalDec, and AspectMember. Most of the qualifiers' names are self-descriptive, but a few require explanation: IDENT is an unqualified name (no dots), while Identifier is a full name of a Java identifier, such as pack.clazz.mem. NamePattern can be either an identifier, or a wildcard, or a combination of both. Pcd is for a pointcut body (e.g., call(* *(..)), as in our example) while PointcutDec is for full pointcut definitions (with names and the AspectJ pointcut keyword).

Although MAJ allows the use of type qualifiers, these are never necessary for uses of quote/unquote, as well as wherever the infer keyword is permitted. The correct types and flavor of the operators can be inferred from the syntax and type information. The goal is to hide the complexity of the explicit type qualifiers from the user as much as possible. Nevertheless, use of types is still necessary wherever the infer keyword cannot be used, notably in method signatures and in definitions of member variables that are not initialized.

3   Applications

There are many ways to view the value of MAJ in the application domain (and, by extension, the value of combining generative and aspect-oriented programming, in general). One can ask why a generator cannot just perform the required modifications to a program without AspectJ, using meta-programming techniques alone. Similarly, one can ask why AspectJ alone is not sufficient for the desired tasks. We address both points below.

3.1   Why Do We Need AspectJ?

Aspect-oriented programming has significant value for building generators. A vidid illustration is our previous work on the GOTECH generator [18]. GOTECH takes a Java program annotated with JavaDoc comments to describe what parts of the functionality should be remotely executable. It then transforms parts of the program so that they execute over a network instead of running on a local machine. The middleware platform used for distributed computing is J2EE (the protocol for Enterprise Java Beans – EJB). GOTECH takes care of generating code adhering to the EJB conventions and makes methods, construction calls, etc. execute on a remote machine. Internally, the modification of the application is performed by generating AspectJ code that transforms existing classes. (We give a specific example later.)

A generator or program transformer acting on Java programs could completely avoid the use of AspectJ and instead manipulate Java syntax directly. Nevertheless, AspectJ gives a very convenient vocabulary for talking about program transformations, as well as a mature implementation of such transformations. AspectJ is a very convenient, higher-level back-end for a generator. It lets its user add arbitrary code in many points of the program, like all references to a member, all calls to a set of methods, etc. If a generator was to reproduce this functionality without AspectJ, the generator would need to parse all the program files, recognize all transformation sites, and apply the rewrites to the syntax. These actions are not simple for a language with the syntactic and semantic complexity of Java. For instance, generator writers often need to use functionality similar to the AspectJ `cflow` construct. `cflow` is used for recognizing calls under the control flow of another call (i.e. while the latter is still on the execution stack). Although this functionality can be re-implemented from scratch by adding a run-time flag, this would be a tedious and ad hoc replication of the AspectJ functionality. It is much better to inherit a general and mature version of this functionality from AspectJ.

Note that using AspectJ as a "bag of program transformation tricks" is perhaps an unintended consequence of its power. AspectJ's main intended use is for cross-cutting: the functionality additions should span several classes. The ability to have one aspect affect multiple classes at once is occasionally useful but secondary when the AspectJ code is generated instead of hand-written. On the other hand, in order to support cross-cutting, aspect-oriented tools need to have sophisticated mechanisms for specifying aspect code separately from the main application code and prescribing precisely how the two are composed. This is the ability that is most valuable to our approach.

3.2   Why Do We Need Meta-programming?

Despite its capabilities, there are several useful operations that AspectJ alone cannot handle. For example, AspectJ cannot be used to create an interface isomorphic to the public methods of a given class (i.e., a new interface whose methods correspond one-to-one to the public methods of a class). This is an essential action for a tool like GOTECH that needs to create new interfaces (home and remote interfaces, per the EJB conventions) for existing classes. GOTECH was used to automate activities that were previously [15] shown impossible to automate with just AspectJ. GOTECH, however, was implemented using text-based templates. With MAJ, we can do much better in terms of expressiveness and safety as the generated code is represented by a typed data structure instead of arbitrary text.

In general, using meta-programming allows us to go beyond the capabilities of AspectJ by adding arbitrary flexibility in recognizing where aspects should be applied and customizing the weaving of code. For instance, AspectJ does not allow expressing joinpoints based on properties like "all native methods", "all classes with native methods", "all methods in classes that extend a system class", etc. Such properties are, however, simple to express in a regular Java program – e.g., using reflection. Similarly, AspectJ does not allow aspects to be flexible with respect to what superclasses they add to the class they affect, whether added fields are private or public, etc. This information is instead hard-coded in the aspect definition. With a meta-program written in MAJ, the generated aspect can be adapted to the needs of the code body at hand.

```
import java.io.*;
import java.lang.reflect.*;
import org.aspectj.compiler.base.ast.*;
import org.aspectj.compiler.crosscuts.ast.*;

public class MAJGenerate {
 public static void genSerializableAspect(Class inClass, PrintStream out)
 {
    // Create a new aspect
    infer serializedAspect = '[aspect SerializableAspect {}];

    // Add Serializable to every method argument type that needs it
    for (int meth = 0; meth < inClass.getMethods().length; meth++) {
      Class[] methSignature =
        inClass.getMethods()[meth].getParameterTypes();
      for (int parm = 0; parm < methSignature.length; parm++) {
        if (!methSignature[parm].isPrimitive() &&
           !Serializable.class.isAssignableFrom(methSignature[parm]))
          serializedAspect.addMember('[ declare parents:
                                      #[methSignature[parm].getName()]
                                      implements java.io.Serializable;
                                  ]
                              );
      } // for all params
    } // for all methods

    infer compU = '[ package gotech.extensions;
                     #serializedAspect
                 ];

    out.print(compU.unparse());
 }
}
```

Fig. 1. A routine that generates an aspect that makes method parameter types be serializable

3.3   Example

The above points are best illustrated with a small example that shows a task that is easier to perform with AspectJ than with ad hoc program transformation, but cannot be performed by AspectJ alone. Consider the MAJ code in Figure 1. This is a complete MAJ program that takes a class as input, traverses all its methods, and creates an aspect that makes each method argument type implement the interface java.io.Serializable (provided the argument type does not implement this interface already and it is not a primitive type). For example, imagine that the class passed to the code of Figure 1 is:

```
class SomeClass {
  public void meth1(Car c) { ... }
  public void meth2(int i, Tire t) { ... }
  public void meth3(float f, Seat s) { ... }
}
```

In this case, the list of all argument types is `int`, `float`, `Car`, `Tire`, and `Seat`. The first two are primitive types, thus the MAJ program will generate the following AspectJ code:

```
package gotech.extensions;
aspect SerializableAspect {
  declare parents: Car implements java.io.Serializable;
  declare parents: Tire implements java.io.Serializable;
  declare parents: Seat implements java.io.Serializable;
}
```

The code of Figure 1 faithfully replicates the functionality of a template used in GOTECH: the system needs to make argument types be serializable if a method is to be called remotely. (We have similarly replicated the entire functionality of GOTECH using MAJ and have used it as a regression test during the development of MAJ.)

This example is a good representative of realistic uses of MAJ, in that the cases where AspectJ alone is not sufficient are exactly those where complex conditions determine the existence, structure, or functionality of an aspect. Observe that most of the code concerns the application logic for finding argument types and deciding whether a certain type should be augmented to implement interface `Serializable`. MAJ makes the rest of the code be straightforward.

The example of Figure 1 is self-contained, but it is worth pointing out that it could be simplified by making use of reusable methods to traverse a class or a method signature. Java allows a more functional style of programming through the use of interfaces and anonymous classes. These let us write general iteration methods like `forAllMethods` or `forAllArguments` that could have been used in this code.

4   Meta-AspectJ Design and Implementation

4.1   MAJ Design

We will next examine the MAJ design a little closer, in order to compare it to other meta-programming tools.

Structured vs. Unstructured Meta-programming. The value of a MAJ quoted code fragment is an abstract syntax tree representation of the code fragment. The MAJ operators ensure that all trees manipulated by a MAJ program are syntactically well-formed, although they may contain semantic errors, such as type errors or scoping errors (e.g., references to undeclared variables). That is, MAJ is based on a context-free grammar for describing AspectJ syntax. The MAJ expressions created using the quote operator correspond to words ("words" in the formal languages sense) produced by different non-terminals of this context-free grammar. Compositions of abstract syntax trees in ways that are not allowed by the grammar is prohibited. Thus, using the MAJ operators, one cannot create trees that do not correspond to fragments of AspectJ syntax. For instance, there is no way to create a tree for an "if" statement with 5 operands (instead of 3, for the condition, then-branch, and else-branch), or a class with a statement as its member (instead of just methods and instance variable declarations), or a declaration with an operator in the type position, etc. The syntactic well-formedness of abstract syntax trees is ensured statically when a MAJ program is compiled. For example, suppose the user wrote a MAJ program containing the declarations:

```
infer pct1 = '[call(* *(..))];
infer progr = '[ package MyPackage;
                   #pct1
               ];
```

The syntax error (pointcut in unexpected location) would be caught when this program would be compiled with MAJ.

The static enforcement of syntactic correctness for the generated program is a common and desirable property in meta-programming tools. It is often described as "the type safety of the generator implies the syntactic correctness of the generated program". The property is desirable because it increases confidence in the correctness of the generator under all inputs (and not just the inputs with which the generator writer has tested the generator). This property is the hallmark of *structured* meta-programming tools – to be contrasted with unstructured, or "text-based", tools (e.g., the C pre-processor or the XDoclet tool [16] for Java). As a structured meta-programming tool, MAJ is superior to text-based tools in terms of safety.

Additionally, MAJ is superior in terms of expressiveness to text-based generation with a tool like XDoclet [16]. MAJ programs can use any Java code to determine what should be generated, instead of being limited to a hard-coded set of attributes and annotations. Compared to arbitrary text-based generation with plain Java strings, MAJ is more convenient. Instead of putting Java strings together with the "+" operator (and having to deal with low-level issues like explicitly handling quotes, new lines, etc.) MAJ lets the user use convenient code templates.

Of course, static type safety implies that some legal programs will not be expressible in MAJ. For instance, we restrict the ways in which trees can be composed (i.e., what can be unquoted in a quote expression and how). The well-formedness of an abstract syntax tree should be statically verifiable from the types of its component parts – if an unquoted expression does not have the right type, the code will not compile even if the run-time value happens to be legal. Specifically, it is not possible to have a single expression take values of two different abstract syntax tree types. For example we cannot create an abstract syntax tree that may hold either a variable definition or a statement and in the cases that it holds a definition use it in the body of a class (where a statement would be illegal).

Qualifier Inference. MAJ is distinguished from other meta-programming tools because of its ability to infer qualifiers for the quote/unquote operators, as well as the ability to infer types for the variables initialized by quoted fragments. Having multiple quote/unquote operators is the norm in meta-programming tools for languages with rich surface syntax (e.g., meta-programming tools for Java [3], C [20], and C++ [7]). For instance, let us examine the JTS tool for Java meta-programming – the closest comparable to MAJ. JTS introduces several different kinds of quote/unquote operators: `exp{...}exp`, `$exp(...)`, `stm{...}stm`, `$stm(...)`, `mth{...}mth`, `$mth(...)`, `cls{...}cls`, `$cls(...)`, etc. Additionally, just like in MAJ, JTS has distinct types for each abstract syntax tree form: `AST_Exp`, `AST_Stmt`, `AST_FieldDecl`, `AST_Class`, etc. Unlike MAJ, however, the JTS user needs to always specify explicitly the correct operator and tree type for all generated code fragments. For instance, consider the JTS fragment:

```
AST_Exp x = exp{ 7 + i }exp;
AST_Stm s = stm{ if (i > 0) return $exp(x); }stm;
```

This written in MAJ is simply:

```
infer x = '[7 + i];
infer s = '[if (i > 0) return #x ;];
```

The advantage is that the user does not need to tediously specify what flavor of the operator is used at every point and what is the type of the result. MAJ will instead infer this information. As we explain next, this requires sophistication in the parsing implementation.

4.2   MAJ Implementation

We have invested significant effort in making MAJ a mature and user-friendly tool, as opposed to a naive pre-processor. This section describes our implementation in detail.

Qualifier Inference and Type System. It is important to realize that although multiple flavors of quote/unquote operators are common in syntax-rich languages, the reason for their introduction is purely technical. There is no fundamental ambiguity that would occur if only a single quote/unquote operator was employed. Nevertheless, inferring qualifiers, as in MAJ, requires the meta-programming tool to have a full-fledged compiler instead of a naive pre-processor. (An alternative would be for the meta-programming tool to severely limit the possible places where a quote or unquote can occur in order to avoid ambiguities.

No tool we are aware of follows this approach.) Not only does the tool need to implement its own type system, but also parsing becomes context-sensitive – i.e., the type of a variable determines how a certain piece of syntax is parsed, which puts the parsing task beyond the capabilities of a (context-free) grammar-based parser generator.

To see the above points, consider the MAJ code fragment:

```
infer l = '[ #foo class A {} ];
```

The inferred type of l depends on the type of foo. For instance, if foo is of type Modifiers (e.g., it has the value '[public]) then the above code would be equivalent to:

```
ClassDec l = '[ #(Modifiers)foo class A {} ];
```

If, however, foo is of type Import (e.g., it has the value '[import java.io.*;]) then the above code would be equivalent to:

```
CompilationUnit l = '[ #(Import)foo class A {} ];
```

Thus, to be able to infer the type of the quoted expression we need to know the types of the unquoted expressions. This is possible because MAJ maintains its own type system (i.e., it maintains type contexts for variables during parsing). The type system is simple: it has a fixed set of types with a few subtyping relations and a couple of ad hoc conversion rules (e.g., from Java strings to IDENTs). Type inference is quite straightforward: when deriving the type of an expression, the types of its component subexpressions are known and there is a most specific type for each expression. No recursion is possible in the inference logic, since the infer keyword can only be used in variable declarations and the use of a variable in its own initialization expression is not allowed in Java.

The types of expressions even influence the parsing and translation of quoted code. Consider again the above example. The two possible abstract syntax trees are not even isomorphic. If the type of foo is Modifiers, this will result in an entirely different parse and translation of the quoted code than if the type of foo is Import (or ClassDec, or InterfaceDec, etc). In the former case, foo just describes a modifier – i.e., a branch of the abstract syntax tree for the definition of class A. In the latter case, the abstract syntax tree value of foo is at the same level as the tree for the class definition.

Parser Implementation. The current implementation of the MAJ front-end consists of one common lexer and two separate parsers. The common lexer recoginizes tokens legal in both the meta-language (Java), and the object language (AspectJ). This is not a difficult task for this particular combination of meta/object languages, since Java is a subset of AspectJ. For two languages whose token sets do not match up as nicely, a more sophisticated scheme would have to be employed.

We use ANTLR [11] to generate our parser from two separate LL(k) grammars (augmented for context-sensitivity, as described below). One is the Java' grammar: Java with additional rules for handling quote and `infer`. The other is the AspectJ' grammar: AspectJ with additional rules for handling `infer`, quote and unquote. Java', upon seeing a quote operator lifts out the string between the quote delimiters (`'[...]`) and passes it to AspectJ' for parsing. AspectJ', upon seeing an unquote, lifts out the string between the unquote delimiters and passes it to Java' for parsing. Thus, we are able to completely isolate the two grammars. This paves way for easily changing the meta or object language for future work, with the lexer caveat previously mentioned.

The heavy lifting of recognizing and type-checking quoted AspectJ is done in AspectJ'. To implement context-sensitive parsing we rely on ANTLR's facilities for guessing as well as adding arbitrary predicates to grammar productions and backtracking if the predicates turn out to be false. Each quote entry point production is preceded by the same production wrapped in a guessing/backtracking rule. If a phrase successfully parses in the guessing mode and the predicate (which is based on the types of the parsed expressions) succeeds, then real parsing takes place and token consumption is finalized. Otherwise, the parser rewinds and attempts parsing by the next rule that applies. Thus, a phrase that begins with a series of unquoted entities might have to be guess-parsed by a number of alternate rules before it reaches a rule that actually applies to it.

The parsing time of this approach depends on how many rules are tried unsuccessfully before the matching one is found. In the worst case, our parsing time is exponential in the nesting depth of quotes and unquotes. Nevertheless, we have not found speed to be a problem in MAJ parsing. The parsing time is negligible (a couple of seconds on a 1.4GHz laptop) even for clearly artificial worst-case examples with a nesting depth of up to 5 (i.e., a quote that contains an unquote that contains a quote that contains an unquote, and so on, for 5 total quotes and 5 unquotes). Of course, more sophisticated parsing technology can be used in future versions, but arguably parsing speed is not a huge constraint in modern systems and we place a premium on using mature tools like ANTLR and expressing our parsing logic declaratively using predicates.

Translation. The MAJ compiler translates its input into plain Java code. This is a standard approach in meta-programming tools [3, 4, 19]. For example, consider the trivial MAJ code fragment:

```
infer dummyAspect = '[ aspect myAspect { } ];
infer dummyUnit = '[ package myPackage;
                     #dummyAspect
                   ];
```

MAJ compilation will translate this fragment to Java code using a library for representing AspectJ abstract syntax trees. The Java compiler is then called to produce bytecode. The above MAJ code fragment will generate Java code like:

```
AspectDec dummyAspect =
  new AspectDec(
    null, "myAspect", null, null, null,
    new AspectMembers(new AspectMember[] {null}));
```

```
CompilationUnit dummyUnit =
  new MajCompilationUnit(
  new MajPackageExpr(new Identifier("myPackage")),
  null, new Decs(new Dec[] { dummyAspect }));
```

The Java type system could also catch ill-formed MAJ programs. If the un-quoted expression in the above program had been illegal in the particular syntactic location, the error would have exhibited itself as a Java type error. Nevertheless, MAJ implements its own type system and performs error checking before translating its input to Java. Therefore, the produced code will never contain MAJ type errors. (There are, however, Java static errors that MAJ does not currently catch, such as access protection errors, uninitialized variable errors, and more.)

Error Handling. Systems like JTS [3] operate as simple pre-processors and delegate the type checking of meta-programs to their target language (e.g., Java). The disadvantage of this approach is that error messages are reported on the generated code, which the user has never seen. Since MAJ maintains its own type system, we can emit more accurate and informative error messages than those that would be produced for MAJ errors by the Java compiler.

Recall that our parsing approach stretches the capabilities of ANTLR to perform context-sensitive parsing based on the MAJ type system. To achieve good error reporting we had to implement a mechanism that distinguishes between parsing errors due to a mistyped unquoted entity and regular syntax errors. While attempting different rule alternatives during parsing, we collect all error messages for failed rules. If parsing succeeds according to some rule, the error information from failed rules is discarded. If all rules fail, we re-parse the expression with MAJ type checking turned off. If this succeeds, then the error is a MAJ type error and we report it to the user as such. Otherwise, the error is a genuine syntax error and we report to the user the reasons that caused each alternative to fail.

Implementation Evolution and Advice. It is worth briefly mentioning the evolution of the implementation of MAJ because we believe it offers lessons for other developers. The original MAJ implementation was much less sophisticated than the current one. The system was a pre-processor without its own type system and relied on the Java compiler for ensuring the well-formedness of MAJ code. Nevertheless, even at that level of sophistication, we found that it is possible to make the system user-friendlier with very primitive mechanisms.

An important observation is that type qualifier inference can be performed even without maintaining a type system, as long as ambiguous uses of the un-quote operator are explicitly qualified. That is, qualifying some of the uses of unquote allows having a single unqualified quote operator and the `infer` keyword. For instance, consider the code fragment:

```
infer s = '[if (i > 0) return #x ;];
```

The syntactic types of s and x are clear from context in this case. Even the early implementation of MAJ, without its own type system, could support the above example. Nevertheless, in cases where parsing or type inference would be truly dependent on type information, earlier versions of MAJ required explicit qualification of unquotes – for instance:

```
infer l = '[ #(Modifiers)foo class A {} ];
```

Even with that early approach, however, parsing required unlimited lookahead, making our grammar not LL(k).

5   Related Work and Future Work Directions

In this section we connect MAJ to other work in AOP and meta-programming. The comparison helps outline promising directions for further research. We will be selective in our references and only pick representative and/or recent work instead of trying to be exhaustive.

In terms of philosophy, MAJ is a compatible approach to that of XAspects [13], which advocates the use of AspectJ as a back-end language for aspect-orientation. Aspect languages in the XAspects framework can produce AspectJ code using MAJ.

It is interesting to compare MAJ to state-of-the-art work in meta-programming. Visser [19] has made similar observations to ours with respect to concrete syntax (i.e., quote/unquote operators) and its introduction to meta-languages. His approach tries to be language-independent and relies on generalized-LR parsing (GLR). We could use GLR technology for MAJ parsing in the future. GLR is powerful for ambiguous grammars as it returns all possible parse trees. Our type system can then be used to disambiguate in a separate phase. Although parsing technology is an interesting topic, we do not consider it crucial for MAJ. Our current approach with ANTLR is perhaps crude but yields a clean specification and quite acceptable performance.

Multi-stage programming languages, like MetaML [17] and MetaOCaml [6] represent state-of-the-art meta-programming systems with excellent safety properties. For instance, a common guarantee of multi-stage languages is that the type safety of the generator implies the type safety of the generated program. This is a much stronger guarantee than that offered by MAJ and other abstract-syntax-tree-based tools. It means that the meta-programming infrastructure needs to keep track of the contexts (declared variables and types) of the *generated program*, even though this program has not yet been generated. Therefore the system is more restrictive in how the static structure of the generator reflects the structure of the generated program. By implication, some useful and legal generators may be harder to express in a language like MetaOCaml. In fact, although there is great value in multi-stage programming approaches, we are not yet convinced that they are appropriate for large-scale, ad hoc generator development. Current applications of multi-stage languages have been in the area of directing the specialization of existing programs for optimization purposes.

An interesting direction in meta-programming tools is that pioneered by *hygienic macro expansion* [10, 8]. Hygienic macros avoid the problem of unintended capture due to the scoping rules of a programming language. For instance, a macro can introduce code that inadvertently refers to a variable in the generation site instead of the variable the macro programmer intended. Similarly, a macro can introduce a declaration (binding instance) that accidentally binds identifier references from the user program. The same problem exists in programmatic meta-programming systems, like MAJ. In past work, we described *generation scoping* [14]: a facility for controlling scoping environments of the generated program, during the generation process. Generation scoping is the analogue of hygienic macros in the programmatic (not pattern-based, like macros) meta-programming world. Generation scoping does not offer any guarantees about the correctness of the target program, but gives the user much better control over the lexical environments of the generated program so that inadvertent capture can be very easily avoided. Adding a generation scoping facility to MAJ is an interesting future work direction.

Other interesting recent tools for meta-programming include Template Haskell [12] – a mechanism for performing compile-time computations and syntax transformation in the Haskell language. Closer to MAJ are tools, like JSE [1], ELIDE [5] and Maya [2] that have been proposed for manipulating Java syntax. Most of these Java tools aim at syntactic extensions to the language and are closely modeled after macro systems. The MAJ approach is different both in that it targets AspectJ, and in that it serves a different purpose: it is a tool for programmatic meta-programming, as opposed to pattern-based meta-programming. In MAJ, we chose to separate the problem of recognizing syntax (i.e., pattern matching and syntactic extension) from the problem of generating syntax (i.e., quoting/unquoting). MAJ only addresses the issues of generating AspectJ programs using simple mechanisms and a convenient language design. Although meta-programming is a natural way to implement language extensions, uses of MAJ do not have to be tied to syntactic extensions at all. MAJ can, for instance, be used as part of a tool that performs transformations on arbitrary programs based on GUI input or program analysis. MAJ also has many individual technical differences from tools like JSE, ELIDE, and Maya (e.g., JSE is partly an unstructured meta-programming tool, Maya does not have an explicit quote operator, etc.).

Complementing MAJ with a facility for *recognizing* syntax (i.e., performing pattern matching on abstract syntax trees or based on semantic properties) is a straightforward direction for future work. Nevertheless, note that the need for pattern matching is not as intensive for MAJ as it is for other meta-programming tools. The reason is that MAJ generates AspectJ code that is responsible for deciding what transformations need to be applied and where. The beauty of the combination of generative and aspect-oriented programming is exactly in the simplicity of the generative part afforded by the use of aspect-oriented techniques. Another promising direction for future work on MAJ is to make it an extension of AspectJ, as opposed to Java (i.e., to allow aspects to generate other aspects). We do not yet have a strong motivating example for this application, but we expect it may have value in the future.

6 Conclusions

In this paper we presented Meta-AspectJ (MAJ): a tool for generating AspectJ programs. The implementation of MAJ was largely motivated by practical concerns: although a lot of research has been performed on meta-programming tools, we found no mature tool, readily available for practical meta-programming tasks in either Java or AspectJ. MAJ strives for convenience in meta-programming but does not aspire to be a heavyweight meta-programming infrastructure that supports syntactic extension, pattern matching, etc. Instead, MAJ is based on the philosophy that generative tools have a lot to gain by generating AspectJ code and delegating many issues of semantic matching to AspectJ. Of course, this approach limits the ability for program transformation to the manipulations that AspectJ supports. Nevertheless, this is exactly why our approach is an aspect-oriented/generative hybrid. We believe that AspectJ is expressive enough to capture many useful program manipulations at exactly the right level of abstraction. When this power needs to be combined with more configurability, generative programming can add the missing elements. We hope that MAJ will prove to be a useful tool in practice and that it will form the basis for several interesting domain-specific mechanisms.

Acknowledgments and Availability

This research was supported by the National Science Foundation under Grants No. CCR-0220248 and CCR-0238289 and by the Yamacraw Foundation/Georgia Electronic Design Center.

MAJ is available at http://www.cc.gatech.edu/~yannis/maj.

References

1. J. Bachrach and K. Playford. The Java syntactic extender (JSE). In *Proceedings of the OOPSLA '01 conference on Object Oriented Programming Systems Languages and Applications*, pages 31–42. ACM Press, 2001.
2. J. Baker and W. C. Hsieh. Maya: multiple-dispatch syntax extension in Java. In *Proceedings of the ACM SIGPLAN 2002 Conference on Programming Language Design and Implementation*, pages 270–281. ACM Press, 2002.
3. D. Batory, B. Lofaso, and Y. Smaragdakis. JTS: tools for implementing domain-specific languages. In *Proceedings Fifth International Conference on Software Reuse*, pages 143–153, Victoria, BC, Canada, 1998. IEEE.
4. D. Batory, J. N. Sarvela, and A. Rauschmayer. Scaling step-wise refinement. In *Proceedings of the 25th International Conference on Software Engineering*, pages 187–197. IEEE Computer Society, 2003.

5. A. Bryant, A. Catton, K. De Volder, and G. C. Murphy. Explicit programming. In *Proceedings of the 1st international conference on Aspect-Oriented Software Development*, pages 10–18. ACM Press, 2002.

6. C. Calcagno, W. Taha, L. Huang, and X. Leroy. Implementing multi-stage languages using ASTs, gensym, and reflection. In *Generative Programming and Component Engineering (GPCE) Conference*, LNCS 2830, pages 57–76. Springer, 2003.

7. S. Chiba. A metaobject protocol for C++. In *ACM Conference on Object-Oriented Programming Systems, Languages, and Applications (OOPSLA'95)*, SIGPLAN Notices 30(10), pages 285–299, Austin, Texas, USA, Oct. 1995.

8. W. Clinger. Macros that work. In *Proceedings of the 18th ACM SIGPLAN-SIGACT symposium on Principles of Programming Languages*, pages 155–162. ACM Press, 1991.

9. G. Kiczales, E. Hilsdale, J. Hugunin, M. Kersten, J. Palm, and W. Griswold. Getting started with AspectJ. *Communications of the ACM*, 44(10):59–65, 2001.

10. E. Kohlbecker, D. P. Friedman, M. Felleisen, and B. Duba. Hygienic macro expansion. In *Proceedings of the 1986 ACM conference on LISP and functional programming*, pages 151–161. ACM Press, 1986.

11. T. J. Parr and R. W. Quong. ANTLR: A predicated LL(k) parser generator. *Software, Practice and Experience*, 25(7):789–810, July 1995.

12. T. Sheard and S. P. Jones. Template meta-programming for Haskell. In *Proceedings of the ACM SIGPLAN workshop on Haskell*, pages 1–16. ACM Press, 2002.

13. M. Shonle, K. Lieberherr, and A. Shah. Xaspects: An extensible system for domain specific aspect languages. In *OOPSLA '2003, Domain-Driven Development Track*, October 2003.

14. Y. Smaragdakis and D. Batory. Scoping constructs for program generators. In *Generative and Component-Based Software Engineering Symposium (GCSE)*, 1999. Earlier version in Technical Report UTCS-TR-96-37.

15. S. Soares, E. Laureano, and P. Borba. Implementing distribution and persistence aspects with AspectJ. In *Proceedings of the 17th ACM SIGPLAN conference on Object-oriented programming, systems, languages, and applications*, pages 174–190. ACM Press, 2002.

16. A. Stevens et al. *XDoclet Web site, http://xdoclet.sourceforge.net/*.

17. W. Taha and T. Sheard. Multi-stage programming with explicit annotations. In *Partial Evaluation and Semantics-Based Program Manipulation, Amsterdam, The Netherlands, June 1997*, pages 203–217. New York: ACM, 1997.

18. E. Tilevich, S. Urbanski, Y. Smaragdakis, and M. Fleury. Aspectizing server-side distribution. In *Proceedings of the Automated Software Engineering (ASE) Conference*. IEEE Press, October 2003.

19. E. Visser. Meta-programming with concrete object syntax. In *Generative Programming and Component Engineering (GPCE) Conference*, LNCS 2487, pages 299–315. Springer, 2002.

20. D. Weise and R. F. Crew. Programmable syntax macros. In *SIGPLAN Conference on Programming Language Design and Implementation*, pages 156–165, 1993.

Splice: Aspects That Analyze Programs

Sean McDirmid and Wilson C. Hsieh

School of Computing, University of Utah
50 S. Central Campus Dr. Salt Lake City UT 84112, USA
{mcdirmid,wilson}@cs.utah.edu

Abstract. This paper describes Splice, a system for writing aspects that perform static program analyses to direct program modifications. The power of an inter-procedural data-flow analysis enables an aspect to examine the flow of data around a program execution point when it determines what code to add or change at that point. For example, an aspect can change the target set of an iteration based on how elements are skipped during the iteration. Splice aspects are written in a rule-based logic programming language with features that help aspect programmers express analyses. We show how a prototype of Splice is used to write two useful aspects in the areas of domain-specific optimization and synchronization.

1 Introduction

Aspect-oriented programming (AOP) systems, such as AspectJ [10], provide mechanisms for organizing code that go beyond conventional objects and functions. An aspect can modify the execution of a program at well-defined points in its execution, which are known as *join points*. The description of join points in AOP systems has generally been limited to their syntactic structure. For example, a set of join points can be described as calls to a particular set of methods. However, current aspect systems cannot describe a join point that depends on what can happen before or after the join point. This paper shows why such join points are useful and how they are supported in Splice, a system for writing aspects that can use static program analysis to identify join points. As a simple example, consider Java code that raises salaries of employees who are programmers:

```
-Iterator i = employees/*jp-1*/.iterator();/* original    code */
+Iterator i = programmers      .iterator();/* transformed code */
 while (i.hasNext())
{ Employee e = (Employee) i.next();
  if (e.isProgrammer()) e.raiseSalary(+20)/*jp-2*/; }
```

The efficiency of this loop can be improved by maintaining and iterating over an extent set of programmers rather than employees. Although this transformation can be performed by hand, implementing it as an aspect could improve modularity by separating a performance concern from base functionality. The aspect would add the `programmers` set to the program and manipulates the program's code at multiple join points. Two of these join points, labeled `jp-1` and `jp-2`, can only be identified with the help of a program analysis. Join point `jp-1` is associated with the `employees` field access used to create an iterator. Identifying `jp-1` requires a data-flow analysis because the

G. Karsai and E. Visser (Eds.): GPCE 2004, LNCS 3286, pp. 19–38, 2004.
© Springer-Verlag Berlin Heidelberg 2004

aspect must discover that each element of the iterator is only updated when an `is-Programmer` method call on the element is true. When `jp-1` is identified, an aspect can replace the `employees` field access with a `programmers` field access. Join point `jp-2` is used to identify `jp-1` by determining when an iterator element is updated, which occurs when a method call can update the field of an `Employee` object. In this example, a call to the `raiseSalary(int)` method can call another method, that sets a `salary` field. Identifying `jp-2` requires an inter-procedural analysis because an aspect must discover that the method being called can either update an instance field or call a method that can update an instance field.

The need for AOP systems with both data-flow and inter-procedural join point identification mechanisms has been mentioned before by Kiczales [9]. Reasoning about inter-procedural data-flow information requires the use of a static program analysis based on abstract interpretation [2], which are commonly used for compilation. Our approach in Splice is to enable an aspect to encode an analysis that determines how a program's execution is transformed by the aspect.

An aspect in Splice is expressed as a collection of rules in a logic programming language with temporal and negation operators. Aspect rules control the propagation of flow information during an analysis; i.e., they can concisely describe flow functions. Aspect rules also operate over a program representation that helps programmers deal with the complexity of variable re-assignment, branches, and loops. The analysis specified by an aspect is automatically divided into multiple passes and stages, which transparently ensures the sound and complete evaluation of rules in the presence of negation. With these features, Splice aspects that perform useful tasks can be expressed with a manageable amount of code; e.g., a Splice aspect that implements the transformation in this section consists of nine rules and 35 logic terms.

The program analysis defined by an aspect is performed over a finite domain of facts that is computed by applying an aspect's rules to a program. A standard gen-kill iterative data-flow analysis algorithm is used to traverse all points in a program repeatedly until fix-points are reached. The analysis supports both forward and backward flows, and is also inter-procedural. Propagation of facts between procedures is flow-insensitive and context-insensitive to enhance scalability. Although flow-insensitive inter-procedural fact propagation sacrifices precision, an aspect can often use static type information to compensate for the precision loss.

We have used a prototype of Splice to write and test complete aspects in the areas of domain-specific optimizations and synchronization. The rest of this paper is organized as follows. Section 2 provides an overview of Splice. Section 3 demonstrates how the transformation in this Section can be implemented in Splice. Section 4 describes Splice's design and implementation. Section 5 presents an informal evaluation of Splice. Related work and our conclusions are presented in Sections 6 and 7.

2   Splice Overview

We introduce Splice by showing how it can be used to write an aspect that implements a synchronization policy. However, before we describe this synchronization policy and show how it is implemented in Splice, we present Splice's basic features.

2.1 Basics

Facts are used in Splice to represent knowledge about a program being processed by an aspect. For example, the fact `Locked([getBalance()],[Accnt.lock])` specifies that the lock `Accnt.lock` must be acquired around `getBalance()` method calls. Aspects are expressed as a collection of rules that manipulate a program by proving and querying facts about the program. A rule is composed out of rule variables, consequents, and antecedents in a form like `rule R0 [x] P(x): Q(x);`, which reads as "for any binding of rule variable x, consequent `P(x)` is a fact whenever antecedent `Q(x)` is a fact." Splice supports bottom-up logic programming, so unlike Prolog the consequents of a rule become facts as soon as the rule's antecedents are facts. By rule R0, `P(5)` is a fact whenever `Q(5)` is a fact, where *unification* binds x to 5 so that the structure of antecedent `Q(x)` is equivalent to the structure of fact `Q(5)`.

Predicates generalize facts like classes generalize objects; e.g., `Locked` is the predicate of fact `Locked([getBalance()],[Accnt.lock])`. Built-in predicates have names that begin with `@`. The built-in predicate `@now` is used to inspect the expressions of the Java program being processed. Consider the definition of a rule from an aspect that implements a synchronization policy:

```
rule S0 [var,lck,obj,args,mthd] Track(var,lck), Needs(var,lck):
                @now(var = obj.mthd(|args)), Locked(mthd,lck);
```

The antecedent `@now(var = obj.mthd(|args))` in rule S0 identifies a call to a method (`mthd`) on an object (`obj`) with arguments (`args`) and a result (`var`). The body of a `@now` antecedent is expressed in a Java-like expression syntax that can refer to rule variables or Java identifiers. An exception to standard Java syntax is the use of the tail operator (`|`), which is used in (`|args`) to specify that `args` is the list of the call's arguments. For unification purposes, the expressions in a Java program are treated as facts, where Java constructs and variables are listed in brackets. When rule S0 is applied to the Java expression `x = accntA.getBalance()`, rule variable var is bound to Java variable `[x]`, obj is bound to `[accntA]`, mthd is bound to method `[getBalance()]`, and args is bound to the empty list.

Although we refer to source code variables `[x]` and `[accntA]` in facts for example purposes, aspects do not directly process source code. Instead, aspects process a control-flow graph (CFG) of a procedure's expressions, where all expression results are assigned to unique temporary variables. The Java syntax bodies of `@now` antecedents are "compiled" to unify with expressions in this representation. A discussion of the program representation aspects process is presented in Section 4.1.

2.2 Temporal Reasoning

The synchronization policy implemented in this section specifies that a certain lock must be acquired before a method call whose result is derived from some protected state. To ensure that a call result remains consistent with the protected state, which could be updated in another thread, the lock must be held as long as the call result can be used. To implement this synchronization policy, an aspect must reason about how and when variables are used. Consider the following three lines of code that withdraw `[z]` amount of money from an account `accntA`:

```
A: x = accntA.getBalance();
B: y = x - z;
C: accntA.setBalance(y);
```

If lock `Accnt.lock` protects `getBalance()` method calls, `Accnt.lock` must be acquired before line A and released after line C because variable `[x]` is assigned at line A and variable `[y]`, which requires the same lock because it is derived from the value of variable `[x]`, is used at line C. Implementing this reasoning in Splice begins by identifying three kinds of facts from the problem description.

First, a `Locked(method, lock)` fact identifies a `method` whose call results must be protected by a `lock`. For the example code, we assume the fact `Locked([getBalance()], [Accnt.lock])` is true. Second, a `Needs(variable, lock)` fact identifies program execution points where a `lock` must be held to ensure a `variable` is consistent with some protected state. For the example code, the fact `Needs([x], [Accnt.lock])` should be true from after line A until just after line B to ensure that the lock is held when variable `[x]` can be used. To implement this behavior, `Needs` facts should *flow forward*; i.e., they should be propagated forward to following CFG points. Third, a `WillUse(variable)` fact identifies program execution points where a `variable` can possibly be used at future execution points. For the example code, the fact `WillUse([y])` should be true before line C because variable `[y]` will be used at line C. To implement this behavior, `WillUse` facts should *flow backward*; i.e., they should be propagated backward to preceding CFG points.

```
global Locked(method,variable); backward WillUse(variable);
forward Needs(variable,lock), Track(variable,lock;)

rule S0a [lck,var,mthd] Needs(var,lck), Track(var,lck):
            @now(var = *.mthd(|*)),  Locked(mthd,lck);
rule S0b [var0,var1,lck,args] Needs(var1,lck), Track(var1,lck):
            @nowi(var1,args), @contains(args,var0), Track(var0,lck);
```

Fig. 1. Predicates and rules that are used to define `Needs` facts.

Predicate declarations involved in the definitions of `Needs` and `WillUse` facts are shown at the top of Figure 1. When a predicate is declared by an aspect, its flow and arguments are specified. The declaration `global Locked(method, variable)` specifies that facts of the `Locked` predicate have two arguments and a global flow, meaning they are true at any point in a program's execution. `WillUse` facts are declared with backward flows, and `Needs` and `Track` facts are declared with forward flows.

Rules S0a and S0b in Figure 1 define how `Needs` facts are proven. Rule S0a specifies that a variable is tracked (`Track(var, lck)`) and a lock needs to be held for the variable (`Needs(var, lck)`) when the variable is assigned from a call (`@now(var = *.mthd(|*))`) and the called method is associated with the lock (`Locked(mthd, lck)`). Wild card values (`*`) are placeholders for "any value." Rule S0b specifies that a variable var1 is tracked and locked when a variable var0 is tracked and locked, and var0 is in the argument list of variables (`@contains(args, var0)`) used by the expression that assigns var1 (@nowi(var1,args)). The @contains antecedent in rule S0b queries the membership of a variable (var1) in a list of variables (args). The @nowi antecedent in rule S0b unifies with all kinds of expressions in the same format; e.g., the expression y = x - z in the example code binds var1 to [y] and args to ([x],[z]).

```
rule S1 [var,args] WillUse(var):
  Track(var,*), @nowi(*,args), @contains(args,var);
rule S2 [var,lck] !Needs(var,lck): !WillUse(var), Needs(var,lck);
```

Fig. 2. Rules that define and use WillUse facts.

Rule S1 in Figure 2 defines how WillUse facts are proven. It specifies that a variable will be used (WillUse(var)) when it is tracked (Track(var,*)) and the current expression (@nowi(*,args)) uses the variable in its arguments (@contains-(args,var)). Track facts proven by rules S0a and S0b and queried by rule S1 address an inefficiency in bottom-up logic programming where all facts are proven as long as they can be derived by the aspect's rules, even if those facts are not useful to the aspect. If Track facts were not used, rule S1 would propagate WillUse facts anytime a variable was used in the program even though most of these facts would never be queried by other rules. Track facts also get around a restriction on how negation can be used in Splice, as will be discussed in Section 2.3.

A rule executes, or *fires*, when all of its antecedents are unified with facts or Java code. When a rule fires, it is associated with a *firing point* in a procedure's CFG. For any rule with a @now or @nowi antecedent, such as rules S0a, S0b, and S1, the firing point is the location of the expression that is unified with the antecedent. When applied to the example code, rule S0a fires at line A, S0b fires at line B, and S1 fires at lines B and C. When a rule fires, the forward and backward-flow facts it proves becomes true after and a backward-flow fact becomes true before the firing point of the rule. When rules S0a, S0b, and S1 are applied to the example code, fact Needs([x],[Accnt-.lock]) becomes true after line A, fact Needs([y],[Accnt.lock]) becomes true after line B, fact WillUse([x]) becomes true before line B, and fact WillUse([y]) becomes true before line C.

2.3 Negation

Rule S2 in Figure 2 specifies that a lock no longer needs to be held for a variable (!Needs(var,lck)) when the variable will no longer be used (!WillUse(var)) and the lock currently needs to be held for the variable (Needs(var,lck)). The negation of an antecedent or consequent occurs using the ! operator. A negated antecedent is true when it does not exist as a fact. Fact WillUse([y]) does not exist at and after line C in the example code at the beginning of Section 2.2, which restricts where rule S2 can fire. A negated consequent stops a fact from being true immediately after or before the firing point if the fact respectively has a forward or backward flow.

Because rule S2 does not have a @now or @nowi antecedent and its Needs consequent has a forward flow, it fires at the earliest point where its antecedents are true.

The firing point of a rule depends on the flow of its consequents; e.g., the firing point of a rule with a backward-flow consequent is the latest point where its antecedents are true. In the example code, line B is the earliest point where WillUse([x]) is false and Needs([x],[Accnt.lock]) is true, and line C is the earliest point where WillUse-([y]) is false and Needs([y],[Accnt.lock]) is true. Therefore, rule S2 fires twice in the example code: at line B to negate the fact Needs([x],[Accnt.lock]), and at line C to negate the fact Needs([y],[Accnt.lock]).

The rules in Figures 1 and 2 collectively describe an analysis whose execution must occur in two stages to ensure soundness. The first stage consists of a forward analysis pass that fires rules S0a and S0b followed by a backward analysis pass that fires rule S1. The second stage consists of a forward analysis pass that fires rule S2. The analysis must execute in two stages because the rule S2 negates a WillUse antecedent, so cannot fire until WillUse facts have been completely proven. Rules S0b and S1 in Figure 1 also refer to Track antecedents rather than Needs antecedents to prevent an invalid cyclic dependency between Needs and WillUse facts that would be rejected as invalid in Splice. As we will describe in Section 4.2, Splice automatically detects invalid dependencies and divides an analysis into multiple stages.

2.4 Advice

Using facts defined by rules in Figures 1 and 2, additional rules can insert code into a program to acquire and release locks. First, we need some way of keeping track of whether or not a lock is held. Forward-flow Has(lock) facts can describe when a lock is held. Rules that insert lock acquisition and release calls are shown in Figure 3. Rule S3 adds code to acquire a lock (@before(lck.[acquire]())) and keeps track of the held lock (Has(lck)) when the lock is not already held (!Has(lck)) and a method associated with the lock (Locked(mthd,lck)) is called (@now(*.mthd-(|*))). A @before consequent performs the before advice of AspectJ: it inserts code specified using a Java-like syntax at a new point that occurs immediately before the rule's firing point. Rule S4 adds code to release a lock (@after(lck.[release()])) and keeps track of the release (!Has(lck)) when the lock is currently held (Has-(lck)) and the lock no longer needs to be held for any variable (!Needs(*,lck)). An @after consequent performs the after advice of AspectJ: it inserts code at a new point that immediately occurs after the rule's firing point.

```
forward Has(lock);
rule S3 [lck,mthd] Has(lck), @before(lck.[acquire]()):
        !Has(lck), Locked(mthd,lck), @now(*.mthd(|*));
rule S4 [lck] !Has(lck), @after(lck.[release]()):
                        Has(lck), !Needs(*,lck);
```

Fig. 3. Two rules and a predicate that are used to insert synchronization code into a program.

When the rules in Figures 1, 2, and 3 are applied to the example code at the beginning of Section 2.2, the following code results:

```
+  Accnt.lock.acquire();
A: x = accntA.getBalance();
B: y = x - z;
C: accntA.setBalance(y);
+  Accnt.lock.release();
```

Rule S3 will fire at line A because lock Accnt.lock is not held. Rule S4 fires after line C because neither fact Needs([x],[Accnt.lock]), negated by rule S2 at line B, nor fact Needs([y],[Accnt.lock]), negated at line C, are true.

2.5   Assignments, Branches, and Loops

The example code described at the beginning of Section 2.2 does not contain branches, loops, or variable re-assignments. At first, these constructs appear to be very problematic because re-assignments create aliases, branches split and merge, and loops create an infinite number of values. However, an aspect programmer can often ignore these constructs because of the way a program is represented to the aspect (described in Section 4.1). Aspects can also specify how facts are propagated through splits and merges and inspect conditional branch tests (demonstrated in Section 3.1).

2.6   Inter-procedural Reasoning

In Section 2.2, we assumed the existence of the fact Locked([getBalance()],-[Accnt.lock]). Although this fact can be manually asserted in an aspect, using rules to prove Locked facts is appealing because an aspect is more reusable when it hard-codes less information. Locked facts have a global flow so when a Locked fact is a consequent of a rule processing the code of one method, that same Locked fact can be used as an antecedent by another rule processing the code of another method. Proving a global-flow fact in one method and querying it in another method is how inter-procedural analysis occurs in Splice.

To prove Locked facts in this example, a programmer manually specifies fields they want protected by a specific lock. Any method that returns the value of these fields directly or indirectly will also be protected by the lock. Also, any method that returns a locked method's call result is transitively protected by the lock. Consider the following code for class Account:

```
class Account {
  int balance;
  int getBalance() { return this.balance; }
  void setBalance(int x) { this.balance = x; }
  int debit(int z) { int y = this.getBalance() - z;
                     this.setBalance(y);  return y; } }
```

We assume that the programmer specifies that account balance state is to be protected by manually asserting the fact Locked([Account.balance],[Accnt.lock]) in an aspect (using the fact keyword). Since the method getBalance() returns the value of the balance field, a rule should prove the fact Locked([getBalance()],-[Accnt.lock]). Since the method debit(int) returns a result derived from a get-Balance() call, a rule should also prove the fact Locked([debit(int)],[Accnt-.lock]). Rules S5 and S6 that implement this behavior are shown in Figure 4. Rule

S5 is like rule S0 in Figure 1 except it identifies field access results, rather than method call results, that are protected by locks. Rule S6 identifies the current method as being protected by a lock (Locked(mthd,lck)) whenever a variable that needs the lock (Needs(var,lck)) is returned by the method (@now(return var)). Antecedents of the built-in predicate @current describe the method currently being processed by the aspect and its arguments; a wild card in rule S6 ignores the current method's arguments.

```
rule S5 [lck,var,fld] Track(var), Needs(var,lck):
               @now(var=*.fld), Locked(fld,lck);
rule S6 [lck,mthd,var] Locked(mthd,lck):
 Needs(var,lck), @current(mthd,*), @now(return var);
rule S3 [lck,mthd0,mthd1] Has(lck), @before(lck.[acquire]()):
 !Has(lck), Locked(mthd0,lck), @now(*.mthd0(|*)),
 @current(mthd1,*), !Locked(mthd1,lck);
rule S7 [lck,fld] Has(lck), @before(lck.[acquire]()):
 !Has(lck), Locked(fld,lck), @now(*.fld=*);
```

Fig. 4. Rules S5 and S6 that prove Locked facts and rule S3 modified from Figure 3 to not acquire locks in locked methods.

Without the modifications to rule S3 in Figure 4, a lock would be acquired inside methods getBalance() and debit(int) because they access fields and call methods protected by the lock. Rule S3 in Figure 4 is modified with two new antecedents that ensures the rule only fires in a method (@current(mthd1,*)) that is not already protected by the lock (!Locked(mthd1,lck)). Rule S7 in Figure 4 ensures that a lock is acquired whenever a protected field is assigned. Unlike the case of reading state, the lock does not need to be held for any duration longer than the point where the field is assigned. When rule S7 is applied to the above code, lock acquisition and release calls are made around the field store in method setBalance(int), but calls to method setBalance(int) are not protected since they do not return protected state.

The synchronization aspect described in this section is ready to do useful work with only nine rules composed of about forty consequents and antecedents. However, many possible program behaviors are not addressed by this aspect. For example, this aspect does not address the storing of data protected by a lock into an unprotected field because the implemented synchronization policy does not mention this behavior. This aspect can serve as a starting point to implement synchronization policies with more advanced features.

3   Loop Compression

The example described in Section 1 is a transformation that we refer to as *loop compression*. A loop compression is enabled by a fact Compress(original,compressed,-filter), which adds and maintains a compressed set that contains those elements of an original set for which the result of a filter method call on the element is true. Loop compression replaces any iteration over the original set with an iteration over the compressed set if elements are updated only when the result of a filter method call on the element is true. Loop compression can be divided into three sub-tasks: identify contexts where iteration replacement should occur (Section 3.1), identify operations that can update state (Section 3.2), and add and maintain the compressed set (Section 3.3).

3.1 Replacement

To understand the organization of the replacement task, consider an elaboration of the example code in Section 1:

```
-L1: Iterator i = this.employees  .iterator();
+L2: Iterator i = this.programmers.iterator();
     while (i.hasNext())
 L3: { Employee e = (Employee) i.next();
 L4:    if (e.isProgrammer())
 L5:      e.raiseSalary(+20);                    }
```

Loop compression rules should be able to replace line L1 with L2 by realizing that an element [e] of the iterator [i] is only updated when an isProgrammer() method call on it is true. Before being implemented in Splice, this description must be re-worded so that it is directly expressible in the temporal logic that Splice supports, where negation must be used to translate terms like "must," "only," and "unless." To do this, we can invert the problem description: if there is any situation where the isProgrammer() method is not called or its result is not conservatively known as true when an element of the iterator is updated, then replacement does not occur.

We first identify the kinds of facts involved in replacement. Compress and Updating(method) facts will be defined by rules in Section 3.2 and Section 3.3, but are needed to express rule antecedents in this section. Filter(object,filter) facts can describe the case where a filter method has been called on an object and the result of this method call is definitely true. Filter facts should have a forward flow because they indicate that the true path of a conditional has been taken. Filter facts should also be merged universally, so they do not remain true when the false path and true path of the conditional merge. Universal facts implement "meet over all paths" propagation semantics, meaning they are true at a point in a procedure's CFG only if they are true on all paths through the point. By default, facts implement "meet over any path" propagation semantics, meaning they are true at a point in a procedure's CFG as long as they are true on one path through the point. NonUpdated(iterator,filter) facts can describe the case where an element of an iterator can be updated when a filter method is not known to be true on that element. NonUpdated facts should have a backward flow because they convey what can happen in the future. Rules CT and NU in Figure 5 respectively prove Filter and NonUpdated facts. Rule RP in Figure 5 then uses these facts to implement field replacement.

Rule CT identifies a filter method whose result is true for an object (Filter(obj,-fltr)) when the true path of a conditional branch is taken that tests the result of a filter method call on the object (@true(obj.fltr())). To prevent unneeded Filter facts from being proven, the filter method must also be involved in a compression (Compress(*,*,fltr)). The @true antecedent used in rule U0 unifies with the first point of a true path for a conditional branch that tests its enclosed expression. Filter

```
global Updating(method), Compress(original,compressed,filter);
universal forward Filter(object,filter);
rule CT [obj,fltr]    Filter(obj,fltr):
 @true(obj.fltr()), Compress(*,*,fltr);

backward NonUpdated(iterator,filter);
rule NU [elm,it,fltr] NonUpdated(it,fltr):
 Compress(*,*,fltr), !Filter(elm,fltr),
 @past(elm=(*) it.[next]()), Updating(mthd), @now(elm.mthd(|*));

rule RP [it,obj,orig,cmps,fltr]
   @replace(it = obj.cmps.[iterator]()): !NonUpdated(it,fltr),
      @now(it = obj.orig.[iterator]()), Compress(orig,cmps,fltr);
```

Fig. 5. Splice code that implements field replacement in a loop compression aspect.

facts have a forward flow and are declared universal, so they are true at points along the true path of the conditional but becomes false as soon as the conditional's true and false paths merge.

Rule NU identifies an iterator whose elements are not updated when a filter method is true (NonUpdated(it,fltr)). This occurs when the next element of the iterator (@past(elm = (*) it.[next]())) is updated (Updating(mthd)), and the call result of a filter method on the iterator element is not known to be true (!Filter(elm,-fltr)). The Compress(*,*,fltr) antecedent is also needed in rule NU because unification cannot bind rule variable fltr through the negated Filter antecedent. Antecedents of the @past predicate inspect expressions like @now antecedents, except an @past antecedent unifies with a statement located at a point that always executes before the rule's firing point.

Rule RP implements the field access replacement portion of the loop compression aspect. The @replace consequent in rule RP performs AspectJ-style around[1] advice by replacing code that occurs at the rule's firing point. Replacement occurs at a field access used to create an iterator when a compression of the field exists (Compress-(orig,cmps,fltr)) and the iterator's elements is not updated when the filter method is not true (!NonUpdated(it,fltr)). Assuming the existence of facts Updating-([raiseSalary(int)]) and Compress([employees],[programmers], [isProgrammer()]), rule RP will replace line L1 with line L2 in the example code because rule NU cannot fire at any point in this code.

3.2 Detecting Updates

To understand the organization of the update identification task, consider the following code that implements a part of class Employee:

```
class Employee
{ private int salary; ...
   void setSalary(int n)   { salary = n; }
   void raiseSalary(int n)  { setSalary((salary*(100+n))/100); }}
```

---

[1] "Proceed" is subsumed in Splice by unification.

```
rule V0 [mthd,fld]   Updating(mthd):
                     @current(mthd,*), @now(this.fld = *);
rule V1 [mth0,mth1]  Updating(mth1):
   @current(mth1,*),Updating(mth0),@now(this.mth0(|*));
```

Fig. 6. Rules that generically prove Updating facts.

Loop compression rules should be able identify method setSalary(int) as an updating method because it sets the salary field of class Employee. The method raise-Salary(int) should also be identified as an updating method because it indirectly sets the salary field by calling the setSalary(int) method. The task of identifying updating methods is similar to the task of identifying methods protected by a lock in Figure 4 of Section 2.6. Rules V0 and V1 in Figure 6 identify updating methods simply by identifying methods whose code can update instance fields (rule V0) or identifying methods whose code can call updating methods (rule V1). Applying rules V0 and V1 to the code for class Employee will prove the facts Updating([setSalary(int)]) and Updating([raiseSalary(int)]).

3.3   Activation

To understand the organization of the task that adds and maintains a compressed set, consider the following code that implements a part of class Company:

```
class Company
{      Set employees   = new HashSet();
+ L0: Set programmers = new HashSet();
   void add(Employee e)
   {    employees.add(e);
+ L3: if (e.isProgrammer()) programmers.add(e); }
   void doit() { ... }                          }
```

The rules of a loop compression aspect add a new programmers field to class Company, initialize it to a set (line L0), and maintain it as a filtered subset of the set referred to by the employees field (line L3). Programmers activate loop compression by asserting DoCompress facts. When a programmer manually asserts a DoCompress-(original,filter) fact, the loop compression will compress an original field according to a filter method; e.g., the fact DoCompress([employees],[isProgrammer()]) directs the loop compression aspect to compress employees into a programmers set. When a DoCompress fact is asserted, the loop compression aspect must add the compressed field, initialize it, and maintain it. Rules that implement this behavior are shown in Figure 7.

Rule C0 introduces a new compressed field into a class with the same attributes of an original field when a programmer asserts a DoCompress fact. The @field antecedent in rule C0 queries the attributes of the original field. The @field consequent in rule C0 introduces a new compressed field into the same class and with the same attributes as the original field. For our example, the compressed field will not actually be named

```
global DoCompress(original,filter);
rule C0 [orig,cmps,fltr,T,name0,name1,flags] @uniqueid(name1),
 @field(cls,flags,T,name1,cmps), Compress(orig,cmps,fltr):
 @field(cls,flags,T,name0,orig), @isa(T, [Set]),
 DoCompress(orig,fltr);

rule C1 [orig,cmps,fltr,T,obj]   @after(obj.cmps = new T()):
        Compress(orig,cmps,fltr), @now(obj.orig = new T());

rule C2 [orig,cmps,fltr,elm]
        @after({ if (elm.fltr()) this.cmps.[add](elm); }):
  Compress(orig,cmps,fltr), @now(this.orig.[add](elm));

rule C3 [orig,cmps,fltr,elm] @after(this.cmps.[remove](elm)):
    Compress(orig,cmps,fltr), @now(this.orig.[remove](elm));
```

Fig. 7. Rules that prove and setup `Compress` facts.

`programmers`, but some unique name (`@uniqueid(name)`). The `@isa` antecedent in rule C0 ensures that the field type is compatible with `java.util.Set`. Rule C1 initializes the new field to an object in the same way an original object is initialized. Rules C2 and C3 ensure the compressed field is a subset of the original field that only contains elements that are true according to a specified filter method.

With nine rules composed of 35 consequents and antecedents, the loop compression aspect described in this section can be used in many situations. However, many details have not been addressed by the aspect's rules that might be significant in specific contexts. For example, this version of the loop compression aspect does not deal with removal through an iterator, alternative set add and remove mechanisms, pointer aliasing, and so on. Therefore, this loop compression aspect is not universally applicable and it is not meant to be a general compiler optimization. Instead, when to use the aspect is under programmer control, and the aspect's rules can be enhanced to handle special cases that may arise. The loop compression aspect can also be modified to accommodate more advanced kinds of filtering; e.g., arithmetic expressions or mapping relationships.

4 Technology

Splice can be described as a bottom-up (forward chaining) logic programming system with Java program manipulation capabilities. In bottom-up logic programming, a rule fires as soon as facts can unify with its antecedents, and facts proven by the firing rule are immediately used to fire other rules. With the addition of temporal logic and negation operators, bottom-up logic programming can express program analyses. Each point in the program's execution is associated with some code, which can be inspected by a rule to determine what facts about the program should propagate to future or past points, or even to points in other methods. Negation allows these rules to reason about what is not true at a point, and also to explicitly prevent the propagation of some facts.

The rest of this section describes Splice's major design and implementation issues. Section 4.1 describes how programs are represented to aspects, which influences how an aspect reasons about assignment, branching, and looping. Section 4.2 describes the role of negation in Splice's design, which is complicated by Splice's support for data-flow analysis. Section 4.3 describes the analysis performed by an aspect. Finally, Section 4.4 discusses the implementation of our Splice prototype.

4.1 Program Representation

Splice aspects analyze programs in a "flat" non-syntax tree representation where the result of every expression is assigned to a unique temporary variable. Because of ambiguity relating to multiple variable assignments, Splice transforms a program into single static assignment (SSA) form, where an SSA variable identifies the result of evaluating a single Java expression [3]. Instead of source code variables, SSA variables are bound to rule variables during unification with @now, @nowi, and @past antecedents. There are two issues with SSA that are addressed in Splice. First, SSA variables assigned in loops are actually reassigned dynamically, so the same SSA variable can refer to different values during an analysis. Second, SSA variables that merge multiple SSA variable together, known as ϕ *variables*, create aliases, so the set of facts true for the ϕ variable and the variable it merges together are related.

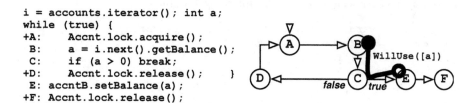

```
i = accounts.iterator(); int a;
while (true) {
+A:    Accnt.lock.acquire();
 B:    a = i.next().getBalance();
 C:    if (a > 0) break;
+D:    Accnt.lock.release();    }
 E:  accntB.setBalance(a);
+F:  Accnt.lock.release();
```

Fig. 8. Code that iterates through a list of accounts (left), and an illustration (right) of when the fact WillUse([a]) is true in the code's CFG (right).

The first issue is dealt with by automatically "expiring" (negating) a forward or backward-flow fact at a point where an SSA variable it refers to is assigned. Expiration of a forward-flow fact occurs immediately at the point of assignment, and expiration of a backward-flow fact occurs by not propagating it to points that precede the assignment. As an example of how expiration works, consider how the synchronization aspect in Section 2 is applied to the code in Figure 8. Variable [a] is assigned at line B in a loop and used at line E outside of the loop. By rule s1 in Figure 2, fact WillUse([a]) will become true before line E, which is then propagated backwards so it is true at lines C and B (illustrated in Figure 8). However, since variable [a] is assigned at line B, the WillUse fact will not be true before line B. This results in fact WillUse([a]) not being true along the false path from line C, so the lock can correctly be released in the loop at line D. Because facts can expire when they refer to values created in loops, aspect programmers must carefully ensure that forward and backward-flow facts are still true when needed by only associating them with values known to still be in use.

The second issue is dealt with by "transferring" forward or backward-flow facts between a ϕ variable and variables it merges together. To explain how fact transferring works, consider a ϕ variable m_1 that merges variables i_0 and i_2 together. When the forward or backward-flow fact P(i_0) is proven in a scope where m_1 exists, fact P(m_1) is automatically proven if P is not universal. If P is universal, then fact P(m_1) is proven true if fact P(i_2) is also proven true. When fact P(m_1) is proven true, facts P(i_0) and P(i_2) are automatically proven true only if P is not universal. The explicit negation of a forward or backward-flow fact is handled in an analogous way. Fact expiration and transferring have an important interaction: fact transferring between a ϕ variable and one of its merged variables only occurs as long as both variables are not reassigned.

The way forward and backward-flow facts expire and are transfered via ϕ variable relationships enables inductive reasoning about loop behavior. Consider the following loop in SSA form that sets elements of an array to 0:

```
i_0 = 0; while (true)
{ m_1 = φ(i_0,i_2);
  if (m_1 >= a.length) break;
  a[m_1] = 0; i_2 = m_1 + 1; }
```

At the point where the above loop breaks, an aspect can recognize that every element of the array has been set to zero using the following three rules:

```
universal forward Zeroed(array,index), Zeroed(array);
rule Z0 [i]     Zeroed(*,i): @now(i=0);
rule Z1 [a,i,j] Zeroed(a,j):
    Zeroed(a,i), @past(a[[i]]=0), @now(j=i+1);
rule Z2 [a,i] Zeroed(a): @false(i>=a.length), Zeroed(a,i);
```

Rule Z0 proves the zeroed base case, where the array index is zero, and rule Z1 proves the zeroed inductive case, where the index is incremented by one. Rule Z2 detects the end of the above loop where the array has been completely zeroed out. When variable m_1 is assigned, the facts Zeroed(*,[i_0]) and Zeroed([a],[i_2]) are true, so fact Zeroed([a],[m_1]) is true. Rule Z1 associates zeroed information with the next index of the loop because any fact that refers to the current index stored in variable m_1 will expire at the beginning of the next loop iteration where m_1 is reassigned.

4.2 Negation

Support for negation is necessary in Splice because it enables reasoning about negative information; i.e., events that cannot occur in a program. Without negation, the aspects described in Sections 2 and 3 and many other useful aspects could not be expressed in Splice. Negation is implemented in Splice with the following constraint: the proof of a fact must not depend on its negation, which is referred to as the *stratified negation* [1] in a logic program. Because forward and backward-flow facts become true after or before, but not at, rule firing points, the proof of these facts can depend on their negation in certain circumstances. However, temporal paradoxes must not occur. Consider the following two rules:

```
backward WillRise(stock); forward Buy(stock);
rule G0 [stck] Buy(stck): WillRise(stck);
rule G1 [stck] !WillRise(stck): Buy(stck);
```

Rules G0 and G1 form a temporal paradox that has no well-defined meaning in Splice. Splice will reject aspect executions when a fact depends on its negation. If the fact is a forward or backward-flow fact, then it can depend on its negation if the negation only occurs through facts of the same flow. These criteria are checked conservatively, and its possible for Splice to reject an aspect execution that actually has a well-defined meaning. However, stratification in Splice is local [13], where facts are stratified dynamically rather than statically, which accepts more aspect executions than more restrictive syntactic stratification.

When no contradictions exist, an aspect's execution has a unique perfect model that ensures soundness [1]: i.e., no facts are proven that are not true. The perfect model ensures that a rule does not fire until it is definitely known where or not that a fact can unify with a non-negated antecedent or no fact can unify with a negated antecedent. For an executing aspect, contradictions are detected and the perfect model is found through a dependency graph that associates facts with the proven and negated facts their proofs or negations can depend on. When the proof or negation of fact f depends on the proof or negation of fact g, the "stage" where the proof or negation of fact f is definitely known is computed according the two following constraints:

1. The proof or negation of fact f is not known at least until proof or negation of fact g is known;
2. If fact f and g are not both forward-flow or are not both backward-flow, then the proof or negation of fact f is not known until after the proof or negation of fact g;

As an example, consider the synchronization aspect in Section 2. When the aspect is applied to a program, the negation of its forward-flow Needs and Has facts are not known until the second stage of the analysis because their proofs depend on negated backward-flow WillUse facts. A rule with negated antecedents cannot fire until the latest stage where the negation of all facts that can unify with its negated antecedents are known. Therefore, rule S2 in Figure 2 and rule S4 in Figure 3 will not fire until the second stage of the aspect's execution.

The fact dependency graph is computed in a pre-processing step of the implementation that applies the rules of an aspect to a program in a flow-insensitive way that ignores negated antecedents. Computing the fact dependency graph is only a secondary by-product of pre-processing, which is essential in simplifying the analysis described in Section 4.3 by narrowing the set of rules that can fire at each point and computing a finite domain of facts that can be true during analysis.

4.3 Analysis

As just described, an analysis in Splice is divided into multiple stages to support the sound execution of any negation used in an aspect, which ensures that analysis execution is monotonic. Each stage is itself divided into multiple forward, backward, and flow-insensitive passes. Rules with forward and backward-flow consequents are only fired respectively during forward and backward analysis passes. Rules with global-flow consequents are fired during a flow-insensitive pass. The direction of an analysis pass determines the order that CFG points are traversed, which will determine the firing point of a rule that can otherwise fire at multiple adjacent points. For a forward analysis pass, a rule will fire at a point closest to the entrance of a procedure. For a backward analysis pass, a rule will fire at a point closest to the exits of a procedure.

For each stage of an analysis, analysis passes are continually performed until no new facts can be proven; i.e., the stage reaches a fix-point. The execution of individual forward and backward analysis passes are very standard finite-domain iterative data-flow analyses. A set of dirty CFG nodes, initially the entry node (forward) or exit nodes (backward) of a method, tracks what CFG nodes need to be traversed. Traversal of a node manages fact expiration and transferring and fires rules according to the code at the node and facts that are true at the node. A set of resulting facts is propagated to the nodes that follow (forward) or precede (backward) the node, adding any node to the dirty set whose set of true facts changes. A fix-point for a forward or backward analysis pass is reached when the dirty set is empty.

4.4   Implementation

Aspect execution in our current prototype of Splice consists of five steps:

1. The Java bytecode of the program is transformed into a CFG-based SSA form.
2. As described in Section 4.2, the rules of an aspect are applied to the program in a flow-insensitive way. Pre-processing computes a fact dependency graph and for each program point, a set of pre-unified rules that can fire at the point. This simplifies the firing of rules in Step four.
3. A fact-dependency analysis described in Section 4.2 detects invalid proof dependencies and computes analysis stages where facts are known.
4. Analysis is performed as described in Section 4.3.
5. Proven code advice facts (e.g., `@after`) are type checked, and compiled into the resulting Java bytecode of the program. Any detected type errors or conflicts will result in an aspect execution error.

5   Discussion

In this section we informally evaluate Splice's design, implementation, and usefulness.

5.1   Usability

Splice is designed to provide aspects with accessible analysis capabilities. As a result, many of Splice's features reduce the amount of effort needed to express an analysis. Splice's internal use of an SSA representation eases reasoning about variable re-assignment, branches, and loops. Stratified negation eliminates concerns about the sound use of negation and the repetition of analysis passes ensures completeness. Soundness and completeness, however, only apply to the execution of an aspect's rules. Splice itself cannot guarantee that the programmer's rules are correct!

Even with its usability features, the task of expressing an analysis in Splice is non-trivial. An aspect programmer must design an analysis using temporal logic, which is not a core programming skill and can be very tricky to use correctly. In the course of developing the two aspects in Section 2 and Section 3, we found that most of our bugs were related to mistakes in understanding the temporal properties of the aspects. Part of this problem arises from the use of negation and multiple rules to encode natural English terms such as "only," "must," and "unless" (Section 3.1), where the encoding often introduces bugs into the aspect.

It is easy to make mistakes in the encoding of an aspect. Therefore, the ability to debug a Splice aspect is very important. The most straightforward way for a programmer to debug an aspect is to view how it transforms a program, and then debug the aspect along with the program. Debugging will also require an inspection of the aspect's reasoning of why it transforms a program in some way. Unfortunately, our current Splice prototype does not provide any debugging support.

5.2 Precision

Aspect programmers can only expect so much precision from an analysis in Splice. Although analysis precision is not significantly limited by branching, looping, and variable re-assignments, an analysis cannot correlate when multiple conditional branches are resolved the same way; e.g., according to whether or not a debug flag is set. The most significant source of imprecision occurs in analyzing how methods interact with each other. By making global facts visible between method implementations in a flow-insensitive way, analysis sacrifices precision so its execution time can scale linearly with the size of a program. Among other things, an inter-procedural analysis is not accurate enough to reason about dynamic dispatch and the effects of execution on memory, including pointer aliasing. Sometimes, this imprecision is acceptable because static information about the program, such as static types, can be used by an aspect to fill in the gaps. However, commonly used programming styles that avoid the use of static information can defeat these assumptions. Examples of these styles in Java include the use of reflection or calling a generic `run()` method in the `Runnable` interface.

One solution to the precision problem is to make analysis in Splice more powerful; e.g., flow-sensitive inter-procedural, context-sensitive, path-sensitive, and capable of performing shape analysis. However, these mechanisms will not scale to analyzing large programs. The other solution relies on the aspect programmer to make up for the lost precision through the encoding of additional rules and manually asserted facts. For example, alias annotations could be encoded in an aspect and verified by its rules in a scalable way. However, this requires more effort from programmers to encode what otherwise could be automatically derived.

5.3 Performance

Automatically ensuring the soundness (Section 4.2) and completeness (Section 4.3) of an aspect requires that a Splice aspect execute about half as fast as a comparable traditional analysis. For example, the analysis expressed by the synchronization aspect in Section 2 requires at least six passes to execute when only three passes are really needed to execute the analysis correctly. The extra passes in our approach are only used to recognize that completeness has occurred.

We believe that the performance of our prototype implementation is adequate. When using our prototype implementation to apply the loop compression aspect in Section 3 to a Java program of 1000 lines, execution takes about 40 seconds[2]. Though not very fast, execution time rises linearly as the size of the program grows, which is not surprising since the inter-procedural analysis used in Splice is flow-insensitive. The bottleneck in our current prototype is not analysis, rather, it is the pre-processing step used to perform the rule unification that simplifies the analysis step. The pre-processing step can become very slow as the number of possibly true global-flow facts increases because they require re-processing of the whole program.

5.4   Applicability

This paper has shown how Splice can be used to write fairly complete synchronization and loop compression aspects. Whereas AspectJ effectively enables the separation of simple concerns related to tracing, logging, security, and instrumentation, Splice expands this domain to include concerns that require data-flow information. Unfortunately, Splice is not dramatically better than AspectJ in addressing complex functionality concerns in real programs where join points must be identified manually. This restriction may negate any advantages Splice has over AspectJ in implementing these concerns.

The synchronization and loop compression aspects shown in this paper provide some evidence that using Splice is worthwhile for implementing concerns that are related to characteristics of a program execution like performance and robustness. Similar to loop compression, Splice can be used to automate domain-specific optimizations that currently need to be performed by hand. Similar to synchronization, Splice can be used to automate the addition of "policy" code into a program, although the programmer will probably need to manually accept these code additions because of constraints on analysis precision. Although not explored in this paper, Splice could also be used to implement better "static-advice aspects" that only check program properties, such as enforcing Law of Demeter rules that ensure loose object coupling [11].

6   Related Work

Aspect-oriented programming based on code transformations at join points is enabled by AspectJ [10]. AspectJ pointcut designators can identify execution events such as a method call and field accesses as they occur in isolation. The cflow pointcut designator provides some inter-procedural reasoning capabilities by allowing an aspect to dynamically inspect program control-flow through the call stack. Splice does not currently provide cflow-like inspection capabilities.

Currently, AspectJ provides no support for static data-flow or inter-procedural analysis. However, proposals have been made to enhance AspectJ with a data-flow pointcut designator dflow and a prediction-based pointcut designator pcflow [9]. The dflow designator is proposed to reason about how a Java value is computed in the data-flow

---

[2] We ran on a Powerbook G4 @ 867 MHz.

of a method. The `pcflow` designator is proposed to reason about what join points can occur in the future of a program's control-flow, including what join points can occur when a method is called. Although the `pcflow` designator has only been mentioned, a version of the `dflow` designator has actually been prototyped and shown to be useful in security applications [12]. Unlike Splice, this `dflow` designator is not implemented using static analysis; instead, special data-flow tags are propagated and inspected at run-time.

Using logic programming features in a meta-programming language is referred to as logic meta-programming (LMP). TyRuBa is a LMP system for manipulating Java code [5]. The Smalltalk Open Unification Language (SOUL) [15] enables Prolog programs to manipulate the execution of Smalltalk programs. Neither system provides meta-programs with data-flow analysis capabilities. The case for expressing program analysis problems in a general logic programming system is made in [4]. Splice does not rely on a general logic programming system—it is designed specifically to support static analysis. Path logic programming extends Prolog with program transformation and static analysis capabilities [6, 14]. Splice differs from path logic programming by concentrating on higher-level transformations needed to do AOP.

Splice can be viewed as an extensible compilation system; e.g., the loop compression aspect in Section 3 is an example of how an aspect can implement domain-specific optimizations. Magik [7] allows programmers to incorporate application-specific extensions into the compilation process. The Broadway compiler [8] can utilize programmer-supplied annotations to optimize library operations. In contrast to these systems, Splice aspects performs anayses and transformations through higher-level LMP abstractions.

7   Conclusions and Future Work

Splice is the first AOP system that provides aspects with static analysis mechanisms to identify join points. Splice aspects are written in a rule-based language with logic programming features that provide convenient access to static analysis mechanisms. Although Splice aspects are not omnipotent, e.g., they cannot reason about pointer aliasing, they can still be useful in improving programmer productivity.

Looking forward, we are currently exploring how join points can be used more expressively once they have been identified. Current mechanisms for expressing advice in Splice and AspectJ are not very declarative and could benefit from more powerful reasoning facilities like those used to identify join points in Splice. Solving this problem of "join point specification" will make AOP systems better platforms for generative programming.

Splice has been implemented and used to write the loop compression and synchronization aspects presented in this paper. We expect to make the prototype publicly available in the near future on our web site at www.cs.utah.edu/plt/splice.

Acknowledgements

We thank Eric Eide, Matthew Flatt, Gary Lindstrom, and the anonymous reviewers for comments on drafts of this paper. Sean McDirmid and Wilson Hsieh were supported in full by NSF CAREER award CCR–9876117.

References

1. K. R. Apt, H. A. Blair, and A. Walker. Towards a theory of declarative knowledge. In *Foundations of Deductive Databases and Logic Programming*, pages 89–147, 1988.
2. P. Cousot and R. Cousot. Abstract interpretation: a unified lattice model for static analysis by construction and approximation of fixpoints. In *Proc. of POPL*, pages 238–252, Jan. 1977.
3. R. Cytron, J. Ferrante, B. K. Rosen, M. N. Wegman, and F. K. Zadeck. Efficient computing static single assignment form and the control dependence graph. In *ACM Transactions on Programming Languages and Systems, 13(4)*, pages 84–97, Oct. 1991.
4. S. Dawson, C. R. Ramakrishnan, and D. S. Warren. Practical program analysis using general logic programming systems - a case study. In *Proc. of PLDI*, pages 117–126, June 1996.
5. K. De Volder. Type-oriented logic meta programming. PhD Thesis, 2001.
6. S. Drape, O. de Moor, and G. Sittampalam. Transforming the .NET intermediate language using path logic programming. In *Proc. of PPDP*, Oct. 2002.
7. D. R. Engler. Incorporating application semantics and control into compilation. In *Proc. of DSL*, pages 103–118, Oct. 1997.
8. S. Z. Guyer and C. Lin. An annotation language for optimizing software libraries. In *Proc. of DSL*, Oct. 1999.
9. G. Kiczales. The fun has just begun, Mar. 2003. Presentation at AOSD.
10. G. Kiczales, E. Hilsdale, J. Hungunin, M. Kersten, J. Palm, and W. Griswold. An overview of AspectJ. In *Proc. of ECOOP*, June 2001.
11. K. Lieberherr, D. H. Lorenz, and P. Wu. A case for statically executable advice: Checking the Law of Demeter with AspectJ. In *Proc. of AOSD*, Mar. 2003.
12. H. Masuhara and K. Kawauchi. Dataflow pointcut in aspect-oriented programming. In *Proc. of APLAS*, Nov. 2003.
13. T. Przymusinski. On the declarative semantics of deductive database and logic programs. In *Foundations of Deductive Databases and Logic Programming*, pages 193–216, 1988.
14. G. Sittampalam, O. de Moor, and K. F. Larsen. Incremental execution of transformation specifications. In *Proc. of POPL*, Jan. 2004.
15. R. Wuyts. Declarative reasoning about the structure of object-oriented systems. In *Proc. of TOOLS USA*, pages 112–124, 1998.

A Generative Approach
to Aspect-Oriented Programming

Douglas R. Smith

Kestrel Institute, Palo Alto, CA 94304, USA
smith@kestrel.edu

Dedicated to the memory of Robert Paige

Abstract. Aspect-Oriented Software Development (AOSD) offers new
insights and tools for the modular development of systems with crosscutting features. Current tool support for AOSD is provided mainly in
the form of code-level constructs. This paper presents a way to express
cross-cutting features as logical invariants and to use generative techniques to produce the kind of code that is usually written manually in
AOSD. In order to state invariants that express cross-cutting features,
we often need to reify certain extra-computational values such as history
or the runtime call stack. The generative approach is illustrated by a
variety of examples.

1 Introduction

Aspect-Oriented Software Development (AOSD) contributes to the broad goal
of modular programming, with a particular focus on cross-cutting concerns [1,
2]. A concern is cross-cutting if its manifestation cuts across the dominant hierarchical structure of a program. A simple example is an error logging policy –
the requirement to log all errors in a system in a standard format. Error logging
necessitates the addition of code that is distributed throughout the system code,
even though the concept is easy to state in itself. Cross-cutting concerns explain
a significant fraction of the code volume and interdependencies of a system. The
interdependencies complicate the understanding, development, and evolution of
the system.

AOSD, as exemplified by AspectJ [3], is based on a key insight: many crosscutting concerns correspond to classes of runtime events. One can think of aspects as providing a kind of "whenever" construct: whenever an event of type e
occurs during execution, perform action a. For example, whenever an exception
is thrown, log it. The runtime events are called *join points*, descriptions of join
points are called *pointcuts*, and the method-like actions to apply at joinpoints
are called *advice*. An *aspect* is a modular treatment of a crosscutting concern
that is composed of pointcuts, advice, and other Java code. The process of detecting when events of type e occur and folding action a into the code may occur
statically (i.e. the actions are folded into the source code), or dynamically (e.g.
in Java, the actions are triggered by tests for the e events in the JVM).

G. Karsai and E. Visser (Eds.): GPCE 2004, LNCS 3286, pp. 39–54, 2004.

AOSD typically has a programming language character in order to attract a wide user community. AspectJ for example [3] targets Java programmers: aspects are written in a Class-like syntax and have a semantics that closely adheres to Java semantics. Despite its attractiveness to programmers, this code-level approach has its disadvantages. First, the intent of an aspect may not be clear, since it is stated operationally. Second, the correctness of an aspect may be difficult to ascertain or to prove. Third, the completeness of the pointcut (i.e. will the pointcut apply to all occurrences of the intended runtime events?) may not be obvious. Fourth, the advice method may need to embody many case distinctions that cater for the various contexts that arise at the joinpoints, giving rise to inefficiency and complexity. Fifth, aspects may interfere with one another – since the order in which they are applied makes a semantic difference, the burden is on the programmer to order them and resolve interferences. Sixth, evolution of the program may require extending the pointcut and advice description to cover any extra cases (which requires an understanding of the modified set of runtime events being targeted, and what code to execute in each specific context of occurrence). In addition, the AspectJ pointcut description language has limited expressiveness; for example, security constraints typically disallow certain behavior patterns which do not correspond to a natural class of run-time events (cf. [4]).

In this paper we present a generative approach to AOSD that aims to overcome these disadvantages. Generative programming has the broad goals of reducing the effort in producing and evolving programs by generating them from high-level models or specifications. The result is higher assurance of correctness, greater productivity through automation, and reduced cost of evolution by allowing change at the model level versus the code level. In a sense, AOSD is a special case of generative programming, with a valuable special emphasis on treatment of crosscutting concerns.

Our approach is (1) to express an aspect by a logical invariant, and (2) to generate code to maintain the invariant throughout the system. The generated maintenance code corresponds to statically woven advice in AspectJ, and could be expressed either directly as AspectJ aspects, or by direct generation and insertion of maintenance code into the system. To state invariants that express cross-cutting features often entails the need to reify certain extra-computational values such as history or the runtime call stack.

The generative techniques in this paper derive from transformational work on incremental computation, in particular Bob Paige's pioneering work on Finite Differencing [5]. Finite Differencing is intended to optimize programs by replacing expensive expressions by new data structures and incremental computation. It achieves this by maintaining invariants of the form $c = f(x)$ where c is a fresh variable, x is a vector of program variables, and $f(x)$ is an expensive expression (usually in a loop). Code to maintain the invariant is automatically generated and inserted at points where the dependent variables change.

After introducing some notation, we work through a variety of examples and conclude with general discussion and directions for future work.

2   Preliminaries

For purposes of this paper, a behavior of a program can be represented graphically as alternating states and actions

$$state_0 \xrightarrow{act_0} state_1 \xrightarrow{act_1} state_2 \xrightarrow{act_2} state_3 \cdots$$

or more formally as a sequence of triples of the form $\langle state_i, act_i, state_{i+1} \rangle$, where states are a mapping from variables to values, and actions are state-changing operations (i.e. program statements). The details of representing an action are not important here, although some form of concrete or abstract syntax suffices. The representation is a system-, language- and application-specific decision. The operators nil and $append$, written $S :: a$, construct sequences, including behaviors. The selectors on behaviors are

$$preState(\langle state_0, act, state_1 \rangle) = state_0$$
$$action(\langle state_0, act, state_1 \rangle) = act$$
$$postState(\langle state_0, act, state_1 \rangle) = state_1$$

If x is a state variable and s a state, then $s.x$ denotes the value of x in s. Further, in the context of the action triple $\langle state_0, act, state_1 \rangle$, x will refer to the value of x in the preState, $state_0.x$, and x' refers to the value in the postState, $state_1.x$.

Several higher-order operators will be useful:

image: Written $f \star S$, computes the image of f over a sequence S:

$$f \star nil = nil$$
$$f \star (S :: a) = (f \star S) :: f(a)$$

filter: Written $p \triangleright S$, computes the subsequence of S comprised of elements that satisfy p:

$$p \triangleright nil = nil$$
$$p \triangleright (S :: a) = if\ p(a)\ then\ (p \triangleright S) :: a\ else\ p \triangleright S$$

always: The temporal logic operator $\Box I$ holds for a behavior when I is true for each state in the sequence.

We specify actions in a pre- and post-condition style. For example, the specification

assume: $x \geq 0$
achieve: $x' * x' = x \ \wedge \ x' \geq 0$

is satisfied by the action $x := \sqrt{x}$.

This paper presents its results in a generic imperative language framework, even though most AOSD approaches target object-oriented languages and even though some of the details of static analysis and code generation are necessarily language-specific. The specifications that we work with are sufficiently abstract that we believe it will not be difficult to generate code in most current programming languages.

3 An Example

A simple example serves to introduce the technique: maintaining an error log for a system. More precisely, whenever an exception handler is invoked, we require that an entry be made in an error log.

The overall approach is to specify an invariant that gives a declarative semantical definition of our requirement, and then to generate aspectual code from it. First, what does the error log mean as a data structure? Informally, the idea is that at any point in time t, the error log records a list of all exceptions that have been raised by the program up to time t. In order to formalize this we need some way to discuss the history of the program at any point in time.

Maintaining a History Variable.

The execution history of the program can be reified into the state by means of a *virtual* variable (also called a shadow or ghost variable). That is, imagine that with each action taken by the program there is a concurrent action to update a variable called *hist* that records the history up until the current state.

$$s_0 \xrightarrow[\;hist := hist::\langle s_0,act_0,s_1\rangle\;]{act_0} s_1 \xrightarrow[\;hist := hist::\langle s_1,act_1,s_2\rangle\;]{act_1} s_2 \xrightarrow[\;hist := hist::\langle s_2,act_2,s_3\rangle\;]{act_2} s_3 \cdots$$

Obviously this would be an expensive variable, but it is only needed for specification purposes, and usually only a residue of it will appear in the executable code.

Invariant.

Given the history variable, $action \star hist$ represents the sequence of actions so far in the execution history. To express the invariant, we need a test for whether an action represents an error; i.e. whether it represents the invocation of an exception handler. Let $error?(act)$ be true when act is an exception, so $error? \triangleright action \star hist$ is the sequence of error actions so far in the execution history.

We can now represent the semantics of the error log:

Invariant: $\Box\; errlog \;=\; error? \triangleright action \star hist$

i.e. in any state, the value of the variable *errlog* is the sequence of error actions that have occurred previously.

The idea is that the programmer asserts this formula as a requirement on the code. It is a cross-cutting requirement since exceptions can be raised anywhere in the code, regardless of its structure.

Disruptive Code and Static Analysis.

In order to enforce the invariance of the asserted formula, we must find all actions in the code that could possibly disrupt the invariant, and then generate new code for maintaining the invariant in parallel with the disruptive action. The set of all code points that could disrupt the invariant corresponds to the AspectJ concept of code points that satisfy a pointcut. The maintenance code that we generate for each such disruptive code point corresponds to a point-specific instance of the advice of an aspect.

Generally, the characterization of disruptive code is based on the Liebniz or substitutivity rule:

$$x = x' \implies I(x) = I(x')$$

where x is the vector of state variables and $I(x)$ is the invariant. The disruptive actions are necessarily those actions in the code that might change the dependent variables of the invariant. A static analyzer would be used to (1) find all actions in the source code that could possibly change the dependent variables of the invariant, and (2) when possible, run inexpensive tests to determine if the invariant is actually violated by the action. For each potentially disruptive action that the static analyzer finds, action-specific maintenance code needs to be generated.

In our example, the dependent variable of the invariant is *hist*, which is changed by every program action. The *error?* predicate serves as an inexpensive test that an action might violate the invariant. A static analyzer would scan the code (i.e. the abstract syntax representation of the code) looking for all actions that satisfy *error?*.

Specification and Derivation of Maintenance Code.

Suppose that *act* is an action such that *error?*(*act*). In order to preserve the invariant, we need to perform a maintenance action that satisfies

assume: $errlog = error? \triangleright action \star hist$
achieve: $errlog' = error? \triangleright action \star hist'$

The postcondition can be simplified as follows:

$errlog' = error? \triangleright action \star hist'$

$\equiv$ {using the definition of *hist*}

$errlog' = error? \triangleright action \star (hist :: \langle \_, act, \_ \rangle)$

$\equiv$ {distributing *action*$\star$ over :: }

$errlog' = error? \triangleright ((action \star hist) :: act)$

$\equiv$ {distributing *error?* $\triangleright$ over ::, using assumption that *error?*(*act*) }

$errlog' = (error? \triangleright action \star hist) :: act$

$\equiv$ {using the precondition/invariant inductively }

$errlog' = errlog :: act$

which is easily satisfied by the simple update

$$errlog := errlog :: act.$$

This maintenance action is to be performed in parallel with *act*. Again, note that this generated maintenance code corresponds to an instance of an aspect's advice that is applicable where *act* occurs in the source code.

More generally, suppose that static analysis has identified an action *act* as potentially disruptive of invariant $I(x)$. If *act* satisfies the specification

    assume : $P(x)$

    achieve : $Q(x, x')$

then the maintenance code *maint* can be formally specified as

    assume : $P(x) \land I(x)$

    achieve : $Q(x, x') \land I(x')$

Code for *maint* often takes the form of a parallel composition

$$act || update$$

of the actions *act* and *update*. Implicit in this specification is the need to preserve the effect of *act* while additionally reestablishing the invariant I. If it is inconsistent to achieve both, then the specification is unrealizable.

By specifying a maintenance action that includes the existing disruptive action, we generalize several options. In AspectJ, programmers must specify whether the maintenance code goes before, after, or replaces the disruptive action. These alternatives all satisfy our specification. A further possibility is that the satisfaction of one constraint may cause the violation of another constraint, triggering an action to maintain it, causing the violation of another constraint, and so on. Our specification may need to be realized by maintenance code that iterates to a solution (as in constraint propagation systems, cf. [6]). Another possibility is that multiple invariants may need to be maintained, and it may be possible (or necessary) to implement the disruptive action and various maintenance actions differently to find a mutually satisfactory solution.

Unfortunately, most programming languages do not have a parallel composition control structure, despite its naturality. This fact has prompted most related work on programming with invariants [7, 8], as well as AspectJ, to prematurely sequentialize the maintenance action – either as a before-method, after-method, or around-method. Conceptually, the maintenance action is parallel to the disruptive action so that the invariant is always observed to hold in all states. The sequentialization of the parallel composition should be treated as an opportunity for machine optimization, not as additional information that must be prescribed by a programmer. However, the sequentialization should take care that no (external) process that depends on the invariant could observe the state between the two actions and notice that the invariant is (temporarily) violated. One technique for assuring that no observation of the intermittent violation can be made is to lock the relevant variables while the maintenance is being performed.

4   More Examples

4.1   Model-View Consistency Maintenance

The classic model-view problem is to maintain consistency between a data model and various graphical views when the program and/or user can change any of them. That is, whenever the program changes the data model, the graphical views should be updated to maintain consistency, and conversely, if the user changes one graphical view interactively, then the data model and the other views must be updated to reflect the change.

Problem: Maintain consistency between a data model and its various views. For simplicity we focus on eager evaluation – maintaining consistency with every change to data models or views.

Domain Theory: At any particular time there are a set of data models of type $Model$. Each model has one or more graphical views of type $View$. Views have an attribute $ModelOf : Model$ that gives the unique model that they display (written $vw.ModelOf$ for view vw). For simplicity, we assume that the data content of $mod : Model$ is given by an attribute $MValue : Model \rightarrow Value$, and, similarly, the data content of a view is given by $Value : View \rightarrow Value$ for $View$. Although we use equality between these values to express consistency, in practical situations, a more complex predicate is needed.

Invariant: $\Box \, \forall (md, vw) \; md = vw.ModelOf \implies vw.Value = md.MValue$

Disruptive Actions: There are two classes of disruptive actions: changes to a view or changes to a model.

Specification and Derivation of Maintenance Code: For each disruptive action act, generate a specification for an action that jointly achieves the effect of act and maintains the invariant:

assume : $vw.Value = md.MValue \land precondition(act)$
achieve : $vw'.Value = md'.MValue \land postcondition(act)$

For example, an action act that updates a view

$$vw.Value := expr$$

results in the maintenance specification

assume : $vw.Value = md.MValue$
achieve : $vw'.Value = md'.MValue \land vw'.Value = expr$

which is satisfied by the concurrent assignment

$$vw.Value := expr \, \| \, md.MValue := expr$$

Similar code is derived for other cases.

4.2   Procedure Calls and Dynamic Context

This exercise treats procedure calls and the reification of dynamic procedure call context.

Problem: Maintain a global that flags when a Sort procedure is executing.

Reification: This problem requires that we reify and maintain the call stack, analogously to the way that history is maintained in *hist*. To reify the call stack, it is necessary to elaborate the model of behavior presented in Section 2. A call to procedure P, $s_0 \xrightarrow{x:=P(x)} s_1$, can be elaborated to a sub-behavior

$$s_0 \xrightarrow{eval\ args} s_{00} \xrightarrow[parms:=argvals]{enter\ P} s_{01} \xrightarrow{execute\ P} s_{02} \xrightarrow[x:=result]{exit\ P} s_1$$

With this elaboration, it is straightforward to maintain a call stack variable cs with operators *Initialize*, *Push*, and *Pop*:

$$s_0 \xrightarrow{eval\ args} s_{00} \xrightarrow[cs:=Push(cs,\langle P,argvals\rangle)]{enter\ P} s_{01} \xrightarrow{execute\ P} s_{02} \xrightarrow[cs:=Pop(cs)]{exit\ P} s_1$$

Procedural languages abstract away these details so a static analyzer must take this finer-grain model into account when appropriate.

Domain Theory: The boolean variable *sorting?* is to be true exactly when a call to *Sort* is on the call stack cs. In the invariant, we use a (meta)predicate $pcall?(act, f)$ that is true exactly when action act is a procedure call to f.

Invariant: $\square\ sorting? = \exists(call)(call \in cs \wedge pcall?(call, Sort))$

Incrementally maintaining a boolean value is difficult, and a standard technique is to transform a quantified expression into an equivalent set-theoretic form that is easier to maintain [5]:

$\square\ sorting? = size(\{call \mid call \in cs \wedge pcall?(call, Sort)\}) > 0$

and introduce a second invariant:

$\square\ sortcnt = size(\{call \mid call \in cs \wedge pcall?(call, Sort)\})$

By maintaining *sortcnt*, we can replace *sorting?* by $sortcnt > 0$ everywhere it occurs.

Disruptive Actions: The static analyzer seeks actions that change the dependent variable cs; i.e. pushes and pops of that call stack cs that satisfy $pcall?(call, Sort)$.

Specification and Derivation of Maintenance Code: There are three basic cases that can arise: *Initialize, Push,* and *Pop* operations. For a push operation of the form

$$cs := Push(cs, \langle Sort, \_ \rangle)$$

the maintenance specification is

assume: $sortcnt = size(\{call \mid call \in cs \ \wedge \ pcall?(call, Sort)\})$
achieve: $sortcnt' = size(\{call \mid call \in cs' \ \wedge \ pcall?(call, Sort)\})$
$\wedge \ cs' = Push(cs, \langle Sort, \_ \rangle)$

which an easy calculation shows to be satisfied by the concurrent assignment

$$cs := Push(cs, \langle Sort, \_ \rangle) \ \| \ sortcnt := sortcnt + 1$$

For a pop operation of the form $cs := Pop(cs)$ where $top(cs) = \langle Sort, \_ \rangle$, the maintenance specification is

assume: $top(cs) = \langle Sort, \_ \rangle$
$\wedge \ sortcnt = size(\{call \mid call \in cs \ \wedge \ pcall?(call, Sort)\})$
achieve: $sortcnt' = size(\{call \mid call \in cs' \ \wedge \ pcall?(call, Sort)\})$
$\wedge \ cs' = Pop(cs)$

which is satisfied by the concurrent assignment

$$cs := Pop(cs) \ \| \ sortcnt := sortcnt - 1$$

The concurrent formulation of the maintenance code can be implemented by sequentializing the *sortcnt* updates into the body of the procedure, just after entry and just before return.

An initialization operation on *cs* will cause *sortcnt* to be set to zero.

4.3   Counting Swaps in a Sort Routine

This problem builds on the previous problem and illustrates the execution of advice within dynamic contexts, a key feature of AspectJ.

Problem: Count the number of calls to a *swap* procedure that are invoked during the execution of a sort procedure *Sort*.

Domain Theory: As in the previous problem, let *cs* be the reified call stack, with operators *Initialize, Push,* and *Pop*.

Invariant: The invariant uses a sequence comprehension notation, so that *swpcnt* is the length of a sequence of actions satisfying various properties. Also, recall that the notation $s_0.cs$ refers to the value of variable *cs* in state s_0.

$$\Box \; swpcnt = length([\, act \mid \langle s_0, act, s_1 \rangle \in hist \;\wedge\; pcall?(act, swap)$$
$$\wedge\; \exists(pc)(pc \in s_0.cs \;\wedge\; pcall?(pc, Sort))])$$

Disruptive Actions: The dependent variable is *hist*. It is easy to statically analyze for $pcall?(act, swap)$. Let's assume that it is not statically determinable whether a particular call to *swap* occurs within the dynamic context of a call to *Sort*. To proceed, we extract the subexpression that cannot be checked statically and formulate an invariant for it:

$$\Box \; sorting? = \exists(call)(call \in cs \;\wedge\; pcall?(call, Sort))$$

Using the result in the previous example allows a simpler formulation for the *swpcnt* invariant:

$$\Box \; swpcnt = length([\, act \mid \langle s_0, act, s_1 \rangle \in hist \;\wedge\; pcall?(act, swap)$$
$$\wedge\; s_0.sortcnt > 0])$$

Specification and Derivation of Maintenance Code: Any call to *swap* is a potentially disruptive action. The following specification jointly achieves the effect of *act* and maintains the invariant:

assume: $hist' = hist :: \langle st_0, act_0, st_1 \rangle$
$\wedge\; pcall?(act_0, swap)$
$\wedge\; swpcnt = length([\, act \mid \langle s_0, act, s_1 \rangle \in hist$
$\qquad\qquad\qquad\qquad \wedge\; pcall?(act, swap)$
$\qquad\qquad\qquad\qquad \wedge\; s_0.sortcnt > 0])$
$\wedge\; precondition(act_0)$
achieve: $swpcnt' = length([\, act \mid \langle s_0, act, s_1 \rangle \in hist'$
$\qquad\qquad\qquad\qquad \wedge\; pcall?(act, swap) \;\wedge\; s_0.sortcnt > 0])$
$\wedge\; postcondition(act_0)$

The postcondition can be simplified as follows (where changes are underlined):

$swpcnt' = length([\, act \mid \langle s_0, act, s_1 \rangle \in hist'$
$\qquad\qquad\qquad\qquad \wedge\; pcall?(act, swap) \;\wedge\; s_0.sortcnt > 0])$

$\equiv$ {using the assumption about $hist'$}

$swpcnt' = length([\, act \mid \langle s_0, act, s_1 \rangle \in \underline{hist :: \langle st_0, act_0, st_1 \rangle}$
$\qquad\qquad\qquad\qquad \wedge\; pcall?(act, swap) \;\wedge\; s_0.sortcnt > 0])$

$\equiv$ {distributing $\in$ over :: }

$swpcnt' = length([\, act \mid \underline{(\langle s_0, act, s_1 \rangle \in hist \;\vee\; \langle s_0, act, s_1 \rangle = \langle st_0, act_0, st_1 \rangle)}$
$\qquad\qquad\qquad\qquad \wedge\; pcall?(act, swap) \;\wedge\; s_0.sortcnt > 0])$

$\equiv$ {driving $\vee$ outward through $\wedge$, sequence-former, and *length*}

$$swpcnt' = \underline{length([\,act \mid \langle s_0, act, s_1 \rangle \in hist}$$
$$\underline{\land\ pcall?(act, swap)\ \land\ s_0.sortcnt > 0\,])}$$
$$+ \underline{length([\,act \mid \langle s_0, act, s_1 \rangle = \langle st_0, act_0, st_1 \rangle}$$
$$\underline{\land\ pcall?(act, swap)\ \land\ s_0.sortcnt > 0\,])}$$

$\equiv$ {using assumption about $swpcnt$, distribute equality in sequence-former}

$$swpcnt' = swpcnt + \underline{length([\,act_0 \mid pcall?(act_0, swap)\ \land\ st_0.sortcnt > 0\,])}$$

$\equiv$ {using assumption about act_0, and simplifying}

$$swpcnt' = swpcnt + \underline{length([\,act_0 \mid st_0.sortcnt > 0\,])}$$

$\equiv$ {using using independence of act_0 from the sequence-former predicate}

$$swpcnt' = swpcnt + \underline{(if\ st_0.sortcnt > 0\ then\ length([\,act_0 \mid true])}$$
$$\underline{else\ length([\,act_0 \mid false]))}$$

$\equiv$ {simplifying}

$$swpcnt' = swpcnt + (if\ st_0.sortcnt > 0\ then\ \underline{1}\ else\ \underline{0}).$$

Consequently, the maintenance specification is satisfied by the parallel statement

$$act_0\ \|\ swpcnt := swpcnt + (if\ sortcnt > 0\ then\ 1\ else\ 0).$$

Note that a residue of the invariant appears in the maintenance code. The test $sortcnt > 0$ could not be decided statically, so it falls through as a runtime test.

4.4   Maintaining the Length of a List

This example does not require the reification of an extra-computational entity. It is presented as an example of our technique that cannot currently be treated in AspectJ because it is handled at the assignment level, rather than method level.

Problem: Maintain the length of a list ℓ.

Domain Theory: The list data type includes constructors (*nil, append, concat*), selectors (*first, rest*), *deleteElt*, as well as a length function and other operators.

Invariant: $\Box\ llength = length(\ell)$

Disruptive Actions: Any action that changes ℓ may disrupt the invariant.

Specification and Derivation of Maintenance Code: For each disruptive action *act*, generate a specification for an action that jointly achieves the effect of *act* and maintains the invariant. For example, an action *act* that appends an element onto ℓ results in the maintenance specification

assume: $llength = length(\ell) \wedge true$
achieve: $llength' = length(\ell') \wedge \ell' = \ell :: elt$

from which one can easily calculate the satisfying concurrent assignment

$$\ell := \ell :: elt \,\|\, llength := llength + 1$$

Other maintenance actions include: when the list ℓ is created, then the variable *llength* is also created; when ℓ is set to *nil*, then *llength* is set to 0; etc.

Notice that in the examples of this section, the generated maintenance code is highly specific to the disruptive action. We start with a single invariant, but in response to its possible violations, we generate a variety of maintenance codes. Programming language approaches to AOSD would have to provide this variety by potentially complex case analysis in the runtime aspect code.

5   Issues

This work may develop in a number of directions, some of which are discussed below.

- *Implementation* – We anticipate implementing the techniques of this paper in our behavioral extension [9] of the Specware system [10]. The calculations for simplifying the maintenance specifications in the examples are comparable in difficulty to those that were performed routinely and automatically in KIDS [11]. However, the simplifier requires the presence of an adequate inference-oriented theory of the language, datatypes, and application domain. As can be seen from the examples, most of the theorems needed are in the form of distributivity laws.

  In general, the problem of synthesizing code from pre/post-conditions is not decidable. However, two factors help to achieve tractability. First, note that the synthesis problem here is highly structured and incremental in nature – the goal is to reestablish an invariant that has just been perturbed by a given action. Second, synthesis can be made tractable by suitable restrictions on the language/logic employed. For example, in Paige's RAPT system, invariants and disruptive actions were restricted to finite-set-theoretic operations from the SETL language, and the corresponding maintenance code could be generated by table lookup.

– *Granularity of Maintenance Code* – It may be convenient to treat a code block or a procedure/method as a single action for purposes of invariant maintenance. The main issue is that no (external) process that depends on the invariant could observe a state in which the invariant is violated. This notion suggests that the possibility of designing a static analyzer to check both (i) change of dependent variables, and (ii) the largest enclosing scope that is unobservable externally. An advantage of using a larger grain for maintenance is the performance advantage of bundling many changes at once, rather than eagerly updating at every dependent-variable-change. This is particularly advantageous when the update is relatively expensive.

A good example arises in the model-view-consistency problem (Section 4.1). If the model is changing quickly (say, due to rapid real-time data feed), then user may not want screen updates at the true change frequency. Instead, aesthetics and user needs may dictate that a time granularity be imposed, e.g. no more frequently than every 100 sec. Where is this granularity-of-observation specified? In open system design, this is a design decision and it can be made precise by means of a specification of environment assumptions. In our behavioral specification formalism, called especs [9], environment assumptions are modeled as parametric behaviors. Under composition, the parametric behavior of a component must be implemented by the rest of the system. In the model-view-consistency problem, the parametric behavior (environmental assumptions) might be that the user observes the display screen with a frequency of at most 0.01Hz. This requirement is satisfied by code that reestablishes the invariant at least once every 100sec.

– *Constraint Maintenance: Maximization Versus Invariance* – Sometimes a cross-cutting feature may not have the form of an invariant for practical reasons. Consider, for example, the quality of service offered by a wireless communications substrate. Ideally, full capacity service is provided invariantly. However, physical devices are inherently more or less unreliable. There are at least two characterizations of the constraint maintenance that make sense in this situation:
1. *Maximize the uptime of the service* – That is, maximize the amount of time that a prescribed level of service is provided. Design-time maintenance might involve composing a fault-adaptive scheme to improve uptime.
2. *Maximize the provided bandwidth*– That is, continually make adjustments that provide maximal bandwidth given the circumstances.

– *Enforcing Behavioral Policies* – This paper focuses on cross-cutting concerns that can be specified as invariants. Behavioral invariants can be equivalently expressed as single-mode automata with an axiom at the mode. It is natural to consider cross-cutting concerns that are specified by more complex automata and their corresponding temporal logic formulas. As mentioned earlier, some security policies disallow certain behavior patterns, as opposed to individual run-time events (see for example [4]). One intriguing direction is to consider generalizing the generation techniques of this paper to classes of policy automata.

– *Maintaining Interacting Constraints* – Many application areas, including active databases with consistency constraints and combinatorial optimization problems with constraint propagation, have the characteristic that a single change $(x := e)$ can stimulate extensive iteration until quiescence (a fixpoint) is reached. In terms of this paper, several invariants can refer to the same variables and their maintenance can interfere with each other's truth. That is, a change to maintain one constraint may cause the violation of another.

A sufficient condition that maintaining such a set of constraints leads to a fixpoint may be found in [12] – constraints over a finite semilattice that are definite (a generalized Horn-clause form $x \sqsupseteq A(x)$ where x is a variable over the semilattice and A is monotone) can be solved in linear time. Using essentially the same theory, in [6, 13] we describe the process of automatically generating a customized constraint solver for definite constraints. The resulting solving process is an iterative refinement of variable values in the semilattice.

This context leads to a generalization of the formalism of this paper when (1) changes to certain variables can be treated as decreasing in a semilattice, and (2) constraints are definite. Then, a disruptive action $(x := e)$ has postcondition $(x' \sqsupseteq e)$ rather than the stronger $(x' = e)$, and all constraint maintenance is downward in the semilattice, until a fixpoint is reached.

– *Comparison with AspectJ* – We conjecture that many aspects in AspectJ can be expressed as invariants, and that their effect can be achieved by means of the general process of this paper. However, the around advice in AspectJ allows the replacement of a method call by arbitrary code, changing its semantics. Our approach is restricted to maintenance that refines existing actions, so it is not complete with respect to AspectJ. On the other hand several of the examples in this paper cannot be carried out in AspectJ, so the two are expressively incomparable.

6   Related Work

The generative techniques in this paper derive from transformational work on incremental computation, especially Paige's Finite Differencing transformation [5, 7]. Finite Differencing, as implemented in the RAPTS system, automatically maintains invariants of the form $c = f(x)$ where c is a fresh variable, x is a vector of program variables, and f is a composite of set-theoretic programming language operations. Maintenance code is generated by table lookup. In the KIDS system [11], we extended Finite Differencing by (1) allowing the maintenance of both language- and user-defined terms, and (2) using automatic simplifiers to calculate maintenance code at design-time. The functional language setting in KIDS naturally reveals the concurrency of disruptive code and maintenance updates.

As in Finite Differencing, other approaches to programming with invariants (e.g. [8]) work exclusively with state variables. This paper introduces the notion of reifying extra-computational information, enabling the expression of system-level cross-cutting features as invariants.

Besides AspectJ, other approaches to AOSD may also be treatable by a generative approach. The Demeter system [14] emphasizes path expressions to provide reusable/context-independent access to data. A typical example is to enumerate all objects that inherit from a superclass *Employee* that have a *Salary* attribute regardless of the inheritance chain from the superclass. Reification of the class graph is essential and is responsible for the support provided for run-time binding of data accessors. HyperJ [15] emphasizes a symmetric notion of aspect, in contrast to the asymmetric approach of AspectJ. The focus of HyperJ is on a cross-product-like composition of features between classes, obtaining a multiplicative generation of code. A foundation for this symmetric composition may be found in the colimit operation of Specware [9, 10].

7   Concluding Remarks

Aspect-Oriented Software Development aims to support a more modular approach to programming, with a special focus on cross-cutting concerns. This paper explores techniques for specifying cross-cutting concerns as temporal logic invariants, and generating the code necessary to maintain them. The reification of extra-computational entities helps in expressing many cross-cutting concerns.

Our invariants provide an abstract yet precise, semantic characterization of cross-cutting concerns. The abstraction should aid in clarifying the intention of a concern and promote stability under evolution. The precise semantics means that the generation of maintenance code can be performed mechanically, with assurance that the result meets intentions.

The generally accepted semantics of AspectJ is based on call-stack reification [16], suggesting that AspectJ cross-cutting concerns can be characterized as actions to take about method calls in a specified dynamic context. Our approach lifts to a more general perspective: what kinds of cross-cutting concerns can be addressed when arbitrary extra-computational information is reified.

This work advocates a design process that focuses on generating a normal-case program from high-level models or specifications, followed by the generation and insertion of extensions to implement various cross-cutting concerns. Code structure simplifies to a clean natural decomposition of the basic business logic together with system-level invariants that specify cross-cutting concerns. The improved modularity should help to ease the cost and effort of development and evolution.

Acknowledgments

Thanks to Cordell Green, Gregor Kiczales, and Kevin Sullivan for discussions of this work. Thanks to Lambert Meertens, Stephen Westfold, and the GPCE reviewers for useful comments on the text.

References

1. Aspect-Oriented Software Development, www.aosd.net.
2. Elrad, T., Filman, R., Bader, A., eds.: Communications of the ACM– Special Issue on Aspect-Oriented Programming. Volume 44(10). (2001)
3. Kiczales, G., et al.: An Overview of AspectJ. In: Proc. ECOOP, LNCS 2072, Springer-Verlag. (2001) 327–353
4. Erlingsson, U., Schneider, F.: SASI enforcement of security policies: A retrospective. In: Proceedings of the New Security Paradigms Workshop, Ontario, Canada (1999)
5. Paige, R., Koenig, S.: Finite differencing of computable expressions. ACM Transactions on Programming Languages and Systems **4** (1982) 402–454
6. Westfold, S., Smith, D.: Synthesis of efficient constraint satisfaction programs. Knowledge Engineering Review **16** (2001) 69–84 (Special Issue on AI and OR).
7. Paige, R.: Programming with invariants. IEEE Software **3** (1986) 56–69
8. Deng, X., Dwyer, M., Hatcliff, J., Mizuno, M.: Invariant-based specification, synthesis and verification of synchronization in concurrent programs. In: Proceedings of the 24th International Conference on Software Engineering. (May 2002)
9. Pavlovic, D., Smith, D.R.: Evolving specifications. Technical report, Kestrel Institute (2004)
10. Kestrel Institute: Specware System and documentation. (2003) http://www.specware.org/
11. Smith, D.R.: KIDS – a semi-automatic program development system. IEEE Transactions on Software Engineering Special Issue on Formal Methods in Software Engineering **16** (1990) 1024–1043
12. Rehof, J., Mogenson, T.: Tractable constraints in finite semilattices. Science of Computer Programming **35** (1999) 191–221
13. Smith, D.R., Parra, E.A., Westfold, S.J.: Synthesis of planning and scheduling software. In Tate, A., ed.: Advanced Planning Technology, AAAI Press, Menlo Park (1996) 226–234
14. Lieberherr, K., Orleans, D., Ovlinger, J.: Aspect-oriented programming with adaptive methods. CACM 44(10) (2001) 39–42
15. Ossher, H., Tarr, P.: Using multidimensional separation of concerns to (re)shape evolving software. CACM 44(10) (2001) 43–50
16. Wand, M., Kiczales, G., Dutchyn, C.: A semantics for advice and dynamic join points in aspect-oriented programming. ACM Transactions on Programming Languages and Systems (2003)

Generic Advice: On the Combination of AOP with Generative Programming in AspectC++

Daniel Lohmann, Georg Blaschke, and Olaf Spinczyk

Friedrich-Alexander-University Erlangen-Nuremberg, Germany
{dl,gb,os}@cs.fau.de

Abstract. Besides object-orientation, generic types or templates and aspect-oriented programming (AOP) gain increasing popularity as they provide additional dimensions of decomposition. Most modern programming languages like Ada, Eiffel, and C++ already have built-in support for templates. For Java and C# similar extensions will be available in the near future. Even though promising, the combination of aspects with generic and generative programming is still a widely unexplored field. This paper presents our extensions to the AspectC++ language, an aspect-oriented C++ derivate. By these extensions aspects can now affect generic code and exploit the potentials of generic code and template metaprogramming in their implementations. This allows aspects to inject template metaprograms transparently into the component code. A case study demonstrates that this feature enables the development of highly expressive and efficient generic aspect implementations in AspectC++. A discussion whether these concepts are applicable in the context of other aspect-oriented language extensions like AspectJ rounds up our contribution.

1 Introduction

Besides object-orientation, most modern programming languages offer *generic types* or *templates* to provide an additional dimension of decomposition. Languages like Ada, Eiffel and C++ already have built-in support for templates. For the Java language, special extensions for generic types have been proposed [6] and will soon be available in Java 1.5 implementations [4]. Template support has also been proposed for the next version of the C# language and the .NET framework [12]. We are convinced that for a long-term and broad acceptance of AOP it is necessary to provide native support for template constructs in current AOP languages.

As AspectC++ [17] supports AOP in the context of C++, which offers highly sophisticated template features, it is an ideal example to study the relation of these two worlds. To familiarize the reader with the terminology used throughout this paper we start with a very brief introduction of the most important AspectC++ language concepts.

1.1 AspectC++ Concepts and Terminology

AspectC++ is a general purpose aspect-oriented language extension to C++ designed by the authors and others. It is aimed to support the well-known AspectJ programming style in areas with stronger demands on runtime efficiency and code density.

G. Karsai and E. Visser (Eds.): GPCE 2004, LNCS 3286, pp. 55–74, 2004.

The AspectC++ terminology is strongly influenced by the terminology introduced by AspectJ [13]. The most relevant terms are *joinpoint* and *advice*. A *joinpoint* denotes a specific weaving position in the target code (often called component code, too). Join-points are usually given in a declarative way by a joinpoint description language. Each set of joinpoints, which is described in this language, is called a *pointcut*. In AspectC++ the sentences of the joinpoint description language are called *pointcut expressions*. For example the pointcut expression

```
call("% Service::%(...)")
```

describes all calls to member functions of the class `Service`[1]. The aspect code that is actually woven into the target code at the joinpoints is called *advice*. Advice is bound to a set of joinpoints (given by a pointcut expression). For example by defining the advice

```
advice call("% Service::%(...)") : before () {
  cout << "Service function invocation" << endl;
}
```

the program will print a message *before* any call to a member function of `Service`. The advice code itself has access to its context, i.e. the joinpoint which it affects, at runtime by a *joinpoint API*. Very similar to the predefined `this`-pointer in C++, AspectC++ provides a pointer called `tjp`, which provides the context information. For example the advice

```
advice call("% Service::%(...)") : before () {
  cout << tjp->signature() << " invocation" << endl;
}
```

prints a message that contains the name of the function that is going to be called.

1.2   Dimensions of Interest

The combination of aspects and templates has two general dimensions of interest. First, there is the dimension of using aspects for the instrumentation of generic code. Second, there is the dimension of using generic code in aspects, that is, to generalize aspect implementations by utilizing generic code. We will see that for the first it is necessary to extend the joinpoint description language while the second leads to specific joinpoint API requirements.

Dimension 1: Using Aspects for the Instrumentation of Generic Code. The most common and popular applications of templates are generic algorithms and container classes, as provided by the C++ standard library STL. To support the modular implementation of crosscutting concerns inside template libraries, a template-aware AOP language should be able to weave aspect code into template classes and functions. This means, for example, that we want to be able to run advice code before and/or after calls to or executions of generic classes or functions. Furthermore, it would be desirable to be able to affect even individual template *instances*. For example, we might want to track element additions to a specific instance of a generic container. Open questions are:

---

[1] % and ... are wildcard symbols in AspectC++ (as * and .. in AspectJ).

– Which extensions to the joinpoint languages are necessary to describe these new kinds of joinpoints?
– Which implementation issues for aspect weavers and compilers arise from such extensions?

As today's aspect-oriented programming languages offer a wide range of language features, finding a common (language-independent) answer for these questions is difficult. However, this paper will answer them in the context of C++/AspectC++ and discuss them in the context of other aspect languages that support similar language features.

Dimension 2: Using Generic Code in Aspects. Generic programming provides an additional dimension for separation of concerns (SoC). Thus, we also want to *use template code* in aspect implementations. This seems easy at first sight. However, an advanced utilization of generic code in advice implementations incorporates (static) type information from the advice context. For example, consider a reusable caching aspect, implemented by advice code that uses a generic container to store argument/result pairs of function invocations. To instantiate the container template from within the advice code, the affected function *argument types* and *result type* are needed, which in turn depend on the joinpoint the advice code affects. As in this case different advice code versions have to be generated, it is reasonable to understand the advice as being *instantiated* for each joinpoint depending on the types it needs for code generation. We will use a new term for this special kind of advice:

We call advice a *generic advice,* if its implementation
depends on joinpoint-specific static type information.

As templates are instantiated at compile time, the type information, which is offered by the run-time joinpoint API of current aspect languages, is not sufficient. Instead, we need a *compile-time* joinpoint API that provides static type information (e.g. the parameter types of the affected function) about the advice instantiation context. The type information provided by the compile-time joinpoint API may then be used to instantiate templates. Open questions concerning dimension 2 are:

– How should aspect languages support the usage of generic code in aspects?
– Which information should be provided by a static joinpoint API?

Besides generic programming, C++ templates are also the base for other advanced and powerful SoC concepts like policy-based design[2] and generative programming[9] that are implemented by template metaprogramming[18]. The ability to use template constructs in advice code promises to forge the link between AOP and these advanced SoC concepts. Aspects may provide great benefit for generative programming and policy-based design by enabling the non-invasive intrusion of template metaprograms. At the same time, generative techniques may be used to implement highly flexible and runtime-efficient aspect implementations.

1.3   Objectives

In this paper we discuss the combination of aspects and templates in AspectC++. From the discussion in this introduction we conclude that weaving in template instances is a consequent and probably useful extension of the target scope of aspects. However, providing advice code with the necessary context information to exploit the power of generic code and metaprograms improves the expressive power of aspect implementations significantly. This promises to be the more interesting research topic[2]. Thus, our work covers both dimensions but concentrates on the second. By presenting a case study we will demonstrate the power of the generic advice feature and the consequences in terms of code quality and performance.

1.4   Outline

The rest is this paper is structured as follows. It starts in section 2 with a description of the template support incorporated into the AspectC++ language and compiler. This is followed by a case study in section 3 that shows how generative techniques can be used for the implementation of a highly flexible and efficient aspect. Furthermore, it evaluates the performance and quality of the solution, which we claim to be unreachable alone with pure template techniques or classic AOP. Section 4 discusses whether similar aspect-oriented language extensions for base languages other than C++ could implement the same concepts. Finally, an overview of related work is given and the results of this paper are summarized.

2   Template Support in AspectC++

This section describes our integration of template support into AspectC++. It is structured according to the two dimensions[3] identified in the introduction. Each of these parts starts with a description of template-related C++ features, which are relevant for the integration, continues with a presentation of our extensions to AspectC++ on the language-level, and ends with a discussion of implementation issues.

2.1   Dimension 1: Using Aspects for the Instrumentation of Generic Code

One possible combination of aspects with templates is the application of advice to template classes and functions as discussed in 1.2.

Relevant Language Features.   C++ templates provide a specific kind of polymorphism which is often referred to as *parametric polymorphism*. While *subclass polymorphism* (based on interface inheritance) defines a runtime substitutability between *object instances*, parametric polymorphism defines a compile-time substitutability between *types*. A formal template parameter can be substituted by a type T1 that provides

---

[2] It is also more appropriate for a conference on generative programming.

[3] In fact, the part on the second dimension is divided into 2a and 2b to handle the very C++-specific template metaprogramming feature separately.

a specific (static) interface. This interface is defined by the set of operations, types and constants used in the template implementation. Note that, in contrast to subclass polymorphism, the parametric substitutability of types T1 and T2 does not lead to any runtime relationship between object instances of T1 and T2. Templates do not break type-safety and induce, in principle, no runtime overhead at all.

In C++, the basic language elements for generic programming are *template classes* and *template functions*. For example, the C++ standard library class

```
template< class T, class U > struct pair {
  T first;
  U second;
  pair() : first(), second() {}
  pair(const T& x, const U& y) : first(x), second(y) {}
  ...
};
```

defines a simple 2-Tuple that can be instantiated with any two types, e.g pair< int, int > or pair< Foo, pair< Bar, int > > that provide at least a default or copy constructor.

Extensions to the Joinpoint Language. Weaving in generic code requires the programmers to describe the set of relevant template instances. Thus, the first step to integrate template support into AspectC++ was to extend the joinpoint description language.

In AspectC++ joinpoints that should be affected by advice are described by so-called *pointcut expressions*. For example

```
call("% Service::%(...)") && cflow(execution("void error_%(...)"))
```

describes all calls to member functions of the class Service . By combining (&& operation) these joinpoints with the cflow pointcut function these joinpoints become conditional. They are only affected by advice if the flow of control already passed a function with a name beginning with error_. Users may define pointcut expressions of arbitrary complexity to describe the crosscutting nature of their aspects. A list of all built-in pointcut functions of AspectC++ is available in the AspectC++ Language Quick Reference Sheet[4].

The core of the joinpoint language are match-expressions. In AspectC++ these expressions are quoted strings where % and ... can be used as wildcards. They can be understood as regular expressions matched against the names of known program entities like functions or classes. To support advice for template class and function instances, the signatures of these instances just have to be considered when match expressions are evaluated. In C++ the signatures of template instances are well-defined and can directly be used to extend the set of known program entities for matching. For example, if a function instantiates template classes with the signatures set<int> and set<float>, the match-expression "% set<int>::%(...)" will only match the member functions of set<int>. Of course, it is also possible to match the member functions of all instances by using "% set<...>::%(...)".

---

[4] The AspectC++ compiler and documentation are available from www.aspectc.org.

Implementation Issues. While this extension is straightforward on the language level it has severe consequences on the weaver implementation. The weaver has to be able to distinguish template instances during the weaving process. Our AspectC++ compiler transforms AspectC++ source code into C++ code[5]. Thus, the compiler has to perform a full template instantiation analysis of the given source code to distinguish template instances and to compare their signatures with match-expressions. To be able to affect only certain instances our compiler uses the explicit template specialization feature of C++. For example, if advice affects only the instance set<int> the template code of set is copied, manipulated according to the advice, and declared as a specialization of set for int[6].

2.2   Dimension 2a: Using Generic Code in Aspects

Templates instances, like pair<int, int> in the example above, can also be used in aspect code. However, for a more elaborate and context dependent utilization of templates in advice code, additional support by the aspect language is necessary.

Relevant Language Features. *Generic advice* uses type information from its instantiation context (the joinpoints). For example, it may instantiate a generic container with the result type of the function the advice is applied to. For this, the argument and result types have to be accessible to the advice code at compile time.

The suitable C++ language concept for this purpose is *type aliases*. In C++, a type alias is defined using the typedef keyword. Type aliases can be used to transport type information through other types or templates:

```
template< class T, class U > struct pair {
  typedef T first_type;
  typedef U second_type;
  ...
};
template<class PAIR> typename PAIR::first_type& get_first(PAIR& p) {
  return p.first;
}
```

The Static Joinpoint API. To support the implementation of generic advice code the AspectC++ joinpoint API had to be extended. It now provides static type information about all types that are relevant for the joinpoint.

Table 1 gives an overview about the new joinpoint API. The upper part (types and enumerators) provides compile-time type information, which can be used by generic code or metaprograms instantiated by advice.

The methods in the lower part of table 1 can only be called at runtime. However, note that the new function Arg<i>::ReferredType *arg() now offers a statically typed

---

[5] AspectC++ is based on our PUMA C++ transformation framework which is beeing developed in line with AspectC++, but may be used for other purposes as well.

[6] C++ does not support the explicit specialization for template functions. However, we can work around this problem by defining a helper template class.

Table 1. The AspectC++ Joinpoint API

types and enumerators:	
`That`	object type
`Target`	target type (call)
`Arg<i>::Type`	argument type
`ARGS`	number of arguments
`Result`	result type
static methods:	
`const char *signature()`	signature of the function or attribute
`unsigned id()`	identification of the join point
`AC::JPType jptype()`	type of join point
`AC::Type type()`	type of the function or attribute
`AC::Type argtype(int)`	types of the arguments
`int args()`	number of arguments
`AC::Type resulttype()`	result type
non-static methods:	
`void proceed()`	execute join point code
`AC::Action &action()`	Action structure
`That *that()`	object referred to by this
`Target *target()`	target object of a call
`void *arg(int)`	actual argument
`Arg<i>::ReferredType *arg()`	argument with static index
`Result *result()`	result value

interface to access argument values if the argument index is known at compile time. `AC::Type` is a special data type that provides type information at runtime, but cannot be used to instantiate templates.

In the future, additional type information, e.g. types of class members and template arguments, will be added to the joinpoint API, as this might allow further useful applications.

Implementation Issues. AspectC++ generates a C++ class with a unique name for each joinpoint that is affected by advice code. Advice code is transformed into a template member function of the aspect, which in turn is transformed to a class. The unique joinpoint class is passed as a template argument to the advice code. Thus, the advice code is generic and can access all type definitions (C++ typedefs) inside the joinpoint class with `JoinPoint::Typename`. Indirectly these types can also be used by using the type-safe argument and result accessor function. The following code fragment shows advice code after its transformation into a template function.

```
class ServiceMonitor {
  // ...
  template<class JoinPoint> void __a0_after (JoinPoint *tjp) {
    cout << "Result: " << *tjp->result () << endl;
  }
};
```

As required for generic advice the C++ compiler will instantiate the advice code with `JoinPoint` as a code generation parameter. Depending on the result type of `tjp->result()` for the joinpoint the right output operator will be selected at compile time.

2.3   Dimension 2b: Using Template Metaprograms in Aspects

The C++ template language provides elaborate features that make it a Turing-complete functional language for static metaprogramming on its own. A C++ template metaprogram works on types and constants and is executed by the compiler at compile time. *Generative Advice* is a special form of generic advice that uses joinpoint-specific type information for the instantiation of template metaprograms.

Relevant Language Features. In addition to types, C++ supports *non-type template parameters*, also frequently referred to as value template parameters. Value template parameters allow to instantiate a template according to a compile-time constant. Apart from the definition of compile-time constants, value template parameters are frequently used for arithmetics and looping in template metaprogramming.

A language that provides a *case discrimination* and a *loop* construct is Touring-complete. In the C++ template metalanguage, case discrimination is realized by *template specialization*. Loops are implemented by *recursive instantiation* of templates. These language features, in conjunction with non-type template parameters, are the building blocks of template metaprograms[7]. This is shown in the most popular (and simple) example of a template metaprogram that calculates the factorial of an integer at compile-time:

```
template< int N > struct fac {
  enum{ res = N * fac< N - 1 >::res }; // loop by rec. instantiation
};
// condition to terminate recursion by specialization for case 0
template<> struct fac< 0 > {
  enum{ res = 1 };
};
// using fac
const fac_5 = fac< 5 >::res;
```

The `fac<int>` template depends on value template parameters and calculates the factorial by recursive instantiation of itself. The recursion is terminated by a specialization for the case `fac<0>`.

Type Sequences. With adequate support by the static joinpoint API metaprograms would be able to iterate over type sequences like the argument types of a joinpoint at compile time. However, these sequences have to be provided in a "metaprogram-friendly" way. Just generating `ArgType0, ArgType1, ..., ArgTypeN` would not allow

---

[7] Non-type template parameters are, strictly speaking, not a mandatory feature for the Turing-completeness of the C++ template language. They "just" allow one to use the built-in C++ operator set for arithmetic expressions.

metaprograms to iterate over these types. For this purpose the generated joinpoint-specific classes contain a template class Arg<I> which contains a the type information for the Ith argument as typedefs.

Implementation Issues. Sequences of types can be implemented by recursive template definitions as in the Loki[1] Typelist. For the AspectC++ we decided for an implementation with less demands on the back-end compiler based on explicit template specialization. The following code shows the generated type for a call joinpoint in the main() function[8].

```
struct TJP_main_0 {
    typedef float Result;
    typedef void That;
    typedef ::Service Target;
    enum { ARGS = 2 };
    template <int I> struct Arg {};
    template <> struct Arg<0> {
        typedef bool Type; typedef bool ReferredType;
    };
    template <> struct Arg<1> {
        typedef int & Type; typedef int ReferredType;
    };
    Result *_result;
    inline Result *result() {return _result;}
};
```

With this type as a template argument for generic advice the advice programmer can now use a metaprogram similar to the factorial calculation to handle each argument in a type-safe way. A further example will be given in the next section.

3   Caching as a Generative Aspect – A Case Study

In this section we demonstrate how the possibility to exploit generic/generative programming techniques for aspect implementations can lead to a very high level of abstraction. Our example is a simple caching policy for function invocations. The implementation idea is straightforward: before executing the function body, a cache is searched for the passed argument values. If an entry is found, the corresponding result is returned immediately, otherwise the function body is executed and the cache is updated.

Caching is a typical example for a crosscutting policy. However, before we extended AspectC++ it was not possible to implement this in a traditional aspect-oriented way. To be generic, the aspect must be able to copy function arguments of arbitrary types into the cache. As C++ lacks good reflection capabilities, it is not possible to do this at runtime.

A caching policy for function invocations is also not easy to implement using sophisticated template techniques like policy-based design[2]. To achieve this, it would

---

[8] The generated code depends on the compiler used as the ac++ back-end.

be necessary to have a generic way to expose the signature (parameter types) of a function at compile time and the invocation context (actual parameter values) at runtime, which is not available. Fortunately, exactly this information is provided by the compile-time and run-time joinpoint API in AspectC++. Hence, it is now possible to implement context-dependent policies, like caching, using generative techniques *together* with aspects.

In the following, we present the implementation of such a generative caching aspect. We introduce the example with an in-place "handcrafted" cache implementation for a single function. A typical AOP implementation of this simple in-place cache gives readers, who are not familiar with AOP, an idea about implementing such a policy by an aspect. We then generalize the AOP implementation to make it independent on the number and types of function arguments using template metaprogramming and the static joinpoint API. This generative aspect is applicable to any function with any number of arguments. Finally, we evaluate our solution and provide a detailed performance analysis.

3.1   Scenario

Consider an application that uses the class Calc (Figure 1). Our goal is to improve the overall application execution speed. With the help of a tracing aspect we figured out that the application spends most time in the computational intensive functions Calc::Expensive(), Calc::AlsoExpensive() and Calc::VeryExpensive(). Furthermore, we detected that these functions are often called several times in order with exactly the same arguments. Therefore, we decided to improve the execution speed by using a simple one-element cache.

Figure 1 demonstrates the implementation principle of such a cache for the function Calc::Expensive(). It uses a local class Cache that implements the caching functionality and offers two methods, namely Cache::Lookup() (line 28) and Cache::Update() (line 32), to access and write the cached data. Cache is instantiated as a static object (line 41) so it stays resident between function invocations.

However, as caching is useful only in certain application scenarios and we have to write almost the same code for Calc::AlsoExpensive() and Calc::VeryExpensive() again, we want to implement this by a reusable aspect.

3.2   Development of a Caching Aspect

The Simple Caching Aspect. Figure 2 shows a typical AOP "translation" of the caching strategy. The class Cache has become an inner class of the aspect Caching. The aspect gives around advice for the execution of Calc::Expensive(), Cache is now instantiated in the advice body (line 22). On each invocation, the function parameters are first looked up in the cache and, if found, the cached result is returned (lines 25–27). Otherwise they are calculated by invoking the original function and stored together with the result in the cache (lines 28–34).

This implementation of a caching aspect is quite straightforward. It uses methods of the runtime joinpoint API (tjp->arg() and tjp->result()) to access the actual parameter and result values of a function invocation. However, it has the major drawback that

```
1   struct Vector                             28    bool Lookup( const Vector& _a,
2   {                                         29                 const Vector& _b ) {
3     Vector( double _x = 0, double _y = 0 )  30      return valid && _a == a && _b == b;
4       : x( _x ), y( _y ) {}                 31    }
5     Vector(const Vector& src){operator =(src);}32   void Update( const Vector& _res,
6     Vector& operator =( const Vector& src ) { 33                 const Vector& _a,
7       x = src.x; y = src.y; return *this;   34                 const Vector& _b ) {
8     }                                       35      valid = true;res = _res; a = _a; b = _b;
9     bool operator==(const Vector& with) const{ 36    }
10      return with.x == x && with.y == y;    37    Vector a, b, res;
11    }                                       38    bool   valid;
12    double x, y;                            39   };
13  };                                        40
14                                            41   static Cache cc;
15  class Calc {                              42
16  public:                                   43   // Lookup value in cache
17    Vector Expensive(const Vector& a,       44   if( cc.Lookup( a, b ) ) {
18                    const Vector& b) const; 45      return cc.res;
19    int AlsoExpensive(double a,double b) const;46   } else {  // Not in cache
20    int VeryExpensive(int a,int b,int c) const;47    Vector Result;
21  };                                        48      // ... do calculations ...
22                                            49
23                                            50      // Store result in cache
24  Vector Calc::Expensive(const Vector& a,   51      cc.Update( Result, a, b ) ;
25                    const Vector& b)const{ 52      return cc.res;
26    struct Cache {                          53   }
27      Cache() : valid( false ) {}           54  }
```

Fig. 1. Elements of the Example Application

it can be applied only to functions with a specific signature, namely functions with two arguments of type Vector which return a Vector. This limited reusability of the caching aspect comes from the fact that both the class Cache and the advice code implementation are built on (implicit) assumptions about the argument and result types.

Generalization. The simple cache class implementation in Figure 2 makes the following implicit assumptions about the advice context it is applied to:

1. The function's result and arguments are of type *Vector*.
2. The function gets *exactly two arguments*. Besides the return value, exactly two values have to be updated by Cache::Update() and compared by Cache::Lookup().

Generalizing from 1 (the result/argument types) can be achieved by passing the types as template parameters. However, to generalize from 2 (the number of arguments) is a bit more complicated. Before weaving time, it is not possible to decide how many parameters have to be stored, updated and compared by Cache. The memory layout of the class Cache, as well as the code of its member functions Lookup() and Update(), has therefore to be *generated* at compilation time. With AspectC++, it is now possible to do this job by a template metaprogram. The new static joinpoint API provides all the necessary context information (number/types of parameters, result type) in a way that is accessible by the C++ template language.

To simplify the implementation of the generative caching aspect (Figure 3), it is mainly based on existing libraries and well-known idioms for template metaprogramming. We used the Loki library[2] by Alexandrescu, especially Loki::Typelist and

```
1   aspect Caching {                              19   advice execution(
2     struct Cache {                              20     "Vector Calc::%( const Vector& %,"
3       Cache() : valid( false ) {}               21     "const Vector& % )" ) : around() {
4       bool Lookup( const Vector& _a,            22     static Cache cc;
5              const Vector& _b ) const {          23
6         return valid && _a == a && _b == b;      24     // Lookup value in cache
7       }                                          25     if( cc.Lookup( *(Vector*)tjp->arg(0),
8       void Update( const Vector& _res,           26          *(Vector*)tjp->arg(1) ) )
9                    const Vector& _a,             27       *tjp->result() = cc.res;
10                   const Vector& _b ) {          28     else {
11        valid = true;                            29       // Not in cache. Calculate and store
12        res = _res;                              30       tjp->proceed();
13        a = _a; b = _b;                          31       cc.Update( *(Vector*)tjp->result(),
14      }                                          32          *(Vector*)tjp->arg(0),
15      Vector a, b, res;                          33              *(Vector*)tjp->arg(1));
16      bool   valid;                              34     }
17    };                                           35   }
18                                                 36 };
```

Fig. 2. Simple Caching Aspect

`Loki::Tuple`[9]. The `Loki::Tuple` construct creates (at compile time) a tuple from a list of types, passed as a `Loki::Typelist`. The resulting tuple is a class that contains one data member for each element in the type-list. The rough implementation idea is, to pass a list of parameter types to the `Cache` template and to store the cache data in a `Loki::Tuple` (instead of distinct data members). The `Lookup()` and `Update()` methods are created at compile time by special generators, because the number of arguments (and therefore the number of necessary comparisons and assignments) is unknown until the point of template instantiation.

In the implementation (Figure 3), the `Cache` class gets only one template parameter (line 32), `TJP`, which is used to pass the actual joinpoint type. The joinpoint type, `JoinPoint`, is created by the AspectC++ compiler and implicitly known in every advice body. It provides the necessary context information. The advice code passes `JoinPoint` as a template argument to `Cache` in the instantiation of the cache object (line 81). Everything else needed for the implementation is retrieved from types and constants defined in `TJP`. The `Cache` class itself is derived from a `Loki::Tuple`, built from the argument types `TJP::Arg<0>::Type, TJP::Arg<1>::Type, ...` (line 34). However, the argument types first have to be transformed into a `Loki::Typelist`. This task is performed by the `JP2LokiTL` metaprogram (lines 13-28), which also removes possible const and reference attributes from the types with a `Traits` helper class. By deriving `Cache` from a tuple constructed this way, it already contains one data member of the correct type for each function argument. The remaining data members (`res` and `valid`) are defined explicitly (lines 64, 65).

The code for the methods `Cache::Lookup()` and `Cache::Update()` is generated by metaprograms. The `Comp_N` metaprogram loops over the function arguments and generates a conjunction of comparisons. Each iteration adds one comparison between the

---

[9] Loki was chosen not only because it provides high level services for our implementation. As a "heavily-templated" library it was also considered being a good real-world test case for the capabilities of our AspectC++ parser.

```
 1   #include "loki/TypeTraits.h"                  46       return *tjp->arg<0>()
 2   #include "loki/Typelist.h"                    47           == Loki::Field<0>(cc);
 3   #include "loki/HierarchyGenerators.h"         48     }
 4                                                 49   };
 5   template< class T > struct Traits {           50
 6     typedef typename Loki::TypeTraits<typename  51   // Copies TJP args into a Loki tuple
 7       Loki::TypeTraits< T >::ReferredType       52   template<class C, int I > struct Copy_N {
 8     >::NonConstType BaseType;                   53     static void proc( TJP* tjp, C& cc ) {
 9   };                                            54       Loki::Field<I>(cc) = *tjp->arg< I >();
10                                                 55       Copy_N< C, I-1 >::proc( tjp, cc );
11   namespace AC {                                56     }
12     // Builds a Loki::Typelist from arg types   57   };
13     template< class TJP, int J >                58   template< class C > struct Copy_N< C, 0 > {
14     struct JP2LokiTL {                          59     static void proc( TJP* tjp, C& cc ) {
15       typedef Loki::Typelist< typename Traits<  60       Loki::Field<0>(cc) = *tjp->arg< 0 >();
16         typename TJP::Arg<                       61     }
17           TJP::ARGS-J >::Type >::BaseType,      62   };
18         typename JP2LokiTL< TJP, J-1 >::Result  63
19       > Result;                                 64   bool valid;
20     };                                          65   typename TJP::Result res;
21     template< class TJP >                       66   Cache() : valid( false ) {}
22     struct JP2LokiTL< TJP, 1 > {                67
23       typedef Loki::Typelist< typename Traits<  68   bool Lookup( TJP* tjp ) {
24         typename TJP::Arg<                       69     return valid && Comp_N< Cache,
25           TJP::ARGS-1 >::Type >::BaseType,      70         TJP::ARGS - 1 >::proc(tjp, *this);
26         Loki::NullType                          71   }
27       > Result;                                 72   void Update( TJP* tjp ) {
28     };                                          73     valid = true;
29   }                                             74     res   = *tjp->result();
30                                                 75     Copy_N< Cache,
31   aspect Caching {                              76         TJP::ARGS - 1 >::proc(tjp, *this);
32     template<class TJP> struct Cache            77   }
33     : public Loki::Tuple< typename              78   };
34     AC::JP2LokiTL< TJP, TJP::ARGS >::Result >   79
35     {                                           80   advice execution("% Calc::%(...)") : around(){
36       // Comp. TJP args with a Loki tuple       81     static Cache< JoinPoint > cc;
37       template<class C,int I> struct Comp_N {   82
38         static bool proc(TJP* tjp,const C& cc){ 83     if( cc.Lookup( tjp ) )
39           return *tjp->arg< I >() ==           84       *tjp->result() = cc.res;
40             Loki::Field< I >( cc ) &&          85     else {
41             Comp_N<C,I-1>::proc(tjp,cc);       86       tjp->proceed();
42       }                                         87       cc.Update( tjp );
43     };                                          88     }
44     template<class C> struct Comp_N<C, 0> {     89   }
45       static bool proc(TJP* tjp,const C& cc){   90   };
```

Fig. 3. Generative Caching Aspect

I^{th} argument, retrieved with `tjp->arg<I>()`, and the cached value stored in the Ith tuple element, retrieved with the `Loki::Field<I>()` helper function. The `Copy_N` metaprogram copies in a similar way the argument values into the cache by generating a sequence of assignments. The implementations of `Cache::Lookup()` and `Cache::Update()` just instantiate these metaprograms and call the generated code (lines 68–71, 72–77).

3.3 Evaluation

The final cache implementation (Figure 3) has indeed become a generic and broadly reusable implementation of a caching strategy. It can be applied non-invasively to functions with 1 to n arguments; each argument being of any type that is comparable and assignable. Type-safety is achieved and code redundancy is completely avoided. The source code complexity, on the other hand, is notably higher. The encapsulation as an aspect may also result in a performance overhead, as the aspect weaver has to create special code to provide the infrastructure for the woven-in advice. In the following, we discuss these specific pros and cons of our approach.

Performance Analysis. Table 2 shows the results of our performance analysis. It displays, from left to right, the runtime overhead induced by a native in-place cache implementation (as in Figure 1), the simple caching aspect (Figure 2), and the generative caching aspect (Figure 3), if applied (as in the example) to the function Calc::Expensive(). The numbers are clock cycles on a Pentium III[10]. For the in-place cache, *cache hit* represent the costs of a successful call to Lookup(), *cache miss* represents the costs of an unsuccessful call to Lookup(), followed by a call to Update(). For the aspect implementations, these numbers include the additional overhead introduced by AspectC++. The numbers in square brackets denote the difference between each implementation and its in-place counterpart. They can be understood as the costs of separating out caching as an aspect.

Table 2. Overhead of the Cache Implementations (clock cycles on a Pentium III)

C++	in-place		simple aspect		generative aspect	
cache hit	38.0	[0.0]	55.0	[17.0]	53.0	[15.0]
cache miss	36.0	[0.0]	70.2	[34.2]	67.0	[31.0]

As expected, the in-place implementation performs best[11]. The additional overhead of the aspect implementations is mainly induced by the fact that AspectC++ needs to create an array of references to all function parameters to provide a unified access to them[12]. If tjp->proceed() is called from within around advice, a function call (to the original code) has to be performed[13]. In the example, this is the case in a cache-miss situation and thereby explains why the overhead for a cache miss (31/34 cycles) is notably higher as the overhead for a cache hit (15/17 cycles).

---

[10] The code was compiled with Microsoft Visual C++ 2003 using /O2 /Ot optimizations. All benchmarks measurements were done on a 700 MHz PIII E ("Coppermine") machine running Windows XP SP1. To reduce multitasking and caching effects, each test was performed 25 times and measured the execution cycles for 1000 repetitions (using the rdtsc instruction). The presented results are averaged from this 25 series and then divided by 1000. The standard derivation is < 0.1 for all series.

[11] The effect that the overhead of a cache miss is even lower than for a cache hit can be explained by the four necessary (and relatively expensive) floating point comparisons to ensure a cache hit, while a cache miss can ideally be detected after the first comparison. The skipped comparisons seem to out-weigh the costs of Update().

[12] As an optimization, AspectC++ creates this array only if it is actually used in the advice body, which is the case here.

[13] For technical reasons, AspectC++ does this indirectly via a function pointer in a so-called action object, the call can therefore not be inlined. As the detour over an action object is not necessary in many cases, this gives room for future improvements of the code generator.

Although we expected the generative aspect implementation to perform not worse than the simple aspect, we were a bit surprised that it actually performs better (2-3 cycles, around 10-12%). We assume that the structure of the code generated by the template-metaprograms accommodates the compiler's optimization strategies.

The additional 40-86% relative overhead for the generative aspect compared to the in-place implementation seems to be remarkably high. However, this is basically caused by the very low costs of our most simple cache implementation, which performs a successful lookup in only 38 cycles. A more elaborated cache implementation (e.g. one that stores more than one cache line) would consume more cycles and thereby lower the effective relative overhead of the aspect-oriented solutions. And finally, the absolute overhead of the generative caching aspect is still very low. If we assume a cache hit rate of only 30%, applying this aspect would even pay off for a function that performs its calculation in 270 cycles ($0.39\mu s$ on a PIII-700)!

Discussion. The caching example has shown, how the combination of AOP with template-related techniques can lead to highly generic and efficient policy implementations. As mentioned above, it is hardly possible to reach the same level of genericity in C++ using templates or aspects alone. Both techniques seem to have their very specific strong points that complement each other.

One strong point of aspects is the *instantiation context* which is available through the joinpoint API. By providing access to the parameter and result types of a function at compile-time, as well as to their actual values at runtime, it offers information that is otherwise not available in a generic way. Another point of aspects is their *non-invasive applicability* by a declarative joinpoint language. While a class or function has to be explicitly prepared to be configurable by templates, aspects can be applied easily and in a very flexible manner "on demand". For instance, by using call advice (instead of execution advice) it is possible to do the caching on the caller side. Hence, the same policy can be applied to selected clients only, or to invocations of third-party code that is not available as source.

However, the easy applicability of aspects leads to high requirements on their genericity and reusability. This forges the link to templates and template metaprogramming. Besides the well known possibility to combine a high level of expressiveness with excellent performance [19], carefully developed generic C++ code is typically instantiable in many different contexts. By using generators, it is even possible to *adapt the structure and the code* depending on the instantiation context.

To summarize, aspects are excellent in defining *where* and under *which circumstances* (context) something should happen, while templates provide the necessary flexibility to define in a generic way *what* should happen at these points. The combination works specifically well for policies which depend on the calling context of a function and/or should be flexibly and non-invasively applicable to clients in configurable program families. Other examples where this technique could be applied are constraint checking, program introspection or marshaling.

While the performance analysis made evident that the resulting flexibility is not payed by a remarkable runtime overhead, it still leads to higher source code complexity. This is a well-known problem of template metaprogramming. However, the development of broadly reusable policies and aspects is anyway a task for experienced library developers. The application developer, who uses the aspect library, is not confronted with the template code.

A Generic Caching Aspect in Java. As an addition to our case study, we also implemented a generic caching aspect in AspectJ. Our goal was to understand, if and how a similar genericity is reachable in a language that does not support static metaprogramming and follows a more runtime-based philosophy.

The Java implementation uses reflection to store the argument and result values in the cache by dynamically creating instances of the corresponding types and invoking their copy-constructors. However, while in C++ the copy-constructor is part of the canonical class interface (and its absence is a strong indicator for a non-copyable and therefore non-cachable class), in Java for many classes copy-constructors are "just not implemented". This limits the applicability of the aspect, and, even worse, it is not possible to detect this before runtime! Another strong issue of a reflection-based solution is performance. On an 1GHz Athlon machine the additional costs of a cache-hit are $0.44\mu s$, a cache miss costs, because of the expensive reflection-based copying, about $26.47\mu s$. Assuming again a cache hit rate of 30%, the Java cache would not pay off for functions that consume less than $63\mu s$ [14]. This "pay-off-number" is significantly higher than the corresponding $0.39\mu s$ (270 ticks on a PIII-700) of the C++ solution[15].

To summarize, the reflection-based "generic" Java solution offers only a limited practical applicability and may even lead to unexpected runtime errors.

4   Applicability to Other Languages

Besides C++, other (imperative) languages like Ada or Eiffel support the template concept. For Java and C# generic extensions have been announced or are on the way into the official language standards[12, 4]. Java, furthermore, provides with AspectJ the most-popular aspect weaver. Several active research projects work on incorporating aspects into the C# language [15, 14] and there are chances that the increasing popularity of AOP also leads to the development of aspect weavers for Ada and Eiffel. This gives rise to the question what kind of combination of AOP with generic programming is feasible in these languages. In this section, we discuss if and how our insights on combining AOP with generic and generative programming in C++ are applicable to other languages.

4.1   Relevant Language Features

In the introduction of this paper, we subdivided the possible combinations of aspects with templates into two dimensions of interest, namely *using aspects to instrument*

---

[14] Java measurements were performed on a 1GHz Athlon 4 ("Thunderbird") running Sun's Java 1.4.2_03 on a Linux 2.6.3 kernel.

[15] We can assume that the 700MHz PIII machine used for the C++ measurements does not perform better than the 1GHz Athlon machine used for the Java measurements.

generic code (dimension 1) and *using generic code in aspects* (dimension 2). We used (in section 2) these dimensions to examine the relevant C++ language elements and derived requirements and implementation ideas for our aspect weaver.

In the following we use the same scheme to examine the other mentioned languages. Table 3 shows the availability of the template-related language features in Generic Java (GJ), Generic C# (GC#), Ada, Eiffel, and C++[16].

Table 3. Language Genericity Features

	GJ	GC#	Ada	Eiffel	C++	Dimension
Template classes/functions	√	√	√	√	√	1
type aliases (typedefs)		(√)			√	
Instantiation with native (build-in) types		√	√	√	√	2a
Non-type template parameters			√		√	
template specialization (condition statement)					√	2b
Recursive instantiation (loop statement)					√	

Dimension 1: Using Aspects to Instrument Generic Code. All of the examined languages provide the feature of template classes and/or functions. A template-aware AOP extension for any of these languages might and should provide the ability to weave aspect code into generic code or certain instantiations of it. While we assume that the necessary extensions to the joinpoint languages are as straightforward as in AspectC++, different consequences on weaver implementations may arise:

- To be able to affect only certain template instances, AspectC++ creates a modified copy of the original template which has been specialized explicitly to promote it to the compiler. Source code weavers for languages that do not support template specialization may run into difficulties here.
- To weave into template code, a weaver has to be able to distinguish between template code and ordinary code. This might become a problem for byte code weavers, if template instances are not visible or distinguishable on this level any more.

Dimension 2: Support for Generic Advice. As explained, we subdivided the relevant language features for dimension 2 into two sets. The language features listed for dimension 2a are helpful to support generic advice code. The language features listed for dimension 2b are additionally necessary to support generative advice code. Up to now, the 2b-features are only available in C++. Only the C++ template language provides elaborate features that make it a Turing-complete functional language on its own which can be used for static metaprogramming. For the other languages we therefore focus on the support of generic advice:

---

[16] The table contains only those features we considered as relevant from perspective of an aspect weaver. A more elaborated comparison of the genericity support in different programming languages can be found in [11].

- To support generic advice, the argument and result types related to a joinpoint have to be accessible by the advice code at compile time. In AspectC++ it was possible to implement this by an extension of the *joinpoint API* which now provides *type aliases* (typedefs) for all relevant types. However, even though the other examined languages do not offer a similar type alias concept[17], aspect weavers for these languages may provide the type information in another way. For instance, an aspect weaver may offer special keywords for this purpose that are resolved to the fully qualified actual parameter and result types at weaving time.
- Generic Java restricts template instantiations to non-primitive types only. This implicitly narrows the applicability of generic advice to functions that do not use the native build-in data types (e.g. int) in their signature. However, aspect weavers for Java may overcome this limitation by providing automatic boxing and unboxing of primitive data types to their corresponding object types (e.g. java.lang.Integer)[18].

4.2 Summary

In principle, all of the examined languages are candidates for template-aware aspect-oriented language extensions. Weaving in generic code (dimension 1) as well as generic advice (dimension 2a) should be feasible in these languages, too. However, while in AspectC++ it was possible to use built-in C++ language features for some important parts of the implementation, weavers for other languages may encounter their own difficulties here. Template-metaprogramming is a very powerful, but unfortunately somewhat C++-specific technique. Even if desirable, it is unlikely that the combination of AOP with generative programming (dimension 2b) is applicable to any of the other examined languages.

5 Related Work

No publications deal with the combination of aspects and templates so far. The few existing work focuses on attempts to "simulate" AOP concepts in pure C++ using advanced template techniques or macro programming [8, 3, 10]. In these publications it is frequently claimed that, in the case of C++, a dedicated aspect language like AspectC++ is not necessary. There is a word of truth in it. Technically speaking, the instantiation of advice code (according to a specific joinpoint at weave time) and the instantiation of a template (according to a set of template parameters at compile time) are similar processes. However, this is a too operational view on the ideas of AOP. The important difference is *where and how* instantiations have to be specified. A class has always to be *explicitly* prepared to be parameterizable by templates. The instantiation and context of a parameterized class, has to be described *explicitly* as well, namely at the point it is actually utilized. The instantiation points of an advice, are, in contrast, described *implicitly*

---

[17] GC# supports type aliases only on local namespace scope. The Ada type keyword, which seems to be somewhat similar to C++ typedef at first sight, actually introduces a new distinct type that is not implicitly convertible to any other type.

[18] AspectJ, for instance, already uses this technique for the argument/result accessors in its runtime joinpoint API.

by a joinpoint description language in the aspect code, outside the class definition and class utilization. The advice context is *implicitly* available through the joinpoint API. To our understanding, this non-invasive, declarative approach is at heart of aspect-oriented programming.

OpenC++ [7] is a MOP for C++ that allows a compiled C++ metaprogram to transform the base-level C++ code. The complete syntax tree is visible on the meta-level and arbitrary transformations are supported. OpenC++ provides no explicit support for AOP-like language extensions. It is a powerful, but somewhat lower-level transformation and MOP toolkit.

Other tools based on C++ code transformation like Simplicissimus[16] and Code-Boost[5] are mainly targeted to the field of domain-specific program optimizations for numerical applications. While CodeBoost intentionally supports only those C++ features that are relevant to the domain of program optimization, AspectC++ has to support all language features. It is intended to be a general-purpose aspect language.

6 Summary and Conclusions

The aim of this work was to investigate the combination of aspects with generic and generative programming in AspectC++. We divided this large topic into mainly two dimensions of interest, namely *using aspects to instrument generic code* and *using generic code in aspects*. We examined the relevant features of the C++ template language, used this to derive the requirements to the AspectC++ language, and presented some details about their incorporation into our AspectC++ weaver[19]. We state that weaving in template instances is not more than a consequent extension of the target scope of aspects. However, providing advice code with additional context information to exploit the power of generic code and metaprograms significantly increases the expressive power of aspect implementations as well as the "on-demand" applicability of template metaprograms. The benefits of such *generic advice* were demonstrated by a case study with a generative implementation of a cache policy. Other useful examples would include introspection, constraint checking or marshaling. Furthermore, we showed that the application of such a policy as a generative aspect does not lead to a significant performance overhead.

We also discussed if and how our insights on combining AOP with generic and generative programming in AspectC++ are applicable to languages that offer a similar model for generic types. We concluded that support to weave in generic code and basic support for generic advice is feasible in these languages, too, even though its implementation into aspect weavers might be difficult. However, even if desirable, it is unlikely that other languages will support the powerful combination of AOP with template metaprogramming in near future. This is a unique feature of AspectC++.

References

1. Loki: A C++ library of designs, containing flexible implementations of common design patterns and idioms. http://sourceforge.net/projects/loki-lib/.

---

[19] The necessary AspectC++ extensions are already implemented and will be published in version 0.9 of the compiler.

2. Andrei Alexandrescu. *Modern C++ Design: Generic Programming and Design Patterns Applied*. Addison-Wesley, 2001. ISBN 0-20-17043-15.
3. Andrei Alexandrescu. Aspect-Oriented Programming in C++. In *Tutorial held on the 17th ACM SIGPLAN Conference on Object-Oriented Programming, Systems, Languages, and Applications (OOPSLA'02)*, November 2002.
4. Calvin Austin. J2SE 1.5 in a Nutshell. Technical report, Sun Microsystems, Inc., February 2004. http://java.sun.com/developer/technicalArticles/releases/j2se15.
5. Otto Skrove Bagge, Karl Trygve Kalleberg, Magne Haveraaen, and Eelco Visser. Design of the CodeBoost transformation system for domain-specific optimisation of C++ programs. In Dave Binkley and Paolo Tonella, editors, *Third International Workshop on Source Code Analysis and Manipulation (SCAM 2003)*, pages 65–75, Amsterdam, The Netherlands, September 2003. IEEE Computer Society Press.
6. G. Bracha and N. Cohen et al. Adding Generics to the Java Programming Language: Participant Draft Specification. Technical Report JSR-000014, Java Community Process, April 2002. http://jcp.org/aboutJava/communityprocess/review/jsr014/index.html.
7. Shigeru Chiba. Metaobject Protocol for C++. In *Proceedings of the ACM Conference on Object-Oriented Programming Systems, Languages, and Applications (OOPSLA)*, pages 285–299, October 1995.
8. Krysztof Czarnecki, Lutz Dominick, and Ulrich W. Eisenecker. Aspektorientierte Programmierung in C++, Teil 1–3. *iX, Magazin für professionelle Informationstechnik*, 8–10, 2001.
9. Krysztof Czarnecki and Ulrich W. Eisenecker. *Generative Programming. Methods, Tools and Applications*. Addison-Wesley, May 2000. ISBN 0-20-13097-77.
10. Christopher Diggins. Aspect-Oriented Programming & C++. *Dr. Dobb's Journal of Software Tools*, 408(8), August 2004.
11. R. Garcia, J. Järvi, A. Lumsdaine, J. Siek, and J. Willcock. A comparative study of language support for generic programming. In *Proceedings of the 18th Conference on Object-Oriented Programming, Systems, Languages and Applications (OOPSLA '03)*, pages 115–134, Anaheim, CA, USA, October 2003.
12. Andrew Kennedy and Don Syme. The design and implementation of generics for the .NET Common Language Runtime. In *Proceedings of the ACM Sigplan Conference on Programming Language Design and Implementation (PLDI'01)*, June 2001.
13. Gregor Kiczales, Erik Hilsdale, Jim Hugonin, Mik Kersten, Jeffrey Palm, and William G. Griswold. An overview of AspectJ. In J. Lindskov Knudsen, editor, *ECOOP 2001 – Object-Oriented Programming*, volume 2072 of *LNCS*. Springer-Verlag, June 2001.
14. Howard Kim. AspectC#: An AOSD implementation for C#. Master's thesis, Trinity College, Dublin, Ireland, September 2002.
15. Donal Lafferty and Vinny Cahill. Language-independent aspect-oriented programming. In *Proceedings of the 18th Conference on Object-Oriented Programming, Systems, Languages and Applications (OOPSLA '03)*, pages 1–12, Anaheim, CA, USA, October 2003.
16. Sibylle Schupp, Douglas Gregor, David R. Musser, and Shin-Ming Liu. Semantic and behavioral library transformations. *Information and Software Technology*, 44(13):797–810, 2002.
17. Olaf Spinczyk, Andreas Gal, and Wolfgang Schröder-Preikschat. AspectC++: An Aspect-Oriented Extension to C++. In *Proceedings of the 40th International Conference on Technology of Object-Oriented Languages and Systems (TOOLS Pacific 2002)*, pages 53–60, Sydney, Australia, February 2002.
18. Todd Veldhuizen. Template metaprograms. *C++ Report*, May 1995.
19. Todd Veldhuizen and Kumaraswamy Ponnambalam. Linear algebra with C++ template metaprograms. *Dr. Dobb's Journal of Software Tools*, 21(8):38–44, August 1996.

Supporting Flexible Object Database Evolution with Aspects

Awais Rashid and Nicholas Leidenfrost

Computing Department, Lancaster University, Lancaster LA1 4YR, UK
{awais,leidenfr}@comp.lancs.ac.uk

Abstract. Object database management systems (ODBMSs) typically offer fixed approaches to evolve the schema of the database and adapt existing instances accordingly. Applications, however, have very specialised evolution requirements that can often not be met by the fixed approach offered by the ODBMS. In this paper, we discuss how aspect-oriented programming (AOP) has been employed in the AspOEv evolution framework, which supports flexible adaptation and introduction of evolution mechanisms – for dynamic evolution of the schema and adaptation of existing instances – governing an object database. We argue that aspects support flexibility in the framework by capturing crosscutting hot spots (customisation points in the framework) and establishing their causality relationships with the custom evolution approaches. Furthermore, aspects help in information hiding by screening the database programmer from the complexity of the hot spots manipulated by custom evolution mechanisms. They also make it possible to preserve architectural constraints and specify custom version polymorphism policies.

1 Introduction

The structure of a database may not remain constant and may vary to a large extent as demonstrated by the measurement of the frequency and extent of such changes [37]. Therefore, it comes as no surprise that the schema, i.e., the class hierarchy and class definitions, governing the objects residing in an object database is often subject to changes over the lifetime of the database. Consequently, a number of models have been proposed to evolve the schema to maintain backward and forward compatibility with applications (in existence before and after the changes respectively). These models can be classified into four categories:

- *Basic schema modification* [3, 16], where the database has only one logical schema to which all changes are applied. No change histories are maintained so the approach only supports forward compatibility with applications.
- *Schema versioning* [22, 27], where a new version of the schema is derived upon evolution hence, ensuring both forward and backward compatibility with applications.
- *Class versioning* [24, 38], where the versioning of schema changes is carried out at a fine, class-level granularity. Like schema versioning, the changes are both forward and backward compatible.

G. Karsai and E. Visser (Eds.): GPCE 2004, LNCS 3286, pp. 75–94, 2004.

- *Hybrid approaches*, which version partial, subjective views of the schema e.g., [1] or superimpose one of the above three models on another e.g., basic schema modification on class versioning as in [30, 35].

The schema evolution models need to be complemented by appropriate mechanisms to adapt instances to ensure their compatibility with class definitions across schema changes. For example, an object might be accessed by a class definition derived by adding a member variable to the definition used to instantiate the object in the first place hence, resulting in incompatibility between the *expected* and *actual* type of the object. Instance adaptation approaches deal with such incompatibilities and can be classified into simulation-based (e.g., [38]) and physical transformation approaches (e.g., [24]). The former simply simulate compatibility between the expected and actual type of the object while the latter physically convert the object to match the expected type.

Traditionally, an ODBMS offers the database application developer/maintainer one particular schema evolution approach coupled with a specific instance adaptation mechanism. For example, CLOSQL [24] is a *class versioning* system employing *dynamic instance conversion* as the instance adaptation mechanism; ORION [3] employs *basic schema modification* and *transformation functions*; ENCORE [38] uses *class versioning* and *error handlers* to simulate instance conversion.

It has been argued that such "fixed" functionality does not serve application needs effectively [34]. Applications tend to have very specialised evolution requirements. For one application, it might be inefficient to keep track of change histories, hence making *basic schema modification* the ideal evolution approach. For another application, maintenance of change histories and their granularity might be critical. Similarly, in one case it might be sufficient that instance conversion is simulated while in another scenario physical object conversion might be more desirable. The requirements can be specialised to the extent that custom variations of existing approaches might be needed.

Such flexibility is very difficult to achieve in conventional ODBMS designs for several reasons:

1. The schema evolution and instance adaptation concerns are overlapping in nature and are also intertwined with other elements of the ODBMS, e.g., the transaction manager, the object access manager, type consistency checker and so on [29]. Any customisation of the evolution concerns, therefore, results in a non-localised impact posing significant risk to the consistency of the ODBMS and, consequently, the applications it services.

2. Even if it is possible to expose the customisation points, such exposure poses a huge intellectual barrier for the database application programmer/maintainer who needs to understand the intricate workings of the ODBMS and its various components in order to undertake any customisation. Furthermore, vendors are, mostly, unwilling to expose the internal operation of their systems to avoid unwanted interference from programmers and maintainers in order to preserve architectural constraints.

3. Customisation of evolution mechanisms has implications for type consistency checking as different schema evolution approaches might have different perceptions of type equivalence, especially in the presence of different versions of the same type or schema.

The AspOEv evolution framework, that we are developing, supports flexible adaptation and introduction of schema evolution and instance adaptation mechanisms in an ODBMS independently of each other and other concerns in the system. AOP [2, 14] has been employed in the framework to capture crosscutting hot spots (customisation points in a framework [15]) and establish their causality relationships with the custom evolution approaches. The pointcuts expose a new interface to the underlying database environment to facilitate flexible tailoring of the schema evolution and instance adaptation approaches. Furthermore, aspects are used to support information hiding by screening the database programmer/maintainer from the complexity of the hot spots manipulated by custom evolution mechanisms. They also make it possible to preserve architectural constraints and specify custom version polymorphism policies.

Section 2, in this paper, provides an overview of the AspOEv architecture and its implementation. Section 3 discusses three key aspects supporting flexibility in the framework namely, Type Consistency and Version Polymorphism, Evolution Primitive Binding and Exception Handling. Section 4 shows the framework in operation and how the aspects in section 3 facilitate customisation of the evolution mechanisms. Section 5 discusses some related work while section 6 concludes the paper and identifies directions for future work.

2 AspOEv Architecture

The architecture of the AspOEv framework is shown in Fig. 1. The framework has been implemented in Java and AspectJ (v1.0) [2].

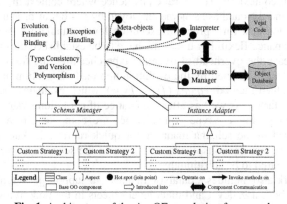

Fig. 1. Architecture of the AspOEv evolution framework

Since most approaches to schema evolution allow several different versions of a class to exist (e.g., individual versions in class versioning or different definitions across schema versions), these versions must be viewed as semantically equivalent and interchangeable. However, most object-oriented (OO) programming languages do not support type versioning. Therefore, the framework employs its own application programming language, Vejal, an OO language with a versioned type system [19, 31]. Vejal has a two-level versioning identifier system (analogous to that used by the popular free source code control system CVS [11]). C<1> indicates class version 1 of class C while C<s=1> implies the class version of C that occurs in schema version 1. In Vejal, one version of a class may be present in multiple schema versions. In order to prevent unworkable schema versions being created, a new version of a class can only be present in all the future schema versions in which it is still compatible with the contracts of the other classes in the schema. Readers should note that, in the rest of the paper, we use the term "type" to refer to both classes and their versions in Vejal.

Traditionally, there has been a natural conflict between language type system constraints and object database evolution approaches, especially those facilitating dynamic evolution and adaptation of types and instances. This is because the constraints of the language type system, which exist to improve safety, act to hinder the required evolution. Consider an example evolution scenario where A and B are the definitions of a particular class before and after the evolution respectively. After evolution it may be desirable that all values of type A now have B as their type. However, such an operation is considered potentially dangerous by the type system (programs already bound to these values may rely on the assumption that they are of type A) which prevents it. The existence of a language with a versioned type system in our framework makes it possible to ensure that important typing constraints are preserved while at the same time facilitating flexible evolution and adaptation of types and instances.

The framework includes an interpreter for Vejal and, like most dynamic schema evolution approaches, employs a meta-object layer to represent persistent data. The existence of an interpreted language introduces some performance overhead – the interoperability of type versions with potentially large differences requires a thorough analysis based on context and structural equivalence where context includes the evolution approach and the database schema employed by it – but affords us the flexibility of customisation at a fine, program execution level granularity. As discussed in [25], such performance-flexibility trade-offs have to be established during framework design. To decrease the overhead of dynamic type checking, the framework creates tables based on 'rules' defined by the evolution approach. Evolution approaches define a boolean valued method, *equals (Type, Type)*, which evaluates the equivalence of two types. At startup, as well as after the change of evolution strategies or execution of evolution primitives, type equivalencies are computed from the database schema and stored in the schema manager for quick runtime lookup. Each type is compared against other versions of the same type in the schema, as well as the versions of types declared to be substitutable.

The framework also includes a database manager to support persistent storage and manipulation of both user-level and meta-level objects in the underlying ODMG 3.0 compliant [7] object database. Currently the framework is being used to facilitate customisable evolution in the commercially available Jasmine object-oriented database [21]; we have implemented an ODMG 3.0 Java binding wrapper for the Jasmine Java binding.

In order to enable the dynamic restructuring of data (e.g., changes to inheritance relationships or class members), the object structure must be kept in the meta-object layer. When coupled with the needs of an interpreted type-versioning language, we are left with two collections of objects to represent the separate concerns of language execution and object structure. The database manager component dealing with database interaction also contains several areas of interest for schema evolution and instance adaptation mechanisms. Therefore, behavioural and structural concerns pertaining to evolution need to be detected and handled across the three components (the interpreter, the meta-object layer and the database manager), which together provide the base OO separation manipulated by three aspects: Type Consistency and Version Polymorphism, Evolution Primitive Binding and Exception Handling. Note that the three base OO components are completely oblivious of the schema evolution and instance adaptation strategies to be plugged in.

The Type Consistency and Version Polymorphism aspect deals with the interpreter's view of typed versions, i.e., whether two different versions of the same class can be considered to be of the same type. This has implications in instance adaptation, type casting and polymorphism – since the class hierarchy can be manipulated at runtime, one version of a type may be assignable to a base type, while another version may not. Schema evolution approaches might also be interested in providing custom version equivalence and substitutability semantics. The aspect, therefore, facilitates customisation of versioned type equality semantics.

The operations used to modify the schema of the database are often referred to as evolution primitives. These primitives range from modification of the class hierarchy, e.g., introduction or removal of classes and modification of inheritance links, to introduction, removal and modification of individual members of a class [3, 26, 35]. The Evolution Primitive Binding aspect monitors the addition and removal of types and their versions from the database schema as well as modification of inheritance links. Schema evolution strategies must decide at these points how to react to the new or deprecated type or to changes in inheritance relationships. Obviously, the action they take must be propagated to instances of the type – an introduced type may become the new standard for the schema, forcing all existing instances to comply before use, or a deprecated type may need all of its instances transferred to another version. The aspect also traps the occurrence of changes to a class and its members. The execution of operations performing such changes provides suitable hotspots for a schema evolution strategy to predict and circumvent any negative impact they might incur. They also allow an instance adaptation strategy to take a wide range of suitable actions.

The Exception Handling aspect allows the application programmer to attempt to preserve behavioural consistency when runtime exceptions are raised. These exceptions may be the result of missing members or type mismatches and could be rectified by handlers provided in custom strategies that have knowledge of the application's inner workings.

The three aspects direct all advice action to method invocations on the two abstract strategy classes (as in the strategy pattern [18]): Schema Manager and Instance Adapter, which are introduced, in the AspectJ sense, into the aspects (to facilitate callbacks). Implementation of custom approaches requires overriding a subset of the callback methods in these classes. This has a number of advantages: Firstly, the application programmer/maintainer is shielded from the complexity of the hot spots in the three base OO components hence, facilitating information hiding and avoiding unwanted interference with those components. Secondly, the programmer/maintainer can create custom strategies without knowledge of AOP and thirdly, strategies can be switched without recompiling the framework. Note that the schema evolution and instance adaptation strategies are independent of each other (cf. section 3.1) so the developer/maintainer is free to choose any combination of strategies as long as they are semantically compatible.

3 Aspects Supporting Flexibility

In this section, we discuss the three aspects introduced in section 2 in more detail. We mainly focus on how the aspects support flexibility in the framework. Note that though the aspects themselves do not change during customisation, nevertheless they help modularise a complex, non-trivial set of crosscutting concerns, namely the schema evolution and instance adaptation strategy to be employed by the underlying ODBMS. In this case, the aspects and the strategy pattern jointly facilitate the flexible customisation and adaptation of these strategies. As demonstrated in [33], aspectisation requires that a coherent set of modules including classes and aspects collaborate to modularise a crosscutting concern – such a view of AOP ensures that aspectisation is not forced and in fact leads to a natural separation of concerns. Therefore, the role of the three aspects in AspOEv is not out of sync with the fundamental aims of aspect-oriented modularity. Furthermore, the design of the framework and the causality relationships between the strategy classes and the other components in the framework would have been very complex without the existence of these aspects. They provide us with a clean, modular design of the framework hence making the framework itself more maintainable and evolvable. They also facilitate separation of the evolution model employed by the ODBMS from the actual implementation of the schema in Vejal.

3.1 Type Consistency and Version Polymorphism Aspect

This aspect supports flexibility in the following three ways:

- It preserves clean design separation between the schema manager and the instance adapter facilitating flexible, semantically compatible, combinations of custom strategies for schema evolution and instance adaptation.
- It captures version discrepancies between the expected and actual type of an object, i.e., between the version in use by the schema and the one to which the object is bound respectively, and provides this information to the schema manager and instance adapter for rectifying action.
- It facilitates the provision of custom version polymorphism policies, i.e., allowing a custom schema manager to specify which type versions are assignable to each other or are substitutable.

Although schema managers and instance adapters work together to achieve stable schema evolution, they are separate concerns, and should not need to know about each other. The instance adapter has the task of adapting an object from its actual type to the schema manager's expected type. From the viewpoint of the instance adapter, it is simply adapting from one type version to another and, therefore, it does not need to be aware of the evolution strategy being employed. The aspect preserves clean design separation by acting as an intermediary between the two concerns. It queries the schema manager for its expected version and passes the resulting information to the instance adapter (cf. shaded code in Fig. 2). Consequently, the instance adapter remains oblivious of the schema manager, yet gets the information it needs to perform its task, while the schema manager receives a converted object of the version it expects.

The code listing in Fig. 2 also shows a simple example of type version discrepancies captured by the aspect and forwarded to the custom schema manager and instance adapter being used. ODMG compliant object databases support binding specific objects to unique names to act as *root entry points* into the database. These persistent roots are retrieved using the lookup method. Since the method only returns a single object, as opposed to other query methods that return collections of matches (and are also monitored by the Type Consistency and Version Polymorphism aspect), it provides a simple example of potential type mismatches in an executing program. The advice in Fig. 2 captures the result of the lookup, queries the schema manager for the type it expects to be returned, and then has the instance adapter perform the proper conversion.

```
pointcut lookup(String name):
    execution(DatabaseManager.lookup(String))
    && args(name);

Object around(String name): lookup(name) {

    MetaObject result = (MetaObject)proceed(name);
    Type resultType = result.getType();
    Type expectedType =
        schemaManager.getActiveType(resultType);
    MetaObject conformed = result;
    if (!resultType.equals(expectedType))
        conformed =
            instanceAdapter.retype(result, expectedType);
    return conformed;

}
```

```
database.bind(new Foo<1.0>,
                    "myFoo");
...
// sometime later
// in execution
Foo<2.0> aFoo =
    database.lookup("myFoo");
```

Fig. 2. Capturing version discrepancies and providing independence of instance adapter and schema manager

Fig. 3. Type mismatch at program execution level (numbers in < > indicate version of Foo used)

Fig. 2 shows an example of type version discrepancies that can be captured at the interface with the database. There are other types of discrepancies that occur at the level of program execution. Consider a class versioning approach to schema evolution when multiple versions of a type are allowed to exist in the execution environment. In this case, the schema manager has no preference to any version[1] and thus the expectedType in Fig. 2 would be the same as the resultType. The code listing in Fig. 3 shows an example of type mismatch at the program execution level. Since the schema manager does not know or care about the version of object aFoo, this can cause serious inconsistencies. Without the use of aspects woven over an interpreted language, this mismatch would be very difficult to catch before an error occurred. However, the type consistency aspect allows instance adapters to monitor assignment in the execut-

---

[1] This is in contrast with, for instance, schema versioning where each schema managed by the schema manager specifies a clear expected version of a type.

ing program. Because schema managers will not always work with a particular version of a type only, flexibility must exist to allow other ways of detecting type mismatch.

The type consistency aspect supports flexible type interchangeability by wrapping type comparison, equality and assignability methods, and allowing a custom evolution strategy to specify how different versions of types are to be treated by the interpreter. Since the evolution framework allows such changes as the addition and removal of classes in the class hierarchy, one version of a type may lose the ability to be assignable to other versions or vice versa. Moreover, one version may be more or less equivalent to a second version, but drastically different from a third. With the ability to evaluate type differences at runtime, the flexibility exists to create a versioned polymorphic environment. In the absence of clear version polymorphism semantics for the evolution approach being employed, there can be lots of potentially unnecessary invocations of the instance adapter resulting in performance overhead.

Consider, for example, the scenarios in Fig. 4. Since Person<2.0> in Fig. 4(a) is derived because of an additive change to Person<1.0>, instances of Person<2.0> could be allowed to be substitutable wherever an instance of Person<1.0> is expected. If a schema manager chooses to allow such substitutability, implicit instance adaptation can be carried out (through version polymorphism) without invoking the instance adapter to do an explicit transformation. This will reduce performance overhead. However, in some cases, the application needs might dictate the schema manager to disallow this substitutability and force an explicit transformation through the instance adapter.

Another scenario where version polymorphism could be required is shown in Fig. 4(b). A schema manager (in response to application requirements) might allow substitution of instances of B<2.0> and C<2.0> wherever an instance of A<1.0> is required, on the grounds that the predecessors of B<2.0> and C<2.0> (B<1.0> and C<1.0> respectively) inherit from A<1.0>. The schema manager might need to evaluate the differences between A<2.0> and A<1.0>before allowing such substitutability.

Equality testing in the Vejal interpreter is similar to that in Java in that it is centred on an equals method defined in types. The typeEquality pointcut in the Type Consistency and Version Polymorphism aspect (cf. Fig. 5) allows a custom strategy to perform a number of tests, including looking for common base classes, hence supporting version polymorphism. Custom version polymorphism is further facilitated by the assignableFrom pointcut[2] (cf. Fig. 5). The default implementation of the method to which the related advice delegates, simply searches for the second type in the first one's supertypes. A custom strategy can alter assignability semantics by overriding the default implementation and searching for a specific base type or performing a more *deep* comparison of the two types, e.g., by searching the supertypes of their predecessor versions.

Note that in class versioning approaches to schema evolution, the execution environment can, potentially, have instances of several versions of a type to manage. Therefore, the schema manager does not necessarily have a default expected type that an instance adapter can convert to when the instance is returned from a database query. Therefore, different type versions could potentially be used interchangeably,

---

[2] The !cflow designator is required because the assignableFrom method is recursive.

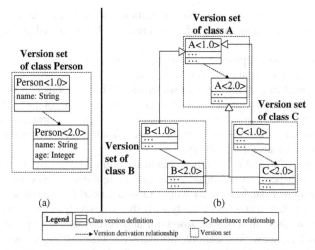

Fig. 4. Potential scenarios involving version polymorphism

```
pointcut typeEquality(Type one, Type two):
    execution(Type.equals(Object))
    && args(two)
    && this(one);

pointcut assignableFrom(Type one, Type two):
    execution(Type.assignableFrom(Type))
    && args(two)
    && this(one)
    && !cflow(Type.assignableFrom(..));
```

Fig. 5. Pointcuts facilitating custom type version polymorphism

without instance adaptation (because of version polymorphism), until a conversion is forced by an incompatible combination or assignment of versions.

3.2 Evolution Primitive Binding Aspect

The execution of evolution primitives, which carry out the schema changes, is of key interest to custom schema managers. Different schema evolution strategies respond to execution of the primitives differently. For instance, schema versioning results in creation of a new schema version upon each change. Class versioning, on the other hand, leads to newer versions of the modified classes. Context versioning [1] only creates newer versions of the partial subjective views in which the modified class participates. Other approaches, e.g., [6], group primitive evolution operations into high-level primitives.

At the same time, each evolution strategy responds to individual evolution primitives differently. For instance, in the class versioning approach proposed in [35], addition, removal or modification of a class member results in creation of a new version of the class. However, if the class version being modified forms a non-leaf node in the hierarchy graph, new versions of all the sub-classes are transitively derived. If a class or class version forming a non-leaf node is removed or repositioned then stubs are introduced to maintain consistency of sub-classes of the removed or repositioned class.

Execution of evolution primitives also has implications for instance adaptation which would almost inevitably be required. Each particular instance adaptation approach will respond to evolution in its own fashion. This variability in the nature of evolution and adaptation approaches, and even in the handling of individual primitives by a particular strategy, makes it essential to allow custom strategies to react to the execution of the primitives in their specialised fashion. The Evolution Primitive Binding aspect facilitates this flexibility.

As an example of evolution primitive binding captured (and passed on to custom strategies) by the aspect, let us consider the case of removing a type from the class hierarchy in an object database. This would raise the need to reclassify (or remove altogether) any existing instances of the type. If the removed type has subtypes, there are further implications in terms of structural and behavioural consistency of their definitions and instances. Furthermore, different evolution strategies would handle type removal differently. For instance, class versioning approaches might only remove a single version of the class while schema versioning and schema modification strategies would, most probably, remove the class altogether from the resulting schema definition. Fig. 6 shows the pointcut, trapping the execution of the type removal primitive, and its associated advice informing the schema manager and instance adapter of this change (note that the two strategies are decoupled and can independently pursue appropriate action in response). By providing a schema evolution strategy with pertinent information at the time of type removal, it can reclassify instances of the removed type appropriately with respect to the schema to avoid information loss. Depending on the evolution strategy being employed, a schema manager could retype existing instances of the removed type to an appropriate base type or retype them to the most similar type version. In either case, the instance adaptation strategy can use the provided information and loaded meta-classes in the interpreter to forward the deprecated type to its replacement.

Note that addition of a new type into the class hierarchy can have similar implications depending on the evolution strategy being employed, i.e., whether subtypes and their existing instances automatically gain functionality provided by the new superclass or new versions of each subtype are required. Similarly, any conflicts between inherited and locally defined members and inheritance paths (Vejal supports multiple inheritance) would need to be resolved in line with preferences of the custom evolution strategy. The aspect captures execution of type addition and other type hierarchy manipulation primitives in a fashion similar to type removal.

For another example of evolution primitive binding, let us consider the modification of class members. The simple evolution scenario shown in Fig. 7 involves *renaming* one of the class members: `surname` to `lastname`. This will result in a behavioural consistency problem as existing references to the renamed member will become invalid. By capturing the state of the member before and after the change, the aspect makes it possible for instance adapters to take corrective action, e.g., by forwarding references. Other class modification primitives are captured and handled in a similar fashion.

```
pointcut removeType(Type removed):
    execution(DatabaseManager+.removeType(Type))
        && args(removed);

before(Type removed): removeType(removed) {
    schemaManager.removeType(removed);
    Type reclassify =
        schemaManager.getReassignedType(removed);
    instanceAdapter.reclassifyType(removed,
                                    reclassify);
}
```

```
class Person<1.0> {

    String firstname,
            surname;

}
                    (a)
class Person<2.0> {

    String firstname,
            lastname;

}
                    (b)
```

Fig. 6. Pointcut and advice pertaining to type removal

Fig. 7. Evolution scenario: renaming a member (a) before evolution (b) after evolution

```
pointcut fieldChanged(Metaclass versionOne,
                       Metaclass versionTwo,
                       MetaField oldField,
                       MetaField newField):
                execution(MetaClass+.changeField(
                            MetaClass,
                            MetaField,
                            MetaField))
                    && args(versionOne,
                            oldField,
                            newField)
                    && target(versionTwo);

Object around(Metaclass versionOne,
              Metaclass versionTwo,
              MetaField oldField,
              MetaField newField):
        fieldChanged(versionOne,
                     versionTwo,
                     oldField,
                     newField) {

    /* Should create bridge if non-existent,
    otherwise retrieve from transient memory. */
    VersionBridge bridge =
        instanceAdapter.getVersionBridge(versionOne,
                                          versionTwo);
    bridge.mapFields(oldField, newField);
}
```

Fig. 8 Pointcut and advice pertaining to version bridges

The aspect also facilitates optimisation of repeated adaptations required in response to an evolution primitive execution. Once again, consider the simple scenario of renaming a member from Fig. 7. While this seems like a simple enough change, references to this member by the handle surname could exist in a number of different places – more so than one could hope to catch and change at the moment of primitive execution. By capturing hot spots in the meta-object layer, the aspect can create a *version bridge* that is aware that the reference to the member surname in Person<1.0> should map to lastname in Person<2.0>. The pointcut and associated around advice corresponding to version bridges is shown in Fig. 8.

Note that a version bridge in the framework is a piece of meta-data that mimics more than one meta-class at once. A type instance can be safely reclassified to reflect its ability to fulfill the requirements of another version, while still maintaining its own type identity. Version bridges know about the meta-classes for both versions, and can thereby easily perform tasks such as forwarding. Obviously, with several existing types, version bridges could quickly become tedious and time consuming for the application programmer/maintainer to generate manually. Therefore, the use of the Evolution Primitive Binding aspect to dynamically create and retype instances in accordance with a general strategy saves a non-trivial amount of work.

3.3 Exception Handling Aspect

Since exceptions are a means of attracting attention to abnormal or incorrect circumstances in program execution, they offer a natural mechanism for a framework designed to preserve consistency during object database evolution in a flexible fashion. In fact, some approaches to instance adaptation, e.g., [36, 38], rely entirely on handling exceptions raised in response to type mismatches to take rectifying action – rigidity affords no other opportunities to capture mismatches. Such approaches, that completely rely on exception handling for instance adaptation, therefore, need to know about a variety of events such as type mismatch, name mismatch and missing, extraneous or incorrect data members and parameters, etc.

While exception handling is by no means a new territory for AOP and AspectJ, the ability to handle exceptions thrown from an interpreter, over which custom evolution strategies have some control, provides additional flexibility. There could arise situations under which even the most well adapted strategy would fail without exception handling. Furthermore, if approaches for schema evolution or instance adaptation change, the new approaches may not have had the opportunity to handle changes that occurred before the switch. The new schema managers and instance adapters cannot rely on their respective previous strategies to inform them of all the changes that might have occurred. By carrying information pertinent to the context of the mismatch, specialised exceptions give instance adaptation strategies a final chance to preserve behavioural consistency. Two examples of such exceptions and the information they carry are shown in Fig. 9. Note that, as discussed in sections 3.1 and 3.2, the AspOEv framework offers other opportunities to detect and handle situations requiring instance adaptation.

Fig. 10 shows a pointcut and its associated around advice from the Exception Handling aspect intercepting such a type mismatch exception and deferring it to the instance adapter and schema manager for rectifying action.

Since the exceptions are raised by consistency issues at runtime, they are unexpected by the program. Therefore, no handling code, aside from that of the custom strategy on which the Exception Handling aspect calls back, is in place. As these exceptions are raised in an interpreted environment, adapters have the opportunity to make changes and retry the failed operation. Execution could effectively be paused, or even taken back a step. Furthermore, due to the nature of the meta-data provided to exception handlers, it is possible to determine the types of changes that have resulted in the inconsistency in question. Members such as meta-fields and meta-methods all have unique identifiers, so it is possible to determine that a member has been renamed, as opposed to it seeming as if a removal and subsequent addition occurred.

throw new
    TypeMismatchException(
        <Type> expected,
        <Type> actual);
 	
throw new
    NoSuchFieldException(
        <FieldReference> field,
        <Type> owner);
	``
	pointcut typeMismatch(MetaObject found,
	                      Type required):
	  call(TypeMismatchException.new(MetaObject,
	                                Type))
	  && args (found, required);
	
	Object around(MetaObject found, Type required):
	  typeMismatch (found, required) {
	    try {
	        proceed(found, required);
	    }
	    catch (TypeMismatchException tme) {
	        instanceAdapter.retype(found, required);
	        schemaManager.typeMismatch(tme);
	    }
	}
	``

Fig. 9. Examples of information provided by exceptions advice

Fig. 10. An exception handling pointcut and associated with callbacks to instance adapter and schema manager

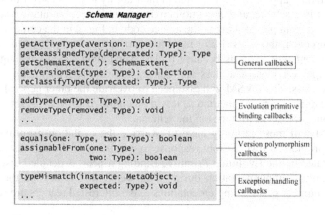

Fig. 11. Callbacks in the abstract Schema Manager strategy class

4   The Framework in Operation

In this section we discuss how two significantly different evolution strategies namely, class versioning and basic schema modification can be implemented using the framework. Before providing an insight into the implementation of the two strategies, it is important to highlight the callback methods available in the abstract Schema Manager class as both evolution strategies would extend this class and override the callbacks of relevance to them. The Schema Manager class is shown in Fig. 11. The callback methods are categorised into *general callbacks*, *evolution primitive binding callbacks*, *version polymorphism callbacks* and *exception handling callbacks*. Here we briefly summarise the role of the general callbacks as the roles of the other three sets are self-explanatory:

- `getActiveType`: returns the active type version (expected type), corresponding to the argument type version, in use by the schema.

- getReassignedType: a simple accessor method to obtain, from the type map in the schema manager, a reference to the type to which instances of a deprecated type have been reassigned.
- getSchemaExtent: to get the set of all classes in a schema or schema version.
- getVersionSet: to get the set of all versions of a class. Note that if a class versioning approach is being used, the getSchemaExtent method will use this method to obtain and return a set of all the version sets of all the classes in the schema.
- reclassifyType: encapsulates the algorithm to identify and specify the *reassigned* type for instances of a deprecated type.

4.1 Implementation of Custom Evolution Approaches

Let us first consider the implementation of class versioning using the framework. We will refer to this as Class Versioning Schema Manager (CVSM).

Class versioning approaches are unique in their ability to permit several versions of a type to exist in a schema and execution environment hence, facilitating active type consistency. For example, looking at the advice code in Fig. 2 in the context of a class versioning approach, the CVSM will need to override getActiveType to simply return the argument type. This is because a class versioning schema manager has to manage multiple versions of a class and hence, does not specify a single expected version of the class. The CVSM will also need to override the other general callbacks especially the getVersionSet method as it will be employed by the getSchemaExtent method to obtain the set of all types in the schema.

The CVSM will most certainly have to override the evolution primitive binding callbacks to provide its own custom response to execution of the various primitives. This is facilitated by the Evolution Primitive Binding aspect. A detailed discussion of evolution primitive implementation during class versioning is beyond the scope of this paper. A number of such implementations exist. Interested readers are referred to [5, 24, 35, 38].

A class versioning implementation also has the responsibility of managing the assignment and accessibility of many versions of a type at the level of the executing program. To ensure consistency at these points, the corresponding instance adapter would be invoked (cf. section 3.1). However, with the flexibility provided by the Type Consistency and Version Polymorphism aspect, the CVSM has the option of overriding the version polymorphism callbacks to stipulate semantics for type equality, assignability and version polymorphism within the executing interpreter, thus preventing unnecessary instance adaptation.

The CVSM may also override the exception handling callbacks (afforded by the Exception Handling aspect) to capture any inconsistencies in type version equivalence or instance adaptation not captured by the version polymorphism callbacks or the instance adapter.

Let us now consider the implementation of the basic schema modification strategy. We will refer to this as Basic Schema Modification Manager (BSMM). The BSMM must first define a working schema, listing all types that will be used (usually the most recent versions of a class), and must override the getActiveType callback to return the correct type defined by the schema. Though this might seem trivial at first glance, this is a vital callback for the BSMM as it facilitates maintenance of consistency of objects by comparing them with the expected types of the schema before they enter execution.

The BSMM must also define how it will deal with the various evolution primitives through the evolution primitive binding callbacks. Interested readers are referred to [3, 16] for a discussion of potential behaviour of basic schema modification primitives that could be implemented by the BSMM, as a detailed discussion is beyond the scope of this paper.

Like the CVSM, the BSMM could specify handlers for any mismatches not captured by other callbacks. However, it will, most likely, not utilise the version polymorphism callbacks as these mainly facilitate an informed evaluation of the need for instance adaptation in an environment with multiple versions. Since the BSMM exercises strict control in the form of having the most recent version of a type in the schema, these callbacks would be of little interest to it.

Note that so far we have not discussed customisation of the instance adapter to suit the CVSM and the BSMM. Though one might think that instance adapters for these two approaches would not be compatible, this is not the case. If an instance adapter is designed to respond to instance adaptation needs at both the program execution level and at the interface with the database, it will certainly service the needs of both. It will serve the BSMM effectively as most of the instance adaptation for this would occur at the interface with the database. This is because a BSMM dictates that the persistent instance retrieved from the database is compliant with the expected type in the schema before it is loaded into the execution environment. Therefore, the instance adapter will adapt the instance to comply with the expected type upon retrieval. Conversely, the instance adapter would not be invoked for the CVSM when query results are received from the database as the need for adaptation is postponed till an actual collision occurs (recall that the CVSM has no default expected type version for a class). Here the ability to monitor join points at program execution level comes into play. Note that this orthogonality of instance adaptation and schema evolution concerns is afforded by the Type Consistency and Version Polymorphism aspect (cf. Section 3.1).

4.2 Handling Structural Consistency Issues

Let us consider the problems arising if an evolution approach prior to customisation may have remapped instances of a type (such as a removed type) to one of its base classes. If the new approach employs the (previously removed) type in its schema, it would want to return the remapped instances to their original type. Also, in the event that data from two different schemas are merged, several types from one schema may have been remapped to their equivalent type in the second schema. The new schema manager will need to know about these type equivalencies in order to continue to serve applications employing the merged data. The framework facilitates the handling of these situations by providing communication between the current and former schema managers when a switch occurs (cf. Fig. 12). The SchemaExtent object is a collection of types utilised by a schema manager (its schema) as well as relationships between types, such as remapped (deprecated) and substitutable (semantically or structurally equivalent) types. The new approach can either immediately convert these types, or convert them lazily. AspOEv facilitates lazy conversion in this case by providing functionality for automatically "enriching" type specific queries with remapped and substitutable types. Objects that have been remapped by another schema, however, must be differentiated from any existing instances of the type they are remapped to. Therefore, in AspOEv, each object has two stored types, the *current* type and the *declaration* type. While schemas may classify an object as many different types during its lifetime, the object's declaration type never changes. Remapped objects can be identified as such by their declaration types.

4.3 Handling Behavioural Consistency Issues

Database evolution primitives can break behavioural consistency by altering types or members that are referenced elsewhere in the program space. The persistent storage of Vejal programs as AbstractSyntaxTree elements in AspOEv facilitates querying for instances of programming components, such as field references, variable declarations, or method invocations in dependent types. This enables the framework to present the programmer with detailed information about where problems might occur. Moreover, this level of granularity in Vejal meta-data allows the framework to create new versions of dependent classes to automatically comply with some changes. If, for example, a member is renamed, the framework can detect and change any field references or method invocations in dependent classes (cf. Fig. 13).

Of course, changes such as renaming are seldom completely free of semantic implications, and any generated versions must be verified by the programmer before being put into effect.

```
SchemaExtent oldSchema =
    oldSchemaManager.getSchema();
schemaManager.transitionFrom(oldSchema);
```

```
// Start a transaction
QueryCursor ageAccesses =
    FieldReference.where("fieldName == \"surname\"");
while (ageAccesses.moreElement( )) {
    FieldReference reference =
        (FieldReference)ageAccesses.nextElement( );
    reference.setFieldName("lastName"); }
// Commit transaction
```

Fig. 12. Communication between old and new schema managers

Fig. 13. Querying and altering program elements

5   Related Work

The SADES object database evolution system [30, 35, 36] employs a declarative aspect language to support customisation of the instance adaptation mechanism. Two instance adaptation strategies, error handlers (a simulation-based approach) [38] and update/backdate methods (a physical transformation approach) [24], have been successfully implemented using the aspect language [36]. Though the work on customisable evolution in AspOEv has been inspired by SADES, there are some marked differences between the two systems. SADES uses aspects to directly plug-in the instance adaptation code into the system. Consequently, the complexity of the instance adaptation hot spots has to be exposed to the developer/maintainer and, at the same time, there is a risk of unwanted interference with the ODBMS from the aspect code. This is in contrast with the framework discussed in this paper as the developer/maintainer is shielded from the complexity of the hot spots. Furthermore, the inner workings of the ODBMS do not have to be exposed hence, facilitating preservation of architectural constraints by avoiding unwanted interference. SADES supports customisation of the instance adaptation approach only – the schema evolution strategy is fixed. It does not support version polymorphism either.

An earlier version of AspOEv [28, 29, 31] also facilitated customisation of both schema evolution and instance adaptation mechanisms. However, like SADES, aspects were employed to specify and directly plug-in the strategies into the system. Also, version polymorphism was not supported.

The composition of aspects in a persistent environment is treated in [32], which discusses various issues pertaining to weaving of aspects which are persistent in nature. Though the three AspOEv aspects discussed here are also operating in a persistent environment, they are not persistent in nature. They, however, do have to account for the fact that the pointcuts they employ span both transient and persistent spaces in the underlying database environment.

The GOODS object-oriented database system [23] employs a meta-object protocol to support customisation of its transaction model and related concerns such as locking and caching. Custom approaches can be implemented by refining existing meta-objects through inheritance. Customisation of the schema evolution and instance adaptation strategies is not supported. Furthermore, though customisation of the transaction model, locking and cache management is supported, the three concerns are not untangled. Consequently, customisation of one of the three concerns has an impact on the others.

Component database systems, e.g., [13, 20] offer special customisation points, similar to hot spots in OO frameworks, to allow custom components to be incorporated into the database system. However, customisation in these systems is limited to introduction of user-defined types, functions, triggers, constraints, indexing mechanisms and predicates, etc. In contrast our framework facilitates customisation or complete swapping of fundamental ODBMS components encapsulating the schema evolution and instance adaptation mechanisms. Our work, therefore, bears a closer relationship with DBMS componentisation approaches such as [4, 8]. However, unlike these works which focus on architectures to build component database systems, the focus of our framework is to provide customisable evolution in existing object database systems without rearchitecting them.

The use of aspects in our framework also bears a relationship with the work on active database management systems [12]. These systems employ event-condition-action (ECA) rules to support active monitoring and enforcement of constraints (and execution of any associated behaviour). If a simple or composite event that a rule responds to is fired, the specified condition is evaluated and subsequently the action is executed provided the condition evaluates to true. Aspects in our framework are similar in that they monitor the hot spots in the three base OO components and, upon detection of an event of interest, invoke the callback methods in the strategy classes. In some instances, the aspects evaluate some conditions before invoking the callbacks, e.g., comparing the expected and actual type (cf. Fig. 2) before invoking the instance adapter. This similarity between the use of aspects in the framework and active databases does not come as a surprise as already work has been undertaken to demonstrate the relationship between the two concepts [9].

[17] discusses the need for application-specific database systems and proposes the use of domain-specific programming languages with embedded, domain-specific database systems for the purpose. Our approach is similar in that it supports application-specific customisation of evolution concerns and employs its own database programming language, Vejal, with a versioned type system to facilitate capturing of behavioural concerns at program execution level. However, the customisation is carried out through a general-purpose OO programming language, i.e., Java, and is facilitated by a general-purpose AOP language, i.e., AspectJ. Furthermore, our framework is motivated by the need to modularise crosscutting evolution concerns.

The work presented in this paper also bears a relationship with the notion of aspect-oriented frameworks, e.g., [10]. However, unlike [10], which describes a general AOP framework, AspOEv is specific to the domain of object database evolution.

6   Conclusion and Future Work

This paper has discussed the use of aspects to support flexibility in an object database evolution framework. Aspects are employed to capture points of interest in three base OO components and to forward information from these points to custom schema evolution and instance adaptation strategies by invoking callback methods. This way aspects establish the causality relationships between the points in the base OO components and the evolution concerns interested in manipulating the behaviour at those points. However, these relationships are established without exposing the complexity of the customisation points hence, promoting information hiding. The benefits of this are twofold. Firstly, the programmer/maintainer does not need to understand the details of the ODBMS design to implement a custom evolution concern. Secondly, the ODBMS is shielded from unwanted interference from the custom concerns hence, ensuring that architectural constraints are preserved and integrity is not compromised. This is significant as quite often AOP attracts criticism because aspects break encapsulation. In this instance, however, aspects are being employed to preserve encapsulation and information hiding.

Another key feature of aspects in the framework is the provision of support for version polymorphism. To the best of our knowledge, substitutability and assignability in a type-versioning environment has not been explored to date let alone application-specific customisation of such semantics. This flexibility would not have been possible without the use of aspects to establish the required causality relationships.

The use of aspects coupled with the strategy pattern makes it possible to swap schema evolution and instance adaptation strategies in the framework without recompilation. This implies that over the lifetime of an application one can choose to employ a different strategy in response to changing requirements. In our future work, we aim to focus on facilitating communication between old and new strategies to ensure that the new strategy can utilise information from changes by the previous one if needed. We are also developing a mechanism whereby the possible set of pointcuts to be captured by the three aspects is provided as a set of *bindings* and the aspects generated from these bindings. This ensures that if some pointcuts are needed for a specific customisation and are not already included in the aspects, they can be introduced without significant effort. Another important area of future interest is exploring the introduction of new, application-specific, evolution primitives by exploiting the flexibility afforded by the three aspects and the bindings. We also aim to carry out further case studies to test drive the customisability of the framework.

Acknowledgements

This work is supported by UK Engineering and Physical Science Research Council (EPSRC) Grant: AspOEv (GR/R08612), 2000-2004. The Jasmine system is provided by Computer Associates under an academic partnership agreement with Lancaster University. The authors wish to thank Robin Green for implementation of the previous version of AspOEv.

References

1. J. Andany, M. Leonard, and C. Palisser, "Management of Schema Evolution in Databases", Proc. VLDB Conf., 1991, Morgan Kaufmann, pp. 161-170.
2. AspectJ Team, "AspectJ Project", http://www.eclipse.org/aspectj/, 2004.
3. J. Banerjee, H.-T. Chou, J. F. Garza, W. Kim, D. Woelk, and N. Ballou, "Data Model Issues for Object-Oriented Applications", *ACM Transactions on Office Inf. Systems*, 5(1), pp. 3-26, 1987.
4. D. S. Batory, "Concepts for a Database System Compiler", Seventh ACM SIGACT-SIGMOD-SIGART Symposium on Principles of Database Systems, 1988, ACM, pp. 184-192.
5. A. Bjornerstedt and C. Hulten, "Version Control in an Object-Oriented Architecture", in *Object-Oriented Concepts, Databases, and Applications*, W. Kim, Lochovsky, F. H., Ed., 1989, pp. 451-485.
6. P. Breche, F. Ferrandina, and M. Kuklok, "Simulation of Schema Change using Views", Proc. DEXA Conf., 1995, Springer-Verlag, LNCS 978, pp. 247-258.
7. R. G. G. Cattell, D. Barry, M. Berler, J. Eastman, D. Jordan, C. Russel, O. Schadow, T. Stenienda, and F. Velez, *The Object Data Standard: ODMG 3.0*: Morgan Kaufmann, 2000.
8. S. Chaudhuri and G. Weikum, "Rethinking Database System Architecture: Towards a Self-tuning RISC-style Database System", Proc. VLDB Conf., 2000, Morgan Kaufmann, pp. 1-10.
9. M. Cilia, M. Haupt, M. Mezini, and A. Buchmann, "The Convergence of AOP and Active Databases: Towards Reactive Middleware", Proc. GPCE, 2003, Springer-Verlag, LNCS 2830, pp.169-188.
10. C. Constantinides, A. Bader, T. Elrad, M. Fayad, and P. Netinant, "Designing an Aspect-Oriented Framework in an Object-Oriented Environment", *ACM Computing Surveys*, 32(1), 2000.
11. CVS, "Concurrent Versions System", http://www.cvshome.org/, 2003.
12. K. R. Dittrich, S. Gatziu, and A. Geppert, "The Active Database Management System Manifesto", 2nd Workshop on Rules in Databases, 1995, Springer-Verlag, LNCS 985, pp. 3-20.
13. K. R. Dittrich and A. Geppert, *Component Database Systems*: Morgan Kaufmann, 2000.
14. T. Elrad, R. Filman, and A. Bader (eds.), "Theme Section on Aspect-Oriented Programming", *Communications of the ACM*, 44(10), 2001.
15. M. E. Fayad and D. C. Schmidt, "Object-Oriented Application Frameworks", *Communications of the ACM*, 40(10), pp. 32-38, 1997.
16. F. Ferrandina, T. Meyer, R. Zicari, and G. Ferran, "Schema and Database Evolution in the O2 Object Database System", Proc. VLDB Conf., 1995, Morgan Kaufmann, pp. 170-181.

17. K. Fisher, C. Goodall, K. Högstedt, and A. Rogers, "An Application-Specific Database", 8th Int'l Workshop on Database Programming Languages, 2002, Springer-Verlag, LNCS 2397, pp. 213-227.
18. E. Gamma, R. Helm, R. Johnson, and J. Vlissides, *Design Patterns - Elements of Reusable Object-Oriented Software*: Addison Wesley, 1995.
19. R. Green and A. Rashid, "An Aspect-Oriented Framework for Schema Evolution in Object-Oriented Databases", AOSD 2002 Workshop on Aspects, Components & Patterns for Infrastructure Software.
20. L. M. Haas, J. C. Freytag, G. M. Lohman, and H. Pirahesh, "Extensible Query Processing in Starburst", Proc. SIGMOD Conf., 1989, ACM, pp. 377-388.
21. Jasmine, *The Jasmine Documentation*, 1996-1998 ed: Computer Associates International, Inc. & Fujitsu Limited, 1996.
22. W. Kim and H.-T. Chou, "Versions of Schema for Object-Oriented Databases", Proc. VLDB Conf., 1988, Morgan Kaufmann, pp. 148-159.
23. Knizhnik, K.A., "Generic Object-Oriented Database System", http://www.ispras.ru/~knizhnik/goods/readme.htm, 2003.
24. S. Monk and I. Sommerville, "Schema Evolution in OODBs Using Class Versioning", *ACM SIGMOD Record*, 22(3), pp. 16-22, 1993.
25. D. Parsons, A. Rashid, A. Speck, and A. Telea, "A 'Framework' for Object Oriented Frameworks Design", Proc. TOOLS Europe, 1999, IEEE Computer Society Press, pp. 141-151.
26. R. J. Peters and M. T. Ozsu, "An Axiomatic Model of Dynamic Schema Evolution in Objectbase Systems", *ACM Transactions on Database Systems*, 22(1), pp. 75-114, 1997.
27. Y.-G. Ra and E. A. Rundensteiner, "A Transparent Schema-Evolution System Based on Object-Oriented View Technology", *IEEE Trans. Knowledge and Data Engg.*, 9(4), pp. 600-624, 1997.
28. A. Rashid, *Aspect-Oriented Database Systems*: Springer-Verlag, 2003.
29. A. Rashid, "Aspect-Oriented Programming for Database Systems", in *Aspect-Oriented Software Development (To Appear)*, M. Aksit, S. Clarke, T. Elrad, and R. Filman, Eds.: Addison-Wesley, 2004.
30. A. Rashid, "A Database Evolution Approach for Object-Oriented Databases", IEEE International Conference on Software Maintenance (ICSM), 2001, IEEE Computer Society Press, pp. 561-564.
31. A. Rashid, "A Framework for Customisable Schema Evolution in Object-Oriented Databases", International Data Engineering and Applications Symposium (IDEAS), 2003, IEEE, pp. 342-346.
32. A. Rashid, "Weaving Aspects in a Persistent Environment", *ACM SIGPLAN Notices*, 37(2), pp. 36-44, 2002.
33. A. Rashid and R. Chitchyan, "Persistence as an Aspect", 2nd International Conference on Aspect-Oriented Software Development, 2003, ACM, pp. 120-129.
34. A. Rashid and P. Sawyer, "Aspect-Orientation and Database Systems: An Effective Customisation Approach", *IEE Proceedings - Software*, 148(5), pp. 156-164, 2001.
35. A. Rashid and P. Sawyer, "A Database Evolution Taxonomy for Object-Oriented Databases", *Journal of Software Maintenance - Practice and Experience (To Appear)*, 2004.
36. A. Rashid, P. Sawyer, and E. Pulvermueller, "A Flexible Approach for Instance Adaptation during Class Versioning", ECOOP 2000 Symp. Objects and Databases, 2000, LNCS 1944, pp. 101-113.
37. D. Sjoberg, "Quantifying Schema Evolution", *Information and Software Technology*, 35(1), pp. 35-44, 1993.
38. A. H. Skarra and S. B. Zdonik, "The Management of Changing Types in an Object-Oriented Database", Proc. OOPSLA Conf., 1986, ACM, pp. 483-495.

A Pointcut Language for Control-Flow

Rémi Douence and Luc Teboul

EMN INRIA Obasco Group
École des Mines, BP 20722, Nantes 44307 Cedex 3, France
{Remi.Douence,Luc.Teboul}@emn.fr

Abstract. In AOP, a pointcut matches base-program execution points
where an advice must be executed. Most pointcut are method signatures.
In AspectJ, pointcuts based on control-flow (e.g. the method foo when
it is called *during* the method bar) can be defined with a cflow operator
which also provides context passing (e.g., when foo is called, print the
argument of the pending call to bar).

In this article, we propose a pointcut language that extends the pointcut language of AspectJ for control-flow. We exemplify how it enables
definition of useful pointcuts based on control-flow with context passing.
We provide both an intuitive semantics based on post-mortem execution traces and an implementation based on program instrumentation.
We also provide analyses for pointcut conflict and instrumentation optimization.

1   Motivations

Aspect-oriented languages provide support for the implementation of crosscutting concerns. Aspects define pointcuts and advice. Pointcuts specify where advice (i.e., pieces of code) must be woven in a base program. In this article, we
propose a pointcut language specialized for control-flow.

AspectJ provides a restricted pointcut language. In an AspectJ tutorial [1],
a move tracking aspect TrackMoves is defined for a simple figure editor based
on points and lines. Its pointcut definition:

```
pointcut moves():   receptions(void Point.setX(int))
                 || receptions(void Point.setY(int))
                 || receptions(void Line.setP1(Point))
                 || receptions(void Line.setP2(Point)); 1
```

matches all method calls that modify coordinates of points or lines. The associated advice sets a boolean flag to true in order to track moves. Such an aspect
can be used to detect when the display must be refreshed.

However, when a line is moved, a point is also moved (i.e., setP1 and setP2
execution call setX and setY) and the display may be uselessly refreshed several
times instead of only once. In this case, the method calls to setP1 and setP2 are
not independent from method calls to setX and setY, but part of a call chain.
In order to detect the start of such a chain, the following pointcut is introduced:

---

1 In recent releases of AspectJ receptions is replaced by execution.

G. Karsai and E. Visser (Eds.): GPCE 2004, LNCS 3286, pp. 95–114, 2004.
© Springer-Verlag Berlin Heidelberg 2004

```
pointcut topLevelMoves(): moves() && !cflow(moves())
```
It can be read as: "method calls that modify coordinates of points or lines when there is no pending call to such a method". It detects top-level only calls to moving methods. So the corresponding aspect refreshes the display only once when a line is moved.

The operator `cflow` of AspectJ allows to pick out method calls based on whether they are in a particular control-flow relationship with other method calls (e.g., `foo` is called during `bar`). It can also be used to pass context between those related method calls (i.e., pass the argument of the pending call `bar` to `foo`). For instance, the same tutorial presents another application that implements a call chain: a caller invokes a service, then the service invokes a worker. In this case, a security aspect `capabilityChecking` passes the caller identity to the worker with the following pointcut:

```
pointcut perCallerCflow(Caller c):
        cflow(invocations(c)) && workPoints(); 2
```
The associated advice can check capabilities of the caller `c` when a worker is invoked. Such control-flow based pointcuts have also been used to pass file opening mode across layers to the prefetching module in a Unix system [4]. In all these examples, the context is passed downward (i.e. from a caller to a sub-callee). Some aspects require to pass context up. For instance, in the service/worker application a `billing` aspect would require the identity of the worker to be passed back to the caller in order to let him pay the charge. In this case, the control-flow relationship must be handcoded in AspectJ: two pointcuts identify points of interest separately, and their associated advice maintain a state to pass context upward.

In this paper, we propose a pointcut language dedicated to express various relations on control-flow. This work provides the following contributions:

- A pointcut language specialized for control-flow. This language enable top-down but also bottom-up and left-to-right context passing. It does not depend on a particular programming language, but it only requires the notion of strict function or method (as provided by C or Java, for instance);
- A formal semantics for our language. This semantics is mandatory for the aspect programmer comprehension, and it enables to design analyses (e.g. aspects interaction);
- An open implementation of our language for experimentations.

This article is structured as follows. In Section 2 we introduce our language for control-flow pointcuts and its formal semantics. Section 3 exemplifies different applications of our pointcut language. Section 4 presents the architecture and implementation of our Java prototype. Formal studies of our language such as an interaction analysis and optimizations are discussed in Section 5. Finally, we review related work (Section 6) and conclude (Section 7). An appendix contains excerpt of the semantics of our language. The full semantics as well as the Java prototype are available at `http://www.emn.fr/x-info/axl`.

---

2 In recent releases of AspectJ `invocations` is replaced by `call`.

2   A Pointcut Language for Control-Flow

In this section, we present a pointcut language for control-flow. First, we introduce a base program as a running example. Second, we define a semantics of our pointcut language.

2.1   A Simple Base Program

Let us consider the base program shown in Figure 1. This Java program defines five methods. When it runs, the method b and the method c are called three times. Such an execution can be represented equivalently either by the n-ary call tree shown in the right of Figure 1, or by the execution trace (i.e. sequence of method calls and returns) as shown below the source code. Note that, a tree node corresponds to a call joinpoint *and* a return joinpoint. For instance, the leftmost b in the tree corresponds to the second and third joinpoints in the trace.

```
class Base {
  public static void main(String[] args) { new Base().a(); }
  void a() { b(); c(1); c(3); }
  void b() { }
  void c(int n) { if (n==1) { c(2); }
                  if (n==2) { b(); d(); } }
  void d() { b(); }
}
```

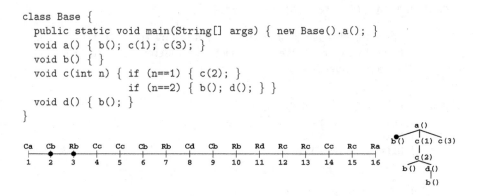

Fig. 1. A Simple Base Program in Java and its Execution

2.2   The Pointcut Language and Its Semantics

We have defined the semantics of our language in Haskell[3] with the help of a post-mortem execution trace (see Appendix). An actual implementation, such as described in Section 4, does not consider a post-mortem execution trace, but it detects matching joinpoints of a pointcut, on the fly, as the base program execution progresses.

We model the base program by its post-mortem execution trace. An execution **Event** is either a method call or a method return:

```
data Event = Call MethodIdent | Ret MethodIdent
```

_____
[3] Haskell [12] is a functional language that allows us to define a declarative yet operational interpreter of our language.

where `MethodIdent` is a method identifier (our prototype described in Section 4 also stores arguments and method receivers). A `Joinpoint` is an execution `Event` numbered in order to distinguish different calls to the same method and a `Trace` is a list of `Joinpoints`.

```
type JoinPoint = (Event,Int)
type Trace = [JoinPoint]
```

The semantics of a pointcut definition is defined by an interpreter function:

```
eval :: Trace -> PcD -> [JoinPoint]
```

that takes the complete post-mortem execution trace of the base program, a pointcut definition and returns the list of joinpoints that match the pointcut. For instance, the program `Base` of the previous section has the following execution trace:

```
traceOfBase=[(Call "a",1),(Call "b",2),(Ret "b",3),(Call "c",4),
(Call "c",5),(Call "b",6),(Ret "b",7),(Call "d",8),(Call "b",9),
(Ret "b",10),(Ret "d",11),(Ret "c",12),(Ret "c",13),
(Call "c",14),(Ret "c",15),(Ret "a",16)]
```

A pointcut is an abstract syntax tree as defined by the data type (a.k.a. grammar) shown in Figure 2. We now review the different constructions and exemplify them on `traceOfBase`.

```
data PcD = Filter      (JoinPoint -> Bool)
         | Inter       PcD PcD
         | Union       PcD PcD
         | Diff        PcD PcD
         | Head        PcD
         | Tail        PcD
         | Cflow       PcD
         | CflowBelow  PcD
         | From        PcD
         | Path        PcD
         | PathAbove   PcD
```

Fig. 2. Grammar of Pointcut Definitions

Filter: The pointcut `Filter` *p*, where *p* is a joinpoint predicate, matches in a trace, every joinpoint that satisfies *p*. For instance, the pointcut:

```
calls = Filter isCall (resp. rets = Filter isRet)
```

matches, in a trace, every call joinpoint (resp. return). The pointcut `calls` is evaluated (i.e. `eval traceOfBase calls`) to:

```
[(Call "a",1),(Call "b",2),(Call "c",4),(Call "c",5),(Call "b",6),
(Call "d",8),(Call "b",9),(Call "c",14)]
```

Those results can be represented graphically as:

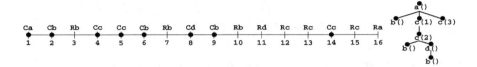

where black dots identify matching joinpoints. For the sake of readability, from here on, we provide only the graphical representation.

Similarly, `Filter (isMethod "foo")` matches in a trace every joinpoint where the method `foo` is called or returns. For instance,

    `isB = Filter (isMethod "b")` matches:

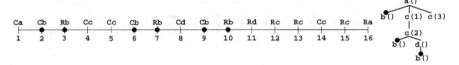

Inter, Union, Diff: A pointcut denotes a list of joinpoints. We provide set-like operators (`Inter`, `Union`, `Diff`) in order to compose these results.

    `callsB = Inter calls isB` matches:

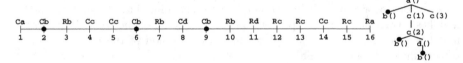

Head, Tail: The pointcut `Head` *pcd* (resp. `Tail` *pcd*) selects the first matching joinpoint (resp. all but the first matching joinpoint) of *pcd*.

    `butFirstCallsB = Tail callsB` matches:

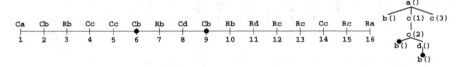

Cflow, CflowBelow: Similarly to AspectJ, we provide a `Cflow` operator. When *pcd* matches a single call joinpoint, say `jp`, `Cflow` *pcd* matches a trace segment: all joinpoints from `jp` to the corresponding return joinpoint. When *pcd* matches several call joinpoints[4], `Cflow` *pcd* matches the union of the corresponding traces segments. For example, `duringC = Cflow callsC` matches every joinpoint that occurs during evaluation of the method c:

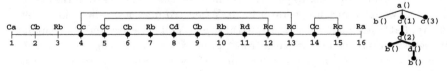

---

[4] Return joinpoints of *pcd* are ignored by `Cflow` *pcd*.

So, invocations of the method b during a call to c are represented by:
`callsBDuringC = Inter duringC callsB` which matches:

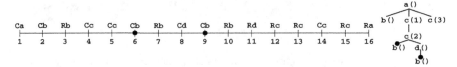

We also offer an alternative operator `CflowBelow` that is similar to `Cflow` but omits the first joinpoint (i.e. call) and the last joinpoint (i.e. return) of each trace segment. `duringC' = CflowBelow callsC` matches:

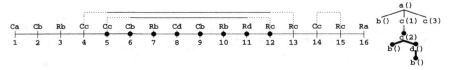

The operator `Cflow` allows us to pass control-flow information downward in the execution tree. Indeed, `callsBDuringC` matches calls to b when c is being executed.

From: In order to pass control-flow information from left to right we introduce the operator `From`. When *pcd* matches a single joinpoint, say jp, `From` *pcd* matches a trace suffix: all joinpoints from jp to the end of the trace. When *pcd* matches several call joinpoints `From` *pcd* matches union of the corresponding trace suffixes. As an example,

`fromSecondCallB = From (Head butFirstCallsB)`

matches every joinpoint that occurs from the second call to b:

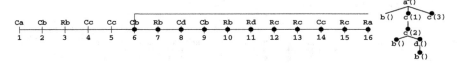

So, we can specify every call to c after the second call to b with
`callsCFromSecondCallB = Inter fromSecondCallB callsC` which is:

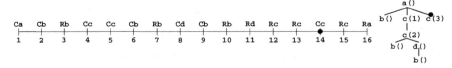

Path, PathAbove: In order to pass control-flow information upward in the execution tree, we introduce an operator `Path`. When *pcd* matches a single joinpoint, say jp, `Path` *pcd* matches a return path: (jp as well as) every return joinpoint in the execution tree on the path, from jp, up to the root. When *pcd* matches several joinpoints, `Path` *pcd* matches union of the corresponding return paths.

`pathCallsB = Path callsB`

matches (`callsB`, i.e., every call to b as well as) every return joinpoint of enclosing methods of method b:

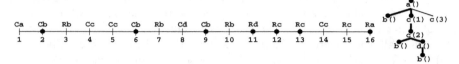

So, we can specify returns of c that call b with
`cOnPathCallsB = Inter pathCallsB (Filter (isMethod "c"))` which is:

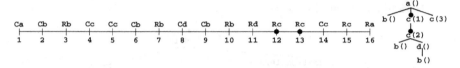

We also offer an alternative operator `PathAbove` *pcd* that is similar to `Path` *pcd* but omits the first joinpoint of each return path (i.e. matching joinpoints of *pcd*). For instance: `pathAboveCallsB = PathAbove callsB` matches:

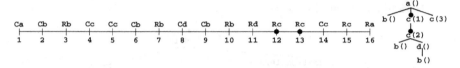

3   Application

In this section, we show how our pointcut language for control-flow can be used to define useful aspects. First, we introduce a base application, then we define different versions of two aspects. A logging aspect illustrates pointcuts based on control-flow and a billing aspect illustrates context passing with pointcuts based on control-flow.

3.1   A Base Application

Let us consider a service allocation system. This base application is inspired from an AspectJ tutorial [1] and can have different instantiations (e.g., a file processing application, a batch system). We focus on three main classes: `Pool` which groups a set of callers, `Caller` which represents a task to be performed by workers and `Worker` which implements a service.

These classes implement the following algorithm: the method `Pool.doAllCallers` iterates until the pool is empty by repeatedly invoking the method `Caller.doService`, which allocates services and calls `Worker.doTask`. This architecture is illustrated by the execution tree of Figure 3. This tree does not display intermediate computations (e.g., a caller may call a service allocator that ultimately invokes `Worker.doService`). In this example, there are two pools of callers. Typically, as exemplified by the leftmost execution branch, a pool invokes

a caller, which invokes a worker. A pool can also directly invoke a worker as in
the second execution branch to perform an *administrative* task. A worker can
delegate its task to another worker as in the third branch. In such a delegation
chain, the top-level doTask is qualified as *principal* (e.g., w3) and bottom-level
doTask (that actually performs the task) is qualified as *executive* (e.g., w5).
We assume all workers are instances of a same class and can perform different
kinds of task (e.g., the second task performed by w4 is executive but not the first
one). Control-flow pointcuts allow to distinguish these tasks. If different classes of
worker are used, the different kinds of task can simply be distinguished by checking the receiver type with joinpoint predicates. Indeed, in this object-oriented
context a joinpoint contains the receiver.

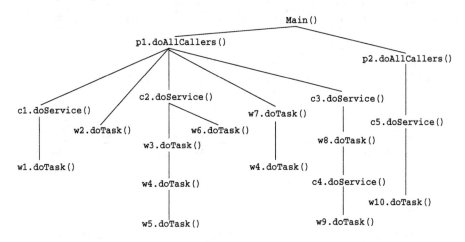

Fig. 3. An Execution Tree of the Base Pool-Caller-Worker Application

3.2   A Logging Aspect

The first aspect we consider is a logging aspect. When a joinpoint matches for
one of its pointcuts, its advice prints the receiver object of the method represented by the matching joinpoint[5]. In this section, we experiment with different
pointcuts in order to generate specific logs.

All workers perform a service when their method doTask is called:
```
allW = Inter (Filter isCall) (Filter (isMethod "doTask"))
```

Administrative workers are not invoked by a caller:
```
adminW = Diff allW (Cflow allC)
```
where allC is similar to allW and matches all callers. So, adminW matches every
worker call but (i.e., Diff) those during Caller.doService (i.e., Cflow allC).

---

[5] We provide a special variable currentJoinPoint to access to the matching joinpoint.
   The advice looks like : System.out.println(currentJoinPoint.getReceiver()).

In this case, we get workers number 2, 7 and (the second invocation of) 4.

Principal workers are top-level workers:
```
principalW = Diff allW (CflowBelow allW)
```
So, `principalW` matches every worker call but (i.e., `Diff`) those during `Worker.doTask` (i.e., `CflowBelow allW`). Note that we have to use `CflowBelow` here because `Cflow allW` includes `allW`, so `Diff allW (Cflow allW)` would be empty. We log workers number 1, 2, 3, 6, 7, 8 and 10.

Principal administrative workers have both properties:
```
principalAdminW = Inter principalW adminW
```
We log workers number 2 and 7.

Executive workers are bottom-most workers in each branch of the execution tree:
```
allRetW = Inter (Filter (isMethod "doTask")) (Filter isRet)
execW = Diff allRetW (PathAbove allW)
```
They can be identified as they return (i.e., `allRetW`) but no (i.e., `Diff`) sub-worker was involved (i.e., `PathAbove allW`). In this case, we log workers number 1, 2, 5, 6, (second invocation of) 4, 9 and 10.

Non executive workers are all workers but executives:
```
noExecW = Inter Path(allW) allRetW
```
They are workers (i.e., `allRetW`) and (i.e., `Inter`) on the path of another worker (i.e., `Path allW`). They are workers 3, 4, 7 and 8.

Executive non administrative workers are bottom-most workers under callers (`Cflow allC`):
```
execNonAdminW = Inter execW (Cflow allC)
```
We get workers number 1, 5, 6, 9 and 10.

Principal executive non administrative workers can be logged with:
```
principalExecNonAdminW = Diff execNonAdminW (CflowBelow allW)
```
They are workers 1, 6 and 10 and they correspond to the standard scenario (a caller invokes directly a worker) as exemplified by the leftmost branch.

Principal callers between first and second administrative worker can be logged with:
```
firstPrincipalAdminW     = Head principalAdminW
secondPrincipalAdminW    = Head (Tail principalAdminW)
betweenAdminW            = Diff  (From firstPrincipalAdminW)
                                 (From secondPrincipalAdminW)
principalC               = Diff allC (CflowBelow allC)
principalCBetweenAdminW = Inter principalC betweenAdminW
```

We get caller 2 only which is invoked between worker 2 and 7.

Finally, note that arbitrary (top, second, third...) level workers can be selected, and a pointcut can have different definitions:

```
topLevelW = Diff allW (CflowBelow allW)              (1, 2, 3, 6, 7, 8, 10)
noTopLevelW = Diff allW topLevelW                    (4, 5, 4, 9)
secondLevelW = Inter (CflowBelow allW) allW          (4, 4, 9)
secondLevelW' = Diff noTopLevel (CflowBelow noTopLevel)
thirdLevelW = Inter (CflowBelow secondLevel) allW    (5)
...
```

3.3   A Billing Aspect

In this section, we experiment with a billing aspect: workers must charge callers. For instance, in the leftmost branch of Figure 3, the worker 1 must bill the caller 1. These non administrative workers can be identified with:

```
Inter (Cflow(Inter(Filter isCall)(Filter (isMethod "doService"))))
      (Inter(Filter isCall)(Filter (isMethod "doTask")))
```

This aspect requires context-passing. Indeed, matching joinpoint of this pointcut represents a call to doTask on a worker and there is a pending call to doService. The advice needs to know the caller to be billed which is not in the current join-point (but in a past joinpoint). To this end, joinpoints are stored as the pointcut is evaluated: occurrences of Filter are replaced by joinpoints in the definition. This incremental instantiation is described in Section 4.3. For example, when this matches for the first time, the corresponding pointcut instance is:

```
Inter (Cflow(Inter(Call "c1.doService")(Call "c1.doService")))
      (Inter(Call "w1.doTask")(Call "w1.doTask"))
```

Such an instance collects joinpoints that contribute to a pointcut. It can be visited by the billing advice to get the client identity when a task is performed.

There may be more than one instance of a pointcut definition at a given joinpoint. For example, when the previous pointcut is true for worker 9, there are one instance for caller 3 and another one for caller 4. Indeed, worker 9 belongs to the Cflow of caller 3 as well as the Cflow of caller 4. In this case, both callers are collected (in a data structure to be visited by the advice). This data structure is a partial execution tree: it contains only caller 3 and its son caller 4. These collected joinpoints enable the advice to implement different billing strategies. For instance, a worker could bill its bottom-most caller (here the worker 9 would bill the caller 4). This is the semantics chosen by AspectJ for Cflow. A worker could also bill all its callers (here the worker 9 would bill caller 3 and caller 4), following simplified Java code inspired from the Java prototype (see Section 4) present how an advice can iterates over all callers collected by the previous pointcut:

```
Worker worker = (Worker)currentJoinPoint.getReceiver();
Iterator it = context.getTree().elements();
while(it.hasNext()){ worker.bill((Caller)it.next()); }
```

A worker could also bill its top-most (a.k.a. principal) caller. In this case, the pointcut could be modified (by replacing `Inter(Filter isCall)(Filter (isMethod "doService"))` by `principalC` of the previous section) so that it collects only the top-most caller.

Finally, let us now consider pools are responsible for billing callers for workers. The (executive non administrative) workers must be passed to the enclosing pool as specified by the following pointcut: `Inter retPool (path execNonAdminW)`. Such a pointcut passes context downward from callers to workers (with `Cflow`), then upward from workers to pools (with `Path`). When `p1.doAllCallers` returns, the advice can visit a tree of (executive non administrative) workers. This tree is constituted of workers number 1, 5, 6 and 9. The advice can then visit a tree of callers for *each worker*.

4   A Prototype for Java

In this section, we describe a prototype for Java that evaluates a pointcut, on the fly, while a base program is being executed. First, we present its overall architecture, then we detail implementation of the operators of our language with simplified excerpt from the actual available implementation. Finally, we discuss context passing implementation.

4.1   Prototype Architecture

Our prototype implements the Interpreter design pattern [9]: each operator of our language is implemented by a class that extends an abstract class `PcD`. A pointcut is an abstract syntax tree built by instantiating these classes (e.g., `new Cflow(new Filter(new IsMethod("foo")))` line 3 below). We use AspectJ as a preprocessor to instrument the base program and call our interpreter:

```
1    aspect MyAspect {
2      pointcut all() : execution(* *.* (..));
3      PcD pcd = new Cflow(new Filter(new IsMethod("foo")));
4      before() : all() {
5        CallJp callJp = new CallJp(thisJoinPoint);
6        pcd.evalCallBefore(callJp);
7        if (pcd.isMatching()) myAdvice(pcd.getContext(), pcd.getCurrentJp);
8        pcd.evalCallAfter(callJp);
9      }
10     after() returning (Object ret) : all() {
11       RetJp retJp = new RetJp(thisJoinPoint, ret);
12       pcd.evalRetBefore(retJp);
13       if (pcd.isMatching()) myAdvice(pcd.getContext(), pcd.getCurrentJp);
14       pcd.evalRetAfter(retJp);
15     }
16     void myAdvice(Context context) { ... }
17   }
```

The abstract class `PcD` defines one boolean member `isMatching` and four interpretative methods `evalCallBefore`, `evalCallAfter`, `evalRetBefore` and `evalRetAfter`. Each time a method of a base program is called, a call joinpoint is created (line 5) and the method `evalCallBefore(CallJp)` is called (line 6) to update `pcd.isMatching`. When `isMatching` is `true` (i.e., the current joinpoint matches the pointcut `pcd`) an advice is executed (line 7) with context information as a parameter. Then `evalCallAfter(CallJp)` is called (line 8) to maintain data structures needed by context passing (see Section 4.3). The same scheme is implemented for method returns (line 10 to 15). This naïve implementation instruments every method (see the pointcut `all()`). A more realistic partial instrumentation is discussed in Section 5.3.

4.2   Implementation of Operators

Because of space constraint, we present only the implementation of four operators. Other operators are implemented similarly.

`Filter` evaluates its predicate for each joinpoint in order to update its `isMatching` field (line 3 and 5):

```
1 class Filter extends PcD {
2   Predicate pred;
3   void evalCallBefore(CallJp jp){isMatching = pred.apply(jp);}
4   void evalCallAfter(CallJp jp) { }
5   void evalRetBefore(RetJp jp)  {isMatching = pred.apply(jp);}
6   void evalRetAfter(RetJp jp)    { }
7 }
```

Each joinpoint predicate implements the interface `Predicate`, hence a method `boolean apply(JoinPoint)`. Our prototype provides different predicates; for instance, `IsMethod` enables to select joinpoints according to a method name (line 4):

```
1 class IsMethod implements Predicate {
2   String methodName;
3   boolean apply(JoinPoint jp) {
4     return methodName.equals(jp.getMethodName());}
5 }
```

Other predicates include: `IsCall, IsRet, IsInClass` which enables to select joinpoints on the declaring type of the method and `IsInstanceOf` which enables to select joinpoints on the dynamic type of the receiver. New predicates can be defined by users.

The operator `Inter` first evaluates its two sub-pointcuts `pcd1` and `pcd2` (line 4, 7 and 9, 12), then it computes the conjunction of the two corresponding booleans (line 5 and 10):

```
1 class Inter extends PcD {
2   PcD pcd1, pcd2;
3   void evalCallBefore(CallJp jp) {
```

```
4      pcd1.evalCallBefore(jp); pcd2.evalCallBefore(jp);
5      isMatching = pcd1.isMatching && pcd2.isMatching; }
6    void evalCallAfter(CallJp jp) {
7      pcd1.evalCallAfter(jp); pcd2.evalCallAfter(jp); }
8    void evalRetBefore(RetJp jp)  {
9      pcd1.evalRetBefore(jp); pcd2.evalRetBefore(jp);
10     isMatching = pcd1.isMatching && pcd2.isMatching; }
11   void evalRetAfter(RetJp jp)   {
12     pcd1.evalRetAfter(jp); pcd2.evalRetAfter(jp); }
13 }
```

For Cflow, isMatching is true from a call joinpoint (line 5) until the corresponding return joinpoint. To detect this return (line 10) a counter nbPendingCalls is maintained (line 6 and 11):

```
1  class Cflow extends PcD {
2    int nbPendingCalls = 0; PcD pcd;
3    void evalCallBefore(CallJp jp) {
4      pcd.evalCallBefore(jp);
5      isMatching = pcd.isMatching || nbPendingCalls >0;
6      if (isMatching) nbPendingCalls++; }
7    void evalCallAfter(CallJp jp) { pcd.evalCallAfter(jp); }
8    void evalRetBefore(RetJp jp) {
9      pcd.evalRetBefore(jp);
10     isMatching = nbPendingCalls > 0;
11     if (isMatching) nbPendingCalls--; }
12   void evalRetAfter(RetJp jp) { pcd.evalRetAfter(jp); }
13 }
```

Finally, Path is true for joinpoints that match its sub-pointcut or on the return of enclosing methods of those joinpoints. In order to detect those joinpoints a counter nbPendingCalls is maintained (line 4 and 9) and it is set to 1 (resp. 0) when a matching joinpoint of the sub-pointcut is a call (resp. a return). Then, isMatching is true for a return joinpoint when nbPendingCalls is negative.

```
1  class Path extends PcD {
2    int nbPendingCalls = 0; PcD pcd;
3    void evalCallBefore(CallJp jp) {
4      pcd.evalCallBefore(jp); nbPendingCalls++;
5      if (pcd.isMatching) nbPendingCalls = 1;
6      isMatching = pcd.isMatching;}
7    void evalCallAfter(CallJp jp) { pcd.evaCallAfter(jp); }
8    void evalRetBefore(RetJp jp) {
9      pcd.evalRetBefore(jp); nbPendingCalls---;
10     if (pcd.isMatching) nbPendingCalls = 0;
11     isMatching = nbPendingCalls < 0 || pcd.isMatching;}
12   void evalRetAfter(RetJp jp) { pcd.evalRetAfter(jp); }
13 }
```

4.3 Implementation of Context Passing

When an advice is executed the current joinpoint is available, but an advice may also require past joinpoints. For example, in Section 3.3, the billing aspect requires the caller identity when the worker is called. This context passing is implemented by `Cflow` as follows:

```
1 class CflowCP extends Cflow {
2   Stack cflowStack = new Stack(); Tree cflowTree = new Tree();
3   void evalCallBefore(CallJp jp) {
4     pcd.evalCallBefore(jp);
5     if(pcd.isMatching) {
6       cflowStack.push(nbPendingsCalls); cflowTree.add(jp); }
7   }
8   void evalCallAfter(CallJp jp) { pcd.evaCallAfter(jp); }
9   void evalRetBefore(RetJp jp)  { pcd.evalRetBefore(jp);}
10  void evalRetAfter (RetJp jp) {
11    pcd.evalRetAfter(jp);
12    if(cflowStack.peek() == nbPendingCalls){
13      cflowStack.pop(); cflowTree.remove(jp); }
14  }
15 }
```

A `Cflow` starts before a call joinpoint and finishes after the corresponding return. We use a stack (line 2, 6 and 13) in order to detect *each* of those return joinpoints (line 12, there is the same number of pending calls before a call and after the corresponding return). Joinpoints are stored in a (partial) execution tree (line 3) and can be accessed by the advice. Matching call joinpoint of *pcd* in `Cflow` *pcd* must be available from the call joinpoint until the corresponding return. It's the reason why joinpoints are stored by `evalCallBefore` (line 6) and discarded by `evalRetAfter` (line 13). Context passing is implemented similarly by operators `From` and `Path`.

5 Formal Study of Properties

In this section, we define an alphabet analysis that characterizes the joinpoints matching a given pointcut. We show how it enables to detect aspects interaction and optimize implementation.

5.1 Alphabet Analysis

A pointcut matches a list of method calls and/or returns. For instance,

```
    Inter (Cflow callsC) callsB
    where callsB = Inter (Filter isCall) (Filter (isMethod "b"))
          callsC = Inter (Filter isCall) (Filter (isMethod "c"))
```

matches calls to b during execution of c. So, it is a safe approximation to state that it matches *some* calls to b. We call such an approximation the alphabet of a pointcut. Those points in the program text which may generate a matching joinpoint are called joinpoint shadows [16]. An alphabet is as a pair of sets of joinpoints shadows. In Figure 4, we define an analysis that computes the alphabet of any pointcut.

$$\alpha : pcd \rightarrow 2^{all_C.all_M} \times 2^{all_C.all_M}$$

$$\alpha(\texttt{Filter isCall}) = (all_C.all_M, \varnothing)$$

$$\alpha(\texttt{Filter isRet}) = (\varnothing, all_C.all_M)$$

$$\alpha(\texttt{Filter (isMethod "m")}) = (all_C.\texttt{m}, all_C.\texttt{m})$$

$$\alpha(\texttt{Filter (isClass "c")}) = (\texttt{c}.all_M, \texttt{c}.all_M)$$

$$\alpha(\texttt{Filter (isInstanceOf "c")}) = (super_C(\texttt{c}).all_M, super_C(\texttt{c}).all_M)$$

$$\alpha(\texttt{Filter } p) = (all_C.all_M, all_C.all_M)$$

$$\alpha(\texttt{Cflow } pcd) = if(fst(\alpha(pcd)) == \varnothing)$$
$$then\ (\varnothing, \varnothing)\ else\ (all_C.all_M, all_C.all_M)$$

$$\alpha(\texttt{Path } pcd) = if(\alpha(pcd) == (\varnothing, \varnothing))$$
$$then\ (\varnothing, \varnothing)\ else\ (fst(\alpha\ pcd), all_C.all_M)$$

$$\alpha(\texttt{From } pcd) = if(\alpha(pcd) == (\varnothing, \varnothing))$$
$$then\ (\varnothing, \varnothing)\ else\ (all_C.all_M, all_C.all_M)$$

$$\alpha(\texttt{Diff } pcd_1\ pcd_2) = \alpha(pcd_1)$$

$$\alpha(\texttt{Union } pcd_1\ pcd_2) = (fst(\alpha(pcd_1)) \cup fst(\alpha(pcd_2)),$$
$$snd(\alpha(pcd_1)) \cup snd(\alpha(pcd_2)))$$

$$\alpha(\texttt{Inter } pcd_1\ pcd_2) = (fst(\alpha(pcd_1)) \cap fst(\alpha(pcd_2)),$$
$$snd(\alpha(pcd_1)) \cap snd(\alpha(pcd_2)))$$

$$\alpha(\texttt{Head } pcd) = \alpha(pcd)$$

$$\alpha(\texttt{Tail } pcd) = \alpha(pcd)$$

where

$$all_C.all_M = \{\texttt{c}.m \mid \forall c \in Classes, \forall m \in Methods(c)\}$$

$$all_C.\texttt{m} = \{\texttt{c}.\texttt{m} \mid \forall c \in Classes, \texttt{m} \in Methods(c)\}$$

$$\texttt{c}.all_M = \{\texttt{c}.m \mid \forall m \in Methods(c)\}$$

$$super_C(\texttt{c}).all_M = \texttt{c}.all_M \cup \{\texttt{c}.m \mid \forall c \in SuperClasses(\texttt{c}),$$
$$\forall m \in Methods(c)\}$$

Fig. 4. Alphabet Analysis

The pointcut `Filter isCall` matches all method calls of the base program (noted $all_C.all_M$) and no method return (noted $\varnothing$). `Filter isRet` matches the opposite. The alphabet of `Filter (isMethod "m")` is calls and returns of methods m in any class. The alphabet of `Filter (isClass "c")` is calls and returns of any method defined in the class c. The alphabet of `Filter (isInstanceOf "c")` is calls and returns of any method defined in the class c or in its super classes. Indeed, an instance of c can only receive invocation of methods defined in c and its super classes. Finally, an arbitrary user predicate p can match any method in any class. The alphabet of `From` pcd (resp. `Cflow` pcd) matches every method as long as the alphabet (resp. call alphabet) of pcd is not empty. The alphabet of `Path` pcd matches every method return and the method calls of pcd

as long as *pcd* is not empty. We omit rules for `CflowBelow` and `PathAbove` which are quite similar. The alphabet of `Diff` pcd_1 pcd_2 is not the difference of sub-pointcuts alphabets. Indeed, let us consider pointcuts `pcd1 = Filter(isMethod a)` (all calls and returns to a) and `pcd2 = Inter (Cflow (Filter (isMethod b))) (Filter (isMethod a))` (calls and returns to a during b), both alphabets of `pcd1` and `pcd2` are calls and returns to method a but `Diff pcd1 pcd2` (calls and returns to a not during b) is not empty in general and its alphabet is the alphabet of `pcd1`. Alphabet of `Union` (resp. `Inter`), is union (resp. intersection) of alphabets. Finally, `Head` *pcd* and `Tail` *pcd* do not alter the alphabet of *pcd* but discard some results.

This analysis provides feedback to aspect programmer: when the resulting alphabet is empty, the pointcut is probably erroneous (i.e., it never matches), when the resulting alphabet is $all_C.all_M$ the pointcut may matches every method which can be quite expensive.

5.2   Interaction Analysis

Two aspects interact when their pointcuts `pcd1` and `pcd2` matches same join-points. When the alphabet of (`Inter pcd1 pcd2`) is empty there is no interaction, otherwise there *may* be interaction. For instance, `pcd1 = Filter isCall` and `pcd2 = Filter isRet` obviously never interact (i.e., α(`Inter pcd1 pcd2`) $= (\varnothing, \varnothing)$). Our analysis can be too conservative. For instance, our analyze detects: `pcd1 = (Inter callsB (Cflow callsA))` and `pcd2 = (Diff callsB (Cflow callsA))` *may* interact because the alphabet of (`Inter pcd1 pcd2`) is not empty (but calls to b). The lack of interaction can be proved manually. Here it is easy to prove there is no conflict (i.e., `Inter pcd1 pcd2` $= \varnothing$) by using the standard laws of set operators (associativity, distributivity, etc. . .).

5.3   Efficient Instrumentation

In the Java prototype described in Section 4, *every* method of the base program is instrumented which can make the woven program very inefficient. It is not always mandatory to instrument every method of the base program. For instance, `Inter callsB (Cflow callsA)` only requires to instrument the methods a and b. In the other hand, `Cflow callsA` matches every joinpoint during a, so it requires every method to be instrumented.

Here is a simple criterion to optimize instrumentation for a pointcut *pcd*. In order to compute when *pcd* matches, it is sufficient to instrument $\alpha(pcd)$ as well as $\alpha(pcd')$ for all *pcd'* where `Cflow` *pcd'*, `Path` *pcd'*, `From` *pcd'*, `Head` *pcd'* and `Tail` *pcd'* are sub-terms of *pcd*. Indeed, *pcd* matches when an advice may be executed, and the different *pcd'* match when a joinpoint must be collected for context passing. So, we detect `Inter callsB (Cflow callsA)` only requires to instrument the methods a and b, while `Inter callsB (Cflow (Cflow callsA))` requires to instrument every method (in order to collect methods which are called during a).

6   Related Work

There is a growing body of work on AOP. In this section, we review this related work and focus on their pointcut languages.

AspectJ [13] is an AOP extension of Java that provides an implementation designed to be efficient. Regarding control-flow, its pointcut language is less expressive than ours: it provides only the `cflow` operator. This operator offers context passing but only the most recent pending call for recursive method is considered. On the other hand, the AspectJ pointcut language offers more kinds of joinpoints than we do (i.e., field reading, field writing, exception handling) and distinguishes method call (caller side) from method execution (callee side). It also deals with static scope (i.e., pointcut on the structure of the code instead of the structure of the execution tree). Regarding semantics, an operational semantics [25] has been proposed. We believe our semantics based on post-mortem trace predicate is simpler for users. AspectJ has been integrated with different IDEs, so that they annotate the base program to show joinpoint shadows. Our alphabet analysis is equivalent to this analysis.

Walker *et al.* have introduced the idea of sequences of events as an extension of AspectJ with a `morecent` pointcut designator [23]. This work was generalized with a context free language (a.k.a. grammar) over past events [24]. Their pointcut language based on grammar is more expressive than ours, but it is less compositional (in particular their tracecut cannot take tracecut as a parameter). Their prototype also provides partial instrumentation.

Sereni *et al.* [21] generalize `cflow` by specifying regular expression of pending calls in the stack. Sequencing operator of regular expressions can be translated in our language by nesting `Cflow`, and the choice operator | is equivalent to `Union`. However, we have no way to translate the * operator of regular expressions in our language. So, their `cflow` is more general than ours. In the other hand, their generalized `cflow` can not express `Path` or `From` because those operators requires past joinpoints which are not (anymore) in the call stack. This work focuses on efficient implementation: a control-flow analysis can be used to detect when an advice can be statically inlined in the base program. Such an analysis can also be used to detect some pointcut conflicts.

In a previous paper, Douence *et al.* [6] use an execution monitor in order to detect sequences of execution events. Their pointcut language makes it easy to monitor several sequences in parallel, however it is Turing-complete and interaction must be proven manually. It provides no control-flow primitive operators although they can be hand coded as exemplified with `cflow`. When the pointcut language is restricted to regular expressions [5], conflict detection can be automated, but `Cflow` and `Path` cannot be expressed.

Other approaches do not focus on control-flow. Hyper/J [18] proposes a language to merge class graphs. The pointcut language of DJ [17] specifies traversals over object graphs. Masuhara *et al.* [15] propose a pointcut language for data-flow. These approaches are complementary to ours: they focus on different views of programs (class graph, object graph, data-flow graph).

Other researchers propose specialized pointcut languages but rely on general programming languages to define relationship between several joinpoints. These work include: method call interceptors (formalized in a type-safe manner by Lämmel [14]), composition filters (a.k.a. wrappers) [2], JAC [19] which relies on Java to define sets of joinpoints. DeVolder *et al.* [22] use Prolog to define pointcuts on an abstract syntax tree. Gybels [10] also use Prolog but takes into account dynamic values.

Finally, execution monitors have been used before AOP to analyze and debug programs. For instance, Opium [8] makes it easy to define dynamic analyses for Prolog applications. This work has been adapted to C applications [7]. In both cases, the monitor is programmed with a Prolog library. PathExplorer [11] uses temporal logic to dynamically detect illegal sequences of execution events for Java programs. All of these provide pointcut languages (to specify sequences of execution events) but do not provide advice languages.

7   Conclusion and Future Work

In this article, we proposed a pointcut language that extends the pointcut language of AspectJ for control-flow. It allows top-down (with `Cflow`) but also bottom-up (with `Path`) and left-to-right (with `From`) context-passing. We provide a simple semantics of our pointcut language based on post-mortem execution trace. We argue such an intuitive semantics is mandatory for aspect programmers. We also provide a prototype for Java, based on instrumentation of the base program. This interpreter can be directly implemented to get a prototype for any programming language that supports strict functions (e.g., C, Java, etc...). Our prototype for Java, allows us to exemplify our language expressiveness by defining complex pointcuts for a generic application. Finally, our specialized language and its semantics promote formal studies. Regarding aspects interaction, we propose an alphabet analysis that enable to detect (lack of) interaction and we discuss manual proofs. We also discuss optimization of the base program instrumentation. Our pointcut language for control-flow offers many future work opportunities. First, it should be studied how our Java prototype could be formally derived from an incremental version of our Haskell semantics. Second, the laws and properties of our operators (e.g. `cflow (cflow` *pcd*) and `cflow` *pcd* match the same joinpoints) should be explored. These laws enable pointcut simplifications and could help to detect interactions. Third, tree (a.k.a. context) visitors should be provided to advice programmer. These visitors could be used to infer *partial* context to be collected (there is no need to pass what is never visited).

Acknowledgments

The authors thank Simon Denier, Jacques Noyé, Marc Ségura, Mario Südholt, Eric Tanter and our reviewers for their comments on this article. Rémi dedicates this work to C., A. and S.

References

1. AspectJ Site. Aspect-oriented programming in java with aspectj, 2001.
   http://www.parc.com/research/csl/projects/aspectj/downloads/OReilly2001.pdf.
2. Lodewijk Bergmans and Mehmet Aksits. Composing crosscutting concerns using composition filters. *Communications of the ACM*, 2001.
3. USA Boston, Massachusetts, editor. *(AOSD 2003)*. ACM Press, 2003.
4. Yvonne Coady, Gregor Kiczales, Mike Feeley, and Greg Smolyn. Using aspectc to improve the modularity of path-specific customization in operating system code. In *(ESEC and FSE 2001)*. ACM Press, 2001.
5. Rémi Douence, Pascal Fradet, and Mario Südholt. A framework for the detection and resolution of aspect interactions. In *(GPCE 2002)*, volume 2487 of *LNCS*. Springer-Verlag, 2002.
6. Rémi Douence, Olivier Motelet, and Mario Südholt. A formal definition of crosscuts. In (Reflection 2001) [20].
7. M. Ducassé. Coca: An automated debugger for C. In *(ICSE 99)*. ACM Press, 1999.
8. M. Ducassé. Opium: An extendable trace analyser for Prolog. *The Journal of Logic programming*, 39, 1999.
9. Eric Gamma, Richard Helm, Ralph Johnson, and John Vlissides. *Design Patterns: Elements of Reusable Object-Oriented Software*. Addison-Wesley, 1994.
10. Kris Gybels and Johan Brichau. Arranging language features for pattern-based crosscuts. In Boston [3].
11. Klaus Havelund and Grigore Rosu. Synthesizing monitors for safety properties. In *(TACAS 2002)*, volume 2280 of *LNCS*. Springer-Verlag, 2002.
12. Paul Hudak, Simon Peyton Jones, and al. Report on the programming language haskell: a non-strict, purely functional language version 1.2. *SIGPLAN Not.*, 27, 1992.
13. Gregor Kiczales, Erik Hilsdale, Jim Hugunin, Mik Kersten, Jeffrey Palm, and William G. Griswold. An overview of AspectJ. *LNCS*, 2072, 2001.
14. Ralf Lämmel. A semantic approach to method-call interception. In *(AOSD 2002)*. ACM Press, 2002.
15. Hidehiko Masuhara and Kazunori Kawauchi. Dataflow pointcut in aspect-oriented programming. In *(APLAS 2003)*, volume 2895 of *LNCS*. Springer Verlag, 2003.
16. Hidehiko Masuhara, Gregor Kiczales, and Chris Dutchyn. Using aspectc to improve the modularity of path-specific customization in operating system code. In *(CC2003)*, volume 2622 of *LNCS*. Springer-Verlag, 2003.
17. Doug Orleans and Karl Lieberherr. Dj: Dynamic adaptive programming in java. In (Reflection 2001) [20].
18. Harold Ossher and Peri Tarr. Multi-dimensional separation of concerns and the hyperspace approach. In *Proceedings of the Symposium on Software Architectures and Component Technology: The State of the Art in Software Development.* Kluwer, 2000.
19. Renaud Pawlak, Lionel Seinturier, Laurence Duchien, and Gerard Florin. Jac: A flexible solution for aspect-oriented programming in java. In (Reflection 2001) [20].
20. *(Reflection 2001)*, volume 2192 of *LNCS*. Springer-Verlag, 2001.
21. Damien Sereni and Oege de Moor. Static analysis of aspects. In Boston [3].
22. Kris De Volder and Theo D'Hondt. Aspect-oriented logic meta programming. In *(Reflection 1999)*, volume 1616 of *LNCS*. Springer-Verlag, 1999.
23. R. J. Walker and G. C. Murphy. Joinpoints as ordered events: Towards applying implicit context to aspect-orientation. In *Advanced Separation of Concerns Workshop at (ICSE 2001)*, 2001.

24. R. J. Walker and G. C. Murphy. Communication history patterns: Direct imple-
    mentation of protocol specifications. Technical report, Department of Computer
    Science, University of Calgary, 2004.
25. Mitchell Wand, Gregor Kiczales, and Chris Dutchyn. A semantics for advice
    and dynamic join points in aspect-oriented programming. In *FOAL Workshop at
    (AOSD 2002)*, 2002.

Appendix: Semantics in Haskell (Excerpt)

```
eval :: Trace -> PcD -> [JoinPoint]
eval t (Filter pred)     = filter pred t
eval t (Inter pcd1 pcd2)= inter (eval t pcd1) (eval t pcd2)
eval t (Cflow pcd)    = foldr union [] (map (cflow t) (eval t pcd))
eval t (Path  pcd)    = foldr union [] (map (path t) (eval t pcd))
eval t (From  pcd)    = foldr union [] (map (from t) (eval t pcd))

from :: Trace -> JoinPoint -> [JoinPoint]
from t p = dropWhile (/= p) t

cflow :: Trace -> JoinPoint -> [JoinPoint]
cflow t p | isCall p = cflow' 0 (from t p)
          | isRet  p = []

cflow' :: Int -> Trace -> [JoinPoint]
cflow' i ((Call id,n):es) = (Call id,n):(cflow' (i+1) es)
cflow' 1 ((Ret  id,n):es) = [(Ret id, n)]
cflow' i ((Ret  id,n):es) = (Ret id, n):(cflow' (i-1) es)

path :: Trace -> JoinPoint -> [JoinPoint]
path t p | isCall p = p:path' 0 (from t p)
         | isRet  p = path' 0 (from t p)

path' :: Int -> Trace -> [JoinPoint]
path' _ []               = []
path' 0 ((Ret  id,n):es) = (Ret id,n):(path' 0 es)
path' i ((Call id,n):es) = path' (i+1) es
path' i ((Ret  id,n):es) = path' (i-1) es
```

SourceWeave.NET:
Cross-Language Aspect-Oriented Programming

Andrew Jackson and Siobhán Clarke

Distributed Systems Group, Department of Computer Science, Trinity College Dublin
Dublin 2, Ireland
{Andrew.Jackson,Siobhan.Clarke}@cs.tcd.ie

Abstract. Aspect-Oriented Programming (AOP) addresses limitations in the Object-Oriented (OO) paradigm relating to modularisation of crosscutting behaviour. In AOP, crosscutting behaviour is expressed as *aspects* that are integrated with a base program through a *weaving* process. Many language-specific AOP models already exist, requiring the programmer to work with a single language for base and aspect programs. The .NET framework, with its multi-language standards and architecture, has presented a new opportunity for *cross-language* AOP within .NET. Advances have been made to take advantage of this opportunity, but at the expense of qualities such as the ability to debug executing code, or define some kinds of weaving capabilities. This paper describes an investigation into providing cross-language AOP in .NET without making such compromises. The approach, called SourceWeave.NET, allows debugging because it weaves source code, and also provides an extensive weaving model. We describe what can be learned from SourceWeave.NET, in terms of both its benefits, and also its limitations.

1 Introduction

When modelling software systems using the Object-Oriented (OO) paradigm, some kinds of behaviours cannot be cleanly modularised into the primary OO encapsulation unit, the object. Behaviour that has an impact on multiple objects in a system (often termed *crosscutting*) is likely to be scattered and tangled throughout the system. Aspect-Oriented (AO) programming addresses this problem by providing constructs to modularise crosscutting behaviour, and to state where in the system this behaviour should be executed [9].

There have been many different approaches to implementing AOP that target a single programming language [3, 4, 7, 8, 17, 6, 36]. The .NET framework opens up a whole new set of opportunities to provide the benefits of AOP in a multi-language environment [22]. .NET is an architecture that enables multi-language programming. It is based on a set of standards that specify a common infrastructure for language implementation, and provides a run-time environment on which supported languages can execute. The architecture is extensive, and offers opportunities for different strategies for employing language independent AOP. Possible strategies include

G. Karsai and E. Visser (Eds.): GPCE 2004, LNCS 3286, pp. 115–135, 2004.

weaving at pre-compile-time, compile-time, load-time or run-time. There has already been a considerable amount of activity related to applying AOP to .NET in different ways. In general for such approaches, programmers lose the ability to debug their source code. Current approaches that work with source code in .NET, such as EOS [25] and Aspect.NET [28] do so by extending a particular language, and lose the benefit of cross-language AOP.

This paper describes SourceWeave.NET, which provides cross-language AOP at the source code level while providing a high level of support for *debugging expressiveness*. Debugging expressiveness relates to the extent to which a developer may step through and inspect woven source code. With a high level of debugging expressiveness, a developer may scrutinise state changes as woven crosscutting behaviour executes. This level of developer support is becoming more important as a number of technological advances further complicate modern application development. For example, advances in wireless network technologies, together with requirements to support user mobility and pervasive computing, pose new challenges to developers that are required to provide mobile, context-aware applications. It is likely that application components in such an environment will be expressed in many different languages (e.g., domain specific languages (DSLs)) and will be required to collaborate and interact to provide the context-aware services a mobile user requires. The highly dynamic nature of pervasive environments also requires applications to deal with unpredictable state changes, compounding the need for complexity management and a high level of debugging expressiveness. AOP can help reduce the inherent complexity of this pervasive environment, and SourceWeave.NET provides an AOP environment that can deal with the multiple languages of collaborating components and also provide debugging expressiveness for dynamic state change scrutiny.

The SourceWeave.Net architecture is based on a .NET standard for representing source code as abstract syntax trees called CodeDOM. Using SourceWeave.NET, a developer can write base and aspect components in standard C#, VB.NET and J#, specify how these components should be woven with an XML descriptor, and step through the original source when debugging woven systems.

Section 2 provides some background into the technologies either used in, or informing, SourceWeave.NET. Section 3 describes the SourceWeave.NET architecture, and how it works. Section 4 provides an assessment of the benefits and liabilities of the approach. Section 5 describes related work, while Section 6 summarises and concludes.

2 Background

This section provides a brief overview of AspectJ and .NET. The AOP model used by AspectJ was considered as a requirements specification for SourceWeave.NET's weaving model. We describe .NET especially in terms of the standards it imposes and uses. The .NET architecture gives considerable scope for different strategies for applying the AO paradigm to the architecture. A brief discussion of some possibilities is included.

2.1 AspectJ

AspectJ extends Java and enables the developer to modularise additional behaviour to run at certain well-defined points of execution in the program, called "crosscutting" behaviour [35]. Handling crosscutting in AspectJ is based on identifying points of execution in the program (*joinpoints*) and specifying additional behaviour to be executed at those execution points (*advice*). This specification of a point of execution in a program is termed a *pointcut* and it identifies joinpoints. A pointcut can be primitive or composite. A primitive pointcut identifies a particular code section based on a singular characteristic of the code. For example, the primitive handler(FooException) pointcut identifies joinpoints at catch constructs where the type or super-type of the exception caught matches the exception-type specified in the handler pointcut. A composite pointcut is a series of pointcuts composed via logical operators. A joinpoint can be mapped to a specific construct in the program code which when executed results in the generation of the joinpoint. The particular construct exists in a code segment called the shadow of the joinpoint (*joinpoint shadow*) [14]. Through comparing the characteristics of pointcuts and the program text, joinpoint shadows are identified. The handler(FooException) pointcut matches catch constructs that refer to the FooException type and its super-types. The executable code segments of catch constructs matched are then joinpoint shadows. At run-time joinpoints are generated based on the positive evaluation of the pointcuts against the joinpoint shadows. Advice is a method-like mechanism used to identify behaviour that should be executed at joinpoints. AspectJ provides a sophisticated model for joinpoints, pointcuts and advice that we considered a good basis from which to conduct our research.

2.2 .NET

The .NET framework is an architecture that enables multi-language programming and is based on a series of ECMA [2] and Microsoft standards. These standards specify a common infrastructure on which different programming languages can be implemented. The layered architecture of the .NET framework is illustrated in Figure 1. There are two high-level layers within the architecture. The first is the compilation layer where source code written in various languages can be compiled to assemblies. The second layer is the run-time environment, which takes the assemblies and executes the Intermediate Language (IL) code packaged within the assemblies.

Fig. 1. .NET Layered Architecture

The compilation layer is defined by the Common Language Specification [23] (CLS) standard. This defines conventions that languages must support in order to be inter-operable within .NET. Any .NET compliant language that conforms to the CLS can compile to a common IL. Each language implementer provides a compiler that takes in source code and outputs IL packaged as assemblies or modules. A Common Class Library [20] (CCL) is a set of base namespaces or libraries that are common to all .NET languages and are available in all .NET compliant languages. A Common Type System [21] (CTS) is a subset of the CLS that defines OO types and values that must be supported by all .NET compliant languages. A CTS is the most critical pre-requisite for language integration.

Assemblies are deployable units that contain IL code executed by the Common Language Runtime (CLR) [15]. The CLR acts as a virtual machine that manages code execution, memory and threads. An assembly forms a security, type, reference scope and version boundary in .NET [18]. It follows a strict format and contains an assembly manifest. This manifest exposes metadata about the assembly, allowing it to be self-describing.

2.3 Applying AOP to .NET

One of the main attractions of the .NET framework is its support for language independence. Approaches to applying AOP to .NET have an opportunity to take corresponding advantage of this to achieve cross-language aspect-oriented programming. There are a number of possible strategies that can be followed to achieve this. These are discussed briefly here and are later expanded in Section 5.

One strategy is to extend the CLR. This strategy has been shown to exhibit several drawbacks including performance degradation; current approaches that have followed this strategy support limited joinpoint models and do not support essential developer tools such as debuggers.

Another strategy is to apply AOP to .NET through weaving assembly packaged IL. IL based approaches have had varying levels of success. This strategy however, suffers a loss of tool support such as debugging. This is due to breaking the bonds that bind the IL to source code through IL weaving. This adversely affects the debugger's ability to step through woven source code.

An extension of the CLS/CTS to introduce AOP at the compilation level is another possible strategy to achieve cross-language AOP. However, changing these specifications means that the .NET language providers have to update their language implementation accordingly. Beyond this, the framework tool-set would also have to be upgraded to handle the new AO constructs. Applying the new AOP extension to the CLS/CTS would be infeasible in the short-to-medium term.

A strategy based on working at the source-code level avoids these problems encountered by other approaches. This strategy ensures language-independent AOP, and provides the rich joinpoint model that AOP developers have come to expect. More importantly this strategy offers the developer facilities, such as debugging expressiveness, currently unique to source-code level AOP.

3 SourceWeave.NET

SourceWeave.NET is a cross-language source code weaver that allows modularisation and re-composition of crosscutting concerns independent of implementation language. SourceWeave.NET supports an extensive joinpoint and aspect model based on AspectJ, but does not require extensions to any .NET languages. Each component, whether base or aspect, is declaratively complete. A separate XML specification describes the pointcuts and advice necessary for weaving.

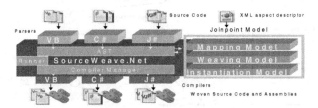

Fig. 2. SourceWeave.NET Architecture

In the following sections we will describe the architecture of SourceWeave.NET as shown in Figure 2. The main components of the architecture are: a component which contains a set of language parsers that converts all input source code to an AST, a joinpoint model component that weaves the input components and aspects, and a compilation component that compiles the woven code into assemblies.

3.1 AST and Parsers

It is the responsibility of the parsers and AST component to produce an object graph representation of the input source code. The Joinpoint Model component works with these object graph representations to perform its weaving process. There is a different parser for each language used, each of which converts the input code to the same object graph format. The object graph format we used is a .NET CCL component called CodeDOM (Code Document Object Model) [19]. The CodeDOM namespace provides interfaces and classes to represent the structure of a source code document, independent of language, as an object graph or tree.

Figure 3 demonstrates how source code is abstracted onto an object graph. The root of all elements of the graph is a CodeCompileUnit, and every source code element is linked to CodeCompileUnit in a hierarchical containment structure (i.e. a CodeCompileUnit contains CodeNamespacees which in turn contain CodeClassees). Figure 3(a) illustrates an example of a C# program that has a method WriteMessage in class MessageWriter that writes a message to the console. Figure 3(b) illustrates an example of a VB program that has a method beforeNewMessage in class VBMessageCounter which writes an integer counter to the console. In the corresponding CodeDOM graphs we can see how the differing source code syntax maps to the similar abstracted types in CodeDOM

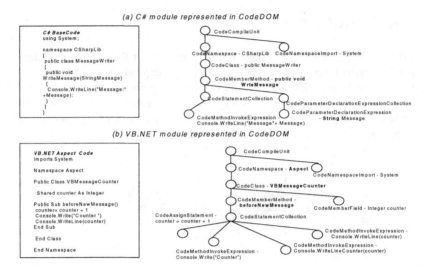

Fig. 3. CodeDOM Source Code Abstraction

Table 1. Supported Joinpoints

Joinpoint Category	Joinpoint types	Supported
Execution	method execution	Yes
	Constructor execution	Yes
	handler execution	Yes
	initializer execution	No
	staticInitializer execution	No
	object initialization	No
Call	method call	Yes
	constructor call	Yes
	object pre-initialization	No
Field Access	field reference	Yes
	field assignment	Yes

3.2   Joinpoint Model

In AOP, joinpoints are described as "well-defined places in the structure or execution flow of a program where additional behaviour can be attached" [9]. Aspect languages have "three critical elements: a join point model, a means of identifying join points, and a means of affecting implementation at join points" [8]. This section describes the joinpoints supported in SourceWeave.NET. Section 3.3 describes the AOP language used to identify joinpoints. Section 3.4 describes how SourceWeave.NET identifies joinpoints and affects implementation at joinpoints. First though, we look at the AspectJ joinpoints that SourceWeave.NET supports.

As listed in Table 1, SourceWeave.NET handles most of the joinpoints supported by AspectJ. Those that are not were deemed to be so similar to other ones that they did not require further research. Joinpoints exist at run-time during program execution. In the following sections we will show how SourceWeave.NET enables join-point identification and how implementation is affected at joinpoints.

3.3 AOP Language

A developer wishing to leverage AOP must have a means of identifying joinpoints and specifying the behaviour modification required at identified joinpoints. Source-Weave.NET allows the developer to achieve this through an XML AOP language, based on the AspectJ language, which was introduced in Weave.NET [11]. The As-pectJ language is an AOP extension of the java language. As raised in section 2.3, it would be impractical to follow the same strategy in .NET. To avoid language exten-sion the developer identifies joinpoints through an XML pointcut specification lan-guage which refers to OO source code.

In the XML schema that defines the AOP language used in SourceWeave.NET, an aspect is considered to be analogous to a class, and methods analogous to advice. XML tags define advice and pointcuts, with refinements to capture the varying sub-tleties required. See [12] for a detailed specification.

3.3.1 Pointcuts

SourceWeave.NET supports primitive signature and type-based pointcuts, control flow pointcuts, contextual pointcuts and compositions of pointcuts. Table 2 lists the primitive pointcuts that SourceWeave.NET supports.

Table 2. Supported Pointcuts

Pointcut Category	Primitive	Supported
Signature and type-based	execution(signature)	Yes
	call(signature)	Yes
	get(signature)	Yes
	set(signature)	Yes
	handler(type pattern)	Yes
	initializer(type pattern)	Yes
	staticInitializer(signature)	Yes
	object initialization(signature)	Yes
	within(type pattern)	Yes
	withincode(signature)	Yes
Control Flow	cflow(pointcut)	Yes
	cflowbelow(pointcut)	Yes
Context	this(type pattern/variable)	Yes
	target(type pattern/variable)	Yes
	args(type pattern/variable)	Yes

Signature and type-based pointcuts identify joinpoints through matching code segments that correspond to the code features described in the pointcut. Source-Weave.NET, like AspectJ, also supports the use of property type-based pointcuts. This is where pointcuts are specified "in terms of properties of methods other than their exact name" [35]. Control flow based pointcuts relate to other pointcuts and not signatures. These pointcuts select joinpoints in the control flow of joinpoints from its related pointcut. Contextual pointcuts expose part of the execution context at their joinpoint. The "context" is information that can be derived at run-time when the code is executing, and can be used within advice. Finally, in SourceWeave.NET pointcuts can be composed with logical and, or and not operators, to form composite point-cuts.

3.3.2 Advice

A developer must also have a means of associating advice with pointcuts, to specify what behaviour change should occur at a joinpoint that matches the associated poin-tuct. The AOP language employed by SourceWeave.NET supports three types of advice before, after and around. Each advice type denotes how advice is woven at a joinpoint. Before for example denotes that the advice behaviour should be introduced before joinpoint execution.

3.3.3 XML Aspect Descriptor

Figure 4 and its accompanying description in Table 3 provide a practical example of the AOP language used in SourceWeave.NET. In the XML aspect descriptor there is a declaration of a pointcut and advice associated with that pointcut. The arrows (in Figure 4) drawn between the XML aspect descriptor and Base/Aspect code (described in Table 3) illustrate the relationship between the XML AOP language and source code. The aspect code is written in VB.NET and the base code is written in C#. The XML advice declaration, typing and pointcut association is separated from source code to ensure AOP language neutrality. Here we see how the XML AOP language brings advice declaration and actual advice implementation together. The example also depicts how the language enables the developer to identify execution points in the program that they wish to crosscut with advice behaviour. This is achieved in this example through the declaration of typed-based pointcut expressed here as a series of XML tags.

Table 3 describes the relationship between the XML elements and the Aspect and Base source code presented in Figure 4.

3.4 Weaver Implementation

The joinpoint model and AOP language supported in SourceWeave.NET is explained in sections 3.2 and 3.3. In this section we illustrate how this model has been imple-mented.

3.4.1 Mapping Model

The mapping model component is responsible for identifying all of the joinpoint shadows in the CodeDOM representation of the base program that correspond to the joinpoints that may match a given pointcut. First, a DOM is created based on the XML Aspect Descriptor file, this is wrapped by a series of interfaces, presented in Figure 5, that map to the XML schema and enables simplified usage of the weaving

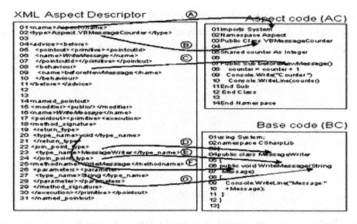

Fig. 4. Cross-language Weaving Specification

Table 3. XML Aspect Descriptor – separating AOP constructs and .NET code

Arrow	XML Line	Code Line	Description
A,B	02	AC 02-03	Arrow A from XML line 02 to AC line 02 and Arrow B to line 03 in the AC code emphasises a match between the declaration of the aspect `Aspect.VBMessageCounter` to the `Aspect` namespace and `VBMessageCounter` class.
C	04-11	AC 07	Arrow C identifies a method named `beforeNewMessage` the signature of which is at line 07 of the AC as advice. The `<before>` tag on line 04 indicates the advice type.
D	20	BC 06	Arrow D from line 20 to line 06 of the BC illustrates a match between the return type of the execution pointcut and the BC.
E	23	BC 04	Arrow E leading from line 23 to 04 of the BC shows the identification of the `MessageWriter` type in which joinpoint may be crosscut.
F	22	BC 06	The `WriteMessage` method name as we see, declared on line 22, identifies the method of the same name on line 06 of the BC. This is again highlighted by arrow F that links the identical names
G	27	BC 06	Arrow G from line 27 to 06 of the BC matches the `String` parameter specified in the pointcut.

specification. For example, the `Aspect` type enables identification of the class in which the crosscutting behaviour is modularised. The `Aspect` type references `Pointcut` and `Advice` types.

Pointcuts match joinpoints at run-time. To enable run-time joinpoint generation the mapping model must firstly identify joinpoint shadows. As discussed in Section 2.1 joinpoint shadows [14] are areas in program text where joinpoints may originate. The declared characteristics of pointcuts are used to discover joinpoint shadows in the CodeDOM AST. Once generated, the CodeDOM graph is traversed and the instances of the `JoinpointShadow` type are created at points where joinpoints could be generated. Instances of the `pointcut` type containing the joinpoint identification criteria are used on a subsequent `JoinpointShadow` traversal. At each joinpoint shadow the pointcut is compared against the relevant CodeDOM information obtained through the `JoinpointShadow` interface. Where comparisons are positive a `PointcutToJoinPointBinding` is created to represent the match.

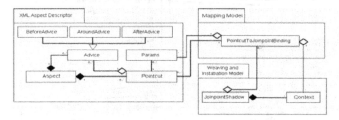

Fig. 5. Mapping Model Structure

Joinpoint shadows are represented as types in SourceWeave.NET, as illustrated in Figure 6. An execution joinpoint shadow, for example, is expressed as a `MethodExecutionJoinpointShadow` type. Each `JoinpointShadow` type references and wraps a CodeDOM object which the joinpoint shadow represents. For example the, `MethodExecutionJoinpointSadow` and wraps the CodeDOM `CodeMemberMethod`.

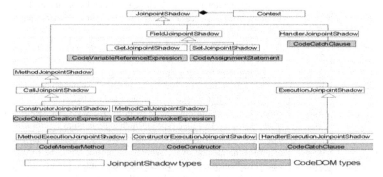

Fig. 6. Joinpoint Shadow Model

3.4.1.1 Signature and Type-Based Pointcuts

Providing mappings to signature and type-based pointcuts is relatively straightforward. SourceWeave.NET matches the attributes exposed by the CodeDOM objects against the signatures declared within the XML signature pointcut representations.

Returning to our example presented in Section 3.3.3, a signature based `MethodExecutionJoinpointShadow` which wraps a `CodeMemberMethod` object that represents the method `void MessageWriter.WriteMessage(String Message)`. The `CodeMemberMethod` is an object created when the source code is parsed to CodeDOM (see Figure 3). The pointcut in Figure 4 describes the features held in the `MethodExecutionJoinpointShadow` instance which when matched against the instance of the `Pointcut` type, representing the declared pointcut, results in a match and the creation of a representative `PointcutToJoin-PointBinding`.

3.4.1.2 Control Flow Pointcuts

To identify joinpoints based on cflow pointcuts, we insert Boolean flags (initially `false`) into the aspect class CodeDOM image to represent the `cflow`. This amounts to a CodeDOM `CodeConditionStatement` representing the test being inserted into the CodeDOM representation. When the joinpoint matches the `cflow`'s associated pointcut, then this flag is activated. Activation takes the form of an invocation at the joinpoint of an inserted CodeDOM `CodeAssignStatement`, where the cflow flag is set to true. At all joinpoint shadows the state of the cflow flags are tested. Joinpoints are then matched by checking to see if they are part of any cflow. At run-time, this is achieved by querying the aspect's cflow activation flags or execution of the inserted `CodeConditionStatement`. If a flag is true then the joinpoint shadow has matched the cflow otherwise there is no match. This joinpoint can then be crosscut by the advice associated with cflow pointcut.

3.4.1.3 Contextual Pointcuts

Context pointcut matching is achieved by matching the type information held within the CodeDOM objects that represent signature based joinpoint shadows. For example, from `MethodExecutionJoinpointShadows`'s encapsulation of the `Code-MemberMethod` instance, this instance exposes a `CodeParameterDeclara-tionExpressionCollection`. The parameter types can be examined for matching against types declared in an `args` pointcut. The context information is represented in the joinpoint shadow as instances of the `Context` type and is matched against `TypedFormalParameters`, which represents the XML declaration of context pointcuts.

Context is exposed at the method execution joinpoint shadow representing the `WriteMessage` method shown in the base code section of Figure 4. This method contains a `String` parameter named `Message` seen at lines 06-07. The method is also declared within the scope of the `MessageWriter` class. The objects of those types can be exposed to the crosscutting behaviour at runtime by using the `args`, `this` or `target` pointcuts. For example, if the XML described a pointcut of the form `String messages:args(message)` the joinpoint shadow would match the pointcut and the message would be exposed to the crosscutting behaviour.

3.4.2 Weaving and Instantiation Model

Once the mapping model has matched all joinpoint shadows in the target code against the pointcuts and the proper bindings have been created, the next step is to affect implementation at the bound joinpoint shadows. The weaving model intersects the matched joinpoint shadows with the appropriate advice for the related pointcut. Each `JoinpointShadow` type encapsulates how advice should be woven at the source code point that it represents. Advice types `before`, `after` and `around` are modelled as types `BeforeAdvice`, `AfterAdvice` and `AroundAdvice`. These types and their relationships with other types used by SourceWeave.NET can seen in Figure 5. Advice types encapsulate information about the advice methods within the class identified as an aspect by the XML Aspect Descriptor.

SourceWeave.NET implements two types of weaving – direct and indirect. With direct weaving, a joinpoint shadow has matched a pointcut and there is advice associated with that pointcut. This advice is the behaviour that is to be introduced at the CodeDOM source code representation in a manner determined by the type of the advice. Indirect weaving is required for control flow joinpoints. Because we can only know at run-time the joinpoint shadows that need to be affected due to `cflow` membership, abstracted code representations are inserted at every joinpoint shadow to check for `cflow` membership and depending on a positive outcome at run-time, behaviour is then introduced at the joinpoint. In either scheme, as the crosscutting code is weaved into the base source code a set of comments is also interwoven around injected code. These comments give a clear and precise understanding of what is happening in the generated advice call and why this code was injected, with reference to the Aspect XML Descriptors weaving specification. This commenting strengthens the provided debugging expressiveness as the developer will be able to gain a quick appreciation of what is occurring in the weaved code.

There are a number of steps required for both direct and indirect weaves. Firstly, if the aspect class is in another `CodeCompileUnit` (i.e. a different aspect or base code module) then a reference between the `CodeCompileUnit` and the aspects `CodeCompileUnit` is made. This ensures that the compiler can find the types used in the woven code at compile-time. Then, the list of imports or using statements is amended if the aspect's namespace is not present. An aspect declaration and instantiation of the aspect are required.

To support debugging expressiveness we used a different instantiation model to AspectJ. An instantiation model dictates when instances of aspects will be created to support the execution of the crosscutting behaviour that is encapsulated by that aspect. Debugging expressiveness partially relates to the investigation of state changes based on operations within a component. Per-advice instantiation involves instantiation of the aspect containing the advice at each advice call. As there is a new instance for each call, there is no scope to maintain any state across calls (and indeed, no corresponding need to debug state changes across calls). However, this restriction does not cater for many requirements, for example, the message counter from Figure 4. AspectJ also has a singleton instantiation model that we considered, where one instance of the aspect is shared through out the system. However, this approach is very state heavy for debugging purposes. SourceWeave.NET's instantiation model is a compromise between the two, and follows a per-method instantiation strategy. A per-method model means the aspect is instantiated once in every method in which advice on that aspect is called. We also investigated instantiation models which were less granular, such as per-class instantiation, but found the flow based state change on a per-method basis more intuitive for a developer when debugging. As well as tracing state changes based on control flows, we also found that the generated source code looked much cleaner when using the per-method instantiation model, which again supports debugging expressiveness.

Once the aspect declaration and instantiation has been inserted into the CodeDOM method representation, we can then insert advice calls on the aspect. Depending on the insertion rules that vary depending on joinpoint type, a CodeDOM `CodeMethodInvokeExpression` is created to introduce the advice at the joinpoint. In this call there may be context information required which is added to the call in the form of arguments that correspond to parameters on the advice method being targeted in the call.

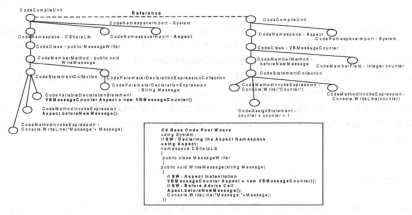

Fig. 7. Woven Code

Figure 7 illustrates the result of weaving the example introduced Section 3.1, expanded in Section 3.3 and referenced through section 3.4.1. The highlighted code represents code that has been woven into the base program. The first thing to note is the introduction of a `using` statement. Within the `WriteMessage` method we can see the aspect type `VBMessageCounter` being declared and also instantiated. Then on the next line the before advice is called on the class identified as an aspect. With the inserted code we can also see the inserted comments which explain the inserted aspect instantiation and advice call.

3.4.3 Compilation

By now, we have a woven CodeDOM abstract representation of the code. The next step is to compile this code into assemblies. Inter-compilation-unit dependencies are created when types in one compilation-unit are referenced in another. These dependencies affect the order in which source code units can be compiled. For example if we are trying to compile source unit A that references types held in (as yet un-compiled) source unit B, then A will not compile as the compiler cannot find the types that A is using. The SourceWeave.NET compiler manager ensures a compilation order that avoids compiler error.

To provide the developer with a consistent view of the potentially cross-language code, each `CodeCompileUnit` unit is converted back to the language in which it was originally expressed and is available for the developer to inspect. A compiler for the original language compiles the `CodeCompileUnit` in to an assembly with the debug information particular to that language. In this manner, the developer can debug the woven code in the original source code language in which it was written. CodeDOM provides a set of tool interfaces for CodeDOM related tasks such as compilation and source code generation from the CodeDOM object graph.

4 Discussion

The motivation for the development of SourceWeave.NET was to investigate cross-language weaving possibilities when working with source code. We wanted to research the extent to which we would have to compromise the joinpoint model in order to support *cross-language* weaving of source code. Since .NET achieves language independence by being very standards driven, we wanted to stay within the .NET standards as far as possible. In so doing, we were able leverage .NET facilities such as CodeDOM and Reflection. In this section, we assess the benefits and limitations of this approach.

4.1 Benefits

The benefits that SourceWeave.NET gives to the developer are: an extensive joinpoint model, support for cross-language development of base code and aspect code, and debugging expressiveness.

- *Joinpoint model*: SourceWeave.NET supports an extensive range of joinpoints described in section 3.2, a comprehensive AOP language described in section 3.3. The separation of the XML AOP language from the CLS also means that code and crosscutting specifications are more reusable and flexible. Moreover, the .NET standards are not altered and developers can express their code in standard .NET languages.
- *Cross language-support*: SourceWeave.NET's weaver works on CodeDOM representation of source code. As part of the .NET Base Class Library, CodeDOM is a standard representation for languages that conform to the CLS. Notwithstanding limitations we will discuss in the next section, any language that provides a parser to CodeDOM can be weaved by SourceWeave.NET. We have evaluated this for C#, VB.NET, and J#.
- *Debugging expressiveness*: SourceWeave.NET weaves at source code level, and as such does not affect the bonds created in assemblies for debugging. During weaving, comments are inserted into the code at weave points, and other interesting points of change within the code, to explain what has happened at that point. The developer will be able to trace through the execution of the woven code in the language in which it was written, where there will be comments to indicate the crosscutting nature of the behaviour. To our knowledge, there is no other approach to cross-language weaving that can achieve this.

4.2 Limitations

SourceWeave.NET also has some limitations, these include: a dependency on Code-DOM, which currently suffers some limitations in expressiveness and an inability to deal with circular CodeDOM dependencies.

- *CodeDOM dependency*: If a .NET language does not have a parser to CodeDOM, then SourceWeave.NET cannot weave code written in that language.
- *CodeDOM limitations:* In its current implementation, CodeDOM has limitations in terms of its expressiveness. C# constructs map reasonably well to CodeDOM, but that is not true of all .NET languages' constructs. For example, Eiffel's pre-conditions, postconditions and invariants are not supported [5]. The following constructs are also not supported [16, 37, 38]: Nested namespaces, variable declaration lists, namespace aliasing, unary expressions, inline conditional expressions, calling base constructors and nested or "jagged" arrays, safety modifiers read-only and volatile, structural safety modifiers virtual and override, event operator members and destructors, add and remove accessors for events, attribute targets and accessors on attributes, unsafe keyword used to denote unmanaged code, break and continue in case statements.
- *Compilation dependency*: SourceWeave.NET is limited because of compilation dependency issues. For example, take three compilation units A, B and C. If A references B and a reference to C is woven into A when B references C, then a circular dependency results. None of these compilation units of source code can compile as each compilation unit needs another to be compiled for itself to be compiled.
- *Source code dependency*: As SourceWeave.NET requires access to source code, pre-compiled, third-party components may not be included in the weaving process.

Two other areas of SourceWeave.NET are currently being addressed. The first is the use of XML for the aspect descriptor. XML was chosen originally because it appeared to be emerging as the de facto standard description language. Currently, SourceWeave.NET developers have to write this XML by hand, which is tedious. We are working on a wizard-like mechanism, similar to that available for EJB Deployment Descriptors [39] that will generate the required aspect descriptor. We also plan to consider languages other than XML, which may be more readable. The second area of concern is with supporting control flow based joinpoints. Nested control flow joinpoints are not yet supported. In the current implementation we are concerned with the performance of the system when supporting control flow activated joinpoints. Our initial attempt was to use Boolean flags inserted into the CodeDOM aspect representations to later determine at each joinpoint shadow whether a cflow is activated and matches a particular joinpoint. This is a solution, but we consider it to be a brute-force effort. There are significant refinements possible, such as code analysis to reduce the set of joinpoint shadows that could possibly be within a particular cflow, which we expect will considerably improve the performance.

There has been a proliferation of approaches to applying AOP to .NET in recent years. We describe them here in the categories outlined in Section 2, and, where appropriate, assess them against criteria similar to those outlined for SourceWeave.NET in the previous section.

5   Related Work

There has been a proliferation of approaches to applying AOP to .NET in recent years. We describe them here in the categories outlined in Section 2, and, where appropriate, assess them against criteria similar to those outlined for SourceWeave.NET in the previous section.

5.1   Altering the Run-Time Environment

AspectBuilder [34] and LOOM.NET [32] are the two main approaches to introducing aspects to .NET by altering the run-time environment. AspectBuilder intercepts calls through transparent proxies that wrap targets of message calls. These transparent proxies are points at which crosscutting behaviour can be introduced during execution. .NET custom metadata are created that act as explicit joinpoints. Custom metadata (or programmer-defined *attributes*) allows a programmer explicitly identify joinpoints. As modified by AspectBuilder, the CLR uses the extended metadata to distinguish points in the execution where normal execution should be suspended and modularised crosscutting behaviour should execute. LOOM.NET also exploits metadata exposed in assemblies to declare joinpoints, modifying the CLR to recognise where crosscutting behaviour should execute. AspectBuilder and LOOM.NET have the significant advantage of being inherently language neutral. All languages that can execute on the CLR are subject to aspect weaving.

We also perceive some drawbacks. Using custom metadata, or attributes, requires an intrusive joinpoint model, which means the programmer must explicitly declare every joinpoint in the base code.

One issue relating to this run-time AOP is the potential for performance degradation. Although, to our knowledge, performance has not been measured within .NET, AOP research on the Java [1] platform reveals AOP implemented in the JVM degrades run-time performance over AspectJ, which is a byte-code based weaver. The similarity in platform architecture of .NET and Java suggests that an AOP run-time implementation would have similar results.

Another issue is the limited joinpoint models currently demonstrated. For example, the joinpoint model in AspectBuilder cannot modularise concerns that crosscut the structures internal to a component interface. The joinpoint model employed by an approach determines its ability to modularise crosscutting concerns, and so an extensive joinpoint model is an important goal for an AOP approach.

Finally, supporting debugging facilities appears difficult, and has not been demonstrated in approaches following this strategy. This is because the .NET run-time environment is altered, which breaks conformance to the standards. Debuggers within a framework such as .NET are dependant on the run-time as this is where execution occurs [27]. A standard debugger expects a run-time environment that conforms to standards similar to that of the debugger. When the run-time is altered this can break the assumptions the debugger was created on. Alteration then prevents correct debugging.

5.2 Weaving at IL Level

There have been a number of attempts to introduce AOP concepts through IL manipulation. Weave.NET [11], AOP.NET [29] and its predecessor AOP# [33], and CLAW [13] weave IL components. LOOM.NET [32] also has a version that weaves IL. For each, weaving is based on information that identifies components with crosscutting behaviour and characterises how the crosscutting behaviour should be distributed across other IL components. CLAW and AOP.NET are run-time weavers that manipulate IL pre-execution time. They use the CLR events exposed through the unmanaged profiling interfaces [24] to trace the execution of a program in the CLR. Unmanaged profiling interfaces allow observation of the CLR, including the loading of code. When the weaver is notified of the activation of a joinpoint, it adds the relevant aspect code to be executed. The IL version of LOOM.NET (an update to Wrapper Assistant [30]) creates component proxies to act as points at which aspect behaviour can be introduced. The joinpoint model is GUI driven, where joinpoints are selected intrusively through a user interface [31]. LOOM.NET supports an aspect specific template mechanism that was initially described in [30]. These aspect templates are structures that have been customised to represent a particular type of concern, fault-tolerance is the example most used. Aspect specific templates provide mechanisms to match declarative expressions in components to macros which create C# aspect framework proxy code. The user can then write their aspects in C# to fit into this framework. Weave.NET delivers the most extensive joinpoint model of these approaches. It is implemented as a managed .NET component that works at loadtime, utilising the .NET reflection libraries to both read and generate assemblies. It also has a specialised IL reader that can read IL to statement and expression levels to discover joinpoints internal to the class construct. This allows it to support more expressive joinpoints than signature and type-based ones, such as joinpoints that expose context.

Approaches that weave at IL level have the advantage of cross-language aspect support. It has yet to be proven, though, how extensive a joinpoint model is possible. Only Weave.NET has achieved close to the set listed in Table 1. There is also a dependency on having assemblies that conform to the CLI. This has shown itself to be restrictive because, for example, assemblies generated by the J# compiler do not expose the standard metadata. This means that IL-based approaches cannot work with J# components. Finally, programmers cannot debug woven source code. For debugging purposes, source code is bound to the IL it relates to at compile time. By manipulating the IL, the bond forged at compile-time is disturbed, removing the binding to the original source. IL weavers do expose their woven IL but developers may not understand IL, or even want to. Adding comments to the IL to help programmers is currently not possible, as comments may not be expressed in IL.

5.3   Working with Source: Extending the CLS and CTS

Each .NET compiler converts source code that conforms to the CLS to standard IL. To support a cross-language AOP the CLS and CTS must be extended to specify AO constructs. This alteration would be difficult, as it would require extending the standard, and enforcing every language that conforms to the standard to include compiler support for the AOP constructs. EOS (formerly IlaC#) and Aspect.NET both take the approach of extending the compilers. Both target the C# compiler and are not focused on seeking language independence. The focus of EOS is instance-level aspect weaving described in [25] and [26].

5.4   Working with Source: Unchanged CLS

Working with source code and weaving pre-compile time was an approach first taken by AspectC# [6]. AspectC#, which is the predecessor of SourceWeave.NET, works with C# source code. Like SourceWeave.NET, it expresses AO constructs in XML, superimposing crosscutting behaviour that is modularised in OO classes. AspectC# was an initial proof of concept project that demonstrated, using a primitive joinpoint model, the possibilities for weaving cross-language source code. It provided an initial platform on which SourceWeave.NET was developed, showing us that decoupling AO constructs from base and aspect languages and expressing the AO concepts in a language neutral fashion, avoids the need to alter the CLS.

6   Summary and Conclusions

SourceWeave.NET has achieved language-independent AOP through cross-language source level weaving. No extensions have been added to any language, as weaving specifications are separated from the input components through the use of XML. Because of this, and because the architecture weaves an AST representation of source code, we can easily support programmers stepping through woven code in the language in which it was written for debugging purposes. A high level of debugging expressiveness in a multi-language environment is becoming increasingly important because of the new challenges emerging for application development in mobile, context-aware, pervasive environments. In such environments, systems are composed of many interacting devices that are driven by software that may be written in various languages, with highly dynamic state changes that are difficult to anticipate prior to run-time. SourceWeave.NET provides an environment that caters for such application development. Its multi-language environment supports a level of complexity management through AOP, and that also supports the debugging expressiveness that developers need to fully assess the operation and possible states of their inter-woven components.

Multi-language debugging expressiveness has been achieved without sacrificing the joinpoint model that is employed, or limiting (at some level) the languages that can be supported. From the perspective of the joinpoint model, SourceWeave.NET supports signature and type-based pointcuts, control flow pointcuts, contextual point-cuts, and composite pointcuts. As for supported languages, any language for which there is a parser to CodeDOM is able to participate in the AOP model. We have evaluated this for C#, VB.NET and J#.

SourceWeave.NET uses .NET's CodeDOM as the AST representation of base and aspect source code. This has turned out to be both a strength and a weakness. It has contributed to the reason why programmers can step through woven code's source for debugging purposes. However, it has limitations in terms of its current expressive-ness, which means that there are a number of language constructs that are not yet supported. We considered extending CodeDOM, but this would alter the standard-ised framework. We have, however, received communication that the relevant stan-dards committees will extend its specification to be as expressive as it is advertised.

Nonetheless, our approach has considerable merit. The ability to step through source code in the language in which it was written is a strong requirement for cross-language AOP approaches. It is difficult to see how approaches that extend the run-time environment can achieve this. On the other hand, if IL weavers could be written to update the source to IL binding created for debugging purposes as part of the weaving process, it seems possible that a similar approach could work for IL. We plan to continue with our refinements to SourceWeave.NET, such as improving how cflow is handled, and making the XML aspect descriptors more accessible. We are also interested in incorporating ideas such as joinpoint encapsulation [10] and in-stance-level aspect weaving [25, 26]. SourceWeave.Net has the potential to provide an AOP environment that makes it easy for programmers to work directly with cross-language source code as written, while still providing support for an exhaustive AOP model.

References

1. Chiba, S., Sato, Y., Tatsubori, M.: Using HotSwap for Implementing Dynamic AOP Sys-tems, ECOOP'03 Work-shop on (ASARTI) Advancing the State of the Art in Runtime In-spection, Darmstadt, Germany (2003)
2. ECMA International.: Standard ECMA-335 Common Language Infrastructure (CLI), ECMA Standard (2003)
3. Gal, A., Mahrenholz, D., Spinczyk, O.:AspectC++, http://www.aspectc.org (2003)
4. Hirschfeld, R.: AspectS – Aspect-Oriented Programming with Squeak. In M. Aksit, M. Mezini, R. Unland, editors, Objects, Components, Architectures, Services, and Applica-tions for a Networked World, pp. 216-232, LNCS 2591,Springer (2003)
5. Holmes, J.: Using the CodeDOM to Wrap, Extend and Generate, Assemble and Load New Code on the Fly, VSLIVE, Visual Studio Developer Conference, Orlando, USA (2003)
6. Howard, K.: AspectC#: An AOSD implementation for C#. M.Sc Thesis, Comp.Sci, Trin-ity College Dublin, Dublin (2002) TCD-CS-2002-56
7. Kiczales, G., Coady.Y.: AspectC, www.cs.ubc.ca/labs/spl/projects/aspectc.html (2003)
8. Kiczales, G., Hilsdale, E., Hugunin, J., Kersten, M., Palm, J., Griswold, W.G.: Getting Started with AspectJ Communications of the ACM, 44 (10), (2001) 59-65.

9. Kiczales, G., Lampoing, J., Mendhekar, A., Maeda C., Lopez, C., Loingteir, J., Irwin, J.: Aspect-Oriented Programming, In proceedings of the European Conference on Object-Oriented Programming (ECOOP), Finland (1997)
10. Koreniowski, B.J.: Microsoft.NET CodeDOM, http://www.15seconds.com/issue (2003)
11. Lafferty, D.: Language Independent Aspect Oriented Programming, In proceedings of the Object-Oriented, Programming, Systems, Languages (OOPSLA), California, USA (2003)
12. Lafferty, D.: W3C XML Schema for AspectJ Aspects, XML Schema, http://aosd.dsg.cs.tcd.ie/XMLSchema/aspect_Schema.xsd (2002)
13. Lam, J.: Cross Language Aspect Weaving, Demonstration, AOSD 2002, Enschede, (2002)
14. Masuhara, H., Kiczales, G. and Dutchyn, C.,A Compilation and Optimization Model for Aspect-Oriented Programs, In Proceedings of Compiler Construction (CC2003), LNCS 2622, pp.46-60, 2003.
15. Meijer, E., Gough, J.: Overview of the Common Language Runtime, Microsoft (2000)
16. Mercy, G.P.: Dynamic Code Generation and CodeCompilation, C# Corner, http://www.c-sharpcorner.com/Code/2002/Dec/DynamicCodeGenerator.asp (2002)
17. Mezini, M., Osterman, K.: Cesar, http://caesarj.org (2003)
18. Microsoft: Assemblies Overview, .Net framework developer's guide, http://msdn.microsoft.com/ (2003)
19. Microsoft.: CodeDOM, http://msdn.microsoft.com/ (2003)
20. Microsoft.: MSDN Library, Common Class Library, http://msdn.microsoft.com/ (2003)
21. Microsoft.: MSDN Library, Common Type System, http://msdn.microsoft.com/ (2003)
22. Microsoft.: .Net, http://www.microsoft.com/net/ (2003)
23. Microsoft.: MSDN Library, What is the Common language Specification ?, http://msdn.microsoft.com (2003)
24. Pietrek, M.: The .NET Profiling API and the DNProfiler Tool, http://msdn.microsoft.com/msdnmag/issues/01/12/hood (2003)
25. Rajan, H., Sullivan, K.: Eos: Instance-Level Aspects for Integrated System Design, In the proceedings of the ESEC/FSE, Helsinki, Finland (2003)
26. Rajan, H., Sullivan, K.: Need for Instance Level Aspects with Rich Pointcut Language, In the proceedings of the Workshop on Software Engineering Properties of Languages for Aspect Technologies (SPLAT) held in conjunction with AOSD 2003, Boston, USA (2003)
27. Rosenberg, J.: How Debuggers Work - Algorithms, Data Structures, and Architecture. John Wiley & Sons, New York, USA, (1996) 77-106
28. Safonov, V.:Aspect.NET- a Framework for Aspect-Oriented Programming for .Net platform and C# language, St, Petersberg, Russia.
29. Schmied, F.: AOP.NET, http://wwwse.fhs-agenberg.ac.at/se/berufspraktika/2002/ (2003)
30. Schult, W., Polze, A.: Aspect-Oriented Programming with C# and .NET. In 5th IEEE International Symposium on Object-oriented Real-time Distributed Computing, (Washington , DC, 2002), IEEE Computer Society Press 241-248
31. Schult, W., Polze, A.: Speed vs. Memory Usage – An Approach to Deal with Contrary Aspects. In 2nd AOSD Workshop on Aspects, Components, and Patterns for Infrastructure Software (ACP4IS) in AOSD 2003, Boston, Massachusetts (2003)
32. Schult, W.: LOOM.NET, http://www.dcl.hpi.unipotsdam.de/cms/research/loom/ (2003)
33. Schüpany, M., Schwanninger, C., Wuchner, E.: Aspect-Oriented Programming for .NET. In First AOSD Workshop on Aspects, Components, and Patterns for Infrastructure Software, Enschede, The Netherlands (2002) 59-64.
34. Shukla, D., Fell, S., Sells, C.: Aspect–Oriented Programming enables better code encapsulation and reuse, http://msdn.microsoft.com/msdnmag/issues/02/03/AOP (2002)
35. The AspectJ Team.: The AspectJ Programming Guide (V1.0.6), http://download.eclipse.org/ technology/ajdt/ aspectj-docs-1.0.6.tgz (2002)

36. Wichman J.C.: ComposeJ, The development of a pre-processor to facilitate Composition Filters in Java, M.Sc the sis, Comp.Sci, University of Twente, Twente (1999)
37. Wiharto,M..: Journal Entry for June 13, The Mars Project, School of Computer Science and Software Engineering, Monash University, Australia, http://www.csse.monash.edu.au/~marselin/archive/2003_06_08_journal_archive.html (2003)
38. Whittington, J.: CodeDOM needs help, http://staff.develop.com/jasonw/weblog (2003)
39. Xdoclet: Attribute-Oriented Programming, http://xdoclet.sourceforge.net/ (2003)

Meta-programming
with Typed Object-Language Representations*

Emir Pašalić and Nathan Linger

OGI School of Science & Engineering
Oregon Health & Science University
{pasalic,rlinger}@cse.ogi.edu

Abstract. We present two case studies demonstrating the use of type-equality constraints in a meta-language to enforce semantic invariants of object-language programs such as scoping and typing rules. We apply this technique to several interesting problems, including (1) the construction of tagless interpreters; (2) statically checking de Bruijn indices involving pattern-based binding constructs; and (3) evolving embedded DSL implementations to include domain-specific types and optimizations that respect those types.

1   Introduction

Meta-programs manipulate object-programs as data. Traditionally, these object-programs are represented with algebraic datatypes that enforce *syntactic invariants* of the object-language: only syntactically valid object programs are representable. In this paper, we explore a method for object-program representation that also enforces the *semantic invariants* of scoping and typing rules. The type system of the meta-language then guarantees that all meta-programs respect these additional object-language properties, thereby increasing our assurance in the correctness of meta-programs.

Although this can be done using an *encoding* of equality types in (standard extensions to) the Haskell 98 type system, the meta-language Ωmega [10] that we use in this paper directly supports the notion of *type equality*. Its type system automatically propagates and solves type-equality constraints, thus implementing a form of Cheney and Hinze's *First Class Phantom Types* [1]. Our case studies show that such support from the type system makes programming with well-typed object programs considerably less tedious than explicitly encoding equality types. Ωmega also supports user-defined kinds and staging. This integration of features makes Ωmega a powerful meta-programming tool.

In this paper, we apply this new meta-programming approach to several interesting problems: (1) the construction of tagless interpreters; (2) statically checking de Bruijn indices involving pattern-based binding constructs; and (3)

---

* The work described in this paper is supported by the National Science Foundation under the grant CCR-0098126.

G. Karsai and E. Visser (Eds.): GPCE 2004, LNCS 3286, pp. 136–167, 2004.

evolving embedded DSL implementations to include domain-specific types and optimizations that respect those types.

Our case studies demonstrate that these techniques support the embedding of the logical frameworks style of judgments into a programming language such as Haskell. This is important because it allows programmers to reason about their programs as they write them rather than separately at the meta-logical level.

Tagless Staged Interpreters. Staging a definitional interpreter written in a staged language (e.g. MetaML) is one way of deriving an implementation that is both reliable and efficient [2]: reliable because the staged interpreter retains a close link with the original (reference) interpreter, and efficient because staging can remove an entire layer of interpretive overhead, thereby yielding a simple compiler.

However, many existing staged interpreter implementations retain at least one significant source of overhead: *tagging* [3]. Unnecessary tagging arises when both the meta-language and the object-language are strongly typed. The meta-language type system forces the programmer to encode object-language values into an universal (tagged) domain, leading to numerous and unnecessary runtime tagging and untagging operations. In previous work [4], we have addressed the problem of tagging by using a dependently typed meta-language which allows the user to type the interpreter without the need for a universal value domain. In this paper, we show how to get the same effect using well-typed object-language representations.

Statically Checked de Bruijn Indices. De Bruijn formulated [5] a technique for handling binding of variables by using a nameless, position dependent naming scheme. While elegant, this framework is notorious for subtle off-by-one errors. Using well-typed object-language representations, these off-by-one errors become meta-program typing errors and are identified earlier. We show that this technique scales gracefully to handle richer binding mechanisms involving patterns.

A Process for Evolving DSL Implementations. The benefits of domain-specific languages (DSLs) are well known, but the cost of design and implementation can outweigh the benefits. The technique of embedding a DSL's implementation in a host language with flexible abstraction mechanisms has proven a good way to reduce these costs.

We illustrate how the features of Ωmega's type system make it well suited as a host language for embedding DSLs. User-defined kinds provide a mechanism for defining a domain-specific type system. Well-typed object-language representations harness the type system to prove type-correctness of domain-specific optimizations to object-programs. Again, staging constructs allow us to define a tagless staged interpreter for our DSL. This combination of language features makes Ωmega a powerful host language for embedding DSL implementation. The process presented here for evolving DSL implementations should be straightforward to reproduce. Parts of it can be automated.

The remaining sections are organized as follows. Section 2 introduces Ωmega. We then develop two comprehensive case studies: First, we implement a tagless staged interpreter for a functional language with pattern matching (Sections 3 and 4). Second, we present a development of a small domain-specific language for describing geometric regions (Sections 5 and 6) where we describe not only an efficient staged interpreter, but also type-preserving optimizations. Section 8 gives an example of using the region language. Sections 9 and 10 discuss related and future work.

2 Ωmega: A Meta-language with Support for Type Equality

In this section we shall familiarize the reader with the most important features of Ωmega: type equality, user-defined kinds and staging. The syntax and type system of Ωmega are descended from Haskell, while its staging support descends from that of MetaML.

Type Equality in Haskell. A key technique that inspired the work described in this paper is the encoding of *equality between types* as a Haskell type constructor (`Equal a b`). Thus a non-bottom value (`p::Equal a b`), can be regarded as a proof of the proposition that a equals b.

The technique of encoding the equality between types a and b as a polymorphic function of type $\forall \varphi.\ \varphi\ a \to \varphi\ b$ was proposed by both Baars & Swierstra [6], and Cheney & Hinze [1] at about the same time, and has been described somewhat earlier in a different setting by Weirich [8]. We illustrate this by the datatype `Equal : * → * → *`

```
data Equal a b = Equal (∀φ. φ a → φ b)
cast :: Equal a b → φ a → φ b
cast (Equal f) = f
```

The logical intuition behind this definition (also known as Leibniz equality [9]) is that two types are equal if, and only if, they are interchangeable in any context. This context is represented by the arbitrary Haskell type constructor φ. Proofs are useful, since from a proof `p :: Equal a b`, we can extract functions that *cast* values of type $C[a]$ to type $C[b]$ for type contexts $C[\ ]$. For example, we can construct functions `a2b::Equal a b → a → b` and `b2a::Equal a b → b → a` which allow us to cast between the two types a and b in the identity context. Furthermore, it is possible to construct combinators that manipulate equality proofs based on the standard properties of equality (transitivity, reflexivity, congruence, and so on).

Equality types are described elsewhere [6], and we shall not further belabor their explanation. The essential characteristic of programming with type equality in Haskell is that programmers must explicitly manipulate proofs of equalities between types using a specific set of combinators. This has two practical drawbacks. First, such explicit manipulation is tedious. Second, while present throughout a program, the equality proof manipulations have no real computational content – they are used solely to leverage the power of the Haskell type system to accept certain programs that are not typable when written without the proofs. With all the clutter induced by proof manipulation, it is sometimes difficult to discern the difference between the truly important algorithmic part of the program and mere equality proof manipulation. This, in turn, makes programs brittle and rather difficult to change.

2.1 Type Equality in Ωmega

What if we could extend the type system of Haskell, in a relatively minor way, to allow the type checker itself to manipulate and propagate equality proofs? Such a type system was proposed by Cheney and Hinze [1], and is one of the ideas behind Ωmega [10]. In the remainder of this paper, we shall use Ωmega, rather than pure Haskell to write our examples. We conjecture that, in principle, whatever it is possible to do in Ωmega, it is also possible to do in Haskell (plus the usual set of extensions, possibly using some unsafe operations), only in Ωmega it is expressed more cleanly and succinctly.

The syntax and type system of Ωmega has been designed to closely resemble Haskell (with GHC extensions). For practical purposes, we could consider (and use) it as a conservative extension to Haskell. In this section, we will briefly outline the useful differences between Ωmega and Haskell.

In Ωmega, the equality between types is not encoded explicitly (as the type constructor `Equal`). Rather, it is built into the type system, and is used implicitly by the type checker. Consider the following (fragmentary) datatype definitions[1].

```
data Exp e t = Lit Int        where t = Int
             | V (Var e t)
data Var e t = ∀γ.  Z         where e = (γ,t)
             | ∀γα. S (Var γ t) where e = (γ,α)
```

Each data constructor in Ωmega may contain a `where` clause which contains a list of equations between types in the scope of the constructor definition. These equations play the same role as the Haskell type `Equal` in Section 2, with one important difference: the user is not required to provide any actual evidence of type equality – the Ωmega type checker keeps track of equalities between types and proves and propagates them automatically.

The mechanism Ωmega uses for this is very similar to the constraints that the Haskell type checker uses to resolve class based overloading. A special qualified type [11] is used to assert equality between types, and a constraint solving system is used to simplify and discharge these assertions. When assigning a type to a

---

[1] *Syntactic and Typographical Conventions.* We adopt the GHC syntax for writing the existential types with a universal quantifier that appears to the left of a data constructor. We also replace the keyword `forall` with the symbol ∀. We shall write explicitly universally or existentially quantified variables with Greek letters. Arrow types (`->`) will be written as →, and so on.

type constructor, the equations specified in the where clause become predicates in a qualified type. Thus, the constructor `Lit` is given the type $\forall$e t. (t=Int) => Int → Exp e t. The equation t=Int is just another form of predicate, similar to the class membership predicate in Haskell (e.g., Show a => a → String).

Tracking Equality Constraints. When type checking an expression, the Ωmega type checker keeps two sets of equality constraints *obligations* and *assumptions*.

Obligations. The first set of constraints is a set of *obligations*. Obligations are generated by the type checker either when (a) the program constructs values with constructors that contain equality constraints; or (b) an explicit type signature in a definition is encountered.

For example, consider type checking the expression (`Lit 5`). The constructor `Lit` is assigned the type $\forall$e t. (t=Int) => Int → Exp e t. Since `Lit` is polymorphic in e and t, the type variable t can be instantiated to `Int`. Instantiating t to `Int` also makes the equality constraint obligation Int=Int, which can be trivially discharged by the type checker.

```
Lit 5 :: Exp e Int     with obligation    Int = Int
```

Data constructors of `Exp` and `Var` have the following types:

```
Lit :: ∀e t.      (t=Int)    => Int → Exp e t
Z   :: ∀e e' t.   (e=(e',t)) => Var e t
S   :: ∀e t e' t'. (e=(e',t')) => Var e' t → Var e t
```

which can be *instantiated* as follows:

```
Lit :: Int → Exp e Int
Z   :: Var (e',t) t
S   :: Var e' t → Var (e',t') t
```

We have already seen this for `Lit`. Consider the case for `Z`. First, the type variable e can be instantiated to (e',t). After this instantiation, the obligation introduced by the constructor becomes (e',t)=(e',t), which can be immediately discharged by the built-in equality solver. This leaves the instantiated type (Var (e',t) t).

Assumptions. The second set of constraints is a set of *assumptions* or *facts*. Whenever, a constructor with a **where** clause is pattern-matched, the type equalities in the where clause are added to the current set of assumptions in the scope of the pattern. These assumptions can be used to discharge obligations. For example, consider the following partial definition:

```
evalList :: Exp e t → e → [t]
evalList exp env = case exp of Lit n → [n]
```

When the expression `exp` of type (Exp e t) is matched against the pattern (Lit n), the equality t=Int (see definition of Lit) is introduced as an assumption. The type signature of `evalList` induces the obligation that the body of the definition has the type [t]. The right-hand side of the case expression, [n], has the type [Int]. The type checker now must discharge (prove) the obligation [t]=[Int], while using the fact, introduced by the pattern (Lit n) that t=Int. The Ωmega type checker uses an algorithm based on congruence closure [12], to discharge equality obligations. It automatically applies the laws of equality to solve such equations. In this case, the equation is discharged using congruence.

2.2   User-Defined Kinds

Another feature of Ωmega that we will use is the facility for *user-defined kinds*. Kinds classify types in the same way that types classify values. Just as value expressions can have varying types, type expressions can have varying kinds. There is a base kind * (pronounced "Star") that classifies all types that classify values such as Int, [Char], Bool → Float. The kind * → * classifies type constructors such as [], the list type constructor, and Maybe, a type constructor for optional values. Note that there are no values of type [] or Maybe.

In addition to kinds built up from * and →, Ωmega allows programmers to define their own kinds. The syntax is analogous to datatype definitions:

```
kind Unit = Pixel | Centimeter
```

This declaration defines a new kind Unit and two new types, Pixel and Centimeter, of kind Unit. Though there are no values of type Pixel or Centimeter, these types can be used as type parameters to other type constructors. This use of type parameters has been called indexed types [13].

2.3   An Introduction to Staging

Staging is a form of meta-programming that allows users to partition a program's execution into a number of *computational stages*. The languages MetaML [14], MetaOCaml [15], and Template Haskell support this partitioning by the use of special syntax called staging annotations. This is also the case with Ωmega, and we will use two such staging annotations in the examples we present in this paper.

Brackets, [| _ |], surrounding an expression, lift the expression into the next computational stage. This is analogous to building a piece of *code* that when evaluated will be equivalent to the bracketed expression. In staged languages, the type system reflects the delay, so that if an expression e has the type Int, the expression [|e|] has the type (Code Int) (pronounced "code of int"). Escape, $(_), can only occur inside of code brackets and drops the expression it surrounds into the previous computational stage. Once the escaped expression is evaluated, its result, which must itself be delayed, is then incorporated at the point at which the escape has occurred. This is analogous to evaluating a computation that builds *code* and then "splices" the resulting code into the larger piece of code being built.

$\tau \in \mathbb{T} ::= \mathsf{Nat} \mid \tau_1 \rightarrow \tau_2 \mid \tau_1 \times \tau_2 \mid \tau_1 + \tau_2$

$\Gamma \in \mathbb{G} ::= \langle \rangle \mid \Gamma, \tau$

$p \in \mathbb{P} ::= \bullet_\tau \mid \mathsf{Inl}_{\tau_1 \, \tau_2} \, p \mid \mathsf{Inr}_{\tau_1 \, \tau_2} \, p \mid (p_1, p_2)$

$e \in \mathbb{E} ::= \mathsf{Lit} \, n \mid \mathsf{Var} \, n \mid \lambda p.e \mid e_1 \, e_2 \mid (e_1, e_2) \mid \mathsf{Inl}_{\tau_1 \, \tau_2} \, e \mid \mathsf{Inr}_{\tau_1 \, \tau_2} \, e \mid \mathsf{case} \, e_1 \mathsf{of} \, \overline{p_n \rightarrow e_n}$

Fig. 1. Syntax of L_1. The notation $\overline{x}$ indicates a sequence of 1 or more x's.

Annotations introduce a notion of *level* into the syntax of programs. The level of an expression is the number of its surrounding brackets minus the number of its surrounding escapes. Levels correspond to stages, roughly, in the sense that an expression at level n is evaluated in the n-th stage. The type system of MetaML (and similar staged languages) statically guarantees that the staged program is free from *phase errors* – situations in which a variable bound at a later stage is used in an earlier stage. By adding staging annotations to an interpreter, we can change its behavior so that *static* computation is performed in an earlier stage. This specializes the interpreter with respect to a particular object-program, and produces a more efficient "residual" program in the next stage, which is free from all interpretive overhead [17]. In effect, this produces a compiler from an interpreter [2].

There are two more staging annotations in Ωmega. The `lift` annotation evaluates an expression of primitive type to a literal value and builds some trivial code that returns that value. The final annotation is `run`. It evaluates its argument (of code type) and executes the resulting code.

3   A Language with Patterns

In this section, we present a simple λ-calculus based language with sums and products, which are eliminated by the use of pattern matching. Variable binding is done with *de Bruijn* indices [5]. In this notation, variables are named by natural number indices. The index of a variable is the number of intervening binding sites between a variable's use and its definition. The notion of binding site is made more complex by the presence of pattern matching, and handling this complication in an elegant and type aware manner is a contribution of this work. The language is based on the simply typed λ-calculus. We shall refer to this language as L_1.

3.1   Syntax

The syntax of the language L_1 is given in Figure 1. Four sets of terms are defined:
(1) A set of *types*, $\mathbb{T}$, consisting of a base (in this case natural numbers), function, product, and sum types.
(2) A set of *type assignments*, $\mathbb{G}$, which are defined as finite sequences of types. The binding convention used in this presentation is that the n-th type from the right in the sequence is the type of the free variable with the index n.

(3) A set of *patterns*, $\mathbb{P}$. The most basic kind of pattern is the (nameless) *variable binding pattern*, $\bullet_\tau$: Patterns can also be sum patterns, $\mathsf{Inl}_{\tau_1\ \tau_2}\ p$ and $\mathsf{Inr}_{\tau_1\ \tau_2}\ p$, or product (pair) patterns (p_1, p_2). Patterns can be nested to arbitrary depth.

(4) A set of *expressions*, $\mathbb{E}$. The mixing of de Bruijn notation and patterns make expressions slightly non-standard. As in standard de Bruijn notation, variables are represented by natural number indices. Variables are bound in patterns, which occur in λ-abstractions and case-expressions. In standard de Bruijn notation the index of a variable indicates the number of intervening binding sites between the use and binding site of the variable, the index 0 being the "most recently bound variable." In this language a pattern might bind several variables, so the notion of "binding site" must choose a particular strategy as to which variables in a pattern are bound "earlier" than others. Sum types are introduced by injection constructs $\mathsf{Inl}\ e$ and $\mathsf{Inr}\ e$. Products are introduced by the pairing construct, (e_1, e_2). Both sum and product types are eliminated by pattern matching. Due to the limited space in this paper, we only show a subset of the language features we have been able to implement. Additional features include recursive definitions, let-bindings, patterns with guards, staging constructs, etc.

3.2   Meta-language Formalization

Figure 1 is a typical formalization of the syntax of a language. A good meta-language should not only capture the syntactic properties of the language, but semantic properties as well. Semantic properties of a language are often captured as judgments over the syntax of the language. Using the equality type extensions of Ωmega, we can implement the object language L_1 in a way which enforces the static semantics as defined in Figures 2 through 4. In this, we shall use the following techniques:

Type Equality Constraints. A key technique is the type equality constraint. Written as equations in **where**-clauses in datatype definitions, these constraints allow the programmer to specify an exact shape of type arguments to type constructors, and to use that shape to encode properties.

Type Indexes. Object language types are represented by meta-language Ωmega types. For example, the L_1 type ($\mathsf{Nat} \rightarrow \mathsf{Nat}$) corresponds to the Ωmega type ($\mathtt{Int} \rightarrow \mathtt{Int}$).

Well-Typed Terms. Each judgment of the static semantics is represented by an Ωmega datatype. A value of each of these datatypes represents a derivation of the corresponding judgment. The actual **data** type definitions for the typing judgments of each syntactic category are found in the corresponding right-hand columns of Figures 2 through 4.

For example, a derivation of the pattern judgment $\Gamma \vdash p : \tau \Rightarrow \Gamma'$ is represented by a value of the type ($\mathtt{Pat\ t\ gammaIn\ gammaOut}$), where $\mathtt{t}$ corresponds to τ, $\mathtt{gammaIn}$ to Γ and $\mathtt{gammaOut}$ to Γ'. Note that only the $\mathtt{t}$, $\mathtt{gammaIn}$ and $\mathtt{gammaOut}$ arguments of the judgment are also in the **data** type, but *not* the pattern argument (p). This is possible because the judgments are syntax directed

$$\frac{}{\Gamma, \tau \vdash 0 : \tau}\text{(Base)} \qquad \frac{\Gamma \vdash n : \tau}{\Gamma, \tau' \vdash (n+1) : \tau}\text{(Weak)}$$

```
data Var e t
  = ∀γ.  Z  where e = (γ,t)
  | ∀γα. S (Var γ t) where  e=(γ,α)
```

Fig. 2. Static semantics of L_1 variables: $(\Gamma \vdash n : \tau \subseteq \mathbb{G} \times \mathbb{N} \times \mathbb{T})$ and `Var e t`.

and the constructors of the derivations encode exactly the same information. This trick is used in the other judgments as well.

Instead of manipulating syntax, the meta-program manipulates data structures representing derivations of the typing judgments. The main advantage of this representation scheme, is that only well-typed L_1 terms can be created and manipulated in an Ωmega program. One might think that constructing and manipulating judgments is more complicated than constructing and manipulating syntax. We will argue that this is not necessarily the case.

3.3 Static Semantics

The static semantics of the language L_1 is defined as a set of three inductive judgment relations for variables, patterns and expressions.

Variables. (Figure 2). The variable typing judgment (Figure 2) is defined inductively on the natural number index of a variable. Its task is to project the appropriate type for a variable from the type assignment: the constructor `Z` projects the 0-th type; iterating the constructor `S` n times projects the n-th type. Not surprisingly, the structure of variable judgments is reminiscent of the structure of natural numbers. In the right-hand column of Figure 2 variable judgments are represented by the type constructor (`Var e t`), whose first argument, `e`, is the typing assignment, and whose second argument, `t`, is the type of the variable expression itself.

The two constructors, `Z` and `S`, correspond to using the Base and Weak rules to construct the variable judgments. The constructor `Z` translates the inductive definition directly: its definition states that there exists some environment γ such that the environment `e` is equal to γ extended by `t`. The constructor `S` takes a "smaller" judgment (`Var γ t`), and asserts the requirement that the environment `e` is equal to the pair (γ, α), where both γ and α are existentially quantified.

Patterns. (Figure 3). The pattern typing judgment *relates* an "input" type assignment Γ, a pattern p which should match a value of type τ, and an extended type assignment Γ' which assign types to variables in p. It is defined in Figure 3. As more than one variable in a pattern can be bound, the judgment specifies how names of variables are related to numerical indices. The choice is expressed in the Pair rule: the "furthest" variable binding site is the leftmost bottommost variable. For example: $\lambda(\bullet, \bullet).(\mathsf{Var}\ 0, \mathsf{Var}\ 1)$ corresponds to the function $\lambda(x, y).(y, x)$.

$$\frac{}{\Gamma \vdash \bullet_\tau : \tau \Rightarrow \Gamma, \tau}\text{(Var)} \quad \frac{\Gamma \vdash p : \tau_1 \Rightarrow \Gamma'}{\Gamma \vdash \mathsf{Inl}_{\tau_1\ \tau_2}\ p : \tau_1 + \tau_2 \Rightarrow \Gamma'}\text{(Inl)}$$

$$\frac{\Gamma \vdash p : \tau_2 \Rightarrow \Gamma'}{\Gamma \vdash \mathsf{Inr}_{\tau_1\ \tau_2}\ p : \tau_1 + \tau_2 \Rightarrow \Gamma'}\text{(Inr)}$$

$$\frac{\Gamma \vdash p_1 : \tau_1 \Rightarrow \Gamma' \quad \Gamma' \vdash p_2 : \tau_2 \Rightarrow \Gamma''}{\Gamma \vdash (p_1, p_2) : \tau_1 \times \tau_2 \Rightarrow \Gamma''}\text{(Pair)}$$

```
data Pat t gin gout =
     PVar  where gout = (gin,t)
  | ∀αβ. PInl (Pat α gin gout)
     where t = (Either α β)
  | ∀αβ. PInr (Pat β gin gout)
     where t = (Either α β)
  | ∀αβγ.PPair (Pat α gin γ)
       (Pat β γ gout)
     where t = (α,β)
```

Fig. 3. Static semantics of L_1 patterns ($\Gamma \vdash p : \tau \Rightarrow \Gamma' \subseteq \mathbb{G} \times \mathbb{P} \times \mathbb{T} \times \mathbb{G}$) and Pat t gin gout.

The pattern typing judgment $\Gamma_{\mathsf{in}} \vdash p : \tau \Rightarrow \Gamma_{\mathsf{out}}$ is encoded by the Ωmega datatype (Pat t gin gout) in the right-hand column of Figure 3.

The constructor function for variable-binding patterns PVar requires an equality constraint that the type of the target type assignment gout is equal to the source type assignment gin paired with the type of the pattern itself (gout=(gin,t)). The constructor functions for building patterns for sum types PInl (respectively PInr) take sub-pattern judgments (Pat α gin gout) (respectively (Pat β gin gout)), and require that t equals (Either α β). The most interesting case is the pattern constructor function for pair types PPair.

```
··· | ∀αβγ. PPair (Pat α gin γ) (Pat β γ gout) where t = (α,β)
```

It takes a pair of sub-pattern judgments. It is worth noting how the target type assignment of the first argument, γ, is then given as a source type assignment to the second argument, thus imposing left-to-right sequencing on type assignment extension for pairs.

Expressions. (Figure 4). The typing judgment for expressions is defined in Figure 4. The expression judgments are represented by the type constructor (Exp e t). Again, e is the type assignment, and t the type of the expression itself. A general pattern emerges: by using existentially quantified variables and type equality constraints, the constructor functions of the datatype mimic the structure of the formal judgments. In the Exp data type there are two interesting constructor functions Abs and Case, which include the Pat sub-judgment. These cases implement the static scoping discipline of the language, and ensure that both the scoping discipline and the typing discipline are maintained by the meta-program.

```
··· | ∀αβγ. Abs (Pat α e γ) (Exp γ β) where t = α → β
```

In the λ-abstraction case, the sub-pattern judgment transforms the environment from e to γ, and the body must be typable in the environment γ. Only then is the whole λ-term well formed. Of course, the type t of the overall λ-abstraction must be equal to a function type between the domain and the codomain ($\alpha \to \beta$).

$$\frac{}{\Gamma \vdash \mathsf{Lit}\ n : \mathsf{Nat}}\text{(Lit)} \qquad \frac{\Gamma \vdash n : \tau}{\Gamma \vdash \mathsf{Var}\ n : \tau}\text{(Var)}$$

$$\frac{\Gamma \vdash p : \tau_1 \Rightarrow \Gamma'}{\Gamma' \vdash e : \tau_2}{\Gamma \vdash \lambda p.e : \tau_1 \rightarrow \tau_2}\text{(Abs)}$$

$$\frac{\Gamma \vdash e_1 : \tau' \rightarrow \tau \quad \Gamma \vdash e_2 : \tau'}{\Gamma \vdash e_1\ e_2 : \tau}\text{(App)}$$

$$\frac{\Gamma \vdash e_1 : \tau_1 \quad \Gamma \vdash e_2 : \tau_2}{\Gamma \vdash (e_1, e_2) : \tau_1 \times \tau_2}\text{(Pair)}$$

$$\frac{\Gamma \vdash e : \tau_1}{\Gamma \vdash \mathsf{Inl}_{\tau_1\ \tau_2}\ e : \tau_1 + \tau_2}\text{(Inl)}$$

$$\frac{\Gamma \vdash e : \tau_2}{\Gamma \vdash \mathsf{Inr}_{\tau_1\ \tau_2}\ e : \tau_1 + \tau_2}\text{(Inr)}$$

$$\frac{\Gamma \vdash e : \tau \quad \Gamma \vdash p_n : \tau \Rightarrow \Gamma_n \quad \Gamma_n \vdash e_n : \tau'}{\mathsf{case}\ e\ \mathsf{of}\ \overline{p_n \rightarrow e_n} : \tau'}\text{(Case)}$$

```
data Exp e t
    =       Lit Int (Equal t Int)
    |       V (Var e t)
    | ∀αβγ. Abs (Pat α e γ) (Exp γ β)
                where t = (α → β)
    | ∀α.   App (Exp e (α → t))
                (Exp e α)
    | ∀αβ.  Inl (Exp e α)
      where t = Either α β
    | ∀αβ.  Inr (Exp e β)
      where t = Either α β
    | ∀αβ.  Pair (Exp e α) (Exp e β)
      where t =(α,β)
    | ∀α.   Case (Exp e α) [Match e α t]

data Match e t' t =
    ∀γ. Match (Pat t' e  γ) (Exp γ t)
```

Fig. 4. Static semantics of L_1 expressions: $\Gamma \vdash e : \tau \subseteq \mathbb{G} \times \mathbb{E} \times \mathbb{T}$ and `Exp e t`.

```
data Exp e t      = ∀α. Case (Exp e α) [Match e α t] | ···
data Match e t' t = ∀γ. Match (Pat t' e  γ) (Exp γ t)
```

A case expression, with a type assignment `e`, of type `t` consists of a discriminated expression of type `Exp e` α, and a number of pattern matches. Each match consists of a pattern which augments the type assignment `e` to some type assignment γ, and a body which produces a value of type `t` in the type assignment γ. Since in each match the pattern can extend the environment differently, the extended environment, γ, is existentially quantified. This use of existential types allows us to give the same type to an entire collection of matches.

4   Dynamic Semantics

We illustrate meta-programming over typed object-language syntax by defining a series of interpreters for the language L_1. We are interested in applying *staging* to interpreters to obtain efficient implementations. The efficiency of such an implementation comes from eliminating *interpretive overhead* and *tagging overhead* from the interpreter. To demonstrate our technique: We sketch out a preliminary *tagged* dynamic semantics for L_1 to illustrate the concept of *tagging overhead*. (Section 4.1). We define an unstaged definitional interpreter. This interpreter avoids tagging altogether by the use of equality constraints (Section 4.2). We then stage the definitional interpreter (Section 4.3). Finally, we apply a *binding time improvement* to the staged interpreter (Section 4.4).

```
eval0 :: Exp e t → [V] → V              data V = VF (V → V) | VI Int
eval0 (Lit i _) env = | VI | i                 | VP V V | VL V | VR V
eval0 (V var) env = evalVar0 var env    unVF (VF f) = f
eval0 (App f x) env =
 | unVF | (eval0 f env) (eval0 x env)   evalVar0 :: Var e t → [V] → V
eval0 (Abs pat e _) env =               evalVar0 (Z _) (v:vs) = v
 | VF | (\v →                           evalVar0 (S s _) (v:vs) = evalVar0 s vs
     eval0 e (unJust(evalPat0 pat v env)))
                                        evalPat0::Pat t i o → V → [V] → Maybe [V]
                                        evalPat0 (PVar _) v env = return (v:env)
```

Fig. 5. The tagging interpreter. These functions are purposely incomplete, and are given only to illustrate the use of tags.

4.1   The Tagging Interpreter

To illustrate the problem with tagging we write a dynamic semantics for L_1 as the function eval0. This interpreter uses a tagged value domain V which encodes in a single sum type all the possible values an L_1 program can return. Runtime environments are then represented by lists of these values. This scheme has been widely used for writing (interpreted) language implementations. In Figure 5 we give a sketch of how such an interpreter is implemented. "Unfolding" this interpreter on the input expression, (app (abs (var z)) (lit 0)), yields the following value: | unVF | (| VF | (\v → v)) (| VI | 0)

The unfolding (we ignore for a moment how such an unfolding can be achieved) has removed the recursive calls of eval0, but the program still contains the *tags* VF, unVF and VI. Such tags may indeed be necessary if the object language is untyped/dynamically typed. However, in our implementation, only well-typed L_1 expressions are ever interpreted. This means that the tagging and untagging operations in the residual programs never do any useful work, since the strong typing of the object language guarantees that no mismatch of tags ever occurs. Practical testing [3] has revealed that the performance penalty exacted on staged interpreters by unnecessary tags may be as high as a factor of 2-3 (in some cases even as high as 3-10 [19]).

4.2   The Tagless Interpreter

A dynamic semantics that takes advantage of well-typed object terms can be given in a "categorical style": by writing a set of semantic functions, one for each of the judgments.

```
eval    :: Exp e t → (e → t)
evalVar :: Var e t → (e → t)
evalPat :: Pat t ein eout → (t → ein → (Maybe eout → a) → a)
```

For example, the semantic function eval is defined inductively on the structure of typing judgments for expressions. Its meaning is an "arrow" (i.e., here a Haskell function) from the meaning of type assignments (the runtime environment) to the meaning of types. For example, the meaning of the type as-

```
1   eval :: (Exp e t) → e → t              25  evalPat (PVar) v e k = k (Just (e,v))
2   eval (Lit i) env = i                   26  evalPat (PInl pt) v e k =
3   eval (V v) env = evalVar v env         27    case v of
4   eval (Abs pat exp) env =               28      Left x → evalPat pt x e k
5     (\x → evalPat pat x env h)           29      Right _ → k Nothing
6     where h Nothing                      30  evalPat (PInr pt) v e k =
7           = error "Glob. Failure"        31    case v of
8           h (Just env) = eval exp env    32      Left _ → k Nothing
9   eval (App f x) env = (eval f env)      33      Right x → evalPat pt x e k
10                       (eval x env)       34  evalPat (PPair pat1 pat2) v e k =
11  eval (Pair x y) env =  (eval x env,    35    case v of
12                          eval y env)    36      (v1,v2) → evalPat pat1 v1 e h
13  eval (Case e branches) env =           37    where h Nothing = k Nothing
14    (evalCase (eval e env)               38          h (Just eout1) = evalPat pat2 v2
15      branches env)                      39                           eout1 k
16                                         40
17  evalVar :: (Var e t) → e → t           41  evalCase :: t1 → [Match ein t1 t2] →
18  evalVar Z env = snd env                42                  ein → t2
19  evalVar (S v) env                      43  evalCase val [] env = error "Empty Case!"
20    = evalVar v (fst env)                44  evalCase val ((Match(pat,body)):rest) env =
21                                         45    (evalPat pat val env k)
22  evalPat :: (Pat t ein eout)            46    where k Nothing = evalCase val rest env
23          → t → ein →                    47          k (Just env2) = eval body env2
24          (Maybe eout → a) → a
```

Fig. 6. Tagless interpreter for L_1. The semantic functions operate over the structure of judgments.

signment $(\langle\rangle, \mathsf{Int}, \mathsf{Int}, \mathsf{Int} \rightarrow \mathsf{Int})$ is a Haskell value of the nested product type $((((()\,,\mathtt{Int})\,,\mathtt{Int})\,,\mathtt{Int} \rightarrow \mathtt{Int})$.

Before we proceed to define the semantics of various judgments of L_1, we digress briefly to discuss *effects* introduced by presence of patterns in the object language L_1. Pattern matching failure may manifest itself in two different (and related) ways:

(1) Global failure. Pattern matching may fail when matched against an incompatible value. This may occur, for example, in λ-expressions, such as $(\lambda(\mathsf{Inl}\,\bullet).\,\mathsf{Var}\,0)\,(\mathsf{Inr}\,10)$. In case of such a failure, the meaning of the program is undefined. In our implementation we will model the global failure by the undefined, bottom value in Haskell (the function **error**). *(2) Local failure.* Pattern matching may also fail in one or more alternatives in a **case** expression. Local failure may, or may not, be promoted into a global failure: if a pattern match in one arm of a case expression fails, the control should be passed to the next arm of the case expression, until one of them succeeds. If there are no more arms, a global failure should take place.

One way to model pattern matching failure is to use a *continuation*. The denotations of patterns that produce an environment of type **eout** are functions of type $(\mathtt{t} \rightarrow \mathtt{ein} \rightarrow (\mathtt{Maybe}\ \mathtt{eout} \rightarrow \mathtt{a}) \rightarrow \mathtt{a})$. In other words, they take a value, and input environment, and a *continuation* κ which consumes the output environment and produces "the rest of the program" of type **a**. The argument to κ is a maybe type so that the continuation can decide how to continue in case of the success or failure of pattern matching.

We now define the function **eval** and its siblings **evalVar** and **evalPat** (we shall refer to the implementation in Figure 6). It is in these functions that the assumptions and obligations of judgment constructors play an essential role.

Expressions: eval. Let us look at several clauses of the function eval (Figure 6) to demonstrate the main points of our technique.

Literals (line 2). Consider the case of evaluating integer literals. Here we see the most elementary use of the equality constraints. The function eval must return a result of type t, but what we have is the integer i. However, pattern matching over the constructor Lit introduces the *fact* that t = Int. The Ωmega type checker uses this fact to prove that i indeed has the type t.

Abstraction (line 4). The abstraction case returns a function of type $\alpha \to \beta$, where α and β are the types of its domain and codomain. In the body of this function, its parameter x is matched against the pattern pat. The continuation h given to evalPat results in global failure if the pattern matching fails. If the pattern matching succeeds, it simply evaluates the function body with the extended environment produced by evalPat. Finally, the fact that t = $\alpha \to \beta$ is used to give the resulting function the required type t.

Application (line 10). The function part of the application is evaluated, obtaining a function value of type $\alpha \to t$; next, the argument is evaluated obtaining a value of type α. Finally the resulting function is applied, obtaining a result of type t. The function eval is a polymorphic recursive function with type eval :: ((Exp e t) → e → t). It is called recursively at two different instances. This is frequently the case in this kind of meta-programming.

Case (line 13). The implementation of case involves an interesting interaction with the semantics of patterns, evalPat. The function eval first evaluates the discriminated expression e, and then calls the auxiliary function evalCase which matches each arm of the case against this value. The function evalCase examines a list of matches. If the list is empty, matching has failed with global failure. Otherwise, in each arm, evalPat matches the pattern against the discriminated value val. The function evalPat is given the continuation k as its argument. The continuation k proceeds to evaluate the body *if the pattern succeeds*, or simply calls evalCase recursively with the next pattern if the pattern matching fails (lines 46-47).

Variables: evalVar. *(line 17).* The variable case of eval passes control directly to the function evalVar, which projects the appropriate value from the runtime environment. The base case for variables casts the runtime environment of type e, using the fact that e=(γ,t), to obtain the pair (γ,t). Then, the function snd is applied, to obtain the correct result value of type t. In the weakening case, the fact that e=(γ,t') is again used to treat the runtime environment as a pair. Then, the function evalVar is called recursively on the predecessor of the variable (v) index together with the first component of the pair (the sub-environment (fst env)).

Patterns: evalPat. The function evalPat has four arguments: a pattern judgment of type (Pat t ein eout); a value of type t against which the pattern matching will be done; an *input* environment of type ein; and a continuation.

The continuation either (a) consumes an extended output environment of type eout to produce some final result of type a or, (b) knows how to produce some alternative result of type a in case the pattern matching fails.

Variable Patterns (line 25). For variable patterns, the value v is simply added to the environment e. This transforms the initial environment into a larger environment, which is then supplied to the continuation k.

Sum Patterns (line 26). The case for Inl (Inr) patterns is more interesting. First, the value v is examined to determine whether it is the left (or right) injection of a sum. If the injection tag of the pattern does not match the injection tag of the value, the continuation k is immediately applied to Nothing indicating pattern match failure. If the injection tag matches, the sub-value x is selected from v and evalPat is recursively invoked with the sub-pattern p, the sub-value x, and the same continuation k. It is this recursive call to evalPat that binds variables.

Pair Patterns (line 34). The case for pair patterns involves taking a pair value apart, and matching the left sub-pattern with the first element of the value. However, this invocation of evalPat is given an enlarged continuation h. The continuation h looks at its argument. If it is Nothing it immediately invokes the initial continuation k with Nothing, thus propagating failure that must have occurred during the pattern matching of the left sub-pattern. If, however, its argument is some output environment eout1 obtained from matching the left sub-pattern, it recursively invokes evalPat on the right sub-pattern with the runtime environment eout1 and the initial continuation k.

Note that the structure of the pattern judgment (specified in Figure 3) forces us to thread the environment correctly: were we to make the mistake of first evaluating the right-hand side pattern and threading its result to the evaluation of the left-hand side pattern, the types simply would not work out. This is an important advantage of using typed object-language representations: *meta-level types catch object-level semantic errors.*

Ubiquitous in these definitions is the implicit use of equality constraints, manipulated behind the scenes by the type checker to ensure that the functions are well-typed. In eval, for example, they are always used to show that although each equation in the definition of eval returns a value of a different type, all of those types can be made equal to the type t from eval's type signature. Thus, the type checker automatically performs precisely the same role as *tags* in an interpreter which uses a universal domain. However, the crucial difference is that while tags are checked *dynamically*, at the runtime of the interpreter, the equality constraint manipulation is performed statically, at type checking time. Thus, unlike tags, it incurs no runtime performance penalty for the interpreter.

4.3   The Staged Interpreter

The interpreter presented in Figure 6 does not rely on a universal domain for its values. Rather, it starts from a well-typed judgment (Exp e t) and ultimately returns a value of type t: such use of polymorphism gives us, in effect, a whole family of evals, one for each resulting type. Instead of tags, the equality

```
1    evalS :: Exp e t → Code e → Code t    13   evalVarS :: Var e t → Code e → Code t
2    evalS (V v) env = evalVarS v env      14   evalVarS Z env = [| snd ($env) |]
3    evalS (Lit i) env =  [| i |]          15   evalVarS (S v) env =
4    evalS (Abs pat exp) env =             16     [| ($(evalVarS v [|fst ($env)|])) |]
5      [| \x → $(evalPatS                  17
6          pat [|x|] env h) |]             18   evalPatS :: (Pat t e1 e2) →
7        where h Nothing                   19           Code t → Code e1 →
8              = [| error "Failure" |]     20           ((Maybe (Code e2)) → Code a) →
9              h (Just env2)               21           Code a
10             = evalS exp env2            22   evalPatS PVar v e k =
11   ... ... ...                           23     k (Just [| ($([| ($e,$v) |])) |]) |])
12
```

Fig. 7. The staged interpreter `eval`, take 1.

constraints partition this family of `eval`s. Thus the tagging overhead has been removed, but the interpreted overhead of traversing the data representing the program remains. Staging can remove this overhead. It is straightforward to add staging to the interpreter of Figure 6: we modify the types of the interpreter, adding `Code` to the types of the runtime environment and the result. Thus, the new types of the modified semantic (interpreter) functions are changed as follows (we also change their names, appending "S" for "staged"):

```
evalS     :: Exp e t → Code e → Code t
evalVarS  :: Var e t → Code e → Code t
evalPatS  :: Pat t ein eout → Code t → Code ein →
             (Maybe (Code eout) → Code a) → Code a
```

Figure 7 gives the relevant definitions of the staged semantics. (Note that, due to limitations of space, we show only those parts of the implementation that differ from the final version of the interpreter in Figure 8). Consider the simplest case, that of literals (Figure 7, line 3). Two things are different from the unstaged version: First, the result of the function is a code value, enclosed in code brackets. Recursive calls to `evalS` are always escaped into a larger piece of code that is being built. Second, the type equalities of the form `t=Int`, introduced as facts by pattern-matching on the judgments (line 3), are used in a richer type context. For example, in line 3 the type checker "converts" a result of `Code Int` to type `Code t`.

Another thing to note is the slightly changed type of the continuation in `evalPat`. The continuation takes an argument of type (`Maybe (Code env)`), i.e., the success or failure portion of the argument is *static*, while the environment itself is dynamic. This means that we can *statically* generate both the success and failure branches of the pattern.

We will not further belabor the explication of this particular staged implementation, since we will rewrite and improve it in the following section. It is instructive, however, to examine the residual code produced by the interpreter from Figure 7 as this will motivate the improvements. Consider the source program $\lambda\bullet. \lambda\bullet. (\text{Var } 0) (\text{Var } 1)$. The code produced by the staged interpreter `evalS` is basically: $\x → \f →$ `(snd (((),x),f))` `(snd (fst (((),x),f)))`.

The two boxed expressions in the residual code above correspond to the variable case of `evalS`: as the interpreter descends under the abstraction terms, it

```
1   data PSE e = EMPTY where e = ()
2        | ∀αβ. EXT (PSE α) (Code β)
3              where e=(α,β)
4
5   eval2S :: Exp e t → PSE e → Code t
6   eval2S (Lit i) env = [| i |]
7   eval2S (V v) env = evalV2S v env
8   eval2S (App e1 e2) env =
9     [| $(eval2S e1 env)
10       $(eval2S e2 env) |]
11  eval2S (EInl e) env =
12    ([|Left ($(eval2S e env))|])
13  eval2S (EInr e) env =
14    ([|Right ($(eval2S e env))|])
15  eval2S (Abs pat body) env =
16    ([| x → $(evalPat2S
17       pat [|x|] env h)|])
18    where h (Nothing)
19            = [| error "fail" |]
20          h (Just e) = eval2S body e
21  eval2S (ECase e matches) env = [|
22    let value = $(eval2S e env)
23    in  $(evalCase2S [|value|]
24              matches env)|]
25
26  evalCase2S ::
27  Code t1 → [Match e t1 t2]
28      → PSE e → Code t2
29  evalCase2S val [] env =

30    [| error "fail" |]
31  evalCase2S val ((Match (pat,body)):rest) env =
32    evalPat2S pat val env h
33    where h (Nothing) = evalCase2S val rest env
34          h (Just env2) = eval2S body env2
35
36  evalVar2S :: Var e t → PSE e → Code t
37  evalVar2S Z   (EXT _ b) = b
38  evalVar2S (S s) (EXT e _ ) = evalVar2S s e
39
40  evalPat2S :: Pat t ein eout → (Code t) →
41      (PSE ein) → (Maybe (PSE eout) → Code ans) →
42      Code ans
43  evalPat2S PVar v ein k = k (Just  (EXT ein v))
44  evalPat2S (PInl pt) v ein k = [|
45    case $v of
46    Left x  →$(evalPat2S pt [|x|] ein k)
47    Right x →$(k Nothing) |]
48  evalPat2S (PInr pt) v ein k = [|
49    case $v of
50    Left x →$(k Nothing)
51    Right x →$(evalPat2S pt [|x|] ein k) |]
52  evalPat2S (PPair pt1 pt2) v ein k =  [|
53    case $v of
54    (v1,v2) →
55      $(evalPat2S pt1 [|v1|] ein (h [| v2 |]))|]
56    where h n Nothing = k Nothing
57          h n (Just eout1) =
58            evalPat2S pt2 n eout1 k
```

Fig. 8. Binding time improved staged interpreter.

builds ever larger runtime environments. At the variable use sites, the interpreter evalVarS then generates projection functions (e.g., snd (fst ···)) to project runtime values from these environments. This leads to variable lookup at runtime which is proportional to the length of the runtime environment, an instance of interpretive overhead *par excellence*.

4.4   Improved Staged Interpreter

The process of (slightly) changing the interpreter to make it more amenable to staging is known as *binding time improvement* [17]. In the remainder of this section, we will apply a binding time improvement to the staged interpreter for L_1 with the goal of removing the dynamic lookup mentioned above. The full implementation of the interpreter with the binding time improvement is given in Figure 8.

The previously presented staged interpreter fails to take advantage of the fact that the runtime environment is *partially static*. Namely, while the values in the environment are not known until stage one, the actual *shape* of the environment is known statically and depends only on the syntactic structure of the interpreted term. Therefore, we should be able to do away with the dynamic lookup of values in the runtime environment. The resulting interpreter should produce residual code for the above example that looks like this: [| \x → \f → f x |]. Recall that environments in the previous definitions of the interpreter are dynamic nested pairs of the form [| ((...,v2),v1) |]. The corresponding partially static environment is a static nested pair tuple, in which each second element is a dynamic value: $((\ldots,[|v2|]),[|v1|])$. This relationship between environment types and the corresponding partially static environments is encoded by the following datatype:

```
data PSE e  = EMPTY where e = ()
            | ∀αβ. EXT (PSE α) (Code β) where e=(α,β)
```

A partially static environment (hence, a PSE) can either empty (EMPTY), or it can be a PSE extended by a dynamic value. In a PSE, constructed using EXT, the *shape* of the environment is known statically, but the actual values that the environment contains are known only at the next stage. This allows us to perform the projections from the PSE statically, while the actual values projected are not known until runtime. The type equality constraint ensures that the type index e is identical in form (i.e. nested pairs) to the form of the environment argument of judgments (the e in (Exp e t) and (Var e t)). Now, we can give a new type to the interpreter, as follows:

```
eval2S :: Exp e t → PSE e → Code t
evalVar2S :: Var e t → PSE e → Code t
```

The interpreter now takes a judgment (Exp e t), and a partially static environment (PSE e), and produces a delayed result of type (Code t). The largest change is in the evaluation function for variables, evalVar2S. The base case takes a zero variable judgment and a PSE (EXT _ b), with b::code β, and introduces the equality e=(α,β). From this fact, the type checker can easily conclude that β is equal to t. A simple congruence then further allows the type checker to conclude that (Code β) is equal to (Code t). The inductive case is similar: the equality constraints introduced by the pattern matching are used to treat the environment as a pair, and then a sub-environment is projected from the environment and used in the recursive call to evalVar2S. Partially static environments are created in the PVar case of evalPat2S.

Now, if we consider the L_1 program $(\lambda \bullet .\lambda \bullet .(\text{Var } 0)(\text{Var } 1))$, the code generated for it by the interpreter in Figure 8 looks like this: $[|\backslash x \rightarrow \backslash f \rightarrow f \ x|]$. All the recursive calls to eval have been unfolded, all the dynamic lookups in the environment have been replaced by just variables in the residual program, and *there are no tags*.

5   The Region DSL: Embedded Implementation

The Region language is a simple DSL whose programs are descriptions of two-dimensional geometric regions. The example is just large enough to show the techniques involved.

5.1   Magnitudes

Recall the user-defined kind Unit we defined in Section 2.2. Using the kind Unit, we can first define a datatype of lengths indexed by a unit of measure:

```
data Mag u  =  Pix  Int    where u = Pixel
            |  Cm   Float  where u = Centimeter
```

Ωmega infers the kind of `Mag` to be `Unit -> *`. Note how the parameter to `Mag` is not of kind `*`, this allows the user to define domain-specific type systems for the DSL within the host languages type system. Magnitudes are lengths with an associated type (unit) index.

As we have seen earlier, equality constraints force the constructors `Pix` and `Cm` to produce values of type `Mag` annotated by the appropriate unit of measurement. Here are some programs manipulating `Mag u` values:

```
scale = 28

pxTOcm            :: Mag Pixel → Mag Centimeter
cmTOpx            :: Mag Centimeter → Mag Pixel

pxTOcm (Pix i)  = Cm (intToFloat (div i scale))
cmTOpx (Cm f)   = Pix (round (f #* intToFloat scale))
```

A note on Ωmega arithmetical operator names: built-in arithmetic functions on floats are prefixed with a hash mark (`#`). Note that these equations define total functions even though the case analysis is not exhaustive. This is because clauses such as, for example, `pxTOcm (Cm f) = ...` would be ill-typed because the obligation `u = Centimeter` cannot be discharged given the assumption `u = Pixel`. For this reason, the type parameter `u` in `Mag u` acts more like a *type index* than a usual parameter.

We lift the following arithmetic operations to be used on Magnitudes.

```
neg                   :: Mag u → Mag u
plus, minus, times    :: Mag u → Mag u → Mag u
leq                   :: Mag u → Mag u → Bool
```

The lifting is straightforward, for example:

```
times (Pix a)  (Pix b)  = Pix (a*b)
times (Cm a)   (Cm b)   = Cm (a#*b)
```

We will also need some other derived operators.

```
square a          = times a a
between a b c     = leq a b && leq b c
```

5.2 Regions

Now we can define an embedded implementation of the Region language. The meaning of a region is a set of points in the two-dimensional plane. In this style of implementation, we shall represent a region by its characteristic function.

```
type Region u = Mag u → Mag u → Bool
```

Primitive Regions. The Region language supports four primitive regions, circles of a given radius (centered at the origin), rectangles of a given width and height (centered at the origin), the all-inclusive universal region, and the empty region.

```
circle      :: Mag u → Region u
rect        :: Mag u → Mag u → Region u
univ        :: Region(u)
empty       :: Region(u)

circle r    = \x y → leq  (plus (square x) (square y)) (square r)
rect w h    = \x y → between (neg w) (plus x x) w &&
                             between (neg h) (plus y y) h
univ        = \x y → True
empty       = \x y → False
```

Region Combinators. The Region language supports the following combinators for manipulating regions: The combinator **trans** (δ_x, δ_y) translates a region by the given amounts along both the X and Y axes; The combinator **convert t** changes the units used to describe a region according to **t**. The combinators **intersect** and **union** perform set intersection and set union, respectively, on regions considered as sets of points.

```
trans          :: (Mag u,Mag u) -> Region u -> Region u
convert        :: (Mag v -> Mag u) -> Region u -> Region v
intersect      :: Region u -> Region u -> Region u
union          :: Region u -> Region u -> Region u

trans (a,b) r     = \x y -> r (minus x a) (minus y b)
convert t r       = \x y -> r (t x) (t y)
intersect r1 r2   = \x y -> r1 x y && r2 x y
union r1 r2       = \x y -> r1 x y || r2 x y
```

6   Intensional Implementation

One problem with the embedded implementation of the previous section is that we can not write programs that manipulate the *intensional form* of a region. Such programs include optimizing transformations, pretty printers, and program analyses (such as computing a bounding box for a region). Because regions are represented by their denotations as functions, their structure is opaque to the rest of the program. The solution to removing this opacity is to use a data structure to represent regions. Consider the following naïve attempt at defining such a data structure.

```
data Len = PixLen Int | CmLen Float

data RegExp = Univ
            | Empty
            | Circle Len
            | Rect Len Len
            | Union RegExp RegExp
            | Inter RegExp RegExp
            | Trans (Len,Len) RegExp
            | Convert CoordTrans RegExp

data CoordTrans = CM2PX | PX2CM
```

While solving one problem, this introduces another: meta-programs can now build ill-typed object programs. Here is one such meaningless program:

```
Convert CM2PX (Convert CM2PX Univ)
```

This is a step backwards from the embedded approach, in which object-language type errors show up as meta-language type errors. Can we achieve both intensional manipulation and object-level type safety? Yes – by using type-equality constraints. This allows us to define an `Unit` indexed intensional representation that captures all the object-level type information present in the embedded function approach.

```
data RegExp u
        =          Univ
        |          Empty
        |          Circle (Mag u)
        |          Rect (Mag u) (Mag u)
        |          Union (RegExp u) (RegExp u)
        |          Inter (RegExp u) (RegExp u)
        |          Trans (Mag u, Mag u) (RegExp u)
        | ∀ v.    Convert (CoordTrans v u) (RegExp v)
```

```
data CoordTrans u v
        =  CM2PX where u = Centimeter,  v = Pixel
        |  PX2CM where u = Pixel,       v = Centimeter
```

This representation enforces typing constraints as in the embedded approach but also supports intensional analysis of Region expressions.

6.1   Type Relations

The definition of the datatype `CoordTrans` is interesting in its own right, demonstrating the technique of embedding *type relations* in types of the host language. The relation encoded by `CoordTrans` would be written in more traditional mathematical notation as

$$\{(Centimeter, Pixel), (Pixel, Centimeter)\}$$

The elements `CM2PX` and `PX2CM` are *witnesses* to the relation. Pattern matching over such witnesses allows the type inference to locally make use of the fact that the relation holds. Consider the following program:

```
opp :: CoordTrans a b -> CoordTrans b a
opp CM2PX = PX2CM
opp PX2CM = CM2PX
```

While type checking the body of the first equation, we have the assumptions `a = Centimeter` and `b = Pixel` at our disposal. We need to check that `PX2CM` has type `CoordTrans b a`. This check results in the obligations `b = Pixel` and `a = Centimeter`, precisely the assumptions we have at our disposal.

The simplest type relation just encodes a single type-equality constraint. For this purpose, the Ωmega prelude defines the following datatype:

$$\text{univ} \cup r = \text{univ} \qquad \text{empty} \cap r = \text{empty}$$

$$\text{empty} \cup r = r = \text{univ} \cap r \qquad (r_1 \cup r_2) \cap (r_1 \cup r_3) = r_1 \cup (r_2 \cap r_3)$$

$$\text{conv } \tau_{12} \, (\text{conv } \tau_{21} \, r) = r \qquad \text{conv } \tau_{12} \, (r_1 \cup r_2) = \text{conv } \tau_{12} \, r_1 \cup \text{trans } \tau_{12} \, r_2$$

$$\text{trans } \delta \, (\text{trans } \delta' \, r) = \text{trans } (\delta + \delta') \, r \qquad \text{trans } \delta \, (r_1 \cup r_2) = \text{trans } \delta \, r_1 \cup \text{trans } \delta \, r_2$$

Fig. 9. Some algebraic identities on region expressions.

```
data Eq a b = Eq where a = b
```

A value of type `Eq a b` is a token representing the fact that `a` equals `b`. We can make use of this fact by pattern matching the value against the pattern `Eq`. We use this technique later. For now, just note that building values of type `Eq a b` is a way to inform the type checker of a fact it wasn't already aware of. The following function shows how one might construct an `Eq a b` value.

```
twoPoint :: CoordTrans a b -> CoordTrans b c -> Eq a c
twoPoint CM2PX PX2CM = Eq
twoPoint PX2CM CM2PX = Eq
```

Once again, these equations are exhaustive because no other combinations type check. In the first equation, we have the assumptions `a = Centimeter`, `b = Pixel`, `c = Centimeter` available when discharging the proof obligation `a = c`.

6.2   Interpreters for Free

We can reuse the combinators from the embedded implementation to define an interpreter for this representation of region expressions. Notice how easy it is to define `interp`: just replace each data constructor with its corresponding combinator.

```
interp                        :: RegExp u -> Region u
interp Univ                   = univ
interp Empty                  = empty
interp (Circle r)             = circle r
interp (Rect w h)             = rect w h
interp (Union a b)            = union (interp a) (interp b)
interp (Inter a b)            = intersect (interp a) (interp b)
interp (Trans xy r)           = trans xy (interp r)
interp (Convert trans r)      = convert (interpTrans trans) (interp r)

interpTrans                   :: CoordTrans u v -> Mag v -> Mag u
interpTrans CM2PX             = pxTOcm
interpTrans PX2CM             = cmTOpx
```

6.3   A Simple Optimizer

Region expressions have a rich algebraic structure. Figure 9 show a handful of identities over region expressions. These identities constitute *domain-specific knowledge* and can be used to optimize object programs for performance. We illustrate the utility of the typed intensional region representation for program transformation by writing a function `simplify` that applies domain-specific region equalities like those in Figure 9 to simplify a region expression.

```
simplify :: RegExp u -> RegExp u
simplify (Union a b)    = mkUnion (simplify a) (simplify b)
simplify (Inter a b)    = mkInter (simplify a) (simplify b)
simplify (Trans xy r)   = mkTrans xy (simplify r)
simplify (Convert t r)  = mkConvert t (simplify r)
simplify t              = t
```

The function `simplify` works by replacing (in a bottom up fashion) each data constructor in a Region expression with its corresponding "smart" constructor. The smart constructor "implements" the algebraic identites for that combinator. Here is the smart constructor for `Convert` expressions.

```
mkConvert :: CoordTrans u v -> RegExp u -> RegExp v
mkConvert t (Convert t' r)   = case twoPoint t' t of Eq -> r
mkConvert t (Univ)           = Univ
mkConvert t (Empty)          = Empty
mkConvert t (Union a b)      = Union  (mkConvert t a)
                                      (mkConvert t b)
mkConvert t (Inter a b)      = Inter  (mkConvert t a)
                                      (mkConvert t b)
mkConvert t (Circle rad)     = Circle (convMag t rad)
mkConvert t (Rect w h)       = Rect (convMag t w) (convMag t h)
mkConvert t (Trans (dx,dy) r) = Trans (convMag t dx,convMag t dy)
                                      (mkConvert t r)
```

```
convMag :: CoordTrans u v -> Mag u -> Mag v
convMag t a = interpTrans (opp t) a
```

In the first equation, we have the typing assignments `t :: CoordTrans u v`, `t' :: CoordTrans v' u`, and `r :: RegExp v'` for some arbitrary (Skolem) type `v'`. We want to return `r`, but the type checker doesn't know that it has the right type, `RegExp v`. In order to inform the type checker of this fact we build a `Eq v' v` witness using the previously defined function `twoPoint` and pattern match it against `Eq`. In the scope of the pattern, the type checker knows `v' = v` and uses this fact to deduce `r :: RegExp v`. An important advantage of using a typed intensional representation is that manipulations of Region expressions must obey the typing invariants of the Region language as captured in the definition of `RegExp`. It is impossible to write a domain-specific optimization function that violates the typing discipline of the object language.

7   Staged Implementation

The intensional approach of the previous section introduces a layer of interpretive overhead into the implementation (a problem we encountered in Section 4.1). In the embedded approach this extra overhead was not present. To remove this overhead [3] we employ the staging techniques already demonstrated in Section 4.3.

The goal of this section is to stage the interpreter `interp` to obtain a simple compiler `comp`. The transition from `interp` to `comp` is accomplished in a few simple steps:

1. Stage the `Mag` datatype so that it contains (`Code Int`) instead of `Int` and (`Code Float`) instead of `Float`. This allows us to know the units of a magnitude at "compile time", even though we will not know its value until "run time". The definition of `CodeMag` accomplishes this staging.

```
data CodeMag u
    =  CodePix  (Code Int)    where u = Pixel
    |  CodeCm   (Code Float)  where u = Centimeter
```

2. Stage the primitive functions on `Mag` values to work with this new type. We follow the convention that the staged versions of helper functions are given the same name but suffixed with an "S".

```
pxTOcmS              :: CodeMag Pixel -> CodeMag Centimeter
cmTOpxS              :: CodeMag Centimeter -> CodeMag Pixel
```

```
pxTOcmS (CodePix i)  =
          CodeCm [| intToFloat (div $i $(lift scale)) |]
cmTOpxS (CodeCm f)   =
          CodePix [| round ($f #* $(lift (intToFloat scale)))|]
```

Note that these definitions differ from their unstaged counterparts only in the addition of the staging annotations [| _ |] , $(_), and (lift _).

```
timesS :: CodeMag u -> CodeMag u -> CodeMag u
timesS (CodePix a)  (CodePix b)  = CodePix  [| $a * $b |]
timesS (CodeCm a)   (CodeCm b)   = CodeCm   [| $a #* $b |]

squareS a       = timesS a a
betweenS a b c = [| $(leqS a b) && $(leqS b c) |]
```

Each of these staged functions is derived from the original in a systematic way. In fact our work on using type annotations as specifications to binding time analysis [20, 21] leads us to believe this process can be completely automated. We also define a lifting function for magnitudes:

```
liftMag          :: Mag u -> CodeMag u
liftMag (Pix i)  = CodePix (lift i)
liftMag (Cm i)   = CodeCm (lift i)
```

3. Stage the `Region` type so that it is defined in terms of `CodeMag` instead of `Mag`. The definition of `CReg` (Compiled Region) accomplishes this staging.

```
type CRegion u = CodeMag u -> CodeMag u -> Code Bool
```

4. Redefine the region combinators and interpreter `interp` to manipulate `CReg` values instead of `Region` values. The updated definition is given in terms of the staged primitives from step 2. This is accomplished by `comp` and its helper functions. First we stage the primitive region constructors:

```
circleS  :: Mag u -> CRegion u
rectS    :: Mag u -> Mag u -> CRegion u
univS    :: CRegion u
emptyS   :: CRegion u

circleS r  x y = leqS (plusS (squareS x) (squareS y))
                              (liftMag (square r))
rectS w h  x y =
     [| $(betweenS (liftMag (neg w)) (plusS x x) (liftMag w)) &&
        $(betweenS (liftMag (neg h)) (plusS y y) (liftMag h)) |]
univS       x y = [| True |]
emptyS      x y = [| False |]
```

Then we stage the region combinators:

```
transS     :: (Mag u,Mag u) -> CRegion u -> CRegion u
convertS   :: (CodeMag v  -> CodeMag u) ->
                        CRegion u -> CRegion v
intersectS :: CRegion u -> CRegion u -> CRegion u
unionS     :: CRegion u -> CRegion u -> CRegion u

transS (dx,dy) r  x y = r (minusS x dx) (minusS y dy)
convertS t r      x y = r (t x) (t y)
intersectS r1 r2  x y = [| $(r1 x y) && $(r2 x y) |]
unionS r1 r2      x y = [| $(r1 x y) || $(r2 x y) |]
```

Then we stage the interpreter:

```
comp                      :: RegExp u -> CRegion u
comp Univ                 = univS
comp Empty                = emptyS
comp (Circle r)           = circleS r
comp (Rect w h)           = rectS w h
comp (Union a b)          = unionS (comp a) (comp b)
comp (Inter a b)          = intersectS (comp a) (comp b)
comp (Trans xy r)         = transS xy (comp r)
comp (Convert trans r)    = convertS (compTrans trans) (comp r)

compTrans :: CoordTrans u v -> CodeMag v -> CodeMag u
compTrans CM2PX = pxTOcmS
compTrans PX2CM = cmTOpxS
```

The structure of each staged definition is the same as the unstaged definition modulo staging annotations. Once we stage the types to reflect what information should be static (known at compile time) versus dynamic (known at run time), the changes made to the definitions are completely systematic. In fact, we have had some success in building automatic tools to accomplish this [20, 21]. These tools borrow from research on staging and binding time analysis from the partial evaluation community. We believe it is possible to completely automate this task once the types are staged.

8   Example Region Language Program

The DSL is still embedded, so we can apply the full power of the host language in constructing region programs. For example, the code below constructs three adjacent circles. The resulting data structure r is relatively large and complicated.

```
f         :: [RegExp Centimeter] -> RegExp Centimeter
f []      = Empty
f (x:xs)  = Union x (Trans (Cm 2.0,Cm 0.0) (f xs))

c = Circle (Cm 1.0)
r = Convert CM2PX (Trans (Cm (#- 2.0),Cm 0.0) (f [c,c,c]))
```

```
prompt> r
(Convert CM2PX (Trans ((Cm -2),(Cm 0))
    (Union (Circle (Cm 1))
           (Trans ((Cm 2),(Cm 0))
                  (Union (Circle (Cm 1))
                         (Trans ((Cm 2),(Cm 0))
                                (Union (Circle (Cm 1))
                                       (Trans ((Cm 2),(Cm 0)) Empty)
                                )))))))  : RegExp Pixel
```

The intensional representation allows for domain-specific transformations like our **simplify** function. Such transformations can dramatically reduce the size and complexity of the region's representation.

```
prompt> simplify r
(Union (Trans ((Pix -56),(Pix 0))
              (Circle (Pix 28)))
    (Union (Trans ((Pix 0),(Pix 0))
                  (Circle (Pix 28)))
           (Trans ((Pix 56),(Pix 0))
                  (Circle (Pix 28)))))  : RegExp Pixel
```

Staging allows the removal of all interpretive overhead incurred by creating an intensional representation, so that our technique is no less efficient than the embedded combinator approach (in fact, once the domain-specific optimizations are used, DSL programs can be implemented *more* efficiently this way).

```
prompt> [| \(Pix a) (Pix b) ->
             $(comp (simplify r) (CodePix [|a|]) (CodePix [|b|])) |]
[| \ (Pix x) (Pix y) ->
     (x + 56) * (x + 56) + (y * y) <= 784 ||
     (x * x) + (y * y) <= 784 ||
     (x - 56) * (x - 56) + (y * y) <= 784
|] : Code ((Mag Pixel) -> (Mag Pixel) -> Bool)
```

A further optimization phase could eliminate common sub-expressions.

```
[| \ (Pix x) (Pix y) ->
     let a = x + 56 in
       let b = 784 - (y * y) in
         let c = x - 56 in
           a * a <= b || x * x <= b || c * c <= b
|] : Code ((Mag Pixel) -> (Mag Pixel) -> Bool)
```

The Region DSL can be interpreted in other ways (besides its denotation as a characteristic function). For example, we can translate Region expressions into PostScript. The PostScript for the following picture was generated by running an alternative interpreter in Ωmega on the region program **r** defined above.

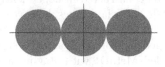

9   Related Work

Interpreters with Equality Proofs. Implementations of simple interpreters that use equality proof objects implemented as Haskell datatypes, have been given by Weirich [8] and Baars and Swierstra [6]. Baars and Swierstra use an untyped syntax, but use equality proofs to encode dynamically typed values.

Phantom Types. Hinze and Cheney [22, 1] have recently resurrected the notion of "phantom type," first introduced by Leijen and Meijer [23]. Hinze and Cheney's phantom types are designed to address some of the problems that arise when using equality proofs to represent type-indexed data. Their main motivation is to provide a language in which polytypic programs, such as generic traversal operations, can be more easily written. Cheney and Hinze's system bears a strong similarity to Xi et al.'s *guarded recursive datatypes* [24], although it seems to be a little more general.

We adapt Cheney and Hinze's ideas to meta-programming and language implementation. We incorporate their ideas into a Haskell-like programming language. The value added in our work is additional type system features (user-defined kinds and arbitrary rank polymorphism, not used in this paper) applying these techniques to a wide variety of applications, including the use of typed syntax, the specification of semantics for patterns, and its combination with staging to obtain tagless interpreters, and the encoding of logical framework style judgments as first class values within a programming language.

Tagless Interpreters and Typeful Object-Language Representations. The problem of tags in interpreters has been addressed in a number of settings. Tag elimination [3] is, in terms of its results, the closest to this work. In this approach, a separate tag elimination phase is introduced into the meta-language. It transforms a tagged residual program into a tagless one, guaranteeing that the meaning of the residual program is preserved. There are two major drawbacks compared to the approach outlined in this paper. First, a separate meta-theoretic proof is required to show that tags will be eliminated from a particular object language interpreter – there is no such guarantee statically. As our sample implementation shows, the staged interpreter we presented is *tagless by construction*. Second, more particularly, we know of no tag elimination for an object language with patterns.

The technique of manipulating well-typedness judgments has been used extensively in various logical frameworks [25, 26]. We see the advantage of our work here in translating this methodology into a more mainstream functional programming idiom. Although our examples are given in Ωmega, most of our techniques can be adapted to Haskell with some fairly common extensions. Tagless interpreters can easily be constructed in dependently typed languages such as Coq [27] and Cayenne [28]. These languages, however, do not support staging, nor have they gained a wide audience in the functional programming community. Construction of tagless staged interpreters has been shown possible in a meta-language (provisionally called MetaD) with staging and dependent types [4].

The drawback of this approach is that there is no "industrial strength" implementation for such a language. In fact, the technique presented in this paper is basically the same, except that instead of using a hypothetical dependently typed language, we encode the necessary machinery in a language which extend Haskell only minimally. By using explicit equality types, everything can be encoded using the standard GHC extensions to Haskell 98.

A technique using *indexed type systems* [13], a restricted and disciplined form of dependent typing, has been used to write interpreters and source-to-source transformations on typed terms [24]. Recently, Xi and Chen have used an encoding similar to ours as a basis for meta-programming [29]: they provide a meta-theoretical translation which embeds MetaML-style code into a datatype similar to Exp: this allows them to use staging syntax, but manipulate well-typed terms judgments "under the hood." Where our work is different and complementary is (a) that we consider an object language with patterns; (b) we use a similar encoding to accomplish a slightly different goal (i.e., rather then give it as a meta-theory for staged programming, we use staged programming to obtain efficient tagless interpreters). It would be interesting to see how our interpreter could be implemented in their meta-language λ_{code}.

Domain Specific Langauges. Hudak introduced the notion of a "domain-specific embedded language" [30]. He argues that DSLs are "the ultimate abstraction", capturing precisely a certain domain of calculation, and suggests embedding a DSL in a host language has the benefits of inheriting the infrastructure of the host language.

The Pan compiler of Elliot et al. [31] uses similar techniques to ours here. They use phantom types to partially ensure the well-typedness of object programs. The safety guarantees are only as strong as the discipline of the programmer who chooses to use the type safe interface constructors. The type system of Ωmega, however, enforces the same constraints at the level of the actual type constructors. Rhiger [32] proves that this style of programming provides safety guarantees about programs that *build* object programs, but notes that all type information is lost when deconstructing object programs in this way. This means that the type checker may not accept certain well-typed transformations of object programs. Cheney and Hinze motivate their work with a similar line of reasoning.

10   Discussion and Future Work

Finally, we discuss some outstanding issues and identify areas of future work.

Constructing Judgments and Other Applications. One final important consideration is whether arbitrary typing judgments could be constructed *at runtime*. In other words, could we write a *parsing* function that takes a string (or other) representation of object-language programs and compute a typing judgment? The problem is that the type of the judgment must be known *statically*, since, strictly speaking, judgments for different object-language terms have different types. Fortunately, there is a technique which allows us to construct just the kind of parsing functions discussed above. The key to this technique is to use an existential type, where the parsing function takes a textual representation of a program and constructs a judgment of the type $\exists \tau.(\text{Exp } e \ \tau)$. We do not have the space here to further discuss the particulars here.

Another interesting set of meta-programs is *source-to-source* transformations. In our setting, source-to-source transformations manipulate proofs of typing-judgments – the Ωmega type system guarantees that all such transformations respect the object-language types. Section 6.3 shows one transformation: an optimizer for a simple DSL. Others we were able to implement, but do not discuss here, include (1) substitution of well-typed terms of type t for a free variable of type t and (2) a big-step evaluator. The key to implementing substitution is to define an encoding for well-typed substitution judgments, as in the typed calculi with explicit substitutions [33, for example].

Meta-language Implementation. The meta-language used in this paper can be seen as a (conservative) extension of Haskell, with built-in support for equality types. It was largely inspired by the work of Cheney and Hinze. The meta-language we have used in our examples in this papers is the functional language Ωmega, a language designed to be as similar to Haskell. We have implemented our own Ωmega interpreter, similar in spirit and capabilities to the Hugs interpreter for Haskell [34]. Recent work on adding staging constructs to Haskell (albeit in a slightly different way [?]) or Objective Caml [15, 35] indicate that adding staging to industrial strength functional language implementation is feasible. Theoretical work demonstrating the consistency of type equality support in a functional language has been carried out by Cheney and Hinze. We have implemented these type system features into a type inference engine, combining it with an equality decision procedure to manipulate type equalities. The resulting implementation has seen a good deal of use in practice, but more rigorous formal work on this type inference engine is indicated.

Ωmega as a DSL Implementation Platform. We have shown how several features of Ωmega allow the programmer to lower the cost of DSL implementations by bridging the gap between embedded and intensional DSL representations. We have advocated the use of well-typed object-language syntax representations, allowing the implementors to write both type safe optimizations and translations into other target languages.

Though the Region language is quite simple, the ideas presented here scale up to larger expression languages with variables and environments. At OGI, we have used these techniques to capture security type systems, temporal properties of APIs, closedness of code, and others.

Polymorphism and Binding Constructs in Types. The language L_1, presented in this paper, is simply typed: there are no binding constructs or structures in any index arguments to Exp. If, however, we want to represent object languages with universal or existential types, we will have to find a way of dealing with *type constructors* or *type functions* as index arguments to judgments, which is difficult to do in Haskell or Ωmega. We are currently working on extending the Ωmega type system to do just that. This would allow us to apply our techniques to object languages with more complex type systems (e.g. polymorphism, dependent types, and so on).

Logical Framework in Ωmega. The examples presented in this paper succeed because we manage to encode the usual logical framework style of inductive predicates into the type system of Ωmega. We have acquired considerable experience in doing this for typing judgments, lists with length, logical propositions, and so on. What is needed now is to come up with a formal and general scheme of translating such predicates into Ωmega type constructors, as well as to explore the range of expressiveness and the limitations of such an approach. We intend to work on this in the future.

Acknowledgment

The work described in this paper is supported by the National Science Foundation under the grant CCR-0098126. We also wish to thank our thesis advisor Tim Sheard for countless hours of discussion on these and similar topics.

References

1. Cheney, J., Hinze, R.: First class phantom types. Technical Report CUCIS TR2003-1901, Cornell University,
   http://techreports.library.cornell.edu:8081/Dienst/UI/1.0/Display/cul.cis/TR2003-1901 (2003)
2. Sheard, T., Benaissa, Z., Pašalić, E.: DSL implementation using staging and monads. In: Second Conference on Domain-Specific Languages (DSL'99), Austin, Texas, USEUNIX (1999)
3. Taha, W., Makholm, H., Hughes, J.: Tag elimination and jones-optimality. Lecture Notes in Computer Science **2053** (2001) 257–??
4. Pašalić, E., Taha, W., Sheard, T.: Tagless staged interpreters for typed languages. In: The International Conference on Functional Programming (ICFP '02), Pittsburgh, USA, ACM (2002)
5. Bruijn, N.G.d.: Lambda calculus notation with nameless dummies, a tool for automatic formula manipulation, with application to the Church-Rosser theorem. Indagaciones Mathematische **34** (1972) 381–392 This also appeared in the Proceedings of the Koninklijke Nederlandse Akademie van Wetenschappen, Amsterdam, series A, 75, No. 5.
6. Baars, A.I., Swierstra, S.D.: Typing dynamic typing. In: Proceedings of the Seventh ACM SIGPLAN International Conference on Functional Programming (ICFP '02), Pittsburgh, Pennsylvania, USA, October 4-6, 2002. SIGPLAN Notices 37(9), ACM Press (2002)
7. Cheney, J., Hinze, R.: Phantom types. Available from
   http://www.informatik.uni-bonn.de/~ralf/publications/Phantom.pdf. (2003)
8. Weirich, S.: Type-safe cast: functional pearl. In: Proceedings of the ACM Sigplan International Conference on Functional Programming (ICFP-00). Volume 35.9 of ACM Sigplan Notices., N.Y., ACM Press (2000) 58–67

9. Nordström, B., Peterson, K., Smith, J.M.: Programming in Martin-Lof's Type Theory. Volume 7 of International Series of Monographs on Computer Science. Oxford University Press, New York, NY (1990) Currently available online from first authors homepage.
10. Sheard, T., Pasalic, E., Linger, R.N.: The ωmega implementation. Available on request from the author. (2003)
11. Jones, M.P.: Qualified Types: Theory and Practice. PhD thesis, Oxford University (1992) Also available as Programming Research Group technical report 106.
12. Nelson, G., Oppen, D.C.: Fast decision procedures based on congruence closure. Journal of the ACM **27** (1980) 356–364
13. Xi, H., Pfenning, F.: Dependent types in practical programming. In: Conference Record of POPL 99: The 26th ACM SIGPLAN-SIGACT Symposium on Principles of Programming Languages, San Antonio, Texas, New York, NY, ACM (1999) 214–227
14. Taha, W., Sheard, T.: MetaML: Multi-stage programming with explicit annotations. Theoretical Computer Science **248** (2000)
15. Taha, W., Calcagno, C., Huang, L., Leroy, X.: MetaOCaml: A compiled, type-safe multi-stage programming language. Available from
    `http://cs-www.cs.yale.edu/homes/taha/MetaOCaml/` (2001)
16. Sheard, T., Jones, S.P.: Template meta-programming for Haskell. ACM SIGPLAN Notices **37** (2002) 60–75
17. Jones, N.D., Gomard, C.K., Sestoft, P.: Partial Evaluation and Automatic Program Generation. Prentice-Hall (1993) Avaiable online from
    `http://www.dina.dk/~sestoft.`
18. Taha, W., Makholm, H., Hughes, J.: Tag elimination and Jones-optimality. In Danvy, O., Filinski, A., eds.: Programs as Data Objects. Volume 2053 of Lecture Notes in Computer Science. (2001) 257–275
19. Huang, L., Taha, W.: A practical implementation of tag elimination. In preperation (2002)
20. Sheard, T., Linger, N.: Search-based binding time analysis using type-directed pruning. In: Proceedings of the ACM SIGPLAN Asian Symposium on Partial Evaluation and Semantics-Based Program Manipulation (ASIA-PEPM), ACM Press (2002) 20–31
21. Linger, N., Sheard, T.: Binding-time analysis for metaml via type inference and constraint solving. Proceedings of TACAS '04 (2004)
22. Cheney, J., Hinze, R.: A lightweight implementation of generics and dynamics. In: Proc. of the workshop on Haskell, ACM Press (2002) 90–104
23. Leijen, D., Meijer, E.: Domain-specific embedded compilers. In: Proceedings of the 2nd Conference on Domain-Specific Languages, Berkeley, CA, USENIX Association (1999) 109–122
24. Xi, H., Chen, C., Chen, G.: Guarded recursive datatype constructors. In Norris, C., Fenwick, J.J.B., eds.: Proceedings of the 30th ACM SIGPLAN-SIGACT symposium on Principles of programming languages (POPL-03). Volume 38, 1 of ACM SIGPLAN Notices., New York, ACM Press (2003) 224–235
25. Harper, R., Honsell, F., Plotkin, G.: A framework for defining logics. In: Proceedings Symposium on Logic in Computer Science, Washington, IEEE Computer Society Press (1987) 194–204 The conference was held at Cornell University, Ithaca, New York.

26. Pfenning, F., Schürmann, C.: System description: Twelf – A meta-logical frame-work for deductive systems. In Ganzinger, H., ed.: Proceedings of the 16th International Conference on Automated Deduction (CADE-16). Volume 1632 of LNAI., Berlin, Springer-Verlag (1999) 202–206

27. Barras, B., Boutin, S., Cornes, C., Courant, J., Filliatre, J., Giménez, E., Herbelin, H., Huet, G., Muñoz, C., Murthy, C., Parent, C., Paulin, C., Saïbi, A., Werner, B.: The Coq Proof Assistant Reference Manual – Version V6.1. Technical Report 0203, INRIA (1997)

28. Augustsson, L., Carlsson, M.: An exercise in dependent types: A well-typed interpreter. In: Workshop on Dependent Types in Programming, Gothenburg (1999) Available online from www.cs.chalmers.se/~augustss/cayenne/interp.ps.

29. Chen, C., Xi, H.: Meta-Programming through Typeful Code Representation. In: Proceedings of the Eighth ACM SIGPLAN International Conference on Functional Programming, Uppsala, Sweden (2003) 275–286

30. Hudak, P.: Building domain-specific embedded languages. ACM Computing Surveys **28** (1996) 196

31. Elliott, C., Finne, S., de Moor, O.: Compiling embedded languages. Journal of Functional Programming **8** (1998) 543–572

32. Rhiger, M.: A foundation for embedded languages. ACM Transactions on Programming Languages and Systems TOPLAS **25** (2003) 291–315

33. Benaissa, Z.E.A., Briaud, D., Lescanne, P., Rouyer-Degli, J.: $\lambda\nu$, a calculus of explicit substitutions which preserves strong normalisation. Journal of Functional Programming **6** (1996) 699–722

34. Jones, M.P.: The hugs 98 user manual (200)

35. Calcagno, C., Taha, W., Huang, L., Leroy, X.: Implementing multi-stage languages using ASTs, gensym, and reflection. In Czarnecki, K., Pfenning, F., Smaragdakis, Y., eds.: Generative Programming and Component Engineering (GPCE). Lecture Notes in Computer Science, Springer-Verlag (2003)

Metaphor: A Multi-stage, Object-Oriented Programming Language

Gregory Neverov and Paul Roe

Centre for Information Technology Innovation
Queensland University of Technology
Brisbane, Australia
{g.neverov,p.roe}@qut.edu.au

Abstract. This paper presents a language (called Metaphor) for expressing staged programs in a strongly-typed, imperative, object-oriented environment. The language is based on a subset of $C^{\#}$ or Java; it is multi-stage and provides static type checking of later stage code. Object-oriented frameworks usually offer a type introspection or *reflection* capability to discover information about types at run-time. Metaphor allows this reflection system to be incorporated into the language's staging constructs, thus allowing the generation of code based on the structure of types – a common application for code generation in these environments. The paper presents the language, gives a formal description of its type system and discusses a prototype implementation of the language as a compiler targeting the .NET Common Language Runtime.

1   Introduction

Multi-stage programming languages [1–4] take the programming task of code generation and support it as a first-class language feature. In a *typed* multi-stage language, type correctness guarantees that all code generated by a meta-program will be type safe. This typing simplifies programming and reduces errors.

Most research to date in the field of typed multi-stage languages has been done in a functional setting. In particular MetaML [1] has proved to be a successful language for expressing staged computation. In this paper we apply the theory and practice of languages like MetaML to mainstream object-oriented languages such as Java and $C^{\#}$. In doing so we can improve the level of abstraction and type-safety offered for run-time code generation in these object-oriented programming environments.

Modern object-oriented run-time environments such as Java and .NET offer run-time introspection of types (called *reflection*), and dynamic code generation and loading. Code generation libraries that provide a higher level of abstraction than raw bytes or strings are also quite popular on these platforms (e.g. the .NET framework's Reflection.Emit library and numerous third party libraries available for both Java and .NET.) These code generation libraries use reflection to refer to types in the code they are generating. To be able to generate the same sort

G. Karsai and E. Visser (Eds.): GPCE 2004, LNCS 3286, pp. 168–185, 2004.

of code as one of these libraries, an object-oriented, multi-stage language needs to incorporate reflection into its staging constructs.

In this paper we present a small object-oriented language called Metaphor which supports multi-stage programming and reflection on types. Multi-stage programming allows the run-time generation of code. Reflection allows the run-time analysis of types. In combination they enable a programmer to write statically-typed programs that dynamically generate code based on the structure of types.

The reflection system in Java or C$^\#$ is dynamically typed; indeed it is often used as a means of performing dynamically-typed operations in the midst of the statically-typed language. If such a reflection system were allowed to interact with staging constructs, then its dynamic typing would destroy the static typing of the multi-stage language. I.e. it would be possible to write a type correct meta-program that generates ill-typed code via reflection. We present a solution to this problem by introducing a type system that statically types reflection operations and therefore prevents them from generating ill-typed code.

Writing code induced by the structure of types is known as generic or polytypic programming [5–7]. Many programs object-oriented programmers write or generate use polytypic code, e.g. object serialisation/deserialisation, value equality of objects, object cloning (deep-copying) and enumerators or iterators for collections. Metaphor allows a programmer to define code-generating functions for these operations that are type-safe and produce code at run-time. Most existing approaches for generating code for these operations either only work at compile-time (e.g. templates, macros) or do not statically-type the generated code (e.g. library-based run-time code generation).

The contributions of this paper are:

1. the design and implementation of a typed, multi-stage programming language extension to a simple object-oriented language;
2. the integration of an object-oriented reflection system with the language's staging constructs such that a programmer can use the reflection system in the type-safe generation of code.

The paper is organised as follows. Section 2 discusses the basics of staging and reflection, and how they interact. Section 3 gives a detailed overview of the language's new constructs and how its type system is used to prevent staging errors. Section 4 gives an example of writing a serialiser generator in Metaphor. Section 5 gives a formal description of the language's type system, and Section 6 gives an account of the current implementation.

2   The Language

We introduce a small object-oriented language in the style of Java or C$^\#$ that supports multi-stage programming and reflection on types. The base language includes common object-oriented constructs such as classes, methods, and fields, as well as general imperative programming constructs for assignment and control flow.

2.1   Staging

The base language is extended with the three staging constructs: brackets, escape and run – as used in MetaML [1]. These staging constructs enable the statically type-safe, run-time generation of code. The classic staged program – the power function – may be written thus:

```
class PowerExample {
  static <|int|> Power(<|int|> x, int n) {
    <|int|> p = <|1|>;
    while(n > 0) {
      p = <|~p * ~x|>;
      n = n - 1;
    }
    return p;
  }

  delegate int Int2Int(int x);

  static void Main() {
    <|Int2Int|> codePower3 =
      <|delegate Int2Int(int x) {
        return ~Power(<|x|>, 3);
      }|>;
    Int2Int power3 = codePower3.Run()
    Console.WriteLine(power3(2));
  }
}
```

Instead of calculating the value of x^n, this power method generates code that will calculate x^n for a given value of n. The brackets <| and |> quote statements or expressions and create *code objects*. A code object of an expression has type <|A|>, where A is the type of the underlying expression; a code object of a statement has type <|void|>. Code objects are first-class values that can be manipulated and passed and returned from methods. The type system is designed to prevent ill-typed code from being produced. The escape construct (~) splices the value of a code object into a surrounding code object. The Run method compiles and executes a code object and returns the result of its execution.

The use of higher-order function values in staged programming is a common idiom. A staged program typically needs to produce code for a function rather than code that just computes a single value (like an integer). Therefore Metaphor supports C#-like *delegates* and *anonymous methods*. Delegates are essentially named function types. An anonymous method is defined by specifying a delegate type, a list of method parameters and a method body.

The Main method generates the code for a function that computes x^3 and invokes it. The call to Power returns the code object <|1*x*x*x|>. The Main method defines a anonymous method using the delegate type Int2Int (which maps integers to integers) and splices this code object as the body of the anonymous method.

2.2   Reflection in Java and .NET

The Java and .NET frameworks include a *reflection* system that allows a program to discover information about its types at run-time. Types can be reified into objects, which a program can then manipulate like any other object. Such objects have type Type. Reflection has two typical uses: firstly, to dynamically perform actions on types or members when it is not possible to do so statically and secondly, for use with a code generation library (e.g. .NET's Reflection.Emit) to describe types and members in generated code.

The Type type has methods that provide information on the type it describes, e.g. name, base class, list of defined fields and methods, etc. Fields and methods are also reified into objects of the Field type and Method type respectively.

```
class A { int i; int j; }
Type t = typeof(A);
Field f = t.GetField("i");
int val = (int) f.GetValue(new A());
```

The above C$^{\#}$ code shows how to use reflection to dynamically access the field i. typeof(A) reifies the type A. GetField gets a reified object for the field named i. GetValue gets the value of the field on a new instance of A. As can be seen reflection is dynamically typed.

2.3   Reflection and Staging

It is desirable to combine reflection with staging so that a staged program may use type analysis to control the generation of code. For example, this is needed in a serialiser generator that uses reflection to get a list of fields on an object and then generates code that accesses those fields. To support this we introduce a new construct called field splice which is written .%. This construct is similar to a field access except that its right operand is an expression that evaluates to a Field value, instead of an identifier. For example:

```
class A { int i; int j; }
Type t = typeof(A);
Field f = t.GetField("i");
<|new A().%f|>
```

This program generates code that accesses a field on an instance of A, but the field to access is computed at run-time. There are two typing problems with this code expression.

1. The type system must statically prevent the generation of ill-typed code. In this code expression the type-checker does not know the run-time value of

f and so cannot check that it is a valid field on the type A. If f describes a field from some other type then this code expression will generate ill-typed code.

2. The code expression must be assigned a code type but the type of the field being accessed is not statically known.

These problems exist because the underlying reflection system is dynamically-typed and so does not maintain the type-safety of the language's statically-typed staging constructs. To solve these problems in Metaphor we have enhanced the type system so that it can statically type-check the use of reflection in a program.

3   The Reflection Type System

We introduce a new type system for reflection that constrains the use of reflection in a staged program such that future stage code is type-safe. For simplicity we will only consider the reflection of types and fields. Methods can be handled as an extension to fields, i.e. fields with function types.

The reflection type system consists of –

1. general constructs that produce values of reflection types;
2. a set of reflection types;
3. staging constructs that consume values of reflection types in the generation of code.

An overview of how these parts fit together in the language is given in Figure 1.

3.1   Reflection Types

The new reflection types are parameterised over types to carry more information about the expressions they are assigned to.

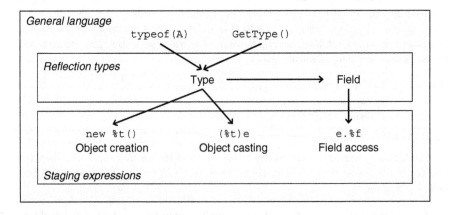

Fig. 1. Overview of reflection/staging language extension

The Type type takes one type parameter, i.e. `Type<A>`. There is only one value that has the type `Type<A>` and that is the value that reifies the type A. A could be a constant type (like `int`, `string`, etc.) or it could be a type variable. Metaphor uses existentially-quantified type variables to encapsulate the dynamic typing of the original reflection system. Hence the type `exists A.Type<A>` is the sum of all Type types and is equivalent to the unparameterised Type type in Java or .NET.

The Field type takes two type parameters, i.e. `Field<A,B>`. The first parameter, A, is the type the field is defined on. The second parameter, B, is the type of the field itself. Similarly, the type `exists A,B.Field<A,B>` is equivalent to the unparameterised Field type.

3.2 Reflection Expressions

A value involving the Type type can be introduced in three ways:

Context	Expression	Type
Static	`typeof(A)`	`Type<A>`
Semi-static	`o.GetType()`	`exists B <: A.Type<A>` where `o :: A`
Dynamic	`GetType(s)`	`exists A.Type<A>` where `s :: String`

Static. The `typeof` operator produces the Type value for a given type. The value of this expression is known statically and these expressions are essentially the constants of the Type type.

Semi-static. The `GetType` method is available on every object and is used to find the object's dynamic (or run-time) type. The dynamic type must be a subtype of the static type of the expression. This information is conveyed in the type of `GetType` using bounded existential quantification. (Note: if the static type of `o` is a *sealed* type (i.e. cannot be inherited) then this case can become the static case, i.e. no existential quantification required.)

Dynamic. It is possible to produce a Type value through some arbitrary means, such as by parsing a string that contains a type name and returning the corresponding Type value. In this scenario no static information is available about the Type value returned from this expression. Hence unbounded existential quantification is used on the type variable A.

The type `Type<A>` contains a method named `GetFields` that returns an array of type `(exists B.Field<A,B>)[]`. The elements of this array are Field values that describe the fields of A. The array is homogeneous in A, because the fields are all defined on the same type, but is heterogeneous in B, because the field type of each field is unknown and is in general different for each field. Existential quantification is used once again to express this information in a type.

Typically a programmer uses many ways to extract fields from types, e.g. getting a field by name or getting all fields of a particular type. These field operations can be given a type in the reflection type system and be implemented using the single primitive `GetFields` method. For example, the type `Type<A>` might be declared like so:

```
class Type<A> {
  exists B.Field<A,B>[] GetFields();
  exists B.Field<A,B> GetFieldByName(string name);
  Field<A,B>[] GetFieldsWithType<B>(Type<B> type);
}
```

A Note on the Invariance of the Type Type. The use of bounded existential quantification instead of subtyping is needed because the Type type is invariant, i.e. `Type<A>` $\leq$ `Type<B>` iff A = B. If the Type type was covariant it would be possible to access a field of a derived class on an object of a base class. E.g., assuming B < A, then value `typeof(B)` could be given the type `Type<A>`. Via this type, the fields returned by `typeof(B).GetFields()` would have type `exists C.Field<A,C>`, which indicates they are available on the supertype A when they may only be available on the subtype B.

3.3   Miscellaneous Expressions

Open. As the language uses existential types, there needs to be a way to *open* existentially-typed values, e.g.

```
open(t = GetType(s) as Type<A>) { ... }
```

Here the existentially-typed expression `GetType(s)` is bound to the variable t having the non-existential type `Type<A>`. The scope of t and the new type variable A is limited to the following statement block. There is no explicit *pack* operation because existential values can only be created by built-in reflection operations.

Typeif. Metaphor also provides a construct to scrutinise the value of a type variable, e.g.

```
typeif(A is int) { ... }
```

If the value of A matches the specified type (in this case `int`) then the typeif block is evaluated. Inside this block the type variable A is substituted with the type that was matched.

3.4   Staging Expressions

Types and fields are used in the syntax of code in three places: accessing a field on an object, creating a new object and casting an object. To make the link between the reflection and staging systems, three new staging constructs are added to consume reflection values and produce these three kinds of code. The syntax for each construct is the syntax for the underlying unstaged construct embellished with a % symbol. Each construct is used to generate code for field access, object creation or object cast when the field or type to use in the code is not known until run-time. The constructs are illustrated in the following example.

```
class Foo { int i; }
class Bar {}

Type<A> t;
Field<A,B> f;
Type<C> u;

<|A|> x1 = <|new %t()|>; // staged object creation
<|B|> x2 = <|~x1.%f|>;   // staged field access
<|C|> x3 = <|(%u)~x2|>;  // staged object casting
```

In this example A, B and C are type variables. x1 is assigned code that creates a new object, where the type of the object to create is defined by the value of t. x2 is assigned code that accesses a field determined by f. This code expression is the example from the beginning of this section but now properly typed. Finally, x3 is assigned code that makes a cast to a type determined by u.

Suppose that at run-time the type variables A, B and C are bound to the types Foo, int and Bar, respectively. Also suppose that t is bound to the Type value for Foo, f is bound to the Field value for Foo.i and u is bound to the Type value for Bar. Then when this code is executed the variables x1, x2 and x3 will have the following values:

```
x1 == <|new Foo()|>
x2 == <|new Foo().i|>
x3 == <|(Bar)new Foo().i|>
```

These code values statically (or literally) refer to the types and fields that were described by the run-time values of t, f and u.

4   Serialiser Generator Example

Serialisation is the process of taking a value and converting it into a stream. An object is typically serialised by recursively serialising each of the object's fields. Writing a serialiser is a fairly mechanical process and therefore serialisers are most often generated rather than hand-written.

Serialiser generators can be compile-time tools that typically produce textual source code, which is then difficult to compose with other generated code. In a multi-stage language a serialiser generator produces a code object that is modular and robust, and can be safely incorporated into a larger code generating application. The need to dynamically generate serialisers arises in distributed application frameworks which provide an infrastructure for applications to communicate data over a network. The types of data to communicate are not known until deployment or run-time and so the framework must dynamically generate serialisers for them.

Below is the code for a serialiser generator in Metaphor – it is a staged program that takes a reified type value and produces code that will serialise that type. The staged serialiser was created by taking an unstaged serialiser and adding staging annotations in the manner of a *staged interpreter* [8].

```
static <|void|> Serialise<A>(Type<A> type, <|A|> obj) {
  typeif(A is int) { return <|WriteInt(~obj);|>; }
  else {
    <|void|> result = <|;|>;
    (exists B.Field<A,B>)[] fields = type.GetFields();
    for(int i = 0; i < fields.Length; i++) {
      open(field = fields[i] as Field<A,B>) {
        Type<B> ft = typeof(B);
        <|B|> fv = <|~obj.%field|>;
        <|void|> code = Serialise<B>(ft, fv);
        result = <|~result; ~code;|>;
      }
    }
    return result;
  }
}
```

The `Serialise` method takes two arguments: the type to be serialised and the code for an object to be serialised. The universally-quantified type parameter A is used to form a relationship between the types of the two arguments, i.e. the type of the object being serialised must match the type the serialiser was generated for.

For simplicity we only consider a single primitive type `int`, which is serialised by the function `WriteInt`. For a non-primitive type, the program opens each field in the `fields` array using the type variable B to represent the abstract type of the current field. B also provides enough typing information to be able to make the recursive call to `Serialise`. The variable `result` accumulates the code for the serialiser. The generated serialiser does not use reflection and is known at compile-time to be type correct. For simplicity this example does not handle recursive types or the possibility of null field values.

To be able to use the generated serialiser we need to create an "invoking" function that we can pass the value we want serialised to. If the type we are going to generate a serialiser for is statically known (i.e. is a compile-time constant) then we can create an invoking function like so:

```
delegate void FooSerialiser(Foo obj);

// generate a serialiser for the type Foo
<|FooSerialiser|> codeFooSerialiser =
  <|delegate FooSerialiser(Foo obj) {
```

```
  ~Serialise<Foo>(typeof(Foo), <|obj|>);
  return;
}|>;
FooSerialiser fooSerialiser = codeFooSerialiser.Run();

//invoke the serialiser
fooSerialiser(new Foo());
```

Here we generate a serialiser for the statically-known type Foo, where foo-Serialiser is the invoking function. If the type Foo is defined as below, then at run-time codeFooSerialiser will be assigned the following code object.

```
class Foo { int x; Bar y; }
class Bar { int z; }

<|delegate FooSerialiser(Foo obj) {
  WriteInt(obj.x);
  WriteInt(obj.y.z);
  return;
}|>
```

If however the type to be serialised is not statically known then the serialiser can only be invoked through a dynamically-typed invoking function, like so:

```
delegate void AnySerialiser(object obj);

// get type to serialise
exists A.Type<A> type = GetType();

// generate a serialiser for an arbitrary type
<|AnySerialiser|> codeAnySerialiser;
open(type = type as Type<A>)
  codeAnySerialiser =
    <|delegate AnySerialiser(object obj) {
      A castObj = (%type) obj;
      ~Serialise<A>(type, <|castObj|>);
      return;
    }|>;
AnySerialiser anySerialiser = codeAnySerialiser.Run();

// invoke the serialiser
anySerialiser(obj);
```

Since we don't know the type of object being serialised, anySerialiser must take an object as its parameter. GetType is a function that computes the type to generate a serialiser for. In codeAnySerialiser, obj is cast to type A which is an abstract representation of the type the serialiser is generated for. castObj has the correct static type to pass in the call to Serialise. Although the invoking function is dynamically-typed, the code inside it is not (except for the initial cast). The purpose of the cast is to prevent an object of the wrong type from being serialised. E.g. if the run-time type of `obj` is not compatible with the type described by the value of `type`, then the cast will fail since it would not be meaningful to serialise that object with this serialiser. The invoking function cannot take a parameter of type A because that type variable cannot escape the scope of the open block.

If `type` has the value `typeof(Foo)` (defined as before), then `codeAnySeri-aliser` will be assigned the following code object.

```
<|delegate AnySerialiser(object obj) {
  Foo castObj = (Foo) obj;
  WriteInt(castObj.x);
  WriteInt(castObj.y.z);
  return;
}|>
```

5   Formalisation

We present a formal language to express the core functionality of Metaphor. The constructs of the language can be divided into three categories:

General. General programming language constructs for an object-oriented language, similar to object-oriented calculi such as Featherweight Java [9] and C$^{\#}$ minor [10].

Staging. Typical meta-programming language constructs for staged computation [1].

Reflection. Constructs that link the reflection system of the object-oriented runtime environment with the staging constructs to achieve typed object-oriented program generation – the chief contribution of this paper.

5.1   Syntax

Figure 2 shows the syntax of the language. The over-line notation, $\overline{X}$, is used to denote a sequence of X's, e.g. a class declaration contains a sequence of field declarations A_1 f_1, A_2 f_2, ..., A_n f_n. A program consists of an expression and a class table, CT, which maps class names to class declarations. A class declaration consists of a class name and a collection of named fields. Methods can be emulated by fields with function types. The domain of types contains class types, type variables, polymorphic function types, existential types, code types and the reflection types Type and Field. Existential quantification is restricted to reflection types as only these types can be existentially quantified in Metaphor. Type variables can only be bound to class types and other type variables.

The general expressions of the language comprise of basic object-oriented expressions as well as a `typeif` for testing the value of a type variable and an `open` for opening an existentially-typed value. Staging expressions are the usual brackets, escape, run and an explicit lift operator. The lift expression $\%E$

Class names	c
Field names	f
Variables	x, y
Type variables	α
Class decl	$C ::= \text{Class } c\ \{\overline{A}\ \overline{f}\}$
Types	$A, B ::= S \mid R \mid \forall \overline{\alpha}.(\overline{A}) \to B \mid \exists \alpha.R \mid \langle A \rangle \mid$ General types
	$R ::= \text{Type } S \mid \text{Field } S_1\ S_2 \mid$ Reflection types
	$S ::= c \mid \alpha$ Simple types
Expressions	$E ::=$

General

$x \mid$	Variable
$\text{fun } B\ y<\overline{\alpha}>(\overline{A\ x})\{E\} \mid$	Func. def.
$E<\overline{S}>(\overline{E}) \mid$	Func. app.
$E.f \mid$	Field access
$\text{new } c \mid$	Obj. creation
$(c)E \mid$	Obj. casting
$\text{typeif}(\alpha \text{ is } S)\ E_1 \text{ else } E_2 \mid$	Type test
$\text{open}(\alpha\ x = E_1) \text{ in } E_2 \mid$	Exist. open

Staging

$\langle E \rangle \mid$	Brackets
$\tilde{\ }E \mid$	Escape
$\text{run } E \mid$	Run
$\%E \mid$	Lift

Reflection

$E_1.\%E_2 \mid$	Staged field access
$\text{new } \%E \mid$	Staged obj. creation
$(\%E_1)E_2 \mid$	Staged obj. casting
$\text{typeof } S$	Type of

Fig. 2. Syntax

evaluates the expression E in the preceding stage and embeds the resulting value as a literal in the current stage.

The reflection expressions incorporate the reflection system into the generation of code. They generalise the unstaged expressions for field access, object creation and casting. Instead of using a literal field or type as in the unstaged case they use a reflection expression that evaluates to a field or type. These reflection expressions must be evaluated at the stage before the code they are used in is executed. Consequently they must appear inside staging brackets.

The typeof expression produces a Type value from a literal type. Other operations on reflection values such as getting fields from types can be typed as a function in the language, e.g.:

$$getFields :: \forall \alpha.(\text{Type } \alpha, \text{String}) \to \exists \beta.\text{Field } \alpha\ \beta$$

5.2   Type Rules

The type system for this formal language is expressed as type rules in Figure 3. The natural numbers m and n define the staging level that a term is typed at. The level of a term is equal to the number of brackets minus the number of escapes and lifts that surround it. The type judgments use two environments:

- Δ is the environment of type variables. It contains the type variables annotated with the level they are declared at. It is not valid to use a type variable at a level less than what it is declared at.

Environments

$$\Delta ::= \emptyset \mid \Delta, \alpha^n \qquad \Gamma ::= \emptyset \mid \Gamma, x : A^n$$

Types

$$\frac{CT(c) = \text{Class } c \ \{\overline{A} \ \overline{f}\}}{\Delta \overset{n}{\vdash} c} \qquad \frac{\alpha^m \in \Delta \quad m \le n}{\Delta \overset{n}{\vdash} \alpha} \qquad \frac{\Delta \overset{n}{\vdash} S}{\Delta \overset{n}{\vdash} \text{Type } S}$$

$$\frac{\Delta \overset{n}{\vdash} S_1 \quad \Delta \overset{n}{\vdash} S_2}{\Delta \overset{n}{\vdash} \text{Field } S_1 \ S_2} \qquad \frac{\Delta, \overline{\alpha}^n \overset{n}{\vdash} \overline{A} \quad \Delta, \overline{\alpha}^n \overset{n}{\vdash} B}{\Delta \overset{n}{\vdash} \forall \overline{\alpha}.(\overline{A}) \to B} \qquad \frac{\Delta, \alpha^n \overset{n}{\vdash} R}{\Delta \overset{n}{\vdash} \exists \alpha.R} \qquad \frac{\Delta \overset{n+1}{\vdash} A}{\Delta \overset{n}{\vdash} \langle A \rangle}$$

General Expressions

$$\frac{x : A^n \in \Gamma}{\Delta; \Gamma \overset{n}{\vdash} x : A} \qquad \frac{\Delta, \overline{\alpha}^n \overset{n}{\vdash} \overline{A} \quad \Delta, \overline{\alpha}^n \overset{n}{\vdash} B \quad \Delta, \overline{\alpha}^n; \Gamma, \overline{x} : \overline{A}^n \overset{n}{\vdash} E : B}{\Delta; \Gamma \overset{n}{\vdash} \text{fun } B \ y < \overline{\alpha} > (\overline{A} \ \overline{x})\{E\} : \forall \overline{\alpha}.(\overline{A}) \to B}$$

$$\frac{\Delta \overset{n}{\vdash} \overline{S} \quad \Delta; \Gamma \overset{n}{\vdash} E : \forall \overline{\alpha}.(\overline{A}) \to B \quad \Delta; \Gamma \overset{n}{\vdash} \overline{E} : \overline{A}[\overline{\alpha}/\overline{S}]}{\Delta; \Gamma \overset{n}{\vdash} E < \overline{S} > (\overline{E}) : B[\overline{\alpha}/\overline{S}]} \qquad \frac{\Delta \overset{n}{\vdash} c}{\Delta; \Gamma \overset{n}{\vdash} \text{new } c : c}$$

$$\frac{\Delta; \Gamma \overset{n}{\vdash} E : c \quad CT(c) = \text{Class } c \ \{\overline{A} \ \overline{f}\} \quad f = \overline{f}_i}{\Delta; \Gamma \overset{n}{\vdash} E.f : A_i} \qquad \frac{\Delta \overset{n}{\vdash} c \quad \Delta; \Gamma \overset{n}{\vdash} E : A}{\Delta; \Gamma \overset{n}{\vdash} (c)E : c}$$

$$\frac{\Delta \overset{n}{\vdash} \alpha \quad \Delta \overset{n}{\vdash} S \quad \alpha \ne S \quad \Delta - \{\alpha\}; \Gamma[\alpha/S] \overset{n}{\vdash} E_1 : A \quad \Delta; \Gamma \overset{n}{\vdash} E_2 : A}{\Delta; \Gamma \overset{n}{\vdash} \text{typeif}(\alpha \text{ is } S) \ E_1 \text{ else } E_2 : A}$$

$$\frac{\Delta; \Gamma \overset{n}{\vdash} E_1 : \exists \beta.A \quad \Delta, \alpha^n; \Gamma, x : A[\beta/\alpha]^n \overset{n}{\vdash} E_2 : B \quad \Delta \overset{n}{\vdash} B}{\Delta; \Gamma \overset{n}{\vdash} \text{open}(\alpha \ x = E_1) \text{ in } E_2 : B}$$

Staging Expressions

$$\frac{\Delta; \Gamma \overset{n+1}{\vdash} E : A}{\Delta; \Gamma \overset{n}{\vdash} \langle E \rangle : \langle A \rangle} \qquad \frac{\Delta; \Gamma \overset{n}{\vdash} E : \langle A \rangle}{\Delta; \Gamma \overset{n+1}{\vdash} {\sim}E : A} \qquad \frac{\Delta; \Gamma \overset{n}{\vdash} E : \langle A \rangle}{\Delta; \Gamma \overset{n}{\vdash} \text{run } E : A} \qquad \frac{\Delta; \Gamma \overset{n}{\vdash} E : A}{\Delta; \Gamma \overset{n+1}{\vdash} \%E : A}$$

Fig. 3. Type Rules

Reflection Expressions

$$\frac{\Delta \vdash^{n} S}{\Delta; \Gamma \vdash^{n} \mathsf{typeof}\ S : \mathsf{Type}\ S} \qquad \frac{\Delta; \Gamma \vdash^{n+1} E_1 : A \quad \Delta; \Gamma \vdash^{n} E_2 : \mathsf{Field}\ A\ B}{\Delta; \Gamma \vdash^{n+1} E_1.\%E_2 : B}$$

$$\frac{\Delta; \Gamma \vdash^{n} E : \mathsf{Type}\ A}{\Delta; \Gamma \vdash^{n+1} \mathsf{new}\ \%E : A} \qquad \frac{\Delta; \Gamma \vdash^{n} E_1 : \mathsf{Type}\ A \quad \Delta; \Gamma \vdash^{n+1} E_2 : B}{\Delta; \Gamma \vdash^{n+1} (\%E_1)E_2 : A}$$

Fig. 3. Type Rules (continued)

– Γ is the environment of regular variables. It contains the names of variables, their types and the level they are declared at. A variable can only be used at the same level it is declared at, but variables from earlier stages can be lifted to the current stage using lift.

The judgment $\Delta \vdash^{n} A$ means that under the environment Δ the type A is valid at level n. The judgment $\Delta; \Gamma \vdash^{n} E : A$ means that under environments Δ and Γ the expression E has type A at level n.

The type rules for general expressions are standard. The type rules for staging expressions are typical for typed multi-stage languages in the style of MetaML. Of particular interest is how these type judgments control the staging level, e.g. brackets increase the level and escape and lift decrease the level and so cannot be used at level zero.

In the typeif expression, the type variable α is tested for equality against the type S. If they are equal then the expression E_1 is evaluated, otherwise E_2 is evaluated. When typing the E_1 branch, α is removed from Δ and any occurrence of α in Γ is substituted with S.

The reflection expressions are typed like specialised versions of lift. The reflection expressions type their Type or Field sub-expression at one level lower than where the reflection expression occurs. The Type or Field sub-expression is also evaluated at an earlier stage and its value is embedded as a literal type or field in the current stage code. Thus these constructs are equivalent to the standard lift construct except that they lift types or fields instead of values.

6 Implementation

We have implemented a prototype compiler for Metaphor that targets the .NET Common Language Runtime. The compiler has a traditional structure divided into three phases: parsing, type checking and code generation. During the first phase the whole source program is parsed including code that lies inside code brackets. The result of the parse phase is a parse tree.

In the next phase, the parse tree is type-checked and transformed into an abstract syntax tree (AST). The AST generated here is important because it also serves as the internal representation of code objects at run-time.

During the code generation phase, the AST is traversed and target language code is emitted for each node in the tree. The code generator emits stage zero code as it would in a unstaged language compiler. The code generator emits stage one and higher code as code that rebuilds the AST. When this compiled code is executed it reconstructs part of the compile-time AST that it was generated from. The run operator is implemented by invoking this code generation phase again at run-time. At run-time, code is compiled into an in-memory code buffer using the .NET framework's support for run-time code generation. Code can be generated and executed in the same process that invoked its generation.

Cross-stage persistence is handled using a global lookup table of objects. Cross-stage persisted objects are added into this table and their table indices are used by compiled code to refer back to the objects. The address of an object cannot be emitted in the generated code because the memory managed environment of the .NET CLR may change the object's location.

Variables in staged code must be renamed to prevent accidental name capture or collision. For example in the code below, the variable x is renamed in the value of c3 to avoid a duplicate local variable declaration.

```
<|int|> c1 = <|int x = 1; x|>;
<|int|> c2 = <|int x = 1; x|>;
<|int|> c3 = <|~c1 + ~c2|>;
```

Therefore when this code is executed the value of c3 would be something like:

```
<|int x1 = 1; int x2 = 1; x1 + x2|>
```

The parameterised reflection types in the source program are erased in the compiled program. They are replaced by the non-parameterised versions of reflection types used by the .NET CLR. In effect the reflection type system is just a compile-time check that has no residue in compiled code.

Metaphor suffers from some well-known problems with the typing of multi-stage languages, such as the unsafety of the run operator and scope extrusion in the presence of imperative side-effects [11]. These problems are areas of active research and current solutions [12, 13] to them could be applied to Metaphor.

7   Related Work

7.1   Generic Programming

Generic programming involves writing *polytypic functions* that implement algorithms that are induced by the structure of a type. Hinze and Peyton Jones [6] present a generic programming extension to Haskell that allows the definition of polytypic functions to produce implementations of Haskell type classes. The code of the type class implementation is expanded at compile-time.

Cheney and Hinze [7] propose a method to implement polytypic functions in Haskell with only minimal language extension. The *representation types* of this system are analogous to the Type type of Metaphor. However this system does not involve the generation of code.

Template Meta-Haskell [14] is a static meta-programming language extension to Haskell. It can be used to generate code for polytypic functions at compile-time.

The reflection and staging constructs of Metaphor enable the definition of polytypic functions that are type-checked at compile-time, but have code generated for them at run-time.

7.2 Typed Multi-stage Languages

The multi-stage programming extensions used in Metaphor were inspired from the language MetaML [1, 2]. MetaML is an extension to ML that supports typed multi-stage programming with cross-stage persistence. MetaML is a functional language and is implemented as an interpreter written in SML.

MetaOCaml [15] is a newer language that has evolved from MetaML. It differs from MetaML in that it safely handles ML's side-effecting constructs with respect to staging and is implemented as a modified OCaml byte-code compiler.

7.3 Higher-Level Imperative Code Generation

A number of imperative programming systems for run-time code generation exist but differ from Metaphor in their balance of type-safety versus expressiveness. `C [16] is fast run-time code generation extension to C. It inherits C's weak type system but allows for more expressive code generation, e.g. functions with a dynamically determined number of parameters.

A run-time code generation extension [17] to Cyclone [18], and DynJava [19] a similar extension to Java offer stronger typing than `C but lose expressiveness. In these languages code values cannot be passed or returned from functions (i.e. lambda-abstracted), have no "run" operator and are not multi-stage. However these languages do cover the full set of their base languages features.

CodeBricks [20] is a software library designed to facilitate code composition in the .NET framework. It exposes a high-level abstraction to the programmer for composing code at the compiled (byte-code) level. Like all code generation/manipulation libraries it cannot statically type later stage code.

8 Conclusion and Future Work

We have described a typed, multi-stage, object-oriented language called Metaphor. The language can express staged programming in object-oriented languages like $C^\#$ or Java. The language has a statically-typed reflection system for run-time type analysis that is used in conjunction with its staging constructs. This allows the programmer to implement type-safe polytypic functions by means of run-time code generation, or in other words to generate code based on the structure of types.

We plan to extend the language with dynamic type generation, i.e. not only can a type be analysed using reflection but a new type can also be created.

With this feature a meta-program could generate a new type and use it in an object-program. The multi-stage type system will prevent types from being used before they are created. The formal calculus presented in this paper will also be extended with this functionality and a soundness proof undertaken for this complete type system.

The prototype Metaphor compiler is available for download at http://sky.fit.qut.edu.au/~neverov/metaphor/.

References

1. Taha, W., Sheard, T.: Multi-stage programming with explicit annotations. In: Partial Evaluation and Semantics-Based Program Manipulation, Amsterdam, The Netherlands, June 1997, New York: ACM (1997) 203–217
2. Taha, W.: Multi-Stage Programming: Its Theory and Applications. PhD thesis, Oregon Graduate Institute of Science and Technology (1999)
3. Sheard, T.: Accomplishments and research challenges in meta-programming. In Taha, W., ed.: Proceedings of the Workshop on Semantics, Applications and Implementation of Program Generation (SAIG'01). (2001) Invited talk.
4. Sheard, T., Benaissa, Z., Martel, M.: Introduction to multi-stage programming using MetaML. Technical report, Pacific Software Research Center, Oregon Graduate Institute (2000)
5. Jansson, P., Jeuring, J.: PolyP – A polytypic programming language extension. In: ACM Symposium on Principles of Programming Languages, POPL'97, Paris, France, 15–17 Jan 1997, New York, ACM Press (1997) 470–482
6. Hinze, R., Peyton Jones, S.: Derivable type classes. In Hutton, G., ed.: Haskell Workshop, Montreal, Canada (2000)
7. Cheney, J., Hinze, R.: A lightweight implementation of Generics and Dynamics. In: Haskell'02, Pittsburgh, Pennsylvania, USA (2002)
8. Sheard, T., Benaissa, Z., Pasalic, E.: DSL implementation using staging and monads. In: Domain-Specific Languages. (1999) 81–94
9. Igarashi, A., Pierce, B., Wadler, P.: Featherweight Java: A minimal core calculus for Java and GJ. In Meissner, L., ed.: Proceedings of the 1999 ACM SIGPLAN Conference on Object-Oriented Programming, Systems, Languages & Applications (OOPSLA'99). Volume 34(10)., N. Y. (1999) 132–146
10. Kennedy, A., Syme, D.: Transposing F to C#. In: Proceedings of Workshop on Formal Techniques for Java-like Programs, Málaga, Spain. (2002)
11. Calcagno, C., Moggi, E., Taha, W.: Closed types as a simple approach to safe imperative multi-stage programming. In: Automata, Languages and Programming. (2000) 25–36
12. Taha, W., Nielsen, M.F.: Environment classifiers. In: Proceedings of the 30th ACM Symposium on Principles of Programming Languages (POPL'03), New Orleans, Louisiana, ACM Press, New York (NY), USA (2003)
13. Calcagno, C., Moggi, E., Taha, W.: ML-like inference for classifiers. In: Proceedings of the European Symposium on Programming (ESOP 2004). LNCS, Springer-Verlag (2004)
14. Sheard, T., Peyton Jones, S.: Template metaprogramming for Haskell. In Chakravarty, M., ed.: ACM SIGPLAN Haskell Workshop 02, ACM Press (2002) 1–16

15. Calcagno, C., Taha, W., Huang, L., Leroy, X.: Implementing multi-stage languages using ASTs, Gensym, and Reflection. In: Generative Programming and Component Engineering. (2003)
16. Engler, D.R., Hsieh, W.C., Kaashoek, M.F.: `C: A language for high-level, efficient, and machine-independent dynamic code generation. In: Symposium on Principles of Programming Languages. (1996) 131–144
17. Hornof, L., Jim, T.: Certifying compilation and run-time code generation. In: Partial Evaluation and Semantic-Based Program Manipulation. (1999) 60–74
18. Jim, T., Morrisett, G., Grossman, D., Hicks, M., Cheney, J., Wang, Y.: Cyclone: A safe dialect of C. In: USENIX Annual Technical Conference, Monterey, CA, June 2002. (2002)
19. Oiwa, Y., Masuhara, H., Yonezawa, A.: DynJava: Type safe dynamic code generation in Java. In: JSST Workshop on Programming and Programming Languages, Tokyo (2001)
20. Attardi, G., Cisternino, A., Kennedy, A.: CodeBricks: Code fragments as building blocks. In: ACM Symposium on Partial Evaluation and Semantics-Based Program Manipulation. (2003)

Optimising Embedded DSLs
Using Template Haskell

Sean Seefried, Manuel Chakravarty, and Gabriele Keller

PLC Research Group
The University of New South Wales, Sydney
National ICT Australia*, ERTOS
{sseefried,chak,keller}@cse.unsw.edu.au

Abstract. Embedded domain specific languages (EDSLs) provide a specialised language for a particular application area while harnessing the infrastructure of an existing general purpose programming language. The reduction in implementation costs that results from this approach comes at a price: the EDSL often compiles to inefficient code since the host language's compiler only optimises at the level of host language constructs. The paper presents an approach to solving this problem based on compile-time meta-programming which retains the simplicity of the embedded approach. We use PanTHeon, our implementation of an existing EDSL for image synthesis to demonstrate the benefits and drawbacks of this approach. Furthermore, we suggest potential improvements to Template Haskell, the meta-programming framework we are using, which would greatly improve its applicability to this kind of task.

1 Introduction

Domain Specific Languages (DSLs) reduce the cost of producing software by providing programming constructs tailored for a particular domain. This reduces the amount of repetitive code that would otherwise be written in a general purpose language and also means that people that have little programming experience, but are nevertheless conversant in the domain can use these languages. Yet in terms of implementation effort, constructing new languages is expensive [14].

Embedded domain specific languages (EDSLs) ([7], [8]) decrease the implementation burden since they are implemented in an existing, feature-rich, general purpose language. This allows the reuse of a substantial portion of the host language's programming environment, such as the lexical analyser, parser, type checker, optimisation phases and code generator of the compiler and the tools surrounding it such as debuggers and profilers. Some host languages are better choices than others: in this paper, we argue that a language with support for compile-time meta-programming is an ideal tool for the implementation of an EDSL due to their ability to express compiler-like optimisations, thus increasing the number of domain specific optimisations that can be written.

* National ICT Australia is funded through the Australian Government's *Backing Australia's Ability* initiative, in part through the Australian Research Council.

The standard approach to the construction of EDSLs involves implementing them as libraries of combinators in a language with support for higher order functions, a rich type system and good syntactic control mechanisms[1]. Unfortunately, EDSLs constructed in this manner often produce inefficient code.

The reason behind this is that domain data types are usually represented as algebraic data types and are *interpreted* by recursive traversal functions ([3], [9], [15], [18]). This interpretive overhead is present in the generated code as the host language compiler has no knowledge of code improvement techniques that may be applied to domain data types and expressions which use them. What is absent is the ability to declare compiler-like optimisations that operate on the syntactic structure of expressions: a capability that *is* offered by a language with compile-time meta-programming features.

An alternative is to *embed a compiler* [5] for the DSL, rather than the DSL itself, in the host language. This was precisely the approach taken by the implementors of Pan, a language for the synthesis of two-dimensional images and animations [4]. In this approach the primitives of the DSL are defined as functions over an abstract syntax tree (AST) representation. The ASTs generated by programs written in the host language are then optimised and fed to a code generator which produces efficient code in a (not necessarily different) target language. The effort involved is equivalent to writing a compiler back-end and although it is considerable, the cost of writing the components of a compiler front-end (such as a lexical analyser, parser, and type checker) is saved.

Approach	Inherit front-end	Inherit back-end	Optimise via
Embedded compiler	yes	no	traditional compiler opts.
Staged interpreter	no	yes	MP: delayed expressions
Extensional meta-programming	yes	yes	MP: transformation (requires code *inspection*)

MP = meta-programming

Fig. 1. A comparison of three approaches to implementing DSLs

The main disadvantage to embedding a compiler is that access to the (often extensive) general optimisations of the host language compiler are lost. Furthermore, if there is disparity between the host language and the target language, generated programs may not be able to use features of the host language. Finally, even though one ostensibly writes programs in the host language it may not be possible to use language constructs which require a base type of the language. (For instance, for *if-then-else* expressions to be valid they typically require an expression of boolean type.) Unfortunately, the representation of expressions as ASTs requires the use of synthetic types, which precludes the use of such language constructs.

---

[1] This has the additional benefit of easing their distribution; it is much easier to distribute and build a module written in a well established language than the sources for an entire compiler.

These disadvantages are automatically avoided by the traditional approach to EDSL implementation (of not embedding a compiler back-end). We assert that the problem of inefficient code is adequately solved by extending this approach with the techniques provided by compile-time meta-programming. Our approach, which we have dubbed *extensional meta-programming* transforms user-written code according to its syntactic structure. The key idea is to represent code as a data structure (preferably an abstract syntax tree), manipulate this data so that it represents equivalent but faster code, and finally turn this data back into code.

Extensional meta-programming differs quite markedly from another popular meta-programming approach: staged interpreters [2]. Staged interpreters use meta-programming annotations to traverse the representation of the interpreted program before the essence of the program is executed at run-time and amounts to a form of domain specific partial evaluation. This approach also inherits the optimisations of the host language (as they will be applied to the generated code) but introduces the expense of having to implement the front-end of a compiler. If this was merely restricted the implementation of a simple lexer and parser this expense would be acceptable. Unfortunately real languages often require significant front-end infrastructure such as a symbol table, a complicated abstract syntax tree representation and analysis phases.

One advantage of the staged interpreter approach is that the meta-language does not require the ability to inspect the structure of code. MetaML and MetaO-Caml both lack this ability. We have summarised the differences between embedded compilers, staged interpreters and extensional meta-programming in Figure 1.

Since our primary motivation is to increase reuse in order to reduce the effort required to create new languages we have chosen extensional meta-programming. To demonstrate the feasibility of our approach, we use Template Haskell[16], a compile-time meta-programming extension to the Glasgow Haskell Compiler [1] to provide an alternative implementation of Pan [4], which we have dubbed PanTHeon. Pan was implemented as an embedded compiler in Haskell, its target language being C. As alluded to earlier, the disparity between these two languages means that the generated programs cannot use features of the host language: in this case laziness and higher-order functions.

To summarise, the main contributions of this paper are:

1. We introduce an approach, extensional meta-programming, to implementing EDSLs offering the following benefits over an embedded compiler:
   - Reduced implementation effort through the sharing of host language's programming environment and the *extension* of its suite of optimisations.
   - Retention of host language features.
   - Inheritance of host language constructs.
2. We investigate the feasibility of extensional meta-programming using Pan-THeon as an example.
3. Template Haskell is evaluated on an example of significant size, and suggested extensions to Template Haskell that will make a wider range of EDSL implementation tasks easier.

The rest of the paper is organised as follows. First, we provide an introduction to meta-programming through Template Haskell. We then give a brief overview of PanTHeon. This comprises a brief introduction to the Pan language and then a description of the transformations we apply to it. Each description is divided into a language independent description (lest readers come to the conclusion the solution is specific to Template Haskell) and one that focuses on the implementation details. Next we present benchmarks that provide evidence of the efficacy of our optimisations followed by an analysis of recurrent problems we have had with Template Haskell and any solutions we devised.

2   An Introduction to Compile-Time Meta-programming via Template Haskell

This section shows how a useful algebraic transformation can be implemented in Template Haskell. Since the optimisations of PanTHeon are treated more than adequately in the rest of the paper we focus on a useful transformation in a well-known domain: linear algebra.

A basic result of linear algebra is that an $n \times n$ matrix, M, multiplied by its inverse, M^{-1}, is equal to the identity matrix, I. This is just the sort of property that we cannot expect most compilers to optimise away, due to the domain-specific knowledge that is required to perform such an optimisation. Consider an expression m * inverse m where m and n are matrices. (The precise details of how matrices are implemented is immaterial.) In order that this expression may be simplified it must first be converted from code into a data structure via a process known as *reification* [6].

Once we have verified that this data structure matches the pattern m * inverse m we can replace it with the data structure that represents identity. We then need to convert the data structure back into code, via a process known as *reflection* [17]. This is also known, particularly in Template Haskell, as *splicing*.

In most meta-programming languages, the reification of m * inverse m * n will take the form of an abstract syntax tree. The transformation of this expression is then simple. We create a new data structure which represents identity * n   and splice it. We now show how this is achieved using Template Haskell on a (rather contrived) lambda expression with body equal to m * inverse m * n.

```
exp_mat = [| \m n -> m * inverse m  * n |]
```

exp_mat makes use of the quasi-quote notation of Template Haskell, denoted by the [| and |] brackets. These brackets reify code within.

Figure 2 presents the function rmMatByInverse which removes the redundancy in the reified expression. Unfortunately, without familiarity with the data structure used for representing expressions the code can be difficult to understand. The first case does the real work; it matches against infix expressions of the form m * inverse m and returns identity, while the second and third (after matching against expressions of the form $\lambda p.e$ and fa respectively) recursively

```
rmMatByInverse (InfixE (Just 'm) 'GHC.Num.* (Just (AppE 'inverse 'm))) =
  VarE (mkName "identity")
rmMatByInverse (LamE pats exp) = LamE pats (rmMatByInverse exp)
rmMatByInverse (AppE exp exp') =
  AppE (rmMatByInverse exp) (rmMatByInverse exp')
rmMatByInverse exp = exp
```

Fig. 2. An example of an arithmetic transformation

call upon sub-expressions. (Note that we have only presented the cases necessary to transform exp_mat.)

Template Haskell's splicing operator, $(...), *runs* meta-programs and converts the resulting data structure back to code. In our case the expression $(rmMatByInverse exp_mat) evaluates to the *code* \m n -> n at compile-time. This is a key aspect of our approach; by using a language which is restricted to compile-time meta-computation we guarantee that there is no run-time overhead in the code generated.

3 PanTHeon

PanTHeon is a direct implementation of the image primitives presented in Elliott's paper [4]. There are three main classes of optimisation: the unboxing of arithmetic expressions, aggressive inlining and algebraic transformations. In the subsections below we describe why each is particularly applicable to our domain, and its realisation in general meta-programming terms, without recourse to Template Haskell specifics. Any language of similar functionality could be used in its place (although we know of no such language yet.) However, Template Haskell is a relatively new extension to Haskell. It is common wisdom that languages change rapidly and substantially early in their lives. This is at least partly motivated by their use in novel situations where it is discovered that additional features would simplify things. As such, we follow the general description of each optimisation with the solution we devised in Template Haskell, highlighting problems we encountered.

But first, to put all this in context, we describe Pan in more detail.

3.1 A Pan Example

Pan is a domain specific language founded upon the concept of modelling an *image* as a function from continuous Cartesian coordinates to colour values. The *animation* extends the image concept; it is simply a function from continuous time to an image.

Figure 3 presents a simple Pan effect that will be used as a running example throughout the rest of the paper and is self contained with respect to Appendix A.

Colours are represented as four-tuples containing red, green, blue and alpha (transparency) components in the range [0, 1]. whiteH and blackH are 50%

```
checker (x,y) = if even e then blackH else whiteH
  where e = floor x + floor y
stripes (x,y) =
  | even (floor x) = blue
  | otherwise = red
checker_on_stripes = checker 'over' (empty 'over' swirl stripes)
```

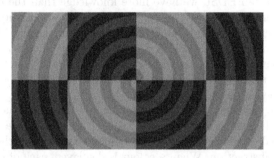

Fig. 3. Checker board imposed over swirled vertical blue and red stripes

transparent. The checker board (checker) is defined as a function which takes a coordinate (x,y) and returns blackH if $\lfloor x \rfloor + \lfloor y \rfloor$ is even and whiteH otherwise. The stripes function is even easier to define. Here we simply check that that $\lfloor x \rfloor$ is even and colour it blue if so, red if not.

In checker_on_stripes we see the use of the *image overlay* combinator, over. This function combines two images pointwise. Depending on the transparency of the top image a portion of the underlying image will show through. swirl is an interesting Pan primitive that warps an image by rotating points a distance proportional to their distance from the origin. The empty image is completely transparent. See Appendix A for their implementation.

3.2 Architecture of PanTHeon

PanTHeon consists of three main parts - the language implementation, the optimisation modules and a client for displaying effects. As mentioned above, the language implementation is a direct implementation of the combinators in [4]. Users write effects in Pan (which is really just Haskell) which can then be loaded directly into the client via conventional file menu widgets. The user written code is imported into an automatically generated module which transforms their code via functions present in the optimisations modules. This file is then compiled in GHC and dynamically loaded using Don Stewart's *hs-plugins* library[13].

3.3 Unboxing Arithmetic

Motivation and Abstract Approach. PanTHeon is a numerically intensive application, almost exclusively using floating-point arithmetic. Hence unboxing can yield significant improvements in speed[2]. Unboxed code also yields better memory locality as the arguments and results do not require an indirection to a heap allocated object. In fact, it may be possible that the arguments are placed directly into registers.

Most compilers optimise away as much unnecessary boxing as is feasible, but as implementors of an EDSL we have more knowledge than the compiler does and can consequently do better. We can be certain of the validity of unboxing assuming that every function in PanTHeon is also monomorphic. Although it is quite possible to define functions this way (and we have done so) a much nicer solution would be to specialise each invocation of a polymorphic function based on the type information gleaned from the context in which it is invoked. We discuss this further in the next subsection.

This begs the question, why do we not simply define all the functions in terms of unboxed arithmetic in the first place? Apart from the fact that the syntax of unboxed arithmetic is ugly and cumbersome to use, there is a more important issue: abstraction. When a colour is displayed, each of its component values is converted to an integral value between 0 and 255 and combined into a single 32-bit integer that is placed into video memory. Efficiency can be gained by converting the functions that operate on colours to their integer arithmetic equivalents behind the scenes, while the user retains their view of the current abstraction (i.e. floats of $[0,1]$)[3].

In general terms this optimisation requires that we traverse the representation of each top level function replacing all boxed arithmetic operators and constants with their unboxed equivalents. The unboxing of arithmetic is an interesting transformation as it changes the semantics of the program. Each type in the resulting program corresponds exactly to a type in the original, but it is clear that the validity of this correspondence relies upon our knowledge of the domain.

Implementation in Template Haskell. The process of replacing all boxed operators and constants with their unboxed equivalents is generally a straightforward process in Template Haskell, although we run into difficulty in the context of polymorphic data structures. Most cases written for the family of unboxing functions merely call `unbox` recursively on sub-objects (be they declarations, types, bodies, expressions, etc). There are only a few interesting cases:

1. Transforming type signatures. It is clear that any type signatures or type annotations that existed in the original declarations will no longer be valid. For each type synonym and data type declared for the boxed declarations we declare an unboxed version. For ease of recognition the name of such types have a _UB suffix appended.

---

[2] Without unboxing, each arithmetic function must first unbox its arguments, perform a primitive arithmetic operation upon these values, and re-box the result.

[3] Although early experiments indicated that this arithmetic conversion measurably improved performance, there were technical reasons that prevented it. We discuss the reasons in the implementation details.

2. Replacing arithmetic operators with unboxed equivalents. This code assumes that all operators will be changed to their unboxed floating point equivalents. We recognise this as a flawed assumption and we discuss this further in this paper.
3. Replacing tuples with stricter versions. We declared two new data types to express points and colours to increase strictness. Unlike the situation with tuples, one can add strictness annotations to the arguments of the constructor.

We now present an example of all three of these cases in action.

```
checker :: ImageC
checker (x,y) = if even e then blackH else whiteH
  where e = floor x + floor y
```

becomes

```
checker :: ImageC_UB
checker (Point_UB x y) =  if evenInt# e then blackH else whiteH
  where e = float2Int# x + float2Int# y
```

Our main problem with the implementation of the unboxing pass has been the lack of easily accessible typing information. It is problematic in three ways.

- It is impossible to know what the type of a literal is. This was first identified by Lynagh [12]. Fortunately, nearly all literals in the definition of Pan functions are instances of Fractional. However there were a few instances where this was not true and special cases had to be written for them.
- In the previous section we stated that we had also considered converting the components of colours to the range $[0, 255]$. This would have necessitated a relatively complex transformation on all functions which manipulated colours.
  For instance consider the definition of cOver (a key component of the definition of image overlay.)

```
cOver (r1,g1,b1,a1) (r2,g2,b2,a2) =
  (h r1 r2, h g1 g2, h b1 b2, h a1 a2)
  where h x1 x2 = a1* x1 + (1 - a1) * x2
```

Under our proposed transformation it would become

```
cOver (Colour_UB r1 g1 b1 a1) (Colour_UB r2 g2 b2 a2) =
  (Colour_UB (h r1 r2) (h g1 g2) (h b1 b2) (h a1 a2))
  where h x1 x2 = (a1 *# x1 +# (255# -# a1) *# x2) `divInt#` 255#
```

Such a transformation is only feasible when one has knowledge of the type of each variable. For instance, in the example above it is necessary to know that a1 is of type ColourBit_UB (i.e. in range $[0, 255]$).

- We have had to define all PanTHeon functions that contain arithmetic operations monomorphically. A restriction that GHC imposes is that a function containing unboxed operations cannot operate on polymorphic data types. With type information we could specialise such polymorphic functions at each call site.

Without the ability to reify the type of a fragment of an expression, some transformations simply cannot be written for the general case, and until a satisfactory solution has been found, we regard this as one of the principle shortcomings of our implementation. We discuss this issue further in Section 5.2.

3.4   Inlining

Motivation and Abstract Approach. The style of embedding used in the original implementation of Pan has the effect of inlining all definitions and β-reducing the resulting function applications before any further simplification occurs. This greatly increases the opportunities for algebraic transformation but has the drawback of introducing the possibility of code replication. Fortunately, the effect of code replication can be mitigated by applying a common subexpression elimination (CSE) pass following this one. Based on the success Elliott, Finne, and de Moore [5] had with it we investigated this approach to code improvement.

However, since GHC has its own passes for performing beta-reduction and CSE, we decided to leave these passes unimplemented and see how well the compiler performed. The results of our experiment are encouraging and we provide a concrete example in next section.

In general terms the ability to inline code relies upon two meta-programming facilities: the ability to reify, transform and splice code, and the ability to look up the definition of a top-level function declaration. Unfortunately, Template Haskell does not (yet) support this second facility. In Section 5.1 we explain our solution to this problem which involves the manual creation of a look-up table.

With this infrastructure in place, the inlining process is relatively straightforward. We take as input the final animation or image function that PanTHeon will display and traverse its definition. Each time we encounter the use of a function that has been defined in PanTHeon[4] we look up its definition, create an equivalent lambda expression and substitute it at that location. We do this recursively.

Clearly, this leads to non-termination in the context of recursion. While we could refuse to inline recursive function definitions, determining whether a function is recursive is an involved process requiring the construction of a call graph and the determination of strongly connected components, and in any case GHC already does this. Unfortunately we do not have access to this information. (Perhaps Template Haskell should provide it.) Instead we have chosen to limit the inlining process to a fixed depth which roughly corresponds to loop unrolling.

---

[4] We do not inline functions that are part of other Haskell libraries.

Implementation in Template Haskell. Most definitions in the inlining transformation are concerned with traversing the components of a declaration. The function that actually does the real work is `mkInlineExp`. Its implementation is quite cluttered with Template Haskell specifics so we have chosen to present a stepwise example of its effect on our running example (introduced in Section 3.1).

The inlining pass traverses the declaration of `checker_on_stripes` until it comes to the *variable* sub-expression `checker`. At this point a look-up is performed upon its name and the declaration for `checker` is retrieved. We then convert this definition to an equivalent lambda expression. Note that *where* declarations are converted to *let* declarations. Note that without typing information we cannot inline functions that have been overloaded using Haskell's type class mechanism.

```
\(x,y) -> let e = floor x + floor y
          in  if even e then blackH else whiteH
```

This expression is then substituted in place of the variable. Function definitions that contain guards are also handled. This occurs during the inlining of `stripes`. It is replaced with

```
\(x,y) -> if even (floor x) then red else blue
```

In the previous section we promised a concrete example of the effect of GHC's common subexpression elimination on inlined code. A fitting example to consider comes from the original paper on the implementation of Pan [5]):

```
swirlP r = \p -> rotate (distO p * (2*pi/r)) p
```

The result of inlining clearly contains much redundancy:

```
(\(x,y) -> (x * cos (sqrt (x*x + y*y) * (2*pi/r))
          - y * sin (sqrt (x*x + y*y) * (2*pi/r)),
          y * cos (sqrt (x*x + y*y) * (2*pi/r))
          + x * sin (sqrt (x*x + y*y) * (2*pi/r)))
```

The following dump of the Core[5] code produced shows that it is capable of removing much of the redundancy.

```
\w_se6i ww_se6l ww_se6m ->
let { a'334 = <core equivalent of x*x + y*y * (2*pi/r)>
} in
(# (GHC.Prim.minusFloat#
    (GHC.Prim.timesFloat# ww_se6l (GHC.Prim.cosFloat# a'334))
    (GHC.Prim.timesFloat# ww_se6m (GHC.Prim.sinFloat# a'334))),
  (GHC.Prim.plusFloat#
    (GHC.Prim.timesFloat# ww_se6m (GHC.Prim.cosFloat# a'334))
    (GHC.Prim.timesFloat# ww_se6l (GHC.Prim.sinFloat# a'334)))
#)
```

GHC also performs β-reduction and constant folding (e.g. 2π is replaced with the constant $6.283\ldots$) which saves us yet more implementation effort.

---

[5] An intermediate representation used by GHC. Adding the flag-ddump-core to the command line will dump the code to standard output.

3.5   Algebraic Transformation

Motivation and Abstract Approach. The principle behind algebraic transformation as an optimisation technique is simple: expressions are substituted for semantically equivalent expressions which compile to faster code, be it universally or only on average. If we consider our running example again, we can see that overlaying the entirely transparent empty image on top of swirl stripes will have no effect. (This is proved by examining the definition of over.)

```
checker_on_stripes = checker 'over' (empty 'over' swirl stripes)
```

The sub-expression may simply be replaced with swirl stripes. That is, the following algebraic identity holds: empty 'over' *image* = *image*. (For more examples of algebraic properties of Pan see Appendix B.)

What is exciting about our use of this technique in PanTHeon (and in the general context of EDSLs) is that we are using it in a fairly novel context: outside the compiler. A key advantage over an embedded compiler is that we only need to implement transformations specific to our EDSL, *extending* rather than overriding the optimisations of the compiler.

In general terms algebraic transformations are easy to implement. For a given expression we attempt to match it against our known algebraic identities. When successful we replace it with the equivalent optimised expression. To ensure that sub-expressions are also optimised we recursively apply to the sub-expressions left unchanged by the original transformation. We also do this when no algebraic transformation is applicable.

Implementation in Template Haskell. Template Haskell's reification of code as algebraic data types in combination with its pattern matching features make algebraic transformations very easy to write (and has been noted by others [2]). Earlier we showed that the expression empty 'over' *image* can be replaced with *image*. This particular case is implemented via the following code.

```
algTrans (AppE (AppE (VarE 'over) (VarE 'empty)) image) =
  algTrans image
```

One of the side effects of the rich syntaxes offered by modern programming languages, including Haskell, is that there is often more than one way to write essentially the same expression. This is very useful for program *generation* but in the context of program *transformation* means that separate cases must be written to transform equivalent expressions. In order to reduce the number of patterns to be matched against, a number of cases were written that put expressions in a canonical form. For instance, the example above matches on the canonical (prefix) form, over empty *image*, of the algebraic identity presented earlier.

Another tedious aspect of all transformations is the recursive cases. Since we wish our transformations to be applicable not just to expressions but sub-expressions also, we must have cases which recursively call on them. These cases are numerous and easily outnumber the cases that actually do interesting work.

However, a recent paper [11] presents a method by which the such boiler-plate code can be "scrapped"; that is the traversal can be done in a handful of lines of code. We have used these techniques in our source code.

An example of the code reductions are shown below. The function `inlineExp` checks whether an expression is a variable and inlines the appropriate function if so and returns the expression unchanged if not.

The function `inline` is defined using the `everywhereM` combinator. It can be used on any code representation data structure and will transform any component of such data strucutre that contains an expression, no matter how deeply nested. For lack of space we have omitted the function `mkInlinedExp` which creates an lambda expression equivalent to the looked up function definition.

```
inlineExp :: [(String, FunDecl)]
          -> ([(String, FunDecl)] -> (forall a. Data a => a -> Q a))
          -> Exp -> Q Exp

inlineExp tbl inline e@(VarE nm) =
 case lookup (nameBase nm) tbl of
  (Just (funDec, _)) -> mkInlinedExp (inline tbl) funDec
  Nothing -> return e
inlineExp _ _ exp = return exp

inline :: [(String, FunDecl)] -> (forall a. Data a => a -> Q a)
inline tbl = everywhereM (mkM (inlineExp tbl inline))
```

4   Benchmarks

Performance testing on PanTHeon has been conducted in two ways - optimised effects have been compared with their unoptimised counterparts as well as against the original Pan implementation.

4.1   PanTHeon vs. Itself

Figure 4 compares the frame rate of an effect for which different combinations of optimisations have been applied. When both unboxing and inlining are applied the effects run at least twice as fast, and for one particular example the optimisations led to a nine-fold speed-up.

The effects were run on a 1Ghz Apple Powerbook G4 with 512MB of RAM. We have left out the effect of algebraic transformations only because our sample size is so small. Naturally, we could contrive an effect with much computational redundancy which would show off its effectiveness, but this would not tell us much. Only by collecting a large number of effects can we say anything about its effectiveness.

4.2   PanTHeon vs. Pan

How well does the performance of PanTHeon compares with that of Pan? Unfortunately, this is difficult to compare because of platform disparity. PanTHeon

Effect	Base	Inlined	Unboxed	Unboxed & Inlined
checker_swirl	8.86 f/s	1.309x	2.190x	2.258x
circle	11.241 f/s	1.324x	2.126x	2.083x
checker_on_stripes	1.302 f/s	1.027x	8.361x	9.003x
four_squares	2.512 f/s	1.366x	4.184x	4.152x
triball	1.244 f/s	1.914x	2.578x	2.707x
tunnel_view	4.62 f/s	1.223x	2.042x	2.661x

Fig. 4. Effect of optimisations on frame rate for effects displayed at 320x200 resolution

has been implemented for *nix[6] platforms while Pan only runs on Microsoft Windows. Nevertheless, we performed measurements on PanTHeon and Pan on the same machine: a 733 MHz Pentium III, 384 MB RAM, at 400x300 resolution.

Pan still outperforms PanTHeon. The `checker_swirl` effect has performance that compares favourably; at a resolution of 400x300 it runs at 4.78 *frames/s* in PanTHeon and at 10.61 *frames/s* in Pan. Other effects such as `triball` and `four_squares` perform far better in Pan (> 18 *frames/s*) and very slowly in PanTHeon (1.68 *frames/s* and 6.54 *frames/s* respectively). Both these effects makes substantial use of the `over` primitive for layering images on top of each other. Pan seems to do substantial unrolling of expressions, which is an optimisation we have not yet implemented in PanTHeon. We suspect that it will significantly improve effects' performance.

However, we have shown that the issue does not lie with any inherent deficiencies in the quality of the code that GHC produces. We hand-coded (and optimised) a very simple effect which ran at a speed comparable to the same effect in Pan (24 million pixels/s).

Another aspect of the Template Haskell implementation that has hindered further tuning or creation of optimisations is the lack of support for profiling of programs which contain splicing.

4.3   Relative Code Base Sizes

Finally, we compare the amount of code needed to implement Pan and PanTHeon as a crude means of comparing implementation effort. Both Pan and PanTHeon have two components – a language definition and a display client. The PanTHeon library, plus optimisations totals at about 3000 lines of code. The client is implemented in under 1000 lines of code. Pan, in its entirety, exceeds 13000 lines of code. The inheritance of a code generator and host language optimisations by PanTHeon is the primary reason for this difference.

5   Template Haskell Specifics

We found Template Haskell to be an excellent language for extensional metaprogramming. It's quasi-quote notation, its novel approach to typing and its

---

[6] It has been successfully built on Debian GNU/Linux and Mac OS X.

ability to represent and inspect code made the task of writing elegant compiler-like optimisations possible. However, we believe that there are ways in which the language could be improved further and in this section we review difficulties we had with the current Template Haskell implementation and any solutions we devised. We envisage that this section will be of most use to other users of Template Haskell and may be skipped safely by those who are not interested.

5.1   Reification of Top-Level Functions

Both unboxing of arithmetic and inlining, require the ability to reify top-level function declarations. Currently, such reification is unsupported in Template Haskell. There is, however, a relatively simple work-around to this problem. We can create a look up table in two steps. First, we place the entire module in declaration reification brackets and call the resulting data structure something appropriate, such as `moduleImageFuns`. We can then create the look-up table for this module by applying a function which creates a list of pairs matching names to function declarations.

An interesting dilemma arises when one wishes to write a module, say M2TH, which refers to functions defined in module M1TH[7]. But the functions in M1TH are not in scope and will only become so if they are spliced in somewhere. So we create a module M1 which splices in the reified functions from this module and then import M1, not M1TH, inside module M2TH. The basic idea is summarised in Figure 5.

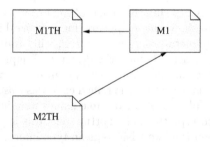

Fig. 5. M2TH imports M1 which splices in declarations in M1TH

There is just one more tiny problem. We wish to transform both the functions in M1TH and M2TH before bringing them into scope for display in the PanTHeon client, but the solution outlined above causes the functions in M2TH to refer to the functions in scope in M1. The reified form of such functions contain *original names* which are of the form M:f (where M and f are module and function names respectively). In order to refer to whatever is in scope at post-transformation splice time we must remove the module prefix from the original names.

---

[7] By convention we append TH to the end of modules constructed in the above manner.

The addition to Template Haskell of a native means to deal with the reification of top-level function declarations would greatly simplify the implementation of PanTHeon and similar programs, and would be less error prone.

5.2   Lack of Type Information

In Section 3.3 we mentioned that lack of type information prevented us from satisfactorily implementing the unboxing transformation. This is for three main reasons:

1. We require the type of literals in order to choose the correct primitive unboxed arithmetic functions.
2. Knowing the type that an invocation of a polymorphic function would be instantiated to is also necessary to choose the correct primitive unboxed arithmetic functions.
3. Polymorphic data structures cannot contain unboxed values. Therefore, specialised data structures are required. Again, types are needed. The next subsection discusses this further.

Template Haskell recently underwent a substantial revision. One of the features that was added was the ability to reify variable names to glean, among other things, their types. Unfortunately, this is only possible if the variable name in question was brought into scope for the one of the following reasons: it came from another module, it was not generated by a splice and appears somewhere in the current module, or it was generated by a top-level splice occurring earlier in the current module.

In fact, this is the only type information that *can* be available without splicing the declaration in which the variable appears, for in general it is undecidable as to whether an arbitrary meta-program, once run, will produce correctly typed code. (This was the motivation behind the design of Template Haskell's typing system which defers type checking until meta-programs have been run.)

However, in the special case that the reified code was *closed*, in the sense that it contained no further splices and all variable names were in scope, it would be possible, in principle, to type the code. Fortunately, this is precisely the sort of declaration in PanTHeon that we wish to glean type information from.

5.3   Unboxing in the Context of Polymorphic Data Structures

Section 3.3 hinted at a problem with unboxed values in the context of polymorphic data structures. One of the restrictions on unboxed values is that they may not be stored in polymorphic data structures. This necessitates the specialisation of polymorphic data structures to monomorphic counterparts. Disregarding the difficulty of doing this in the absence of typing information there is an additional difficulty. While it is possible to reify data type declarations in other modules (using the Template Haskell primitive `reifyDecl`) it is not possible to reify the definitions of functions in those modules. The following example illustrates some of the difficulty arising from this.

```
weird :: Point
weird = head (zipWith (,) [1] [0.5])
```

Without the ability to reify the definitions of `zipWith` and `head`, and specialise them to work on a monomorphic version of the list data type the only other solution is to marshal data to and from unboxed/monomorphic representations at key points within the function definition, which to be feasible also requires access to type information. At present, it is not clear whether the ability to reify entire modules or functions in other modules will be added to Template Haskell or not. The latter solution will be necessary in case it does not.

5.4   The Question of Rewrite Rules

In our implementation we have chosen not to use rewrite rules to perform algebraic transformation of programs, even though it would, in principle, be possible. Template Haskell provides full control over the timing of the application of transformations unlike GHC's rewrite rules [10]. Experience suggests that it is notoriously difficult to ensure that rewrite rules will be applied when one intends them to be. Because of their complex interaction with the other optimisations of GHC it can often be the case that they are not nearly as applicable as one would like. Also, since we cannot apply the unboxing transformation to rewrite rules we would have to do this by hand.

6   Future Work

We have identified a number of ways in which PanTHeon could be further improved. However, the latter two suggestions are not limited to this particular EDSL; they benefit the extensional meta-programming approach we have taken.

Conversion of Domain Data Types. We are still interested in converting the components that make up the colour data type to integers in the range $[0, 255]$ and converting all functions which manipulate colour to operate upon this range. As we noted before, this is not feasible without being able to ascertain the type of individual components of a functional declaration. We believe that this type information would allow more radical conversion. A key function in PanTHeon is `toRGB32` which takes a colour, converts each component to be in the range $[0, 255]$ (which fits in 8 bits) and then packs the four components into a 32-bit integer using bitwise operations. It would be interesting to see if the colours could be represented by this 32-bit representation at all times. This would require colour manipulating functions to use bitwise operations on the colours instead of the native pattern matching facilities of the Haskell language.

Moving Optimisation Phases of the Host Language Compiler into Libraries. There is a subtle problem with the interaction between GHC's optimisations and those presented in this paper: our optimisations are performed before any of GHC's. Unfortunately the order in which optimisations are done is often important; some increase the effectiveness of others if performed at the correct time. While we have not (yet) encountered this problem with PanTHeon, we feel this problem would benefit from closer scrutiny.

The solution to this problem is tantalising. One proposal is that *all* optimisations are written in Template Haskell. This would have the effect of shifting a large portion of the compiler into its support libraries and would arguably simplify the implementation considerably.

However this raises new problems. Many of the optimisations in GHC depend upon information gleaned from the structure of the input program; examples include strictness analysis, various forms of data flow analysis, and call graphs. Further, these optimisations are applied to the Core language, a simplified intermediate representation of Haskell programs, that is nonetheless *not* Haskell. (Since it is syntactically simpler and has less complicated semantics, writing optimisations in Core is easier.) The idea of adding meta-programming facilities to Core has been put forward but it is far from clear how this would be implemented. Nonetheless, the potential benefits almost certainly outweigh the difficulty of this proposal.

Access to Type Information Before Execution of Meta-programs. We are interested in implementing a modest extension to the type checker of Template Haskell that allows *closed* reified code to be typed. It would also be interesting to see whether declarations that are not closed could at least be partially typed.

7   Related Work and Conclusion

Many languages have been developed using the embedded approach to domain specific language construction. Examples include an XML translation language [18] , Fran [3], FranTk [15], and Haskore [9]. These languages are written in an interpretive style in which domain types are modelled as algebraic data types and language primitives as functions which recursively traverse over them. This leads to inefficient code and was the original motivation behind the embedded compiler approach of Pan.

But we feel the embedded compiler approach sacrifices too much. Apart from having to write the entire back-end of a compiler, one also introduces a disparity in the semantics of the host language and the target language which can lead to such problems as the loss of host language features, and the burden of having to duplicate the effect of some constructs, such as *if-then-else* expressions, due to the synthetic nature of the *types* used in the embedded compiler.

Much of the inefficiency of EDSLs results from the host compiler not being able to *see* at the level of the new language. Compilers often have intimate knowledge of semantics of their primitive constructs, and such knowledge allows them to perform sophisticated optimisations to improve the performance of code. But they cannot understand an EDSL in such a manner.

Meta-programming solves this problem by allowing the programmer to use their knowledge of the EDSL to write domain specific optimisations. In this paper we have demonstrated that:

- Optimisations are easy to write. This is facilitated by the quasi-quote notation and pattern matching facilities of Template Haskell. Incidentally, this affirms the half-serious remark that Haskell is a domain specific language for writing compilers.
- Extensional optimisations work well with those inherited from the host language.
- The optimisations are effective. There was at least a factor of two speed up in all the examples we tested on.
- The implementation effort, in terms of raw lines of code, is significantly less.
- Additional meta-programming facilities would increase the power of extensional meta-programming. In particular, more type information is the key to writing more sophisticated transformations.

The source code of PanTHeon, along with instructions for building it, can be found at http://www.cse.unsw.edu.au/~sseefried/pantheon.html.

The comments and suggestions of a number of people helped improve the presentation of this paper. In chronological order of contribution, the authors would very much like to thank Ian Lynagh, Simon Peyton Jones, John O'Donnell, Anthony Sloane, Donald Stewart, Nicolas Magaud and André Pang.

A Listing of module Image

Below is a listing of just the parts of module Image needed to understand the examples presented in this paper.

```
module Image
where

type Point = (Float, Float)
type Colour = (Float, Float, Float, Float)
type Image c = Point -> c
type ImageC = Image Colour
type Warp = Point -> Point

whiteT :: Colour
whiteT = (0,0,0,0)

whiteH, blackH :: Colour
whiteH = (1,1,1,0.5)
blackH = (0,0,0,0.5)

lift0 h       = \p -> h
lift1 h f1    = \p -> h (f1 p)
lift2 h f1 f2 = \p -> h (f1 p) (f2 p)
```

```
empty :: ImageC
empty = lift0 whiteT

distO :: Point -> Float
distO (x,y) = sqrt (x*x + y*y)

swirl :: Float -> Warp
swirl r p = rotateP ((distO p) * (2*pi/r)) p

cOver :: Colour -> Colour -> Colour
cOver (r1,g1,b1,a1) (r2,g2,b2,a2) = (h r1 r2, h g1 g2, h b1 b2, h a1 a2)
    where h x1 x2 = a1* x1 + (1 - a1) * x2

over :: ImageC -> ImageC -> ImageC
over = lift2 cOver
```

B   Some Algebraic Properties of Pan

```
empty 'over' image = image
image 'over' image = image
translate (x1,y1) (translate (x2,y2) im) = translate (x1+x2, y1+y2) im
rotate a im = rotate (a - n*2*pi) im   (where n = a 'div' 2*pi)
rotate a1 (rotate a2 im) = rotate (a1 + a2) im
scale (x1,y1) (scale (x2,y2) im) = scale (x1*x2, y1*y2) im
fromPolar  (toPolar f) = f
```

References

1. The Glasgow Haskell Compiler. http://haskell.org/ghc.
2. Krzysztof Czarnecki, John O'Donnell, Jörg Striegnitz, and Walid Taha. DSL Implementation in MetaOCaml, Template Haskell, and C++.
   URL: http://www.cs.rice.edu/~taha/publications.html, 2003.
3. Conal Elliott. Functional implementations of continuous modeled animation. *Lecture Notes in Computer Science*, 1490:284–, 1998.
4. Conal Elliott. Functional Image Synthesis. In *Proceedings Bridges 2001, Mathematical Connections in Art, Music, and Science*, 2001.
5. Conal Elliott, Sigbjorn Finne, and Oege de Moor. Compiling embedded languages. *Journal of Functional Programming*, 13(3):455–481, May 2003.
6. Daniel P. Friedman and Mitchell Wand. Reification: Reflection without Metaphysics. In *Proceedings of the 1984 ACM Symposium on LISP and functional programming*, pages 348–355, 1984.
7. Paul Hudak. Building domain-specific embedded languages. *ACM Computing Surveys (CSUR)*, 28(4es):196, 1996.
8. Paul Hudak. Modular domain specific languages and tools. In P. Devanbu and J. Poulin, editors, *Proceedings: Fifth International Conference on Software Reuse*, pages 134–142. IEEE Computer Society Press, 1998.
9. Paul Hudak, Tom Makucevich, Syam Gadde, and Bo Whong. Haskore music notation - an algebra of music. *Journal of Functional Programming*, 6(3):465–483, 1996.

10. Simon Peyton Jones, Andrew Tolmach, and Tony Hoare. Playing by the Rules: Rewriting as a practical optimisation technique in GHC. *International Conference on Functional Programming (ICFP 2001). Haskell Workshop.*, September 2001.
11. Ralf Lämmel and Simon Peyton Jones. Scrap your boilerplate: a practical design pattern for generic programming. *ACM SIGPLAN Notices*, 38(3):26–37, March 2003. Proc. of the ACM SIGPLAN Workshop on Types in Language Design and Implementation (TLDI 2003).
12. Ian Lynagh. Unrolling and simplifying expressions with Template Haskell. URL: http://web.comlab.ox.ac.uk/oucl/work/ian.lynagh/papers/ Unrolling_and_Simplifying_Expressions_with_Template_Haskell.ps, May 2003.
13. André Pang, Donald Stewart, Sean Seefried, and Manuel Chakravarty. Plugging Haskell In. To be published in *Haskell Workshop 2004*, June 2004.
14. Arch D. Robinson. The Impact of Economics on Compiler Optimization. In *Proceedings of the ACM 2001 Java Grande Conference, Standford*, pages 1–10, June 2001.
15. Meurig Sage. FranTk – a declarative GUI language for Haskell. *ACM SIGPLAN Notices*, 35(9):106–117, 2000.
16. Tim Sheard and Simon Peyton Jones. Template Meta-Programming for Haskell. *ACM SIGPLAN Notices: PLI Workshops*, 37(12):60–75, 2002.
17. Brian Cantwell Smith. Reflection and Semantics in Lisp. *Conf. Rec. 11th ACM Symp. on Principles of Programming Languages*, pages 23–35, 1984.
18. Malcolm Wallace and Colin Runciman. Haskell and XML: Generic combinators or type-based translation? In *Proceedings of the Fourth ACM SIGPLAN International Conference on Functional Programming (ICFP'99)*, volume 34–9, pages 148–159, N.Y., 27–29 1999. ACM Press.

A Fresh Calculus for Name Management

Davide Ancona and Eugenio Moggi*

DISI, Univ. of Genova, v. Dodecaneso 35, 16146 Genova, Italy
{davide,moggi}@disi.unige.it

Abstract. We define a basic calculus for name management, which combines three ingredients: extensible records (in a simplified form), names (as in FreshML), computational types (to allow computational effects, including generation of fresh names). The calculus supports the use of symbolic names for programming in-the-large, e.g. it subsumes Ancona and Zucca's calculus for module systems, and for meta-programming (but not the intensional analysis of object level terms supported by FreshML), e.g. it subsumes (and improves) Nanevski and Pfenning's calculus for meta-programming with names and necessity. Moreover, it models some aspects of Java's class loaders.

1 Introduction

We introduce a basic calculus, called MML_ν^N, providing name management abilities, like those needed for programming in-the-large [Car97,AZ02]. In MML_ν^N names play the same role as in CMS [AZ02] (and in record calculi): they are used to name components of a module and to refer to external components which need to be provided from the outside (by a name resolver).

In CMS (and record calculi) names are taken from some infinite set Name. In MML_ν^N the idea is to move from ordinary set theory to Fraenkel and Mostowski's set theory, where there is an alternative choice for Name, namely the *FM-set* of atoms (which is potentially infinite). By taking Name as the FM-set of atoms, we can have, as in FreshML [SPG03], a construct that generates a fresh name. In FreshML names are terms (and there is a type of names), so generation of a fresh name is denoted by $\nu x.e$, where x is a term variable which gets bound to the fresh name, and e is the term where the fresh name can be used. In MML_ν^N names occur both in types and in terms, and using x in place of a name X would entail a type system with dependent types (which would be problematic), thus we must use a different binder $\nu X.e$ for names.

To understand the type system and operational semantics of MML_ν^N (and FreshML) there is no need to be acquainted with FM-sets [GP99]. However, some key mathematical properties of FM-sets, like *equivariance* (i.e. invariance w.r.t. name permutations), are manifest in the type system and the operational semantics. Besides names $X \in \mathsf{Name}$, the calculus has

---

* Supported by EU project DART IST-2001-33477 and thematic network APPSEM II IST-2001-38957

- terms $e \in \mathsf{E}$, a closed term corresponds to an *executable* program;
- name resolvers denote partial functions $\mathsf{Name} \overset{fin}{\to} \mathsf{E}$ with finite domain. We write $r.X$ for the term obtained by applying r to *resolve* name X.

Terms include fragments $b(r)e$, i.e. term e abstracted w.r.t. resolver r, which denote functions $(\mathsf{Name} \overset{fin}{\to} \mathsf{E}) \to \mathsf{E}$. We write $e\langle r \rangle$ for the term obtained by *linking* fragment e using resolver r.

Remark 1. If resolvers were included in terms, we would get a λ-calculus with extensible records [CM94], indeed a record amounts to a partial function mapping names (of components) to their values. More precisely, $b(r)e$ would become an abstraction $\lambda r.e$ and $e\langle r \rangle$ an application $e\ r$. We would also gain in expressivity. The main reasons for considering resolvers as second class terms, is to have a simpler type system (no need of subtyping), and to show that the embedding of CMS (and $\nu^{\square}$) is possible under very limited assumptions about resolvers.

The ability to generate a fresh name is essential to prevent accidental overriding of a resolver. If we know in advance what names need to be resolved within a fragment (we call such a fragment closed), then we can statically choose a name which is fresh (for that fragment). However, generic functions manipulating *open* fragments will have to generate fresh names at run-time. There are several reasons for working with open fragments: increase reusability, reduce the need for naming conventions (between independent developers), delay decisions.

MML^N_ν is able to express also run-time code generation (as formalized in [DP01,Nan02]), partial evaluation [JGS93,Dav96] and staging [Tah99,She01] (but formal embedding results appear difficult to establish).

We present MML^N_ν as a monadic metalanguage, i.e. its type system makes explicit which terms have computational effects. Its operational semantics is given according to the general pattern proposed in [MF03], namely we give local simplification rules applicable non-deterministically (because semantic preserving), and computation steps executed in a deterministic order (because they may have computational effects). Generation of fresh names is a computational effect, as in FreshML[1], thus typing $\nu X.e$ requires computational types. However, we consider other monadic operations (for imperative computations), for two reasons:

- to show that generation of fresh names co-exists smoothly with other computational effects;
- to allow arbitrary interleaving of software assembly activities (such as linking) and normal computational activities.

The calculus MML^N_ν subsumes the name management features of CMS and $\nu^{\square}$, while overcoming some deficiencies and unnecessary complexities (see Section 5), and can encode some aspects of Java multiple loaders [LY99] (see Section 3).

---

[1] A previous version of FreshML [PG00] uses a more elaborate type system, which is able to mask the computational effects due to generation of fresh names.

Summary. Section 2 presents syntax, type system and operational semantics of MML_ν^N, a monadic metalanguage for name management (and imperative computations). Section 3 gives several programming examples: programming with open fragments, benchmark examples for comparison with other calculi, and sample encoding of Java class loaders. Section 4 introduces ML_Σ^N, a sub-extension of MML_ν^N with records and recursive definitions, and shows that in it one recovers in a natural way all (mixin) module operations of CMS. Finally, Section 5 discusses related calculi and compares them to MML_ν^N.

Notation. In the paper we use the following notations and conventions.

- m range over the set $\mathcal{N}$ of natural numbers. Furthermore, $m \in \mathcal{N}$ is identified with the set $\{i \in \mathcal{N} | i < m\}$ of its predecessors.
- Term equivalence, written $\equiv$, is α-conversion. $\mathrm{FV}(e)$ is the set of variables free in e, while $e[x_i : e_i \mid i \in m]$ denotes parallel capture avoiding substitution.
- $f : A \overset{fin}{\rightharpoonup} B$ means that f is a partial function from A to B with a finite domain, written $\mathsf{dom}(f)$. $A \to B$ denotes the set of total functions from A to B. We use the following operations on partial (and total) functions:
  - $\{a_i : b_i | i \in m\}$ is the partial function mapping a_i to b_i (where the a_i must be different, i.e. $a_i = a_j$ implies $i = j$); in particular $\emptyset$ is the everywhere undefined partial function;
  - $f_{\backslash a}$ denotes the partial function f' defined as follows: $f'(a') = b$ iff $b = f(a')$ and $a' \neq a$;
  - $f\{a : b\}$ denotes the (partial) function f' s.t. $f'(a) = b$ and $f'(a') = f(a')$ otherwise;
  - f, f' denotes the union of two partial functions with disjoint domains.
- $A\#B$ means that the sets A and B are disjoint.

2   A Basic Calculus with Names: MML_ν^N

This section introduces a monadic metalanguage MML_ν^N with *names*. Names X are syntactically pervasive, i.e. they occur both in types and in terms. Moreover, the term $\nu X.e$ allows to generate a *fresh* name for private use within e. Following FreshML [SPG03], we consider generation of a fresh name a computational effect, therefore for typing $\nu X.e$ we need computational types. In order to investigate the interactions of names with other computational effects, the metalanguage supports also imperative computations.

We parameterize typing judgements w.r.t. a finite set of names, namely those that can occur (free) in the judgement. The theoretical underpinning for manipulating names is provided by [GP99]. In particular, names can be permuted (but not unified), which suffices to consider terms up to α-conversion of bound names.

The operational semantics is given according to the general pattern proposed in [MF03], namely Section 2.3 specifies a confluent *simplification* relation $\longrightarrow$ (defined as the *compatible closure* of a set of rewrite rules), and Section 2.4

specifies a *computation* relation $\longmapsto$ describing how *configurations* may evolve. Most of the technical properties of MML_ν^N (and their proofs) are similar to those given in [MF03] for MML. Therefore, we shall skip most of the proof details.

The syntax is abstracted over symbolic names $X \in \mathsf{Name}$, basic types b, locations $l \in \mathsf{L}$, term variables $x \in \mathsf{X}$ and resolver variables $r \in \mathsf{R}$. The syntactic category of types and signatures (i.e. the types of resolvers) is parameterized w.r.t. a finite set $\mathcal{X} \subseteq_{fin} \mathsf{Name}$ of names that can occur in the types and signatures.

- $\boxed{\tau \in \mathsf{T}_\mathcal{X} ::= b \mid \tau_1 \to \tau_2 \mid [\Sigma|\tau] \mid M\tau \mid R\tau}$ $\mathcal{X}$-types, where

  $\Sigma \in \Sigma_\mathcal{X} \stackrel{\Delta}{=} \mathcal{X} \stackrel{fin}{\to} \mathsf{T}_\mathcal{X}$ is a $\mathcal{X}$-signature $\{X_i : \tau_i | i \in m\}$

- $\boxed{\begin{aligned} e \in \mathsf{E} ::= {}& x \mid \lambda x.e \mid e_1\, e_2 \mid \theta.X \mid e\langle\theta\rangle \mid b(r)e \mid \\ & ret\ e \mid do\ x \leftarrow e_1; e_2 \mid \nu X.e \mid \\ & l \mid get\ e \mid set\ e_1\, e_2 \mid ref\ e \end{aligned}}$ terms, where

  $\theta \in \mathsf{ER} ::= r \mid ? \mid \theta\{X : e\}$ is a name resolver term.

We give an informal semantics of the language (see Section 3 for examples).

- The type $[\Sigma|\tau]$ classifies fragments which produce a term of type τ when linked with a resolver for Σ. The terms $\theta.X$ and $e\langle\theta\rangle$ use θ to *resolve* name X and to *link* fragment e. The term $b(r)e$ *represents* the fragment obtained by abstracting e w.r.t. r.
- The resolver ? cannot resolve any name, while $\theta\{X : e\}$ resolves X with e and *delegates* the resolution of other names to θ.
- The monadic type $M\tau$ classifies programs computing values of type τ. The terms $ret\ e$ and $do\ x \leftarrow e_1; e_2$ are used to terminate and sequence computations, $\nu X.e$ generates a *fresh* name for use within the computation e.
- The reference type $R\tau$ classifies locations with values of type τ (locations l are instrumental to the operational semantics). The following monadic operations act on locations: $get\ e$ returns the contents of a location, $set\ e_1\, e_2$ updates the contents of location e_1 with e_2, and $ref\ e$ generates a new location with e as initial value.

As a simple example, let us consider the fragment $b(r)(r.X*r.X)$ which can be correctly linked by resolvers mapping X to integer expressions and whose type is $[X:int|int]$. Then we can link the fragment with the resolver $?\{X:2\}$, as in $b(r)(r.X*r.X)<?\{X:2\}>$, and obtain $2*2$ of type int. Note that $b(r)(r.X*r.X)$ is not equivalent to $b(r)(r.Y*r.Y)$, whose type is $[Y:int|int]$. This is in clear contrast with what happens with variables and λ-abstractions: $\x->x*x$ and $\y->y*y$ are equivalent and have the same type. The sequel of this section is devoted to the formal definition of MML_ν^N. More interesting examples (with informal explanatory text) can be found in Section 3.

One can define (by induction on τ, e and θ) the following syntactic functions:

- the set $\mathrm{FV}(\_) \subseteq_{fin} \mathsf{Name} \uplus \mathsf{X} \uplus \mathsf{R}$ of free names and variables in $\_$, in particular
  $\mathrm{FV}(\{X_i : \tau_i | i \in m\}) = (\cup_{i \in m}\mathrm{FV}(\tau_i)) \cup \{X_i | i \in m\}$
- the capture-avoiding substitution $\_[x_0 : e_0]$ for term variable x_0.

– the capture-avoiding substitution $\_[r_0 : \theta_0]$ for resolver variable r_0.
– the action $\_[\pi]$ of a name permutation π (with finite *support*) on $\_$.

2.1 Type System

The typing judgments are $\mathcal{X}; \Pi; \Gamma \vdash_\Omega e : \tau$ (i.e. e has type τ) and $\mathcal{X}; \Pi; \Gamma \vdash_\Omega \theta : \Sigma$ (i.e. θ resolves the names in the domain of Σ, and only them, with terms of the assigned type), where

– τ is a $\mathcal{X}$-type and Σ is a $\mathcal{X}$-signature
– $\Pi : \mathsf{R} \xrightarrow{fin} \Sigma_\mathcal{X}$ is a signature assignment $\{r_i : \Sigma_i | i \in m\}$ for resolver variables
– $\Gamma : \mathsf{X} \xrightarrow{fin} \mathsf{T}_\mathcal{X}$ is a type assignment $\{x_i : \tau_i | i \in m\}$ for term variables
– $\Omega : \mathsf{L} \xrightarrow{fin} \mathsf{T}_\mathcal{X}$ is a type assignment to locations.

The typing rules are given in Table 1. All the typing rules, except that for $\nu X.e$, use the same finite set $\mathcal{X}$ of names in the premises and the conclusion. The typing rule for $e\langle\theta\rangle$ supports a limited form of *width* subtyping, namely it allows to link a fragment $e : [\Sigma|\tau]$ with a resolver θ whose signature Σ' includes Σ. All the other rules are standard.

We give the key properties of the type system. We write $\boxed{J ::= e : \tau \mid \theta : \Sigma}$, when it is unnecessary to distinguish between terms and name resolvers.

Lemma 1 (Equivar). *If* $\mathcal{X}; \Pi; \Gamma \vdash_\Omega J$, *then* $(\mathcal{X}; \Pi; \Gamma \vdash_\Omega J)[\pi]$, *with* π *name permutation.*

Equivariance is a key property of names (the action of a name permutation is extended in the obvious way to typing judgments). The property cannot be improved, e.g. substitution of names with names fails to preserve typability. In fact, if we replace X_1 with X_2 in the signature $\{X_1 : \tau_1, X_2 : \tau_2\}$ (for simplicity assume $\mathrm{FV}(\tau_1, \tau_2) = \emptyset$) we get $\{X_2 : \tau_1, X_2 : \tau_2\}$, which is not a signature. However, if we swap X_1 and X_2 we get the signature $\{X_2 : \tau_1, X_1 : \tau_2\}$.

Lemma 2 (Weaken). *If* $\mathcal{X} \subseteq \mathcal{X}'$ $\Pi \subseteq \Pi' : \mathsf{R} \xrightarrow{fin} \Sigma_{\mathcal{X}'}$, $\Gamma \subseteq \Gamma' : \mathsf{X} \xrightarrow{fin} \mathsf{T}_{\mathcal{X}'}$, $\Omega \subseteq \Omega' : \mathsf{L} \xrightarrow{fin} \mathsf{T}_{\mathcal{X}'}$ *and* $\mathcal{X}; \Pi; \Gamma \vdash_\Omega J$, *then* $\mathcal{X}'; \Pi'; \Gamma' \vdash_{\Omega'} J$

Weakening is a standard property of type systems. The statement is cumbersome, because we have to ensure that Π', Γ' and Ω' use only names in $\mathcal{X}'$.

Lemma 3 (Subsume). *The following rules are admissible*

– *If* $\mathcal{X}; \Pi, r : \Sigma_r; \Gamma \vdash_\Omega e : \tau$ *and* $\Sigma_r \subseteq \Sigma_r' \in \Sigma_\mathcal{X}$, *then* $\mathcal{X}; \Pi, r : \Sigma_r'; \Gamma \vdash_\Omega e : \tau$
– *If* $\mathcal{X}; \Pi, r : \Sigma_r; \Gamma \vdash_\Omega \theta : \Sigma$ *and* $\Sigma_r \subseteq \Sigma_r' \in \Sigma_\mathcal{X}$, *then*
  $\mathcal{X}; \Pi, r : \Sigma_r'; \Gamma \vdash_\Omega \theta : \Sigma'$ *for some* $\Sigma \subseteq \Sigma' \in \Sigma_\mathcal{X}$

Subsumption is peculiar of this type system, and is related to *width* subtyping.

Lemma 4 (Subst). *The following rules are admissible*

$$\mathrm{Sub}_x \frac{\mathcal{X}; \Pi; \Gamma \vdash_\Omega e_0 : \tau_0 \quad \mathcal{X}; \Pi; \Gamma, x_0 : \tau_0 \vdash_\Omega J}{\mathcal{X}; \Pi; \Gamma \vdash_\Omega J[x_0 : e_0]} \qquad \mathrm{Sub}_r \frac{\mathcal{X}; \Pi; \Gamma \vdash_\Omega \theta_0 : \Sigma_0 \quad \mathcal{X}; \Pi, r_0 : \Sigma_0; \Gamma \vdash_\Omega J}{\mathcal{X}; \Pi; \Gamma \vdash_\Omega J[r_0 : \theta_0]}$$

Table 1. Type System for MML_ν^N

$$x \;\; \frac{\Gamma(x) = \tau}{\mathcal{X};\Pi;\Gamma \vdash_\Omega x : \tau} \qquad \mathrm{lam} \;\; \frac{\mathcal{X};\Pi;\Gamma,x:\tau_1 \vdash_\Omega e : \tau_2}{\mathcal{X};\Pi;\Gamma \vdash_\Omega \lambda x.e : \tau_1 \to \tau_2}$$

$$\mathrm{app} \;\; \frac{\mathcal{X};\Pi;\Gamma \vdash_\Omega e_1 : \tau_1 \to \tau_2 \quad \mathcal{X};\Pi;\Gamma \vdash_\Omega e_2 : \tau_1}{\mathcal{X};\Pi;\Gamma \vdash_\Omega e_1 e_2 : \tau_2}$$

$$\mathrm{resolve} \;\; \frac{\begin{array}{c}\mathcal{X};\Pi;\Gamma \vdash_\Omega \theta : \Sigma \\ \tau = \Sigma(X)\end{array}}{\mathcal{X};\Pi;\Gamma \vdash_\Omega \theta.X : \tau} \qquad \mathrm{link} \;\; \frac{\begin{array}{c}\mathcal{X};\Pi;\Gamma \vdash_\Omega e : [\Sigma|\tau] \\ \mathcal{X};\Pi;\Gamma \vdash_\Omega \theta : \Sigma'\end{array}}{\mathcal{X};\Pi;\Gamma \vdash_\Omega e\langle\theta\rangle : \tau} \;\; \Sigma \subseteq \Sigma'$$

$$\mathrm{box} \;\; \frac{\mathcal{X};\Pi,r:\Sigma;\Gamma \vdash_\Omega e : \tau}{\mathcal{X};\Pi;\Gamma \vdash_\Omega b(r)e : [\Sigma|\tau]}$$

$$r \;\; \frac{\Pi(r) = \Sigma}{\mathcal{X};\Pi;\Gamma \vdash_\Omega r : \Sigma} \qquad ? \;\; \frac{}{\mathcal{X};\Pi;\Gamma \vdash_\Omega ? : \emptyset} \qquad \mathrm{extr} \;\; \frac{\begin{array}{c}\mathcal{X};\Pi;\Gamma \vdash_\Omega \theta : \Sigma \\ \mathcal{X};\Pi;\Gamma \vdash_\Omega e : \tau\end{array}}{\mathcal{X};\Pi;\Gamma \vdash_\Omega \theta\{X:e\} : \Sigma\{X:\tau\}}$$

$$\mathrm{ret} \;\; \frac{\mathcal{X};\Pi;\Gamma \vdash_\Omega e : \tau}{\mathcal{X};\Pi;\Gamma \vdash_\Omega \mathrm{ret}\, e : M\tau} \qquad \mathrm{do} \;\; \frac{\begin{array}{c}\mathcal{X};\Pi;\Gamma \vdash_\Omega e_1 : M\tau_1 \\ \mathcal{X};\Pi;\Gamma,x:\tau_1 \vdash_\Omega e_2 : M\tau_2\end{array}}{\mathcal{X};\Pi;\Gamma \vdash_\Omega \mathrm{do}\, x \leftarrow e_1 ; e_2 : M\tau_2}$$

$$\nu \;\; \frac{\mathcal{X},X;\Pi;\Gamma \vdash_\Omega e : M\tau}{\mathcal{X};\Pi;\Gamma \vdash_\Omega \nu X.e : M\tau} \;\; X \notin \mathrm{FV}(\Omega,\Pi,\Gamma,\tau)$$

$$l \;\; \frac{\Omega(l) = \tau}{\mathcal{X};\Pi;\Gamma \vdash_\Omega l : R\tau} \qquad \mathrm{get} \;\; \frac{\mathcal{X};\Pi;\Gamma \vdash_\Omega e : R\tau}{\mathcal{X};\Pi;\Gamma \vdash_\Omega \mathrm{get}\, e : M\tau}$$

$$\mathrm{set} \;\; \frac{\mathcal{X};\Pi;\Gamma \vdash_\Omega e_1 : R\tau \quad \mathcal{X};\Pi;\Gamma \vdash_\Omega e_2 : \tau}{\mathcal{X};\Pi;\Gamma \vdash_\Omega \mathrm{set}\, e_1\, e_2 : M(R\tau)} \qquad \mathrm{new} \;\; \frac{\mathcal{X};\Pi;\Gamma \vdash_\Omega e : \tau}{\mathcal{X};\Pi;\Gamma \vdash_\Omega \mathrm{ref}\, e : M(R\tau)}$$

2.2 Polymorphic Extension

Although the technical development will be restricted to the simply typed language, we sketch how to extend the type system with polymorphism, since it is essential for the example on open fragments generators (see Section 3). Basically we need to add type polymorphism (like that available in ML and Haskell) and row polymorphism [Rém93] (available in O'Caml). First we add type variables α and signature variables $p \in \mathsf{P}$. Then we extend the BNF for types and signatures and add the BNF for type schema:

- $\boxed{\tau \in \mathsf{T}_\mathcal{X} ::= b \mid \alpha \mid \tau_1 \to \tau_2 \mid [\Sigma|\tau] \mid M\tau \mid R\tau}$
- $\boxed{\Sigma \in \Sigma_\mathcal{X} ::= \{X_i : \tau_i | i \in m\} \mid p, \{X_i : \tau_i | i \in m\}}$ where $X_i \in \mathcal{X}$ and $\tau_i \in \mathsf{T}_\mathcal{X}$
  for any $i \in m$.
- $\boxed{\sigma \in \mathsf{S}_\mathcal{X} ::= \tau \mid \forall \alpha.\sigma \mid \forall p \# \mathcal{X}'.\sigma}$ where $\mathcal{X}' \subseteq \mathcal{X}$.

Intuitively, $p \# \mathcal{X}'$ means that p can be instantiated with a signature Σ provided $\mathrm{dom}(\Sigma) \# \mathcal{X}'$ (this is like the sorting of row variables in [Rém93]). The typing judgments $\mathcal{X}; \Delta; \Pi; \Gamma \vdash_\Omega e : \tau$ have an additional component $\Delta : \mathsf{P} \to \mathcal{P}_{fin}(\mathcal{X})$, which assigns to every signature variable p its *sort*, moreover $\Gamma : \mathsf{X} \overset{fin}{\to} \mathsf{S}_\mathcal{X}$ assigns type schema instead of types. The typing rules of Table 1 are mostly unchanged, i.e. Δ is the same in premises and conclusion, the only exceptions are

- the typing rule for a variable x, where the type and signature variables quantified in $\Gamma(x)$ get instantiated. The definition of substitutions $\_[\alpha : \tau]$ and $\_[p : \Sigma]$ are straightforward.

For instance x $\dfrac{\Gamma(x) = \forall p\#\mathcal{X}'.\tau \qquad \mathcal{X}; \Delta \vdash \Sigma\#\mathcal{X}'}{\mathcal{X}; \Delta; \Pi; \Gamma \vdash_\Omega x : \tau[p : \Sigma]}$

where $\mathcal{X}; \Delta \vdash \Sigma\#\mathcal{X}'$ means $\Sigma \in \Sigma_\mathcal{X}$ and one of the following holds
  - $\Sigma \equiv \{X_i : \tau_i | i \in m\}$ and $\{X_i | i \in m\}\#\mathcal{X}'$, or
  - $\Sigma \equiv p, \{X_i : \tau_i | i \in m\}$ and $\{X_i | i \in m\}\#\mathcal{X}' \subseteq \Delta(p)$.

- link $\dfrac{\mathcal{X}; \Pi; \Gamma \vdash_\Omega e : [\Sigma|\tau] \qquad \mathcal{X}; \Pi; \Gamma \vdash_\Omega \theta : \Sigma' \qquad \mathcal{X}; \Delta \vdash \Sigma \subseteq \Sigma'}{\mathcal{X}; \Pi; \Gamma \vdash_\Omega e\langle\theta\rangle : \tau}$

where $\mathcal{X}; \Delta \vdash \Sigma \subseteq \Sigma'$ holds only in one of the following cases
  - $\Sigma \equiv \{X_i : \tau_i | i \in m\}$ and $\Sigma' \equiv \{X_i : \tau_i | i \in m+n\}$, or
  - $\Sigma \equiv \{X_i : \tau_i | i \in m\}$ and $\Sigma' \equiv p, \{X_i : \tau_i | i \in m+n\}$, or
  - $\Sigma \equiv p, \{X_i : \tau_i | i \in m\}$ and $\Sigma' \equiv p, \{X_i : \tau_i | i \in m+n\}$ and $X_{m+j} \in \Delta(p)$
    for any $j \in n$.

- ν $\dfrac{\mathcal{X}, X; \Delta^X; \Pi; \Gamma \vdash_\Omega e : M\tau}{\mathcal{X}; \Delta; \Pi; \Gamma \vdash_\Omega \nu X.e : M\tau}$ $X \notin \mathrm{FV}(\Omega, \Pi, \Gamma, \tau)$ with $\Delta^X(p) = \Delta(p) \uplus \{X\}$.

We add a typing rule for let-binding. We give only an instance of it, to exemplify the effect on Δ let $\dfrac{\mathcal{X}; \Delta\{p : \mathcal{X}'\}; \Pi; \Gamma \vdash_\Omega e : \tau \qquad \mathcal{X}; \Delta; \Pi; \Gamma, x : \forall p\#\mathcal{X}'.\tau \vdash_\Omega e' : \tau'}{\mathcal{X}; \Delta; \Pi; \Gamma \vdash_\Omega \text{let } x = e \text{ in } e' : \tau'}$ $p \notin \mathrm{FV}(\Pi, \Gamma, \Omega)$.

2.3   Simplification

We define a confluent relation on terms, called *simplification*. There is no need to define a deterministic simplification strategy, since computational effects are *insensitive* to further simplification. Simplification $\longrightarrow$ is the compatible closure of the following rules

beta) $(\lambda x.e_2)\, e_1 \longrightarrow e_2[x : e_1]$
resolve) $(\theta\{X : e\}).X \longrightarrow e$
delegate) $(\theta\{X : e\}).X' \longrightarrow \theta.X'$ if $X' \neq X$
link) $(b(r)e)\langle\theta\rangle \longrightarrow e[r : \theta]$

Simplification enjoys the following properties.

Theorem 1 (CR). *The simplification relation* $\longrightarrow$ *is confluent.*

Theorem 2 (SR).

- If $\mathcal{X}; \Pi; \Gamma \vdash_\Omega e : \tau$ and $e \longrightarrow e'$, then $\mathcal{X}; \Pi; \Gamma \vdash_\Omega e' : \tau$.
- If $\mathcal{X}; \Pi; \Gamma \vdash_\Omega \theta : \Sigma$ and $\theta \longrightarrow \theta'$, then $\mathcal{X}; \Pi; \Gamma \vdash_\Omega \theta' : \Sigma$.

Table 2. Computation Relation

Administrative steps

(A.0) $(\mathcal{X}|\mu, ret\ e, \Box) \longmapsto$ done
(A.1) $(\mathcal{X}|\mu, do\ x \leftarrow e_1; e_2, E) \longmapsto (\mathcal{X}|\mu, e_1, E[do\ x \leftarrow \Box; e_2])$
(A.2) $(\mathcal{X}|\mu, ret\ e_1, E[do\ x \leftarrow \Box; e_2]) \longmapsto (\mathcal{X}|\mu, e_2[x : e_1], E)$

Name generation step

(ν) $(\mathcal{X}|\mu, \nu X.e, E) \longmapsto (\mathcal{X}, X|\mu, e, E)$ with X renamed to avoid clashes, i.e. $X \notin \mathcal{X}$

Imperative steps

(new) $(\mathcal{X}|\mu, ref\ e, E) \longmapsto (\mathcal{X}|\mu\{l : e\}, ret\ l, E)$ where $l \notin dom(\mu)$
(get) $(\mathcal{X}|\mu, get\ l, E) \longmapsto (\mathcal{X}|\mu, ret\ e, E)$ with $e = \mu(l)$
(set) $(\mathcal{X}|\mu, set\ l\ e, E) \longmapsto (\mathcal{X}|\mu\{l = e\}, ret\ l, E)$ with $l \in dom(\mu)$

2.4 Computation

The computation relation $Id \longmapsto Id'$ | done is defined using evaluation contexts, stores and configurations $Id \in$ Conf. A configuration records the current name space as a finite set $\mathcal{X}$ of names. The computation rules (see Table 2) consist of those given in [MF03] for the monadic metalanguage MML (these rules do not change the name space) plus generation of a fresh name (this is the only rule that extends the name space).

- $\boxed{E \in \text{EC} := \Box \mid E[do\ x \leftarrow \Box; e]}$ evaluation contexts

- $\mu \in \text{S} \overset{\Delta}{=} \text{L} \overset{fin}{\to} \text{E}$ stores map locations to their contents

- $(\mathcal{X}|\mu, e, E) \in$ Conf $\overset{\Delta}{=} \mathcal{P}_{fin}(\text{Name}) \times \text{S} \times \text{E} \times \text{EC}$ configurations consist of the current name space $\mathcal{X}$ (which grows as computation progresses) and store μ, the program fragment e under consideration, and its evaluation context E

- $\boxed{rc \in \text{RC} ::= ret\ e \mid do\ x \leftarrow e_1; e_2 \mid \nu X.e \mid get\ l \mid set\ l\ e \mid ref\ e}$
computational redexes.

Simplification $\longrightarrow$ is extended in the obvious way to a confluent relation on configurations (and related notions). The Bisimulation property, i.e. computation is insensitive to further simplification, is like that stated in [MF03] for MML.

Theorem 3 (Bisim). *If $Id \equiv (\mathcal{X}|\mu, e, E)$ with $e \in$ RC and $Id \overset{*}{\longrightarrow} Id'$, then*

1. *$Id \longmapsto D$ implies $\exists D'$ s.t. $Id' \longmapsto D'$ and $D \overset{*}{\longrightarrow} D'$*
2. *$Id' \longmapsto D'$ implies $\exists D$ s.t. $Id \longmapsto D$ and $D \overset{*}{\longrightarrow} D'$*

where D and D' range over Conf $\cup$ {done}.

One can also show that simplification and computation are equivariant, i.e.

- if $Id \longrightarrow Id'$, then $Id[\pi] \longrightarrow Id'[\pi]$;
- if $Id \longmapsto D$, then $Id[\pi] \longmapsto D[\pi]$.

Table 3. Well-formed Evaluation Contexts

$$\frac{}{\mathcal{X};\square : M\tau \vdash_\Omega \square : M\tau} \quad \square \qquad \frac{\mathcal{X};\square : M\tau_2 \vdash_\Omega E : M\tau' \quad \mathcal{X};\emptyset; x : \tau_1 \vdash_\Omega e : M\tau_2}{\mathcal{X};\square : M\tau_1 \vdash_\Omega E[do\ x \leftarrow \square; e] : M\tau'}$$

where $\mathcal{X};\square : M\tau \vdash_\Omega E : M\tau'$ is such that τ and τ' are $\mathcal{X}$-types and $\Omega : \mathsf{L} \xrightarrow{fin} \mathsf{T}_\mathcal{X}$.

2.5   Type Safety

Type safety, i.e. Subject Reduction and Progress properties, is like that established for MML in [MF03]. We expand only the case for $\nu X.e$, which relies on the equivariance property.

Definition 1 (Well-formed configuration). $\vdash_\Omega (\mathcal{X}|\mu, e, E) : \tau' \overset{\Delta}{\iff}$

- $\exists \tau \in \mathsf{T}_\mathcal{X}$ s.t. $\mathcal{X};\emptyset;\emptyset \vdash_\Omega e : M\tau$ and $\mathcal{X};\square : M\tau \vdash_\Omega E : M\tau'$ (see Table 3)
- $\mathcal{X};\emptyset;\emptyset \vdash_\Omega e_l : \tau_l$ is derivable when $e_l = \mu(l)$ and $\tau_l = \Omega(l)$

Lemma 5 (Equivar). If $\mathcal{X};\square : M\tau \vdash_\Omega E : M\tau'$, then $(\mathcal{X};\square : M\tau \vdash_\Omega E : M\tau')[\pi]$.

Lemma 6 (Weaken). If $\mathcal{X} \subseteq \mathcal{X}'$, $\Omega \subseteq \Omega' : \mathsf{L} \xrightarrow{fin} \mathsf{T}_{\mathcal{X}'}$ and $\mathcal{X};\square : M\tau \vdash_\Omega E : M\tau'$, then $\mathcal{X}';\square : M\tau \vdash_{\Omega'} E : M\tau'$.

Theorem 4 (SR).

- If $\vdash_\Omega Id_1 : \tau'$ and $Id_1 \longrightarrow Id_2$, then $\vdash_\Omega Id_2 : \tau'$.
- If $\vdash_{\Omega_1} Id_1 : \tau'$ and $Id_1 \longmapsto Id_2$, then exists $\Omega_2 \supseteq \Omega_1$ s.t. $\vdash_{\Omega_2} Id_2 : \tau'$.

Proof. The second implication is proved by case analysis on the derivation of $Id_1 \longmapsto Id_2$. For the case (ν) we have $\vdash_{\Omega_1} Id_1 : \tau'$ and

$$Id_1 \equiv (\mathcal{X}|\mu, \nu X.e, E) \longmapsto (\mathcal{X}, X|\mu, e, E) \equiv Id_2$$

We take $\Omega_2 = \Omega_1$ and derive $\vdash_{\Omega_2} Id_2 : \tau'$ by weakening (Lemma 2 and 6).

Theorem 5 (Progress). If $\vdash_\Omega (\mathcal{X}|\mu, e, E) : \tau'$, then

1. *either* $e \notin \mathsf{RC}$ *and* $e \longrightarrow$
2. *or* $e \in \mathsf{RC}$ *and* $(\mathcal{X}|\mu, e, E) \longmapsto$

3   Programming Examples

We demonstrate the use and expressivity of MML^N_ν with few examples:

- the first exemplifies programming with *open* fragments;

- the second and third are classical examples, to allow a comparison with other calculi for run-time code generation and staging;
- the forth exemplifies the analogies with Java class loaders.

To improve readability we use ML-like notation for functions[2] and operations on references, and Haskell's do-notation do {x1 <- e1; ...; xn <- en; e}. In the sequence of commands of a do-expression we allow computations ei whose value is not bound to a variable (because it is not used by other commands) and non-recursive let-bindings like xi = ei (which amounts to replace xi with ei in the commands following the let-binding).

Example 1. We consider an example of generative programming, which motivates the use for fresh name generation. In our calculus a component is identified with a fragment of type $[\Sigma|\tau]$, where Σ specifies what are the parameters that need to be provided for deployment. Generative programming support dynamic manufacturing of customized components from elementary (highly reusable) components. In our calculus the most appropriate building block for generative programming are polymorphic functions $G : \forall p.[p, \Sigma_i|\tau_i] \rightarrow M[p, \Sigma|\tau]$. The result type of G is computational, because generation may require computational activities, while the *signature variable* p classifies the information passed to the arguments of G, but not directly used or provided by G itself. Applications of G may instantiate p with different signatures, thus we say that G manipulates *open* fragments. An over-simplified example of open fragment generator is

```
Ac: [p|a->a] -> M[p|{add: a -> M unit, update: M unit}]
```

it creates a data structure to maintain an (initially empty) set of accounts. Since we don't really need to know the structure of an account, we use a type variable a. The generator makes available two functionalities for operating on a set (of accounts): add inserts a new account in the set, and update modifies all the accounts in the set by applying a function of type a->a, which depends on certain parameters (e.g. interest rate) represented by the signature variable p. These parameters are decided by the bank after the data structure has been created, and they change over time. In many countries bank accounts are taxed, according to criteria set out by local authorities. So we need to provide a more refined generator

```
TaxedAc: [p'|a->a] -> [p|a->a] ->
           M[p'|[p|{add: a -> M unit, update: M unit}]]
```

the extra parameter computes the new balance based on the state of the account after the bank's update. We could define TaxedAc in terms of Ac as follows

```
fun TaxedAc tax upd = nu Tax.
    do {m <- Ac(b(r2) fn x => r2.Tax (upd<r2> x));
        ret (b(r') b(r1) m<r1{Tax:tax<r'>}>)};
```

---

[2] In monadic metalanguages β-reduction is a sound simplification.

Note that it is essential that the name `Tax` is fresh and private to `TaxedAc`, otherwise we may override some information in `r1`, which is needed by `upd`. In fact, `TaxedAc` is an open fragment generator that does not know in advance how the signature variable `p` could be instantiated. On the other hand, with *closed* fragment generators $G : [\Sigma_i|\tau_i] \to M[\Sigma|\tau]$ the problem does not arise, but reusability is impaired. For instance, it is not reasonable to expect that all banks will use the same parameters to update the accounts of their customers.

Example 2. We consider the classical power function `exp:int->real->M real`, which takes an exponent n and a base x, then it computes x^n by making recursive calls. Then we show how to get specialized versions (for fixed n) by unfolding the recursion at specialization time. The result type of `exp` is computational, because we consider recursion a computational effect.

```
(* standard power function *)
fun exp n x = if n=0 then ret(1.0)
              else do {x' <- (exp (n-1) x); ret(x*x')};
>    exp = ... : int -> real -> M real
(* exp_c generates a fragment with hook X for base, its type says
   that recursive calls are at fragment generation time *)
fun exp_c n = if n=0 then ret(b(r) 1.0)
              else do {u <- exp_c (n-1); ret(b(r) (r.X * u<r>))};
>    exp_c = ... : int -> M[X:real | real]
(* optimized version, its type differs from that of exp,
   to reflects the different timing of recursive calls *)
fun exp_o n = do {u <- exp_c n; ret(fn x => u<?{X:x}>)};
>    exp_o = ... : int -> M(real -> real)
do  sq <- exp_o 2; (*  unfolds the recursive calls to exp_c *)
>    sq = (fn x => x*(x*1.0)) : real -> real
```

In comparison to [NP03, Example 3], we don't need fresh names and support polymorphism to give a simple definition of `exp_c` (in fact, we could avoid the use of names altogether). In comparison to MetaML [CMS03], we don't face the problems due to execution of *potentially open* code.

Example 3. We consider a variant of the power function that uses imperative features `p:int->real->(real ref)->M unit`, and show that we can recover the specialized version given in [CMS03, Section 4.1] without facing the problems due to *scope extrusion* (which were the main motivation for the introduction of closed types). The function `p` takes an exponent n, a base x and a reference `y`, then it initializes y with 1.0 and repeatedly multiplying the content of y with x until it becomes x^n. Therefore, the computational effects used by the imperative power function are recursion and side-effects.

```
(* imperative power function *)
fun p n x y = if n=0 then y:=1.0
              else do {p (n-1) x y; y' <- !y; y:=x*y'};
>    p = ... : int -> real -> (R real) -> M unit
```

```
(* p_c generates a fragment with hooks X and Y for base and
   location, its type says that recursive calls are at fragment
   generation time, while side-effects are after linking *)
fun p_c n = if n=0 then ret(b(r) r.Y:=1.0)
            else do {u <- p_c (n-1);
                     ret(b(r) do {u<r>; y' <-!r.Y; r.Y:=r.X*y'})};
>   p_c = ... : int -> M [X:real, Y:R real | M unit]
(* optimized version p_o, its type differs from that of p,
   to reflects the different timing of recursive calls *)
fun p_o n = do u <- p_c n in (fn x,y. u<?{X:x, Y:y}>);
>   p_o = ... : int -> M(real -> (R real) -> M unit)
do sq_i <- p_o 2; (* unfolds the recursive calls to p_c *)
>   sq_i = (fn x,y => do {y:=1.0; y' <- !y; y:=x*y';
                          y' <- !y; y:=x*y'})
        : real -> (R real) -> M unit
```

Example 4. This example establishes a correspondence between our calculus and
some key concepts behind Java class loaders [LY99]. Loaders are a powerful
mechanism which allows dynamic linkage of code fragments, management of
multiple name spaces and code instrumentation [LB98]. Some of the basic notions concerning Java multiple loaders can be encoded naturally in MML_ν^N, as
suggested by the following table (we identify a class file f with a location containing a fragment):

Java	MML_ν^N
a loader	a resolver θ
loader delegation	$\theta\{X : e\}$
the content of a class file	$b(r)e$
a symbolic reference to a class X	$r.X$
loading of class file f with initiating loader θ	$do\ u \leftarrow get\ f; u\langle\theta\rangle$

As shown in the table, MML_ν^N resolvers play the role of class loaders which
replace symbolic references with (concrete references [LY99] to) classes, and the
ability to extend resolvers corresponds to a primitive form of delegation between
loaders. As an example, consider the following code, where class files contain
fragments of type M int, rather than class declarations.

```
(* create three class files *)
do f1 <- ref (b(r) return 1);
>   f1 = ... : R [ | M int]
do f2 <- ref (b(r) return 2);
>   f2 = ... : R [ | M int]
    f3 <- ref (b(r) do {x <- r.X; y <- r.Y; return (x+y)});
>   f3 = ... : R [X:M int, Y:M int | M int]
(* load class file f3 *)
do u  <- !f3;
>   u = ... : [X:M int, Y:M int | M int]
```

```
(* with initiating loader ?{X:c1, Y:c3} *)
do {c1 = do {u <- !f1; u<?>};
    c3 = do {u <- !f3;
             c2 = do {u <- !f2; u<?>};
             u<?{X:c2, Y:c2}>};
    u<?{X:c1, Y:c3}>};
>  5
```

There are three class files, f1, f2 and f3; the execution of the program starts from class file f3. The *initiating loader* [LB98] for the main program is defined by ?{X:c1, Y:c3}. According to the standard definition [LY99], the initiating loader of a given loaded class file f is the loader that will eventually try to resolve all symbolic references contained in f. A class file can be loaded more than once for resolving different symbolic references as happens in Java. For instance, in the program above the class file f3 is loaded twice; the first time for starting execution of the main program, the second for resolving the symbolic reference X in the main program. Indeed, the two loaded code fragments are kept distinct and represent different entities as happens in Java when the same class is loaded by two different loaders. In this case the same symbolic reference in the same class file can be resolved in different ways. For instance, in the program above Y is resolved with f1 in the main program and with f2 when f3 is loaded again.

A clear advantage of modeling Java loaders in MML_ν^N is a better support for code instrumentation (that is, the ability to change class bytecode at load-time), since in Java this feature is implemented at a very low level and basically consists in arbitrary and uncontrolled manipulation of bytecode. However not all aspects of Java loaders can be modeled in MML_ν^N, for instance there is no counterpart to dynamic typing.

4   Relating MML_ν^N with CMS

In this section we introduce ML_Σ^N a sub-extension of MML_ν^N. Then we define a translation of CMS [AZ02] in ML_Σ^N preserving CMS typing and reduction up to Ariola's equational axioms [AB02] for recursion. We mention briefly the main differences between MML_ν^N and CMS (for those already familiar with CMS).

- CMS has a fixed infinite set of names (but a program uses only finitely many of them) and no fresh name generation facility.
- CMS is a pure calculus, thus we can restrict to the fragment of MML_ν^N without computational types (and monadic operations), called ML^N.
- In CMS recursion is bundled in mixin, and removing it results in a very inexpressive calculus. On the contrary, ML^N is an interesting calculus even without recursion, and one can add recursion following standard approaches.

The syntax of ML_Σ^N is defined in two steps. First, we remove from MML_ν^N computational and reference types (and consequently monadic operations, like $\nu X.e$, and locations). In the resulting calculus, called ML^N, the computation relation disappears (CMS is a pure calculus and its reduction semantics corresponds to

Table 4. Additional Typing Rules for ML_Σ^N

$$o \quad \frac{\{\mathcal{X}; \Pi; \Gamma \vdash e_i : \tau_i \mid i \in m\}}{\mathcal{X}; \Pi; \Gamma \vdash \{X_i : e_i | i \in m\} : \{X_i : \tau_i | i \in m\}} \qquad \text{select} \quad \frac{\Sigma(X) = \tau \quad \mathcal{X}; \Pi; \Gamma \vdash e : \Sigma}{\mathcal{X}; \Pi; \Gamma \vdash e.X : \tau}$$

$$\text{plus} \quad \frac{\mathcal{X}; \Pi; \Gamma \vdash e_1 : \Sigma_1 \quad \mathcal{X}; \Pi; \Gamma \vdash e_2 : \Sigma_2}{\mathcal{X}; \Pi; \Gamma \vdash e_1 + e_2 : \Sigma_1, \Sigma_2} \quad \text{dom}(\Sigma_1) \# \text{dom}(\Sigma_2)$$

$$\text{delete} \quad \frac{\mathcal{X}; \Pi; \Gamma \vdash e : \Sigma}{\mathcal{X}; \Pi; \Gamma \vdash e \setminus X : \Sigma \setminus X}$$

$$\text{rec} \quad \frac{\{\mathcal{X}; \Pi; \Gamma, \Gamma' \vdash \rho(x) : \Gamma'(x) \mid x \in \text{dom}(\rho)\} \quad \mathcal{X}; \Pi; \Gamma, \Gamma' \vdash e : \tau}{\mathcal{X}; \Pi; \Gamma \vdash \text{let } \rho \text{ in } e : \tau} \quad \text{dom}(\Gamma') = \text{dom}(\rho)$$

---

simplification), the typing judgements are simplified $\mathcal{X}; \Pi; \Gamma \vdash e : \tau$ (there is no need to have a type assignment to locations), and $\mathcal{X}$ could be left implicit, since the typing judgements of a derivation must use the same $\mathcal{X}$. Then we add records and mutual recursion:

- $\boxed{\tau \in \mathsf{T}_{\mathcal{X}} + = \Sigma}$ types, where $\Sigma \in \Sigma_{\mathcal{X}} \triangleq \mathcal{X} \overset{fin}{\to} \mathsf{T}_{\mathcal{X}}$ is a $\mathcal{X}$-signature

- $\boxed{e \in \mathsf{E} + = o \mid e.X \mid e_1 + e_2 \mid e \setminus X \mid \text{let } \rho \text{ in } e}$ terms, where

  $o : \mathsf{Name} \overset{fin}{\to} \mathsf{E}$ is a record $\{X_i : e_i | i \in m\}$ and

  $\rho : \mathsf{X} \overset{fin}{\to} \mathsf{E}$ is a (recursive) binding $\{x_i : e_i | i \in m\}$.

The type $\Sigma \equiv \{X_i : \tau_i | i \in m\}$ classifies records of the form $\{X_i : e_i | i \in m\}$, i.e. with a fixed set of components. Notice that records should not be confused with resolvers. In particular, a fragment of type $[\Sigma | \tau]$ can be linked to a resolver of any signature $\Sigma' \supseteq \Sigma$. The operations on records correspond to the CMS primitives for mixins: $e.X$ selects the component named X, $e_1 + e_2$ concatenates two records (provided their component names are disjoint), and $e \setminus X$ removes the component named X (if present). The let construct allows mutually recursive declarations, which are used to encode the local components of a CMS module. The order of record components and mutually recursive declarations are immaterial, therefore o and ρ are not sequences but functions (with finite domain).

Table 4 gives the typing rules for the new constructs. The properties of the type system in Section 2 extend in the obvious way to ML_Σ^N. We define simplification $\longrightarrow$ for ML_Σ^N as the compatible closure of the simplification rules for MML_ν^N (see Section 2.3) and the following simplification rules for record operations and mutually recursive declarations:

select) $o.X \longrightarrow e$ if $e \equiv o(X)$
plus) $o_1 + o_2 \longrightarrow o_1, o_2$ if $\text{dom}(o_1) \# \text{dom}(o_2)$
delete) $o \setminus X \longrightarrow o_{\setminus X}$
unfolding) $\text{let } \rho \text{ in } e \longrightarrow e[x : \text{let } \rho \text{ in } \rho(x) \mid x \in \text{dom}(\rho)]$

Simplification for ML_Σ^N enjoys confluence and subject reduction (Theorem 1 and 2).

Table 5. Translation of CMS in ML_{Σ}^{N}

CMS typing	ML_{Σ}^{N} typing
$\Gamma \vdash_{\mathsf{CMS}} E : \tau$	$\mathcal{X}; \emptyset; \Gamma' \vdash E' : \tau'$
CMS type	ML_{Σ}^{N} type
$[\Sigma_1; \Sigma_2]$	$[\Sigma_1' \mid \Sigma_2']$
CMS term	ML_{Σ}^{N} term
x	x
$[\iota; o; \rho]$	$b(r)(let \; \rho' \; in \; o')[x : r.X \mid \iota(x) = X]$
$E_1 + E_2$	$b(r)E_1'\langle r \rangle + E_2'\langle r \rangle$
$E \setminus X$	$b(r)E'\langle r \rangle \setminus X$
$E.X$	$E'\langle ? \rangle.X$
$E!X$	$b(r)let \; \{x_1 : x_2.X, x_2 : E'\langle r\{X : x_1\}\rangle\} \; in \; x_2$
$C\{\rho\}$	$C'[\rho']$

The translations of Γ, Σ, o and ρ are defined pointwise.

4.1   Translation of CMS into ML_{Σ}^{N}

We refer to [AZ99,AZ02] for the definition of the CMS calculus. The key idea of the translation consists in translating a mixin type $[\Sigma_1; \Sigma_2]$ in $[\Sigma_1' \mid \Sigma_2']$, in this way we obtain a compositional translation of CMS terms. In contrast, a translation based on functional types, where $[\Sigma_1; \Sigma_2]$ is translated in $\Sigma_1' \rightarrow \Sigma_2'$, is not compositional (the problem is in the translation of $e_1 + e_2$, which must be driven by the type of e_1 and e_2).

Table 5 gives the translation of CMS in ML_{Σ}^{N}. Since CMS is parametric in the core language, the translation depends on a translation of core terms and types.

In the translation of a basic mixin $[\iota; o; \rho]$ the variables x in $dom(\iota)$ (called *deferred*) are replaced with the resolution $r.X$ of the corresponding name $X = \iota(x)$, whereas the variables x in $dom(\rho)$ (called *local*) are bound by the let construct for mutually recursive declarations. (A similar translation would not work in $\nu^{\square}$, because of the limitations in typing discussed in Section 5).

The translation of selection $E.X$ uses the empty resolver ?, since in CMS selection is allowed only for mixins without deferred components.

The freeze operator $E!X$ resolves a deferred component X with the corresponding output component. This resolution may introduce a recursive definition, since the output component X could be defined in terms of the corresponding deferred component. Therefore, the translation defines the record x_2 by resolving the name X with the X component of the record x_2 itself.

The typing preservation property of the translation can be proved easily, under the assumption that the property holds at the core level.

Theorem 6 (Typing preservation). *If* $\Gamma \vdash_C C : c\tau$ *implies* $\emptyset; \Gamma' \vdash C' : c\tau'$ *for every typing at the core level, then* $\Gamma \vdash_{\mathsf{CMS}} E : \tau$ *implies* $\mathcal{X}; \emptyset; \Gamma' \vdash E' : \tau'$, *where* $\mathcal{X}$ *includes all names occurring in the derivation of* $\Gamma \vdash_{\mathsf{CMS}} E : \tau$.

The translation preserves also the reduction semantics of CMS, but this can be proved only up to some equational axioms for mutually recursive declarations

$$\mathsf{C}[let\ \rho\ in\ e] = let\ \rho\ in\ \mathsf{C}[e] \tag{lift}$$
$$let\ \rho_1, x : (let\ \rho_2\ in\ e_2)\ in\ e_1 = let\ \rho_1, \rho_2, x : e_2\ in\ e_1 \tag{merge}$$
$$let\ \rho, x : e_1\ in\ e_2 = let\ \rho[x : e_1]\ in\ e_2[x : e_1]\ if\ x \notin \mathrm{FV}(e_1) \tag{sub}$$

The (lift) axiom corresponds to Ariola's lift axioms, in principle it can be instantiated with any ML_Σ^N context $\mathsf{C}[\ ]$, but for proving Theorem 7 it suffices to consider the contexts $\boxed{\mathsf{C}[\ ] ::= \square + e \mid e + \square \mid \square \setminus X \mid \square.X}$. The (merge) axiom is Ariola's internal merge, whereas (sub) is derivable from Ariola's axioms.

Let R denotes the set of the three axioms above, and S denotes the set of equational axioms corresponding to the simplification rules for ML_Σ^N; then the translation is proved to preserve the CMS reduction up to $=_{S \cup R}$ (i.e. the congruence induced by the axioms in $S \cup R$).

Theorem 7 (Semantics preservation). *If* $E_1 \xrightarrow[\mathrm{CMS}]{} E_2$, *then* $E_1' =_{S \cup R} E_2'$.

The translation of the non-recursive subset of CMS (i.e. no local declarations ρ and no freeze $E!X$) is a lot simpler, moreover its reductions are mapped to plain ML_Σ^N simplifications.

5 Conclusions and Related Work

This section compares MML_ν^N with two related calculi $\nu^\square$ and MMML.

- The $\nu^\square$ calculus of [Nan02,NP03] is a refinement of $\lambda^\square$ [DP01], which provides better support for symbolic manipulation. The stated aim is to combine safely the best features of $\lambda^\square$ (the ability to execute closed code) and $\lambda^\bigcirc$ [Dav96] (the ability to manipulate open code). The work on MetaML has similar aims, but adopt the opposite strategy, i.e. it starts from $\lambda^\bigcirc$.
- The monadic metalanguage MMML of [MF03] provides an operational semantics sufficiently detailed for analyzing subtle aspects of multi-stage programming [Tah99,She01,CMS03]), in particular the interactions between code generation and computational effects.

MML_ν^N *Versus* $\nu^\square$. Typing judgments of $\nu^\square$ take the form $\Sigma; \Delta; \Gamma \vdash e : \tau[\mathcal{X}]$, where $\mathcal{X} \subseteq \mathrm{dom}(\Sigma)$ includes the names occurring *free* in e, and Δ has declarations of the form $u_i : \tau_i[\mathcal{X}_i]$ with $\mathcal{X}_i \subseteq \mathrm{dom}(\Sigma)$.

In $\nu^\square$ the type of a name X is fixed at name generation time. This is a bad name space management policy, which goes against common practice in programming language design (e.g. modules and records). MML_ν^N follows the approach of mainstream module languages, where different modules can assign to the same name different types (and values). Therefore, programming in $\nu^\square$ forces an overuse of name generation, because the language restricts name reuse.

In $\nu^\square$ terms includes names, so our $\theta.X$ is replaced by X, in other words there is a *default resolver* which is left implicit. Linking $u\langle\Theta\rangle$ uses a function $\Theta \equiv \langle X_i \to e_i | i \in m \rangle$ to modify the default resolver. The typing judgments for explicit substitutions take the form $\Sigma; \Delta; \Gamma \vdash \Theta : \mathcal{X}[\mathcal{X}']$, where $\mathcal{X}'$ includes the names *used* by the modified resolver to resolve the names in $\mathcal{X}$, e.g. $\mathcal{X} \subseteq \mathcal{X}'$ when Θ is empty. The following explicit substitution principle is admissible

$$\frac{\Sigma; \Delta; \Gamma \vdash \Theta : \mathcal{X}[\mathcal{X}'] \quad \Sigma; \Delta; \Gamma \vdash e : \tau[\mathcal{X}]}{\Sigma; \Delta; \Gamma \vdash e[\Theta] : \tau[\mathcal{X}']}$$

Our type $[\Sigma|\tau]$ corresponds to $\Box_{\mathcal{X}}\tau$ with $\mathcal{X} = \mathsf{dom}(\Sigma)$. Typing rules for $\Box_{\mathcal{X}}\tau$ are related to those for necessity of S4 modal logic, e.g. $\Box_{\mathcal{X}}\tau$ introduction is

$$\frac{\Sigma; \Delta; \emptyset \vdash e : \tau[\mathcal{X}]}{\Sigma; \Delta; \Gamma \vdash box\ e : \Box_{\mathcal{X}}\tau[\mathcal{X}']}$$

This rule is very restrictive: it forbids having free term variables x in e, and acts like an *implicit binder* for the free names X of e (i.e. it binds the default resolver for e). Without these restrictions substitution would be unsound in the type system of $\nu^{\Box}$. Such restrictions have no reason to exist in MML_{ν}^{N}, because we allow multiple name resolvers, and fragments $b(r)e$ are formed by abstracting over one name resolver. Furthermore, making name resolvers explicit, avoid the need to introduce *non-standard* forms of substitution.

The observations above are formalized by a CBV translation $\_'$ of $\nu^{\Box}$-terms[3] into MML_{ν}^{N}, where the resolver variable r corresponds to the default resolver, which is implicit in $\nu^{\Box}$.

$e \in \nu^{\Box}$	$e' \in \mathrm{MML}_{\nu}^{N}$	$e \in \nu^{\Box}$	$e' \in \mathrm{MML}_{\nu}^{N}$
x	$ret\ x$	X	$r.X$
$\lambda x : \tau.e$	$ret\ (\lambda x.e')$	$u\langle X_i \rightarrow e_i\rangle$	$u\langle r\{X_i : e_i'\}\rangle$
$e_1\ e_2$	$do\ x_1 \leftarrow e_1'; x_2 \leftarrow e_2'; x_1 x_2$	$box\ e$	$ret\ (b(r)e')$
$\nu X : \tau.e$	$\nu X.e'$	$let\ box\ u = e_1\ in\ e_2$	$do\ u \leftarrow e_1'; e_2'$

We do not define the translation on types and assignments, since in $\nu^{\Box}$ the definition of well-formed signatures $\Sigma \vdash$ and types $\Sigma \vdash \tau$ is non-trivial.

In conclusion, the key novelty of MML_{ν}^{N} is to make name resolvers explicit and to allow a multiplicity of them, as a consequence we gain in simplicity and expressivity. Moreover, by building on top of a fairly simple form of extensible records, we are better placed to exploit existing programming language implementations (like O'Caml).

MML_{ν}^{N} *Versus* MMML. We compare MMML and MML_{ν}^{N} at the level of the operational semantics. At the level of types, one expects an MMML code type $\langle\tau\rangle$ to correspond to a fragment type $[\Sigma|\tau]$, but it is unclear what signature Σ one should take.

In MML_{ν}^{N} linking $e\langle\theta\rangle$ and name resolution $\theta.X$ affect only the simplification relation. On the other hand in MMML code generation, e.g. $\lambda_M x.e$, affects the computation relation, i.e. it requires the generation of fresh names (moreover

---

[3] In [NP03] the operational semantics (and the typing) of $\nu X.e$ differs from that adopted by (us and) FreshML. To avoid unnecessary complications, we work as if $\nu^{\Box}$ is FreshML compliant.

compilation may cause a run-time error, but this could be viewed as a weakness of the type system of MMML). In our calculus the computational effects due to code generation can be expressed as follows

- $\lambda_M x.e$ is a computation generating code for a λ-abstraction. In MML_ν^N it becomes $\nu X.do\ u \leftarrow e[x : (b(r')r'.X)]; ret\ (b(r)\lambda x.u\langle r\{X : x\}\rangle)$.
  This term first computes a fragment u by evaluating e with x replaced by a fragment needing a resolver r' for the fresh name X (and possibly other names), then it returns a fragment for a λ-abstraction. Note that r does not have to resolve X, since u is linked to the modified resolver $r\{X : x\}$ (one also expects r' to be replaced by the modified resolver).
- $op_M(e)$, where op is a unary operation, is a computation generating code for a term of the form $op(...)$, and does not generate fresh names. Thus in MML_ν^N it becomes $do\ u \leftarrow e; b(r)op(u\langle r\rangle)$. Note that in this case u is linked directly to r.

However, it is unclear how to device a whole translation from these two examples. Another feature of MMML (and MetaML) is cross-stage persistence $up(e)$, a.k.a. binary inclusion. The terms 0_V and $up(0)$ of code type $\langle int\rangle$ are different, i.e. they cannot be simplified to a common term, and in *intentional analysis* one wants to distinguish them, since $up(e)$ is a black box for intentional analysis. In MML_ν^N it seems impossible to capture this difference. In conclusion, MML_ν^N might be as expressive as MMML, and its operational semantics appears to be at a lower level of detail.

References

[AB02]   Z. M. Ariola and S. Blom. Skew confluence and the lambda calculus with letrec. *Annals of pure and applied logic*, 117(1-3):95–178, 2002.

[AZ99]   Davide Ancona and Elena Zucca. A primitive calculus for module systems. In *Proc. Int'l Conf. Principles & Practice Declarative Programming*, volume 1702 of *LNCS*, pages 62–79. Springer-Verlag, 1999.

[AZ02]   D. Ancona and E. Zucca. A calculus of module systems. *J. Funct. Programming*, 12(2):91–132, March 2002. Extended version of [AZ99].

[Car97]   Luca Cardelli. Program fragments, linking, and modularization. In *Conf. Rec. POPL '97: 24th ACM Symp. Princ. of Prog. Langs.*, pages 266–277, 1997.

[CM94]   L. Cardelli and J. C. Mitchell. Operations on records. In C. A. Gunter and J. C. Mitchell, editors, *Theoretical Aspects of Object-Oriented Programming: Types, Semantics, and Language Design*, pages 295–350. The MIT Press, Cambridge, MA, 1994.

[CMS03]   C. Calcagno, E. Moggi, and T. Sheard. Closed types for a safe imperative MetaML. *J. Funct. Programming*, 13(3):545–571, 2003.

[Dav96]   R. Davies. A temporal-logic approach to binding-time analysis. In *the Symposium on Logic in Computer Science (LICS '96)*, pages 184–195, New Brunswick, 1996. IEEE Computer Society Press.

[DP01]   Rowan Davies and Frank Pfenning. A modal analysis of staged computation. *Journal of the ACM*, 48(3):555–604, 2001.

[GP99]   Murdoch J. Gabbay and Andrew M. Pitts. A new approach to abstract syntax involving binders. In *Proc. 14th Ann. IEEE Symp. Logic in Comput. Sci.*, pages 214–224, July 1999.

[JGS93]   Neil D. Jones, Carsten K. Gomard, and Peter Sestoft. *Partial Evaluation and Automatic Program Generation.* Prentice Hall, 1993.

[LB98]   S. Liang and G. Bracha. Dynamic class loading in the Java Virtual Machine. In *ACM Symp. on Object-Oriented Programming: Systems, Languages and Applications 1998*, volume 33(10) of *Sigplan Notices*, pages 36–44. ACM Press, October 1998.

[LY99]   T. Lindholm and F. Yellin. *The Java Virtual Machine Specification.* The Java Series. Addison-Wesley, Second edition, 1999.

[MF03]   E. Moggi and S. Fagorzi. A monadic multi-stage metalanguage. In *Proc. FoSSaCS '03*, volume 2620 of *LNCS*. Springer-Verlag, 2003.

[Nan02]   Aleksandar Nanevski. Meta-programming with names and necessity. In *Proceedings of the Seventh ACM SIGPLAN International Conference on Functional Programming (ICFP-02)*, ACM SIGPLAN notices, New York, October 2002. ACM Press.

[NP03]   A. Nanevski and F. Pfenning. Meta-programming with names and necessity. Submitted, 2003.

[Ore]   Oregon Graduate Institute Technical Reports. P.O. Box 91000, Portland, OR 97291-1000,USA. Available online from `ftp://cse.ogi.edu/pub/tech-reports/README.html`.

[PG00]   Andrew M. Pitts and Murdoch J. Gabbay. A metalanguage for programming with bound names modulo renaming. In R. Backhouse and J. N. Oliveira, editors, *Proc. Mathematics of Program Construction, 5th Int'l Conf. (MPC 2000)*, volume 1837 of *LNCS*, pages 230–255, Ponte de Lima, Portugal, July 2000. Springer-Verlag.

[Rém93]   Didier Rémy. Type inference for records in a natural extension of ML. In Carl A. Gunter and John C. Mitchell, editors, *Theoretical Aspects Of Object-Oriented Programming: Types, Semantics and Language Design.* MIT Press, 1993.

[She01]   T. Sheard. Accomplishments and research challenges in meta-programming. In W. Taha, editor, *Proc. of the Int. Work. on Semantics, Applications, and Implementations of Program Generation (SAIG)*, volume 2196 of *LNCS*, pages 2–46. Springer-Verlag, 2001.

[SPG03]   Mark R. Shinwell, Andrew M. Pitts, and Murdoch J. Gabbay. Freshml: Programming with binders made simple. In *Proc. 8th Int'l Conf. Functional Programming.* ACM Press, 2003.

[Tah99]   W. Taha. *Multi-Stage Programming: Its Theory and Applications.* PhD thesis, Oregon Graduate Inst. of Science and Technology, 1999. Available from [Ore].

Taming Macros

Ryan Culpepper and Matthias Felleisen

Northeastern University
Boston, MA, USA
ryanc@ccs.neu.edu

Abstract. Scheme includes a simple yet powerful macro mechanism. Using macros, programmers can easily extend the language with new kinds of expressions and definitions, thus abstracting over recurring syntactic patterns. As with every other powerful language mechanism, programmers can also easily misuse macros and, to this day, broken macro definitions or macro uses pose complex debugging problems to programmers at all levels of experience.

In this paper, we present a type system for taming Scheme-like macros. Specifically, we formulate a small model that captures the essential properties of Scheme-style macros. For this model, we formulate a novel type system to eliminate some of these problems, prove its soundness, and validate its pragmatic usefulness.

1 The Power of Macro-programming

Over the past 20 years, the Scheme community has developed an expressive and easy-to-use standard macro system [1]. To introduce a new construct via a macro, a programmer simply writes down a rewriting rule consisting of a pair of syntactic patterns [2]. The left-hand side is called a *pattern*; the right-hand side is referred to as a *template*. Collectively the set of rules specifies how the macro expander must translate the surface syntax into core syntax. The macro expander eliminates each instance of the pattern in the program by replacing it with an instance of the template where all pattern variables have been appropriately substituted.

Scheme implementors often use the macro system to equip the language with additional forms of expressions. Programmers use the macro system for similar reasons. Many define small domain-specific notations and then formulate their program in a mix of Scheme and domain-specific expressions [3, 4]. The macro system thus empowers them to follow the old Lisp maxim on problem-solving via language definition, which says that programmers should formulate an embedded programming language for the problem domain and that they should express their solution for the domain in this new language.

Naturally, every powerful programming construct invites misuse. For example, a programmer may pass the wrong number of arguments to a function or attempt to apply an operation on the wrong kind of value (such as destructuring a number as if it were a pair or dividing by zero). These errors may cause

G. Karsai and E. Visser (Eds.): GPCE 2004, LNCS 3286, pp. 225–243, 2004.
© Springer-Verlag Berlin Heidelberg 2004

incorrect program results or run-time exceptions. A programmer may misuse macros in similar ways. Misuse of macros may cause the generation of an incorrect program or the triggering of errors during compilation. Given the weak programming environments for macro expansion, debugging macro misuses is extremely difficult compared to other constructs.

With this paper, we attempt to reconcile type checking with powerful syntactic abstractions in the spirit of Scheme. Naturally, the type system reduces the power of the macro system, but we believe that it retains enough for Scheme programmers with ordinary problems. We discuss the one exception to this claim in the conclusion. In the meantime, we briefly introduce macros; illustrate potential misuses; and present our unusual type system and a model for macro expansion so that we can prove type soundness. The penultimate section shows how we can extend our model to accommodate most of Scheme's expressive powers. Finally, we discuss related and future work toward taming macros.

Note: A preliminary version of this paper appeared in the Scheme and Functional Programming Workshop 2003 [5].

2   Why Macros?

Macros enable programmers to abstract over syntactic patterns. The most common uses of macros involve introducing new binding forms, changing the order or context of evaluation, and imposing static constraints on program fragments.

Suppose we wish to write a testing library and want a mechanism to test that an expression raises a specific run-time exception. For example, a programmer should be able to write a test case that looks like this:

   (**assert/exception** (/ 1 0) div-by-zero-exception?)

The meaning of this expression can be described as follows: Evaluate the test expression (/ 1 0). If an exception is raised during the evaluation, test the exception value with the div-by-zero-exception? predicate. If the predicate holds, return true. Otherwise, if the predicate fails or if no exception was thrown, return false.

In Scheme (or any eager language), a programmer must use a macro to introduce this abstraction. Since the test expression must be evaluated in the context of new exception-handling code, **assert/exception** cannot be defined as a function.

In PLT Scheme [6], the macro might be defined as follows, using **with-handlers** to handle exceptions:

```
(define-syntax assert/exception
  (syntax-rules ()
    ((assert/exception test-expression expected-exn?)
     (with-handlers ((expected-exn? (lambda (exn) true))
                     ((lambda (exn) true) (lambda (exn) false)))
       test-expression
       false))))
```

Note how the first macro argument is placed into an exception handling context constructed from the second macro argument, before it is evaluated.

3   Macros Are Too Powerful

Given their purpose, Scheme-style macros suffer from a critical problem. A macro can misapply the language's syntactic constructors, thus creating surface syntax that cannot be parsed into an AST or interpreted. The problem comes in two forms: an error in the macro use and an error in the macro definition.

First, the user of a macro may use it on syntactic forms that the creator of the macro didn't anticipate or intend to allow. Here is an increment macro, which is supposed to function in the context where everything else has its conventional Scheme meaning:

```
(define-syntax incr
  (syntax-rules ()
    ((incr x) (begin (set! x (+ x 1)) x))))
```

While the creator of the macro didn't expect anyone to use the macro with anything but an identifier[1], the user – perhaps someone used to a different syntax – can misapply it to a vector-dereferencing expression:

```
... (incr (vector-ref a 0)) ...
```

The situation is particularly bad when a macro is imported from a module and the user is not able to understand or even access the macro definition.

Second, consider this macro definition:

```
(define-syntax where
  (syntax-rules (is)
    ((where body lhs is rhs) (let ((rhs lhs)) body))))
```

The intention is to define a **where** macro, which could be used like this[2]:

```
(where (+ x y)
  y is 5)
```

Unfortunately, the right-hand side of the rewriting rule for **where** misuses the rhs pattern variable as a **let**-bound identifier and thus creates an ill-formed expression.

At first glance, the situation is seemingly analogous to that of applying a programmer-defined Scheme function outside of its intended domain or defining a function improperly. In either case, the programmer receives an error message and needs to find the bug. Many Scheme systems offer sophisticated debugging aids for run-time exceptions. In contrast, programmers debugging macros have no such support. For example, in Chez Scheme [7], the misuse of **incr** generates the report that the syntax

```
(set! (incr (vector-ref v 0)) (+ (incr (...)) 1))
```

---

[1] Scheme's **set!** is only a variable assignment; it cannot mutate vectors, pairs, or other structures.

[2] Or like this in PLT Scheme: ((+ x y) . **where** . y **is** 5).

is invalid; the user of **where** finds out that

(**let** ((5 x)) (+ x 1))

is invalid syntax, without any clue of which portion of the program introduced this bug. Even in DrScheme [8], a sophisticated IDE that employs source code tracing and highlighting to provide visual clues, a programmer receives difficult-to-decipher error messages. The misuse of **incr** macro highlights the `vector` dereferencing expression and reports that some **set!** expression is ill-formed, which at least suggests that the error is in the use of **incr**. In contrast, for the use of **where**, DrScheme highlights the 5 and suggests that the **let** expression expects identifiers instead of numbers on the left. This leaves the programmer with at most a hint that the macro definition contains an error.

4   A Model of Scheme Macros

This section defines a small programming language with macros, inspired by Scheme. The macro expansion process is formalized with a rewriting semantics, because we consider this style of semantics the best suited to the syntax of macro definitions. The model omits certain properties of Scheme's macro system, including hygiene [9] and referential transparency [10]; they are not relevant for our purposes. Finally, we specify the goal of type checking in this context.

4.1   Syntax

Figure 1 specifies the syntax of our model programming language. It consists of a core language plus macro definitions and macro applications. More precisely, a program consists of a sequence of macro definitions followed by a sequence of top-level terms, which must be either definitions or expressions. Programs in the surface language are expanded into programs in the core language.

This model eliminates several complications from Scheme's macro system and syntax. In particular, there are no local macros (**let-syntax**), and identifiers are a different lexical class from macro keywords. A **lambda** term contains a single formal parameter. Finally, our model does not support literals or ellipses in macro patterns. We discuss in section 8 how to scale our model to a full-fledged version of Scheme.

We use the metavariables x, y to range over syntax in the language (but not macro definitions), m for macro keywords, and P, G, T for macro patterns, guards, and templates, respectively. We require that a pattern variable appear at most once in a pattern. Frequently we use m and the word "macro" to include primitive syntax (such as **lambda** and **quote**) as well; the meaning is always clear from the context.

4.2   Reduction Semantics for Expansion

Figure 2 specifies macro expansion with a reduction semantics. It consists of two relations and some auxiliary functions that deal with macros.

		Surface	Core
program	::=	*macro-def* *top-level**	*top-level**
top-level	::=	*def*	*def*
	|	*expr*	*expr*
def	::=	(**define** *id expr*)	(**define** *id expr*)
	|	(*macro s-expr*)	
expr	::=	*id*	*id*
	|	*number*	*number*
	|	(*expr expr*)	
	|	(**lambda** (*id*) *expr*)	(**lambda** (*id*) *expr*)
	|	(**quote** *s-expr*)	(**quote** *s-expr*)
	|	(*macro s-expr**)	
	|		(**app** *expr expr*)
<u>*macro-def*</u>	::=	(**define-syntax** *macro* (**syntax-laws** *type* (*pattern guards s-expr*)*))	
<u>*pattern*</u>	::=	*pvar* | (*pattern**)	
<u>*guards*</u>	::=	((*pvar shape*)*)	
tag	::=	unspecified countable set	unspecified countable set
keyword	::=	**lambda**	**lambda**
	|	**define**	**define**
	|	**quote**	**quote**
	|	**define-syntax**	
	|	**syntax-laws**	
macro	::=	disjoint subset of *tag*	disjoint subset of *tag*
i ∈ *id*	::=	disjoint subset of *tag*	disjoint subset of *tag*
pvar	::=	disjoint subset of *tag*	disjoint subset of *tag*
x, y ∈ *s-expr*	::=	*keyword*	*keyword*
	|	*macro*	*macro*
	|	*id*	*id*
	|	*pvar*	*pvar*
	|	*number*	*number*
	|	(*s-expr**)	(*s-expr**)

Underlined nonterminals are part of the macro language, not the core language.

Fig. 1. The languages

The first relation $\xrightarrow{Prog}$ defines the expansion of an entire program. Macro definitions are collected into a macro environment ρ. The environment contains all the information from the macro definition, including type annotations. The reduction rules show, however, that the type annotations do not affect expansion.

Each top-level term is expanded in the macro environment ρ using the reduction relation $\xrightarrow{\rho}$ (note that ρ is a parameter of the relation). This reduction relation is defined for numbers, identifiers, applications, the three primitive keywords, and macro applications. The relation is compatible with expansion contexts (E), which allow expansion inside of **lambda**, **define**, and **app** terms but not inside of macro applications. The final result of a successful reduction sequence is a term of the core language (*CoreTerm*).

The recursive structure of expansion contexts (E) shows where expansion occurs, and the matching structure of core terms (*CoreTerm*) shows what expansion may produce in that context. Expansion only occurs in expression and definition contexts. Furthermore, macros must expand into expressions or definitions.

In our language, any parenthesized term in expansion position that is not a special form application must be a procedure application. In our reduction semantics, these are explicitly tagged with **app** after they have been recognized as such. In particular, macro applications cannot expand into keywords and cause expansion of the containing term:

Bad: $((\textbf{id } \textbf{id}) \ 5) \xrightarrow{\rho} (\textbf{id } 5) \xrightarrow{\rho} 5$

is forbidden, just as it is in Scheme.

The single-step macro expansion is described via the auxiliary functions **match** and **transcribe**. If the macro arguments match a pattern, **match** produces a substitution (σ) that maps pattern variables to terms. Then **transcribe** applies the substitution to the template, which produces the replacement term for the macro application. If none of the macro's patterns matches its arguments, the macro is not expanded.

4.3   Stuck Terms

Our goal is to prevent macro expansion from getting stuck. Stuck terms represent those terms for which macro expansion goes awry. Technically, they are terms that are not in the core language and yet they cannot be further expanded. Stuck terms come in three groups.

The first class contains pattern variables, macro keywords, and primitive keywords. These terms have no meaning outside of a macro template or a macro application of the right form. For example, the term **quote** by itself is stuck.

The second class of stuck terms includes all macro applications (and procedure applications) that do not match a clause in ρ or a grammar clause in the core language. For example, (**lambda** x x) is stuck, because **lambda** requires its single formal parameter to be enclosed in parentheses.

The third class of stuck terms are those that have been completely expanded but are not terms of the core language. Thus, (**lambda** (x) (**define** xyz 5)) is stuck because the core grammar does not allow a definition within a **lambda** term[3].

In a syntax closer to Scheme there would be additional classes of stuck terms. For instance, the formal parameters of **lambda** should be distinct, so (**lambda** (x x) 17) would be illegal. We believe, however, that errors such as this one are analogous to division-by-zero errors, which conventional type systems do not catch. For this reason, we have eliminated this complication from our grammar.

5   Shape Types

The semantics for macro expansion guides the development of the type system in two ways. First, the core language grammar and syntax of macro patterns determines the structure of our types. Second, since expansion happens only in certain contexts, the recursive structure of the type checker must respect these contexts.

5.1   Why Shapes?

Syntactically, our language consists of two essential syntactic categories: expressions and definitions. These are also the only two types into which macro applications can expand. The syntax that macros consume, however, cannot be described in terms of just expressions and definitions. After all, our grammar contains many other kinds of syntactic categories. For example, in the case of **lambda**, the first argument is an identifier within parentheses, which should not be typed as either an expression or a definition. If we wish to design a type language that describes all these intermediate *shapes* of syntax, it must cope with the basic identifiers, expressions, and definitions, and shapes built up by grouping with parentheses. We call these descriptions *shape types*.

Shape types provide a way of describing the terms that macros *and* primitive syntax constructors consume and produce. The type checker therefore treats macro applications and primitive keyword applications identically. In particular, an initial type environment contains types for primitive keywords.

Figure 3 defines the language of shape types. We use the term *type* to refer to only expr and def. The term *shape* refers to simple *types* and complex, structured shapes. We use t to range over types and s to range over arbitrary shapes.

The success of a single expansion step of a macro application is determined only by the *shape* of its input. The shape type of the macro's input represents a guarantee that if the actual arguments match the shape type, then they also match one of the macro's patterns, and thus expansion does not get stuck in that step.

If all macro templates contain only macro applications of the correct shape, then expansion never becomes stuck. It is impossible to prove that a template

---

[3] Scheme allows some internal definitions, though not this one. Our model omits internal definitions to simplify the presentation and the proof.

PROGRAM

$$md_i = (\textbf{define-syntax } m_i \ (\textbf{syntax-laws } t_i \ (P_{i,1}G_{i,1}T_{i,1})\cdots)) \qquad i \leq m$$
$$\rho(m_i) = ([(P_{i,1}, G_{i,1}, T_{i,1}), \cdots], t_i) \qquad i \leq m$$
$$\frac{x_k \xrightarrow{\rho}{}^* x_k' \qquad k \leq n \qquad\qquad\qquad}{x_k' \in CoreTerm \qquad k \leq n}$$
$$md_1 \cdots md_m \ x_1 \cdots x_n \xrightarrow{Prog} x_1' \cdots x_n'$$

REDUCTION

$$
\begin{array}{lll}
E & ::= [] \ | \ (\textbf{lambda } (i) \ E) \ | \ (\textbf{app } E \ x) \ | \ (\textbf{app } x \ E) \ | \ (\textbf{define } i \ E) \\
CoreExpr & ::= n \ | \ i \ | \ (\textbf{lambda } (i) \ CoreExpr) \ | \ (\textbf{app } CoreExpr \ CoreExpr) \\
& \quad | \ (\textbf{quote } x) \\
CoreDef & ::= (\textbf{define } i \ CoreExpr) \\
CoreTerm & ::= CoreExpr \ | \ CoreDef
\end{array}
$$

$$\frac{x \xrightarrow{\rho} x'}{E[x] \xrightarrow{\rho} E[x']}$$

$$(x_1 \ x_2) \xrightarrow{\rho} (\textbf{app } x_1 \ x_2) \qquad\qquad\qquad\qquad x_1 \notin macro$$
$$(m \ x_1 \cdots x_n) \xrightarrow{\rho} \textbf{expand } \rho m(x_1 \cdots x_n) \qquad \text{if the right-hand side exists}$$

MATCH

$$
\begin{array}{rl}
\textbf{match } \rho m x = & (\sigma, T_k) \\
& \text{where } \rho(m) = ([(P_1, G_1, T_1) \cdots (P_n, G_n, T_n)], t) \\
& \text{and } \textbf{transcribe } P_k \sigma = x \text{ for minimal } k \\
\textbf{expand } \rho m x = & \textbf{transcribe } T\sigma \quad \text{where } (\sigma, T) = \textbf{match } \rho m x \\
\textbf{transcribe } x\sigma = & x \qquad \text{when } x \in datum \cup id \cup keyword \cup macro \\
\textbf{transcribe } p\sigma = & \sigma(p) \qquad \text{when } p \in \textbf{dom}(\sigma) \\
\textbf{transcribe } (x_1 \cdots x_n)\sigma = & (\textbf{transcribe } x_1\sigma \cdots \textbf{transcribe } x_n\sigma)
\end{array}
$$

Fig. 2. Reduction semantics

has the correct shape if pattern variables be replaced with arbitrary terms, so we allow guards on the macro patterns to constrain the shapes of terms that pattern variables can match. The guards give the macro a more restrictive input shape, and they generate additional information for checking the templates.

In order to check a macro application, there must be a correspondence between terms and shapes. A particular term may be used in many ways, so it must have many potential shapes. Consider the following term:

$$t \in type \quad ::= \quad \textsf{expr} \mid \textsf{def}$$
$$s \in shape \quad ::= \quad type \mid \textsf{ident} \mid \textsf{any}$$
$$\mid \quad (shape^*)$$
$$\mid \quad (\textbf{mclauses} \; (shape \; shape) \cdots (shape \; shape))$$
$$\mid \quad shape \rightarrow type$$

Fig. 3. Shape Types

(define (a b) **(let** ((a b)) (a b)))

The subterm (a b) occurs three times, each time used in a different way. The first occurrence is used as the shape (ident ident), the second as the shape (ident expr), and the third as just expr. Put differently, the assignment of shapes to terms is not unique and poses some complex problems.

5.2   Shape Types Guide Recursive Type Checking

Conventional type checkers synthesize the type of a phrase from the types of its pieces. For example, if the type checker encounters a term of the form $(e_1 \; e_2)$, it recognizes an application and knows to recursively type check the two subterms. If e_1 is of type $a \rightarrow b$ and e_2 is of type a then $(e_1 \; e_2)$ is of type b.

The conventional type checker can make this deduction for any $(e_1 \; e_2)$ that occurs in an *expression position*. Clearly, no type checker would reject a program containing the string "never write (car 17)" on the grounds that 17 is not a list. The conventional type checker operates after the parser has determined the syntactic roles of all program fragments. Thus it knows that in the above string (car 17) does not occur in an expression context and does not require type checking.

In our system, type checking happens before macro expansion and thus before parsing. Rather than the parser determining the syntactic roles of program fragments, in our system the shape types of special forms dictate how to recursively type check the arguments to those special forms.

Consider this example:

(moo (quo rem) (div x y) (= rem 0))

Without some information about **moo**'s legal input shapes, it is impossible to determine the shape type of (quo rem) in **moo**'s argument, since **moo** may destructure and rearrange its arguments in arbitrary and unknown ways. If the type checker knows, however, that **moo** has shape

((ident ident) expr expr) → expr

then it can recursively check the appropriate arguments to **moo** as expressions. First it makes sure there are three arguments. Then it checks that the first argument is a group of two identifiers and that the second and third can be validated to be expressions.

The shape associated with the macro is exactly the information necessary to perform type checking without expansion. Even when code has no macro applications and thus parsing could be done without expansion steps, shape types are still powerful enough to describe how to recursively type check uses of primitive keywords like **define** and **lambda**. In other words, the type checker itself does not need special rules for core keywords.

6   The Shape Type System

Type checking an entire program consists of building a macro type environment for the macro definitions and then type checking the macro templates and the subsequent top-level terms. Type checking a term ($\blacktriangleright$) requires auxiliary two auxiliary relations. One relates S-expressions with shapes ($\circ$), and the other defines an ordering on shapes ($\sqsubseteq$).

6.1   Checking a Complete Program

Figure 4 presents the type rules for programs. A program is typable ([Program]) if each top-level term is typable in the initial type environment augmented with the macro type environment from the macro definitions.

The [Environment] rule defines the "respects" relation $\vdash_{\mathcal{R}}$, which ensures that the macro type environment reflects the patterns and annotations of the macro definitions. It checks each macro clause with [Macro Type] for each macro definition as well as the templates (rule [Templates]) using $\Gamma \cup \Gamma_0$ and the guards.

The [Macro Type] rule relates patterns and shapes with the [Guarded] and [Unguarded] rules. The relation $\vdash_{\mathcal{U}} P : u$ indicates that terms with shape u match the pattern, and $\Phi \vdash_{\mathcal{G}} P : s$ says that when a term of shape s matches P, the resulting substitution satisfies Φ. The overlap relation ($\bowtie$) rejects macro definitions with overlapping patterns. Ensuring that the patterns do not overlap is necessary for the type soundness theorem.

6.2   From Terms to Shape Types

Figure 5 introduces the proof rules that relate S-expressions with their shapes. The rules use two kinds of environments: Γ for the macro type environment, mapping *macro* to *shape*, and Φ for the pattern variable environment, mapping *pvar* to *shape*. Top-level terms are type checked in the empty pattern variable environment, and macro templates are checked in the pattern variable environment corresponding to the guards of that clause.

A judgment $\Gamma; \Phi \vdash x \circ s$ means that in the type environments Γ and Φ, term x has shape s and can be used in any position that expects a term of shape s. Two of the rules deserve an explanation:

PROGRAM
$md_i = (\textbf{define-syntax}\ m_i\ (\textbf{syntax-laws}\ t_i\ (P_{i,1} G_{i,1} T_{i,1}) \cdots))$
$$\rho(m_i) = ([(P_{i,1}, G_{i,1}, T_{i,1}), \cdots], t_i)$$
$$\frac{\Gamma \vdash_\mathcal{R} \rho \qquad \Gamma \cup \Gamma_0; \Phi \vdash x_k \blacktriangleright t_k \quad t_k \in type}{\vdash_\mathcal{P} md_1 \cdots md_n\ x_1 \cdots x_{n'}\ \textbf{correct}}$$

$$\Gamma_0(\textbf{lambda}) = ((\text{ident})\ \text{expr}) \to \text{expr}$$
$$\Gamma_0(\textbf{define}) = (\text{ident expr}) \to \text{def}$$
$$\Gamma_0(\textbf{quote}) = (\text{any}) \to \text{expr}$$
$$\Gamma_0(\textbf{app}) = (\text{expr expr}) \to \text{expr}$$

ENVIRONMENTS
$$\frac{\forall m \in \textbf{dom}\,(\Gamma) \cap macro : \Gamma(m) \vdash_\mathcal{R} \rho(m) \quad \forall m \in \textbf{dom}\,(\rho) : \Gamma \vdash_\mathcal{T} \rho(m)}{\Gamma \vdash_\mathcal{R} \rho}$$

MACRO TYPE
$$\rho(m) = ([(P_0, G_0, T_0), \cdots (P_n, G_n, T_n)], t)$$
$$\Gamma(m) = (\textbf{mclauses}\ (u_1\ s_1) \cdots (u_n\ s_n)) \to t$$
$$\frac{\forall i \le n : G_i \vdash_\mathcal{G} P_i : s_i \quad \forall i \le n : \vdash_\mathcal{U} P_i : u_i \quad \forall i \ne j : u_i \not\bowtie u_j}{\Gamma(m) \vdash_\mathcal{R} \rho(m)}$$

TEMPLATES
$$\frac{\Gamma \cup \Gamma_0; G_i \vdash T_i \blacktriangleright t \quad \forall i \le n \quad \rho(m) = ([(P_0, G_0, T_0), \cdots (P_n, G_n, T_n)], t)}{\Gamma \vdash_\mathcal{T} \rho(m)}$$

GUARDED1
$$\frac{p \in pvar \quad \Phi(p) = s}{\Phi \vdash_\mathcal{G} p : s}$$

GUARDED2
$$\frac{\forall i \le n : \Gamma; \Phi \vdash_\mathcal{G} x_i : s_i}{\Phi \vdash_\mathcal{G} (x_1 \cdots x_n) : (s_1 \cdots s_n)}$$

UNGUARDED1
$$\frac{p \in pvar}{\vdash_\mathcal{U} pvar : \text{any}}$$

UNGUARDED2
$$\frac{\forall i \le n :\vdash_\mathcal{U} x_i : u_i}{\vdash_\mathcal{U} (x_1 \cdots x_n) : (u_1 \cdots u_n)}$$

$$u \in unguarded\ shapes ::= \text{any} \mid (u_1 \cdots u_n)$$

OVERLAP1
$$\forall u : \text{any} \bowtie u$$

OVERLAP2
$$\frac{\forall i \le n : u_i \bowtie u_i'}{(u_1 \cdots u_n) \bowtie (u_1' \cdots u_n')}$$

Fig. 4. Program Correctness

SHAPE1
$$x \in id$$
$$\overline{\Gamma; \Phi \vdash x \circ \mathsf{ident}}$$

SHAPE2
$$x \in number$$
$$\overline{\Gamma; \Phi \vdash x \circ \mathsf{expr}}$$

SHAPE3
$$x \in macro \cup keyword$$
$$x \in \mathbf{dom}\,(\Gamma)$$
$$\overline{\Gamma; \Phi \vdash x \circ \Gamma(x)}$$

SHAPE4
$$x \in pvar$$
$$x \in \mathbf{dom}\,(\Phi)$$
$$\overline{\Gamma; \Phi \vdash x \circ \Phi(x)}$$

SHAPE5
$$x \in macro \cup pvar \cup keyword$$
$$x \notin \mathbf{dom}\,(\Gamma) \cup \mathbf{dom}\,(\Phi)$$
$$\overline{\Gamma; \Phi \vdash x \circ \mathsf{any}}$$

SHAPE6
$$\Gamma; \Phi \vdash x \circ s$$
$$s \sqsubseteq s'$$
$$\overline{\Gamma; \Phi \vdash x \circ s'}$$

SHAPE7
$$\Gamma; \Phi \vdash x_i \circ s_i \qquad i \leq n$$
$$\overline{\Gamma; \Phi \vdash (x_1 \cdots x_n) \circ (s_1 \cdots s_n)}$$

Fig. 5. From Terms to Shapes

[**Shape3**] If a macro keyword has a definition, then it has the shape (an arrow shape type) recorded in the type environment.

[**Shape5**] If a keyword or pattern variable is not bound, it has shape any. It can be used only in positions that place no constraints on the shape; for example, the argument to **quote** takes a term of any shape.

Any S-expression can be given some shape type. In particular, any S-expression can be given the shape type any.

6.3   Ordering Shapes

The judgment $s \sqsubseteq s'$ means that shape s generalizes to shape s'. Put differently, s' reveals fewer details than s. The ordering rules are introduced in fig. 6.

ORDER1
$$\mathsf{ident} \sqsubseteq \mathsf{expr}$$

ORDER2
$$s \sqsubseteq \mathsf{any}$$

ORDER3
$$\forall k \leq n : s_k \sqsubseteq s'_k$$
$$\overline{(s_1 \cdots s_n) \sqsubseteq (s'_1 \cdots s'_n)}$$

ORDER4
$$(s_1 \cdots s_n) \sqsubseteq s$$
$$\overline{(s \rightarrow t\ s_1 \cdots s_n) \sqsubseteq t}$$

ORDER5
$$\overline{(\mathsf{expr}\ \mathsf{expr}) \sqsubseteq \mathsf{expr}}$$

ORDER6
$$s \sqsubseteq s_k \qquad \forall i \neq j : u_i \not\sqsubseteq u_j$$
$$\overline{s \sqsubseteq (\mathbf{mclauses}\ (u_0\ s_0) \cdots (u_k\ s_k) \cdots (u_n\ s_n))}$$

ORDER7
$$s \sqsubseteq s$$

ORDER8
$$s \sqsubseteq s' \qquad s' \sqsubseteq s''$$
$$\overline{s \sqsubseteq s''}$$

Fig. 6. Ordering Relation on Shapes

The rule [Order4] says that groupings that look like macro applications (and satisfy certain constraints) may be interpreted as the result type of the macro. [Order5] applies to procedure applications and expr. Analogous rules are included in the actual type checking rules.

CHECK1
$x \in id \cup number$
$$\Gamma; \Phi \vdash x \blacktriangleright \mathsf{expr}$$

CHECK2A
$x \in pvar \qquad \Phi(x) \sqsubseteq \mathsf{expr}$
$$\Gamma; \Phi \vdash x \blacktriangleright \mathsf{expr}$$

CHECK2B
$x \in pvar \qquad \Phi(x) \sqsubseteq \mathsf{def}$
$$\Gamma; \Phi \vdash x \blacktriangleright \mathsf{def}$$

CHECK3A
$m \in macro \cup keyword \qquad \Gamma; \Phi \vdash m \circ s \rightarrow \mathsf{expr}$
$(s_1 \cdots s_n) \sqsubseteq s \qquad \forall i \leq n : \Gamma \vdash x_i \circ s_i$
$$\Gamma; \Phi \vdash (m\ x_1 \cdots x_n) \blacktriangleright \mathsf{expr}$$

CHECK3B
$m \in macro \cup keyword \qquad \Gamma; \Phi \vdash m \circ s \rightarrow \mathsf{def}$
$(s_1 \cdots s_n) \sqsubseteq s \qquad \forall i \leq n : \Gamma \vdash x_i \circ s_i$
$$\Gamma; \Phi \vdash (m\ x_1 \cdots x_n) \blacktriangleright \mathsf{def}$$

CHECK4
$\Gamma; \Phi \vdash x_i \circ \mathsf{expr}$
$$\Gamma; \Phi \vdash (x_0\ x_1) \blacktriangleright \mathsf{expr}$$

Fig. 7. Type Checking

The final rule [Order6] governs matching shapes of the arguments to macros against the shapes derived from the clauses in a macro definition. The kth clause of a macro definition yields a pair $(u_k\ s_k)$ in the **mclauses** shape type. The first is the unguarded pattern shape; the second is the guarded pattern shape. By construction, the guarded pattern shape is always below the unguarded pattern shape. A shape is below the shape of the clause if it matches (exactly) one of the guarded shapes. The antecedent that requires macro not to overlap guarantees that it does not match more than one. This allows us to establish a definite correlation between the clause that causes the shape checking to succeed and the clause that matches during expansion.

6.4 Type Checking

The goal of type checking is to ensure that top-level terms have each have a type, not just a shape. Type checking takes place in the context of the type environments $\Gamma; \Phi$, in the same way shape checking does.

A judgment of the form $\Gamma; \Phi \vdash x \blacktriangleright t$, where $t \in type$, means that x has type t in the context described by $\Gamma; \Phi$. A macro template is type checked in a pattern variable environment derived from the guards. The typing rules in fig. 7 have the following meaning:

1. Identifiers and numbers are both expressions.
2. If a pattern variable contains a term of expression or definition shape, then that term is an expression or a definition.
3. A macro application has the macro's declared result type if all of its arguments are of the right shape.
4. Two expressions grouped together constitute a procedure application, which is an expression.

7   Soundness

We prove type soundness for this system via subject reduction [11]. Following preservation and progress theorems, we discuss the untypability of stuck terms.

7.1   Preservation and Progress

The main theorems are conventional theorems about type systems. The Preservation Theorem proves that if a program has a type then the expanded program has the same type. The Progress Theorem shows that a typed term is either a term in the core language or expandable.

While the theorems look familiar, the proofs require different lemmas and techniques. Lemma 1 allows us to switch back and forth between proofs of the ∘ relation and ▶ relation. We use this lemma for inductive proofs where the hypotheses involve a different relation than the conclusion. Lemma 2 says that a macro application that type checks always has an expansion, and that the expansion also type checks. Lemma 3 shows that transcriptions of macro templates preserve type if the substitutions respect the template's guards. Lemma 4 guarantees that shape types that do not overlap have no terms in common. This implies that if the unguarded pattern shapes do not overlap, then a term matches a unique pattern.

Theorem 1 (Preservation). *If* $x \xrightarrow{\rho} x'$, $\Gamma \vdash_{\mathcal{R}} \rho$, *and* $\Gamma; \emptyset \vdash x \blacktriangleright t$, *then* $\Gamma; \emptyset \vdash x' \blacktriangleright t$.

Proof. The proof for redexes in the empty evaluation context is by case analysis of the reduction rules. If $x = (x_1 \; x_2)$ then we must have $t = \mathsf{expr}$ and x_1 and x_2 both have shape expr, so the term $(\mathbf{app} \; x_1 \; x_2)$ also has type expr. The case of macro applications is handled by Lemma 2.

Once we have proved subject reduction for empty contexts, we can use induction on the structure of the context, aided by Lemma 1.   □

Theorem 2 (Progress). *If* $\Gamma \vdash_{\mathcal{R}} \rho$, *and* $\Gamma; \emptyset \vdash x \blacktriangleright t$, *then either* $x \in CoreTerm$ *or there is an* x' *such that* $x \xrightarrow{\rho} x'$.

Proof. The proof is by induction on the proof $\Gamma; \emptyset \vdash x \blacktriangleright t$ and case analysis of the last proof step.

[**Check1**] If x is a number or identifier, then x is a core term.

[**Check2**] The pattern variable environment is empty, so this case cannot occur.

[**Check3**] *on primitive syntax:* We prove the claim for **lambda**; **define** is similar, and **quote** is trivial.

Assume $x = (\mathbf{lambda} \; (i) \; y)$. The type of **lambda** ensures that $\Gamma; \emptyset \vdash y \circ \mathsf{expr}$ and Lemma 1 gives us $\Gamma; \emptyset \vdash y \blacktriangleright \mathsf{expr}$. We can apply the induction hypothesis to get $y \xrightarrow{\rho} y'$ or $y \in CoreTerm$. Then we have either a reduction $x \xrightarrow{\rho} (\mathbf{lambda} \; (i) \; y')$ or $(\mathbf{lambda} \; (i) \; y) \in CoreTerm$.

[Check3] *on macros:* If $x = (m \; x_1 \cdots x_n)$, then Lemma 2 guarantees that the expansion succeeds, so x is a redex.

[Check4] If $x = (x_1 \; x_2)$ then we have a reduction $(x_1 \; x_2) \xrightarrow{\rho} (\mathbf{app} \; x_1 \; x_2)$. □

Lemma 1. $\Gamma; \emptyset \vdash x \blacktriangleright t$ *iff* $\Gamma; \emptyset \vdash x \circ t$.

Proof. The proof of the forward implication is a simple case analysis of the last proof step of $\Gamma; \emptyset \vdash x \blacktriangleright t$ and a translation into the Shape and Order rules.

The proof of the reverse implication is by induction on the proof $\Gamma; \emptyset \vdash x \circ t$, including both Shape and Order rules. □

Lemma 2. *If* $\Gamma; \emptyset \vdash (m \; x_1 \cdots x_n) \blacktriangleright t$ *and* $\Gamma \vdash_{\mathcal{R}} \rho$ *then* $\mathbf{expand} \; \rho m(x_1 \cdots x_n)$ *exists and* $\Gamma; \emptyset \vdash \mathbf{expand} \; \rho m(x_1 \cdots x_n) \blacktriangleright t$.

Proof. We use Lemma 4 to show that $(x_1 \cdots x_n)$ matches a unique pattern. Then since $(x_1 \cdots x_n)$ matches the macro input shape, the resulting substitution σ maps pattern variables to terms with the shapes that satisfy the guard. The macro correctness condition requires that templates type check under the pattern variable environment of their guards. Then by Lemma 3 the transcribed template type checks in an empty pattern environment. □

Lemma 3. *Let* σ *be a substitution. If* $\Gamma; \Phi \vdash x \circ s$ *and* $\forall p \in \mathbf{dom}(\Phi) : \Gamma; \emptyset \vdash \sigma(p) \circ \Phi(p)$, *then* $\Gamma; \emptyset \vdash \mathbf{transcribe} \; x\sigma \circ s$.

Proof. The proof is by straightforward induction on the proof of $\Gamma; \Phi \vdash x \circ s$ and case analysis on the last proof step. □

Lemma 4. *For any fixed* Γ, $u_1 \bowtie u_2$ *if and only if there exists a term* x *such that* $\Gamma; \emptyset \vdash x : u_1$ *and* $\Gamma; \emptyset \vdash x : u_2$.

Proof. The forward direction is by induction on the derivation of $u_1 \bowtie u_2$. The reverse direction is by induction on the structure of x and case analysis of u_1 and u_2. □

7.2   Stuck Terms Revisited

Now we can examine the three classes of stuck terms in the shape type system. By inspection we easily see that the type system does not type check stuck terms as either expr or def, meaning that well-typed programs produce proper syntax.

The first class of stuck states consists of pattern variables and keywords. The only shape the type checker assigns to these is any. The second class is the set of macro applications with incorrectly shaped arguments. These cannot be assigned a *type*, because the rules for type checking require correctly shaped arguments. The third class contains expanded terms that are not core terms. These terms violate the shape types of the primitive keywords, so these terms are not typed.

8   Extensions and Pragmatics

Standard Scheme allows programmers to write macros that process arbitrary sequences of inputs, expressed using ellipses in the rewrite rules. For example, the **or** form can be applied to zero or more expressions. Standard Scheme macros can also match on literal data and keywords in patterns. For example, the **cond** form recognizes the keyword **else**.

Extending our model with sequences introduces two kinds of complications. First, a form like **lambda** imposes additional context-sensitive constraints on expressions, which the type system cannot express. In particular, the parameter list may not contain the same identifier twice. As mentioned, we consider such errors analogous to division-by-zero or out-of-bounds array referencing, which type systems in ordinary languages also cannot eliminate. Similarly, various kinds of ellipsis mismatch are beyond the scope of a shape type system. Second, we need to extend the type system to cope with keywords and ellipses in macros.

Keywords in patterns require the extension of our type system. Specifically, it requires the addition of a collection of singleton shape types, each representing one keyword. To preserve the non-overlapping property, these keywords must be a lexical class separate from identifiers and unusable as expressions.

Macros that process sequences also require an extension of the shape language with shapes of the form $(s_r \ldots . s_f)$. The shape $(s_r \ldots . s_f)$ contains all terms of shape s_f as well as all terms of shape $(s_r . (s_r \ldots . s_f))$. This allows us to express shapes describing a sequence of definitions followed by a nonempty sequence of expressions. We can then use Amadio-Cardelli style recursive subtyping [12] to handle sequence shapes.

To test the pragmatics of our type system, we have reformulated the definitions for the collection of macros dubbed "derived syntax" in R^5RS. A reformulation is necessary so that we can annotate the pattern variables with the correct shapes in this extended system. In particular, the $(p0\ p \ldots)$ idiom must be replaced when the sequence is not homogeneous such as with the body of a **lambda** expression where all internal definitions must occur before the (nonempty) sequence of expressions. The appendix provides one example from this test and shows that the difference are minor and do not impose an extraordinary amount of work on the programmer.

9   Related Work

Over the past ten years, other language communities have recognized the value of macro systems and have started to explore their use. Ganz, Sabry, and Taha [13] have designed and implemented MacroML, a version of OCaml with macros. Peyton-Jones has investigated the use of macros in conjunction with Haskell [14]. Other researchers have explored macro-like systems for languages with conventional C-style syntax [15–18]. None of the systems achieves the expressive power of Scheme macros.

The system for C presented in [15] introduces quasiquotation for conventional syntax and appears to statically check *most* templates for correctness. No definition of soundness is given, and no proof is attempted.

Maya, a syntactic extension system for Java[18], allows programmer to extend the syntax of Java using grammar extensions and associated transformers ("semantic actions"). Maya uses types and other pattern annotations to control the parsing of macro arguments. The authors claim to catch syntax errors in macro definitions, but the paper does not include proof of correctness.

The MacroML system by Ganz et al is a type-safe macro system based on MetaML. In fact, their type discipline guarantees that ML-style macros generate proper, well-typed ML code. MacroML achieves soundness, however, by severely restricting the expressive power of the macro system, beyond the point of our own constraints.

10 Conclusion

In this paper, we have presented a type system for macros and proved its soundness. We are now exploring the problem of scaling this system up to handle the complexities of advanced Scheme macros.

We are now developing a prototype implementation of the type checker, exploring its practicality for full Scheme. We are also investigating how to overcome the one major restriction of our system that we haven't addressed yet: macro-generating macros. While such abstractions appear to be esoteric at first, they do occur on occasion in real programs and we believe that a full-fledged shape type system must eventual address this issue.

Our shape system also fails to handle programmed macro systems, such as the **syntax-case** system [19]. We are investigating the use of contracts (as described by Findler [20, 21]) for taming programmed macros.

Acknowledgments

We are grateful to Robby Findler for helping simplify the reduction semantics, and to Matthew Flatt and the anonymous reviewers for many suggestions and improvements.

References

1. Kelsey, R., Clinger, W., Rees (Editors), J.: Revised[5] report of the algorithmic language Scheme. ACM SIGPLAN Notices **33** (1998) 26–76
2. Kohlbecker, E.E., Wand, M.: Macros-by-example: Deriving syntactic transformations from their specifications. In: ACM SIGPLAN-SIGACT Symposium on Principles of Programming Languages. (1987) 77–84
3. Bentley, J.: Programming pearls: little languages. Commun. ACM **29** (1986) 711–721
4. Shivers, O.: A universal scripting framework, or lambda: the ultimate little language. In: Concurrency and Parallelism, Programming, Networking, and Security. Springer Lecture Notes in Computer Science, Springer-Verlag (1996) 254–265

5. Culpepper, R., Felleisen, M.: Well-shaped macros. In: Proceedings of the Fourth Workshop on Scheme and Functional Programming. (2003) 59–68
6. Flatt, M.: PLT MzScheme: Language manual. Technical Report TR97-280, Rice University (1997) http://www.plt-scheme.org/software/mzscheme/.
7. Dybvig, R.K.: Chez Scheme User's Guide. Cadence Research Systems (1998)
8. Findler, R.B., Clements, J., Flanagan, C., Flatt, M., Krishnamurthi, S., Steckler, P., Felleisen, M.: DrScheme: A programming environment for Scheme. Journal of Functional Programming 12 (2002) 159–182 A preliminary version of this paper appeared in PLILP 1997, LNCS volume 1292, pp. 369–388.
9. Kohlbecker, E.E., Friedman, D.P., Felleisen, M., Duba, B.F.: Hygienic macro expansion. In: ACM Symposium on Lisp and Functional Programming. (1986) 151–161
10. Clinger, W., Rees, J.: Macros that work. In: ACM SIGPLAN-SIGACT Symposium on Principles of Programming Languages. (1990) 155–162
11. Wright, A., Felleisen, M.: A syntactic approach to type soundness. Information and Computation (1994) 38–94 First appeared as Technical Report TR160, Rice University, 1991.
12. Amadio, R., Cardelli, L.: Subtyping recursive types. In: ACM Transactions on Programming Languages and Systems. Volume 15. (1993) 575–631
13. Ganz, S.E., Sabry, A., Taha, W.: Macros as multi-stage computations: Type-safe, generative, binding macros in macroml. In: International Conference on Functional Programming. (2001) 74–85
14. Sheard, T., Peyton Jones, S.: Template metaprogramming for Haskell. In Chakravarty, M.M.T., ed.: ACM SIGPLAN Haskell Workshop 02, ACM Press (2002) 1–16
15. Weise, D., Crew, R.: Programmable syntax macros. In: ACM SIGPLAN Conference on Programming Language Design and Implementation. (1993) 156–165
16. Batory, D., Lofaso, B., Smaragdakis, Y.: JTS: tools for implementing domain-specific languages. In: Proceedings Fifth International Conference on Software Reuse, Victoria, BC, Canada, IEEE (1998) 143–153
17. Bachrach, J., Playford, K.: The Java syntactic extender (jse). In: Processdings of the Conference on Object-Oriented Programming Systems. (2001) 31–24
18. Baker, J., Hsieh, W.: Maya: Multiple-dispatch syntax extension in java. In: Proc. ACM Conference on Programming Language Design and Implementation. (2002) 270–281
19. Dybvig, R.K., Hieb, R., Bruggeman, C.: Syntactic abstraction in Scheme. Lisp and Symbolic Computation 5 (1993) 295–326
20. Findler, R.B., Felleisen, M.: Contracts for higher-order functions. In: ACM SIGPLAN International Conference on Functional Programming. (2002)
21. Findler, R.B.: Behavioral Software Contracts. PhD thesis, Rice University (2002)
22. Cardelli, L., Matthes, F., Abadi, M.: Extensible syntax with lexical scoping. Research Report 121, Digital SRC (1994)
23. Dybvig, R.K.: The Scheme Programming Language. 1 edn. Prentice-Hall (1987)
24. Flatt, M.: Composable and compilable macros: You want it *when?* In: ACM SIGPLAN International Conference on Functional Programming. (2002)
25. Queinnec, C.: Macroexpansion reflective tower. In Kiczales, G., ed.: Proceedings of the Reflection'96 Conference, San Francisco (California, USA) (1996) 93–104

A   R5RS Macro Example

The following code is a reformulation of the R^{5}RS macro for **cond** with shape annotations. We use ellipses to write sequence types and **kw:else** for the singleton shape containing the keyword **else**, and likewise for =>. We also use named shape abbreviations.

```
(type expr+ (expr ... expr))
(type cond-clause (union (expr kw:=> expr) expr+))
(type cond-clauses
  (cond-clause ... (union cond-clause (kw:else . expr+))))

(define-syntax cond
  (syntax-laws expr
    ((cond (else . result)
     ([result expr+])
     (begin . result)))
    ((cond (test => result))
     ([test expr] [result expr])
     (let ((temp test))
       (if temp (result temp))))
    ((cond (test => result) . clauses)
     ([test expr] [result expr] [clauses cond-clauses])
     (let ((temp test))
       (if temp
           (result temp)
           (cond . clauses))))
    ((cond (test))
     ([test expr])
     test)
    ((cond (test) . clauses)
     ([test expr] [clauses cond-clauses])
     (let ((temp test))
       (if temp
           temp
           (cond . clauses))))
    ((cond (test . result))
     ([test expr] [result expr+])
     (if test (begin . result)))
    ((cond (test . result) . clauses)
     ([test expr] [result expr+] [clauses cond-clauses])
     (if test
         (begin . result)
         (cond . clauses)))))
```

A Unification of Inheritance
and Automatic Program Specialization

Ulrik P. Schultz

DAIMI/ISIS
University of Aarhus
Denmark

Abstract. The object-oriented style of programming facilitates program adaptation and enhances program genericness, but at the expense of efficiency. Automatic program specialization can be used to generate specialized, efficient implementations for specific scenarios, but requires the program to be structured appropriately for specialization and is yet another new concept for the programmer to understand and apply. We have unified automatic program specialization and inheritance into a single concept, and implemented this approach in a modified version of Java named JUST. When programming in JUST, inheritance is used to control the automatic application of program specialization to class members during compilation to obtain an efficient implementation.

This paper presents the language JUST, which integrates object-oriented concepts, block structure, and techniques from automatic program specialization to provide both a generative programming language where object-oriented designs can be efficiently implemented and a simple yet powerful automatic program specializer for an object-oriented language.

1 Introduction

Inheritance is fundamental to most object-oriented programming languages. Inheritance can add new attributes or refine existing ones. Using covariant specialization, fields and method parameters can even be refined to more specific domains [14, 27]. Equivalent mechanisms for refining the behavior of a method however only allow additional behavior to be added (e.g., method combination such as "inner" and "around"); there is no mechanism for declaratively refining the behavior of methods to something more specific – here, the programmer must override the method with manually implemented code.

Partial evaluation is an automatic program specialization technique that from a general program automatically generates an implementation specialized to specific values from the usage context. Partial evaluation and covariant specialization are intuitively similar: the domain of the entity that is being specialized is restricted. Nevertheless, existing work in partial evaluation for object-oriented languages has failed to bridge the gap between inheritance and partial evaluation [1, 8, 15, 30–32]. Moreover, the object-oriented programmer faces a steep learning curve when using partial evaluation, and applying partial evaluation requires the target program to be structured appropriately for specialization.

G. Karsai and E. Visser (Eds.): GPCE 2004, LNCS 3286, pp. 244–265, 2004.

In this paper we present a unification of inheritance and partial evaluation in a novel generative programming language, JUST (Java with Unified Specialization). The key concept in JUST is that conceptual classification using covariant specialization can control automatic specialization of the program. To provide a unified view of inheritance and partial evaluation, JUST relies on concepts found in the object-oriented paradigm, such as covariant specialization, block structure and customization, combined with techniques from partial evaluation.

Contributions. The primary contribution of this paper is a unification of inheritance and partial evaluation, embodied by the generative programming language JUST: From an object-oriented programming point of view, JUST allows the programmer to easily express an efficient implementation without compromising the object-oriented design of the program. From a partial evaluation point of view, JUST represents a novel approach to specialization of object-oriented programs that sidesteps many of the complications otherwise associated with specializing object-oriented programs, and that eliminates the need for separate declarations to control the specialization process. Moreover, we have implemented a JUST-to-Java compiler, and we use this compiler to demonstrate the efficiency of JUST programs.

Organization. The rest of this paper is organized as follows. First, Sect. 2 compares inheritance and partial evaluation. Then, Sect. 3 presents the language JUST and shows several examples of JUST programs, and Sect. 4 describes the compilation of JUST to Java and several experiments. Last, Sect. 5 discusses related work, and Sect. 6 presents our conclusions and future work.

2   Comparing Partial Evaluation and Inheritance

2.1   Partial Evaluation

Partial evaluation is a program transformation technique that optimizes a program fragment with respect to information about a context in which it is used, by generating an implementation dedicated to this usage context. Partial evaluation works by aggressive inter-procedural constant propagation of values of all data types [21]. Partial evaluation thus adapts a program to known (*static*) information about its execution context, as supplied by the programmer. Only the program parts controlled by unknown (*dynamic*) data are reconstructed (residualized). Compared to more standard forms of optimization, partial evaluation can potentially give larger speedups, but only when guided by the programmer.

Partial evaluation of an object-oriented program is based on the specialization of its methods [32]. The optimization performed by partial evaluation includes eliminating virtual dispatches with static receivers, reducing imperative computations over static values, and embedding the values of static (known) fields within the program code. The specialized method thus has a less general

```
class Color {                      class ColorPoint {
 int r, g, b, a;                    int x, y;
 int pixel() {                      Color c;
  return a<<24                      void draw(Paint p) {
   | r<<16 | g<<8 | b;               p.set(x,y,c.pixel());
 }                                  }
}                                  }
```

Fig. 1. Java implementations of Color and ColorPoint.

```
specclass RedDraw {                aspect RedDraw {
 c: RedC;                           private int Color.pixel_0() {
 void draw(Paint b);                 return a<<24 | 11674146;
}                                   }
                                    private void ColorPoint.draw_0(Paint b) {
specclass RedC                       b.set(x,y,c.pixel_0());
specializes Color {                 }
 r==178; g==34; b==34;              ... around advice for ColorPoint.draw
}                                  }
```

(a) declaring specialization   (b) specialized program

Fig. 2. Specializing colors using Pesto and JSpec.

behavior than the unspecialized method, and it accesses only those parts of its parameters (including the this object) that were considered dynamic.

Typically, an object-oriented program uses multiple objects that interact using virtual calls. For this reason, the specialized methods generated for one class often need to call specialized methods defined in other classes. Thus, partial evaluation of an object-oriented program creates new code with dependencies that tend to cross-cut the class hierarchy of the program. This observation brings aspect-oriented programming to mind; aspect-oriented programming allows logical units that cut across the program structure to be separated from other parts of the program and encapsulated into an aspect [22]. The methods generated by a given specialization of an object-oriented program can be encapsulated into a separate aspect, cleanly separating the specialized code from the generic code (the specialized code is woven into the generic program during compilation).

Motivating Example #1: Colors. Consider the classes Color and ColorPoint shown in Fig. 1 (for readability, we use int rather than byte to store color components). If we often need to draw points with the color "firebrickred" (RGB values 178, 34, and 34), it can be worthwhile to specialize the methods of these classes for this usage context. We use the JSpec partial evaluator with the Pesto declarative front-end [2, 32]. The usage context is specified declaratively using the two specialization classes shown in Fig. 2(a). The specialization class RedDraw indicates that the method draw should be specialized for the color described by the specialization class RedC; this specialization class declares the known RGB values (the alpha value is unknown and can still vary). Based on this information, the partial evaluator generates specialized methods encapsulated into an aspect, as shown in Fig. 2(b). The aspect uses an "around" advice on the method `ColorPoint.draw` to invoke the specialized method `draw_0` in the right context, e.g., when the RGB values are 178, 34 and 34.

Partial evaluation for object-oriented languages (as embodied by JSpec with the Pesto front-end) enables the programmer to easily exploit many kinds of specialization opportunities, but nonetheless has some significant limitations. First, the separate (declarative) control language is yet another language for the programmer to learn. Second, relying on aspect-oriented programming to express the residual program is conceptually unsatisfying compared to partial evaluation for functional, logical, and imperative languages where residual programs can be generated in the same language as the source program. Third, the complexity associated with keeping track of side-effects on heap-allocated objects hampers the understandability of the specialization process and makes it difficult for the partial evaluator to support features such as multithreading and reflection. Last, the propagation of specialization invariants follows the control and data flow of the program, which can be obscured by the mix of loops, recursion, and complex heap-allocated data structures often found in realistic programs.

2.2   Inheritance and Covariance

Inheritance is fundamental to most object-oriented languages. From a conceptual point of view, inheritance supports hierarchical classification of entities in the problem domain. Several concepts (classes) can be generalized into one concept (the superclass), and conversely a single concept (a class) can be specialized (subclassed) into a new concept (the subclass). From a technical point of view, inheritance allows the implementation of one class to be derived from another class: the subclass inherits all members of the superclass except those that the class overrides locally. In some languages, inheritance can also covariantly specialize the type of attributes such as fields and method parameters [28]. In the Beta language, where there is a strong focus on conceptual soundness, virtual attributes are used to represent types that can be covariantly specialized in subclasses [26]. Here, covariant specialization is considered essential when modeling domain concepts as inheritance hierarchies.

As a simple example of covariant specialization, consider the class `Vector`:

```
class Vector {
  type T = Object; // covariant type attribute
  T[] elements = new T[10];
  T get(int index) { ... }
  ...
}
```

The type attribute `T` is declared to be `Object`, and in this respect this mechanism is similar to parameterized classes as seen e.g. in GJ [4]. However, when this class is subclassed, the attribute can be specialized covariantly:

```
class ColorVector extends Vector { type T = Color; }
```

The class `ColorVector` can now only contain elements of type `Color` (or any subclass). Conceptually, `ColorVector` is a more specific concept than `Vector` and *should* therefore be a subclass of `Vector`. Covariant specialization is normally associated with either lack of static typing or lack of subclass substitutability [25], but recent work indicates that by imposing restrictions on the use of classes that can be specialized covariantly, this need not be the case [20, 34–36].

2.3   Unifying Inheritance and Partial Evaluation

Partial evaluation specializes a method by constraining the domain of its parameters (including the `this`) from types to partially known values. Partial evaluation can also specialize programs for abstract properties such as types [5, 18]. For an object-oriented program, such specialization would typically generate a covariantly specialized method.

A subclass represents a more specific domain than its superclass. By definition, inheritance always specializes the type of the `this`, but, as noted above, the types of the class members such as fields can also be (covariantly) specialized.

This similarity leads us to investigate whether inheritance and partial evaluation can be unified. Specifically, inheritance could be used to control how the program is specialized using partial evaluation. Partial evaluation could then automatically derive efficient method implementations according to the declaration of each class. However, some partial evaluation scenarios require information about concrete values to be specified, and thus covariant specialization would have to be generalized to allow the programmer to express attributes that are constrained to be equal to a given value. Moreover, mutual dependencies between classes may necessitate that classes be specialized together.

Motivating Example #2: Polygons. Consider the hierarchy of geometric figures shown in Fig. 3. The class `RegularPolygon` is a generic implementation that can draw a regular polygon with any number of edges, any size (represented by radius), and any orientation (angle). The corner points of the polygon are represented using an array of point objects.

From a regular polygon, we wish to derive efficient implementations of the `Square`, `Triangle`, and `Diamond` classes. In the classes `Square` and `Triangle` the

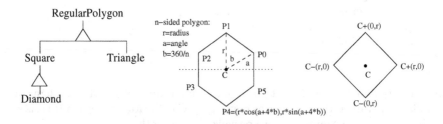

Fig. 3. Efficient implementation of `Diamond` from `RegularPolygon`?

number of points is fixed, and thus the coordinates of the corner points can be directly stored in fields as floating-point values. Instances of the class Diamond are always drawn with a fixed angle, and hence no trigonometric computations are needed. No previous automatic specialization technique that the author is aware of can both specialize the representation (array vs. fields) and the implementation (the use of trigonometric functions) of a class such as RegularPolygon such that it is made efficient in usage contexts that correspond to Square, Triangle, and Diamond (see related work in Sect. 5 for a comparison with existing techniques).

3   JUST

3.1   Overview

The JUST generative programming language unifies inheritance and partial evaluation into a single abstraction. Covariant specialization with singleton types is used to control specialization for both types, primitive values, and partially static objects. Block structure is used to predictably propagate specialization invariants using lexical scoping and furthermore allows a hierarchy of inner classes to be specialized together for common invariants.

Partial evaluation is used to specialize all members of all classes for invariants from type attributes visible in the lexical context, invariants from method calling contexts, and constants embedded inside methods. Covariant specialization allows type attributes to be refined in subclasses and hence allows partial evaluation to incrementally specialize the implementation of each method as new subclasses are added to the program. In effect, conceptual modeling using covariant specialization defines additional invariants that further optimizes the implementation of each class.

One of the primary goals in the design of JUST has been to balance the power of the built-in specialization mechanisms with simplicity of use, in order to make the semantics of the language easy to understand for the programmer. In particular, since partial evaluation for object-oriented languages normally requires expensive and complicated static analyses to determine how the program can be specialized [1, 29, 31, 32], limitations have been imposed on the specialization process. Specifically, specialization is done based on a combination of mutable local variables and immutable object values reified as types. The restriction to immutable object values alleviates the partial evaluator from tracing side-effects on heap-allocated data.

The specialization performed automatically by JUST is highly aggressive, can give a massive increase in code size, and is not guaranteed to terminate[1]. Thus, the programmer must understand the principles of automatic program specialization (just like programmers must have a basic understanding of types to

---

[1] As is common in partial evaluation, there is no limit on the amount of resources that can be used to optimize the program; imposing a limit would in some cases result in overly conservative behavior.

```
class Draw {
 class Color {
  type RT, GT, BT, AT = int;
  RT r; GT g; BT b; AT a;
  int pixel() {
   return a<<24|r<<16|g<<8|b;
  }
 }

 class ColorPoint {
  type ColorT = Color;
  ColorT c;
  int x, y;
  void draw(Paint b) {
   b.set(x,y,c.pixel());
  }
 }
}

class RedDraw extends Draw {
 class Red extends Color {
  type RT=178, GT=34, BT=34;
 }

 class RedPoint extends ColorPoint {
  type ColorT = @Red;
 }
}
```

```
class RedDraw extends Draw {
 class Color { ... }
 class ColorPoint { ... }

 class Red extends Color {
  type RT=178, GT=34, BT=34, AT=int;
  AT a;
  int pixel() {
   return a << 24 | 11674146;
  }
 }

 class RedPoint extends ColorPoint {
  type ColorT = @Red;
  ColorT c;
  int x, y;
  void draw(Paint b) {
   b.set(x,y,c.Red::pixel());
  }
 }
}
```

(a) programmer-written code   (b) compiler-generated code

Fig. 4. Specialized color example, in JUST.

use generics). For example, to avoid generating inefficient code, the programmer has to control the amount of specialization performed by the compiler, through the use of covariant type declarations. For this reason, JUST is only appropriate for implementing performance-critical parts of programs.

3.2   Basic Example

We now revisit the color and colored point example of the previous section. The classes Color and ColorPoint are nested within the top-level class Draw, as shown in Fig. 4(a). In JUST, nested classes can be specialized together for a common set of invariants by subclassing their enclosing class.

In the class Color, the type attributes RT, GT, BT, and AT are used to constrain the types of the fields that hold the RGB and alpha values. In JUST, the implementation of any method that refers to values qualified by type attributes can be specialized by covariantly specializing these type attributes. Indeed, the fields r, g, b, and a are all declared using type attributes. Similarly, in the class ColorPoint the reference to the Color object is qualified by a type attribute.

An implementation that draws "firebrickred" points can be declared by covariantly specializing the type attributes, as shown in the class RedDraw. Here, the types of the fields that hold the RGB values are specialized to concrete integers, and the type of the field that references a color is specialized to a "firebrickred" color (the syntax "@T" means an exact reference to an instance of the class T, i.e., subclasses of T are not allowed). The intermediate result of compiling RedDraw is shown in Fig. 4(b). For each class, the members of the superclass are inherited and specialized. Fields that have constant values are no longer needed, and are eliminated. A direct call is generated to the specialized pixel method from within the draw method (using the "class::name" syntax, which indicates a statically bound, non-virtual call).

The JUST compiler works by first performing a source-to-source specialization, exactly as was illustrated in this example, and then compiling the specialized source code to Java. This approach allows the programmer to easily verify the quality of the specialization performed by the compiler.

3.3 Syntax

The syntax of JUST is a fairly minimal Java subset extended to support unified specialization. A JUST program consists of block-structured classes with fields and methods. Methods can use basic statements such as assignment, conditionals, and while-loops. For simplicity, JUST currently omits many elements of the Java language, such as constructors, try/catch, interfaces, switch statements etc. Some of these elements have already been explored in the context of partial evaluation and would be trivial to implement (e.g., constructors and switch statements), whereas others remain unexplored and would require new techniques to be developed (e.g., try/catch).

JUST extends Java with type members which are used to specify types that can be covariantly specialized by subclasses. A *type member* is declared as a class member using the syntax "type NAME=EXP;" which assigns the value of EXP to the type named NAME. The expression EXP can refer to type members and classes from the lexical scope. If NAME was defined in a superclass, the type is covariantly specialized: the value of EXP must be a subtype of the value denoted by NAME in the superclass. Syntactic elements used to denote types can be manipulated as values, e.g., "type x=int;" is valid syntax; similarly the Java expression "C.class" is simply written "C" in JUST. The intermediate source programs produced by the JUST compiler use an extended syntax where values are substituted for uses of type members everywhere in the program; this syntax is not currently supported in the input language.

JUST also introduces three new operators, @, ::, and lift. The operators @ and :: have already been described in the context of the colors example. The operator lift converts its argument to a dynamic value (in the sense of partial evaluation), which inhibits aggressive operations over the value (see the description of semantics in Sect. 3.5 for details).

$$C <: C \qquad \frac{C <: D \quad D <: E}{C <: E} \qquad \frac{\text{class } C \text{ extends } D \ \{\ldots\}}{C <: D}$$

$$\frac{\text{class } C \text{ extends } D \ \{\ldots\}}{C.E <: D.E} \qquad 1, 2, 3, \ldots <: \text{ int} \text{ , similarly for boolean, float etc.}$$

$$\text{new } C(\ldots) <: C \qquad \frac{\forall f_i \in C : v_i \ <: \ v'_i}{\text{new } C(\ldots, f_i = v_i, \ldots) <: \text{new } C(\ldots, f_i = v'_i, \ldots)}$$

$$\text{new } C[n] = \{\ldots\} <: C[] \qquad \frac{n = n' \wedge \forall i \in 0 \ldots n - 1 : v_i \ <: \ v'_i}{\text{new } C[n] = \{\ldots, v_i, \ldots\} <: \text{new } C[n'] = \{\ldots, v'_i, \ldots\}}$$

Fig. 5. JUST subtyping rules.

3.4   Types

In JUST, classes and methods can be overridden by a subclass, and type attributes can be specialized covariantly by a subclass. Although the specialization process propagates information from type declarations, JUST does not currently have a type system and thus the covariant declarations are not checked. The intention is that the type rules should be based on those found in the Beta family of languages [14, 26]. These languages provide static typing in the presence of covariant specialization using type attributes, and have block structure similar to although not identical to JUST. Covariant specialization of fields and parameters is known to complicate type checking, and features such as singleton types implies that a type system would be undecidable unless restrictions were imposed on the language; we return to these issues Sect. 6.

The subtype relation used in JUST is shown in Fig. 5. Briefly, subclasses are subtypes (nominal subtyping), the subtyping relationship of inner classes follows the subclassing relationship of their enclosing classes, and primitive values are subtypes of their type (which, as in Java, is *not* a subtype of Object). Object instances are subtypes of their class, and an object instance is a subtype of another instance of the same class if the values of each of their fields are subtypes (structural subtyping). Subtyping for arrays works in a similar fashion.

3.5   Semantics

Evaluation of JUST programs takes place both at compile-time and at run-time, so there are two parts to the semantics: the compile-time (specialization) semantics and the run-time semantics. We use partial evaluation terminology to describe the semantics of JUST. We say that an expression which during compilation evaluates to a concrete value (an object, array, or a primitive value such as an integer or a boolean) has a *static type*. Conversely, an expression which during compilation evaluates to a class or a type that describes primitive data (e.g., the type int) has a *dynamic type*.

A critical property of JUST is that types help control side-effects both at compile-time and at run-time. Specifically, when a field has a static type, its value

1. *Propagate types and members.*
   (a) All `type` members in the program are evaluated and transformed into immutable values.
   (b) All uses of type members are resolved, and all classes and all superclass fields not overwritten locally are copied down.
2. *Inline objects and arrays.*
   (a) For each class, each field with a static type of an array instance is replaced by fields that represent the contents of the array.
   (b) Similarly, each field with a static type of an object instance is replaced by fields that represent the contents of the object. The methods of the object are inlined into the class under fresh names.
   (c) The process is applied recursively to the fields that are generated at each step.
3. *Specialize methods and remove static fields.*
   (a) For each class, copy down those methods of the superclass that are not overwritten locally.
   (b) For each method, specialize the statement that it contains based on the types of its parameters, any types from the lexical context, and any constants contained within the method. Imperative statements are specialized using standard techniques. A method invocation with a known receiver is transformed into a direct invocation of the receiver method specialized for its arguments. Access to fields with static types is removed, access to the subcomponents of arrays or objects that have been inlined is replaced with direct access to the corresponding field.
   (c) Any field qualified by a static type is removed.

Fig. 6. Compile-time semantics of JUST.

is determined by the type: assignment to the field is not allowed, and the value read from the field is given by the type. Conversely, when a field has a dynamic type, assignments to and reads from the field can simply be residualized by the specialization process. For this reason, side effects on fields are not relevant to the specializer, and an alias analysis is not needed (unlike standard approaches to program specialization for imperative languages [3, 21, 32]).

We do not explicitly define a run-time semantics, but rather refer to the compilation of JUST into Java described in Sect. 4. Basically, a JUST program written without the use of type members and with `lift` operators around all embedded constants evaluates almost exactly like the equivalent Java program (which would be obtained simply by removing all uses of the `lift` operator). The difference is that in JUST methods and inner classes are customized (based on dynamic types) for each class, so calls to the reflection API might return different results in JUST and Java.

The compile-time semantics of JUST are summarized in Fig. 6. The first step is to propagate types and members. For each class, the expression associated with each type member is evaluated. Such expressions can only refer to lexically visible type members and classes, but can contain arbitrary computations that are evaluated using standard execution semantics. Side-effects are allowed on objects when evaluating these expressions, but are always local to the expression since it can only refer to classes and types from the lexical context. After evaluating the type expression, the compiler can simply inspect the computed value and the local heap that it resides in. The resulting value is converted into a type value through a recursive process that extracts objects and arrays from the heap and converts them into values, in effect converting the value into an immutable tree structure later used as a template for recreating copies of the data. For example, the type declaration

```
type L = (new Line()).setEndPoints(new Point(),new Point());
```

causes the type L to be bound to an immutable representation of a Line object with two specific Point objects as its endpoints:

```
type L = Line(Point(*,*),Point(*,*));
```

(Note that the coordinates of the Point objects are unspecified, and hence appear as dynamic in the value, denoted "*".) Tree structures are usually sufficient for representing the invariants needed for partial evaluation [2], but have the disadvantage that cyclic data and aliasing cannot be represented. Cyclic data causes a compile-time error, whereas aliased objects are duplicated (e.g., DAGs are converted into trees by duplicating shared nodes); since the object structures represented by type expressions in practice often are quite simple, this has so far not been a problem. As a last step, after all type members have been resolved, all classes and fields not overridden are copied down.

The second step is to inline objects and arrays with static types into the class in which they are used as qualifiers on fields. (Allowing inlining of objects into methods is considered future work). A field that is qualified by an object or array static template value is transformed by replacing it with the dynamic parts of the object or array value. For example, given the declaration of the type L from the previous paragraph and the declaration "L lin1, lin2;" a number of new fields are introduced at the same program point:

```
int lin1$p1_x, lin1$p1_y, lin2$p2_x, lin2$p2_y;
```

(assuming that the class Point contains two fields, x and y). Any methods from the objects are also introduced as new members, e.g.

```
int lin1$p1_getX() { return #(C,lin1$p1).x; }
```

where #(C,lin1_p1) is a placeholder object value manipulated during specialization and eliminated during the last compilation step. Arrays are transformed similarly, with each field being numbered according to its index.

The last step is to specialize methods and remove fields bound to static values (such fields will not be referred to from the specialized program). The methods of the superclass, which have already been specialized for any types in the superclass, are copied down. Delaying method copy-down until this point makes specialization incremental. The body of each method is specialized in an environment defined by the types of its lexical context and its formal parameters.

Constants embedded within the method are also considered static for special-ization (the unary operator `lift` can be used by the programmer to convert any static value into a dynamic value, thus limiting the amount of specialization). As described earlier, at this level side effects to fields are always residualized, so only local variables are modified during specialization.

The specialization of imperative computations is standard (loops are un-rolled, conditionals reduced, constants are propagated aggressively, etc.). The specialization of constructs that manipulate objects is as follows. A method in-vocation with a known receiver is specialized by generating a direct call to a specialized version of this method; the specialized method is generated based on the bindings of its formal parameters. A method cache indexed by the concrete types of the formal parameters is used to allow reuse of specialized methods (and enable specialization of recursive methods), as is common in partial evaluation. A method invocation with an unknown receiver is simply residualized (it can be ignored since it cannot have side-effects that affect the specialization process). Field access to dynamic objects is residualized, and field access to static objects is transformed based on the placeholder object value. For example, the method `lin1$p1_getX()` above becomes:

```
int lin1$p1_getX() { return C.this.lin1$p1_x; }
```

This transformation is not legal if the placeholder object value escapes the scope in which the field to which it refers is defined. In this case, a compile-time error is generated. Similarly, a compile-time error is generated if references to a static object are residualized in the program. We observe that since static objects only exist at compile-time, an object identity comparison between a static object and a dynamic object always evaluates to false and hence can be reduced by the compiler. Handling compile-time errors induced by the specialization process is obviously non-trivial for the programmer, and JUST offers no improvement over standard partial evaluation techniques in this sense; we envision that a specialization-time debugger integrated into the compiler can help the program-mer understand the source of the error, but such a tool is future work.

Regarding the amount of specialization performed by the JUST compiler, we note that JUST is sufficiently powerful for specializing interpreters. In fact, interpreter specialization can be performed in at least two different ways. First, consider a bytecode interpreter written as a recursive method parameterized by the program counter [33]. Given that the program counter is static, a specialized method can be generated for each value of the program counter, which allows the interpreter to be specialized. Second, consider an interpreter for a structured lan-guage implemented with a separate class for each syntactic construct [2]. Given that the program is static, object inlining reduces the entire object structure to a set of mutually recursive methods (one for each AST node) that call each other in a fixed manner. In both cases, the interpretive overhead is eliminated.

3.6   Example Resolved: Regular Polygons

Regular polygons were introduced as a motivating example in Sect. 2.3. Using JUST, an efficient implementation of the `Diamond` class can be derived from the

```
class Polygon extends Object {
 type CornersT = Point[];
 CornersT corners;
 type AngleT = int;
 AngleT a;
 ...
 void fix() {
  int c=corners.length;
  int s=360/ncorn;
  int j=0, dx, dy;
  while(j<c) {
   dx=Math.cos(a+(j*s))*radius;
   dy=Math.sin(a+(j*s))*radius;
   corners[j].setX(center.x+dx);
   corners[j].setY(center.y+dy);
   j=j+1;
  }
 }
}

class Square extends Polygon {
 type CornersT = new Point[] {
  new Point(), new Point(),
  new Point(), new Point() };
}

class Diamond extends Square {
 type AngleT = 0;
}
```

(a) programmer-written code

```
class Diamond extends Square {
 int corners$0_x;
 int corners$0_y;
 // more pairs of inlined fields
 ...
 void fix() {
  int dx, dy;
  dx=radius;
  corners$0_Point_setX(center.x+dx);
  corners$0_Point_setY(center.y);
  dy=radius;
  corners$1_Point_setX(center.x)
  corners$1_Point_setY(center.y+dy);
  ...
  // more unrolled loop bodies
  ...
 }

 void corners$0_Point_setX(int i) {
  corners$0_x=i;
 }

 void corners$0_Point_setY(int i) {
  corners$0_y=i;
 }
 // more pairs of inlined methods
 ...
}
```

(b) compiler-generated code for Diamond

Fig. 7. The regular polygons example resolved, using JUST.

Polygon class. The method fix shown in Fig. 7(a) fixes the points of the regular polygon, based on the number of points, the orientation (angle), and the radius. The class Square specifies that the array of points has length four and contains concrete point instances. The class Diamond further specifies that the orientation is zero degrees. Based on these declarations, the compiler generates the specialized implementation of the fix method shown in Fig. 7(b). All coordinates are stored in local fields, and the use of trigonometric functions has been eliminated. As described in Sect. 4, in our experiments the optimized implementation is from 12 to 21 times faster than the generic implementation.

3.7   Large Example: Linear Algebra

The OoLaLa linear algebra library has been designed according to an object-oriented analysis of numerical linear algebra [24]. Compared to traditional linear algebra libraries, OoLaLa is a highly generic, yet simple and streamlined, im-

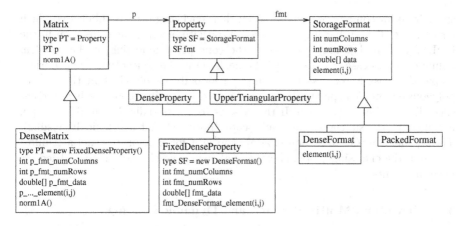

Fig. 8. Efficient implementation of matrices in OoLaLa.

plementation. However, as the designers point out, the genericness comes at a cost in terms of performance.

In the OoLaLa library, matrices are classified by their mathematical properties, for example dense or sparse upper-triangular. A matrix is represented using three objects from different class hierarchies, as illustrated in Fig. 8. The class `Matrix` acts as an interface for manipulating matrices, by delegating all behavior specific to mathematical properties to an aggregate object of class `Property`. Subclasses of the abstract class `Property` define, for example, how iterators traverse matrix elements (e.g., by skipping zero elements in sparse matrices). The `Property` classes delegate the representation of the matrix contents to an object of class `StorageFormat`. The concrete subclasses of the abstract class `StorageFormat` all store the matrix elements in a one-dimensional array, and define a mapping from ordinary matrix coordinates to an index in this array. This decoupling of a single matrix into three objects from separate class hierarchies is a use of the bridge design pattern [16].

To optimize for the case where matrices are dense, we define the classes `FixedDenseProperty` and `DenseMatrix`. In `FixedDenseProperty` the storage format is a `DenseFormat` instance which is inlined into the class definition. Similarly, in `DenseMatrix`, the property is a `FixedDenseProperty` instance which is inlined into the class definition. In the resulting implementation of `DenseMatrix`, all data is available locally in the object, and all virtual method calls can be replaced with direct procedure calls. Any standard use of the bridge design pattern can be specialized in this way. As described in Sect. 4, in our experiments the optimized implementation is from 2 to 5 times faster than the generic implementation.

3.8 Modularity

JUST requires that classes which need to be specialized together must also be declared together as inner classes. Declaring classes together allows them to be specialized for common invariants when their enclosing class is subclassed. Such structuring of the program, although appropriate in some cases (as seen in the OOLALA example), may go against the conceptual modeling of the problem domain. In this case, a class *should* be declared in the conceptually appropriate scope; the class Point was for example a globally visible class in the regular polygons example. Type attributes can be used to specify "hooks" where further specialization can take place. If the class is to be specialized in a given scope, it can simply be subclassed into this scope (provided that it is lexically visible). The type attributes can be bound as appropriate, for example to other attributes visible in the enclosing scope, effectively allowing the class to be specialized for local invariants.

3.9   Reflection, Multithreading, and Dynamic Loading

Reflection allows the program to dynamically decide what methods to call or fields to operate on, based on data computed while the program is running, Partial evaluation can be used to reify reflective operations as efficient, direct operations, as demonstrated for Java by Braux and Noyé, semi-automatically using a generating extension [5]. However, the dynamic nature of reflection and its ability to cause unpredictable control flow and side-effects make static analysis of such programs very difficult, and no partial evaluators that the author is aware of can specialize both (imperative) program operations and reflective operations together. Nonetheless, JUST specialization is based on immutable data, and control flow is determined on-line during specialization, for which reason reflection *can* be specialized in JUST, essentially using the rules proposed by Braux and Noyé. In principle, any Java-style reflective operation based on static values can be reified into equivalent non-reflective operations. Currently, JUST only supports reifying Java-style operations for reading and writing the values of fields; completely supporting the full Java reflection API requires addressing numerous technical issues which are out of the scope of this paper.

Multithreading is used pervasively in modern applications, but is a problem for traditional partial evaluators, since side-effects between threads can cause unpredictable modifications of the store that cannot be performed in advance at compile time. However, since JUST specialization is based on immutable heap data (side-effects to local variables are thread-local since JUST uses Java's thread model), each thread implementation can be specialized individually based on the invariants declared in its lexical context. In addition to specializing individual threads, JUST can specialize the interaction between multiple threads, since invariants specified using covariant type declarations can be safely propagated between threads.

Dynamic class loading poses a problem for traditional partial evaluators, since they essentially rely on a whole-program assumption in order to track side-effects. Some partial evaluators only target a program slice, and require the user to specify the behavior of the code outside the program slice, including any code that could be dynamically loaded [9, 32]. Nonetheless, since JUST specialization is based on immutable data and furthermore is local to each class, dynamic class loading does not invalidate the specialization performed by the JUST compiler, and can be performed safely in specialized programs.

4   Compiling JUST to Java

4.1   Compilation Process

JUST has been designed to aggressively and unconditionally optimize the code provided by the programmer to generate a specialized implementation of each class. While specialization can be useful when applied to performance-critical parts of programs, applying specialization globally would normally result in either non-termination or code explosion. For this reason, it must be possible to only apply specialization to selected parts of the program, a feature normally referred to as modular specialization [9]. Since JUST programs are compiled to Java, the performance-critical parts of a program can be written in JUST, and the other parts of the program in Java.

The translation from JUST to Java source code works as follows. In a specialized JUST program, all class members have been customized and cloned in every class. This code duplication simplifies the JUST to Java compilation process, since inheritance between classes can be substituted for interface inheritance. Each JUST class compiles to a Java class that by default inherits from `java.lang.Object` (a thread class would inherit from `java.lang.Thread`). All methods are made `public`, and all fields have package visibility. Every JUST class implements a Java interface that has the same methods as the JUST class. This interface extends the interface generated for the JUST superclass. If the JUST class overrides a class from the superclass of the enclosing class, the interface also extends the interface of this class. Type attributes are not needed in the Java program, and are ignored by the JUST to Java compiler. Fields are compiled directly to Java fields: since there is no Java inheritance between the generated classes, fields are declared anew in each class, and can thus be covariantly specialized. Methods require special care since covariant specialization of the formal parameters and return type is not possible in Java. For this reason, the most general type (the one found highest in the hierarchy of Java interfaces) is used; downwards casts are inserted where needed for parameters and the return value. Most statements and expressions translate straightforwardly to equivalent Java counterparts. Direct method calls are represented using a class cast to the type in question (this is needed since the callee method might not be visible in the declared interface of the receiver object).

Inlining is not performed by the JUST to Java compiler, since most Java virtual machines perform aggressive inlining dynamically, adapted to the characteristics of the physical machine that the program runs on. To facilitate inlining, methods that are not overridden are declared `final` by the compiler. Nonetheless, performing inlining in the compiler would probably be advantageous in some cases.

Table 1. Benchmark programs and how they are specialized (†: micro-benchmarks).

Benchmark	Specialization target	Primary effect of specialization
Polygons	calls to `fix`	trigonometric operation elimnation, object inlining
OoLaLa	`norm1A` operation[3]	object inlining, decision removal
Reflect†	reflective field access	reification of reflection as normal operations
Multi†	access to shared data	shared data inlining, synchronization elimination
Visitor	visitor traversal tree	inlining of visitor into binary tree [32]

4.2 Experiments

To test the performance of programs written in JUST, we have compared the examples presented in Sect. 3, a program based on the visitor design pattern, and microbenchmarks where reflection and access to thread-shared data can be eliminated, to equivalent programs implemented from scratch in Java. These benchmark programs are summarized in Table 1 (note that two of the benchmarks are microbenchmarks)[2]. The Java programs are run both in their unmodified form and (where possible) after specialization with the JSpec partial evaluator for Java [32]. The unspecialized versions of the JUST classes have performance roughly equivalent to the unspecialized Java programs, and are not included in the experiments.

The experiments are performed on an x86 and a SPARC. The x86 is running Linux 2.4 and has a single 1.3GHz AMD Athlon processor and 512Mb of RAM. The SPARC is a Sun Enterprise 450 running Solaris 2.8, with four 400MHz Ultra-SPARC processors and 4Gb of RAM. Compilation from Java source to Java bytecode is done using Sun's JDK 1.4 `javac` compiler. All programs are run on x86 using IBM's JDK 1.3.1 JIT compiler and on SPARC using Sun's JDK 1.4.0 HotSpot compiler in "server" compilation mode. Each benchmark program performs ten iterations of the benchmark routine, and discards the first five iterations to allow adaptive compilers to optimize the program. All execution times are reported as wall-clock time measured in milliseconds.

The benchmark results are shown in Table 2. As can be seen, the performance of JSpec-specialized Java programs and JUST programs exceed that of the original Java programs (the micro-benchmarks could not be specialized using JSpec since it does not support reflection and multi-threading). The microbenchmarks for reflection and multithreading show extreme speedups that are *not* representative of the kinds of speedups that can be expected on realistic programs, but nonetheless serve to illustrate the relevance of specializing such operations. A

---

[2] We do not use standard benchmarks, because programs from standard benchmark suites (e.g., SpecJVM98) usually either contain no opportunities for specialization or are structured in a way that is incompatible with specialization.

[3] Compared to the example of Sect. 3, the OoLaLa library is also specialized for a specific mode of iteration. Note that all versions of the OoLaLa library used in these experiments were (re)implemented faithfully by the author based on information from Luján's MS [23], since the implementation described by Luján et. al. [24] is not publicly available.

Table 2. Benchmark results (times are reported in seconds, †: micro-benchmark).

	Results for x86						Results for SPARC					
	Java			Speedups			Java			Speedups		
	Gen.	JSpec	JUST	G/JS	JS/JU	G/JU	Gen.	JSpec	JUST	G/JS	JS/JU	G/JU
Polygons	9.40	0.78	0.78	12.01	1.00	12.01	59.28	2.77	1.85	21.40	1.50	32.04
OoLaLa	6.22	2.81	1.17	2.21	2.40	5.32	47.84	21.23	11.76	2.30	1.81	4.01
Reflect†	49.77		0.14			355.5	97.70		0.481			203.12
Multi†	9.17		0.30			30.56	18.30		0.08			228.75
Visitor	2.15	1.32	1.32	1.63	1.00	1.63	14.11	4.14	4.14	3.40	1.00	3.40

thorough investigation of the issues related to specializing programs based on multithreading and reflection are out of the scope of this paper. For the real programs, the most significant speedups (12 times and 32 times) are observed for the Polygons benchmark, where the use of trigonometric computations is eliminated. Furthermore, in the Polygons benchmark on SPARC and in the OoLaLa benchmark on both architectures, JUST provides a significant speedup over the JSpec-specialized programs (from 1.5 to 2.4 times). Last, we note that for the visit example JUST generates almost exactly the same Java code as the specialized code output by JSpec, and therefore offers no additional advantage.

5   Related Work

JUST is directly inspired by programming languages that support covariant specialization [14, 20, 26–28, 34]. Like these languages, JUST allows the types of fields and method parameters to be covariantly specialized. But unlike these more standard programming languages, covariant specialization can be done to specific values, which allows more precise specifications to be declared, similar to Cardelli's power type [6]. An obvious limitation of JUST compared to these other languages is the lack of a type system (see future work). Unification of inheritance and partial evaluation is also seen in the language Ohmu, where function invocation, subclassing, object instantiation, and aspect weaving all are captured by a single mechanism, the structure transformation, which is based on partial evaluation techniques [19]. Compared to JUST, manual meta-programming is however often needed to achieve specialization effects. Moreover, Ohmu has only been implemented as a source-to-source transformation system.

C++ templates can be used as a generative programming language: by combining template parameters and C++ const constant declarations, arbitrary computations over primitive values can be performed at compile time [10, 37]. Although the declaration of how to specialize is effectively integrated with the program in the form of template declarations, this approach is more limited in its treatment of objects than what we have proposed. For example, objects cannot be dynamically allocated and manipulated. Furthermore, the program must be written in a two-level syntax, thus implying that static and dynamic code must be separated manually, and functionality must be implemented twice if both generic and specialized behaviors are needed.

JUST only specializes for immutable object values, similarly to partial evaluation for functional languages, where there is no need to keep track of side-effects on heap-allocated data [21]. The object and array inlining performed by JUST is similar to arity raising for functional languages and structure splitting in C-Mix [3, 21]. However, in both cases, complex data is replaced with local variables, which is only appropriate for stack allocated data (global variables can also be used for structure splitting, but are inappropriate for storing information associated with individual object instances). Partial evaluation for object-oriented languages as embodied by JSpec was described in Sect. 2; its technical and conceptual limitations was a primary motivation for this work. We note that the control-flow simplifications performed by JSpec are a superset of those found in JUST, but JSpec does not perform any simplifications of the data representation, which limits the degree of optimization. Most other approaches to partial evaluation for object-oriented languages typically residualize specialized programs by unfolding all method calls into a single method, and hence do not address issues related to inheritance in the residual program, although object splitting and caching of statically allocated objects has been investigated [1, 8, 15].

Type specialization is an alternative approach to partial evaluation based on type inference, where a functional program can be specialized for the type of the data that it manipulates [13, 18]. Similarly to JUST, singleton types are used to specialize for concrete values; both the implementation of functions, their types, and the datatypes that they manipulate are specialized. To some extent, JUST can be considered as type specialization for the object-oriented paradigm. Nonetheless, JUST automatically infers the binding time of each operation, whereas type specialization requires the programmer to manually control specialization of the entire program using binding-time annotations.

The triggering of optimization in JUST and the propagation of type information is similar to *customization* [7] and its generalization *selective argument specialization* [12]. Here, a method is optimized based on profile information by propagating type information about the `this` argument and the formal parameters throughout the method, and using this type information to reduce virtual dispatches. JUST is more aggressive than selective argument specialization, since it specializes both for type information and concrete values and also specializes the data representation, but it has no similar automatic provisions for detecting invariants and limiting the amount of specialization.

6   Conclusion and Future Work

In this paper, we have presented JUST, a language that unifies inheritance and partial evaluation. By using covariant type declarations, the programmer can be guaranteed an efficient implementation of highly generic program parts, where both computations and data representation are optimized to the task at hand. Ideally, the covariant declarations that one would normally perform when programming would automatically result in an efficient implementation; this idea remains to be tested in large-scale experiments, however.

JUST offers a new perspective on inheritance: covariant specialization can be used to declare information that gives a more precise description of the intention of a given subclass and at the same time automatically triggers the generation of an efficient implementation of this class. Conversely, JUST also offers a new perspective on partial evaluation for object-oriented languages: integration with the inheritance structure opens new opportunities for specialization, which can be exploited using simple and predictable techniques. In effect, we have unified two concepts until now considered different in a novel and useful way.

In terms of future work, we are interested in developing a type system for JUST. Covariant singleton types for e.g. method parameters are inferred by the specialization process, so type checking must either include the complete specialization process (and hence risk non-termination) or perform an approximation. A useful compromise which we are currently investigating is to allow the type checker to consume a fixed number of resources. If type checking cannot be done within the predetermined limit, the program is considered "unsafe," and the programmer can then either accept the program as such, or increase the resource limit. Alternatively, multimethods may be more appropriate for safely implementing the use of covariant types found in JUST. Another issue is controlling the degree of specialization performed by the partial evaluator. We believe it would be useful to separate the declaration of *how* to specialize (that is, the covariant type declarations in JUST) from *what* to specialize. Different scenarios may require exploiting different invariants for optimal performance, for example depending on the physical characteristics of the processor. To this end, we are currently investigating the use of aspect-oriented programming to allow the programmer to explicitly declare what program parts to specialize.

References

1. R. Affeldt, H. Masuhara, E. Sumii, and A. Yonezawa. Supporting objects in runtime bytecode specialization. In *Proceedings of the ASIAN symposium on Partial evaluation and semantics-based program manipulation*, pages 50–60. ACM Press, 2002.
2. H.M. Andersen and U.P. Schultz. Declarative specialization for object-oriented-program specialization. In *ACM SIGPLAN Symposium on Partial Evaluation and Semantics-Based Program Manipulation (PEPM'04)*. ACM Press, 2004. To appear.
3. L.O. Andersen. *Program Analysis and Specialization for the C Programming Language*. PhD thesis, Computer Science Department, University of Copenhagen, May 1994. DIKU Technical Report 94/19.
4. G. Bracha, M. Odersky, D. Stoutamire, and P. Wadler. Making the future safe for the past: adding genericity to the java programming language. In *Proceedings of the 13th ACM SIGPLAN conference on Object-oriented programming, systems, languages, and applications*, pages 183–200. ACM Press, 1998.
5. M. Braux and J. Noyé. Towards partially evaluating reflection in Java. In *ACM SIGPLAN Workshop on Partial Evaluation and Semantics-Based Program Manipulation (PEPM'00)*, Boston, MA, USA, January 2000. ACM Press.
6. Luca Cardelli. Structural subtyping and the notion of power type. In *Conference Record of the Fifteenth Annual ACM Symposium on Principles of Programming Languages, San Diego*, pages 70–79, San Diego, California, 1988.

7. C. Chambers and D. Ungar. Customization: Optimizing compiler technology for SELF, A dynamically-typed object-oriented programming language. In Bruce Knobe, editor, *Proceedings of the SIGPLAN '89 Conference on Programming Language Design and Implementation (PLDI '89)*, pages 146–160, Portland, OR, USA, June 1989. ACM Press.

8. A.M. Chepovsky, A.V. Klimov, A.V. Klimov, Y.A. Klimov, A.S. Mishchenko, S.A. Romanenko, and S.Y. Skorobogatov. Partial evaluation for common intermediate language. In *Perspectives of System Informatics*, volume 2890 of *Lecture Notes in Computer Science*, pages 171–177, 2003.

9. C. Consel, L. Hornof, F. Noël, J. Noyé, and E.N. Volanschi. A uniform approach for compile-time and run-time specialization. In Danvy et al. [11], pages 54–72.

10. K. Czarnecki and U.W. Eisenecker. *Generative Programming: Methods, Tools, and Applications*. Addison-Wesley, 2000.

11. O. Danvy, R. Glück, and P. Thiemann, editors. *Partial Evaluation, International Seminar, Dagstuhl Castle*, number 1110 in Lecture Notes in Computer Science, Dagstuhl Castle, Germany, February 1996. Springer-Verlag.

12. J. Dean, C. Chambers, and D. Grove. Selective specialization for object-oriented languages. In *Proceedings of the ACM SIGPLAN '95 Conference on Programming Language Design and Implementation (PLDI'95)*, pages 93–102, La Jolla, CA USA, June 1995. ACM SIGPLAN Notices, 30(6).

13. D. Dussart, J. Hughes, and P. Thiemann. Type specialisation for imperative languages. In *Proceedings of the second ACM SIGPLAN international conference on Functional programming*, pages 204–216. ACM Press, 1997.

14. Erik Ernst. Propagating class and method combination. In Guerraoui [17], pages 67–91.

15. N. Fujinami. Determination of dynamic method dispatches using run-time code generation. In X. Leroy and A. Ohori, editors, *Proceedings of the Second International Workshop on Types in Compilation (TIC'98)*, volume 1473 of *Lecture Notes in Computer Science*, pages 253–271, Kyoto, Japan, March 1998. Springer-Verlag.

16. E. Gamma, R. Helm, R. Johnson, and J. Vlissides. *Design Patterns: Elements of Reusable Object-Oriented Software*. Addison-Wesley, 1994.

17. R. Guerraoui, editor. *Proceedings of the European Conference on Object-oriented Programming (ECOOP'99)*, volume 1628 of *Lecture Notes in Computer Science*, Lisbon, Portugal, June 1999. Springer-Verlag.

18. J. Hughes. Type specialisation for the λ-calculus or a new paradigm for partial evaluation based on type inference. In Danvy et al. [11], pages 183–215.

19. DeLesley Hutchins. The power of symmetry: unifying inheritance and generative programming. In *Companion of the 18th annual ACM SIGPLAN conference on Object-oriented programming, systems, languages, and applications*, pages 38–52. ACM Press, 2003.

20. A. Igarashi and M. Viroli. On variance-based subtyping for parametric types. In *Proceedings of the European Conference on Object-oriented Programming (ECOOP'02)*, Lecture Notes in Computer Science, pages 441–469, Malaga, Spain, June 2002. Springer-Verlag.

21. N.D. Jones, C. Gomard, and P. Sestoft. *Partial Evaluation and Automatic Program Generation*. International Series in Computer Science. Prentice-Hall, June 1993.

22. G. Kiczales, J. Lamping, A. Mendhekar, C. Maeda, C. Lopes, J. Loingtier, and J. Irwin. Aspect-oriented programming. In M. Aksit and S. Matsuoka, editors, *Proceedings of the European Conference on Object-oriented Programming (ECOOP'97)*, volume 1241 of *Lecture Notes in Computer Science*, pages 220–242, Jyväskylä, Finland, June 1997. Springer.

23. M. Luján. Object oriented linear algebra. Master's thesis, University of Manchester, December 1999.
24. M. Luján, T.L. Freeman, and J.R. Gurd. OoLaLa: an object oriented analysis and design of numerical linear algebra. In M.B. Rosson and D. Lea, editors, *OOPSLA'00 Conference Proceedings*, ACM SIGPLAN Notices, pages 229–252, Minneapolis, MN USA, October 2000. ACM Press, ACM Press.
25. O.L Madsen. Open issues in object-oriented programming – a scandinavian perspective. *SOFTWARE. Practice and Experience*, 25(4), December 1995.
26. O.L. Madsen, B. Møller-Pedersen, and K. Nygaard. *Object-oriented programming in the Beta programming language*. Addison-Wesley, Reading, MA, USA, 1993.
27. O.L. Madsen and B.M. Pedersen. Virtual classes: a powerful mechanism in object-oriented programming. In *Conference proceedings on Object-oriented programming systems, languages and applications (OOPSLA'89)*, volume 24(10) of *SIGPLAN Notices*, pages 397–406, New Orleans, Louisiana, United States, 1989. ACM Press.
28. B. Meyer. *Eiffel: The language*. Object-Oriented Series. Prentice Hall, New York, NY, 1992.
29. U.P. Schultz. *Object-Oriented Software Engineering Using Partial Evaluation*. PhD thesis, University of Rennes I, Rennes, France, December 2000.
30. U.P. Schultz. Partial evaluation for class-based object-oriented languages. In O. Danvy and A. Filinski, editors, *Symposium on Programs as Data Objects II*, volume 2053 of *Lecture Notes in Computer Science*, pages 173–197, Aarhus, Denmark, May 2001.
31. U.P. Schultz, J. Lawall, C. Consel, and G. Muller. Towards automatic specialization of Java programs. In Guerraoui [17], pages 367–390.
32. U.P. Schultz, J.L. Lawall, and C. Consel. Automatic program specialization for Java. *TOPLAS*, 25:452–499, July 2003.
33. S. Thibault, C. Consel, R. Marlet, G. Muller, and J. Lawall. Static and dynamic program compilation by interpreter specialization. *Higher-Order and Symbolic Computation (HOSC)*, 13(3):161–178, 2000.
34. K.K. Thorup and M. Torgersen. Unifying genericity – combining the benefits of virtual types and parameterized classes. In Guerraoui [17].
35. M. Torgersen. Virtual types are statically safe. In *5th Workshop on Foundations of Object-Oriented Languages*, January 1998.
36. M. Torgersen, C.P. Hansen, E. Ernst, P. von der Ahé, G. Bracha, and N. Gafter. Adding wildcards to the Java programming language. In *Proceedings of the 2004 ACM symposium on Applied computing*, pages 1289–1296. ACM Press, 2004.
37. T.L. Veldhuizen. C++ templates as partial evaluation. In *ACM SIGPLAN Workshop on Partial Evaluation and Semantics-Based Program Manipulation (PEPM'98)*, pages 13–18, San Antonio, TX, USA, January 1999. ACM Press.

Towards a General Template Introspection Library

István Zólyomi and Zoltán Porkoláb

Department of Programming Languages and Compilers, Eötvös Loránd University
Pázmány Péter sétány 1/C H-1117 Budapest, Hungary
{scamel,gsd}@elte.hu

Abstract. To ensure the correctness of template based constructions in C++, constraints on template parameters are especially useful. Unlike other languages (Ada, Eiffel, etc.), C++ does not directly support checking requirements on template parameters (i.e., concept checking). However, many articles introduce ad hoc solutions based on special language features. In this paper we propose a structure for a general introspection library which supports easy expression and combination of basic orthogonal requirements, providing the possibility to avoid reimplementation of simple checks for every similar concept. Based on these building blocks, it is possible to express highly complex constraints on template parameters, contrary to languages having builtin support for a limited set of constraints only. Our library enables a checking method that takes the advantages of previous solutions, such as REQUIRE-like macros and static interfaces. Our implementation is non-intrusive, relies only on standard C++ language features and results no runtime overhead.

1 Introduction

1.1 Generative Programming in C++

Generative programming is a rapidly developing and expanding area. It includes generic programming, that aims to create general and reusable components, and template metaprogramming, that tries to move calculations from runtime to compile-time. In C++ these paradigms are based on the template facility of the language, which provides parametric polymorphism. Templates have many unique properties unlike other constructs of the language. By definition, parts of the template are instantiated only when used in the code. Unfortunately this may cause surprising behaviour of our code during the development process. For instance, if we add a legal method call on an object of a template class, our previously accepted code may not compile anymore. This is a result of lazy instantiation: defects in the template argument are encountered only during instantiation of the required feature.

Let us clarify this with an example: using a class T that has no comparison operator< as type parameter for a given C container template, C<T> is legal

G. Karsai and E. Visser (Eds.): GPCE 2004, LNCS 3286, pp. 266–282, 2004.

even if C defines a `sort()` operation, which depends on comparison of objects of type T. Because of the lazy instantiation strategy, the compiler does not try to instantiate the sort operation, therefore does not detect the lack of `operator<` in T. Later, when a user happens to call the `sort()` function and the function is instantiated, the compiler flags the lack of `operator<` in T and raises an error. This holds even for misspelled functions, e.g., a call `srot()` instead of `sort()` in a function template body would not be recognized until instantiation is attempted. Thus the compiler may accept code that is expected to be refused and may raise errors later unexpectedly.

1.2   Previous Approaches

There is no built-in language support in C++ to ensure that features of a template argument exist. Template arguments are not constrained in any way. Instead, all type checking is postponed to template instantiation time. The lack of language support is intentional (see [7]). According to Stroustrup, the flexibility of the C++ template construct makes concepts unnecessary. He considered concept checking to be even harmful. Indeed, a lazy instantiation strategy allows a larger number of types to be used as arguments for a given template: our code will be valid (also for otherwise illegal types) as long as we do not try to refer to any nonexisting member of that template parameter.

Contrary, there were heavy efforts to implement concept checking on template parameters since the introduction of templates in C++. It is especially essential in the Standard Template Library where some limited solutions are currently widely used. It would be similarly useful to verify the correctness of an implementation against a predefined specification: if the users create e.g., a bidirectional iterator, they would like to be able to check the existence of the required features, like `operator--`. This way he could detect wrong or incomplete implementations.

In many cases, instantiation of templates can be explicitly forced, thus drawbacks of lazy instantiation can be avoided. Early ad hoc solutions were based on forcing instantiation of required template features manually, e.g., in constructors. This caused a runtime overhead because of calling the instantiated features directly.

Later, an improved version of this technique by Siek [2] was able to avoid runtime overhead for such instantiations. It was based on instantiating, but not calling functions that contain calls to required features. This solution is currently used in several libraries, e.g., in the STL implementation of g++. Further in the article, we will refer to this solution as REQUIRE-like macros or traditional concept checking.

Another approach was presented by Smaragdakis and McNamara [1]. They introduced a framework called static interfaces, which is based on explicitly specifying concepts that a class conforms to. This is very similar to interfaces in e.g., Java, but has the advantage that checks do not raise errors, but return compile-time constants which can be inspected and used later in the code.

1.3   Our Results

In this paper we aim to provide a general and comprehensive, non-intrusive framework for expressing basic concepts in C++. Our checks result compile-time constants instead of compile errors, thus allowing compile-time adaptation techniques to be used. Adaptations can use different types or algorithmic strategies or may choose to abort compilation with a user-defined error message. The structure of our framework is intended to be orthogonal. Later, based on these building blocks we present a way of concept checking that tries to take the advantages of both traditional concepts and static interfaces.

2   Introspection Library Design

It would be very important and profitable to have a standard, well designed concept checking library: it would largely increase the chance of early detection of many conceptual errors in our program design. Despite the heavy efforts, there are still many deficiencies in current work on concept checking.

Firstly, most concept checking libraries (e.g., boost::concept [10]) raise compile-time errors when the inspected type does not meet its requirements. Introspection and feature detection on type arguments (returning compile-time constants instead of raising errors) would allow us to use more sophisticated programming techniques, such as compile-time adaptation. As an advantage of compile-time adaptation techniques, e.g., a container would be able to store comparable types in a binary tree for efficient access, while it could store other types in a vector. Algorithmic strategies also could be decided, e.g., a sort method could use quicksort for random access containers, while a merge sort could be used otherwise.

Furthermore, we would be able to express relationships between existing concepts using arbitrary logical operations. Note that previous libraries used an implicit *and* connection between all conditions. Contrary, a type could be serialized to `cout` if it has `operator<<` *or* member function `print()`. Another example can be a type having *no* public constructor (e.g., singletons). Using either builtin logical operators or custom metaprogramming calculations, we are even able to exploit the lazy evaluation of logical expressions (i.e., short-cut semantics of the `&&` and `||` connectives).

Secondly, most of the previous works were concentrating on checking particular concepts, but no comprehensive work was made on implementing elementary concepts themselves. Most examples verify the existence of a member type (e.g., `T::iterator`) or a simple function (e.g., comparision operator) in a type parameter. We can easily implement such checks for a single function, but without reusable basic concepts, they must be completely rewritten for any other function, even similar ones. (E.g. concepts EqualityCheckable and LessThanComparable are verifying operators with the same signature, but they are both have to be written from scratch using current libraries if they are not already implemented).

Thirdly, until now, no discussion was made about what would be useful to be expressed as a concept and what minimal orthogonal set of (meta)operations would be required to cover all possible checks. Relying on an orthogonal and complete set of basic concept implementations, we would be able to create a well designed concept library.

Finally, despite having several concept libraries, there are many concepts that seemingly cannot be implemented in C++. Such a concept is already mentioned above, when a type should have *no* public constructor. Note that boost [10] is able to require its existence, but it raises a compile error for check failure, and negation of this condition (e.g., for singletons) is impossible. We cannot be sure if we're searching for the solution in the wrong place, or it is theoretically impossible to implement such concepts based on features of the current language standard. The limitations of concept checking in C++ is still *terra incognita*.

Therefore, we propose the following strategies for a well-designed concept library:

1. Concept checking should be factorized to orthogonal, elementary conditions. We should give tools for assembling compound concepts from such basic conditions.
2. Introspection of code and actions based on check results should be separated: check failures should not be bound to aborting compilation. Instead, an elementary action should be provided to interrupt compilation with custom error message if needed. Of course, any other action also could be triggered.
3. The library should be non-intrusive and extensible.

3   Elementary Conditions

In this section we introduce solutions for several basic conditions. The following set of basic concepts is aimed to be orthogonal. Having a template argument, we have language support to use the type itself, or reference to one of its nested types, data members or member functions. Accordingly, we support the following atomic concepts:

- Constraints on the type, e.g., size, modifiers, etc. These constraints already have an appropriate solution as presented in [4] and [3], hence we suggest to use them instead of reimplementing their functionality.
- Existence of a dependent name (e.g., T::iterator) for
  - nested types
  - members (unified for member functions and attributes)
- For an existing name, the exact type for that name for
  - nested types
  - member functions (both static and non-static)
  - attributes (both static and non-static)

We can see that this list is far from being complete. Because of difficulties of implementation, we cannot check if a type is abstract, if a function is virtual, etc. There are many concepts that would be useful to have, but seemingly impossible to implement using current language features. They are discussed in section 9.

Checking atomic concepts is quite user-friendly. Still, inspecting dependent names require some macro magic:

```
// --- Defines checker functions
PREPARE_TYPE_CHECKER(iterator);

...

// --- Call checker function later
bool result = CONFORMS( TYPE_IN_CLASS(iterator, MyContainer) );
```

In the first call we prepare our checker function: the macro is expanded into a function definition that searches for a dependent type with name `iterator`. Because we have to define a new checker function for each inspected name, we think this is the most comfortable way to provide such definitions. Certainly, this has to be done only once, before making any calls. Later a call to the defined checker can be done. In the example we verify if our container class has an iterator defined. We can inspect dependent member names similarly using macros `PREPARE_MEMBER_CHECKER()` and `MEMBER_IN_CLASS()`.

If we know that such a dependent name exists, remaining inspections are much more natural without many macros. E.g. the search for a comparision operator looks as follows:

```
bool result = CONFORMS(
    Function<bool (const T&, const T&)>::Static(&operator==) );
```

In the above code, `Function<bool (const T&, const T&)>` specifies that we expect to have a function with this signature. We call function `Static()` on this type indicating that we expect to have a global comparision operator. Finally we specify `&operator==` as the inspected function. If the function parameter is exactly the same as we expected, `result` evaluates to true, otherwise it's false.

We can verify attribute types similarly. For a detailed explanation of atomic concept implementations see section 6.

4   Assembling Concepts

In section 3 we have created our basic concepts. However, they are not really useful by themselves. For practical use, we have to combine several elementary conditions to express the actual requirements for a type parameter. In this section we present our approach for assembling our basic conditions into practically used, complex concepts.

Because all of our concept checks result in a boolean value, assembly means a simple application of logical operations in our case. In other libraries there was an implicit *and* between listed conditions, which does not apply for all the cases. In most cases we use *logical and* (`operator &&`), indeed, but other logical operators, such as `operator!` and `operator||` should be supported, too. For example, concept `LessThanComparable` may require that a type must have a member comparision (T::operator<) *or* a global comparision operator ::operator<). Raising an error for check failures, this concept can be expressed as follows[1]:

```
template <class T> struct LessThanComparable
{
    enum { Conforms =
        // --- Check appropriate type for member
        CONFORMS( Function<bool (const T&) >::NonStatic(&T::operator<) )
    ||
        // --- or global operator
        CONFORMS( Function<bool (const T&, const T&)>::Static(&operator<) )
    };
};


// --- Example of usage
template <class Num> struct MyClass
{
    STATIC_CHECK( LessThanComparable<Num>::Conforms,
        TYPE_DOESNT_MEET_ITS_REQUIREMENTS);
    ...
}
```

We can see that the introspection code and the usage of the result is clearly separated. In `LessThanComparable`, we define our introspection criterias and calculate the result. In `MyClass`, we define our action utilizing the result, which is raising a compile-time error in our case. For this we use the `STATIC_CHECK` macro of Loki which enables custom error messages as its second parameter. We could also define any other action, e.g., use compile-time adaptation techniques depending on the result.

5   Programming Techniques

Throughout in our implementation we use several special language features and techniques. In this part we give an introduction to our "tricks".

Firstly, we have two distinct classes `Yes` and `No` marking true and false values by their different size[2]. These classes will be return types of functions, thus marking which variety of overloaded functions is actually chosen for the current function arguments.

```
typedef char No;                        // --- Type meaning false
typedef struct { char dummy[2]; } Yes;  // --- Type meaning true
```

The size of `Yes` is clearly more than the size of `No`, therefore using the `sizeof` operator we can distinguish these classes during compilation time. Instead of manual calls of operator `sizeof`, it is easier to read the code that uses the following class and macro:

---

[1] Note that we did not consider the case when name `operator<` does not exist. A check failure leads to compilation error anyway because of the static assertion.

[2] For a detailed explanation of this technique, see [4].

```
// --- Type to return result as a bool constant
template <int> struct Conforms;

template <> struct Conforms< sizeof(No) >
    { enum { Result = 0 }; };

template <> struct Conforms< sizeof(Yes) >
    { enum { Result = 1 }; };

// --- Provide more readable form of checking result
#define CONFORMS(PARAM) Conforms< sizeof(PARAM) >::Result
```

Class `Conforms` uses template specialization which allows us to use different bodies for templates with different parameters. `Conforms` does not have an implementation for the general case, providing that any parameter other than `sizeof(No)` or `sizeof(Yes)` leads to compilation error. For an actual argument `sizeof(No)`, the class holds 0 as an enumerated value (being equivalent to a `bool` with a `false` value), otherwise it holds 1 for `sizeof(Yes)` (same as `true`). Finally we define macro `CONFORMS` to give a shortcut for the result.

Another common technique is using ellipses (marked as "..." in function signatures). Ellipses mean "match all number and type of parameters". It enables creation of default rescue branches while overloading functions: when the match for all other signatures fail, it surely succeeds. Because ellipses have a minimal priority, it is matched only if no other signature matches the actual arguments. Though ellipses are often considered to be dangerous, we do not actually try to access the parameters of such functions. Ellipses are used to decide whether the actual parameters match the signature of another function or not, hence our library remains safe.

```
Yes f(double);          // --- use different return types
No  f(...);             // --- use ellipse in rescue case

bool a = CONFORMS( f(2) );     // --- calls first, results true
bool b = CONFORMS( f("two") ); // --- calls rescue case, results false
```

Using the `sizeof` operator (in the implementation of macro `CONFORMS`) on the result of the function call, the function itself is no actually executed, because size of the result type can be deducted anyway. Not executing any function body, we have no runtime overhead penalty for checking. Since no implementation for the function is needed, a single declaration is enough, no definition is required.

We also use the so-called SFINAE rule of C++, an acronym for "substitution failure is not an error" (see [3]). It is also often referenced as "two phase lookup". This principle is applied when the compiler tries to instantiate a function template, but deduction of template parameters results in a type error. In this case, instead of raising an error, it tries to use other overloaded instances of the same function. If the compiler finally succeeds, the failure is suppressed and is not considered as an error; it will be flagged only if all instantiation attempts have failed.

```
template <class T>
typename T::iterator f(T t) { return t.begin(); }

void f(...) {}      // --- rescue case

f( list<int>() );  // --- calls first
f( 2 );            // --- no int::iterator, calls second
```

Above we defined two functions to check the existence of type `iterator` declared inside a class. Calling function `f()` with a `list<int>` argument, the first variety of the function is used: type `T` is deduced from the type of the argument, and it has an iterator type, thus the signature is valid. This doesn't hold for the second call: `int` has no nested types at all, thus the signature is invalid and instantiation of the template function fails. According to the SFINAE rule, the compiler struggles on to search for other overloaded versions of the function, and finds our rescue function with the ellipses. Therefore the last line calls this rescue function and the instantiation error will be suppressed.

We can exploit the SFINAE rule directly with the definition and use of the following template class[3]:

```
template <bool, class> struct enable_if {};
template <class T> struct enable_if<true,T> { typedef T Result; };
```

Class `enable_if` provides the possibility of checking arbitrary compile-time conditions on any type. It defines the second parameter as `Result` inside the class, if the condition (as its first parameter) is true; otherwise it does not contain anything. Type `enable_if` has to be included in the signature of a function, and additionally a rescue function is needed in the following manner:

```
// --- Declare function with enable_if specifying custom condition
template <class T> enable_if<MY_CONDITION, Yes>::Result f(T);

No f(...);                          // --- rescue case
bool result = CONFORMS( f(1) );    // --- verify condition on type int
```

If `MY_CONDITION` is true, the result type of `enable_if` will be `Yes`, thus the signature of the first function will be legal and preferred. If the condition is false, the signature is illegal, and the rescue case is found. Hence the result type will be `No`. We can use the above defined `CONFORMS` macro to check the result type of the selected function variety.

6   Implementation

Many specific basic checks already have an appropriate solution. These checks vary from checking the modifiers of the type of a variable (pointer, reference, const, etc.) to verifying the presence of a nested type in a class. These works

---

[3] Class `enable_if` is explained in detail in [8], and is part of the Boost library [9].

provide good and comprehensive libraries, hence we do not intend to reinvent the wheel: we concentrate on concepts that still do not have a comprehensive or general solution. Furthermore, many of our ideas were inspired by these libraries so effective details and solutions are similar at some places.

6.1   Attributes

Solutions based on partial template specialization exist for checking whether a type is reference or const, discussed in [4] and [3]. In a similar manner we can check the *exact type* of an attribute. In this part we introduce our solution for this problem, which is based on function overloading instead of partial specialization.

Based on techniques discussed above, we can check the exact type for any member (being static or non-static member) in the following way:

```
template <class VarType>
struct Attribute
{
    // --- Check static member
    static Yes Static(VarType*);

    // --- Rescue for static member
    static No Static(...);

    // --- Check non-static member
    template <class Class>
    static Yes NonStatic(VarType Class::*);

    // --- Rescue functions for non-static member
    static No NonStatic(...);
    template <class> static No NonStatic(...);
};

// --- Example of usage (results false)
bool result = CONFORMS( Attribute<int>::NonStatic( &list<int>::size ) );
```

The functionality of `Attribute` consists of two main parts: checking static and non-static members[4]. To understand how the above described programming techniques work altogether, let us explain the compilation steps of the usage example in the last line:

1. Classes `Attribute<int>` and `list<int>` are instantiated.
2. A member pointer is set to `list<int>::size`. However, it still has a currently unknown type since it can be either a member function or a data member. (Note that if `size` is a static member, a conventional pointer is gained instead.)

---

[4] Global and namespace variables (and later, functions) could also be checked using function `Static()`.

3. `Attribute<int>::NonStatic()` is chosen according to overloading rules. If the type of the pointed member matches the type argument of the `Attribute` template (actually `int`), our template function is preferred; otherwise the `NonStatic(...)` rescue function is found.
4. The `sizeof` operator is applied on the result type of the previous function call by the `CONFORMS` macro, while the function itself is not actually called. We gain the size of class `Yes` or `No`.
5. The result size is checked and a compile-time boolean constant is finally achieved.

For a deeper understanding of class `Attribute`, we introduce all different functionalities of the class through examples.

```
struct Base { int var; };
struct Derived : public Base {};


// --- Possible forms of calls (without CONFORMS to save space)
Attribute<const int>::Static( &Derived::var );      // --- results No
Attribute<int>::NonStatic( &Derived::var );         // --- results Yes
Attribute<int>::NonStatic<Base>( &Derived::var ); // --- results Yes
```

Function `Static()` returns true only if the parameter is a static member of its class, non-static members are checked the same way by `NonStatic()`. However, this does not limit the usability of our class: if we do not care whether the member is static or non-static, we can check both and connect the results with a *logical or* (e.g., `operator ||`).

Function `NonStatic()` has an interesting feature, shown in the last two examples. Since it is a template function, we do not need to specify its type parameter, it is automatically deduced by the compiler. We allow the examined attribute to be a member of *any* class this way. Though we do not have to, we may explicitly specify the type parameter of `NonStatic()`. In this case we check whether the inspected attribute is a member of the *specified* class.

Note that as a consequence of our implementation technique, this solution has an important property: we have to specify all type modifiers when inspecting types, because they are part of the exact type to be checked. If we check whether an attribute of type `const int` is of type `int`, we get false as result. We must always specify the *exact* type to be checked.

6.2 Implement Attributes, Get Functions for Free

Checking the exact type of functions is a more complicated, but still very similar problem to checking attributes as in 6.1. Functions have a more complex type: they have a return type, a signature and may have several qualifiers (`const`, etc). However, syntaxes for defining the type of a data member and a member function are similar and closely related. Here, we can take advantage of this fact: the exact type of a function can be inspected using the very same method as with attributes. We use only a typedef on our previous `Attribute` class to create

`Function` and change nothing inside the class. Now we can make the following checks:

```
struct Base {
    static string classId();
    double calc(double);
};

struct Derived : public Base {
    void f(int, int);
};

// --- All examples return type Yes
Function<string ()>::Static( &Derived::classID );
Function<void (int,int)>::NonStatic( &Derived::f );
Function<double (double)>::NonStatic( &Derived::calc );
```

Though we have changed nothing in the implementation of our class, it also can be used for functions in a consistent manner. (Because there is no difference between the implementation of checking functions and attributes, we decided to join classes `Attribute` and `Function` into a `Member` class in our final solution.) The only difference occurs when we're parameterizing our template: we specify function types instead of attribute types. Function qualifiers, such as `const`, naturally fit into this construction:

```
// --- const signature
typedef void Signature(int) const;

struct S {
    Signature f; // --- also can be written as void S::f(int) const
};

// --- Example resulting true
bool result = CONFORMS( Function<Signature>::Member<S>(&S::f) );
```

The type definition may be surprising: keyword `const` is meaningless except for member functions. However, the language standard allows such definitions so that member functions can be defined later, such as `f()` in class `S`. (Note that despite the standard, many compilers do not accept such type definitions). Exploiting possibilities of this feature, we gain a consistent way to check function signatures with modifiers.

Unfortunately this construction leads to compile-time errors in some cases. If a function has several overloaded instances, and none of them matches the required signature, the compiler flags the function pointer (e.g., `&S::f`) as ambiguous. The solution for this limitation needs further work.

6.3 Types

It is often required for a template parameter to define a type, e.g., a container should have a dependent iterator type. This concept can be implemented using the SFINAE rule[5], as shown in section 5. Because the name of the type must not be hardwired in a general solution, we are forced to use macros to solve the problem. One macro is required to ease the definition of the checker functions, the other is to provide readable and comfortable usage.

```
// ----- Macros for easier definition
#define PREPARE_TYPE_CHECKER(NAME) \
template <class T> \
typename enable_if< sizeof(typename T::NAME), Yes >::Result \
check_##NAME(Type2Type<T>); \
\
No check_##NAME(...)

// ----- Macro for easier usage
#define TYPE_IN_CLASS(NAME,TYPE)  check_##NAME( Type2Type<TYPE>() )

// --- Definition in global or accessable namespace
PREPARE_TYPE_CHECKER(iterator);

// --- Call check anywhere where variables can be defined
bool result = CONFORMS( TYPE_IN_CLASS(iterator, MyContainer) );
```

Class **Type2Type** is part of the Loki library [4], and is used to differentiate between overloaded function variants without instantiating objects of the template argument, that may have huge costs and unknown side effects. **Type2Type** provides a lightweight type holder with a typedef inside and allows argument type deduction the same way as a conventional parameter.

We use class **enable_if** to provide return type **Yes** for every conforming case. For the first argument of **enable_if**, we have to specify a boolean template parameter, hence we use **sizeof()** to "convert" the inspected type into an integer value, which can be interpreted as a boolean.

Because a checker function for each type name must be declared before it can be used, the **PREPARE_TYPE_CHECKER** macro must be called in advance with the name to be checked as an argument, at any place in the program where global functions can be defined. After preparation, the check can be made similarly to other checks using the **TYPE_IN_CLASS** macro. In the last line of the example, we check whether our container class has a nested type with name **iterator**.

6.4   Member Names

Unfortunately all of our previously implemented data member and member function checks were based on the assumption that at least the name of the inspected member exists in the class. Otherwise, a compile-time error occurs since the referenced member (e.g., **&Derived::var**) cannot be found inside the class. Therefore

---

[5] A similar solution for this problem was already introduced in [3], but it was usable only for a predefined name and had to be rewritten for each other name.

it is essential to check the existence of member names, i.e., the existence of a attribute or function (of any type) with a given name.

The solution for this problem is very similar to the one for inspecting nested types in section 6.3. The only difference is in the conversion to a boolean parameter for enable_if. For functions and attributes, we are able to use the address operator&[6] instead of sizeof(). For nested types, sizeof() was our only choice, because pointers cannot be set to types.

Based on the very same principles, we can define our functions to check member names:

```
// ----- Macros for easier definition
#define PREPARE_MEMBER_CHECKER(NAME) \
template <class T> \
typename enable_if< &T::NAME, Yes >::Result \
checkName_##NAME( Type2Type<T> ); \
\
No checkName_##NAME(...)

// ----- Macro for easier usage
#define MEMBER_IN_CLASS(NAME, CLASS) \
    checkName_##NAME( Type2Type<CLASS>() )

// --- Definition in global or accessible namespace
PREPARE_MEMBER_CHECKER(size);

// --- Call check anywhere where variables can be defined
bool result = CONFORMS( MEMBER_IN_CLASS(size, MyContainer) );
```

In the last line, we are able to check whether our container class has a function *or* attribute with name size.

7   Other Languages

Concept checking and introspection is clearly not a problem specific to C++. Concept checking has been supported in many languages for a long time, e.g., in Ada, in Eiffel or recently in Java. These languages use generics to support parametric polymorphism.

To support concept checking, Eiffel allows constraints on type parameters of generics. Constraints are always related to inheritance: we can restrict a parameter to be derived from a custom class.

```
class SORTED_LIST [T -> COMPARABLE] ...
```

This means that any actual generic parameter can only be a type that is a descendant of COMPARABLE. You cannot apply your custom type C (if it is not derived from COMPARABLE) as a valid parameter of SORTED_LIST, but you can

---

[6] Note that in C++, all non-null pointers are accepted as true.

circumvent this in most cases using e.g., multiple inheritance. The best way is to create a new class COMPARABLE_C by inheriting from both COMPARABLE and C.

This technique allows only a minimal reuse of concepts. Predefined concepts like COMPARABLE are reusable. Fulfilling more complex conditions, even simple conjunction of criteria COMPARABLE *and* HASHABLE expressed as base class COMPARABLE_HASHABLE requires inheriting *not* from COMPARABLE and HASHABLE but from COMPARABLE_HASHABLE. This *structural inheritance* problem is widely discussed in [15].

The case is very similar in Java, though a bit more complex. Early attempts were made in Pizza [13] and Generic Java [14]. Since version 1.5, generics are a part of the language standard. Opposite to other languages, the Java solution was based on *type erasure* rather than instantiation. During compilation, Java applies type checks and ensures proper type matches, but type information is erased after that: all type parameters are transformed into Object, the base of all classes. This prevents code bloat, but makes generics almost nothing more than a safe typecast. Additionally, primitives (e.g., int or double) are not allowed in generics, because they are not descendants of Object.

```
class SortedList <T extends Sortable> ...
```

In both cases, restrictions on type parameters are expressed by inheritance. Note that due to the lack of support for multiple inheritance, Java permits the usage of a class which *implements* an interface, but you still have to use the keyword extends.

Though being older, Ada provides a more sophisticated solution for expressing concepts, i.e., constraints on generic parameters. Since generic is part of the language standard since 1983, it was less influenced by the object oriented paradigm.

```
generic
    type T is private;
    with function "<" (X,Y: T) return Boolean is <>;
package Sorted_List
    ...
end

--- Generics are always instantiated explicitly
package SList is new Sorted_List(MyType, "<=");
```

As you can see, constraints like existence of the comparison operator can be explicitly listed. Similarly to C++, there is no requirement on a common base class: comparable classes can be unrelated by the inheritance relationship. Moreover, any custom function can be specified at instantiation: as in the example above, we can use operator <= as comparison function referred to as < in the definition of the generic.

As a characteristic of concept checking in Eiffel, Java and Ada, there is a common strategy of "fulfill or die". Whenever the parameter does not conform to the constraint, compilation is aborted with an error, therefore there is no way of compile-time adaptation. Furthermore, concepts are simply conjunction of elementary requirements (such as a method in an interface).

8   Further Work

8.1   Platforms

Our production code was placed into a single header file *concept.h*[7]. To minimize dependencies from other libraries, we did not use any third party code. However, two code fragments were used without modification from other projects: class **Type2Type** from Loki and **enable_if** from boost. To avoid dependencies from these libraries, we also placed these very simple class definitions into header *concept.h*.

Altough we used only standard C++ features in our implementation, compilers are still far behind the current language standard. We were able to compile our whole framework on compilers Intel 8.0 and Visual C++ .Net 7.1. Most of the code can be compiled on Gnu C++ 3.3, but failed to implement SFINAE in an appropriate way. Unfortunately, we did not have the possibility to test Comeau C++.

The only compiler that compiled flawless code was Intel 8.0. Visual C++ was not able to correctly interpret **MEMBER_IN_CLASS**, however accepted it syntactically. Features compiled successfully by GNU C++ were interpreted according to the language standard.

We should be able to port a working framework to widely used compilers, hence features supported by most compilers should be used whenever possible.

8.2   Improvements

Based on discussed methods, we can check the exact type for members. However, we often do not care about the exact type in practice. Instead, we want to know if a variable is *usable* (i.e., convertible[8]), which cannot be expressed using the **Attribute** class above. E.g. we would like to require that when we expect a **short**, it can be also a **long** or any class that can be cast to **short**. Our framework should support expression of such non-strict conditions. Note that there is no inheritance relationship between these types. In those cases when there is inheritance relationship, even the conventional tests of our previous **Attribute** class provide the desired answers. These kind of non-strict expressions should also apply to function signatures, where a **void (long)** signature may conform to a **void (int)** restriction (such conversions are possible in **boost::function**, see [9]).

We should also get rid of the drawbacks of the current implementation, such as compilation error for ambigous operators. This would require a change in the

---

[7] This file can be downloaded from **gsd.web.elte.hu/Publications**.

[8] Note that this is a different problem than the one that has been solved with macro SUPERSUBCLASS in [4].

library structure, because this drawback is a direct consequence of referencing members by name when using them as function arguments.

9   Open Questions

Although checking many kinds of concepts has an appropriate solution, there are several questions left open in this area. Perhaps the most important is checking the existence of a public constructor for a class, e.g., a default constructor. Unlike destructors, constructors are not conventional members of the belonging class (e.g., no member pointer can be set to a constructor), therefore they cannot be referenced explicitly as a function. This forbids the use of our above presented method for constructors.

Similarly, we could find no solution for many template introspection issues. Is a function virtual? How many descendents and ancestors does a class have? Is it abstract? Is it a POD type? Does it require memory in the heap?

This kind of problems raise the question: what are the limitations of C++ template introspection? We need a theoretical work inspecting:

- What is the minimal orthogonal implementation for covering already solved concept checking problems?
- What other concepts are expected to have a solution based on standard C++ language features?
- What are the concepts that are *theoretically impossible* to be solved (if there is any)?

10   Summary

Template introspection has serious advantages compared to previous solutions, like **requires** macros of g++, the more sophisticated concept library of boost [10] or static interfaces [1].

Conventional concept checks forced the instantiation of template features by manual calls to required features, which yielded compile-time errors in cases of missing features. Our library does better than that: it provides compile-time boolean values as check results. At the same time, this approach has the advantage of being non-intrusive.

Static interfaces provide similar compile-time boolean results as our framework does. On the other side, they have the drawback of being intrusive since all conforming concepts have to be explicitly specified, similarly to implementing Java interfaces.

Our solution unites the advantages of previous solutions: we have a non-intrusive introspection method providing boolean results, while we are able to express the very same constraints on our classes as these previous libraries and more. Instead of providing a large set of concrete concept checks, we implemented elementary building blocks and construction facilities. This way users can specify and express their own custom concept conditions that can be used for both compile-time adaptation and issuing diagnostics under the process of compilation.

References

1. Brian McNamara, Yannis Smaragdakis: Static interfaces in C++. In First Workshop on C++ Template Metaprogramming, October 2000
2. J. Siek and Andrew Lumsdaine: Concept checking: Binding parametric polymorphism in C++. In First Workshop on C++ Template Metaprogramming, October 2000
3. David Vandevoorde, Nicolai M. Josuttis: C++ Templates: The Complete Guide. Addison-Wesley (2002)
4. Andrei Alexandrescu: Modern C++ Design: Generic Programming and Design Patterns Applied. Addison-Wesley (2001)
5. Krzysztof Czarnecki, Ulrich W. Eisenecker: Generative Programming: Methods, Tools and Applications. Addison-Wesley (2000)
6. Bjarne Stroustrup: The C++ Programming Language Special Edition. Addison-Wesley (2000)
7. Bjarne Stroustrup: The Design and Evolution of C++. Addison-Wesley (1994)
8. Jaakko Jarvi, Jeremiah Willcock, Andrew Lumsdaine: Concept-Controlled Polymorphism. In proceedings of GPCE 2003, LNCS 2830, pp. 228-244.
9. The Boost Library. http://www.boost.org
10. The Boost concept checking library.
    http://www.boost.org/libs/concept_check/concept_check.htm
11. Matthew H. Austern: Generic Programming and the STL. Addison-Wesley (1999)
12. Jarvi, J., Willcock, J., Hinnant, H., Lumsdaine, A.: Function overloading based on arbitrary properties of types. C/C++ Users Journal 21 (2003) pp. 25-32.
13. Pizza Java extension. http://pizzacompiler.sourceforge.net/
14. Generic Java. http://www.cis.unisa.edu.au/~pizza/gj/
15. István Zólyomi, Zoltán Porkoláb: An extension to the subtype relationship in C++ implemented with template metaprogramming. Proceedings of GPCE 2003, vol. 2830 of LNCS, pp. 209-227. Springer (2003)

Declaring and Enforcing Dependencies Between .NET Custom Attributes

Vasian Cepa and Mira Mezini

Software Technology Group, Department of Computer Science
Darmstadt University of Technology, Germany
{cepa,mezini}@informatik.tu-darmstadt.de

Abstract. Custom attributes as e.g., supported by the .NET framework complemented by pre- or post-processing tools can be used to integrate domain-specific concepts into general-purpose language technology, representing an interesting alternative to domain-specific languages in supporting model-driven development. For this purpose, it is important that dependency relationships between custom attributes, e.g., stating that a certain attribute requires or excludes another attribute, can be specified and checked for during model processing (compilation). Such dependencies can be viewed as an important part of expressing the meta-model of the domain-specific concepts represented by custom attributes.

In this paper, we present an approach to specifying and enforcing dependencies between .NET custom attributes, which naturally extends the built-in .NET support. In this approach, dependencies are specified declaratively by using custom attributes to decorate other custom attributes. Once the dependency declaration is made part of the custom attribute support, one can write tools that enforce dependencies based on .NET meta-program API-s like CodeDom or Reflection. In this paper, we present such a tool, called ADC (for attribute dependency checker).

1 Introduction

.NET [24] has native support for introducing custom attributes [13] which can be used to decorate program elements. Elsewhere [26], we have argued that custom attributes combined with API-s like `Reflection` and `CodeDom`[1] provide built-in support for integrating domain specific abstractions without the burden of rewriting the parser and/or the compiler of the language.

For illustration, assume that we want to extend an object-oriented language with constructs that facilitate building web services. In the simple example of Fig. 1 we have introduced two new keywords `webservice` and `webmethod` for this purpose which are used to define the `TravelAgent` as a web service component. While nice to have, this extension requires that the programmer understands and modifies the existing grammar rules to add support for the new keywords to the parser.

---

[1] All non cited references about .NET come from MSDN [22] documentation.

G. Karsai and E. Visser (Eds.): GPCE 2004, LNCS 3286, pp. 283–297, 2004.

```
webservice TravelAgent {
  ...
  webmethod GetHotels(){...}
  ...
}
```

Fig. 1. A domain-specific extension to implement web services

With attributes being built-in elements of the general purpose .NET programming framework, new (domain specific) abstractions can be expressed by annotating existing language elements. Meta-programming APIs can than be used to build transformers that identify decorated elements and transform the AST to integrate the semantics of the attributes. Hence, a language framework with support for attributes is capable of expressing executable (domain-specific) models, representing an interesting alternative to implementing domain-specific languages by means of traditional compiler development tools.

In a .NET language that supports attributes like C# we would write the same web service extensions of Fig. 1 by introducing two custom attributes as shown in Fig. 2. The `TravelAgent` class itself is decorated with the attribute `[WebService]`, whereas its public methods that constitute the web service interface should have a `[WebMethod]` attribute. Introducing new attributes is supported by .NET compilers, thus, we do not need to deal with grammar modification issues which makes it easier to extend a .NET language like C# with domain-specific constructs.

```
[WebService]
class TravelAgent {
  ...
  [WebMethod]
  public void GetHotels(){...}
  ...
}
```

Fig. 2. A web service class with two inter-depended attributes

.NET follows a hybrid approach with respect to attributes: It distinguishes between *predefined* and *custom* attributes. Predefined attributes are used by various API-s of the .NET platform. For example, `[System.Diagnostics.ConditionalAttribute]` is used by the preprocessor to condition the inclusion of methods in the compiled version. The compiler relies on *attribute provider* libraries to interpret the predefined attributes. In contrast to predefined attributes, custom attributes do not, in general, have a meaning to the compiler. Code to interpret a custom attribute has to be implemented by the developer that uses the attribute to introduce domain-specific concepts. Given that in .NET an attribute is defined in a class, the interpretation code can be placed inside the attribute class itself; however, when we need a bigger context to properly interpret the attribute, we place the interpretation code in a separate module.

We observe that there is some custom attribute interpretation code which is so common place and general that we may need to repeat it over and over. An example which we are concerned with in this paper is code needed to enforce dependencies between attributes, requiring e.g., that a certain attribute is present in the program hierarchy before another attribute can be used. A grammar rule such as `webservice := webmethod+` explicitly defines a context relation between `webservice` and `webmethod`. That is, a web method will appear only inside a web service and vice-versa, a web service will contain web methods. Depending on whether we consider the class or its methods, there are two constrains we want to enforce: (a) public methods of a class decorated as `[WebService]` should be decorated with the `[WebMethod]` attribute, (b) any method decorated with a `[WebMethod]` attribute should be declared within a class decorated with the `[WebService]` attribute. That is, the two attributes are inter-dependent. In general, however, the dependency relation need not be symmetric.

Specifying dependency relationships between custom attributes and checking for them during model processing (compilation) is important, in order to make effective use of custom attributes for supporting modeling with domain-specific abstractions directly at the code level. Such dependencies can be viewed as an important part of expressing the meta-model of the domain-specific concepts represented by custom attributes. Furthermore, specifying such dependencies is important to support feature-oriented modeling [15]. If we assume that feature-specific models are expressed in terms of custom attributes corresponding to domain-specific concepts, then expressing feature dependency relationships, requires a means to express and enforce respective dependencies between attributes.

How can attributed dependencies specified and checked? One can leave it to each specific transformer tool which will process the tag-decorated code to check dependencies between attributes. However, with this alternative the dependencies are not explicitly specified and we have to repeat the same checking logic in every transformer. A better alternative would be to declaratively specify dependencies as we do with grammar rules and process such specifications in a generic way before/after the compilation of the decorated code, but before the attributes are processed. Extending the .NET support for attributes to enable declaring and checking dependency constraints between custom attributes based on the second alternative is the main contribution of this paper. We do so in a way that is natural for .NET attribute programmers, without introducing any external notation apart from what is already present in .NET.

Instead of requiring that developers of transformation tools repeat dependency checks over and over, we propose to extend .NET with a new custom attribute, that allows to express such relations declaratively by decorating the involved attributes. This is similar to the use of the predefined `[System.AttributeUsageAttribute]` used in .NET to decorate a custom attribute, providing information about the lexical scope in which the attribute at hand can be used. Based on these usage attributes, any time a custom attribute is encountered in a program, the compiler can check, if it is being used in the right lexical context and report an error if this is not the case.

We adopt the idea underlying [System.AttributeUsageAttribute] to introduce new custom checks, now using custom attributes. That is, given that in .NET attributes are themselves program elements, we recursively use the mechanism of decorating program elements with attributes to extend the .NET support for attributes with dependency declarations. Using custom attributes to decorate other custom attributes is a natural way to extend .NET's attribute support. Given that we cannot change the compiler, we need a way to interpret such dependency attributes. This can be done with a *pre-processor* tool which applies the checks before the compilation using CodeDom[2], or with a *post-processor* tool which applies the checks after the compilation, given that .NET saves the attribute information as part of the IL (Intermediate Language) meta-data.

The technique frees the programmer that writes attribute interpreters from repeating code by centralizing checks to be part of the compilation process; the programmer only declares the dependencies without taking care of how they are resolved and enforced. There are of course many ways to declare and enforce such architectural dependencies [21]. However, using attributes to decorate other attributes is a very natural way for .NET.

The remainder of the paper is organized as follows. Sec. 2 presents our dependency constraint model, and shows by means of examples how our model can be used to specify dependency relationships between domain specific concepts expressed via attributes. Sec. 3 presents ADC - an attribute dependency checker tool for enforcing dependencies based on our dependency model. Sec. 4 presents related work. We summarize the paper in Sec. 5.

2   The Attribute Dependency Model

We distinguish between (a) *required* dependencies - stating that a given attribute requires another one in order to be used, and (b) *disallowed* dependencies - stating that a given attribute cannot be used, if another attribute is present. Furthermore, children nodes in a program's structural hierarchy can declare dependency constrains for parents of any level, and vice-versa. An attribute of a certain program element instance may require that certain attributes are present in the set of the attributes of the structural children of the program element at hand. For example, a *Class* attribute may require a certain attribute to be present in the class' *Methods*. The reverse is also true: An attribute of a child structural element instance may require a certain attribute to be present in the set of the attributes specified for the parent instance. In our model, we generalize these notions to any depth of the structural tree.

On the contrary, sibling nodes in a program's structural hierarchy are not allowed to put constraints on their respective attributes. The attributes of a program element instance cannot place any constrain on the attributes of sibling instances. For example, the attributes that a *Field* instance is decorated with

---

[2] When ICodeParser is implemented.

cannot imply anything about the attributes of *Method* instances or attributes of other *Field* instances. In the same structural level we cannot say anything about the siblings that will be there. However, the attributes of a program element instance can place constrains on other attributes of the same instance. For example, a method attribute a_{m1} of a method m may require another attribute a_{m2} to be present for m.

The semantics of the *disallowed* relation on the structural tree elements and instances can be specified similarly and will not be repeated here.

2.1   The [DependencyAttribute] Class

.NET custom attributes are classes derived from the class `System.Attribute`. They may have arguments specified either as constructor parameters - unnamed arguments -, or as properties of the attribute class which generate *getter* and *setter* methods in C# - named arguments. Attribute classes may also contain methods and state like any other class. Using properties to specify attribute arguments is more flexible than using constructors. The reason is that .NET does not support complex types to be passed as parameters to the constructors[3]. Hence, we define an attribute class `DependencyAttribute`[4] which has one `Required*` and one `Disallowed*` property for each program element type for which attributes are supported, as shown in Fig. 3. Given that the number of the node types in a program's structural tree (`Assembly`, `Class`, `Method`, etc.) is limited, it makes sense to enumerate such operations. This makes the code easier to understand compared to having a single dependency property for all meta-element types.

```
[AttributeUsage(AttributeTargets.Class)]
public class DependencyAttribute : System.Attribute {
    ...
    public DependencyAttribute() {...}
    public Type[] RequiredAssemblyAttributes {...}
    public Type[] DisallowedAssemblyAttributes {...}
    public Type[] RequiredClassAttributes {...}
    public Type[] DisallowedClassAttributes  {...}
    public Type[] RequiredMethodAttributes {...}
    public Type[] DisallowedMethodAttributes {...}
}
```

Fig. 3. The implementation of dependency attribute

---

[3] Only basic constant types and `System.Type` can be used. `System.Object` is also listed in the documentation because it is the parent of simple types and of `System.Type`. However, this does not mean that arbitrary objects can be passed as constructor parameters.

[4] When used in code the suffix `Attribute` may be omitted from the name of an attribute class.

However, the current .NET implementation seems to restrict the complexity of the validation logic that one can implement inside a property of a custom attribute. It is unclear in the .NET documentation whether that code is ever activated. Furthermore, we found that if the code inside a property is more than a simple assignment, that property may be not included in the attribute class without warnings from the compiler. Thus, we must keep the code of the `DependencyAttribute` properties simple and postpone checks, e.g., that the attributes passed as a parameter to a property have the right [System.AttributeUsageAttribute] target[5], until the dependency checking is performed.

The `DependencyAttribute` only stores the required/disallowed attribute arrays and implements only code for printing these arrays as strings needed for error and log reporting. It does not implement any code to interpret the dependencies and its implementation has no other module dependencies. As a consequence, `DependencyAttribute` is independent of any particular dependency checker implementation and can be distributed and used alone to decorate attribute libraries.

The current implementation of our dependency model only supports **Assemblies**, **Classes** and **Methods**. Adding support for **Fields** is trivial (see the implementation details in the next section). Readers familiar with .NET may note that we have skipped **namespace-s**[6] in the list above. The reason is that a **namespace** is a logical rather than a physical concept, so even though we can theoretically decorate a **namespace** with attributes, practically there is not a single physical place where to store the attributes, since a **namespace** may be expanded in many modules and assemblies[7].

2.2   Using the Dependency Attribute

Fig. 4 shows how the `DependencyAttribute` can be used in code to enforce the dependency semantics of the attributes [WebService] and [WebMethod] from the example in Fig. 2. Note the use of the C# 'typeof' operator to obtain an instance of the class type of each attribute.

The following example shows how other checks involving declarative attributes can be expressed using the dependency attribute. It is motivated by implementation restrictions of the EJB [7] container programing model. The EJB specification states, among other restrictions, that components whose instances will be managed as *virtual instances* [20] should not pass *this* as a parameter or return value; the underlying idea is that it makes no sense to return a direct pointer to an object that will be reused with other internal state later by the container.

---

[5] E.g., `AttributeTargets.Method` should be present in the declaration of an attribute included in the list `RequiredMethodAttributes`.

[6] For readers with a Java background **namespace** maps roughly to a **package**; an **Assembly** maps roughly to a JAR file; the **Assembly** attributes map roughly to custom JAR manifest entries.

[7] This is the reason why .NET does not list **namespace** as an entry in the `AttributeTargets` enumeration.

```
[Depedency(RequiredMethodAttributes(new Type[]{typeof(WebMethod)}))]
[AttributeUsage(AttributeTargets.Class)]
class WebService : System.Attribute { ... }

[Depedency(RequiredClassAttributes(new Type[]{typeof(WebService)}))]
[AttributeUsage(AttributeTargets.Method)]
class WebMethod : System.Attribute { ... }
```

Fig. 4. Using the dependency attribute

While the EJB implementations currently do not rely on tags, we can imagine that tags are used in the same way as EJB marking interfaces [14][8]. Let us suppose that the lifetime of an instance of a class is going to be managed by the container only when the class declaration is decorated with the tag [VirtualInstance] (Fig. 5). For a class C tagged with the attribute [VirtualInstance], the restriction about *this* must hold. We express this requirement explicitly by means of a new tag [NoThis]. Let us suppose that the method initialize() of class C is invoked by the container when a virtual instance need to be initialized. We place no restrictions on this method's signature, but annotate it with a [InitInstance] attribute to distinguish it for later processing. In this context, we use [NoThis] as an attribute for decorating program elements and use the dependency attribute to state that it is required whenever [VirtualInstance] and/or [InitInstance] are used, as in Fig. 6.

```
[VirtualInstance]
class C {
  ...
  [InitInstance]
  public C initialize(Id id){...}
  ...
}
```

Fig. 5. A class that requires virtual instance support

That is, we require [NoThis] to be used explicitly in order to check this restriction. Optimally, [NoThis] should be used as a meta-attribute to decorate the attributes [VirtualInstance] and [InitInstance], i.e., at the same abstraction level as [DependencyAttribute], letting an extra tool to check for it. However, this is out of the scope of the discussion here, since all we are interested in is to use the EJB restriction "not allowed to pass this" only as a means to illustrate the dependency attribute. The less declarative notation by using the [DependencyAttribute] does not remove the need that the corresponding container transformer must later enforce [NoThis] semantics in the appropriate way. It only offers a first and quick automated test of the correct usage, which saves us from defining a tool for only enforcing declaratively the

---

[8] Actually, Java 1.5 annotations will be used in EJB 3.0 instead of marking interfaces.

```
[AttributeUsage(AttributeTargets.Class | AttributeTargets.Method)]
class NoThis : System.Attribute { ... }

[Depedency(RequiredMethodAttributes(new Type[]{typeof(NoThis)})]
[AttributeUsage(AttributeTargets.Class)]
class VirtualInstance : System.Attribute { ... }

[Depedency(RequiredClassAttributes(new Type[]{typeof(VirtualInstance)}),
    RequiredMethodAttributes(new Type[]{typeof(NoThis)})]
[AttributeUsage(AttributeTargets.Method)]
class InitInstance : System.Attribute { ... }
```

Fig. 6. Using dependency attribute to check [NoThis] constraints

[NoThis] attribute semantics. Of course, the price of this convenience is that the programmer must then use [NoThis] explicitly in code.

The example illustrates also the non-symmetry of the dependency relation as the [VirtualInstance] class attribute requires [NoThis] method attribute to be present, but [NoThis] method attribute can be used also in methods inside classes that do not have a [VirtualInstance] attribute.

3   The Attribute Dependency Checker (ADC) Tool

The Attribute Dependency Checker (ADC) tool, which can be downloaded from [27], is implemented as a *post-processor* using the **Reflection** API. After the code is compiled and linked one can run the ADC tool over the IL binaries to detect dependency errors, if any. Alternatively, ADC could be implemented as a *pre-processor* tool to be run before the source is compiled using the **CodeDom** API[9].

Fig. 7 shows the classes of ADC and their relations. Almost all the logic of the dependency checker is found in the abstract class **AttributeDependency-Checker**. It uses several helper classes and interfaces (a) to filter the processed elements (**IDependencyFilter**), (b) to log information about the progress of the checking process (**ICheckLogger**), and (c) to report errors (**ErrorReport**). The **IContextMap** class encapsulates the meta-model structure in a single place using a special internal coding. For illustration, Fig. 8 shows how the ADC library can be used to check the attribute dependency constrains for all elements of a given .NET assembly.

In order to implement the semantics of the dependency attribute we need to first build the dependency sets for each structural element by processing the element and all its structural children. After the dependency sets are constructed, we can check the dependency constrains of the element. That is, we need a post-order transversal of the structural tree. A boolean flag in **AttributeDependencyChecker** controls whether the inherited attributes of the structural elements are processed. The actions performed during a call to the **Check(t)**

---

[9] A third party implementation of **ICodeParser** for C# is presented in [12].

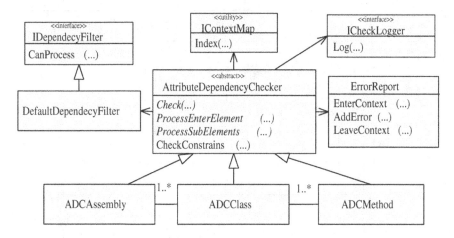

Fig. 7. The run-time attribute dependency checker structure

```
Assembly a = ...; // obtain an assembly
ADCAssembly c = new ADCAssembly();
c.Filter = ...;
c.Logger = ...;
c.Check(a);
if(c.errors.HasWarnings())
{ // process: c.errors.GetWarnings() ... }
if(c.errors.HasErrors())
{ // process: c.errors.GetErrors()   ... }
```

Fig. 8. Using the run-time attribute dependency checker in code

method, where t is the current program element whose attribute dependencies are being checked for, are illustrated in Fig. 9.

First, the filter object is used to check whether the element at hand should be processed (step (2) in Fig. 9). Filters can be used to put arbitrary constrains on the elements that will be processed, e.g., using pattern matching on names. The `DefaultDependencyFilter` processes all the elements. The ADC tool uses a customized filter called `ClassDependecyFilter` derived from `DefaultDependencyFilter` that can restrict checking to a subset of classes whose names are given in the command line. More sophisticated filters can be written and used in a programmatic way. Filters can also be used to implement profiling by keeping track of various counters; e.g., `ClassDependecyFilter` counts the number of classes and methods processed.

Next, the call to `ProcessEnterElement()` (step (3) in Fig. 9) sets the proper `ErrorReport` context (explained later) (step (4) in Fig. 9) to be used when processing the sub-elements of the element at hand. The `ProcessSubElements()` method (step (6) in Fig. 9) calls the `Check()` method of all sub-elements. As shown in Fig. 7, the specific attribute checkers for different meta-elements, e.g.,

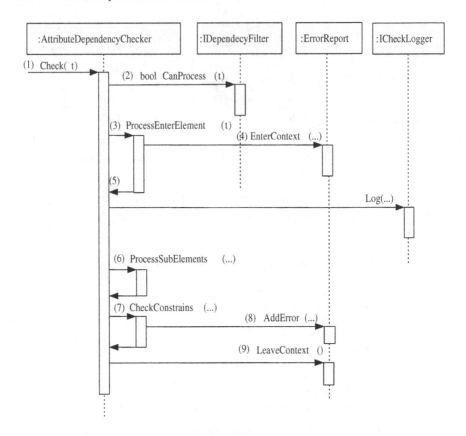

Fig. 9. UML sequential diagram of `Check()` method call

ADCAssembly, ADCClass, etc., are derived form `AttributeDependencyChecker`, by implementing the abstract methods: `Check(object t)`, `ProcessEnterElement(object t)`, and `ProcessSubElements(ref ArrayList ctx, object t)`. For illustration, Fig. 10 shows the implementation of the `ProcessSubElements` method in `ADCClass`. As we see, only the browsing logic of finding the sub elements is part of this method.

The context to be used during the processing of a node and its descendants (the parameter `ctx` in the signature of `ProcessSubElements`) is managed in an `ArrayList` similarly to the method call stack frames in a compiler [2]. A frame in a context contains the attributes and the dependency attributes of a particular element. When we browse the structural tree (by calling `ProcessSubElements`), we fill up the context passing it to every processed sub-element. Each element, when it is processed, can modify the dependency information of context frames of its parents. When we leave a sub-element its frame is removed from the context. After all sub-elements of a given element are processed we have all the required information in the context stack frames to check the dependencies of

```
protected override void ProcessSubElements(ref ArrayList ctx, object t) {
  MethodInfo[] m = ((Type)t).GetMethods(
    BindingFlags.Instance |
    BindingFlags.Public |
    BindingFlags.DeclaredOnly |
    BindingFlags.NonPublic);

  foreach(MethodInfo mi in m) {
    ADCMethod adc = new ADCMethod();
    CopyStateTo(adc);
    adc.InitialContext = ctx;
    adc.Check(mi);
  }
}
```

Fig. 10. ADCClass implementation of ProcessSubElements method

the given element. We compare then the actually present attributes with the total dependency attributes for the current frame, using set operations, in the CheckConstrains() method (step (7) in in Fig. 9).

The :ErrorReport object maintains its own context (set up in step (4) in in Fig. 9) so that when an error is reported (step (8) in in Fig. 9) it can be embedded within the proper structural context. The ErrorReport context is used to report messages in a useful way, as illustrated by the error message:

```
| Required CLASS attribute missing:
| adctests.CA01Attribute @ adctests->adctests.nunit.TDependencyUtils
```

This error message specifies that the required class attribute adctests.CA01-Attribute is missing in class adctests.nunit.TDependencyUtils, part of adctests assembly.

By default ErrorReport accumulates the errors, but this behavior can be changed via a switch, so it will break the checker execution if an error happens by throwing a ADCException. ErrorReport contains also logic to accumulate or immediately report the improper usages in code of the parameters passed to the DependencyAttribute itself. An example is passing an attribute declared with a class lexical scope as an argument to a RequiredMethodAttribute property.

Finally, the ICheckLogger interface (see step (5) in Fig. 9) allows the programmer to associate a customized logger with the checker. If the logger is not null, a hierarchy of the processed elements with details about their attributes and attribute dependencies is printed. A filter could also be used for custom logging. All objects shown in Fig. 9, but :AttributeDependecyChecker, are singletons and are passed to the processing of the sub-elements as part of the context.

The implementation of the class AttributeDependencyChecker is generic w.r.t the implementation of both DependencyAttribute and the meta-model elements, which means that we can reuse its implementation with new attributes as well as with other meta-models. The `AttributeDependencyChecker` achieves this generality by using a combination of the following three techniques:

- First, all the hierarchy information of the supported meta-model is factored out into two static methods (tables) of the `IContextMap` utility class. `AttributeDependencyChecker` uses `IContextMap` to implement a strategy pattern [6]. By changing the `IContextMap` class, users can change the supported meta-model. Theoretically, the information in `IContextMap` would be enough to check the dependencies, i.e., no specific checker classes for different elements of the meta-model, e.g., `ADCClass` would be needed. However, the .NET Reflection API design is not consistent in browsing the meta-elements hierarchy. Unlike other API-s, e.g., XML DOM [4], that have a single base interface, `Node`, from which all elements are derived, the .NET Reflection API does not expose a single generic interface for meta-element types. The rationale being that the number of meta-elements is limited. However, this requires that when adding new meta-elements to the ADC library, we need to derive special classes for them which contain only sub-element browsing code, as described above.
- Second, given the structure of the meta-model is present in the `DependencyAttribute` properties, we use reflection inside the `Check(...)` method over any `DependencyAttribute` properties and map them to the internal `IContextMap` context. The use of the reflection ensures that if we add or remove attributes to the `DependencyAttribute` class, the implementation of the `AttributeDependencyChecker` does not need to be changed. Another generic alternative would be to generate this code based on the `DependencyAttribute` implementation, but this would require to re-generate and re-compile the `AttributeDependencyChecker` for every different version of the `DependencyAttribute` implementation.
- Third, we use the template method pattern [6] to call abstract methods that need to be implemented in the derived classes, like the `ProcessSubElements` method required to browse the sub-elements. The entire checking logic is part of the abstract class `AttributeDependencyChecker`.

The resulting ADC library can be easily extended to support new meta-elements. If we need to add a new type of checker for attributes of another meta-element, we need to derive a class from `AttributeDependencyChecker`, implementing the abstract methods discussed above. In addition, the `IContextMap` class needs to be modified to accommodate the hierarchical structural relation of the new element with the existing elements.

4   Related Work

Using attributes to denote additional custom semantics about an entity is intuitive and is used all around in computer science [16]. Different names used for attributes, range from *tags* to *annotations*. Explicit annotation [1] of source code elements with attributes falls between domain specific languages [3] and generative programming techniques. Explicit attributes can extend the model supported by a generic language, without changing its front-end compiler tools [28] and can be used to drive code transformations [25]. In OMG MDA [5] *tags* are used to *mark* model elements. In the MDA MOF [29] and UML [8] standards, tags have no semantics to the standards themselves. They are used during model transformations as hints by the transformation tools.

Hedin [9] describes how attribute extension grammars can be used to enforce properties about library components that can not be enforced otherwise with object-oriented systems. The work is superseded by language technologies like .NET that directly support attributes and offer API-s to access the AST information along with the decorated attributes. Our approach is situated at a higher abstraction level, using attributes to define declarative rules that must hold between attributes.

Declaring and checking attribute dependencies is one example of explicitly enforcing architectural principles [21]. In fact, attributes offer a unified way to express evolution invariants in languages that support explicit annotations, given that any structural entity can be decorated independently of the syntax. This makes attributes attractive for expressing law-governed system evolution rules. We can express architectural principles that must hold between program entities, as attribute dependencies between architectural attributes used to decorate program entities. System wide invariants can be expressed as `Assembly` attributes and rules can be expressed by meta-attributes over architectural attributes.

Abadi *et al* [17] state that there is a central notion of dependency and abstract any kind of dependency into a Dependency Code Calculus (DCC) based on a computational lambda calculus. Such a formal abstraction can be interesting for proving properties of dependent system elements, but it must be specialized to a specific domain to be of real usage, yielding in different special purpose calculuses. However, some of the dependency problems mentioned in [17] like slicing calculus do not map directly into source code program dependencies and cannot be expressed as source code attributes.

Aspect-oriented programing (AOP) [11] techniques can be also used to enforce architectural decisions. Its usefulness in program generation [15] is based on its global view of the system, which is required to enforce system wide properties. An example how AspectJ [10] (an AOP tool for Java) can be used to enforce system constrains is given in [18]. However as noted there, there are some system wide constrains like name capitalization which cannot be enforced directly with AspectJ. This is because AspectJ abstracts program meta-information between: (a) pointcut declarations - that encapsulate meta-element selection and context; and (b) advice implementations - that make implicit meta-element manipulation. Since the enumeration of all possible meta-operations as declarative constructs is impossible and was not a design goal of AspectJ, there are meta-level programs that cannot be expressed as AspectJ programs.

Our declarative attribute approach is a new natural generative pattern [19] to enforce domain-specific [3] meta-models over attributes. Other problems apart of attribute dependency can be also generalized at the attribute level. However we must note that currently .NET supports only structural elements to be decorated with attributes. We cannot place attributes inside methods, liming rules that can be enforced by our approach.

There are also many generic tools like [30, 31] designed for enforcing rules about a program not covered directly by the programming language mechanisms used. We demonstrated how declarative dependencies can be expressed as attributes to decorate custom attributes, providing a natural way to extend language technologies like .NET where attributes are full status entities. Our approach is however not suited for checking arbitrary program restrictions, which may require customized imperative implementations.

5   Summary

The .NET compiler support for checking custom attributes is limited. We took advantage of the fact that .NET attributes are full status types in the .NET framework, and extended the .NET compiler attribute support with custom declarative checks using attributes themselves. We showed how to decorate custom attribute declarations with other attributes that define additional declarative semantics about the custom attributes. This is a natural way to extend .NET attribute support using pre-processor or post-processor tools, being thus a convenient alternative for supporting domain-specific language constructs [3] and various program transformation techniques [23].

We showed how the attribute dependency problem can be formalized and expressed declaratively as an custom attribute. We described the implementation of the ADC [27] tool designed to check such dependencies. ADC is implemented in a very generic and extensible way. Other attribute enforcement checks can be expressed declaratively in the same way for .NET-like language technologies.

References

1. K. De Volder G. C. Murphy A. Bryant, A. Catton. Explicit Programming. *In Proc. of AOSD '02, ACM Press*, pages 10–18, 2002.
2. A. V. Aho, R. Sethi, J. D. Ullman. *Compilers Principles, Techniques and Tools*. Addisson Wesley, 1988.
3. A. van Deursen, P. Klint, J. Visser. Domain-Specific Languages. *ACM SIGPLAN Notices, Volume 35*, pages 26–36, 2000.
4. B. McLaughlin. *Java and XML*. O'Reilly, Second edition, 2001.
5. D. S. Frankel. *Model Driven Architecture - Applying MDA to Enterprise Computing*. Wiley, 2003.
6. E. Gamma, R. Helm, R. Johnson, J. Vlissides. *Design Patterns*. Addison-Wesley, 1995.
7. E. Roman, S. Ambler, T. Jewell. *Mastering Enterprise JavaBeans*. Wiley, 2001.
8. G. Booch, I. Jacobson, J. Rumbaugh. *The Unified Modeling Language User Guide*. Addison-Wesley, 1998.
9. G. Hedin. Attribute Extension - A Technique for Enforcing Programming Conventions. *Nordic Jounral of Computing*, 1997.

10. G. Kiczales, E. Hilsdale, J. Hugunin, M. Kersten, J. Palm, W. G. Griswold. An Overview of AspectJ. *In Proc. of ECOOP '01, Springer-Verlag, LNCS 2072*, pages 327–353, 2001.
11. G. Kiczales, J. Lamping, A. Menhdhekar, C. Maeda, C. Lopes, J. Loingtier, J. Irwin. Aspect-Oriented Programming. *In Proc. ECOOP '97, Springer-Verlag, LNCS 1241*, pages 220–243, 1997.
12. I. Zderadicka. CS CODEDOM Parser. http://ivanz.webpark.cz/csparser.html, 2002.
13. J. Liberty. *Programming C#*. O'Reilly, 2001.
14. J. Newkirk, A. Vorontsov. How .NET's Custom Attributes Affect Design. *IEEE SOFTWARE, Volume 19(5)*, pages 18–20, September / October 2002.
15. K. Czarnecki, U. W. Eisenecker. *Generative Programming*. Addison-Wesley, 2000.
16. D. Knuth. The Genesis of Attribute Grammars. *In Proc. of International Workshop WAGA*, 1990.
17. M. Abadi, A. Banerjee, N. Heintze, J. G. Riecke. A Core Calculus of Dependency. *In Proc. of the 26th ACM SIGPLAN-SIGACT on Principles of Programming Languages (POPL)*, pages 147–160, 1999.
18. M. Shomrat, A. Yehudai. Obvious or Not? Regulating Architectural Decisions Using Aspect-Oriented Programming. *In Proc. of Aspect-Oriented Software Development - AOSD 01*, 2001.
19. M. Voelter. A Collection of Patterns for Program Generation. *In Proc. EuroPLoP*, 2003.
20. M. Voelter, A. Schmid, E. Wolf. *Server Components Patterns, Illustrated with EJB*. Wiley & Sons, 2002.
21. N. H. Minsky. Why Should Architectural Principles be Enforced? *In Proc. of IEEE Computer Security, Dependability, and Assurance: From Needs to Solutions*, 1998.
22. .NET Framework MSDN Documentation. ms-help://MS.VSCC/MS.MSDNVS/Netstart/html/sdkstart.htm, 2002.
23. R. Paige. Future Directions in Program Transformations. *ACM Computing Surveys, Volume 28*, pages 170–170, 1996.
24. J. Prosise. *Programming Microsoft .NET*. Microsoft Press, 2002.
25. V. Cepa. Implementing Tag-Driven Transformers with Tango. *Proc. of 8th International Conference on Software Reuse - LNCS 3107*, pages 296–307.
26. V. Cepa, M. Mezini. Language Support for Model-Driven Software Development. *(Editor M. Aksit) Special Issue Science of Computer Programming (Elsevier) on MDA: Foundations and Applications Model Driven Architecture*, 2004.
27. .NET Attribute Dependency Checker (ADC) Tool. http://www.st.informatik.tu-darmstadt.de/static/staff/Cepa/tools/adc/index.html, 2003.
28. W. Taha, T. Sheard. Multi-stage Programming. *ACM SIGPLAN Notices*, 32(8), 1997.
29. Meta Object Facility (MOF) Specification Version 1.4. http://www.omg.org, 2002.
30. PMD Java Source Code Scanner. http://pmd.sourceforge.net, 2003.
31. Borland TogetherJ. http://www.borland.com/together/, 2003.

Towards Generation of Efficient Transformations

Attila Vizhanyo, Aditya Agrawal, and Feng Shi

Institute for Software Integrated Systems, Vanderbilt University
Nashville, TN 37235, USA
{viza,aditya,fengshi}@isis.vanderbilt.edu

Abstract. In this paper we discuss efficiency related constructs of a graph rewriting language, called Graph Rewriting and Transformation (GReAT), and introduce a code generator tool, which together provide a programming framework for the specification and efficient realization of graph rewriting systems. We argue that the performance problems frequently associated with the implementation of the transformation can be significantly reduced by partial evaluation and adopting language constructs that allow algorithmic optimizations.

1 Introduction

The Model Driven Architecture (MDA) [3] advocates the use of models in software development through either Unified Modeling Language (UML) [2] or through domain specific languages supported by Meta Object Facility (MOF) [4]. In the later approach, transformations are to bridge the semantic gap between domain specific models and implementation. Other software engineering areas such as Model-Integrated Computing [1] and tool integration also have a requirement of model transformations that bridge semantic gaps between design tools.

Such transformations can be formally specified and automatically implemented using Graph Rewriting/Transformation (GRT) languages [5]. A GRT language typically consists of transformation rules where a pattern graph is matched in the host graph and replaced with a replacement graph. The time complexity of such transformation systems is determined by (1) the sub graph isomorphism algorithm, known to be NP complete and (2) the algorithm to keep track of ready to fire productions. The complexity of such transformation system becomes unacceptable for complex transformations and large graphs. We conjecture that these concerns can be addressed at various places in a transformation system ranging from the language to its implementation.

This paper presents runtime-optimization related features of Graph Rewriting and Transformation (GReAT) [12][13][14] a graphical rewriting/ transformation language and its compiler called Code Generator (CG) that is used to implement the transformations. The optimizations have been classified into two categories, (1) language and algorithmic optimization and (2) partial evaluation and implementation optimizations.

Language and algorithmic optimizations are based on language constructs that have optimized implementation algorithms. While partial evaluation and implementation optimization are performed by the Code Generator (CG) which produces code specific to a given transformation and input/output domains. The generated code provides a significant performance boost over GRE, GReAT's generic graph rewrite/transformation engine. Since the CG does not partially evaluate the transformation based on input/output graph, the generated transformation can be reused for any graph in the input/output domains. There is some overhead associated with regenera-

G. Karsai and E. Visser (Eds.): GPCE 2004, LNCS 3286, pp. 298–316, 2004.

tion and recompilation of the transformation code if the transformation is changed, but those transformations that are still under development can be executed and debugged using a generic rewrite/transformation engine. Once the transformation reaches a mature state, the transformation can be compiled into a high-performance executable that is capable of performing transformations on large models.

Paper organization: Section 2 reviews the area of graph grammars and transformations. Section 3 briefly describes Graph Rewriting and Transformation (GReAT) a metamodel based model-to-model transformation language and discusses language and algorithm level optimizations in GReAT. Section 4 describes GReAT's Code Generator (CG) and implementation level optimizations. Section 5 provides some experimental results comparing the runtime performance of transformations using CG and GRE. Conclusions and proposals for future research are presented in Section 6.

2 Background

2.1 Graph Rewriting and Transformations

There are a variety of graph transformation techniques described in [5–11]. Prominent among these are node replacement grammars, hyper edge replacement grammars, single/double pushout and programmed graph replacement systems. The next few paragraphs will discuss each approach and point out some complexity issues [5].

Node replacement grammars are a class of graph grammars that are based primarily upon the replacement of nodes in a graph. The basic production of every node replacement grammar has a LHS subgraph (called mother graph) that produces an RHS subgraph (called daughter graph). Usually the LHS subgraph consists of only one node, making this class of grammars context free. The productions can be applied whenever a mother node is found in the host graph. If two productions can be applied at the same time then the order of application is non-deterministic [5].

The execution time of node replacement grammars is bounded by graph search and tracking of ready-to-execute productions. If all the subgraphs contain only one node in the mother graph then the worst case complexity of finding a ready-to-execute production is $O(n \times r)$, where n is the number of nodes in the graph and r is number of productions. Single node mother graphs are suitable for defining and parsing graphical languages but are restrictive and not suitable for defining complex "algorithmic" transformations.

Hyperedge replacement grammars deal with the productions that replace hyper edges by subgraphs. Each production has a hyperedge on the LHS, which is replaced by a subgraph on the RHS. Hyperedge replacement by definition is confluent, associative and parallelizable. The time complexity and shortcomings are similar to the node replacement grammars [5].

Another approach to graph grammars is the algebraic one. The approach is based on a generalization of Chomsky grammars from strings to graphs. The main goal was to generalize the string concatenation to a gluing construction of graphs. The gluing of graphs is defined by algebraic constructions called pushouts. The pushout approach has been borrowed from a more general field of category theory. Significant research has been done on pushouts and how productions can be parallelized. The algebraic approach is more powerful and has concepts for sequencing and parallelizing the rules [6].

The algebraic approaches, in the general case, have subgraphs in the LHS and thus subgraph isomorphism algorithms are required to find a particular LHS subgraph in the host graph. Subgraph isomorphism is known to have an order complexity of $O(n^p)$ where, n is the number of host graph nodes and p is the number of nodes in the subgraph. The time complexity of finding a ready-to-execute transformation, in the general case, is $O(r \times n^p)$ where r is the number of transformations in the system. In the algebraic approaches it is possible to specify a sequence of the transformation rules. This eliminates the need for finding the next ready-to-fire transformation. The sequencing of rules is limited only to sequential and parallel execution of the rules. It lacks high-level sequencing constructs such as conditional branching of productions, looping and recursion. The lack of high-level sequencing means that the user cannot represent and/or choose between depth-first search and breadth-first search.

The last approach to be discussed is that of programmed replacement systems, which are the most practical of all the approaches discussed so far. The leading research result is the PROgrammed GRaph REplacement System (PROGRES) [6]. The major breakthrough of PROGRES is that it concentrates equally on productions and sequencing of the productions. Thus the system has a graph replacement language that defines the productions and also programming constructs that define the order of application of the productions. The PROGRES system consists of two parts - the first is a logic based structure replacement system that describes graph transformation productions of the language, and the second is a collection of programming constructs such as recursion, non-deterministic application of productions, conditions and loops. Apart from these PROGRES can also specify static integrity constraints on the graphs. The time complexity of PROGRES based transformations is in the hands of the user [5][6][7].

3   Language and Algorithmic Optimizations

3.1   GReAT: Graph Rewriting and Transformation

Graph Rewriting and Transformation (GReAT) [12][13][14] is the transformation language developed for model-to-model transformations/rewriting. This section provides a brief overview of GReAT, while [12] provides a more detailed description. The operational semantics of GReAT is formally defined in [14]. GReAT is based on the theoretical work of graph grammars and transformations [5] and belongs to the set of practical graph transformations systems, like AGG [8] and PROGRES [7]. GReAT has two parts: (1) graph transformation language, and (2) control flow language. The graph transformation language is used to specify transformations on localized subgraphs and follows the Single Pushout (SPO) algebraic approach [5]. However in SPO, many pattern objects can be mapped to the same graph object, while this is not allowed in GReAT.

A production (also referred to as rule) is the basic unit of transformation and it contains a pattern graph that consists of pattern vertices and edges. Each pattern element has an attribute called role that specifies what happens during the transformation step. A pattern element can play one of three roles: Bind, Delete, CreateNew. The execution of a rule involves matching every pattern object marked either Bind or Delete. The pattern matcher will return all possible matches for the given pattern and host graph. The returned matches are evaluated with the (optional) guard condition, and matches for which the guard evaluates to false are discarded. Then for each match the pattern objects marked Delete are deleted from the graph and objects marked New are created. Finally, the attributes of the graph objects can be manipulated by an optional *AttributeMapping* (AM) specification. The AM specification consists of code based on a C++ API that accesses the graph objects.

GReAT uses the UML [2] class diagram notation for the specification of patterns. For example, in Fig. 2(a), *OrState, SubOrState, State, SubOrState/State* composition and *OrState/SubOrState* composition have the **Bind** role while *NewState, OrState/NewState* composition and *State/NewState* association have the **CreateNew** role. The semantics of the rule is: find the pattern marked **Bind**, in this case the *OrState, SubOrState, State, SubOrState/State* composition and *OrState/SubOrState* composition pattern. Then, for every such pattern evaluate the *Guard* expression. Let the guard expression be "SubOrState.name = State.name". Thus only those matches that have this property will pass the guard and the rest will be discarded. Then create the objects marked *CreateNew*, in this case *NewState, OrState/NewState* composition and *State/NewState* association. Finally, use *AttributeMapping* to fill in the attributes of the newly created objects.

The order complexity of the pattern matching is $O(n^p)$ and if there are many rules to choose from, then the complexity of finding the correct transformation is $O(r \times n^p)$.

Traditionally, in graph grammars and transformations there is no ordering imposed on the productions, but practical model-to-model transformations often require strict control over the execution sequence. GReAT has a high-level control flow language built on top of the graph transformation language to allow users to specify algorithmic transformations.

The control flow constructs have been useful in the development of the following transformations: (1) Simulink/Stateflow to Hybrid Automata [20], (2) Embedded System Modeling Language (ESML) to Boeing's Boldstroke Configuration, (3) Khoral Inc.'s KHOROS to Grand Unified Dataflow Modeling Language (GUDML), (4) OMG's Meta Object Facility (MOF) to MetaGME.

The following language constructs have been developed to improve the efficiency of the transformations: (1) pivoting and (2) sequencing.

3.2 Typed Patterns

It is well known that the worst case execution time for the identification of subgraph isomorphism is exponential in terms of the input graph and the pattern graph. In order to reduce the average case execution time a number of steps can be taken.

One of the well known optimization techniques is to type the pattern vertices and edges, this restrict the search to a subgraph of the host that only contains the particular types used in the pattern [8][18]. If we consider a host graph having say T types of vertices and if we assume that the vertices have even distribution with respect to its type then the time complexity of matching a pattern with P_t types of vertices is $(\frac{P}{T} \times n)^p$. Even though the worst case execution time is $O(n^p)$ the expected case execution will have a saving. On an average, graphs contain ~30 vertex types while a pattern graph uses ~3 vertex type and thus in the average case the saving should be ~10x.

3.3 Pivoted Pattern Matching

Another optimization technique is to start the pattern matcher with an initial binding and we have named it "pivoted pattern matching". In this technique the programmer provides an initial binding for some of the models in the pattern graph to the host graph nodes. The pattern matching is then performed in the context of the initial binding.

In Fig. 1, the pattern vertex *Pv* is initially bound to the host vertex *Hv*. This restricts the search to the area shown within dotted line. This particular optimization works well for sparsely connected graphs. For example, graph has an average connectivity, the number of edges incident on a vertex, of 3 and the greatest distance from the pivot to a vertex in the pattern graph to be 2. Then the matching algorithm will only search within a tree of depth 3 starting from the pivoted node. In general the number of host graph vertices included in the search will be c^d where c is the connectivity and d is the depth of the pattern. Hence the order complexity of the matching algorithm is $O(n^p)$, where $n = c^d$ and p is the number of unbound vertices.

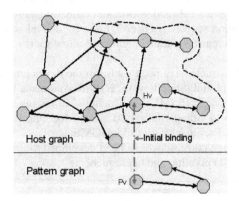

Fig. 1. Pivoted Matching

This optimization technique, when added to the typed pattern vertex technique gives a significant saving because in this case the connectivity of the restricted graph is even less. Fig. 2(b) shows the same rule as in Fig. 2(a) with the addition of *In* and

Out ports used to provide the initial binding. The *OrState* pattern vertex is bound to a host graph vertex supplied by the port labeled *In*.

3.4 Reusing Previously Matched Objects

The next optimization technique used in GReAT is the one called "Reusing previously matched objects". The idea here is to cache previously found results and pass it on to subsequent rules as the initial binding.

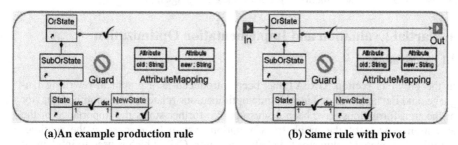

(a)An example production rule   (b) Same rule with pivot

Fig. 2. Transformation rule specification

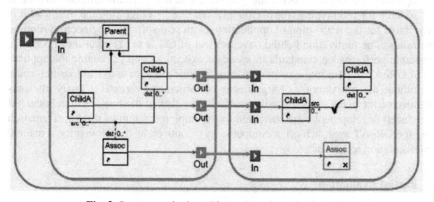

Fig. 3. Sequence of rules with passing of previous results

For example, in Fig. 3, there are two rules, the first rule gets an input binding for *Parent* and finds all *ChildA, ChildB, Assoc* triples that correspond to the pattern. In the subsequent rule these triples are required to perform an action. Instead of finding the pattern again, the first rule passes the triples along to the next rule. For the next rule they serve as the initial binding. When a rule executes it can produce multiple matches. Each match produces a host graph object for each output port and this coherent set of objects is called a packet. These packets are sent to the subsequent rules as one unit.

GReAT supports hierarchical specification of transformation rules. High-level rules can be created by composing a sequence of primitive rules. There are two kinds of high-level rules in GReAT: *Block* and *ForBlock*. The execution semantics of the

Block is to pass all input packets to the first contained rule, the outputs packets created by it are passed to subsequent rules and so on. After all packets have been processed and all output packets of the Block have been generated the Block returns control to its parent. Semantics for the *ForBlock* is to pass one input packet at a time through all the contained rules. After the first packet has been processed all the way to the output of the *ForBlock* the next packet is processed. These two constructs enables user to choose different traversal strategies. A *Test/Case* is also available in GReAT. It can be used to choose between different execution paths, during the transformation and is similar to 'if' statements in programming languages.

4 Partial Evaluation and Implementation Optimization

4.1 Motivation

In the previous section, GReAT has been introduced as a graphical rewriting language, and the language and algorithmic optimizations related to the runtime behavior of the transformations have been discussed. We further stress the importance of the execution aspects of the graph transformation system by discussing the runtime-optimization related features of the Code Generator (CG), which is used to implement the transformations.

Graph Rewrite Engine (GRE), the generic graph rewrite/transformation engine is [12] suitable for prototyping transformations but due to a high runtime overhead it is not suitable for the realization of applications with real software engineering runtime constraints. The motivation behind development of CG is to (1) meet the criteria for acceptable performance standards in speed of execution, and (2) enable the application of GReAT system implementations as a feasible alternative to hand written code, i.e. without the introduction of significant performance overhead. Clearly, the performance of the generated code will remain below that of the hand written code, but the reduced development time attributed to the implementation of the transformation using the GReAT approach often compensates or outweighs the conventional manual implementation techniques.

4.2 Partial Evaluation

If we write the Graph Rewriting Engine (GRE) of GReAT as a function it will have the following signature:

$$GRE : (I \times M_I \times M_O \times T) \rightarrow O \text{, where}$$

- M_I, M_O - metamodels. A Metamodel is a graph that defines the graph grammar of the input/output models.
- I – input model. A graph that conforms to the metamodel M_I.
- O- output model. A graph that conforms to the metamodel M_O.
- T - transformation. Is a graph rewrite/transformation specification.

The Code Generator performs a partial evaluation of the GRE function to produce code specific to a given transformation and input/output metamodels.

$$CG : (M_I \times M_O \times T) \rightarrow (T_C : (I) \rightarrow O)$$

The justification for the partial evaluation is that the transformation and the metamodels make up the invariant part of transformation system. The same transformation is typically run on multiple inputs over a course of time. We argue that once the transformation and the modeling paradigm(s) reach a mature state, the transformation can be compiled into a high-performance executable that is capable of performing transformations in an efficient way.

By treating the metamodels as invariants, the CG can generate code that manipulate input and output models using paradigm-specific API's. These API's are generated by Universal Data Model (UDM), a framework that provides object-oriented C++ interfaces to programmatically access input/output models. UDM can generate a domain specific custom API with type-safe access methods for object creation/removal, link creation/removal, and attribute setters/getters [15]. The transformation executable can be built by compiling the generated transformation files and the paradigm-specific API files.

4.3 Implementation of Algorithmic Optimizations

The transformation rules are compiled into C++ class definitions. Although from the point of view of the language semantics, the procedural programming paradigm would suffice, we will see later in this section that introducing user-defined types for the transformation rules results in a much cleaner design. In C++, data abstraction is implemented by classes, and the class is also the unit of encapsulation, which OO concept will assist in the implementation of the packet passing mechanism.

The only function exposed in the public interface of each class definition is the function operator. Calling the function operator of a given class triggers the execution of the corresponding rule.

GReAT trans. Rule	Generated C++ class definition

Rule	*class Rule {*
	public:
	    void operator( )( )(const Packets_t& In1, const Packets_t& In2,
	        Packets_t& Ou1, Packets_t& Ou2, Packets_t& Ou3);
	};

Fig. 4. Mapping GReAT transformation rules to C++ classes

GReAT introduces the optimization *"Reusing Previously Matched Objects"*, which is basically the idea of passing graph objects attached to *ports* from one rule to another.

The function operator argument list implements the facility for passing vertices of already matched subgraphs between a set of rules. *Packets_t* is a list of objects, which is the common base class for all classes that represent the graph objects. In this context, the *Packets_t* arguments represent a list of graph objects directed to a specific port. Subgraphs can be derived by taking together the input or output packets of the corresponding rule.

The implementation of *operator( )* depends on the type of the GReAT rule:

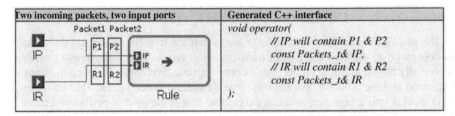

Fig. 5. A graph object passing use-case

- For rules of type *Block*, the function operator executes the contained rules in the sequencing order for all incoming packets.
- For rules of type *ForBlock*, the function operator executes each contained rule for each incoming packet, one-by-one.
- For rules of type *Test*, the contained cases are executed for all incoming packets in a deterministic order, which is derived from the physical placement of the cases, until a match has been found in a case.
- For rules of type *ForTest*, the contained cases are executed in the same way as in the case of the *Test*, but each case is executed for each incoming packet, one-by-one.
- For rules of type *Rule*, the incoming packets representing a host subgraph are tested against the pattern graph, then for each match new objects are created and matched objects deleted according to the rule semantics specified in Section 3.1. The pattern objects connected to the output port are then used to create output packets, as specified in Section 3.4.
- For rules of type *Case*, incoming packets representing a host subgraph are tested against the pattern graph, and the pattern objects connected to the output port are then used to create output packets.

4.4   Rule Execution and Sequencing

The generated transformation code can be initiated starting from any rewriting rule; rules contained in that rule will be executed. The execution sequence of contained rules is maintained by *rule callers*. Rule callers are protected member functions of composite rules, and are designed to implement three important tasks:

1. Calling rules with the necessary arguments.
2. Calling the rule callers of *destination rules*. *Destination rules* are defined as the set of those rules, whose inputs are supplied by the current rule.
3. Forwarding packets to the output ports of the parent rule.

Let block *Block* contain *Rule0, Rule1, Rule2*. The class definition generated for block *Block*, will contain one rule caller for each rules: *Rule0, Rule1, Rule2*. Fig. 6 shows the code for the rule caller of *Rule0*. Observe, how packets are passed from caller to caller through the function argument lists.

To solve task 3, each contained rule must be able to append its own outputs to the parent block's outputs. The block's outputs should be visible only for those rules which are contained in that block. If every block output were passed as an individual argument to each rule caller function, the interface would quickly become very

GReAT rule sequencing pattern	Generated C++ code
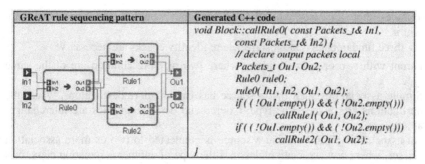	*void Block::callRule0(const Packets_t& In1,* * const Packets_t& In2) {* * // declare output packets local* * Packets_t Ou1, Ou2;* * Rule0 rule0;* * rule0(In1, In2, Ou1, Ou2);* * if((!Ou1.empty()) && (!Ou2.empty()))* * callRule1(Ou1, Ou2);* * if((!Ou1.empty()) && (!Ou2.empty()))* * callRule2(Ou1, Ou2);* *}*

Fig. 6. Rule execution and sequencing via rule callers

bloated. Our preferred approach to this problem is to represent the block output ports as member variables. Initially, rule callers had been implemented as procedures, but the design constraint described above led us to rely on OO encapsulation and C++ classes. Restricting data visibility to a set of functions automatically entails the conversion of those functions to class member functions. Classes are the primary language elements in C++ that represent concepts in the application domain. Thus in the process of seeking a good representation of the GReAT rules, we eventually employed *abstract data types*.

4.5 Pattern Matcher

The graph rewriting/transformation process starts with the *pattern matching*, where an input subgraph and pattern graph are used to perform subgraph isomorphism on the input graph. The pattern graph can be described as a set of graph objects each with specific type, connected together with specific containment and association relationships. Therefore the task of the generated pattern matcher code is to (1) type-check all input subgraph elements and (2) check for the existence of the pattern vertices and edges in the input graph. If any type mismatch is found, then the pattern matching fails for the current input, and the processing proceeds to the next input. The pattern matching algorithm used in CG traverses the relationships specified in the pattern graph and generates code for each relationship. Traversed relationships are marked bound. The code generation process stops when all relationships in the pattern have been marked bound.

Specification of the types of the graph objects is fully exploited in the code generation process in the following way. In contrast with a naïve and general pattern matching implementation, we utilize strongly typed interfaces in the generated code, which leads to the restriction of the candidate objects and relations. This brings about the performance gain consequence of checking smaller number of graph objects and relations in the input host graph.

The GReAT definition of a match enforces that each pattern object must refer to a unique host graph object. The brute force approach would check a newly matched graph object with all previously matched objects before actually making the match. However, *identity checks* need not be so thorough, because in many cases different pattern objects cannot possibly refer to the same graph object. Objects of different types cannot be identical, objects of different parents cannot be either, and so on.

Nevertheless there are cases, when they can, and they would, if *identity checks* did not prevent it.

The three fundamental relationships where identity checks are necessary:

1. Parent with two or more children, where two or more children are of the same type.
2. Simple associations such that a source has two or more destinations, where the destinations are of the same type; (source and destination roles are interchangeable).
3. An association class such that a source is connected to two or more association classes, where any association class has the type of another association class, or a source is connected to two or more different type association classes, but connected to destinations, where any destination has the type of another destination; (source and destination roles are interchangeable)

GReAT pattern	Generated UDM API C++ pseudo-code

Paradigm::BoundParent / Paradigm::UnboundChild	//get children of type UnboundChild only
	set< Paradigm::UnboundChild> unboundChilds=
	       boundParent.UnboundChild_kind_children();
	for(set< Paradigm::UnboundChild>::const_iterator it=
	       unboundChilds.begin();it!= unboundChilds.end(); ++it){
	       Paradigm::UnboundChild currUnboundChild = *it;
	       ...
	}

Paradigm::UnboundParent / Paradigm::BoundChild	Udm::Object& boundChildParent= boundChild.container();
	// UDM RTTI
	if(false== Uml::IsDerivedFrom(boundChildParent.type(),
	       Paradigm::UnboundParent::meta))
	       continue;
	Paradigm::UnboundParent unboundParent=
	       Paradigm::UnboundParent::Cast(boundChildParent);
	...

Fig. 7. Composite relationships and the respective generated code fragments

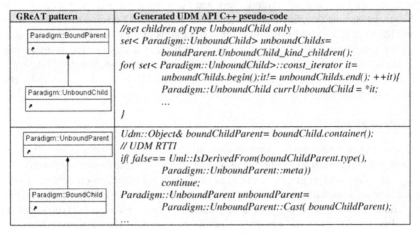

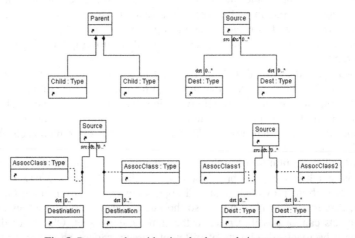

Fig. 8. Patterns where identity checker code is necessary

The performance gain resulting from the application of identity checkers is apparent for large pattern graphs along with those relationships described above. The brute force approach that checks each object for uniqueness would impose a significant performance overhead in the runtime.

In the generated code the identity checks are performed if and only if the objects in the match have the same type, and they are connected to some identical object (such as a parent, or other end of an association). ('Has the type' means same type, or direct or indirect descendant of, as in OO terminology.)

4.6 Effector

Pattern graphs can have pattern objects with roles set to *CreateNew* or *Delete*, as described in Section 3.1. The actions are executed for each match found by the pattern matcher. Fig. 9 presents some examples of consequence code generation.

Another specification element of consequences is the *Attribute Mapping Code*. These are code snippets provided by the user to manipulate the attributes of the graph objects. The specification language for these snippets is C/C++, hence the code can be directly copied into the generated code. The CG provides the context for the *Attribute Mapping Code* by instantiating variables with pattern object names within the scope of the *Attribute Mapping Code*.

GReAT consequence	Generated UDM API C++ pseudo-code
Paradigm::Parent → Paradigm::Child	// Create Pattern Object *Paradigm::Child newChild= Paradigm::Child::Create(Parent);*

Paradigm::Object	// Delete Pattern Object
	*if (Object) // if Object exists
	     Object.DeleteObject();*

Source src 0..* dst 0..* Destination	// create multiple cardinality simple association link
	Source.dst()+= Destination;
	// create single cardinality simple association link
	Source.dst()= Destination;

Fig. 9. GReAT consequences and the respective generated code fragments

4.7 Architecture of the CG

Having illustrated some required features of the generated code, we now focus our attention on the design aspects of the CG tool. We present a way of using the *composite* design pattern to produce the inherently complex transformation code. But before going into details we present the architectural overview of the CG tool.

The most fundamental design challenges along with their resolutions regarding the generated C++ code are:

1. *Simplicity and Clarity:* Introducing the OO programming paradigm, that results in a faithful representation of the architecture of the application domain. Dependen-

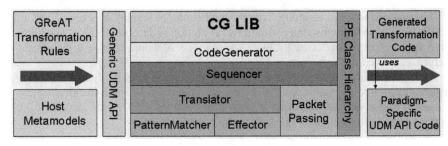

Fig. 10. The overall architecture diagram of the CG tool

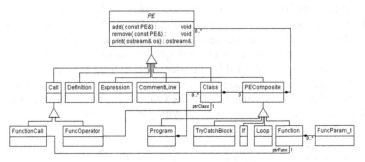

Fig. 11. The PE Class Hierarchy

cies between different parts of the program are minimized by the use of well-defined interfaces.

2. *Correctness and Safety:* The generated code is built up from small validated code blocks in an iterative manner. Type safety is ensured by performing run-time type checks previous to executing type casts. Application of STL containers and iterators, which are not only safe but also predictably efficient with the STL complexity guarantees.

3. *Efficiency:* Prudent application of language-level efficiency guidelines such as passing objects by references, omission of creation objects on the heap, elimination of implicit temporary objects, etc.

The approach we have taken to achieve these goals is to build a C++ syntax tree like structure from various abstract data types representing C++ language primitives, For instance, we created a class to embody the representation of a C++ class definition or a C++ for-loop. This family of classes can also be thought of as the metamodel for the output code, where each metamodel element corresponds to a specific code fragment. In the code generation process we essentially construct the appropriate objects and compose these objects into tree structures to represent the generated program hierarchy. Finally the resulting hierarchical structure (or part of) can be serialized in to C++ source file(s). This is an application of the *Composite* design pattern [16].

The key to this design is the class *PE*, which is declared abstract, and represents both primitives and containers. *PE* (Program Element) declares composite operations for managing its children, and a *print()* function, which prints the object to the stream, which is the function argument of *print()*.

All these operations are declared as virtual to take advantage of *polymorphism* in a variety of cases where type dependent run-time discrimination is needed. One example is the *print()* function of the composite class, which performs recursive serialization through the polymorphic container *_elems*.

```
std::ostream& PEComposite::print( std::ostream &os) const {
    typedef std::list< const PE*> PEs_t;
    // print children
    for( PEs_t::const_iterator it= _elems.begin(); it != _elems.end(); ++it) {
        const PE* pe= *it;
        os= pe->print( os);
    }
    return os;
}
```

The CG tool generates human readable code -featuring formatted output and separate header/source serialization-, by simply invoking the *print()* method on the topmost object in the container hierarchy. Therefore, the fundamental challenge is rather the *creation* of the *PE* hierarchy. In this sense, the CG tool can be thought of as a translator, which translates the GReAT program hierarchy into the *PE* syntax hierarchy. In this respect the current version of CG can be used to develop the next generation CG in GReAT.

The various modules of the Code Generator perform this translation in different stages during the generation process. Each class encapsulates a set of algorithms specific to a given task. If one class uses some services of another class, we made that first class configurable with the behavior of the other class. This design first and foremost supports runtime configuration of the various components, but it also enhances reusability and advocates extensibility in the future. This is the *Strategy* design pattern [16]. For example, the Sequencer class can be configured with a Translator class, therefore the same sequencer can be (re)used with different translator implementations. The key components of the CG tool are described below:

- *CodeGenerator:* This class provides the main user interface for the code generation. It offers the family of strategy objects (see below) that support the default translation course. The class also contains a *Program* object, which represents the target of the translation. The primary design goal was to make this class as easy to use as possible; if the user wants to perform more sophisticated code generation, he can implement his own strategy classes and plug them in the existing code generation framework.

- *Sequencer:* The structure of the GReAT rules can be represented by a possibly cyclic directed graph. The Sequencer performs a Breadth-first traversal on this graph starting from the root rule. Already visited vertices are marked to prevent infinite traversals of the graph. For every sequenced rule, the Sequencer calls the Translator to generate code which implements that particular rule.

- *Translator:* This is the class that is primarily responsible for the translation. Each rule is translated to its equivalent C++ class definition. The translation procedure depends on the type of the rule, i.e. the implementation of the class is rule-type-dependent. It is the Translator that generates the rule callers, and it also keeps track of the mapping between the rules and the corresponding generated class definitions. The Translator uses PacketPassing, PatternMatcher and Effector modules to perform those subtasks that are not directly related to the generic translation process.

- *PacketPassing:* This module defines a set of data structures that keep track of the mapping between ports of a rule and the function argument list generated for that rule. PacketPassing plays an indispensable role in the generation of the rule callers, where function operators are to be called with the correct function argument list to support the passing of already matched subgraphs between various rules.

- *PatternMatcher:* The class PatternMatcher encapsulates all the translation logic which is associated with the pattern matching code generation. The pattern matching algorithm traverses the edges of the pattern graph, and produces optimized pattern matching program code which implements the pattern specification. The generated code checks the types of the graph objects and the existence of specific type relationships in the host subgraph in an efficient way which is described in Section 4.5. The input subgraph gets entered into the pattern matching context through the use of the PacketPassing data structures. The PatternMatcher also generates an embedded class definition which represents the match specific for the given rule. If a match has been found, a container of the matches is appended with the match. This container is going to be used in the implementation of consequences, which is generated by the Effector.

- *Effector:* Consequences, such as object creation, deletion, and creation or deletion of relationships are implemented by the Effector class. This class is also responsible for printing out the Attribute mapping code and creating output packets from those pattern objects which are connected to the output ports of the related rule.

The generated code compiles without any custom modifications, and it is also ISO Standard C++ compliant, consequently platform independent.

4.8   Related Work

In the area of model based software engineering, XSLT is the tool of choice for transforming models represented in XML [21]. XSLT is a tree rewriting language and many interpreters are available that execute the XSLT program.

The PROGRES environment developed at Aachen University of Technology solves the pattern matching efficiency problem with the help of a simple heuristic optimization algorithm, which is based on the implementation of a sophisticated cost model. PROGRES, similarly to GReAT, introduces various language elements to restrict the number of possible search paths, like node and edge types and edge cardinality assertions [18]. PROGRES also offers an interpreter and a cross-compiler, the later of which generates efficient Modula-2 or C code for PROGRES specifications [7].

OPTIMIX is a flexible optimizer generator developed by Uwe Aßman at University of Karsruhe. Its input language is based on Datalog and graph rewriting systems such as edge addition rewrite systems (EARS) and stratified graph rewrite systems (stratified GRS). The transformation can manage data models specified in heterogeneous syntax formats like Java, AST and CoSy-fSDL. OPTIMIX is capable of generating C or JAVA code based on the type of the input data models [17].

CLEAN, created by the Software Technology department of the University of Nijmegen, is a functional programming language with explicit graph rewriting semantics. A CLEAN program basically consists of a number of graph rewrite rules with the common graph transformation semantics, but the left-hand side graph being required to be a tree. CLEAN is not primarily designed to be a sophisticated graph transformation specification language. Rather it is a modular and general purpose programming language offering I/O libraries and diverse type systems [19].

The FUJABA Environment generates Java code from UML class diagrams and a combination of statecharts, activity diagrams and collaboration diagrams [22].

Whereas GReAT, PROGRES,OPTIMIX and FUJABA generate code in other programming languages and use external general-language compilers to generate executables, CLEAN provides its own compiler and code generator, producing efficient native object code optimized for graph rewriting programs.

Currently we have no performance benchmarks to compare GReAT with the tools mentioned above. Developing such a benchmark would require comparing the tools on many transformations and various inputs. Furthermore, the comparison would not contribute to the paper, because the aim is to showcase how language constructs and their implementation can improve the runtime performance of a given graph transformation language.

5   Comparison of CG with GRE

The CG has been specified as a partial evaluation of the GRE with the promise of significant performance gains over the GRE. In this section we present a comparison of the execution times to evaluate whether the claims are justified. Two transformation problems have been chosen for the comparison. These transformations are: (1) *Df→Fdf:* Transform Hierarchical dataflow to its equivalent Flat dataflow representation. (2) *Hsm→Fsm:* Transform Hierarchical Concurrent State Machine (HCSM) to its equivalent Finite State Machine (FSM).

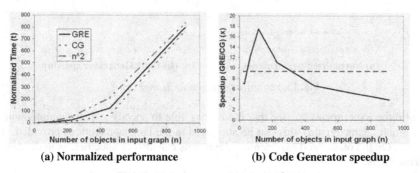

(a) Normalized performance   (b) Code Generator speedup

Fig. 12. Performance graphs for Df→Fdf

To evaluate the performance of CG in comparison with GRE, the Df→Fdf transformation was executed on 7 different input graphs. The size of these graphs varied from 24 vertices to 914 vertices. Execution times of GRE and CG were measured for all the inputs. Fig. 12(a) is a plot of the input graph size (n) vs. normalized execution time for both GRE and CG. Matlab's polyfit function was used to find the closest fitting polynomial or exponential to the results and the second order polynomial yielded the best results. For this reason the n^2 plot is also shown in Fig. 12. From the graph we can see that the order complexity of the transformation doesn't change significantly between GRE and CG and is governed by the complexity of the transformation algorithm. Experimentally we have seen that the transformation algorithms complexity is ~ $O(n^2)$. Fig. 12(b) shows the graph of n vs. speedup achieved by the code generator. The dashed line in the graph represents the average speedup of 9.3x. From the graph we can see that the speedup varies within a bound ranging from 4x to 18x.

For $Hsm \rightarrow Fsm$, 4 input graphs were used. These graphs only had parallel states and varied from 11 vertices to 27 vertices. Execution times of GRE and CG were measured for all the inputs. Fig. 13(a) is a plot of the input graph size (n) vs. normalized execution time for both GRE and CG. The polyfit function was again used and this time an exponential to the base 10 yielded the closest results. For this reason Fig. 13 also shows the 10^n plot. From the graph we can see that the order complexity of the transformation doesn't change between GRE and CG and is governed by the complexity of the transformation algorithm. In this case we see that that transformation algorithms complexity approaches ~ $O(10^n)$. Fig. 13(b) shows the graph of n vs. speedup achieved by the code generator. The dashed line in the graph represents the average speedup of 83.3x. From the graph we can see that the speedup varies within a bound ranging from 14x to 119x. The 14x speed up was observed for very small models and could be because of a constant runtime overhead. A speedup of ~100x was observed consistently for larger models.

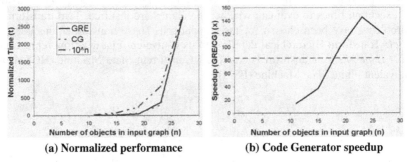

(a) Normalized performance (b) Code Generator speedup

Fig. 13. Performance graphs for $Hsm \rightarrow Fsm$

From the experiments we see that the user is able to specify transformations with polynomial characteristics, this can be attributed to the language features provided in GReAT. On the other hand exponential algorithms can also be specified as in the case of $Hsm \rightarrow Fsm$.

The second conclusion is that the order complexity of the transformation remains the same for both GRE and CG. This is an expected result because the code generator does not perform any modifications that can provide a gain in order complexity.

The speedup doesn't seem to have a definitive trend with respect to the input size but vary a lot from one kind of transformation to another. Df$\rightarrow$Fdf, an $O(n^2)$ transformation yielded an average speedup of ~9x while the Hsm$\rightarrow$Fsm, an $O(10^n)$ transformation yielded an average speedup of ~85x. These results make us believe that the speedup is dependent on the complexity of the transformation. For higher complexity transformations the speedup is also higher.

One possible reason for such a result can be based on the percentage of the total execution time spent in the pattern matching as opposed to the packet passing and other housekeeping work. Since a higher order complexity algorithm will spend more time in the pattern matcher, and the code generator partially evaluates the pattern matcher, a better speedup is observed. When the time complexity of the algorithm is small and the size of the models is large, the packet-passing/housekeeping overhead is a large percentage of the total execution time and the observed speedup is less.

6 Conclusion and Future Work

Specification of Graph transformations using high-level transformation languages has many advantages in Model Driven Architecture (MDA), tool integration and other areas in software engineering. The major bottleneck associated with graph rewriting systems is poor runtime performance. Performance issues need to be tackled at all levels of the transformation system, ranging from the language to low-level implementations. There are two major categories of optimizations that can be applied to graph transformation languages: (1) language and algorithmic, that may yield an improvement in the order complexity and (2) partial evaluation and implementation optimization that produce a constant time improvement.

Three language-level optimizations have been described in the paper – (a) Typed patterns, (b) Pivoted pattern matching and (c) Reusing previously found objects. These optimizations on an average can produce a significant speedup in the execution time of the transformations. As shown in the comparison section, the Df$\rightarrow$Fdf transformation had an order complexity of only n^2 for both GRE and CG.

Although the reduced development time attributable to the graph specific language semantics is an obvious benefit, efficiency drawback in the execution time can still prevent the application of graph transformations in many real systems. We have described how partial evaluation and other implementation techniques can considerably speed up the transformations. In the case of Hsm$\rightarrow$Fsm transformation the CG provided a speedup of ~100x over the generic graph rewrite engine.

Though many solutions have been presented in this paper to address the performance needs, there are still some transformations that are exponential. In these cases, though we cannot change the order complexity of the transformation, we should be able to further optimize the implementations such that they produce much better results in the average case. Until the generated code does not do better than its hand coded counterpart in speed of execution, there will be always room for improvement. The generator can factor out repetitive transformations and reuse parts of the pattern matching code.

Acknowledgement

The DARPA/IXO MOBIES program, Air Force Research Laboratory under agreement number F30602-00-1-0580 and NSF ITR on "Foundations of Hybrid and Embedded Software Systems" programs have supported, in part, the activities described in this paper.

References

1. J. Sztipanovits, and G. Karsai, "Model-Integrated Computing", Computer, Apr. 1997, pp. 110-112.
2. J. Rumbaugh, I. Jacobson, and G. Booch, "The Unified Modeling Language Reference Manual", Addison-Wesley, 1998.
3. "The Model Driven Architecture", http://www.omg.org/mda/, OMG, Needham, MA, 2002.
4. "Request For Proposal: MOF 2.0 Query/Views/Transformations", OMG Document: ad/2002-04-10, 2002, OMG, Needham, MA.
5. Grzegorz Rozenberg, "Handbook of Graph Grammars and Computing by Graph Transformation", World Scientific Publishing Co. Pte. Ltd., 1997.
6. Blostein D., Schürr A., "Computing with Graphs and Graph Rewriting", Technical Report AIB 97-8, Fachgruppe Informatik, RWTH Aachen, Germany.
7. A. Schürr, "PROGRES for Beginners", Technical Report, Lehrstuhl für Informatik III, RWTH Aachen, Germany.
8. H. Gottler, "Attributed graph grammars for graphics", H. Ehrig, M. Nagl, and G. Rosenberg, editors, Graph Grammars and their Application lo Computer Science, LNCS 153, pages 130-142, Springer-Verlag, 1982.
9. J. Loyall and S. Kaplan, "Visual Concurrent Programming with Delta-Grammars," Journal of Visual Languages and Computing, Vol 3, 1992, pp. 107-133.
10. G. Engels, H. Ehrig, G. Rozenberg (eds.), "Special Issue on Graph Transformation Systems", Fundamenta Informaticae, Vol. 26, No. 3/4 (1996), No. 1/2, IOS Press (1995).
11. H.Ehrig, M. Pfender, H. J. Schneider, "Graph-grammars: an algebraic approach", Proceedings IEEE Conference on Automata and Switching Theory, pages 167-180 (1973).
12. Agrawal A., Karsai G., Shi F., "A UML-based Graph Transformation Approach for Implementing Domain-Specific Model Transformations", Technical report, (ISIS), Vanderbilt University, Nashville, TN, 2003.
13. Agrawal A., Karsai G., Ledeczi A., "An End-to-End Domain-Driven Software Development Framework", 18th Annual ACM SIGPLAN Conference on Object-Oriented Programming, Systems, Languages, and Applications (OOPSLA), Anaheim, California, October 26, 2003.
14. Karsai G., Agrawal A., Shi F., Sprinkle J., "On the Use of Graph Transformations for the Formal Specification of Model Interpreters", JUCS, November 2003.
15. Magyari E., Bakay A., Lang A., Paka T., Vizhanyo A., Agrawal A., Karsai G., "UDM: An Infrastructure for Implementing Domain-Specific Modeling Languages", The 3rd OOPSLA Workshop on Domain-Specific Modeling, OOPSLA 2003, Anaheim, California, October 26, 2003.
16. Gamma, R. Helm, R. Johnson and J. Vlissides, "Design Patterns", Addison-Wesley, 1995.
17. Aue Aßmann, "OPTIMIX, A Tool for Rewriting and Optimizing Programs", Technical Report, University of Karslruhe, Germany, 1998.
18. Albert Zundorf: "Graph Pattern Matching in PROGRES", Graph Grammars and Their Application to Computer Science, 5h International Workshop, Williamsburg, VA, 1994.
19. "CLEAN: Version 2.0 Language Report", Software Technology department, University of Nijmegen, The Netherlands,
20. Agrawal A., Simon G., Karsai G.: "Semantic Translation of Simulink/Stateflow models to Hybrid Automata using Graph Transformations", International Workshop on Graph Transformation and Visual Modeling Techniques, Barcelona, Spain, March 27, 2004.
21. W3C. XSL Transformations (XSLT), 1999. http://www.w3.org/TR/xslt
22. U. Nickel and J. Niere and A. Zundorf, "Tool demonstration: The FUJABA environment", Proc. ICSE: The 22nd International Conference on Software Engineering, Limerick, Ireland, ACM Press, 2000.

Compiling Process Graphs into Executable Code

Rainer Hauser and Jana Koehler

IBM Zurich Research Laboratory
CH-8803 Rüschlikon, Switzerland
{rfh,koe}@zurich.ibm.com
http://www.zurich.ibm.com/csc/ebizz/bpia.html

Abstract. Model-driven architecture envisions a paradigm shift as dramatic as the one from low-level assembler languages to high-level programming languages. In order for this vision to become reality, algorithms are needed that compile models of software systems into deployable and executable implementations. This paper discusses two algorithms that provide such transformations for process graph models in a business process or workflow environment and produce executable programs based on Web services and orchestration languages. The reverse transformations back from executable programs to process graphs are also described.

1 Introduction

The model-driven architecture (MDA) initiative introduced by the Object Management Group (OMG) [1] is slowly becoming mature and is being given appropriate tool support [2]. However, there is still a long way to go before complex software systems can be completely described as models and deployed automatically [3]. In this respect, software engineering is far behind hardware development.

Model-driven development (MDD) for arbitrary software systems is still not possible, and – even if it were – the danger is that creating the complete set of models for a complex system may turn out to be more difficult than realizing it with traditional programming methods. Thus, MDD may not be considered worth the effort despite potential savings of maintenance costs. Applied to the field of business process engineering, the problems of MDD are simpler than those for general software systems thanks to the componentization and composition structure where the parts that are difficult to describe in models have already been implemented by other means. The basic building blocks for business processes (i.e., the components) are either services directly implemented as Web services or legacy systems wrapped as a Web service [4]. These building blocks are combined to form complex business logic (i.e., the composition) using orchestration languages such as BPEL4WS [5] and datatype definitions specified using WSDL [6]. Therefore, applying MDD to business processes means modeling a complex business process in terms of available Web services and transforming this model (or set of models) into executable and deployable orchestrations.

G. Karsai and E. Visser (Eds.): GPCE 2004, LNCS 3286, pp. 317–336, 2004.

Complete business process models consist of a process model to describe the execution logic, an information model for the datatypes used in the process model, an organizational model with a role or authorization model, and possibly other models. The compilation from a model describing a complex business process to a deployable BPEL4WS implementation has to transform the process model into BPEL4WS activities, the role or authorization model into BPEL4WS partners, and the information model into BPEL4WS variables specified using WSDL. In this paper, we will concentrate on transforming the process model's control flow into BPEL4WS activities. We specify process models using a subset of UML 2.0 activity diagrams [7], which is sufficiently rich to allow concurrency and arbitrary cycles in the control flow. For the orchestration, we simplified the BPEL4WS specification to contain only those elements needed to describe the execution logic extracted from the process model. UML 2.0 activity diagrams and BPEL4WS have been selected because both are widely accepted, de-facto standards.

UML activity diagrams (and most of the other modeling languages for business processes) allow specification of cyclic behavior. However, these cycles are unstructured, and BPEL4WS only allows structured cycles in the form of while-loops. Therefore, when going from the UML process model to the BPEL4WS implementation, unstructured cycles have to be resolved into structured cycles. Our discussion traces such transformations of process graphs into executable code, and we present two algorithms in detail. We also show the transformation in the other direction, which is important for reconciliation if the process graph and the executable code can be modified independently[1].

This paper is structured as follows: We define the subset of UML 2.0 activity diagrams used to model business processes (process graphs) in Section 2, and the simplified BPEL4WS used to describe the orchestration (executable code) in Section 3. We discuss in Sections 4 and 5 the transformation (compilation) from process graphs into executable code and the transformation (decompilation) of executable code back into a process graph, respectively. Finally, we conclude the paper in Section 6 with a discussion of this approach and an outlook.

2   Process Graph Model

Several modeling languages for business processes (such as BPMN [8]) have been proposed. We selected a subset of the UML 2.0 activity diagram meta-model [7] as the basis for this work. (BPMN and UML 2.0 activity diagrams are similar and may converge in the future [9].) In order to remove redundancy

---

[1] It is not yet clear how important reconciliation in MDA/MDD will turn out to be. Software engineers these days rarely look at the machine code produced by the compiler of a high-level programming language. When MDA/MDD has become reality and the compilation of models into deployable code has become mature, there will be no need to modify the deployed code except through recompilation and redeployment. However, there may still be a need for decompiling deployed code into a business process model.

and architectural elements not needed for modeling the control flow of a business process or workflow, we restrict the UML 2.0 activity diagrams to a subset shown in Figure 1.

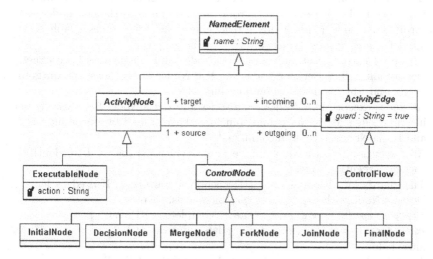

Fig. 1. Abstract syntax of process graph models.

According to the abstract syntax, a process graph consists of nodes and edges represented as instances of the abstract classes ActivityNode and ActivityEdge. A node is either an ExecutableNode or a ControlNode. An executable node is supposed to perform an action represented as a string that is not specified further. An edge can only be a ControlFlow whose guard is also represented as a string. The relation between nodes and edges is modeled as bidirectional associations. A node can have multiple incoming and outgoing edges, but an edge has always exactly one source and one target node. The start node of a process graph is an InitialNode, and the end node is a FinalNode. The XOR-splits and -joins (alternatives) are represented as DecisionNodes and MergeNodes. The AND-splits and -joins (concurrency) are modeled as ForkNodes and JoinNodes.

Basically, a process graph is a connected, directed graph with a single start and a single end node. Such a graph is called reducible if (informally speaking) "there are no jumps into the middle of loops from outside" [10]. A node n_1 is said to dominate a node n_2 if all paths from the start node to n_2 go through n_1 [10]. A fork-join pair is properly nested if (again informally speaking) there are no jumps into and out of the corresponding concurrent threads nor any interactions between the threads[2]. A formal definition will be given in Section 4.4.

For a process graph to be valid, there are further well-formedness constraints not shown in the class diagram:

---

[2] It is not possible to design more sophisticated synchronization mechanisms between threads in this simplified model.

1. The process graph is finite.
2. A process graph must have exactly one InitialNode and one FinalNode. (A process graph has a single entry and a single exit.)
3. A process graph and every thread contains at least one ExecutableNode.
4. For every node, there is a path from the start node to the end node going through this node. (This avoids unreachable areas of the process graph, which are detectable through static analysis of the graph.)
5. All nodes except DecisionNodes, ForkNodes and FinalNodes have exactly one outgoing edge. DecisionNodes and ForkNodes have at least two outgoing edges, and FinalNodes have no outgoing edge.
6. All nodes except MergeNodes, JoinNodes and InitialNodes have exactly one incoming edge. MergeNodes and JoinNodes have at least two incoming edges, and InitialNodes have no incoming edge.
7. All ExecutionNodes have a unique name, which can be used to identify a specific ExecutionNode.
8. The guards for all nodes except DecisionNode are $true$. If n edges leave a DecisionNode with $expr_1, \ldots, expr_n$ as guards, then
   $$expr_1 \vee expr_2 \vee \ldots \vee expr_n = true \quad \text{complete} \quad \text{(PM1)}$$
   $$expr_i \wedge expr_j = false \text{ (for } i \neq j \text{)} \quad \text{deterministic} \quad \text{(PM2)}$$
   must hold[3].
9. All fork-join pairs are properly nested (see Section 4.4).

When transforming a process graph with the algorithms introduced below, these constraints can be checked automatically except for PM1 and PM2 in Constraint 8 which would require domain knowledge of the model's data types[4].

The above list of constraints expresses a set of necessary conditions for a process graph to be valid, but the list is not sufficient. It is still possible to define valid process graphs that do not make sense.

Figure 2 shows the simple and artificially created example of a process graph, which will be used throughout this paper, because it contains all the features needed to explain the transformation algorithms. It introduces at the same time the graphical notation for the types of nodes in UML 2.0 activity diagrams used in this paper. The InitialNode on the left side is connected to a Fork-Node, and the corresponding JoinNode on the right side leads to the FinalNode. There are two threads between fork and join. The upper one is more complex and contains DecisionNodes with guards (e.g., $exprSA$) and MergeNodes. The ExecutableNode A is contained in a cycle. The lower thread is a simple sequence of the two ExecutableNodes C and D. If $exprSB = \neg exprSA$ is true (to enforce PM1 and PM2), this example process graph is valid according to the above well-formedness constraints. There is exactly one start and one end node, the

---

[3] We also assume that each $expr_i$ is sometimes true in order to avoid areas of the process graph whose unreachability cannot solely be detected by static analysis of the process graph.

[4] We can always enforce PM1 by adding an 'else'-edge going to the FinalNode (or its corresponding MergeNode), and PM2 by modifying the guards with $expr_i' = expr_i \wedge \neg expr_1 \wedge \ldots \wedge \neg expr_{i-1}$.

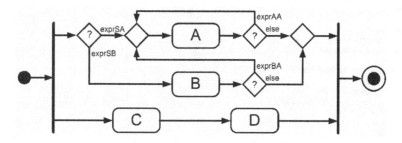

Fig. 2. Process graph example.

fork-join pair is properly nested, and the two sequential threads satisfy the other constraints.

3   Executable Code Model

The orchestration language BPEL4WS [5] describes the execution logic for business processes composed of Web services. Figure 3 shows the simplified subset used for the purpose of demonstrating compilation and decompilation.

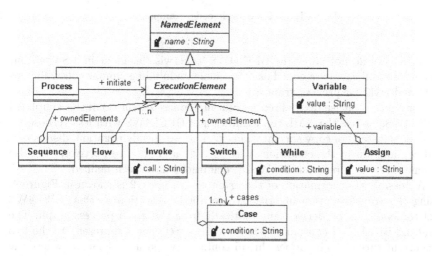

Fig. 3. Abstract syntax of executable code models.

A model contains a Process with one ExecutionElement initiating the execution. ExecutionElements can be Sequences (sequential), Flows (concurrent), the structural elements Switch (case-statement) and While (loop), Assign (variable assignment) and Invoke. The Invoke is merely a placeholder for synchronous and asynchronous Web service invocations with an action attribute (call). For

```
<process>
  <flow>
    <sequence>
      <assign 'SA:=exprSA' />
      <assign 'SB:=exprSB' />
      <switch>
        <case condition= 'SB'>
          <sequence>
            <invoke B />
            <assign 'BA:=exprBA' />
          </sequence>
        </case>
      </switch>
      <switch>
        <case condition= 'SA | (SB & BA)'>
          <sequence>
            <assign 'loopA:=true' />
            <while condition= 'loopA'>
              <invoke A />
              <assign 'AA:=exprAA' />
              <assign 'loopA:=AA' />
            </while>
          </sequence>
        </case>
      </switch>
    </sequence>
    <sequence>
      <invoke C />
      <invoke D />
    </sequence>
  </flow>
</process>
```

Fig. 4. Executable code example.

simplicity, we do not allow the BPEL4WS 'otherwise' element in a Switch but assume that all cases are coded as Case elements fulfilling similar constraints as PM1 and PM2 for process graphs.

For a more concise textual representation (concrete syntax) of this simplified BPEL4WS, we use the XML representation of BPEL4WS with less verbose assignments instead of copy specifications [5], and we encode negation, disjunction and conjunction in the conditions with "!", "|" and "&", respectively. We also assume that the corresponding WSDL definitions have been defined.

A possible transformation of the example in Figure 2 is shown in Figure 4. Using the transformation algorithms described in Section 4, this BPEL4WS skeleton code can be derived automatically from the given process graph. The resulting BPEL4WS contains a Flow with two Sequences representing the two concurrent threads. The upper thread contains two switch elements, where the second one consists of a while-loop. The second thread contains simply two invocations called one after the other without further control logic.

4   Compilation of Process Graphs

Among the model transformation approaches [11], graph transformation methods are quite popular [12, 13]. Work on signal flow graph compilers is relevant as well [14]. The problem we need to solve can – independent of the actual transformation approach – use techniques from compiler theory [15] because a sequential process graph can be compiled into a program with gotos. After this initial transformation, goto-elimination methods for sequential programming languages can be applied. We look at non-concurrent process parts first and examine concurrency later.

4.1   Initial Transformation for a Sequential Part

The general pattern of an activity in a sequential part of a process graph (either a completely sequential process graph or a sequential thread) is – as shown in Figure 5 – a MergeNode followed by an ExecutableNode followed by a DecisionNode, where the MergeNode collects the incoming edges (XOR-join), and the DecisionNode routes the control flow to the next activity (XOR-split). However, MergeNodes with only one incoming edge and DecisionNodes with only one outgoing edge are eliminated. (The lower thread in Figure 2, for example, shows the two activities C and D without MergeNodes and DecisionNodes.) Similarly, the InitialNode is followed by a DecisionNode, and the FinalNode is preceeded by a MergeNode. InitialNodes and FinalNodes (or the ForkNodes and JoinNodes as the start and end nodes of a thread) can be interpreted as no-op action.

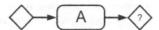

Fig. 5. General pattern of an activity.

Thus, a sequential process graph (or a sequential thread) can be translated into an initial program with guarded gotos for the edges using the rules:

1. A MergeNode – even if eliminated – becomes a label in the program. (Especially, the always missing MergeNode of the start node – interpreted as a no-op action – becomes the start label of the program.)
2. A node representing an action – usually an ExecutionNode – becomes an executable action that is not further specified. (In particular, the start node becomes a no-op action, and the end node an exit action.)
3. A DecisionNode – even if eliminated – becomes a set of guarded gotos (one per edge).

If a MergeNode is directly connected to a DecisionNode, we also insert a no-op action.

The result of this initial transformation applied to the upper thread of Figure 2 is shown in Figure 6 in a simple programming language[5] and with the labels S and T used for the invisible start and end node of the thread.

---

[5] Instead of extending the executable code model with a goto ExecutionElement or defining an intermediate model, we use a familiar but not formally specified programming language with simple if-statements and repeat-while-loops instead of the more complicated switch-construct and the while-loop in BPEL4WS.

```
S: if (exprSA) goto A;            // left-most DecisionNode
   if (exprSB) goto B;
A: invoke A;                      // MergeNode and ExecutionNode A
   if (exprAA) goto A;            // DecisionNode after A
   if (!exprAA) goto T;          // instead of "else goto T;"
B: invoke B;                      // ExecutionNode B
   if (exprBA) goto A;            // DecisionNode after B
   if (!exprBA) goto T;          // instead of "else goto T;"
T: exit;                          // right-most MergeNode
```

Fig. 6. Initial transformation result.

This initial program consists of blocks, where a block starts with a label and ends either before the next label or at the program's end. Because of PM1, there is no implicit flow of control from one block to the next, and the blocks (except for the first one) can be arbitrarily reordered. Because of PM2, the order of the guarded goto-statements in a block is irrelevant, and they can be arbitrarily reordered as well[6]. Both properties are important as will be shown below.

4.2   Finite State Machine Transformation for a Sequential Part

There is a straightforward translation of this initial program into a single loop, which basically transforms the sequential process graph into a finite state machine. Figure 7 shows the result for the upper thread of the example shown in Figure 2. The gotos become assignments to the variable $nextNode$, the initial block becomes the initialization, the terminal block dissolves into an implicit exit at the program end, and the other blocks become cases in the switch.

This compilation method, which obviously could be directly applied to a sequential process graph instead of going through the initial transformation first, has the advantage that it is easy to implement. However, it has two disadvantages. First, performance is an issue for process graphs with a large number of nodes because the switch testing of which node comes next has to test $n/2$ guards on average if n is the number of nodes in the graph. Second, the program does not show the inherent program structure with the different phases of a business process, the nesting of cyclic activities and the order of sequential activities[7]. For

---

[6] Without PM2, there are three semantics possible for the DecisionNode: (1) The guards are tested in a certain order, and the first true one gets control. (2) The set of guards is executed nondeterministically (e.g., as a set of Dijkstra's guarded commands). (3) All edges whose guards are enabled are followed concurrently. Note that for the second case, the initial transformation preserves the behavior if we interpret the set of guarded gotos in a block as a set of Dijkstra's guarded commands.

[7] It is rather subjective to determine which program structure best represents a process graph. However, we believe that business processes are often designed as a sequence of various phases. A shopping application, for example, starts with an authentication phase, continues with a product configuration and selection phase, and ends with a negotiation of terms and conditions. These phases should be made visible in the executable code model and should not be merged into a single loop.

```
<sequence>
  <switch>
    <case condition= 'exprSA'>
      <assign 'nextNode:=A' />
    </case>
    <case condition= 'exprSB'>
      <assign 'nextNode:=B' />
    </case>
  </switch>
  <while condition= 'nextNode!=T'>
    <switch>
      <case condition= 'nextNode=A'>
        <sequence>
          <invoke A />
          <switch>
            <case condition= 'exprAA'>
              <assign 'nextNode:=A' />
            </case>
            <case condition= '!exprAA'>
              <assign 'nextNode:=T' />
            </case>
          </switch>
        </sequence>
      </case>
      <case condition= 'nextNode=B'>
        <sequence>
          <invoke B />
          <switch>
            <case condition= 'exprBA'>
              <assign 'nextNode:=A' />
            </case>
            <case condition= '!exprBA'>
              <assign 'nextNode:=T' />
            </case>
          </switch>
        </sequence>
      </case>
    </switch>
  </while>
</sequence>
```

Fig. 7. Finite state machine transformation result.

these two reasons we do not consider the result of this transformation method satisfactory. Note, however, that this transformation would allow nondeterminism to be preserved if we relax PM2 and if the underlying platform supports nondeterminism (e.g., in the form of Dijkstra's guarded commands).

4.3   Goto-Elimination Method for a Sequential Part

The method by Ammarguellat [16] for eliminating gotos in program languages to achieve single-entry, single-exit while-loops has two main steps called "derecursivation" for removal of self-references (self-loops) and "substitution" for merging two activities into one activity. Note that these two steps correspond to the T1 and T2 rule, respectively, in the T1-T2 analysis [17]. The substitution step may need "if-distribution" and "factorization" as additional steps at the end. We adapted this method for process graphs and describe the different steps in the following.

Pre-calculation: We start from the initial program and introduce additional variables in order to save the current state of the expressions. The reason for this step is explained below. The input to this step (and the other steps later on) is shown on the left, the output on the right:

```
L: invoke L;                    L: invoke L;
   if (exprLM1) goto M1;           if (exprLM1) nextNodeFromL:=M1;
   ...                             ...
   if (exprLMm) goto Mm;           if (exprLMm) nextNodeFromL:=Mm;
                                   if (nextNodeFromL=M1) goto M1;
                                   ...
                                   if (nextNodeFromL=Mm) goto Mm;
```

Common Block Structure: After every transformation step, we bring each block in the program back into a structure where the structured elements appear before the unstructured guarded goto-statements. After pre-calculation, the program is in this structure. The *invoke L* and the first set of if-statements with assignments for *nextNodeFromL* are the structured part. We will call the structured part of block L *bodyL* in the following steps.

Substitution and Elimination: Because there is no implicit control flow from one block to another, we can replace all occurences of *goto M* with the complete block M if block M does not itself contain a *goto M*:

```
L: bodyL;                       L: bodyL;
   if (exprL1) goto M1;            if (exprL1) goto M1;
   ...                             ...
   if (exprLi) goto M;            if (exprLi) {
   ...                               bodyM;
   if (exprLm) goto Mm;              if (exprM1) goto N1;
...                                  ...
M: bodyM;                            if (exprMn) goto Nn;
   if (exprM1) goto N1;           }
   ...                             ...
   if (exprMn) goto Nn;           if (exprLm) goto Mm;
```

If-Distribution: With the substitution step, the label M together with all *goto M* statements have been eliminated. However, we have lost the common block structure. In order to regain it, we have to apply another step:

```
if (exprLi) {                   if (exprLi) {
  bodyM;                          bodyM;
  if (exprM1) goto N1;          }
  ...                           if (exprLi & exprM1) goto N1;
  if (exprMn) goto Nn;          ...
}                               if (exprLi & exprMn) goto Nn;
```

This step is only allowed if $exprLi$ is not changed by $bodyM$. (Ammarguellat introduces an additional variable because of the general applicability of her method, but we will show below how to ensure in the special context of our transformation that the logic is not changed by if-distribution.)

After substitution and if-distribution, we can move the structured parts of the source and the target block of the substitution together because the guards of the if-statements are mutually exclusive owing to PM2. Note also that the resulting guarded gotos are still mutually exclusive and complete.

Factorization: If the unstructured part of a block contains two guarded gotos to the same label, the two statements can be combined into one:

```
L: bodyL;                         L: bodyL;
     if (exprL1) goto M1;              if (exprL1) goto M1;
     ...                               ...
     if (exprLi) goto M;               if (exprLi | exprLj) goto M;
     ...                               ...
     if (exprLj) goto M;               if (exprLm) goto Mm;
     ...
     if (exprLm) goto Mm;
```

Derecursivation: Self-references have to be resolved through derecursivation after moving the self-referencing goto to the top of the unstructured part:

```
L: bodyL;                         L: repeat {
     if (exprLs) goto L;                   bodyL;
     if (exprL1) goto M1;             } while (exprLs);
     ...                              if (exprL1) goto M1;
     if (exprLm) goto Mm;             ...
                                      if (exprLm) goto Mm;
```

The complete repeat-while-loop becomes the new structured part $bodyL$ for the next step. Note also here that the guards of the unstructured gotos are still complete and mutually exclusive, but may no longer form a logical tautology, even if they did before. (After the loop, $exprLs$ must be false, and therefore $exprL1 \lor \ldots \lor exprLm$, without $exprLs$, must be true.)

A repeat-while-loop with the test at the end can be converted into an ordinary while-loop with the test at the beginning – as needed for BPEL4WS – but requires the introduction of one additional variable per loop:

```
repeat {                          loopL:=true;
  bodyL;                          while (loopL) {
} while (exprLs);                   bodyL;
                                    loopL:=exprLs;
                                  }
```

Obsolete-Guard-Removal: Because of PM1 the set of guarded gotos in any block of the initial program is complete in the sense that every possible case is covered. This property is preserved by all the transformation steps discussed above. Therefore, if only one guarded goto is left in a block, the guard must be true and can be removed:

```
L: bodyL;                          L: bodyL;
     if (expr) goto M;                  goto M;
```

The Complete Algorithm for Reducible Process Graphs: These transformation steps can be applied in different order. Before we describe in which sequence the goto-elimination algorithm will apply them, we make some observations: (1) The derecursivation step can be applied to a block with self-references at any time, but if it is applied right before it is substituted, the number of while-loops is minimized. (2) Substituting a block for more than one goto-statement leads to code duplication. (3) Blocks can be substituted in any order.

Ammarguellat proves that there is a substitution sequence for reducible graphs where each block is only substituted once. This property together with the observations above determines the sequence in which the various steps are applied for reducible process graphs. The pre-calculation is the first step. Next, one block after the other (except the blocks corresponding to the start and end node in the graph) is selected in a loop for substitution such that there is only one goto to the label of this block. In the loop, when we have selected a block, we apply derecursivation if necessary and perform the substitution. With if-distribution we bring the target block back into the common block structure, and with factorization we reduce the number of gotos in a block to at most one for each remaining label. If at this point only one guarded goto is left in a block, it can be removed using the obsolete-guard-removal step. After elimination of all labels and gotos with exception of the ones corresponding to the start and end block, the label for the start node can be removed[8]. Next, the guard for the remaining $goto\,T$ can be removed with obsolete-guard-removal, the block corresponding to the end node dissolves into an implicit *exit* at the end of the program, and *bodyS* becomes the resulting program:

```
S: bodyS;                          bodyS;
     if (expr) goto T:
T: exit;
```

The algorithm in pseudo-code is shown in Figure 8. Note that in a final step, *bodyS* has to be converted into the simplified BPEL4WS encoding.

The result of the transformation algorithm applied to the upper thread in Figure 2 is shown in Figure 9. For space reasons we cannot show larger examples, but we applied this algorithm to real-world business processes with very promising results for the program structure. The method of Ammarguellat nicely

---

[8] A start node has no incoming edges. If this restriction is relaxed, a derecursivation step would remove all remaining gotos to the label of the start node.

$blocks \leftarrow preCalculation(processGraph)$
while $blocks \backslash \{startBlock, endBlock\} \neq \emptyset$ **do**
  $sourceBlock \leftarrow selectBlockForSubstitution(blocks \backslash \{startBlock, endBlock\})$
  $blocks \leftarrow blocks \backslash \{sourceBlock\}$
  if $sourceBlock \in sourceBlock.gotoTargets$ **then**
    $derecursivation(sourceBlock)$
  end if
  for all $targetBlock \in blocks$ **do**
    if $sourceBlock \in targetBlock.gotoTargets$ **then**
      $substitution(sourceBlock, targetBlock)$
      $ifDistribution(targetBlock)$
      $factorization(targetBlock)$
      if $\mid targetBlock.gotoTargets \mid = 1$ **then**
        $obsoleteGuardRemoval(targetBlock)$
      end if
    end if
  end for
end while

Fig. 8. Goto-elimination algorithm.

structures the execution logic of the original graph but has the disadvantage of duplicating code if the graph is irreducible.

Note also that this method – unlike the finite state machine translation – does not preserve nondeterminism, because the guarded gotos (initially interpretable as a set of Dijkstra's guarded commands) get separated by substitution and derecursivation. We finally mention without further elaboration that the two transformation methods can be combined in various ways (e.g., by applying the goto-elimination method until code duplication would be necessary, and completing with the finite state machine method.)

Discussion of Additional Variables: The method described above works only for reducible process graphs because the if-distribution can be dangerous as mentioned when we introduced the if-distribution step. In Ammarguellat's original method, if-distribution is safe but always adds a new variable to the program. Additional variables must be meaningful for a reader of the program if the program is intended to be read by a human user. The variable $nextNode$ in the finite state machine transformation method (Figure 7) and the variables $nextNodeFromX$ as well as $loopX$ in the goto-elimination transformation method (Figure 9) have an obvious meaning[9].

We outline a proof that if-distribution is legal if every substitution step replaces only a single goto with a block (which is always possible for reducible graphs). We define for each block of the initial program after the pre-calculation step a set called $Modifies(block, step)$ that shows which variables can be modi-

---

[9] Instead of a variable $nextNodeFromX$, we used a set of Boolean variables XY in Figure 4 to express $nextNodeFromX = Y$ in an alternative, more compact form.

```
<sequence>
  <switch>
    <case condition= 'exprSA'>
      <assign 'nextNodeFromS:=A' />
    </case>
    <case condition= 'exprSB'>
      <assign 'nextNodeFromS:=B' />
    </case>
  </switch>
  <switch>
    <case condition= 'nextNodeFromS=B'>
      <sequence>
        <invoke B />
        <switch>
          <case condition= 'exprBA'>
            <assign 'nextNodeFromB:=A' />
          </case>
          <case condition= '!exprBA'>
            <assign 'nextNodeFromB:=T' />
          </case>
        </switch>
      </sequence>
    </case>
  </switch>
  <switch>
    <case condition= 'nextNodeFromS=A |
                      (nextNodeFromS=B & nextNodeFromB=A)'>
      <sequence>
        <assign 'loopA:=true' />
        <while condition= 'loopA'>
          <invoke A />
          <switch>
            <case condition= 'exprAA'>
              <assign 'nextNodeFromA:=A' />
            </case>
            <case condition= '!exprAA'>
              <assign 'nextNodeFromA:=T' />
            </case>
          </switch>
          <assign 'loopA:=(nextNodeFromA=A)' />
        </while>
      </sequence>
    </case>
  </switch>
</sequence>
```

Fig. 9. Goto-elimination transformation result.

fied by the body of block *block* in step *step*. Initially, the set is $Modifies(L,0) = \{nextNodeFromL\}$ for each block L. If block M is substituted in block L in step n, the set becomes $Modifies(L,n) = Modifies(L,n-1) \cup Modifies(M,n-1)$. Because the problematic expression in the if-condition references only variables in $Modifies(L,n-1)$ and *bodyM* modifies only variables in $Modifies(M,n-1)$, if-distribution is allowed if $Modifies(L,n-1) \cap Modifies(M,n-1) = \emptyset$. This intersection can only be nonempty if a block N previously has been substituted in blocks L and M.

The easiest solution to make if-distribution safe in the case of irreducible graphs is what is called node-splitting in compiler theory. For each *goto M* in the initial program, a copy of the block M is created with new labels M_1, M_2 and so on. This leads to different additional variables $nextNodeFromM_i$.

4.4   Separation of Sequential and Concurrent Parts

The compilation of a single pair of ForkNode and JoinNode in the process graph model into a Flow element in the executable code model is trivial if each thread between them contains only one ExecutableNode. Based on this observation, we outline an algorithm to decompose a process graph into sequential and concurrent subgraphs.

Areas of a process graph with only one edge leading from the outside into the area and one edge leading from the area to the outside are of special interest because they can be abstracted into a single node as a structured activity. The incoming and the outgoing edge define the interfaces to such an abstractable area or subgraph. A fork-join pair is called properly nested if all threads are such abstractable areas, and their incoming edges come from the same fork, and the outgoing edges lead to the same join. In the following paragraphs, we give formal definitions that a reader may skip if satisfied with the informal descriptions.

We define a process graph $G(N, E, n_i, n_f)$ with a set of nodes N, a set of edges E, the InitialNode n_i and the FinalNode n_f as usual. We write $e(n_1, n_2)$ for the edge from $n_1 \in N$ to $n_2 \in N$. A subgraph $G'(N', E')$ with $N' \subseteq N \setminus \{n_i, n_f\}$ and $\forall e = e(n_1, n_2) \in E (n_1 \in N' \vee n_2 \in N' \leftrightarrow e(n_1, n_2) \in E')$ is called abstractable if there exist two edges $e(n_1, n_1')$ and $e(n_2, n_2')$ in E' such that $n_1 \in N \setminus N'$, $n_1' \in N'$, $n_2 \in N'$ and $n_2' \in N \setminus N'$, whereas all the other edges in E' lead from a node in N' to a node in N'. In other words, the subgraph contains all edges between its own nodes, and there is exactly one edge coming in from outside and exactly one edge going out. (For all process graphs $G(N, E, n_i, n_f)$, the subgraph $G(N \setminus \{n_i, n_f\}, E)$ is an abstractable subgraph because there is one edge with n_i as source and one edge with n_f as target.)

The source of the incoming edge of an abstractable subgraph $G(N', E')$ dominates all nodes in N'. Note also that if the original graph was valid, an abstractable subgraph is also valid when completed with an additional InitialNode and FinalNode to replace the source and target of the incoming and outgoing edges, respectively.

To define when fork-join pairs are properly nested, we select one ForkNode f, which must have at least two outgoing edges to be valid. We follow one of them, come to node n_i (the first node of thread i) and compute N_i, the set of nodes dominated by n_i. We determine further the set of edges where source and/or target belong to N_i and call this set E_i. We do this for all threads. If $G(N_i, E_i)$ for all threads i are abstractable subgraphs whose outgoing edges lead to the same JoinNode j, which does not have any other incoming edge, then the corresponding fork-join pair is properly nested.

The abstractable subgraph $G(N_i, E_i)$ for each thread i can be combined into an abstract sequential node s_i hiding all nodes in N_i and all edges in E_i except for the incoming edge from f and the outgoing edge to j. The subgraph $G(N_{\parallel}, E_{\parallel})$ with $N_{\parallel} = \{f, j\} \cup \bigcup_i \{s_i\}$ and $E_{\parallel} = \bigcup_i \{e(f, s_i), e(s_i, j)\}$ is also an abstractable node, which can be combined into an abstract concurrent node.

By recursively combining threads into abstract sequential nodes and fork-join pairs with already abstracted threads into abstract concurrent nodes, a complete valid process graph can be transformed into sequences and flows in the simplified version of BPEL4WS.

5   Reverse Engineering of Process Graphs

The result of the two transformation methods can be decompiled back into a process graph if its structure has not been modified manually. For the flows, this is trivial. Thus, we only have to outline the decompilation of a sequence without flows but possibly with abstract concurrent nodes hiding flows.

5.1   Reverse Finite State Machine Transformation

The initialization before the while-loop determines the start node and its sucessor or successors with transition conditions. The loop-condition determines the end node. The cases in the switch of the loop determine the successor or successors for each node with transition conditions. Thus, we can obtain all edges with their transition conditions and create the process graph. This is not very surprising because a process graph can be interpreted as a graphical representation of a finite state machine.

5.2   Reverse Goto-Elimination Method

Decompilation after the goto-elimination method is based on two observations. First, substitution (together with if-distribution) adds an if-statement to the end of the target block's structured part, and derecursivation wraps a structured part into a while-loop. Factorization affects only the unstructured part. Second, if the conditions in the loops and if-statements are brought into disjunctive normal form $C_1 \vee \ldots \vee C_n$, all C_i are of the form $nextNodeFromX_1 = X_2 \wedge nextNodeFromX_2 = X_3 \wedge \ldots \wedge nextNodeFromX_{n-1} = X_n$, and they all lead from the same X_1 to the same X_n. Thus, these conditions encode possible paths in the process graph from X_1 to X_n. Not all paths may be shown explicitly because some conditions may have been eliminated by obsolete-guard-removal.

To reverse the goto-elimination method, the statements $invoke\, X$ and the variables $nextNodeFromX$ are used to determine the ExecutableNodes with their names, and the program is recursively brought back into the form it had after the initial transformation and the pre-calculation step, which obviously can be transformed into a process graph. The program – after conversion from the simplified BPEL4WS back into the simple programming language with if-statements and repeat-while-loops – becomes:

```
S: bodyS;
   if (expr) goto T;
T: exit;
```

We set $expr$ to true and mark it as temporary because it may have to be modified in order to fulfill PM2 (reverse obsolete-guard-removal).

Also for the reverse transformation, we keep the blocks in the common block structure, and a block therefore has the form:

```
L: bodyL;
   if (expr1) goto L1;
   ...
   if (exprn) goto Ln;
```

The last statement in *bodyL* is either an *invoke X*, an if-statement or a repeat-while-loop. If the last statement is not the only statement in *bodyL*, we split the block into two blocks, one with all the statements except for the last one (*rest*), and one with only the last statement (*last*):

```
L: rest;
   if (expr) goto M;
M: last;
   if (expr1) goto L1;
   ...
   if (exprn) goto Ln;
```

We set *expr* again to true and mark it as temporary. The body of block M now contains only one statement. If it is an *Invoke X*, we are done. If it is a loop, we undo derecursivation:

```
M: repeat {                      M: body;
     body;                          if (cond) goto M;
   } while (cond);                  if (expr1) goto L1;
   if (expr1) goto L1;              ...
   ...                              if (exprn) goto Ln;
   if (exprn) goto Ln;
```

If the body of block M is an if-statement, we undo substitution:

```
N: ...                           N: ...
   if (expr) goto M;                if (expr & cond) goto M;
   ...                              ...
M: if (cond) {                   M: body;
     body;                          if (expr1') goto L1;
   }                                ...
   if (expr1) goto L1;              if (exprn') goto Ln;
   ...
   if (exprn) goto Ln;
```

In order to determine *expr1'*, we have to undo if-distribution (i.e., remove the conjunction with *cond*) and factorization (i.e., split disjunctions).

After each step, we have to rename previously introduced labels such that the label for *Invoke L* is L, and the logical expressions marked as temporary must be resolved if possible. For space reasons, we will not go into more details of the reverse goto-elimination method.

6   Summary and Outlook

This paper describes two methods for compiling process graphs into executable code and vice versa. We concentrated on the algorithmic aspects of the transformations between business process models and executable models with an emphasis on the implementation. Other aspects such as some background from theoretical computer science and an alternative algorithm based on continuation semantics are discussed in [15].

Transformation methods like the ones discussed here are a step in the direction of OMG's MDA vision. However, the simplified models used to demonstrate the transformations have to be extended to the full power of control and data flow available in BPEL4WS, including fine-grained synchronization between concurrent threads. Organizational models for roles and authorizations as well as information models have to be included, together with additional deployment information. Only then will the completely automatic translation and deployment of business processes encoded as BPEL4WS be possible.

As an intermediate step on the way to fulfilling the complete MDA vision, the executable model may have to be refined manually before deployment. In this case, reconciliation of business process models and executable models is important in order to preserve manual changes on the side of the executable models when the business process models are modified. The transformations from the executable models back into the business process models is only one part, but keeping track of the mapping between the elements in the two model sets is also crucial. This has been recognized by the community discussing the upcoming OMG Q/V/T standard for MOF 2.0 query, views and transformations [18].

The two models shown in Figures 1 and 3 as well as the not formally specified intermediate model (the simple programming language used to describe the two transformation methods) can be represented as MOF 2.0 models [19]. The Object Constraint Language OCL [20], which is regarded as an important part of the Q/V/T standard, is powerful enough – though rather verbose and difficult to read – to specify the well-formedness constraints on a process graph to be valid. Therefore, we can imagine that the final Q/V/T language will be capable of defining complex transformations such as the ones described in this paper. There are two reasons why this may not be the right way to go.

First, the examples in the Q/V/T proposals are all very simple, and there is a big class of transformations needed in the MDA-space with a similar complexity. A Q/V/T language designed for this class of problems can be made simple, easy to use and purely declarative. If a Q/V/T language tries to solve all possible transformation problems, it may become just another imperative, general-purpose programming language. In the goto-elimination method, defining the mapping for process graph and executable code elements as well as the transformation logic itself is far from being trivial.

Second, we are not sure how much of the transformations as described in this paper will still be needed for MDA in the long run. To explain what we mean we have to step back and examine why we are today where we are. Software projects in general and business process or workflow projects in particular require bridging the gap between the customer (business people) and the IT team. These two groups speak different languages and think in terms of different concepts. Informal drawings have helped and still help them find a common understanding to design such software systems. These graphical aids evolved into modeling languages and have become quite mature by now. The fact that we can define algorithms such as the ones discussed in this paper, which compile business process models automatically into executable code, makes it clear that these business process model languages are – or can be made – precise, complete and formal enough, although there is no formally defined semantics for UML 2.0 yet.

Thus, why not develop formally defined semantics for these modeling languages – if not yet available – together with execution engines that allow deployment and execution of business models directly [21]? If a model contains all information needed to simulate it and to compile it automatically into orchestration languages, an appropriate execution engine should also be able to run it. Efficiency may be a problem, and there are other open issues, but they may be solved in the future. Thus, algorithms to transform unstructured cycles into structured loops may in the long run disappear or only remain needed for analysis and validation purposes, and orchestration languages such as BPEL4WS may turn out to be only an interim step on the way to directly deployable and executable models.

Acknowledgments

We thank the anonymous reviewers for their encouraging comments and valuable suggestions, and Jochen Küster, Shane Sendall, Markus Stolze and Michael Wahler for their advice, which helped to improve this paper significantly.

References

1. OMG: Model-Driven Architecture (MDA). http://www.omg.org/mda/.
2. Uhl, A.: Model Driven Architecture Is Ready for Prime Time. IEEE Software 20(5), September/October 2003, pp. 70-73.
3. Ambler, S.: Agile Model Driven Development Is Good Enough. IEEE Software 20(5), September/October 2003, pp. 71-73.
4. W3C: Web Services Activity. http://www.w3.org/2002/ws/.
5. OASIS: Business Process Execution Language for Web Services (BPEL4WS) 1.1. http://www-106.ibm.com/developerworks/webservices/library/ws-bpel/. May 5, 2003.
6. W3C: Web Services Description Language (WSDL) 1.1. http://www.w3.org/TR/wsdl. March 15, 2001.
7. OMG: Unified Modeling Language 2.0. http://www.omg.org/uml/.
8. BPMI: BPMN 1.0 working draft. http://www.bpmi.org/.
9. White, S.: Process Modeling Notations and Workflow Patterns. In The Workflow Handbook 2004. Fischer, L. (Ed.). Future Strategies Inc., Lighthouse Point, FL, USA, 2004.
10. Aho, A. et al.: Compilers. Principles, Techniques, and Tools. Addison-Wesley, 1986.

11. Czarnecki, K., Helsen, S.: Classification of Model Transformation Approaches. Report of 2nd OOPSLA Workshop on Generative Techniques in the context of Model Driven Architecture, Anaheim, California, October 2003.
   http://www.softmetaware.com/oopsla2003/czarnecki.pdf.
12. Karsai, G., Agrawal, A.: Graph Transformations in OMG's Model-Driven Architecture. Proc. Applications of Graph Transformations with Industrial Relevance, Charlotsville, Virginia, September 2003.
13. Heckel, R. et al.: Towards Automatic Translation of UML Models into Semantic Domains. Proc. APPLIGRAPH Workshop on Application of Graph Transformation (AGT 2002), Grenoble, France, April 2002, pp. 11-22.
14. Wess, B.: Optimizing Signal Flow Graph Compilers for Digital Signal Processors. Proc. 5th International Conference on Signal Processing Applications and Technology, Dallas, Texas, October 1994.
15. Koehler, J., Hauser, R.: Untangling Unstructured Cyclic Flows - A Solution based on Continuations. Submitted for publication, 2004.
16. Ammarguellat, Z.: A Control-Flow Normalization Algorithm and Its Complexity. Software Engineering 18(3), pp. 237-251, 1992.
17. Hecht, M.S., Ullman, J.D.: Flow Graph Reducibility. SIAM J. Comput. 1(2), pp. 188-202, 1972.
18. Gardner, T. et al.: A Review of OMG MOF 2.0 Query / Views / Ttransformations Submissions and Recommendations Towards the Final Standard. Workshop on MetaModelling for MDA, York, England, November 2003.
19. OMG: Meta Object Facility 2.0. http://www.omg.org/docs/ad/03-04-07.pdf.
20. Warmer, J., Kleppe, A.: The Object Constraint Language – Second Edition. Getting Your Models Ready for MDA. Addison-Wesley, 2003.
21. Rumpe, B.: Executable Modeling with UML. A Vision or a Nightmare? In: Issues & Trends of Information Technology Management in Contemporary Associations, Seattle. Idea Group Publishing, Hershey, London, pp. 697-701. 2002.

Model-Driven Configuration and Deployment
of Component Middleware Publish/Subscribe Services*

George Edwards, Gan Deng, Douglas C. Schmidt,
Aniruddha Gokhale, and Bala Natarajan

Department of Electrical Engineering and Computer Science, Vanderbilt University
Nashville, TN 37235, USA
{edwardgt,dengg,schmidt,gokhale,bala}@dre.vanderbilt.edu

Abstract. Quality of service (QoS)-enabled publish/subscribe services are available in component middleware platforms, such as the CORBA Component Model (CCM). Today, however, these platforms lack a simple and intuitive way to integrate publish/subscribe service configurations and deployments. This paper illustrates how generative model-driven techniques and tools can automate many service configuration and deployment tasks associated with integrating publish/-subscribe services into QoS-enabled component-based systems. We evaluate these techniques in the context of a real-time avionics mission computing problem involving a system with over 50 components. Our evaluation finds that an automated model-driven configuration of a reusable component middleware framework not only significantly reduces handwritten code and but also simultaneously achieves high reusability and composability of CCM components.

Keywords: Real-time Publish/subscribe Service, Component Middleware, CORBA Component Model, Model-based Systems.

1 Introduction

Emerging Trends. To reduce the complexity of designing robust, efficient, and scalable distributed real-time and embedded (DRE) software systems, developers increasingly rely on *middleware* [1], which is software that resides between applications and lower-level run-time infrastructure, such as operating systems, network protocol stacks, and hardware. Middleware isolates DRE applications from lower-level infrastructure complexities, such as heterogeneous platforms and error-prone network programming mechanisms. It also enforces essential end-to-end quality of service (QoS) properties, such as low latency and bounded jitter; fault propagation/recovery across distribution boundaries; authentication and authorization; and weight, power consumption, and memory footprint constraints.

Over the past decade, middleware has evolved to support the creation of applications via composition of reusable and flexible software *components* [2]. Components are implementation/integration units with precisely-defined interfaces that can be installed

---

* This work was sponsored in part by grants from NSF ITR CCR-0312859, Siemens, and
  DARPA/AFRL contract #F33615-03-C-4112.

G. Karsai and E. Visser (Eds.): GPCE 2004, LNCS 3286, pp. 337–360, 2004.

in application server run-time environments. Examples of conventional commercial-off-the-shelf (COTS) component middleware include the CORBA Component Model (CCM) [3] and Java 2 Enterprise Edition (J2EE) [4].

Component middleware generally supports two models for component interaction: (1) a *request-response* communication model, in which a component invokes a point-to-point operation on another component, and (2) an *event-based* communication model, in which a component transmits arbitrarily-defined messages, called *events*, to other components [5]. Event-based communication models are particularly relevant for large-scale DRE systems[1] (such as avionics mission computing [6, 7], distributed audio/video processing [8, 9], and distributed interactive simulations [10, 11]) since they help reduce software dependencies and enhance system composability and evolution. In particular, the *publish/subscribe* architecture [12] of event-based communication allows application components to interact anonymously and asynchronously [13]. The publish/-subscribe communication model defines the following three software roles:

- **Publishers** generate events to be transmitted. Depending on the architecture design and implementation, publishers may need to describe the events they generate *a priori*.
- **Subscribers** receive events via hook operations. Subscribers also may need to declare the events they receive *a priori*.
- **Event channels** accept events from publishers and deliver events to subscribers. Event channels perform event filtering and routing, QoS enforcement, and fault management. In distributed systems, event channels propagate events across distribution domains to remote subscribers.

Figure 1 illustrates the relationships and information flow between these three types of components.

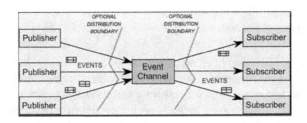

Fig. 1. Relationships Between Components in a Publisher/subscribe Architecture

Applying Model-Driven Middleware to Publish/Subscribe Architectures. Our previous work on publish/subscribe architectures focused on the patterns and performance optimizations of event channels in the context of QoS-enabled *distributed object computing* (DOC) middleware [14], specifically a highly scalable [11] and real-time [15, 6] CORBA Event Service [16]. This paper extends our previous work on DOC middleware as follows:

---

[1] In this context, *systems* include the OS/hardware/network, middleware, and applications.

- We describe key challenges associated with configuring and deploying publish/-subscribe services in QoS-enabled *component middleware*. Component middleware enhances DOC middleware to enable the composition, configuration, and deployment of reusable services and applications more rapidly and robustly.
- We present a methodology for resolving these challenges based on *Model-Driven Middleware* (MDM) [17], which is a generative programming paradigm that integrates (1) model-driven development technologies, such as Model-Integrated Computing [18, 19] and the OMG's Model Driven Architecture [20], and (2) QoS-enabled component middleware technologies, such as Real-time CORBA [21] and the *Component-Integrated ACE ORB* (CIAO), which is our QoS-enabled implementation of CCM.
- We describe the *Event QoS Aspect Language (EQAL)*, which is an MDM tool that supports graphical representations of crosscutting concerns (such as component event port connections and event channel configuration) associated with publish/-subscribe QoS configurations and federated publish/subscribe service deployments. This paper explores EQAL support for two generative aspects – service configuration and deployment – that help automate much of the integration of publish/-subscribe services into QoS-enabled component-based DRE systems.
- We evaluate empirically how MDM reduces the amount of handwritten code in developing component applications that utilize publish/subscribe services. Our results applying MDM to a 50 component avionics mission computing scenario show that it dramatically reduces handwritten code via automated configuration of a reusable component framework, while simultaneously eliminating accidental complexities incurred when hand-crafting 100+ XML-based descriptor files, which are the standard way to describe configure and deploy publish/subscribe services in CCM.

Paper Organization. The remainder of this paper is organized as follows: Section 2 outlines the deployment and configuration capabilities in the CORBA Component Model (CCM) that is leveraged by our work; Section 3 describes the key challenges and solution approaches associated with configuring and deploying publish/subscribe services in QoS-enabled component middleware; Section 4 demonstrates in detail how our EQAL MDM tool addresses the publish/subscribe configuration and federation deployment challenges; Section 5 empirically evaluates the extent to which EQAL reduces the amount of handwritten code in developing component-based avionics mission computing systems that utilize publish/subscribe services; Section 6 compares our MDM approach with related work; and Section 7 presents concluding remarks and outlines future work.

2   Overview of CCM Configuration and Deployment Capabilities and DAnCE

The CORBA Component Model (CCM) [3] specification describes a component architecture and standardizes component implementation, packaging, and deployment mechanisms [22]. Components in DRE systems may need to be configured differently, depending on the context in which they are used. For example, it might be necessary to collocate or replicate related components to improve performance or resilience to failures by distributing functionality encapsulated as components. CCM implementations provide the capabilities described below that DRE systems can use to (1) collocate and/or distribute components depending on application QoS needs, (2) make the necessary connections between communicating components, (3) group components together to form reusable artifacts, and (4) deploy groups of components on various nodes in a target environment.

Component packaging groups implementations of component functionality (typically stored in a dynamic link library) together with metadata that describes the features available in it (*e.g.*, its properties) or the features that it requires (*e.g.*, its dependencies). A component package is the vehicle for deploying a single component implementation. The CCM Component Implementation Framework (CIF) uses the Component Implementation Definition Language (CIDL) to generate the component implementation skeletons and persistent state management automatically.

Component assembly groups components and characterizes the metadata that describes these components in an assembly [22] via a *component assembly descriptor*, which specify how components are connected together, on what hosts they will run, how the components are instantiated, among numerous other properties. A component assembly package is the vehicle for deploying a set of interrelated component implementations. CCM assemblies are defined via XML Schema templates, which provide an implementation-independent mechanism for describing component properties and generating default configurations for CCM components. These assembly configurations can preserve the required QoS properties and establish the necessary configuration and interconnections among groups of related components.

Component deployment installs and connects a logical component topology to form a physical computing environment. The component topology is specified by an assembly package. A *deployment tool* deploys individual components and assemblies of components to an installation site, *e.g.*, a set of hosts on a network. Based on an assembly descriptor and user input, a CCM deployment tool installs and activates component homes and instances. It also configures component properties and connects components together via interface and event ports, as designated by an assembly descriptor.

Figure 2 illustrates the Deployment and Configuration Engine (DAnCE) [23], which is our implementation of the OMG deployment and configuration (DnC) specification [22], addressing the DnC crosscutting concerns of DRE systems, DAnCE supports the creation, control, and termination of components on the nodes of the target environment. DAnCE takes the DnC XML descriptors and creates an in-memory representation of the metadata. Run-time services in DAnCE then populate a global deployment plan, which provides an in-memory representation. Depending on the number of nodes needed for a particular deployment, DAnCE splits the global plan into multiple local deployment plans that are optimally configured for deployment on that platform.

3   Meeting the Challenges of Configuring and Deploying Publish/Subscribe Systems

QoS-enabled component middleware platforms, such as the CIAO [24] and Qedo [25], leverage the benefits of component-based software development and preserve the optimization patterns and principles of DOC middleware. Before developers of event-based DRE systems can derive benefits from QoS-enabled component middleware, however,

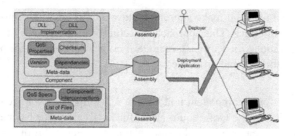

Fig. 2. DAnCE Deployment and Configuration Engine

they must reduce the complexity of configuring and deploying publish/subscribe services. In particular, DRE system developers must resolve the following challenges associated with publish/subscribe mechanisms provided by conventional component middleware:

1. **Configuring publish/subscribe service QoS**, where there are currently no standard means of configuring component middleware mechanisms to deliver appropriate QoS to DRE systems, and
2. **Deploying federated publish/subscribe services**, where there are currently no standard policies and mechanisms to deploy a federation of publish/subscribe services for DRE systems.

This section explains the context in which each challenge outlined above arises, identifies the specific problems that must be addressed, and outlines solution approaches that help resolve the challenge. Section 4 then illustrates how we have applied these solutions using Model-Driven Middleware (MDM).

3.1 Challenge 1: Configuring Publish/Subscribe Quality-of-Service

Context. *Configurability* is an important requirement for many publish/subscribe services developed using middleware. For example, various operating policies (such as threading and buffering strategy) of the CORBA publish/subscribe services can be customized programmatically via invocations on a configuration interface. The drawbacks with DOC middleware approaches to configurability, however, are (1) *reduced flexibility* due to tight coupling of application logic with crosscutting configuration and deployment concerns, such as publish/subscribe relationships and choice of various types of publish/subscribe services, such as the CORBA-based Event, Real-time Event, and Notification Services. and (2) *impeded reuse* due to tight coupling of application logic with specific QoS properties, such as event latency thresholds and priorities.

In contrast, component middleware publish/subscribe services enhance flexibility and reuse by using meta-programming techniques (such as the XML descriptor files in CCM) to specify component configuration and deployment concerns. This approach enables QoS requirements to be specified *later* (*i.e.*, just before run-time deployment) in a system's lifecycle, rather than *earlier* (*i.e.*, during component development). For example, the configuration framework provided by the CIAO component middleware parses

XML configuration files and make appropriate invocations on a publish/subscribe service configuration interface. This approach is useful for DRE systems that require custom QoS configurations for various target OS, network, and hardware platforms that have different capabilities and properties.

Problem. Conventional component middleware relies upon *ad hoc* techniques based on *manually* specifying the QoS requirements for DRE component systems. Unfortunately, configuring component middleware manually is hard [26] due to the number and complexity of operating policies, such as transaction and security properties, persistence and lifecycle management, and publish/subscribe QoS configurations. These policies exist at multiple layers of middleware and often employ non-standard legacy specification mechanisms, such as configuration files that use proprietary text-based formats.

Moreover, given component interoperability needs across various platforms (*e.g.*, CCM and J2EE) and the existence of multiple publish/subscribe services within individual platforms (*e.g.*, the CORBA Event Service and Notification Service), a component-based application may use several publish/subscribe services. To further complicate matters, certain combinations of policies are semantically invalid and can result in system failure. For example, if multiple levels of priorities for events are supported, a priority-based thread pool model should be used rather than a reactive threading model [27]. Care should be taken to ensure that lower level configurations support end-to-end priorities, *e.g.*, using Real-time CORBA priority-banded connections [28].

Most publish/subscribe services based on DOC middleware (including the CORBA Event and Notification Services) do not validate QoS specifications automatically. It is hard, moreover, to *manually* validate QoS configurations for semantic compatibility. This process is particularly daunting for large-scale, mission-/safety-critical DRE systems, where the cost of human error is most egregious.

Solution Approach → Develop MDM Tools to Create Publish/Subscribe Service Configuration Models. MDM tools can help application developers create QoS specifications for DRE systems more rapidly and correctly by automatically generating configuration descriptor files and enforcing constraints among publish/subscribe policies via model checkers [29]. These benefits are particularly important when component applications are maintained and evolved over an extended period of time since (1) QoS configurations can be modified more easily to reflect changing OS, network, and hardware platforms and (2) QoS configurations for system enhancements can be checked systematically for compatibility with legacy specifications.

To attain these benefits, we developed the *Event QoS Aspect Language* (EQAL), which is an MDM tool that models configurations for three CORBA-based publish/-subscribe services: (1) the Event Service [16], (2) Real-time Event Service [6, 15], and (3) Notification Service [30]. EQAL informs users if invalid combinations of QoS policies are specified. After publish/subscribe QoS models are complete and validated, EQAL can also synthesize the XML configuration files used by the underlying component middleware to configure itself. Section 4.2 illustrates how we applied EQAL to configure key QoS properties of component middleware publish/subscribe services.

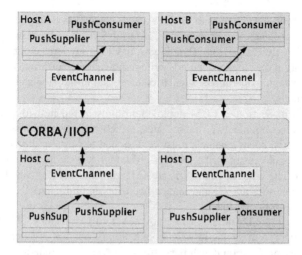

Fig. 3. Federated Event Channels in CIAO

3.2 Challenge 2: Deploying Publish/Subscribe Services in Target Networks

Context. *Scalability* is another important requirement for many publish/subscribe systems. Large-scale publish/subscribe systems consist of many components and event channels distributed across network boundaries and possibly different administrative domains, and each event channel may have many consumers. Naive implementations of publish/subscribe services send a separate event across the network for each remote consumer, which can transmit the same data multiple times (often to the same target host) and incur network and host overhead that is excessive for many resource-constrained DRE applications. As the number of channels and/or consumers grows, these types of publish/subscribe services can become a bottleneck.

To minimize the overhead of publish/subscribe services, multiple event channels can be linked together to form *federated* configurations [11, 15], where event channels are assigned to particular hosts and events received by one channel are propagated automatically to other channels in the federation. Figure 3 illustrates how CIAO's publish/-subscribe services support federated event channels. In CIAO's federated publish/-subscribe services, suppliers and consumers that are collocated on the same host connect to a local event channel. Each local event channel communicates with other event channels when events sent by suppliers are destined for consumers on remote hosts. This design reduces latency in large-scale DRE systems when consumers and suppliers exhibit *locality-of-reference*, *i.e.*, where event consumers are on the same host as event suppliers. In such cases, only local C++ method calls are needed instead of remote CORBA operation calls. Moreover, if multiple remote consumers are interested in the same event, only one message is sent to each remote event channel, thereby reducing network utilization.

In CIAO's federated publish/subscribe services, event channel *gateways* are used to mediate the communication between remote event channels, while suppliers and consumers communicate with each other via local event channels. Each gateway is a

CORBA component that connects to the local event channel as a supplier and connects to the remote event channel as a consumer. CIAO supports three types of event channel gateways: CORBA IIOP, UDP, and IP multicast. In CIAO's federated publish/subscribe services, application developers need not write tedious and error-prone code manually to perform bookkeeping operations, such as creating and initializing gateways that federate event channels.

As discussed in Section 2, CCM deployment tools install individual components and assemblies of components on target sites, which are normally a set of hosts on a network. Similarly, event channels must be assigned to hosts in the target network. CIAO's federated publish/subscribe services are integrated via its DAnCE component deployment tool. The input to DAnCE is an XML data file that (1) specifies the event channel deployment sites and (2) automatically creates and initializes the event channel gateways at the appropriate sites.

Problem. Although the DAnCE CCM deployment tool provided by CIAO shields application developers from having to write bookkeeping code for its federated publish/-subscribe services, application developers still must *hand-craft* federation deployment descriptor metadata using an XML schema based on the OMG Deployment and Configuration specification [22]. Hand-crafting descriptor metadata involves determining information about the type of federations (*i.e.*, CORBA IIOP, UDP, or IP multicast), identifying remote event channels, and identifying local event channels. Moreover, the metadata must address the following deployment requirements: (1) each host could have its own event channels, event consumers, event suppliers, and event channel gateways, (2) each event consumer and event supplier only communicates with a event channel collocated in the same host, (3) event channels distributed across network boundaries are connected through event channel gateways, (4) each connection between an event channel and an event supplier should be uniquely identified, (5) each connection between an event channel and an event consumer should be identified by using existing events, as defined in step (4), and (6) each connection between an event channel and an event channel gateway should also be identified by using existing events, as defined in step (4).

Experience has shown [31, 32] that it is hard for DRE developers to keep track of many complex dependencies when deploying federated publish/subscribe services. Without tool support, therefore, the effort required to deploy a federation involves hand-crafting deployment descriptor metadata in an *ad hoc* way. Since large-scale DRE systems may involve many different types of events and event channels, *ad hoc* ways of writing metadata to deploy publish/subscribe services are tedious and error-prone. Addressing this challenge requires techniques that can analyze, validate, and verify the correctness and robustness of federated event channel deployments.

Solution Approach → Develop MDM Tools to Deploy Event Channel Federations in a Visual, Intuitive Way. MDM tools can synthesize the metadata for deploying a federated publish/subscribe service from *models* of the interactions among different event-related components (*e.g.*, event suppliers, event consumers, event channels, and various types of event channel gateways). MDM tools can also generate the metadata needed to deploy federated publish/subscribe services that are syntactically and semantically valid. Section 4.3 shows how the EQAL MDM tool was applied to deploy publish/subscribe service federations more effectively than existing approaches.

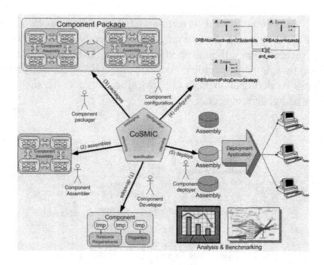

Fig. 4. CoSMIC MDM Toolsuite

4 Resolving Publish/Subscribe Service Configuration and Deployment Challenges in CoSMIC

This section describes how we have employed Model-Driven Middleware (MDM) techniques to address the challenges of publish/subscribe service configuration and federated deployment discussed in Section 3. We present an overview of the *Event QoS Aspect Language* (EQAL) and show how EQAL helps to resolve the challenges of (1) publish/subscribe configuration described in Section 3.1 and federated event service deployment described in Section 3.2. As shown in Figure 4, EQAL is part of the configuration generative tools of the *Component Synthesis via Model Integrated Computing* (CoSMIC) [23] MDM toolsuite. CoSMIC contains a collection of domain-specific modeling languages and their associated analysis/synthesis tools that support various phases of DRE system development, assembly, configuration, and deployment. CoSMIC generates crosscutting concerns, such as XML descriptors, that can be woven into component applications via the DAnCE deployment and configuration engine outlined in Section 2.

4.1 Overview of the Event QoS Aspect Language (EQAL)

Conventional component middleware frameworks use XML files to describe publish/-subscribe service configurations and deployments. These textual specifications are unnecessarily complex and error-prone, however, as discussed in Sections 3. To address these problems we created the EQAL MDM tool, which supports graphical representations of QoS configurations and federated deployments of publish/subscribe services.

EQAL is developed using the Generic Modeling Environment (GME) [33], which is a generative technology for creating domain-specific modeling languages and tools [18]. GME can be programmed via *metamodels* and *model interpreters*. Metamodels define modeling languages (called *paradigms*) that specify the syntax and semantics of the modeling element types, their properties and relationships, and presentation abstractions defined by a domain-specific modeling language. Model interpreters can traverse a paradigm's modeling elements and perform various actions, such as analyzing model properties and generating code.

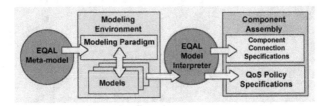

Fig. 5. The Event QoS Aspect Language Architecture

The EQAL paradigm in GME consists of the two complementary entities shown in Figure 5 and described below:

• **EQAL metamodel**, which defines a modeling paradigm in which modelers specify the desired publish/subscribe service (*e.g.*, the CORBA Event Service, Notification Service, or Real-time Event Service) and the configuration of that service for each component event connection. Based on application needs, modelers can also specify how event channels are assigned to different hosts and whether/how they must be linked together to form federations.

• **EQAL model interpreters** that can (1) validate configuration and deployment models and (2) synthesize text-based middleware publish/subscribe service and federation service configuration- and deployment-specific descriptor files from models of a given component assembly. Component deployers can build publish/subscribe service configurations for component applications using the EQAL modeling paradigm and its model interpreters.

The remainder of this section describes how EQAL addresses the challenges presented in Section 3.

4.2 Configuring Publish/Subscribe Quality-of-Service in EQAL

To address the publish/subscribe service configuration challenge described in Section 3.1, the EQAL *configuration paradigm* specifies publish/subscribe QoS configurations, parameters, and constraints. For example, the EQAL metamodel contains a distinct set of modeling constructs for each publish/subscribe service supported by CIAO. Example policies and strategies that can be modeled include filtering, correlation, timeouts, locking, disconnect control, and priority.

Publish/subscribe service policies can have different scopes, ranging from a single port to an entire event channel. EQAL's publish/subscribe service configurations can therefore be provisioned at the following three levels of granularity:

- **Channel scope**, which applies to all components using the channel. Each event channel is specified with a number of policies that control its behavior, such as event filtering, event correlation, timeouts, and locking. These policies control how the channel handles all connections and events.
- **Proxy scope**, which applies to a single component port. Each event port is associated with a proxy object. Certain QoS policies are configured at the proxy level, such as threading control settings, average execution time, and worst-case execution time. QoS parameters can be provided for each connection by configuring the proxy. Naturally, connection-level parameters for a proxy must be consistent with channel-level policies.
- **Event scope**, which applies to an event instance. A limited number of QoS settings, such as timeouts, can be specified for an individual event instance.

The EQAL metamodel allows modelers to provision reusable and sharable configurations at each level of granularity outlined above. Modelers assign configurations to individual event connections and then construct filters for each connection. EQAL supports two forms of event generation using the push model: (1) a component may be an exclusive supplier of an event type or (2) a component may supply events to a shared channel.

Dependencies among publish/subscribe QoS policies, strategies, and configurations can be complex. Ensuring coherency among policies and configurations is therefore a non-trivial source of complexity in component middleware [34]. During the modeling phase, EQAL ensures that dependencies between configuration parameters are enforced by declaring constraints on the contexts in which individual options are valid, *e.g.*, priority-based thread allocation policies are only valid with component event connections that have assigned priorities. EQAL can then automatically validate configurations and notify users of incompatible QoS properties during model validation, rather than at component deployment- and run-time.

To ensure semantically consistent configurations, violation of constraint rules should be detected early in the modeling phase rather than later in the component deployment phase. To support this capability, EQAL provides a constraint model checker that validates the syntactic and semantic compatibility of event channel configurations to ensure the proper functioning of publish/subscribe services. EQAL's model checker uses GME's constraint manager, which is a lightweight model-checker that implements the standard OMG Object Constraint Language (OCL) specification [35].

EQAL's model interpreters perform the following two distinct configuration aspects:

● **XML Descriptor Generation.** EQAL contains an interpreter that synthesizes XML descriptors used by the DAnCE component deployment framework to indicate the QoS requirements of individual component event connections. Since the CCM specification does not explicitly address the mechanisms for ensuring component QoS properties, the EQAL-generated descriptors are based on a schema developed for the Boeing Bold Stroke project for their Prism [34] extensions to CCM (the XML descriptors remain compliant with the CCM specifications, however). Boeing's Bold Stroke schema has been carefully crafted, refined, tested, and optimized in the context of production DRE avionics mission computing systems [31, 32].

EQAL generates the XML descriptors for one service at a time. To complete the interpretation process, EQAL makes multiple passes through the model hierarchy, corresponding to each different type of publish/subscribe services, until all the service connections are configured. To simplify the interpreter implementation, EQAL [36] uses the Visitor pattern [37], which utilizes a double-dispatch mechanism to apply file-generation operations to different type of modeling elements.

• **Service Configuration File Generation.** EQAL also contains an interpreter that generates event channel service configuration files, called `svc.conf` files, that are used by the underlying publish/subscribe services to select the appropriate behaviors of event channel resource factories [11]. These factories are responsible for creating many strategy objects that control the behavior of event channels. CIAO supports many (*i.e.*, more than 40) options/policies for different types of publish/subscribe services, which increases the complexity for application developers who must consider numerous design choices when configuring the publish/subscribe services. Interactions between event channel policies are complex due to the possibility of incompatible groupings of options, making hand-crafting these files hard, *e.g.*, priority-based thread allocation policies are only valid with component event connections that have assigned priorities.

Much of the complexity associated with validating event channel QoS configurations is accomplished by EQAL's modeling constraints and GME's lightweight model checker. These constraints prevent application developers from specifying inconsistent or invalid combinations of policies. After a set of policy settings is validated via modeling constraints, EQAL generates an *event channel descriptor* (`.ecd`) file that contains valid combinations of policy settings chosen for a particular service configuration.

4.3   Deploying Publish/Subscribe Service Federations in EQAL

To address the publish/subscribe federation service deployment challenge outlined in Section 3.2, the EQAL *deployment paradigm* specifies how components and event channels are assigned to hosts on a target network. To address the scalability problem in any large-scale event-based architecture, CIAO provides publish/subscribe services that supports event channel federation. With CIAO's publish/subscribe services, an event channel federation can be implemented via CORBA gateways. Application developers can configure the location of the gateways to utilize network resources effectively.

For example, collocating a gateway with its consumer event channel (*i.e.*, the one it connects to as a supplier) eliminates the need to transmit events that have no consumer event channel subscribers. Application developers can also choose different types of gateways based on different application deployment scenarios with different networking and computing resources. These deployment decisions have no coupling with, or bearing on, component application logic. The same set of components can therefore be reused and deployed into different scenarios without modifying application code manually.

The EQAL modeling paradigm allows three types of federation (*i.e.*, CORBA IIOP, UDP, or IP multicast) to be configured in a deployment. For event channel federation models, the EQAL metamodel defines two levels of syntactic elements:

- The **outer-level**, which contains the host elements as basic building blocks and allows users to define the hosts present in the DRE system and

– The **inner-level**, which represents a host containing a set of elements (including event channels, CORBA IIOP gateways, UDP senders and receivers, IP multicast senders and receivers, and event type references) that allow users to configure the deployment of these artifacts inside a host.

These two levels are associated with each other via *link parts*, which act as connection points between two different views of a model (such as adjacent layers of a hierarchical model) to indicate some form of association, relationship, or dataflow between two or more models. The inner-level elements are exposed to the outer-level in the form of link parts from the outside view, which can be used to connect them to form a federation.

Figure 6 (a) is a screenshot that illustrates how we used EQAL to model the outer-level view of CIAO federated publish/subscribe service in the real-time avionics mission computing application outlined in Section 1. This figure shows the outer-level model of the deployment of the federated publish/subscribe service, which includes nine physically distributed locations that host CCM components. Figure 6 (b) shows the inner-level of the federation configurations, which establish four CORBA gateways in the track center module to form a federation that reduces network traffic.

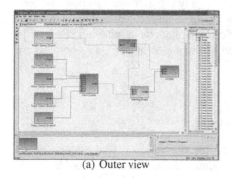 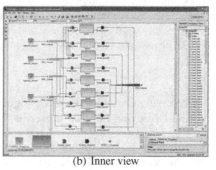

(a) Outer view   (b) Inner view

Fig. 6. EQAL Deployment Model for a Real-time Avionics System

To ensure the validity of event channel federation models during the deployment phase, each event channel's configurations and settings must be model-checked to ensure that they are consistent with the federation types. For example, IP multicast uses the Observer pattern [37] capabilities of CIAO's event channels. When a user chooses IP multicast as the type of event channel federation, this observer functionality must be enabled for IP multicast to work properly. These constraints can be checked automatically using EQAL.

Section 4.2 described how EQAL's model interpreters handle configuration aspects. EQAL also contains a model interpreter for the deployment aspect, which synthesizes the federated publish/subscribe service assembly and deployment descriptor XML files. The information captured in these files includes the relationship between each artifact, the physical location of each supplier, consumer, event channel, and CORBA gateway. This file is subsequently fed into the DAnCE CCM deployment tool, which deploy the federated system to its designed target nodes.

5 Evaluating the Merits of Model-Driven Middleware

The EQAL MDM tool described in Section 4 is designed to reduce the configuration and development effort of DRE applications. This section evaluates how the EQAL MDM tool helps alleviate common sources of complexity in a representative DRE application based on QoS-enabled component middleware. We conduct this evaluation in the context of Boeing Bold Stroke, which is an open experimental platform (OEP) [34] in the DARPA PCES [38] program for real-time avionics mission computing. The Bold Stroke OEP integrates and demonstrates model-based, language-based, and middleware-based technologies to productively program and evolve crosscutting aspects that support composable DRE middleware for publish/subscribe-based avionics systems. Crosscutting concerns addressed by the Bold Stroke OEP include synchronization, memory management, fault tolerance, real-time deadlines, end-to-end latencies, and bandwidth and CPU management.

We implemented the OEP's *Medium-sized* (MediumSP) scenario, which is a challenge problem product scenario in the DARPA PCES OEP [38], using EQAL and CIAO CCM middleware platform. The MediumSP scenario is representative of real-time avionics mission computing systems that employ event-driven data flow and control [31, 32]. This scenario consists of 50+ components with complex event dependencies that control embedded sensors and perform calculations to maintain displays. In this type of mission-critical DRE system, reliability and stringent QoS assurance are essential.

5.1 Resolving Complexities of Configuring and Deploying Publish/Subscribe Services

The configuration and deployment of publish/subscribe services is an example *crosscutting concerns* that need to be refactored, modularized, and then composed back into the middleware. EQAL helps to automate this process by enabling different types of services to be configured based on application needs and available resources. For example, EQAL's integrated model checker and model interpreters can flag invalid configurations at design- and/or deployment-time, thereby eliminating sources of accidental complexity that would otherwise manifest themselves at run-time. EQAL also significantly increases component reusability and maintainability by decoupling (1) the type of publish/subscribe service configured into the system from (2) the functionality of application components.

In the Bold Stroke MediumSP scenario, there are over 50 components and most components act as both suppliers and consumers of events. Without automated support from an MDM tool like EQAL, application developers would face the following challenges when implementing the MediumSP scenario:

No Systematic Approach to Specify Policies/Options. Manually configuring the publish/subscribe services via *ad hoc* techniques can overwhelm application developers since configuration of each service is intertwined with 20+ configuration parameters spread throughout different subsystems and layers of the component middleware and applications. For example, configuration parameters in the CIAO Real-time Event Service include the number of threads, cached execution time, worst-case execution time, average execution time, level of importance, entry point name, etc.

Low-Level, Complex Glue Code. Application developers would either have to write/-maintain special-purpose "glue code" manually for different types of publish/subscribe services or treat the different services in the same way, *e.g.*, write different publish/-subscribe-related glue code for different types of publish/subscribe services (such as Event Service, Real-time Event Service, and Notification Service) or a degenerate case of components communicating directly with each other.

Potential Run-Time Errors. If the component middleware was configured improperly, application functionality and QoS behavior can be incorrect. For example, if a component server and its containers were not configured with support for real-time priorities and concurrency, it would be hard for an *ad hoc* configuration and deployment process to detect erroneous conditions, such as an application developer configuring a real-time event channel within the component middleware. These conditions would be detected only when the system was actually deployed and operating, at which point it might be too late to prevent serious run-time errors.

5.2   Evaluating How Component Middleware Minimizes Handwritten Code

In earlier generation of DOC middleware, developers had to explicitly handle the complexity of connecting to, and configuring the policies of, the underlying middleware. For example, in the CORBA 2.x DOC model, developers often manually configured the policies of middleware entities, such as publish/subscribe services, transaction services, and security services. Moreover, event channels were deployed by hand-crafting DOC middleware application servers to create and destroy event channels and gateways.

Figure 7 shows how application developers using CORBA DOC middleware must write code manually in the "Server" and "Impl" files. These manual programming activities result in the production of considerable repetitive boilerplate code, which may actually be larger than the application logic requiring publish/subscribe functionality! Moreover, these activities are error-prone since they require application developers to wrestle with middleware details, which are often low-level and proprietary.

In contrast, CCM middleware defines the container and component server elements to handle most of the glue code. Moreover, CCM shields component developers from low-level details of the underlying middleware via containers that provide the execution context in which application components run and mediate access to underlying middleware services. Likewise, generic component servers provide a standardized OS process in which components and event channels can be composed and run, thereby alleviating the need to write and deploy custom servers.

As illustrated in Figure 8, CCM middleware increases the amount of generated code compared with handwritten code because much of the boilerplate component server code, XML component descriptors, servants, and other glue code can be generated automatically. Likewise, the configuration and deployment of publish/subscribe services can be automated by CCM middleware. Below we highlight concretely how EQAL can automatically generate code for the MediumSP scenario that would otherwise be written manually.

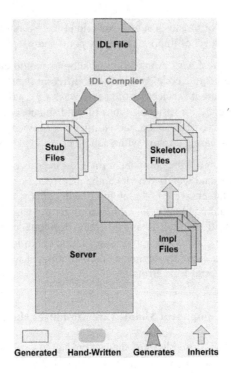

Fig. 7. Generated vs. Handwritten Code in the CORBA DOC Model

Creating Event Channels. To create an event channel, the following steps must be carried out: (1) *declaring the channel,* where a name is assigned to the channel, (2) *setting channel attributes,* where the appropriate service configurator file is specified to configure the channel, (3) *instantiating the channel,* where memory is allocated for the channel and its constructor is called, (4) *activating the channel,* where the channel's servant is enabled, and (5) *registering the channel,* where the channel is registered with a CORBA server. The implementation of the event channel creation member function requires 22 lines of C++.

Specifying Service Policies. When configuring a real-time service, the QoS requirements for a supplier or consumer must be specified. This specification process involves the following steps: (1) *building a filter,* where a consumer specifies the logical conditions (*e.g.,* based on the supplier and type of an event) under which an event should be delivered, and (2) *specifying real-time properties,* where desired QoS properties (*e.g.,* priorities and required execution times) are given for each event supplier and consumer. The implementation for specifying service policies requires 334 lines of C++.

Connecting Suppliers and Consumers. Connecting a supplier or consumer to a channel invokes the following steps: (1) *obtaining an administrative object,* where the channel supplies a reference to a configuration entity known as an admin object, (2) *obtaining a proxy,* where the admin supplies a reference to a connection point, known as a proxy object, (3) *creating a consumer/supplier servant,* where a servant is declared, instanti-

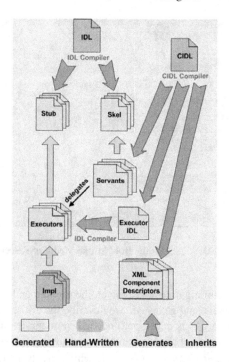

Fig. 8. Generated vs. Handwritten Code in the CORBA Component Model

ated, and activated, and (4) *connecting to the event channel*, where a reference to the servant is passed to the proxy object. The implementations of connection methods for suppliers and consumers required 45 and 54 lines of C++, respectively.

Implementing Supplier and Consumer Servants. Implementing a supplier or consumer servant involves inheriting from an abstract base class and implementing several hook methods. The supplier and consumer servant methods are then dispatched by an event channel when an event is pushed or when a disconnection occurs. Code to handle these occurrences in accordance with specific requirements of an application must be provided by application developers. The amount of code necessary is heavily dependent on application requirements, but required 94 lines of C++ in the Bold Stroke MediumSP scenario.

5.3   Applying EQAL to Real-Time Avionics Mission Computing

Based on the discussions in Sections 5.1 and 5.2, we now focus on applying EQAL to model the Bold Stroke MediumSP scenario, which is shown in Figure 9. We use this scenario to further qualify the code reduction that results from employing the EQAL MDM tool and CIAO component middleware instead of handwritten glue-code and DOC middleware.

Based on the particular assignment of components to host sites, different event channel federations are possible. For the scenario depicted in Figure 9, our EQAL model

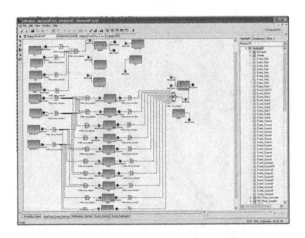

Fig. 9. EQAL Model for the Bold Stroke MediumSP Scenario

distributes components among nine hosts. Given the number and location of suppliers, consumers, event channels, and gateways, we describe the effort (measured roughly in terms of the number of artifacts developed) needed to integrate publish/subscribe services in the following phases of the MediumSP scenario:

Phase 1: Managing Event Channel Lifecycles, which involves creating and destroying event channels. Since EQAL's MediumSP model incorporates multiple publish/subscribe services, multiple event channels of differing types must be managed. In the MediumSP example, more than 10 event channels must be managed.

Phase 2: Initializing Gateways, Suppliers, and Consumers, which involves (1) making interconnections between supplier/consumer components, event channels, and gateways and (2) implementing supplier/consumer servants. There are a total of 42 event suppliers and 38 event consumers in the MediumSP scenario that must be created and initialized. Based on the deployment scenario, we have set up 12 gateways to federate these event channels (other types of gateways may chose to form different types of federations).

Phase 3: Specifying Service Policies, which involves establishing control strategies, such as filter criteria and QoS parameters. All 42 suppliers and 38 consumers of events specify real-time rate requirements and 8 of the consumers require filter specifications to correlate events. Each supplier and consumer must be configured individually with the appropriate policies, such as filtering, correlation, timeouts, locking, disconnect control, and priority.

In each phase above, glue-code and XML descriptors must be provided to configure and deploy the required publish/subscribe services. To avoid hand-crafting boilerplate software, EQAL combines component middleware with MDM technology to synthesize glue-code and XML descriptors. The resulting reduction in complexity for the MediumSP scenario is summarized below:

The assembly of 50+ components for the MediumSP scenario requires a complicated *component assembly* file that stores the connection information between component ports as XML descriptors, partitions for process collocation, and interrelationships with other descriptors (*e.g.*, the relationship between the interface definitions and component implementations) whose details are spread across other assembly files, such as the *implementation artifact descriptor* (.iad) file. EQAL shields DRE system developers from these low-level details by ensuring that all this metadata and dependencies are captured appropriately in various descriptor files it generates in conjunction with other CoSMIC tools, such as PICML [23].

Every component requires two descriptor files: (1) the *software package descriptor* for the component, which contains general information about the software (such as author, description, license information, and dependencies on other software packages), followed by one or more sections describing implementations of that software, and (2) the *servant software descriptor*, which CIAO deployment tools use to load the desired servant library. For ~50 components, ~100 files are therefore required. Once again, EQAL shields DRE system developer from these low-level details by generating these files automatically, thereby ensuring that all interdependencies are captured appropriately in the descriptor files.

For the publish/subscribe service in the MediumSP component assembly, a *component property descriptor* (CPF file) is generated for each component event port, an *event channel descriptor* (ECD file) will be generated for each real-time event channel filter, and CIAO's service configuration file (svc.conf) file) will be generated for each event channel configuration. As a result, 12 ECD files, 53 CPD files, and 1 svc.conf file are generated by EQAL. Figure 10 summarizes the lines of code saved by not having to hand-craft these files.

File Type	# of Files	Average # Lines/File	Total Lines
CAD	1	750	750
CSD	50	46	2300
SSD	50	43	2150
CONF	3	6	18
ECD	12	8.58	103
CPF	53	43	2279
Total	**169**	**44.97**	**7600**

CAD: Component Assembly Descriptor   CONF: Service Configuration File
CSD: Software Package Descriptor   ECD: Event Channel Descriptor
SSD: Servant Software Descriptor   CPF: Component Property File

Fig. 10. Amount of Code Reduction for Metadata in Bold Stroke MediumSP Scenario

Each component, event service, and their servants are distinguished via a unique identifier (called a UUID) within the descriptor files mentioned above. Moreover, it is necessary to ensure that when referring to a specific component or event service, the same UUID is referenced across the different descriptor files. This requirement can yield accidental complexities when descriptor files are hand-crafted manually. In the MediumSP scenario, this results in ~100 UUIDs that are referred to across the ~100 descriptor files. EQAL's generative tools eliminate these accidental complexities by synthesizing the proper UUID references in the descriptor files.

The XML tags used to represent real-time properties and resulting configurations in component middleware for integrating real-time event channels are not standardized by OMG yet. Different QoS-enabled component middleware, such as CIAO, therefore define their own XML tags using either XML DTDs or XML Schema definitions. For the MediumSP scenario, this results in enhancing the above-mentioned descriptor files with CIAO-specific real-time properties, and configuration XML tags and data. EQAL shields DRE system developers from these low-level details by synthesizing the proper middleware-specific tags and data in the appropriate descriptor files.

The XML output shown below illustrates an EQAL-generated *component property descriptor* (.cpf) file for a BMDevice component in the MediumSP scenario. This file contains the port real-time QoS properties, such as the number of threads and worst-case execution time.

```xml
<?xml version="1.0" encoding="UTF-8" ?>
<!DOCTYPE properties SYSTEM "properties.dtd">
<properties>
  <struct name="BMDevice-data_available-" type="ACEXML_RT_Info">
    <description>Real-time Scheduler info for
                BMDevice::data_available</description>
  <simple name="port" type="string">
                <value>data_available</value> </simple>
  <simple name="period" type="string">
                <value>0</value> </simple>
  <simple name="entry_point" type="string">
                <value></value> </simple>
  <simple name="criticality" type="string">
    <value>MEDIUM_CRITICALITY</value></simple>
  <simple name="enabled" type="string">
    <value>DEPENDENCY_NON_VOLATILE</value></simple>
  <simple name="importance" type="string">
    <value>MEDIUM_IMPORTANCE</value></simple>
  <simple name="quantum" type="string">
                <value>0</value> </simple>
  <simple name="threads" type="string">
                <value>1</value> </simple>
  <simple name="cached_execution_time" type="string">
                <value>0</value> </simple>
  <simple name="worst_case_execution_time" type="string">
                <value>0</value> </simple>
  <simple name="info_type" type="string">
                <value>OPERATION</value> </simple>
  <simple name="typical_execution_time" type="string">
                <value>0</value> </simple>
  </struct> </properties>
```

In summary, EQAL dramatically reduces an application developer's effort for an event-based DRE application, such as the Bold Stroke MediumSP scenario, by generating a considerable amount of glue-code and XML descriptors that are then used by other CCM-related tools, such as DAnCE [23], to configure and deploy the CIAO publish/subscribe service middleware.

6   Related Work

This section reviews related work on model-based software development and describes how modeling, analysis, and generative programming techniques have been used to model and provision QoS capabilities for QoS-enabled component middleware and applications.

Cadena [29] is an integrated development environment for modeling and model-checking component-based DRE systems. Cadena's model checking environment is particularly well suited to event-based inter-component communication via real-time event channels. Cadena also provides an Event Configuration Framework (EMF) [39] that allows modeling event channel properties, which can be model checked. We are integrating our CoSMIC toolsuite with Cadena to leverage its model checking capability. Both Cadena and CoSMIC have been used in the context of Boeing's OEP on avionics mission computing and for CCM-based applications.

Publish/subscribe service modeling research is also provided by Ptolemy II [40], which is a tool for modeling concurrent hybrid and embedded systems based on the actor-oriented design approach [41]. This approach uses the abstraction of actors, ports, interfaces, and model of computations to model the system. Publish/subscribe is a model of computation in Ptolemy II. Our efforts with CoSMIC are relatively orthogonal with Ptolemy II, *e.g.*, our target is QoS-component middleware and could fit in various families of applications.

The Aspect Oriented Middleware (AOM) research at the University of Toronto, is focusing on the extension and refinement of publish/subscribe service for effectively supporting information dissemination applications, such as modeling of uncertainty [42] or semantic matching [43] in publish/subscribe services. Compared with our work on EQAL, the AOM project focuses on enhancing the publish/subscribe services with uncertainty capabilities because in some situations exact knowledge to either specify subscriptions or publications is not available. Although this approach proposes a new publish/subscribe model based on possibility theory and fuzzy set theory to process uncertainties for both subscriptions and publications, it does not provide a visual modeling language to model the QoS-enabled DRE systems, which is provided by EQAL.

Zanolin et. al. [44] propose an approach to support the modeling and validation of publish/subscribe service architectures. Application-specific components are modeled as UML statechart diagrams while the middleware is supplied as a configurable predefined component. As to validation, properties are described with live sequence charts (LSCs) and transformed into automata. Components, middleware, and properties are translated into Promela [44] and then passed to SPIN (linear temporal logic) to validate the architecture. The main difference between this approach and our work is that Zanolin et. al.'s approach is based on standard UML statecharts to model and validate the publish/subscribe service, but unlike EQAL they do not model the QoS properties and the federation aspect in the publish/subscribe architecture.

7   Concluding Remarks

This paper showed how a Model-Driven Middleware (MDM) tool called the *Event QoS Aspect Language* (EQAL) can automate and simplify the integration of publish/-

subscribe services into QoS-enabled component-based systems. EQAL verifies model validity and generates XML metadata to configure and deploy publish/subscribe service federations in QoS-enabled component middleware. Our experience applying EQAL in the context of DRE systems (such as the avionics mission computing system analyzed in Section 5) is summarized below:

- EQAL allows DRE system deployers to create rapidly and synthesize publish/-subscribe QoS configurations and federation deployments via *models* that are much easier to understand and analyze than hand-crafted code.
- EQAL decouples configuration and deployment decisions from application logic, which enhances component reusability by allowing QoS specifications (and their associated implementations) to change based on the target network architecture.
- EQAL helps alleviate the complexity of validating the QoS policies of publish/-subscribe services for DRE component applications, which is particularly important for large-scale DRE systems that evolve over long periods of time.
- EQAL reduces the amount of code written by application developers for event-based DRE systems by employing a configurable publish/subscribe service framework, which eliminates the need to write code that handles event channel lifecycles, QoS configurations, and supplier/consumer connections.

EQAL, CoSMIC, and CIAO are open-source software available for download at www.dre.vanderbilt.edu/cosmic/.

References

1. Schantz, R.E., Schmidt, D.C.: Middleware for Distributed Systems: Evolving the Common Structure for Network-centric Applications. In Marciniak, J., Telecki, G., eds.: Encyclopedia of Software Engineering. Wiley & Sons, New York (2002)
2. Heineman, G.T., Councill, B.T.: Component-Based Software Engineering: Putting the Pieces Together. Addison-Wesley, Reading, Massachusetts (2001)
3. Object Management Group: CORBA Components. OMG Document formal/2002-06-65 edn. (2002)
4. Sun Microsystems: Java^{TM} 2 Platform Enterprise Edition. java.sun.com/j2ee/index.html (2001)
5. Pietzuch, P.R., Shand, B., Bacon, J.: A Framework for Event Composition in Distributed Systems. In Endler, M., Schmidt, D., eds.: Proceedings of the 4th ACM/IFIP/USENIX International Conference on Middleware (Middleware '03), Rio de Janeiro, Brazil, Springer (2003) 62–82
6. Harrison, T.H., Levine, D.L., Schmidt, D.C.: The Design and Performance of a Real-time CORBA Event Service. In: Proceedings of OOPSLA '97, Atlanta, GA, ACM (1997) 184–199
7. Gill, C.D., Levine, D.L., Schmidt, D.C.: The Design and Performance of a Real-Time CORBA Scheduling Service. Real-Time Systems, The International Journal of Time-Critical Computing Systems, special issue on Real-Time Middleware **20** (2001)
8. Loyall, J., Gossett, J., Gill, C., Schantz, R., Zinky, J., Pal, P., Shapiro, R., Rodrigues, C., Atighetchi, M., Karr, D.: Comparing and Contrasting Adaptive Middleware Support in Wide-Area and Embedded Distributed Object Applications. In: Proceedings of the 21st International Conference on Distributed Computing Systems (ICDCS-21), IEEE (2001) 625–634

9. Karr, D.A., Rodrigues, C., Krishnamurthy, Y., Pyarali, I., Schmidt, D.C.: Application of the QuO Quality-of-Service Framework to a Distributed Video Application. In: Proceedings of the 3rd International Symposium on Distributed Objects and Applications, Rome, Italy, OMG (2001)

10. Noseworthy, R.: IKE 2 – Implementing the Stateful Distributed Object Paradigm . In: 5th IEEE International Symposium on Object-Oriented Real-Time Distributed Computing (ISORC 2002), Washington, DC, IEEE (2002)

11. O'Ryan, C., Schmidt, D.C., Noseworthy, J.R.: Patterns and Performance of a CORBA Event Service for Large-scale Distributed Interactive Simulations. International Journal of Computer Systems Science and Engineering 17 (2002)

12. Buschmann, F., Meunier, R., Rohnert, H., Sommerlad, P., Stal, M.: Pattern-Oriented Software Architecture – A System of Patterns. Wiley & Sons, New York (1996)

13. Carzaniga, A., Rosenblum, D.S., Wolf, A.L.: Design and Evaluation of a Wide-Area Event Notification Service. ACM Transactions on Computer Systems 19 (2001) 332–383

14. Schmidt, D.C., Natarajan, B., Gokhale, A., Wang, N., Gill, C.: TAO: A Pattern-Oriented Object Request Broker for Distributed Real-time and Embedded Systems. IEEE Distributed Systems Online 3 (2002)

15. Schmidt, D.C., O'Ryan, C.: Patterns and Performance of Real-time Publisher/Subscriber Architectures. Journal of Systems and Software, Special Issue on Software Architecture - Engineering Quality Attributes (2002)

16. Object Management Group: Event Service Specification Version 1.1. OMG Document formal/01-03-01 edn. (2001)

17. Gokhale, A., Schmidt, D.C., Natarajan, B., Gray, J., Wang, N.: Model Driven Middleware. In Mahmoud, Q., ed.: Middleware for Communications. Wiley and Sons, New York (2004)

18. Karsai, G., Sztipanovits, J., Ledeczi, A., Bapty, T.: Model-Integrated Development of Embedded Software. Proceedings of the IEEE 91 (2003) 145–164

19. Gray, J., Bapty, T., Neema, S.: Handling Crosscutting Constraints in Domain-Specific Modeling. Communications of the ACM (2001) 87–93

20. Object Management Group: Model Driven Architecture (MDA). OMG Document ormsc/2001-07-01 edn. (2001)

21. Krishna, A.S., Schmidt, D.C., Klefstad, R., Corsaro, A.: Real-time CORBA Middleware. In Mahmoud, Q., ed.: Middleware for Communications. Wiley and Sons, New York (2003)

22. Object Management Group: Deployment and Configuration Adopted Submission. OMG Document ptc/03-07-08 edn. (2003)

23. Gokhale, A., Balasubramanian, K., Balasubramanian, J., Krishna, A., Edwards, G.T., Deng, G., Turkay, E., Parsons, J., Schmidt, D.C.: Model Driven Middleware: A New Paradigm for Deploying and Provisioning Distributed Real-time and Embedded Applications. The Journal of Science of Computer Programming: Special Issue on Model Driven Architecture (2004)

24. Wang, N., Schmidt, D.C., Gokhale, A., Rodrigues, C., Natarajan, B., Loyall, J.P., Schantz, R.E., Gill, C.D.: QoS-enabled Middleware. In Mahmoud, Q., ed.: Middleware for Communications. Wiley and Sons, New York (2003)

25. Ritter, T., Born, M., Unterschütz, T., Weis, T.: A QoS Metamodel and its Realization in a CORBA Component Infrastructure. In: Proceedings of the 36th Hawaii International Conference on System Sciences, Software Technology Track, Distributed Object and Component-based Software Systems Minitrack, HICSS 2003, Honolulu, HW, HICSS (2003)

26. Memon, A., Porter, A., Yilmaz, C., Nagarajan, A., Schmidt, D.C., Natarajan, B.: Skoll: Distributed Continuous Quality Assurance. In: Proceedings of the 26th IEEE/ACM International Conference on Software Engineering, Edinburgh, Scotland, IEEE/ACM (2004)

27. Schmidt, D.C.: Evaluating Architectures for Multi-threaded CORBA Object Request Brokers. Communications of the ACM Special Issue on CORBA 41 (1998)

28. Pyarali, I., Schmidt, D.C., Cytron, R.: Techniques for Enhancing Real-time CORBA Quality of Service. IEEE Proceedings Special Issue on Real-time Systems **91** (2003)
29. Hatcliff, J., Deng, W., Dwyer, M., Jung, G., Prasad, V.: Cadena: An Integrated Development, Analysis, and Verification Environment for Component-based Systems. In: Proceedings of the 25th International Conference on Software Engineering, Portland, OR (2003)
30. Object Management Group: Notification Service Specification. Object Management Group. OMG Document formal/2002-08-04 edn. (2002)
31. Sharp, D.C.: Reducing Avionics Software Cost Through Component Based Product Line Development. In: Proceedings of the 10th Annual Software Technology Conference. (1998)
32. Sharp, D.C.: Avionics Product Line Software Architecture Flow Policies. In: Proceedings of the 18th IEEE/AIAA Digital Avionics Systems Conference (DASC). (1999)
33. Ledeczi, A., Bakay, A., Maroti, M., Volgysei, P., Nordstrom, G., Sprinkle, J., Karsai, G.: Composing Domain-Specific Design Environments. IEEE Computer (2001)
34. Sharp, D.C., Roll, W.C.: Model-Based Integration of Reusable Component-Based Avionics System. In: Proceedings of the Workshop on Model-Driven Embedded Systems in RTAS 2003. (2003)
35. Object Management Group: Unified Modeling Language: OCL version 2.0 Final Adopted Specification. OMG Document ptc/03-10-14 edn. (2003)
36. Edwards, G., Schmidt, D.C., Gokhale, A., Natarajan, B.: Integrating Publisher/Subscriber Services in Component Middleware for Distributed Real-time and Embedded Systems. In: Proceedings of the 42nd Annual Southeast Conference, Huntsville, AL, ACM (2004)
37. Gamma, E., Helm, R., Johnson, R., Vlissides, J.: Design Patterns: Elements of Reusable Object-Oriented Software. Addison-Wesley, Reading, MA (1995)
38. Office, D.I.E.: Program Composition for Embedded Systems (PCES). www.darpa.mil/ixo/ (2000)
39. Singh, G., Maddula, B., Zeng, Q.: Event Channel Configuration in Cadena. In: Proceedings of the IEEE Real-time/Embedded Technology Application Symposium (RTAS), Toronto, Canada, IEEE (2004)
40. Liu, J., Liu, X., Lee, E.A.: Modeling Distributed Hybrid Systems in Ptolemy II. In: Proceedings of the American Control Conference. (2001)
41. Lee, E.A., Neuendorffer, S., Wirthlin, M.J.: Actor-Oriented Design of Embedded Hardware and Software Systems. Journal of Circuits, Systems, and Computers (2003) 231–260
42. Liu, H., Jacobsen, H.A.: Modeling uncertainties in Publish/Subscribe System. In: Proceedings of The 20th International Conference on Data Engineering (ICDE04), Boston, USA (2004)
43. Petrovic, M., Burcea, I., Jacobsen, H.A.: S-ToPSS: Semantic Toronto Publish/Subscribe System. In: Proceedings of the 29th VLDB Conference, Berlin, Germany (2003)
44. Zanolin, L., Ghezzi, C., Baresi, L.: An Approach to Model and Validate Publish/Subscribe Architectures. In: Proceedings of the SAVCBS'03 Workshop, Helsinki, Finland (2003)

Model-Driven Program Transformation
of a Large Avionics Framework

Jeff Gray[1], Jing Zhang[1], Yuehua Lin[1], Suman Roychoudhury[1], Hui Wu[1],
Rajesh Sudarsan[1], Aniruddha Gokhale[2], Sandeep Neema[2], Feng Shi[2], and Ted Bapty[2]

[1] Dept. of Computer and Information Sciences, University of Alabama at Birmingham
Birmingham, AL 35294-1170
{gray,zhangj,liny,roychous,wuh,sudarsar}@cis.uab.edu
http://www.gray-area.org
[2] Institute for Software Integrated Systems, Vanderbilt University
Nashville, TN 37235
{gokhale,sandeep,fengshi,bapty}@isis.vanderbilt.edu
http://www.isis.vanderbilt.edu

Abstract. Model-driven approaches to software development, when coupled
with a domain-specific visual language, assist in capturing the essence of a
large system in a notation that is familiar to a domain expert. From a high-level
domain-specific model, it is possible to describe concisely the configuration
features that a system must possess, in addition to checking that the model preserves semantic properties of the domain. With respect to large legacy applications written in disparate programming languages, the primary problem of
transformation is the difficulty of adapting the legacy source to match the
evolving features specified in the corresponding model. This paper presents an
approach for uniting model-driven development with a mature program transformation engine. The paper describes a technique for performing widespread
adaptation of source code from transformation rules that are generated from a
domain-specific modeling environment for a large avionics framework.

1 Introduction

A longstanding goal of software engineering is to construct software that is easily
modified and extended. A desired result is to achieve modularization such that a
change in a design decision is isolated to one location [24]. The proliferation of software in everyday life (e.g., embedded systems found in avionics, automobiles, and
even mobile phones) has increased the level of responsibility placed on software applications [9, 29]. As demands for such software increase, future requirements will
necessitate new strategies to support the requisite adaptations across different software artifacts (e.g., models, source code, test cases, documentation) [2].

Research into software restructuring techniques, and the resulting tools supporting
the underlying science, has enhanced the ability to modify the structure and function
of a software representation in order to address changing stakeholder requirements
[16]. As shown in Figure 1, software restructuring techniques can be categorized as
either horizontal or vertical. The research into horizontal transformation concerns
modification of a software artifact at the same abstraction level. This is the typical
connotation when one thinks of the term *transformation* [33], with examples being

G. Karsai and E. Visser (Eds.): GPCE 2004, LNCS 3286, pp. 361–378, 2004.
© Springer-Verlag Berlin Heidelberg 2004

code refactoring [10] at the implementation level, and model transformation [4] and aspect weaving at a higher design level [13]. Horizontal transformation systems often lead to invasive composition of the software artifact [1]. In contrast, vertical transformation is typically more appropriately called *translation* (or synthesis) [33] because a new artifact is being synthesized from a description at a different abstraction level (e.g., model-driven software synthesis [12], [23], and reverse engineering). Vertical translations often are more generative in nature [8].

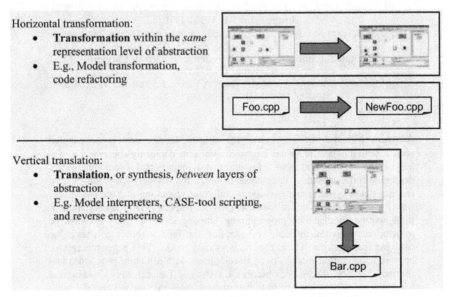

Horizontal transformation:
- **Transformation** within the *same* representation level of abstraction
- E.g., Model transformation, code refactoring

Vertical translation:
- **Translation**, or synthesis, *between* layers of abstraction
- E.g. Model interpreters, CASE-tool scripting, and reverse engineering

Fig. 1. Two directions of software transformation and translation

The most popular model-driven approach is the Object Management Group's (OMGs) Model-Driven Architecture (MDA), which separates application domain logic from the underlying execution platform [5, 11]. The overwhelming majority of early MDA efforts are of the translational, or synthesis style. That is, new software artifacts are generated whole-scale from properties that are refined from platform-independent models, down to platform-specific models, eventually leading to code. The challenge arises when MDA is to be applied to literally several hundred billion lines of legacy code in production use today [30]. To apply model-based techniques to such systems, it is beneficial to have an approach that is also transformational (i.e., one that actually modifies the source code representation) in order to add features to an existing code base. There are two primary factors that make it difficult to achieve true transformation of legacy source code from models:

- If pre-existing code is to be transformed from models, the model interpreters (existing within the modeling environment) must possess the ability to parse the underlying source. Thus, complex parsers must be built into the model interpreter. If a goal of the modeling environment is to achieve language-independence, then a new parser must be integrated into the model interpreter for each programming language that is to be supported. This is very time consuming, if not unfeasible [20].

- Even if a mature parser is constructed for the underlying source, it is then necessary to provide a transformation engine to perform the adaptations to the source that are specified in the model. This is also a laborious task and was not needed by previous translators that only generated *new* artifacts from models. Yet, the need to synchronize model properties with pre-existing code requires the invasive capability for altering the code base.

We observe that the two difficulties enumerated above can be ameliorated by integrating the power of a program transformation system, which provides the required parsers and transformation engine, within a modeling tool chain. This paper describes our investigation into a synergistic technique that unites model-driven development (MDD) with a commercially available program transformation engine. Our approach enables adaptation of a large legacy system from properties described in a high-level model. A model interpreter generates the low-level transformation rules that are needed to provide a causal connection between the model description and the representative legacy source code. A video demonstration of the approach is available (please see Section 4 for details).

The rest of the paper is organized as follows: Section 2 provides an overview of the case study and the two technologies that are integrated to provide the realization of *Model-Driven Program Transformation (MDPT)*. A domain-specific visual modeling environment for embedded systems is introduced in Section 3. The heart of the approach is contained in Section 4. The fourth section also presents two illustrative examples of the approach applied to concurrency control and a black-box flight data recorder. The conclusion offers summary remarks, as well as related and future work.

2   Background: Supporting Technologies and Case Study

This paper unites the descriptive power provided by MDD (Section 2.1) with the invasive modification capabilities of a mature program transformation system (Section 2.2). Specifically, representative approaches from MDD and program transformation are described in this section to provide the necessary background to understand other parts of the paper. The mission computing framework that will be used as a case study is also introduced in Section 2.3.

2.1   Model-Integrated Computing

A specific form of MDD, called Model-Integrated Computing (MIC) [28], has been refined at Vanderbilt University over the past decade to assist the creation and synthesis of computer-based systems. A key application area for MIC is those domains (such as embedded systems areas typified by automotive and avionics systems [29]) that tightly integrate the computational structure of a system and its physical configuration. In such systems, MIC has been shown to be a powerful tool for providing adaptability in frequently changing environments. The Generic Modeling Environment (GME) [21] is a meta-modeling tool based on MIC that can be configured and adapted from meta-level specifications (called the *modeling paradigm*) that describe the domain [18]. When using the GME, a modeling paradigm is loaded into the tool to define an environment containing all the modeling elements and valid relationships that can be constructed in a specific domain. Thus, the approach provides a meta-environment for constructing system and software models using notations that are familiar to the modeler. The mission-computing avionics modeling environment described in Section 3 is implemented within the GME.

2.2 The Design Maintenance System

The Design Maintenance System (DMS) is a program transformation system and re-engineering toolkit developed by Semantic Designs (www.semdesigns.com). The core component of DMS is a term rewriting engine that provides powerful pattern matching and source translation capabilities [3]. In DMS parlance, a language domain represents all of the tools (e.g., lexer, parser, pretty printer) for performing translation within a specific programming language. DMS provides pre-constructed domains for several dozen languages. Moreover, these domains are very mature and have been used to parse several million lines of code, including the millions of lines of the targeted system explored in our research (i.e., Boeing's Bold Stroke [26], which is introduced in Section 2.3). Utilization of mature parsers that have been tested on industrial projects offers a solution to the two difficulties mentioned earlier; i.e., in addition to the available parsers, the underlying rewriting engine of DMS provides the machinery needed to perform invasive software transformations on legacy code [1]. Examples of DMS transformation rules will be given in Section 4.3.

2.3 The Bold Stroke Mission Computing Avionics Framework

Bold Stroke is a product-line architecture written in several million lines of C++ that was developed by Boeing in 1995 to support families of mission computing avionics applications for a variety of military aircraft [26]. As participant researchers in DARPA's Program Composition for Embedded Systems (PCES), we have access to the Bold Stroke source code as an experimental platform on which to conduct our research on MDPT. The following section describes the Bold Stroke concurrency mechanism that will be used later as an example to demonstrate the possibilities of our approach.

Bold Stroke Concurrency Mechanisms. To set the context for Sections 3 and 4, the Bold Stroke concurrency mechanism is presented to provide an example for the type of transformations that can be performed in order to improve better separation of concerns within components that have been specified in a domain-specific modeling language.

There are three kinds of locking strategies available in Bold Stroke: Internal Locking, External Locking and Synchronous Proxy. The Internal Locking strategy requires the component to lock itself when its data are modified. External Locking requires the user to acquire the component's lock prior to any access of the component. The Synchronous Proxy locking strategy involves the use of cached states to maintain state coherency through a chain of processing threads.

Figure 2 shows the code fragment in the "Update" method of the "BM_PushPull-Component" in Bold Stroke. This method participates in the implementation of a real-time event channel [17]. In this component, a macro statement (Line 3) is used to implement the External Locking strategy. When system control enters the Update method, a preprocessed guard class is instantiated and all external components that are trying to access the BM_PushPullComponent will be locked.

```
1  void BM__PushPullComponentImpl::Update (const UUEventSet& events)
2  {
3      UM__GUARD_EXTERNAL_REGION(GetExtPushLock());  // <-Locking Macro
4
5      BM_CompInstrumentation::EventConsumer(GetId(), "Update", events);
6      unsigned int tempData1 = GetId().GetGroupId();
7      unsigned int tempData2 = GetId().GetItemId();
8
9      //* REMOVED: code for implementing Real-time Event Channel
10
11     UM__GUARD_INTERNAL_REGION;  // <-Locking Macro
12     data1_ = tempData1;  //* REMOVED: actual var names (proprietary)
13     data2_ = tempData2;
14 }
```

Fig. 2. Update method in Bold Stroke BM_PushPullComponentImpl.cpp

After performing its internal processing, the component eventually comes to update its own data. At this point, another macro (Line 11) is used to implement the Internal Locking strategy, which forces the component to lock itself. Internal Locking is implemented by the Scoped Locking C++ idiom [25], which ensures that a lock is acquired when control enters a scope and released automatically when control leaves the scope. Specifically, a guard class is defined to acquire and release a particular type of lock in its constructor and destructor. There are three types of locks: Null Lock, Thread Mutex, and Recursive Thread Mutex. The constructor of the guard class stores a reference to the lock and then acquires the lock. The corresponding destructor uses the pointer stored by the constructor to release the lock.

The Problem with Macro-customization. The existence of locking macros, as shown in Figure 2, is representative of the original code base for Bold Stroke. During the development of that implementation, the concurrency control mechanisms implemented as locking macros occur in many different places in a majority of the components comprising Bold Stroke. In numerous configuration scenarios, the locking macros may evaluate to null locks, essentially making their existence in the code of no consequence. The presence of these locks (in lines 3 and 11 of Figure 2), and the initial effort needed to place them in the proper location, represents a point of concern regarding the manual effort needed for their initial insertion, and the future maintenance regarding this concern as new requirements for concurrency are added. The macro mechanism also represents a potential source of error for the implementation of new components – it is an additional design concern that must be remembered and added manually in the proper place for each component requiring concurrency control.

In Section 4, we advocate an approach that permits the removal of the locking macros (as well as other crosscutting properties) and offers automated assistance in adding them back into the code only in those places that are implied by properties described in a model. Before describing that approach, however, it is essential to introduce the modeling language that is used to specify embedded systems like Bold Stroke.

3 Embedded Systems Modeling Language

In this section, the Embedded Systems Modeling Language (ESML) is described as a domain-specific graphical modeling language for modeling real-time mission computing embedded avionics applications. Its goal is to address the issues arising in system integration, validation, verification, and testing of embedded systems. ESML has been defined within the GME and is being used on several US-government funded research projects sponsored from DARPA. The ESML was primarily designed by the Vanderbilt DARPA MoBIES team, and can be downloaded from the project website at http://www.isis.vanderbilt.edu/Projects/mobies/. There are representative ESML models for all of the Bold Stroke usage scenarios that have been defined by Boeing.

3.1 ESML Modeling Capabilities

From the ESML meta-model (please see [21] for details of meta-model creation), the GME provides an instantiation of a new graphical modeling environment supporting the visual specification and editing of ESML models (see Figures 3 and 4). The model of computation used for ESML leverages elements from the CORBA Component Model [12] and the Bold Stroke architecture, which also uses a real-time event channel [17].

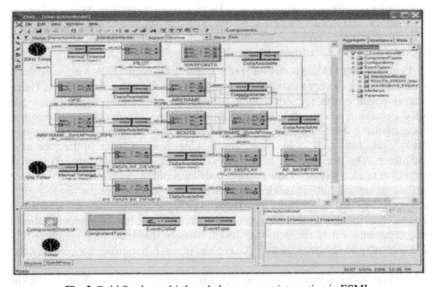

Fig. 3. Bold Stroke multi-threaded component interaction in ESML

The ESML provides the following modeling categories to allow representation of an embedded system: a) Components, b) Component Interactions, and c) Component Configurations. Figure 3 illustrates the components and interactions for a specific scenario within Bold Stroke (i.e., the MC_ConcurrencyMP scenario, which has components operating in a multi-processor avionics backplane). This higher-level diagram captures the interactions among components via an event channel. System timers and their frequencies are also specified in this diagram.

Figure 4 illustrates the ESML modeling capabilities for specifying the internal configuration of a component. The BM_PushPullComponent is shown in this figure. For this component, the concurrency control mechanism is specified, as well as facet descriptors, internal data elements, and a logging policy.

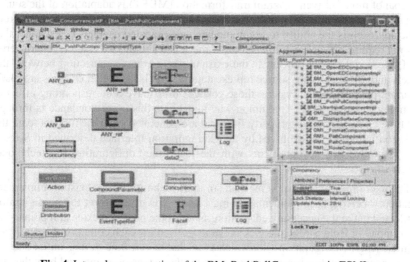

Fig. 4. Internal representation of the BM_PushPullComponent in ESML

3.2 ESML Model Interpreters

The result of modeling in ESML is a set of diagrams that visually depict components, interactions, and configurations, as shown in Figures 3 and 4. The objective of the design is to create, analyze, and integrate real systems; thus, we had to define a number of interfaces to support these activities.

A very important part of domain modeling within the GME is the capability of creating model interpreters. The modeling environment stores the model as objects in a database repository, and it provides an API for model traversal using a standard integration mechanism (i.e., COM) provided by the GME. Using the API, it is possible to create interpreters that traverse the internal representation of the model and generate new artifacts (e.g., XML configuration files, source code, or even hardware logic) based on the model properties. It is possible to associate multiple interpreters to the same domain.

Three model interpreters have been created for the ESML. The Configuration Interface interpreter is responsible for generating an XML file that is used during load-time configuration of Bold Stroke. The locking macros of Figure 2 are configured from this generated file. The Configuration Interface provides an example of vertical translation that is more aligned with the synthesis idea for generating new artifacts, rather than a pure transformation approach that invasively modifies one artifact from descriptions in a model (as in Section 4). A second interpreter for ESML is the Analysis Interface, which assists in integrating third-party analysis tools. A third ESML interpreter has been created to invasively modify a very large code base from properties specified in an ESML model. This third interpreter enables the ideas of model-driven program transformation.

4 Model-Driven Program Transformation

The goal of model-driven program transformation (MDPT) is adaptation of the source code of a legacy system from properties described in high-level models. A key feature of the approach is the ability to accommodate unanticipated changes in a manner that does not require manual instrumentation of the actual source. An essential characteristic of the model-driven process is the existence of a causal connection between the models and the underlying source representation. That is, as model changes are made to certain properties of a system, those changes must have a corresponding effect at the implementation level. A common way to achieve this correspondence is through load time configuration of property files that are generated from the models (e.g., the XML configuration file deployed by the Configuration Interface described in Section 3.2). There are two key problems with the load-time configuration file technique, however:

- The load time configuration mechanism must be built into the existing implementation. The source implementation must know how to interpret the configuration file and make the necessary adaptations at all of the potential extension points. For example, in Bold Stroke the locking strategy used for each component is specified in an XML configuration file, which is loaded at run-time during initial startup. The component developer must know about the extension points and how they interact with the configuration file at load time.
- A typical approach to support this load-time extension is macro tailorability, as seen in Figure 2. At each location in the source where variation may occur, a macro is added that can be configured from the properties specified in the XML configuration file. However, this forces the introduction of macro tags in multiple locations of the source that may not be affected under many configurations. The instrumentation of the source to include such tailoring is often performed by manual adaptation of the source (see lines 3 and 13 of Figure 2). This approach also requires the ability to anticipate future points of extension, which is not always possible for a system with millions of lines of code and changing requirements.

These problems provide a major hurdle to the transfer of model-based and load-time configuration approaches into large legacy systems. As an example, consider the two hundred billion lines of COBOL code that are estimated to exist in production systems [30]. To adopt the load-time configuration file approach to such systems will require large manual modifications to adjust to the new type of configuration. We advocate a different approach, based upon the unification of a program transformation system (DMS) with a modeling tool (GME).

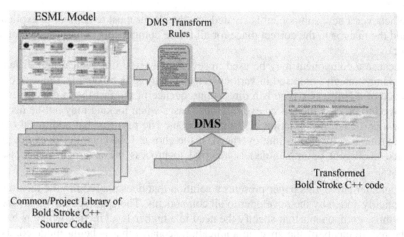

Fig. 5. Overview of Model-Driven Program Transformation

Figure 5 presents an overview of the idea of model-driven program transformation. The key to the approach is the construction of model interpreters that generate transformation rules from the model specifications. The rules are then fed into a program transformation system (represented in the top-left of Figure 5 that shows the path of generation from the models to the DMS transformation rules), along with the base implementation of a large application (e.g., Bold Stroke, as depicted in the bottom-left of the figure). The overall benefit of the approach is large-scale adaptation across multiple source files. The adaptation is accomplished through minimal changes to the models. Such super-linearity is at the heart of the abstraction power provided by model-driven techniques [14], [29].

In summary of Figure 5, the modeler simply makes changes to models using a higher-level modeling language, like the ESML. Those models are then interpreted to generate transformation rules that will invasively modify a large cross-section of an application. It should be noted that the modeler does not need to understand the accidental complexities of the transformation rule language. That process is transparent and is generated by the model interpreter. The following two sub-sections provide a description of crosscutting properties that have been weaved into the Bold Stroke C++ code from the model descriptions. The two examples represent crosscutting concerns related to concurrency control and recording of flight data information. A final sub-section introduces the idea of two-level weaving, which allows aspects at the modeling level to drive widespread adaptations of the representative source code.

4.1 Weaving Concurrency into Bold Stroke

Recall the concurrency mechanism supported within Bold Stroke, as described in Section 2.3. In particular, consider the code fragment in Figure 2. There are a few problems with the macro tailorability approach, as used in this example code fragment:

- Whenever a new component is created, the developer must remember to explicitly add the macros in the correct place for all future components (a large source of error).
- Because a component may be used in several contexts, it is typical that different locking strategies are used in various usage scenarios. For example, the very existence of a Null Lock type is a direct consequence of the fact that a component is forced to process the macro even in those cases when locking may not be needed for a particular instantiation of the component. The result is that additional compile-time (or, even run-time overhead, if the chosen C++ compiler does not provide intelligent optimizations) is incurred to process the macro in unnecessary cases.

As an alternative, this paper presents a solution that does not require the locking to be explicitly added by the developer to all components. The approach only adds locking to those components that specify the need in a higher-level model, which is based on the requirements of the specific application scenario that is being modeled. This can be seen in the bottom-right of Figure 4, where the type of concurrency is specified for the selected "Concurrency" modeling atom (an internal null-lock is specified in this particular case). Suppose that all of the locking strategies did not exist in the component code (i.e., that lines 3 and 13 were removed from Figure 2 in ALL Bold Stroke components), and the component developers want to add the External Locking strategy to all of the hundreds of components that also require concurrency control. Completing such a task by hand is time-consuming and error-prone.

The DMS reengineering toolkit provides a powerful mechanism to transform code written in C++ and many other languages. In our investigation into the model driven program transformation approach, we initially removed the concurrency macros from a large set of components. We were able to insert different kinds of lock statements back into all of the Bold Stroke components that needed concurrency, as specified in the ESML models. This was accomplished by applying DMS transformation rules that were generated by a new ESML interpreter (see Section 4.3 for details).

4.2 Supporting a Black Box Data Recorder

In avionics systems, an essential diagnostic tool for failure analysis is a "black box" that records important flight information. This device can be recovered during a failure, and can reveal valuable information even in the event of a total system loss. There are several factors that make development of such a data recording device difficult:

- During ground testing and simulation of the complete aircraft system, it is often useful to have a liberal strategy for collecting data points. The information that is collected may come from a large group of events and invocations generated during testing of a specific configuration of Bold Stroke.
- However, an actual deployed system has very limited storage space to record data. In a deployed system, data may be collected from a small subset of the points that were logged during simulation. For example, only a few components may be of interest during specific phases of a mission. Also, only a subset of events may be recorded in an operational fighter jet.

It is a desirable feature to support the various types of recording policies that may be observed throughout development, testing, and deployment. Currently, the development tools associated with Bold Stroke do not support a capability to plug recording policies easily into the code base. The manual effort that would be required to plug/unplug different data recording policies throughout all components would be unfeasible in general practice. It is possible to transform existing Bold Stroke code by adding the black box flight recorder concern. The recorder information is specified by a logging policy (as can be seen in the "Log" modeling element of Figure 4). Within the logging policy, a modeler can specify policies such as "Record the values upon <entry/exit> of <a set of named methods>" or "Record the value upon every update to the <data variable>."

4.3 An Example of the Generated Transformation

The DMS Rule Specification Language (RSL) provides basic primitives for describing numerous transformations that are to be performed across the entire code base of an application. The RSL consists of declarations of patterns, rules, conditions, and rule sets using the external form (concrete syntax) defined by a language domain. Typically, a large collection of RSL files, like those represented in Figure 6 and Figure 7, are needed to describe the full set of transformations (we provide these two specifications as an illustration of the style of RSL that is generated from the ESML models). The patterns and rules can have associated conditions that describe restrictions on when a pattern legally matches a syntax tree, or when a rule is applicable on a syntax tree.

Figure 6 shows the RSL specification for performing two kinds of transformations: insertion of an External Locking Statement and an Internal Locking Statement. This RSL file was generated from the MDPT interpreter that we created, which extends the capabilities of ESML. The first line of the figure establishes the default language domain to which the DMS rules are applied (in this case, it is the implementation environment for Bold Stroke – Visual Studio C++ 6.0). Eight patterns are defined from line 3 to line 26, followed by two transformation rules. The patterns on lines 3, 6, 9, 13, 26 – along with the rule on line 28 – define the external locking transformation. Likewise, the patterns on lines 16, 19, 22 – and the rule on line 36 – specify the internal locking transformation.

Patterns describe the form of a syntax tree. They are used for matching purposes to find a syntax tree having a specified structure. Patterns are often used on the right-hand side (target) of a rule to describe the resulting syntax tree after the rule is applied. In the first pattern (line 3, Figure 6), a very simple pattern is described. This pattern matches the inserted macro (named **UM_GUARD_EXTERNAL_RE-GION**) to the syntax tree expression that is defined as **identifier_or_template_id** in the grammar definition of the DMS VC++6.0 domain. The third pattern (line 9) is used to combine the first and second pattern into a larger one, in order to represent the full macro statement along with its parameters. The target rule that describes the form of the resulting syntax tree is specified in the fourth pattern (line 13). This fourth pattern scopes the protected region and places the external locking statement as the first statement within the scope. Similarly, the pattern on line 22 describes the form of the resulting syntax tree after inserting an internal locking statement in front of any

```
1    default base domain Cpp~VisualCpp6.
2
3    pattern UM_GUARD_EXTERNAL_REGION_as_identifier_or_template_id():
4      identifier_or_template_id = "UM__GUARD_EXTERNAL_REGION".
5
6    pattern GetExternPushLock_as_identifier_or_template_id():
7      identifier_or_template_id = "GetExternalPushLock".
8
9    pattern ExternLockStmt(): expression_statement =
10     "\UM_GUARD_EXTERNAL_REGION_as_identifier_or_template_id\(\)
11     (\GetExternPushLock_as_identifier_or_template_id\(\)());".
12
13   pattern ExternLockAspect(s: statement_seq): compound_statement =
14                            "{\ExternLockStmt\(\) {\s}}".
15
16   pattern InternLockStmt(): expression_statement =
17                            "UM__GUARD_INTERNAL_REGION;".
18
19   pattern InternLockJoinPoint(expr:logical_or_expression): statement =
20                            "data1_= \expr;".
21
22   pattern InternLockAspect(expr:logical_or_expression, s:statement_seq):
23     statement_seq = "\s {\InternLockStmt\(\)
24                           \InternLockJoinPoint\(\expr\)}".
25
26   pattern JoinPoint(id:identifier): qualified_id = "\id :: Update".
27
28   rule insert_extern_lock(id:identifier, s: statement_seq,
29                           p:parameter_declaration_clause):
30     function_definition -> function_definition =
31           "void \JoinPoint\(\id\)(\p) {\s} " ->
32           "void \JoinPoint\(\id\)(\p) {\ExternLockAspect\(\s\)}"
33   if ~[modsList:statement_seq. s matches
34           "\:statement_seq \ExternLockAspect\(\modsList\)"].
35
36   rule insert_intern_lock(expr:logical_or_expression, s:statement_seq):
37     statement_seq -> statement_seq =
38           "\s \InternLockJoinPoint\(\expr\)" ->
39           "\InternLockAspect\(\expr\,\s\)"
40   if s ~= "\:statement_seq \InternalLockStmt\(\)".
41
42   public ruleset applyrules={insert_extern_lock, insert_intern_lock}.
```

Fig. 6. A set of generated locking transformation patterns and rules in the DMS Rule Specification Language

update of data1_. The last pattern (line 26) provides the context in which the transformation rules will be applied. Here, the rules will be applied to all of the components containing an Update method. This pattern is similar to a *Join Point* in AspectJ [19]. Although this last pattern is very simple, it quantifies over the entire code base and selects all of those syntax trees matching the pattern.

The RSL rules describe a directed pair of corresponding syntax trees. A rule is typically used as a rewrite specification that maps from a left-hand side (source) syntax tree expression to a right-hand side (target) syntax tree expression. As an example, the rule specified on line 28 of Figure 6 represents a transformation on all Update methods (specified by the JoinPoint pattern). The effect of this rule is to add an external locking statement to all Updates, regardless of the various parameters of each Update method. Notice that there is a condition associated with this rule (line 33). This condition describes a constraint that this rule should be applied only when there already does not exist an external locking statement. That is, the transformation rule will be applied only once. Without this condition, the rules would be applied iteratively and fall into an infinite loop. The rule on line 36 applies the transformations associated with inserting an internal locking statement just before modification of the internal field named data1_. Rules can be combined into *sets* of rules that together form a transformation strategy by defining a collection of transformations that can be applied to a syntax tree. In the ruleset defined on line 42, the two locking rules are aggregated to perform a sequence of transformations (i.e., External/Internal Locking).

The logging transformation is much simpler and can be found in Figure 7. For this example, the "Log on Method Exit" logging policy is illustrated (this is specified as an attribute in the "Log" modeling element of Figure 4). The patterns on lines 3, 5, 8 – with the rule on line 10 – denote the update logging transformation. The pattern on line 5 shows the resulting form after inserting a log statement on all exits of the Update method. The corresponding rule on line 10 inserts the logging statement upon the exit of every Update method of every component.

It is important to reiterate that the modeler/developer does not create (or even see) the transformation rules. These are created by the ESML interpreter and directly applied toward the transformation of Bold Stroke code using DMS, as shown in Figure 5.

```
1   default base domain Cpp~VisualCpp6.
2
3   pattern LogStmt(): statement = "log.add(\"data1_=\" + data1_);".
4
5   pattern LogOnMethodExitAspect(s: statement_seq): statement_seq =
6                               "\s \LogStmt\(\)".
7
8   pattern JoinPoint(id:identifier): qualified_id = "\id :: Update".
9
10  rule insert_log_on_method_exit(id:identifier, s:statement_seq,
11                              p:parameter_declaration_clause):
12      function_definition -> function_definition =
13          "void \JoinPoint\(\id\)(\p) {\s} " ->
14          "void \JoinPoint\(\id\)(\p) {\LogOnMethodExitAspect\(\s\)}"
15  if ~[modsList:statement_seq. s matches
16          "\:statement_seq \LogOnMethodExitAspect\(\modsList\)"].
17
18  public ruleset applyrules={insert_log_on_method_exit}.
```

Fig. 7. A set of generated logging transformation patterns and rules in the DMS Rule Specification Language

With respect to the generalization of the process for supporting new concerns (other than concurrency and logging strategies as indicated above) in the Bold Stroke application through the MDPT technique, the following two steps are involved:

- If the current ESML metamodel does not provide the paradigm to specify the new concern of interest, it has to be extended to include the new model concepts in order to support the new requirements.
- The MDPT interpreter itself also has to be updated to generate the corresponding DMS transformation rules for the new concerns.

4.4   Transformation at the Modeling Level

It is interesting to note that the specification of modeling concerns can also cut across a domain model [13], in the same way that aspects cut across code [19]. That is, the specification of concurrency and logging concerns in a model may require the modeler to visit multiple places in the model. This is undesirable because it forces the modeler to spend much time adapting model properties. We have previously worked on a model transformation engine called the Constraint-Specification Aspect Weaver (C-SAW), which allows high-level requirements to be weaved into the model before the model interpreter is invoked [14].

The C-SAW transformation engine unites the ideas of aspect-oriented software development (AOSD) [19] with MIC to provide better modularization of model properties that are crosscutting throughout multiple layers of a model. Within the C-SAW infrastructure, the language used to specify model transformation rules and strategies is the Embedded Constraint Language (ECL), which is an extension of Object Constraint Language (OCL). ECL provides many common features of the OCL, such as arithmetic operators, logical operators, and numerous operators on collections. It also provides special operators to support model aggregates, connections and transformations that provide access to modeling concepts within the GME. There are two kinds of ECL specifications: an aspect, which is a starting point in a transformation process, describes the binding and parameterization of strategies to specific entities in a model; and a strategy is used to specify elements of computation and the application of specific properties to the model entities.

Utilizing C-SAW, a modeler can specify a property (e.g., "Record All updates to All variables in All components matching condition X") from a single specification and have it weaved into hundreds of locations in a model. This permits plugging/unplugging of specific properties into the model, enabling the generation of DMS rules resulting in code transformations. We call this process *two-level weaving* [14].

As an example, Figure 8 contains the ECL specification to connect "Log" atoms (of type "On Method Exit") to "Data" atoms in ESML models (see Figure 4). The transformation specification finds all of the "Data" atoms (line 3 to line 6) in every component whose name ends with "Impl" (line 21 to line 25). For each "Data" atom, a new "Log" atom is created, which has its "MethodList" attribute as "Update" (line 17). Finally, it connects this new "Log" atom to its corresponding "Data" atom (line 18). As a result, after using C-SAW to apply this ECL specification, "LogOnMethodExit" atoms will be inserted into each component that has a "Data" atom. As a front-end design capability, model weaving drives the automatic generation of the DMS rules in Figure 7 to transform the underlying Bold Stroke C++ source program.

Video Demonstration. The web site for this research project provides the software download for the model transformation engine described in Section 4.4 Additionally, several video demonstrations are available in various formats of the Bold Stroke transformation case study presented in this paper. The software and video demonstrations can be obtained at http://www.gray-area.org/Research/C-SAW.

```
1   defines Start, logDataAtoms, AddLog;
2
3   strategy logDataAtoms()
4   {
5     atoms()->select(a | a.kindOf() == "Data")->AddLog();
6   }
7
8   strategy AddLog()
9   {
10    declare parentModel : model;
11    declare dataAtom, logAtom : atom;
12
13    dataAtom := self;
14    parentModel := parent();
15    logAtom := parentModel.addAtom("Log", "LogOnMethodExit");
16    logAtom.setAttribute("Kind", "On Method Exit");
17    logAtom.setAttribute("MethodList", "Update");
18    parentModel.addConnection("AddLog", logAtom, dataAtom);
19  }
20
21  aspect Start()
22  {
23    rootFolder().findFolder("ComponentTypes").models().
24              select(m|m.name().endWith("Impl"))->logDataAtoms();
25  }
```

Fig. 8. ECL code for adding "LogOnMethodExit" to "Data" in ESML models

5   Conclusion

A distinction is made in this paper between *translational* approaches that generate new software artifacts, and *transformational* techniques that modify existing legacy artifacts. The model-driven program transformation technique introduced in Section 4 offers a capability for performing wide-scale source transformation of large legacy systems from system properties described in high-level models.

The major difficulty encountered in this project centered on the initial learning curve for DMS. Much time was spent in understanding the capabilities that DMS provides. After passing the initial learning curve, we believe that DMS offers a powerful engine for providing the type of language-independent transformation that is required for large-scale adaptation using model-driven techniques.

Related Work – There are related investigations by other researchers that complement the model-driven program transformation (MDPT) approach described in this paper. The general goals of MDA [5, 11], and the specific implementation of MIC with GME [21, 28], are inline with the theme of our paper. The main difference is that most model-driven approaches synthesize new artifacts, but the approach advocated in this paper provides an invasive modification of legacy source code that was designed without anticipation of the new concerns defined in the models.

The properties described in the models are scattered across numerous locations in the underlying source. Hence, there is also a relation to the work on aspect-orientation [19], adaptive programming [22], and compile-time meta-object protocols [6]. The manner in which the MDPT approach transforms the legacy code has the same intent as an aspect weaver. Our early experimentation with OpenC++ [6] and AspectC++

[27], however, suggest that the parsers in these tools are not adequate to handle the complexities that exist in the million lines of C++ code in Bold Stroke. However, DMS was able to parse the Bold Stroke component source without any difficulty. As an aside, we have also used DMS to define an initial approach for constructing aspect weavers for legacy languages [15]. With respect to aspects and distributed computing, the DADO project has similar goals [34], but does not focus on modeling issues.

As an alternative to DMS, there are several other transformation systems that are available, such as ASF+SDF [31], TXL [7], and Stratego [32]. We chose DMS for this project due to our ongoing research collaboration with the vendor of DMS (Semantic Designs). From this collaboration, we were assured that DMS was capable of parsing the millions of lines of Bold Stroke code. We have not verified if this is possible with other transformation systems.

Future Work – With respect to future work, there are several other concerns that have been identified as targets for Bold Stroke transformation (e.g., exception handling, fault tolerance, and security). We will also explore the transformation of Bold Stroke to provide the provisioning to support adaptation based on Quality of Service policies. Our future work will focus on adding support to the ESML and the associated interpreter in order to address such concerns. In addition, the generalization of a process for supporting legacy system evolution through MDPT will be explored.

Acknowledgements

This project is supported by the DARPA Program Composition for Embedded Systems (PCES) program. We thank David Sharp, Wendy Roll, Dennis Noll, and Mark Schulte (all of Boeing) for their assistance in helping us with specific questions regarding Bold Stroke. Our gratitude also is extended to Ira Baxter for his help during our group's initiation to the capabilities of DMS.

References

1. Uwe Aßmann, *Invasive Software Composition*, Springer-Verlag, 2003.
2. Don Batory, Jacob Neal Sarvela, and Axel Rauschmeyer, "Scaling Step-Wise Refinement," *IEEE Transactions on Software Engineering*, June 2004, pp. 355-371.
3. Ira Baxter, Christopher Pidgeon, and Michael Mehlich, "DMS: Program Transformation for Practical Scalable Software Evolution," *International Conference on Software Engineering (ICSE)*, Edinburgh, Scotland, May 2004, pp. 625-634.
4. Jean Bézivin, "From Object Composition to Model Transformation with the MDA," *Technology of Object-Oriented Languages and Systems (TOOLS)*, Santa Barbara, California, August 2001, pp. 350-354.
5. Jean Bézivin, "MDA: From Hype to Hope, and Reality," *The 6th International Conference on the Unified Modeling Language*, San Francisco, California, Keynote talk, October 22, 2003. (http://www.sciences.univ-nantes.fr/info/perso/permanents/bezivin/UML.2003/UML.SF.JB.GT.ppt)
6. Shigeru Chiba, "A Metaobject Protocol for C++," *Object-Oriented Programming, Systems, Languages, and Applications (OOPSLA)*, Austin, Texas, October 1995, pp. 285-299.
7. James Cordy, Thomas Dean, Andrew Malton, and Kevin Schneider, "Source Transformation in Software Engineering using the TXL Transformation System," Special Issue on Source Code Analysis and Manipulation, *Journal of Information and Software Technology* (44, 13) October 2002, pp. 827-837.

8. Krzysztof Czarnecki and Ulrich Eisenecker, *Generative Programming: Methods, Tools, and Applications*, Addison-Wesley, 2000.
9. Eric Evans, *Domain-Driven Design: Tackling Complexity at the Heart of Software*, Addison-Wesley, 2003.
10. Martin Fowler, *Refactoring: Improving the Design of Existing Programs*, Addison-Wesley, 1999.
11. David Frankel, *Model Driven Architecture: Applying MDA to Enterprise Computing*, John Wiley and Sons, 2003.
12. Aniruddha Gokhale, Douglas Schmidt, Balachandran Natarajan, Jeff Gray, and Nanbor Wang, "Model-Driven Middleware," in *Middleware for Communications*, (Qusay Mahmoud, editor), John Wiley and Sons, 2004.
13. Jeff Gray, Ted Bapty, Sandeep Neema, and James Tuck, "Handling Crosscutting Constraints in Domain-Specific Modeling," *Communications of the ACM*, Oct. 2001, pp. 87-93.
14. Jeff Gray, Janos Sztipanovits, Douglas C. Schmidt, Ted Bapty, Sandeep Neema, and Aniruddha Gokhale, "Two-level Aspect Weaving to Support Evolution of Model-Driven Synthesis," in *Aspect-Oriented Software Development*, (Robert Filman, Tzilla Elrad, Mehmet Aksit, and Siobhán Clarke, eds.), Addison-Wesley, 2004.
15. Jeff Gray and Suman Roychoudhury, "A Technique for Constructing Aspect Weavers Using a Program Transformation System," *International Conference on Aspect-Oriented Software Development (AOSD)*, Lancaster, UK, March 22-27, 2004, pp. 36-45.
16. William G. Griswold and David Notkin, "Automated Assistance for Program Restructuring," *Trans. on Software Engineering and Methodology*, July 1993, pp. 228-269.
17. Tim Harrison, David Levine, and Douglas C. Schmidt, "The Design and Performance of a Hard Real-Time Object Event Service," *Conference on Object-Oriented Programming Systems, Languages & Applications (OOPSLA)*, Atlanta, Georgia, October 1997, pp. 184-200.
18. Gábor Karsai, Miklos Maroti, Ákos Lédeczi, Jeff Gray, and Janos Sztipanovits, "Type Hierarchies and Composition in Modeling and Meta-Modeling Languages," *IEEE Trans. on Control System Technology* (special issue on *Computer Automated Multi-Paradigm Modeling*), March 2004, pp. 263-278.
19. Gregor Kiczales, John Lamping, Anurag Mendhekar, Chris Maeda, Cristina Videira Lopes, Jean-Marc Loingtier, and John Irwin, "Aspect-Oriented Programming," *European Conference on Object-Oriented Programming (ECOOP)*, LNCS 1241, Springer-Verlag, Jyväskylä, Finland, June 1997, pp. 220-242.
20. Ralf Lämmel and Chris Verhoef, "Cracking the 500 Language Problem," *IEEE Software*, November/December 2001, pp. 78-88.
21. Ákos Lédeczi, Arpad Bakay, Miklos Maroti, Peter Volgyesi, Greg Nordstrom, Jonathan Sprinkle, and Gábor Karsai, "Composing Domain-Specific Design Environments," *IEEE Computer*, November 2001, pp. 44-51.
22. Karl Lieberherr, Doug Orleans, and Johan Ovlinger, "Aspect-Oriented Programming with Adaptive Methods," *Communications of the ACM*, October 2001, pp. 39-41.
23. Sandeep Neema, Ted Bapty, Jeff Gray, and Aniruddha Gokhale, "Generators for Synthesis of QoS Adaptation in Distributed Real-Time Embedded Systems," *Generative Programming and Component Engineering (GPCE)*, LNCS 2487, Pittsburgh, Pennsylvania, October 2002, pp. 236-251.
24. David Parnas, "On the Criteria To Be Used in Decomposing Systems into Modules," *Communications of the ACM*, December 1972, pp. 1053-1058.
25. Douglas C. Schmidt, Michael Stal, Hans Rohnert, and Frank Buschmann, *Pattern-Oriented Software Architecture: Patterns for Concurrent and Networked Objects*, John Wiley and Sons, 2000.
26. David Sharp, "Component-Based Product Line Development of Avionics Software," *First Software Product Lines Conference (SPLC-1)*, Denver, Colorado, August 2000, pp. 353-369.

27. Olaf Spinczyk, Andreas Gal, Wolfgang Schröder-Preikschat, "AspectC++: An Aspect-Oriented Extension to C++," *International Conference on Technology of Object-Oriented Languages and Systems (TOOLS Pacific 2002)*, Sydney, Australia, February 2002, pp. 53-60.

28. Janos Sztipanovits and Gábor Karsai, "Model-Integrated Computing," *IEEE Computer*, April 1997, pp. 10-12.

29. Janos Sztipanovits, "Generative Programming for Embedded Systems," *Keynote Address: Generative Programming and Component Engineering (GPCE)*, LNCS 2487, Pittsburgh, Pennsylvania, October 2002, pp. 32-49.

30. William Ulrich, *Legacy Systems: Transformation Strategies*, Prentice-Hall, 2002.

31. Mark van den Brand, Jan Heering, Paul Klint, and Pieter Olivier, "Compiling Rewrite Systems: The ASF+SDF Compiler," *ACM Transactions on Programming Languages and Systems*, July 2002, pp. 334-368.

32. Eelco Visser, "Stratego: A Language for Program Transformation Based on Rewriting Strategies. System Description of Stratego 0.5," *12th International Conference on Rewriting Techniques and Applications (RTA)*, Springer-Verlag LNCS 2051, Utrecht, The Netherlands, May 2001, pp. 357-361.

33. Eelco Visser, "A Survey of Rewriting Strategies in Program Transformation Systems," *Workshop on Reduction Strategies in Rewriting and Programming (WRS'01) - Electronic Notes in Theoretical Computer Science*, vol. 57, Utrecht, The Netherlands, May 2001. (http://www1.elsevier.com/gej-ng/31/29/23/93/27/33/57007.pdf)

34. Eric Wohlstadter, Stoney Jackson, and Premkumar T. Devanbu, "DADO: Enhancing Middleware to Support Crosscutting Features in Distributed, Heterogeneous Systems," *International Conference on Software Engineering*, Portland, Oregon, pp. 174-186.

Automatic Remodularization and Optimized Synthesis of Product-Families

Jia Liu and Don Batory

Department of Computer Sciences
University of Texas at Austin
Austin, Texas, 78712 USA
{jliu,batory}@cs.utexas.edu

Abstract. A *product-family* is a suite of integrated tools that share a common infrastructure. Program synthesis of individual tools can replicate common code, leading to unnecessarily large executables and longer build times. In this paper, we present remodularization techniques that optimize the synthesis of product-families. We show how tools can be automatically remodularized so that shared files are identified and extracted into a common package, and how isomorphic class inheritance hierarchies can be merged into a single hierarchy. Doing so substantially reduces the cost of program synthesis, product-family build times, and executable sizes. We present a case study of a product-family with five tools totalling over 170K LOC, where our optimisations reduce archive size and build times by 40%.

1 Introduction

Compositional programming and automated software engineering are essential to the future of software development. Arguably the most successful example of both is *relational query optimization (RQO)*. A query is specified in a declarative domain-specific language (SQL); a parser maps it to an inefficient relational algebra expression; the expression is optimized; and an efficient query evaluation program is generated from the optimized expression. RQO is a great example of *automatic programming* – transforming a declarative specification into an efficient program, and *compositional programming* – a program is synthesized from a composition of algebraic operators.

Our research is *Feature Oriented Programming (FOP)* which explores feature modularity and program synthesis [3]. We believe that FOP generalizes the paradigm exemplified by RQO so that compositional programming and automated software development can be realized in any domain. FOP supports the paradigm of mapping declarative specifications (where users specify the features they want in their program) to an actual implementation. This is possible because programs are synthesized by composing implementations of the required features. The novelty of FOP is that it models software domains as algebras, where each feature is an operation. Particular programs that can be synthesized are compositions of operations.

The hallmark of the RQO paradigm is the ability to optimize algebraic representations of programs using identities that relate domain operators. The commutability of joins and the distributivity of project over joins are examples in relational algebra. In this paper, we demonstrate an interesting example of automatic algebraic optimization

G. Karsai and E. Visser (Eds.): GPCE 2004, LNCS 3286, pp. 379–395, 2004.

and reasoning to accomplish the remodularization and optimized synthesis of product-families.

A *product-family* is a suite of integrated tools that share a common code base. A Java *Integrated Development Environment (IDE)* is an example: there are tools for compiling, documenting, debugging, and visualizing Java programs. Engineers perform two tasks when these tools are designed and coded *manually*: (1) they create and implement a design for each tool and (2) integrate each design with the design of other tools to minimize code replication. A paradigm for automated software development achieves the same result in a similar way. Individual tools are synthesized from declarative specifications. This allows, for example, multiple tools to be developed simultaneously because their implementations are completely separate. This is possible because the common code base for these tools is replicated. However, to achieve the "optimized" manual design where common code is not replicated requires an *optimization* that (1) breaks the modular encapsulations of each synthesized tool and (2) identifies the infrastructure shared by all tools and factors it out into common modules. So not only must tools be synthesized automatically, so too must the post-synthesis remodularization optimisation be done *automatically*.

In this paper, we present two optimizations that remodularize tool applications automatically. The first resembles the common practice of extracting shared classes into a common library, but is more efficient with algebraic analysis than brute-force file comparisons. The second merges isomorphic class inheritance hierarchies into a single hierarchy, which delivers better results than extracting shared classes. Both optimisations substantially reduce the size of executables, the cost of tool synthesis, and product-family build times.

We present a case study of a product-family with five tools totalling over 170K LOC. Our optimizations reduce its generation and build times by 40%. Although the percentage reductions are specific to the case study, the techniques we present are general and are applicable to product-families in arbitrary domains.

2   FOP and AHEAD

AHEAD (Algebraic Hierarchical Equations for Application Design) is a realization of FOP based on step-wise refinement, domain algebras, and encapsulation [1].

2.1   Refinements and Algebras

A fundamental premise of AHEAD is that programs are constants and refinements are functions that add features to programs. Consider the following constants that represent base programs with different features:

```
f // program with feature f
g // program with feature g
```

A *refinement* is a function that takes a program as input and produces a refined or feature-augmented program as output:

```
i(x) // adds feature i to program x
j(x) // adds feature j to program x
```

A multi-featured application is an *equation* that corresponds to a refined base program. Different equations define a family of applications, such as:

```
app1 = i(f) // app1 has features i and f
app2 = j(g) // app2 has features j and g
app3 = i(j(f)) // app3 has features i, j, f
```

Thus, the features of an application can be determined by inspecting its equation.

An *AHEAD model* or *domain model* is an algebra whose operators are these constants and functions. The set of programs that can be synthesized by composing these operators is the model's *product-line* [2].

2.2 Encapsulation

A base program typically encapsulates multiple classes. The notation:

```
P = { A, B, C }
```

means that program **P** *encapsulates* classes **A**, **B**, and **C**.

When a new feature **R** is added to a program **P**, any or all of the classes of **P** may change. Suppose refinement **R** modifies classes **A** and **B** and adds class **D**. We write that **R** encapsulates these changes:

```
R = {ΔA, ΔB, ΔD }
```

The refinement of **P** by **R**, denoted **R(P)** or **R•P**, composes the corresponding classes of **R** and **P**. Classes that are not refined (**C**, **D**) are copied:

$$R•P = \{ΔA, ΔB, D \} • \{ A, B, C \}$$
$$= \{ΔA•A, ΔB•B, C, D \} \tag{1}$$

That is, class **A** of program **R•P** is generated by composing **A** with **A**, class **B** of **R•P** is ΔB•B, etc. **(1)** illustrates the *Law of Composition*, which defines how the composition operator • distributes over encapsulation [1]. It tells us how to synthesize classes of a program from the classes that are encapsulated by its features (e.g., base programs and refinements).

2.3 AHEAD Tool Suite (ATS)

ATS is a product-family that implements the AHEAD model. All ATS source files are written in the Jak (short for Jakarta) language; Jak is Java extended with refinement declarations, metaprogramming, and state machines. Jak programs are indistinguishable from Java programs, except those that express refinements and state machines.

As examples of Jak source, Figure 1a shows class **c** (which is identical to its Java representation). Figure 1b shows a refinement Δ**c** which adds variable **y** and method **h** to **c**. In general, a class refinement can add new data members, methods or constructors to a class, as well as extend existing methods and constructors. The composition of Δ**c** and **c**, denoted Δ**c(c)** or Δ**c•c**, is shown in Figure 1c; composi-

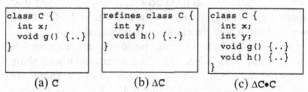

```
class C {            refines class C {      class C {
    int x;               int y;                 int x;
    void g() {..}        void h() {..}          int y;
}                    }                          void g() {..}
                                                void h() {..}
                                            }
        (a) c               (b) Δc                (c) Δc•c
```

Fig. 1. Class Definition, Refinement, and Composition

tion merges the changes of Δc into c yielding an updated class. See [1] for more details about Jak specifications.

In general, an AHEAD constant encapsulates a set of classes (as in Figure 1a). An AHEAD function encapsulates a set of classes and class refinements (as in Figure 1ab). That is, an AHEAD function refines existing classes and can add new classes that can be subsequently refined. Thus, an AHEAD function typically encapsulates a *crosscut*, meaning that it encapsulates fragments (refinements) of multiple classes. Composing AHEAD constants and functions yields packages of fully formed classes [2]. As AHEAD deals with cross-cuts, it is related to Aspect-Oriented Programming. We explore this relationship in Section 4.

ATS has five core tools that transform, compose, or introspect Jak files:

- **jak2java** translates a Jak file to its corresponding Java file,
- **jampack** and **mixin** are different implementations of the composition operator for Jak files,
- **unmixin** uncomposes a composed Jak file, and
- **mmatrix** provides code browsing capabilities.

These tools are fairly large, the sum of their individual sizes exceeds 170K LOC in Java.

ATS has been bootstrapped, so that each ATS tool has its own AHEAD equation and the tool itself is synthesized from this equation. The AHEAD synthesis process expands a tool's equation $T = j \bullet i \bullet \ldots \bullet k$ using (1) so that each tool is equated with a set of expressions $\{e_1, \ e_2, \ e_3, \ \ldots\}$, one expression e_i for each class that the tool encapsulates:

$$T = j \bullet i \bullet \ldots \bullet k$$
$$= \{e_1, \ e_2, \ e_3, \ \ldots\}$$

Evaluating each of the e_i generates a particular file of the target tool.

2.4 Optimizing Product-Families

Although different tools or members of a product-family are specified by different feature sets, tools can share features, and thus share a significant code base. In object-oriented systems this corresponds to shared classes or shared methods. For example, when a tool is synthesized from an AHEAD equation, all the classes that comprise that tool – both common and tool-specific – are generated. Thus, if there are n tools, each common class will be generated n times. Not only does this result in longer build times, it also leads to code duplication in tool executables, since every tool has its own package where the classes are replicated.

For example, each ATS tool performs an operation – composition, translation, or introspection – on a Jak file. This means each tool shares the same parser (which comprises 4 classes). ATS tools also share the same parse tree classes, which are represented by an inheritance hierarchy of *abstract syntax tree (AST)* nodes.

Both the parser and the inheritance hierarchy are generated from the grammar of the Jak language. Parser generation from a grammar is well-known; less well-known is our algorithm for synthesizing the AST inheritance hierarchy. Consider Figure 2a which shows grammar productions **Rule1** and **Rule2**, where **C1**, **C2** and **C3** are terminals. From this, the inheritance hierarchy of Figure 2b is inferred. Each production and pattern is mapped to a distinct AST class. Production-pattern relations are captured by inheritance.

The generated AST hierarchy corresponds to a single AHEAD feature that is shared by all tools. Its classes have bare-bones methods and data members that allow ASTs to be printed and edited. These classes are subsequently refined with new data members and methods that implement tool-specific actions.

The Jak grammar has 490 rules, so the inheritance hierarchy that is generated has 490 classes. After refinement, over 300 of these classes are identical across Jak tools; those that are different result in the different actions per tool. Clearly, such redundancies increase the generation time and build time for ATS, and lead to larger executables. In the following sections, we present two ways to automatically eliminate such redundancies.

2.5 Shared Class Extraction (SCE)

A common practice to eliminate redundancies is to factor files into tool-specific and tool-shared (or common) packages. For example, in ATS tools domain-knowledge tells us that the common parser files can be manually extracted into a common package, but these are just 4 files. The vast majority of the common classes reside at various locations in the AST hierarchy, and which files are common depends on the tools being considered. A brute-force way to identify common classes is by "diffing" source files. This way one can only recognize identical files *after* all files have been composed and generated. To make the problem worse, the corresponding composed Java files have different **package** declarations, so the **diff** utility that is used in file comparison would have to ignore differences in package names. This involves a lot of unnecessary work.

Ideally, we want a procedure that automatically identifies all common files *before* they are generated, and extracts them into a common library. *No* knowledge about productfamily design (e.g., common parser) should be needed for this optimization. This ideal can be achieved using algebraic reasoning.

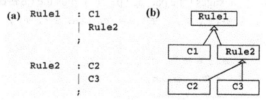

Fig. 2. Grammars and Inheritance Hierarchies

Solution. We introduce an operator to compute the common classes from multiple tools:

$$\text{Common} = \mathbf{T}_1 \oplus \mathbf{T}_2 \oplus \ldots \oplus \mathbf{T}_n \tag{2}$$

The operator is both associative and commutative, meaning that the order in which tools are applied does not matter:

$$(\text{T1} \oplus \text{T2}) \ \oplus \ \text{T3} = \text{T1} \oplus (\text{T2} \oplus \text{T3}) \tag{3}$$

$$\text{T1} \oplus \text{T2} = \text{T2} \oplus \text{T1} \tag{4}$$

Each tool of ATS is defined by a set of equations, one equation for each artifact (Jak file, grammar file) that the tool encapsulates. Suppose tools **T1** and **T2** both encapsulate files **x**, **y**, **z**, and **w**. Further suppose the equations for these files for **T1** are:

```
x = x3•x2•x1
y = y2•y1
z = z1
w = w2•w1
```

and the equations for these files for **T2** are:

```
x = x3•x2•x1
y = y3•y1•
z = z1
w = w3•w1
```

Without generating the files, we conclude from these definitions that files **y** and **w** are different across the two tools, because their equations differ. On the other hand, file **x** in **T1** is the same as in **T2**, because both equations are identical[1]. By the same reasoning, file **z** is also identical in **T1** and **T2**. Thus, files **x** and **z** are shared by **T1** and **T2** and can be placed in a shared package. Hence:

```
Common= T1 ⊕ T2
```
$$= \{ \text{ x3•x2•x1, y2•y1, z1, w2•w1 } \} \oplus \{ \text{ x3•x2•x1, y3•y1, z1, w3•w1 } \}$$
$$= \{ \text{ x3•x2•x1, z1 } \}$$

In effect, we are comparing the *specifications* of files to test for file equality, rather than the files themselves. The efficiency of doing so is significant: equational specifications are short (10s of bytes), and simple string matching is sufficient to test for equality. In contrast, the files that they represent are more expensive to generate and are long (1000s of bytes) where simple string matching is inefficient.

The algorithm, called *shared class extraction (SCE)*, finds the common equations in an arbitrary set of tools. It maps a set of n packages (one package per tool) to a set of $n+1$ packages (one package per tool, plus the **Common** package):

$$\text{SCE}(\{\text{T}_1, \ \text{T}_2, \ \dots \ \text{T}_n\}) \ \rightarrow \{\text{Common, } \ \text{T}_1', \ \text{T}_2', \ \dots \ \text{T}_n'\}$$

where:

$$\text{Common} = \text{T}_1 \oplus \text{T}_2 \oplus \dots \oplus \text{T}_n$$
$$\text{T}_1' = \text{T}_1 - \text{Common}$$
$$\text{T}_2' = \text{T}_2 - \text{Common}$$
$$\dots$$
$$\text{T}_n' = \text{T}_n - \text{Common}$$

and – is the set difference operator. Of course, there are variations of this algorithm. A file, for example, can be shared by some but not all of the input packages. For our study, we found the additional savings of these variants not worth the complexity.

The SCE optimization produces the same results as file diffing in terms of code archives. But SCE is more efficient because instead of diffing generated files, it identi-

---

[1] Package names are implicit in AHEAD specifications.

fies all common files by comparing file equations. In Section 3, we present our experimental results and a comparison between file diffing and our SCE optimization. It is worth noting that the SCE optimization does *not* rely on the fact that AHEAD tools are being built. The SCE algorithm imposes *no* interpretation on equations, which means it should be able to optimize the synthesis of *arbitrary* product-families in *arbitrary* domains. The same holds for our next optimization.

2.6 Merging Class Hierarchies (MCH)

A more sophisticated optimization relies on the knowledge that ATS tools are variants of a common design. Namely, all tools could be built using a common parser and a single AST class hierarchy. Each class of the hierarchy would have the form:

```
class typical extends ... {
    common methods and variables;
    jampack-specific methods and variables;
    mixin-specific methods and variables;
    ...
}
```

That is, each class would have a set of common methods and variables for traversing and editing ASTs, plus methods and variables that are specific to each tool. This might be the design of choice if ATS tools were developed manually. However, in typical FOP designs we generate a distinct class hierarchies for each tool by composing corresponding features. As a result common methods and variables are replicated in each class hierarchy, and consequently common code are shared by the generated tools. In this section, we show how the former design can be realized – and therefore the tool suite optimised – automatically using algebraic reasoning.

Consider the following general problem. Given tools T_1, T_2, ..., T_n, we want an operator $\otimes$ that *merges* their designs so that a single tool T_{n+1} has the union of the capabilities of each individual tool:

$$T_{n+1} = T_1 \otimes T_2 \otimes ... \otimes T_n \tag{5}$$

T_{n+1} has, in essence, all the features of all the tools that are merged. Like the common class extraction operator , the merge operator $\otimes$ is also associative and commutative:

$$(T1 \otimes T2) \otimes T3 = T1 \otimes (T2 \otimes T3) \tag{6}$$

$$T1 \otimes T2 \qquad = T2 \otimes T1 \tag{7}$$

Further, $\otimes$ distributes over encapsulation. That is, the merge of two tools is the same as the merge of its corresponding artifacts; tool-specific artifacts are just copied:

$$T3 \otimes T4 = \{ a3, b3, c3 \} \otimes \{ b4, c4, d4 \}$$
$$= \{ a3, b3 \otimes b4, c3 \otimes c4, d4 \} \tag{8}$$

That is, **(8)** is a special case of **(1)**.

Example. Consider the merge of the `jak2java` and `mixin` tools. The class hierarchies that are synthesized for `jak2java` and `mixin` are depicted in Figure 3a-b. A typical class from **jak2java** has a set of common methods plus the **re-duce2java()** method among others that translate or "reduce" an AST in Jak to an AST in Java. A typical class from the **mixin** tool has the same common methods. However, it has a **compose()** method among others that compose ASTs of different Jak files. The result of **jak2java mixin** is a class hierarchy where each class has the union of the methods in the corresponding classes in each tool (Figure 3c). Merging is not limited to classes in the AST hierarchy; all classes in these tools participate. The parser classes, for example, do not belong to the AST hierarchy but are merged also. Since the parser classes in both tools are identical, they are simply copied to the merged tool.

In the following, we explain how class inheritance hierarchies are merged. We consider the same issues and make similar assumptions as Ernst [4] and Snelting and Tip [10], who studied the semantic issues of merging class inheritance hierarchies prior to our work.

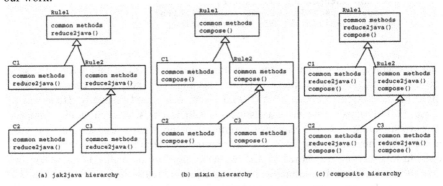

Fig. 3. Tool-Specific and Merged Class Inheritance Hierarchies

2.6.1 Conflict-Freedom

Two classes can be merged into a single class if they agree on the contents (variables, methods, and constructors) that they share. Equivalently, *classes cannot be merged if they have different definitions for a shared variable, method, or constructor*. The property that two classes can be merged is called *conflict-freedom* or *static non-interference* [10].

In general, two AHEAD sets are *conflict free* if they agree on the specifications of the artifacts that they share. Consider sets A_1, A_2, and A_3:

$$A_1 = \{\ r_1,\ s_1\ \}$$
$$A_2 = \{\ r_1,\ t_1\ \}$$
$$A_3 = \{\ r_2,\ t_1\ \}$$

Sets A_1 and A_2 are conflict free because they share artifact r and the definitions for r are the same (both are r_1). However, sets A_1 and A_3 conflict because they share artifact r and have different definitions for r (r_1 is different than r_2). Similarly, sets A_2 and A_3 conflict. They have r and t in common; the t's are the same but their r's differ.

We can automatically deduce if two classes are conflict free in the following way. Each tool to be merged is defined by a set of equations, one equation for each Jak class to synthesize. From a previous page, we defined an equation for class **w** for tool **T1** as:

```
w = w2 • w1
```
(9)

And the corresponding equation for **w** in tool **T2** was:

```
w = w3 • w1
```
(10)

Each w_i is a class or a class refinement that encapsulates a set of members. Suppose **w1**, **w2**, and **w3** are:

```
w1 = { a1, b1 }
w2 = { c2, b2 }
w3 = { d3, b3 }
```
(11)

That is, **w1** encapsulates members **a1** and **b1**; **w2** encapsulates **c2** and **b2**, etc[2]. We use (11) and the law of composition (1) to expand equations (9) and (10) to synthesize class specifications:

```
w = { a1, b2•b1, c2 } // tool T1
w = { a1, b3•b1, d3 } // tool T2
```

That is, class **w** for tool **T1** has data members or methods **a**, **b**, and **c**; class **w** for tool **T2** has data members or methods **a**, **b**, and **d**. Given these specifications, we see that they conflict – the two tools differ on their definitions for member **b**. This means the specifications of the **w** classes cannot be merged, and thus the **w** classes are placed in their tool-specific packages. If specifications can be merged, we merge them and place the merged class into a shared package.

Reflection. Java's reflection mechanism allows programs to do various kinds of self-inspection, e.g. to retrieve the name of an object's class and to determine the number of methods in a given class. Although reflection was not used in ATS tools, merged classes that use reflection may execute differently before and after a merge. There is no easy solution other than "rewriting existing code on a case by case basis as is deemed necessary" [14]. In our approach, a user can specify the classes that use reflection by listing them in a configuration file; these classes are not merged and are placed into tool-specific packages [12]. We discuss how to merge specifications in the next section.

2.6.2 The Merge Operator ⊗

Suppose the equations for class **y** in tools **T1** and **T2**, shown below, are expanded and are found not to conflict:

```
y = y2 • y1 // tool T1
y = y3 • y1 // tool T2
```

What is the merge (**y3•y1**) ⊗ (**y2•y1**) of these equations?

The merge operator exploits the fact that its equations do not conflict and that it integrates equations by preserving the partial order relationships of individual equations. For example, the equations of **y** show that **y2** and **y3** are refinements of **y1**. Hence we have:

---

[2] We do *not* compare the source code of method and data member definitions. b_i means the definition of member b in file i. We assume $b_i \neq b_j$ for all $i \neq j$.

```
y2 > y1,
y3 > y1
```

where $>$ indicates a partial order relationship between the class refinements. A merge of these partial orders yields another partial order[3]. The merge operator generates an equation that contains every term in its input and preserves the order imposed by each equation. If no order is specified for a particular pair of elements, then both permutations are legal. Thus, either of the following equations produce equivalent output:

```
(y2•y1)  ⊗ (y3•y1)= y3•y2•y1
               = y2•y3•y1
```

The correctness of a merge comes directly from its specification. Since there is no conflict, different refinements for a class in different tools are orthogonal – they do not affect each other and the order of their composition does not matter. So the merging of class specifications is correct as long as the compositional ordering in each equation is preserved. Thus, the result of $T1 \otimes T2$ is:

```
Common = T1  ⊗ T2
       = {x3•x2•x1, y2•y1, z1, w2•w1}  ⊗ {x3•x2•x1, y3•y1, z1, w3•w1}
       = { (x3•x2•x1)  ⊗ (x3•x2•x1), (y2•y1)  ⊗ (y3•y1), z1  ⊗ z1,
           (w2•w1)  ⊗ (w3•w1) }
       = { x3•x2•x1, y3•y2•y1, z1 }
```

For files that are not merged (like w above) because of conflicts, they do not appear in the merged result but do appear in the tool-specific packages $T1'$ and $T2'$:

```
T1' = { w2•w1 }
T2' = { w3•w1 }
```

Thus, three packages $Common$, $T1'$ and $T2'$ are synthesized.

Once tools are merged, it remains to be shown that the merged code is type correct and that each merged tool has the same behavior as its unmerged counterpart [10]. We demonstrate type correctness and semantic equality of the merged tools in the appendix.

3 Experiments

We applied the two optimizations on the synthesis on the five ATS tools described earlier. Currently the size of these tools is 170K LOC. In our experiments, we used a desktop com-

Table 1. Product-Family Statistics w/o Optimization

Package	Classes	LOC(K)	Archive(KB)
jak2java	511	38	546
jampack	496	38	556
mixin	495	35	483
mmatrix	499	34	467
unmixin	496	34	457
total	2497	178	2,509

---

[3] This is true for all ATS tools and for all tools that we can imagine. If a cycle were created by a merge, it would indicate either that the cycle could be eliminated by permuting features without changing tool semantics, or that there is a fundamental error in the design of the domain model. We have encountered the former which is easy to fix [2], but never the latter. In either case, the merge of the equations would fail, just as if the equations were recognized to be in conflict.

puter with an Intel Pentium III 733 Mhz microprocessor, 128 MB main memory running Microsoft Windows 2000 and Java SDK 1.4.1. Table 1 shows the number of classes, *lines of code (LOC)* and archive size of each ATS tool. The LOC measurement is calculated from the Java source code of each tool, and the archive size is obtained from the generated Java JAR files. In the original build without optimizations, a package is compiled for each tool.

Table 2 demonstrates the results of shared class extraction optimization. The first five rows summarize each tool-specific package while the last row is the shared package. Nearly 70% of the classes in each tool are shared. Factoring these classes into a common package reduces the volume of code and executables by over 45%.

Table 3 lists the corresponding results for the merging class hierarchy optimization. All conflict-free classes are merged into the shared package, which leaves only conflicting classes in each tool-specific package. Conflicts in ATS tools are rare – of 500 classes in each tool, only 10 or 11 (including 5 dynamic interferences discussed in the appendix) conflict. This yields

Table 2. Product-Family Statistics of SCE Optimization

Package	Classes	LOC(K)	Archive(KB)
jak2java	165	13	246
jampack	150	13	257
mixin	149	10	189
mmatrix	153	9	170
unmixin	150	9	160
shared	347	25	294
total	1,114	80	1,316

Table 3. Product-Family Statistics of MCH Optimization

Package	Classes	LOC(K)	Archive(KB)
jak2java	10	2	32
jampack	11	3	46
mixin	11	3	35
mmatrix	10	2	25
unmixin	10	2	24
shared	510	43	689
total	562	55	851

Table 4. Build Time Comparisons

Build Time	Original	Diff	SCE	MCH
optimize	0	24	3	15
compose	170	170	134	110
compile	300	150	150	129
jar	26	14	14	7
total	496	358	301	261

even greater reductions – more than 65% – in code and archive volume. Note that in Table 2 and Table 3, the number of classes in a tool-specific package plus the shared package is slightly larger than that of the original tool package shown in Table 1. For example, in Table 2 the total number of **jak2java** classes (165) and **shared** classes (347) is 512, whereas the original **jak2java** package has 511 classes as Table 1 shows. This is because some classes are not needed by all the tools, but they still can be factored out by SCE or merged by MCH optimization processes.

Table 4 illustrates the times of the unoptimized and optimized builds *that include overhead for optimizations*. It also shows the brute-force method to find common files by diffing generated files (**Diff**). In an unoptimized build, each class has to be composed from its featured source, compiled and finally packaged into jar files. Brute-force diffing reduces build times by 28%. SCE eliminates the need for unnecessary file generation and reduces build times by 39%. Comparing file specifications takes only three seconds since there is no file I/ O. MCH has better performance as it reduces build times by 47%.

4 Related Work

Three topics are relevant to our work: composing class hierarchies, on-demand modularization, and AOP.

4.1 Composing Class Hierarchies

Refining a class hierarchy is equivalent to hierarchy composition. AHEAD, Hyper/J[7], and AspectJ[6] are among the few tools that can compose class hierarchies. Few papers address the semantic issues of hierarchy composition.

Snelting and Tip present algorithms for merging arbitrary class hierarchies [10]. Our work is a subproblem of what they addressed, and there are four basic differences. First, there is no known implementation of their algorithms [11]. Second, inheritance hierarchies that we merge are isomorphic by design. As mentioned earlier, the features that are composed in AHEAD have an implementation that conforms to a master design; this is how we achieve a practical form of interoperability and composability. Without pragmatic design constraints, features that are not designed to be composable won't be (or arbitrarily difficult problems may ensue). This is a variation of the architectural mismatch problem [5]. Third, the algorithm in [10] requires assumptions about the equivalence of methods in different hierarchies; we can deduce this information automatically from equational specifications. Thus our representations lead to more practical specifications of program relationships. Fourth, the means by which semantic equivalence is achieved in [10] requires verifying that each method call in the original and merged tools invoke the same method. Thus, if there are n tools, c is the number of classes per tool, m the number of methods per class, and k the number of calls per method, the cost of their algorithm to verify behavioral equivalence is $O(n*c*m*k)$. We achieve the same effect by comparing method signatures of each class to test for dynamic interference; our algorithm is faster $O(n*c*m)$ because it is more conservative.

Ernst considered a related problem of merging and reordering mixins [4]. Mixins approximate class refinements; the primary difference is that refinements can add and refine existing constructors, whereas mixins cannot. Ernst defines how mixins can be composed and how compositions of mixins can be merged. The technique of merging compositions is based on preserving partial orderings of compositions, just like our work. However, the concept of composition is implicit in [4], and merging is the only explicit operator to "glue" mixins together. To us, composition and merge are very different operators that are *not* interchangeable – $(A \bullet B)(B \bullet C) \neq (A \bullet B) \bullet (B \bullet C)$. Thus, our model is more general.

4.2 On-Demand Remodularization

Ossher and Tarr were the first to recognize and motivate the need for *on-demand remodularization (ODM)*, which advocates the ability to translate between different modularisations [7]. While Hyper/J and AHEAD are tools that can be used for ODM, there are few published results or case studies on the topic.

Mezini and Ostermann proposed language constructs called *collaboration interfaces* to mix-and-match components dynamically [8]. The approach is object-based, where objects that fulfill contracts specified in collaboration interfaces are bound. The loose couplings of the implementations and interfaces allow collaborations to be reused independently. Here the purpose of remodularization is to meet the needs of different client programs, where in contrast we remodularize to optimize the program synthesis.

Lasagne [13] defines an architecture that starts with a minimal functional core, and selectively integrates extensions, which add new features to the system. A feature is implemented as a wrapper and can be composed incrementally at run-time. Dynamic remodularization is supported by the context sensitive selection on a per collaboration basis, enabling client specific customizations of systems. Our work also composes features, but it is done statically and AHEAD equations are algebraically optimized.

Our work remodularizes packages automatically by extracting common files into a shared package, thus eliminating redundancy and improving system build times. A similar result is described by Tip et al. [12], where Java packages are automatically optimised and compressed through the compaction of class inheritance hierarchies and the elimination of dead-code. Our work and [12] allows the user to specify where reflection occurs so that the corresponding classes may be properly handled to avoid errors. Our work is different because we split class inheritance hierarchies into multiple packages in order to optimize program achieve size and build time.

4.3 Aspect-Oriented Programming

AHEAD refinements have a long history, originating in collaboration-based designs and their implementations as mixins and mixin-layers (see [9] for relevant references). They also encapsulate *cross-cuts*, a concept that was popularized by *Aspect-Oriented Programming (AOP)* [6]. There are three differences between AOP and AHEAD. First, the concept of refinement in AHEAD (and its predecessor GenVoca) is virtually identical to that of extending object-oriented frameworks. Adding a feature to an OO framework requires certain methods and classes to be extended. AHEAD takes this idea to its logical conclusion: instead of having two different levels of abstraction (e.g., the abstract classes and their concrete class extensions), AHEAD allows arbitrary numbers of levels, where each level implements a particular feature or refinement [1].

Second, the starting points for AHEAD and AOP differ: product-lines are the consequence of pre-planned designs (so refinements are designed to be composable); this is not a part of the standard AOP paradigm. Third, the novelty and power of AOP is in quantification. Quantification is the specification of where advice is to be inserted (or the locations at which refinements are applied). The use of quantification in AHEAD is no different than that used in traditional OO frameworks.

5 Conclusions

The synthesis of efficient software from declarative specifications is becoming increasingly important. The most successful example of this paradigm is relational query optimisation (RQO). Replicating this paradigm in other domains and exploring its capabilities is the essence of our research.

In this paper, we focused on a key aspect of the RQO paradigm, namely the optimization of algebraic representations of programs. We showed how algebraic representations of the tools of a product-family could be automatically remodularized (refactored) so their shared infrastructure need not be replicated. We presented two optimisations that remodularized synthesized tool packages: extracting shared files and merging class hierarchies. Our optimizations are examples of equational reasoning; they were defined algebraically, were automatic, and required minimal domain knowledge. Further, our optimizations were efficient and practical: in both cases, we improved upon algorithms that previously existed. We presented a case study of a product-family of five tools and achieved a reduction of 40% in build times and archive size.

We believe our results contribute further evidence that algebraic representations of programs coupled with algebraic reasoning is a powerful way to express software designs and manipulate them automatically.

Acknowledgements

We thank Jacob Sarvela, Kurt Stirewalt, William Cook, and Mark Grechanik for their helpful comments on earlier drafts of this paper.

References

1. D. Batory, J.N. Sarvela, and A. Rauschmayer, "Scaling Step-Wise Refinement", *IEEE Transactions on Software Engineering*, June 2004.
2. D. Batory, J. Liu, J.N. Sarvela, "Refinements and Multi-Dimensional Separation of Concerns", *ACM SIGSOFT 2003 (ESEC/FSE2003)*.
3. D. Batory, "The Road to Utopia: A Future for Generative Programming". Keynote presentation at *Dagstuhl for Domain-Specific Program Generation*, March 23-28, 2003.
4. E. Ernst, "Propagating Class and Method Combination", *ECOOP 1999*.
5. D. Garlan, R. Allen, and J. Ockerbloom, "Architectural Mismatch: Why it is hard to Build Systems from Existing Parts", *ICSE 1995*.
6. G. Kiczales, E. Hilsdale, J. Hugunin, M. Kirsten, J. Palm, W.G. Griswold. "An overview of AspectJ", *ECOOP 2001*.
7. H. Ossher and P. Tarr, "On the Need for On-Demand Remodularization", Position Paper for Aspects and Dimensions of Concern Workshop, *ECOOP 2000*.
8. M. Mezini and K. Ostermann. "Integrating independent components with on-demand remodularization", In *Proceedings of OOPSLA '02*, 2002.
9. Y. Smaragdakis and D. Batory, "Mixin Layers: An Object-Oriented Implementation Technique for Refinements and Collaboration-Based Designs", *ACM TOSEM*, March 2002.
10. G. Snelting and F. Tip, "Semantics-Based Composition of Class Hierarchies", *ECOOP 2002*, 562-584.
11. G. Snelting, personal communication.

12. F. Tip, C. Laffra, P. F. Sweeney, and D. Streeter. "Practical experience with an application extractor for Java", In *Proceedings of OOPSLA*, pages 292–305, November 1999.
13. E. Truyen, B. Vanhaute, W. Joosen, P. Verbaeten, and B. N. Jrgensen. "Dynamic and Selective Combination of Extensions in Component-Based Applications". In *Proceedings of the 23rd International Conference on Software Engineering (ICSE'01)*, Toronto, Canada, May 2001.
14. O. Agesen. *Concrete Type Inference: Delivering Object-Oriented Applications*. Ph.D. thesis, Stanford University, 1995.

Appendix

This appendix demonstrates type correctness and semantic equality of the merged tools. Static type correctness is simple. All ATS tools are variants of a master design. A design defines a set of class hierarchies; AHEAD refinements add more members to existing classes or add new classes only as bottom-level leaves to pre-defined hierarchies. Changing superclass relationships in inheritance hierarchies is not permitted, nor is deleting classes. Thus, the inheritance hierarchies that are present in a tool prior to merging remain the same after merging. Similarly, since methods are never deleted, the set of method *signatures* that are present in a class prior to merging are present afterwards. Thus, all objects created in an unmerged tool will be of the same type as that in the merged tool; all methods in the unmerged tool are present in the merged tool. If the unmerged tool is type correct, its corresponding code in the merged tool is type correct.

Proving behavioral equivalence between the unmerged and merged tools is more difficult. Although the general problem is undecidable, Snelting and Tip [10] have shown for merging class hierarchies, behavior equivalence can be checked via static analysis of *dynamic interference*. To verify that two tools (before and after merging) do not have dynamic interference, [10] requires us to show that (a) both define methods in the same way and (b) both invoke the same methods in the same order.

Same Method Definitions. The only problematic scenario is that in an unmerged program a class inherits a method from its superclass, but after merging this method is overridden. Figure 4a illustrates a class hierarchy before merging, where the method **foo()** is inherited by class **Two**. After merging, a different version of **foo()** is inserted in class **Two** that overrides the inherited method.

```
class One {                    class One {
    void foo() {...}               void foo() {...}
}                              }

class Two extends One {        class Two extends One {
    void main() {                  void main() {
        Two t = new Two();             Two t = new Two();
        t.foo();                       t.foo();
    }                              }
}                                  void foo() {...}
                               }

        (a)                            (b)
```

Fig. 4. Method Overridden in a Class Composition

A variant of (1) allows us to propagate the contents of class ancestors to its sub-classes. Figure 5a shows a hierarchy of three classes and the members that they locally encapsulate. Figure 5b shows the contents of class encapsulation after propagation. Note that a method refinement (Δm_1 for example) extends the original method m_1 by performing some task intermixed with a *super* call.

$$(a)\ X = \{ m_1,\ m_2 \} \qquad (b)\quad X = \{ m_1,\ m_2 \}$$
$$\uparrow \qquad\qquad\qquad \uparrow$$
$$Y = \{ \Delta m_1,\ m_3 \} \qquad Y = \{ \Delta m_1 \bullet m_1,\ m_2,\ m_3 \}$$
$$\uparrow \qquad\qquad\qquad \uparrow$$
$$Z = \{ \Delta m_2 \} \qquad\quad Z = \{ \Delta m_1 \bullet m_1,\ \Delta m_2 \bullet m_2,\ m_3 \}$$

Fig. 5. Propagating Contents Down A Hierarchy

Given this, we can determine the variables and methods of every class in each tool and the merged tool, along with their specifications by tracing back along the inheritance chains. Let c_i denote a class from tool T_i and c_m denote the corresponding class in the merged tool. If c_i does not conflict with c_m, we know c_m includes the same variables and methods of c_i *and* defines them in the same way. By performing this test over all classes in all original tools, we can prove that all methods in the original tools are present and are defined in the same way as in the merged tool.

Same Methods Called. We still need to prove that the same methods are called. Consider the class hierarchy of Figure 6a. When the **main** method is executed, the **foo(One x)** method is invoked. Now consider the addition of a specialized **foo(Two x)** method in Figure 6b. When **main** is now executed, **foo(Two x)** is called. Here is an example where all of the original methods in Figure 6a are present in Figure 6b, but at run-time a different, more specialized method is invoked, thus leading to different behavior. This is the problem of ambiguous method invocations.

```
(a)  class One {                    (b)  class One {
        void foo(One x) {...}               void foo(One x) {...}
     }                                    }

     class Two extends One {              class Two extends One {
        void main() {                        void main() {
           Two t = new Two();                   Two t = new Two();
           t.foo(t);                            t.foo(t);
        }                                    }
     }                                       void foo(Two x) {...}
                                          }
```

Fig. 6. The Problem of Method Specialization

To detect this problem, we again return to the members that we computed for class c_i and c_m. Although we have been using simple names, like "m_1", to denote a class member, the actual name of a member is its type signature. By comparing type signatures of two methods we can tell whether one method is a specialization of another. If there is any method in the set difference $c_m - c_i$ (i.e., the methods in the merged class that are not members of the original class) that could be a specialization of a method in c_i, ambiguous invocation as in Figure 6 is possible. In our optimization process, potential ambiguous invocations are detected, and the corresponding classes are not merged and are put in tool-specific packages.

So assuring that all methods in the original tools are present and are defined in the same way as in the merged tool, and ambiguous method invocations are not possible, we guarantee the absence of dynamic interference, thus behavior equivalence between the unmerged and merged tools.

VS-Gen: A Case Study of a Product Line for Versioning Systems

Jernej Kovse and Christian Gebauer

Department of Computer Science
Kaiserslautern University of Technology
P.O. Box 3049, D-67653 Kaiserslautern, Germany
kovse@informatik.uni-kl.de, gebauer@gmx.com

Abstract. This paper describes our experience with developing a product line for middleware-based versioning systems. We perform a detailed domain analysis and define a DSL for configuring individual systems. Afterwards, we present a template-based approach for generating versioning systems from UML models. The presented approach is evaluated from two perspectives. We first use diverse measures to determine the properties of code templates used by the generator. Afterwards, we compare the performance of a generated versioning system to a system that has been developed by means of a framework and thus has to rely on a set of generic implementation components.

1 Introduction

Versioning systems are generally used to manage data objects that change frequently over time. Their main function is to represent intermediate stages in the object's evolution path as *versions* and allow users to revert to these stages afterwards. Versioning is useful in a variety of different applications: In a software project, developers will want to version their specifications, data and process models, database schemas, program code, build scripts, binaries, server configurations, and test cases. In an editorial department of a magazine, authors will want to version the text of their articles, images, tables, teasers, and headlines before submitting the final version of their contribution.

This paper summarizes the practical experience gathered with our *VS-Gen (Versioning Systems Generator)* project. The goal of the project is to support a product line of versioning systems. A specific system from the product line is specified by describing its data model in UML and afterwards selecting the features desired for the system on the basis of this model. Feature selection is supported by a UML profile. The resulting UML model is analyzed by a template-driven generator that delivers a complete middleware-based implementation of the versioning system.

The rest of the paper is organized as follows. The features of versioning systems will be presented in Sect. 2 which provides a detailed domain analysis for the product line. Sect. 3 will first examine the implementation components of versioning systems

G. Karsai and E. Visser (Eds.): GPCE 2004, LNCS 3286, pp. 396–415, 2004.

to illustrate what has to be generated automatically and then outline the generation approach. We evaluate our product line from two perspectives: First, in Sect. 4, we use diverse measures to examine both the properties of generated code for an exemplary system from the domain as well as the properties of code templates used by the generator. Afterwards, in Sect. 5, we examine the performance of a sample versioning system generated with VS-Gen in comparison to a system developed using a framework that relies on a number of generic implementation components. This framework can be considered as an alternative implementation of the product line. Finally, Sect. 6 gives an overview of related work while Sect. 7 summarizes the presented results and gives some ideas for the future work related to VS-Gen.

2   Domain Analysis

A versioning system stores objects and relationships between these objects. Each object and each relationship is an instance of some object or relationship type. Object and relationship types are defined by the versioning system's *information model* [3]. For example, the OMG's MOF Model can be used as an information model in case the users want to store and version MOF-based metamodels, or the UML Metamodel can be used as an information model for storing and versioning UML models. Fig. 1 illustrates a very simple information model from the domain of content management, which will be used as an example for VS-Gen throughout this paper.

Obviously, it would be possible to come up with a generic implementation of a versioning system capable of dealing with any information model without needing any change in the implementation. In such an extreme case, even attribute values could be stored in a single relational table as name-value pairs. Even though such generic solutions represent performance drawbacks, certain variants prove useful due to their simplicity (we compare the performance of one selected variant to a system generated by VS-Gen in Sect. 5).

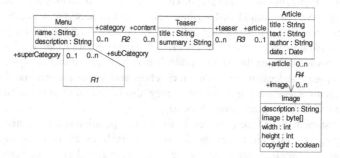

Fig. 1. A simple information model

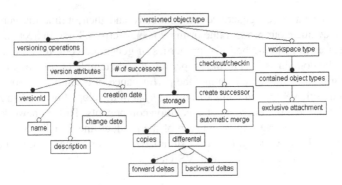

Fig. 2. Feature diagram for versioned object types

In VS-Gen, the information model represents a basis for configuring the desired versioning system. This is done by *selecting features* related to the model elements, as described in the following sections.

2.1 Object Types

An *object type* may or may not support versioning. For every object type, the versioning system provides only the basic operations *create*, *copy*, *delete* and the so-called *finders*. In case an object type supports versioning, each object (instance) of this type is also a version that belongs to some version graph. A corresponding feature diagram for versioned object types is illustrated in Fig. 2. A versioned type provides an identifying attribute *versionId* for referencing a version within the graph. Each graph is equipped with an *objectId*. A version can also be referenced directly using a *globalId* that comprises both identifiers. For a type that supports versioning, the user may require additional attributes for storing *version name*, *description*, last *change date* and *creation date*. Using the feature *# of successors*, it is possible to limit the number of direct successors for a version in the version graph. The storage of versions may proceed in copies that duplicate even the unmodified attribute values for fast access or using the so-called *forward* or *backward deltas* (storing only the differences from the predecessor to the successor version or vice versa). The *checkout/checkin* operations are used to lock/unlock the version for the exclusive use mode. It may be required that the system always creates a separate successor version upon checkout and leaves the original version unadorned (*create successor*). In this case, it may also be useful to *automatically merge* this version with the original upon checkin.

Each versioned object type provides the following operations (not depicted in Fig. 2) for managing versions and traversing the version graph: *createSuccessor*, *deleteVersion*, *merge*, *getAncestor*, *getSuccessors*, *getAlternatives*, and *getRoot*. Some of these carry further subfeatures, e.g., *prevent deletion of ancestors* is an optional subfeature of *deleteVersion* that we also use in the UML profile in Sect. 2.4. It marks whether a version can be deleted in case it already has some successors in the version graph.

2.2 Workspace Types

Workspace types (also see Fig. 2) are versioned object types with special properties. Workspaces (instances of workspace types) contain many objects (of diverse types). However, only one version of a particular object may be present in a workspace at a time – in this way, a workspace acts as a version-free view to the contents of a versioning system, allowing the user to navigate among the contained objects without explicitly referring to versions. A version arrives in a workspace using the *attach* operation. A workspace can possess an exclusive ownership for the attached versions, meaning that they cannot be attached to another workspace at the same time.

2.3 Relationship Types

The majority of interesting behavior in a versioning system is captured by properties of *relationship types*. Each type consists of two relationship ends that connect to object types. The features for an end are illustrated by the feature diagram in Fig. 3. An end is primarily characterized by the defined *role name*, whether it is *navigable*, and its *multiplicity*. More interestingly, in case an end connects to a versioned object type, the user can define the end as *floating*. A floating end contains a subset of versions that can be reached when navigating to this object. This subset is called a *candidate version collection (CVC)* and can be either *system-* or *user-managed*. In a system-managed CVC, the CVC is initialized by a version specified by the user; afterwards, the system adds every successor of this version (obtained either by invoking *createSuccessor* or by merging) to the CVC. In a user-managed CVC, the user explicitly adds versions from the version graph to the CVC.

There are two possible ways of using a CVC when navigating between objects. In *unfiltered navigation*, the user requests all versions from the CVC when navigating from some origin object (note that if the multiplicity of the end is *many*, there will be many CVCs, one for each connected object). In *filtered navigation*, the system automat-

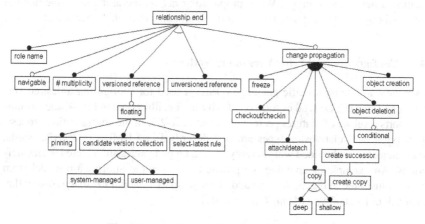

Fig. 3. Feature diagram for relationship ends

ically selects a version for the user. In case filtered navigation is carried out within a workspace, a version from the CVC that is attached to the workspace will be returned. Outside a workspace, the system first checks whether there is a *pinned version* in the CVC (this is the version the user has explicitly marked as default using the *pin* operation). Otherwise, the system selects the *latest (newest) version* from the CVC. Floating relationship ends prove useful for managing configurations of versions, but also represent a large performance overhead due to special properties. For this reason, we consider them optional, so the user can define the relationship end that connects to a versioned object type as non-floating and use it to connect to versions as if they were regular objects.

To illustrate the concepts of floating relationship ends, consider the following example based on Fig. 1. Suppose that the relationship end *content* which belongs to the relationship type *R2* and connects to the object type *Teaser* is floating. The multiplicity of the end is many. This means that a given version of a menu *m* connects to many CVCs for the teasers. Each of these teaser-CVCs is bound to a version graph for some teaser and contains a subset of versions from this version graph. Within each teaser-CVC, there is a latest version and there can be a pinned version. The following situations can arise where navigating from *m* across the relationship R2 towards *Teaser*.

- *Filtered navigation outside a workspace.* For every teaser-CVC related to *m*, a pinned version is returned, in case it exists. Otherwise, the latest version is returned.
- *Filtered navigation within a workspace w.* For every teaser-CVC related to *m*, we check whether there is a teaser version attached to *w* and return this version. Note that a CVC that connects to *m* does not have to contain a version attached to *w*. For such a CVC, no version is returned.
- *Unfiltered navigation.* All versions from all teaser-CVCs related to *m* are returned. It is up to the client application to decide which versions to use.

As illustrated in Fig. 3, relationship ends can also be used to propagate operations from the object the operation got invoked on towards its connected objects. When propagating *createSuccessor*, the user can choose to invoke *copy* on a connected object, thus initiating a new version graph. When propagating *delete*, the user can define that the connected object is to be deleted only if it does not connect to any other objects.

2.4 A Configuration DSL for Versioning Systems

In VS-Gen, a domain-specific language (DSL) is used for configuring a desired versioning system. The DSL takes form of a UML profile, illustrated in Fig. 4, and currently supports a subset of features presented in Sect. 2.1-2.3. In the configuration process, object types and relationship types are first described in a UML model. Afterwards, model elements are branded with stereotypes and tagged values are selected for tag definitions. An example of applying the profile to our sample information model from Fig. 1 is illustrated in Fig. 5. We also added a workspace type *EditorialDepartment* that can attach objects of type *Menu*, *Teaser*, and *Article*.

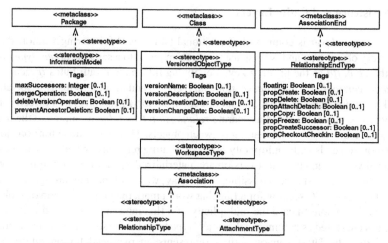

Fig. 4. A UML Profile for information models in VS-Gen

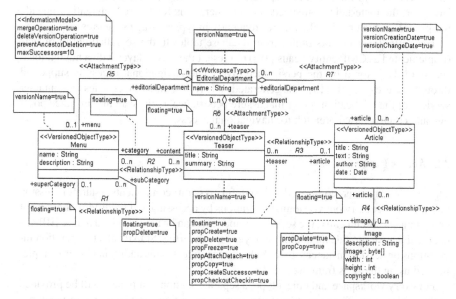

Fig. 5. A sample information model branded with stereotypes and tagged values

3 Generated Components

This section outlines the implementation components of a versioning system and the template-based approach used to generate these components. The target platform for generated systems is J2EE [20] with a RDBMS as a persistent storage for objects and relationships.

3.1 Persistence and Entity Layers

The *persistence layer* is composed of relational tables used for storing versioned objects. Every object type and workspace type gets mapped to a separate *object type table* using the *globalId* as the primary key. Versioning information (attributes *frozen*, *versionName*, *versionCreationDate*, *versionChangeDate*, and the one-to-many association for linking a predecessor version to its direct successors) gets integrated directly into the table. If possible, we avoid a separate *relationship type table* to minimize the number of joins required when navigating between objects. This can be done for non-floating relationship ends with multiplicity *one*. For floating relationship ends, references to the pinned version and the latest version are materialized as additional foreign key values to assure the fastest access possible. In this way, we avoid running through all target version keys in a CVC seeking for a flag that would mark the pinned version or looking for the latest version. In case the multiplicity of a floating relationship end is *one*, the two values are stored as columns in the object type table for the source of the navigation. Materializing the latest version setting represents an overhead for operations that change the state of the CVC, i.e., operations for creating or deleting the relationships. However, the materialization speeds up the operations for filtered navigation outside workspaces, which are invoked more frequently in typical usage scenarios.

The *entity layer* mirrors tuples from database tables to the so-called entity objects (implemented as CMP entity beans [19]) to present the access layer with a navigational access to data stored by the persistence layer. The navigational access is supported through the use of CMR [19]. The generated code for the entity layer relies on container services of the application server that assure persistence, entity caching, instance pooling, and context-based prefetch for navigational access.

3.2 Access Layer

The access layer is comprised of stateful session components (stateful session beans [19]) that carry out versioning operations by accessing and modifying the state of entity objects. Technically, the session components can be accessed by a native EJB client or, since we provide an additional layer for converting SOAP calls to operation invocations on session instances, by a Web Services client. This additional layer is implemented using the Axis framework [2].

For every workspace and object type, a separate session component will be provided in the access layer. The core object management operations provided by every component include *createObject*, *copyObject*, *deleteObject*, *findAll* and *findByObjectId* and the *get/set* operations for the defined attributes. Session components for versioned object types provide operations *createSuccessor*, *deleteVersion*, *merge*, *getRoot*, *getAncestors*, *getSuccessors*, and *getAlternatives*. Since an instance of a session component is never bound to a particular object, operations that perform work on an existing object require the object's *globalId* as parameter, e.g., given a session component instance *menuAccess* for the object type *Menu* from Fig. 5, *menuAccess.createSuccessor(393218)* will create a successor to the menu with the *globalId 393218* and return the *globalId* of the successor version to the client. In this way, a single session component instance can answer diverse operation calls for different objects of the same type thus saving server-side resources. Operations also come in variants that provide value-based return, e.g., *createSuccessor_Value*, returning a serializable representation of an object to the client.

Session components in the access layer also provide operations for managing and traversing relationships. For example, invoking operations *addCategory* or *removeCategory* on a session component instance *teaserAccess* for the object type *Teaser* creates or deletes a relationship among a teaser and a menu (note that *Menu* is referred to from the *Teaser* using the role name *category*). Both operations maintain CVCs on the corresponding relationship ends. The operation *getCategory* performs a filtered navigation from the teaser to the menu, returning either the pinned version from each connected CVC on the side of the menu or the latest version, in case the pinned version does not exist. For a session component instance a current workspace can be set (this is the reason for session components being stateful) in case an attachment relationship type has been defined among a corresponding object type and the workspace type. For example, the operation *setCurrentEditorialDepartment* can be invoked on *teaserAccess*. With a current workspace set, the operation *getCategory* will return only the connected versions of the menu that are attached to this workspace. The operations *getCategoryPinned*, *pinCategory*, and *unpinCategory* are used for explicitly navigating to the pinned menu versions and manipulating the pin settings. Unfiltered navigation is supported using the operation *getCategoryUnfiltered*.

Taking advantage of the specified operation propagation properties, the generator hardwires the application logic for propagation directly in the implementation of session components in the access layer. For the example in Fig. 5, creating a copy of an article automatically creates copies of associated teasers and images and connects these copies with relationships.

3.3 Content Browser

In addition to the programmatic access described in the previous section, the versioning system can also be accessed using a content browser. This access is convenient for manually invoking the operations of a versioning system. The browser is a Web application based on the JSP Model 2 Architecture [17]. It consists of generated JSPs, which contain no Java scriptlet code and serve only as views to the requested information. In addition, for each object type, we generate a servlet that takes the role of a Web controller. These servlets invoke operations on the access layer and dispatch the returned information to the JSPs.

3.4 Example

To illustrate the concepts described by Sect. 3.1-3.3, we take a look at an example scenario for the system generated from the information model illustrated in Fig. 5. Suppose that in the content browser, the user gets an overview of a specific article version. From this overview, the *createSuccessor* operation is invoked on this version. The invocation

```
1:   public ArticleLocal createSuccessor_Local(ArticleLocal object, HashMap recursionMap) throws Exception {
2:       if (!object.getFrozen()) { // ... Exception throwing code }
3:       if (getSuccessors_Local(object).size() >= 10) { // ... Exception throwing code }
4:       ArticleLocal newCopy = null;
5:       newCopy = mHomeInterface.create(object.getObjectId());
6:       object.getSuccessors().add(newCopy);
7:       newCopy.setTitle(object.getTitle());
8:       newCopy.setText(object.getText());
9:       newCopy.setAuthor(object.getAuthor());
10:      newCopy.setDate(object.getDate());
11:      recursionMap.put(object.getGlobalId(), newCopy);
12:      TeaserAccessLocal teaserAccessBean = getTeaserAccessBean();
13:      for (Iterator it=getTeaser_Local(object).iterator(); it.hasNext();) {
14:          TeaserLocal linked = (TeaserLocal)it.next();
15:          if (linked.getFrozen()) {
16:              TeaserLocal newLinked = null;
17:              if (!recursionMap.containsKey(linked.getGlobalId()))
18:                  newLinked = teaserAccessBean.createSuccessor_Local(linked, recursionMap);
19:              else newLinked = (TeaserLocal)recursionMap.get(linked.getGlobalId());
20:              addTeaser_Local(newCopy, newLinked);
21:          }
22:      }
23:      return newCopy;
24: }
```

Fig. 6. *createSuccessor_Local* operation for the *Article* object type

is accepted by the Web controller servlet for the *Article* object type. The servlet calls the method *createSuccessor_Value* on the stateful session bean object in the access layer that is responsible for the *Article* object type. As mentioned in Sect. 3.2, this method returns a serializable representation of the newly created version. The method relies on the method *createSuccessor_Local*, which actually creates the successor version. This method is illustrated by Fig. 6. *newCopy* (line 5) is a reference to an entity bean for the newly created version. Lines 7–10 copy the attribute values to this version. Lines 11–22 implement the propagation of the *createSuccessor* operation from an article version towards connected teaser versions. A hash map *recursionMap* is used to keep track of already visited versions to prevent cycles in operation propagation.

3.5 Generation Process

The generation process in VS-Gen is based on a set of code templates. Nearly all existing template-based code generation approaches work in the same way. First, a template that consists of static parts, placeholders for user-defined values, and control flow statements that drive the evaluation of the output of the template is prepared. Afterwards, in a process called *merging*, a context of values that will replace placeholders is prepared and the control flow of the template is executed by a template engine. To separate it from the *static code* parts in the template, we refer to context references and control flow as *metacode*. The template engine used in VS-Gen is Velocity [1]. No generated code is produced by means other than templates. Table 1 gives an overview of the 25 code templates used in VS-Gen and the implementation parts they generate.

Code generation from UML models often requires flexible access to model information that is dispersed across many model elements due to fine-grained nature of the UML Metamodel. Following the idea described by Sturm et al. [18], this problem is solved by implementing the so-called *prepared classes* that aggregate model information from diverse model parts. VS-Gen uses XMI to import an information model from

Table 1. Velocity templates used by VS-Gen

Temp-Id	Template name	Used to generate...
1	VSObjAccBean	a class implementation for components in the access layer
2	VSObjAccLocal	local component and home interfaces for components in the access layer
3	VSObjAccLocalHome	
4	VSObjAccRemote	remote component and home interfaces for components in the access layer
5	VSObjAccRemoteHome	
6	VSObjBean	a class implementation for components in the entity layer
7	VSObjLocal	local component and home interfaces for components in the entity layer
8	VSObjLocalHome	
9	VSObjRemote	remote component and home interfaces for components in the entity layer
10	VSObjRemoteHome	
11	VSObjValue	serializable representations of object types
12	ControllerServlet	request dispatcher servlets (Web controllers) for the content browser
13	ShowInstance	a JSP page that displays information on a stored object
14	ShowTypeInfo	a JSP page that displays type information (metadata, i.e., attributes and relationship types) for an object type
15	ShowList	a JSP page that displays the matching objects as a result of a finder method or a navigation operation
16	ShowIndex	a JSP page that displays the navigation bar in the content browser
17	Web-xml	a Web deployment descriptor
18	EJB-jar-xml	an EJB deployment descriptor
19	Application-xml	a deployment descriptor for the entire enterprise application
20	AS-application-xml	an application server specific deployment descriptor for the application
21	Deploy-wsdd	a Web services deployment descriptor
22	Undeploy-wsdd	a file to undeploy previously deployed Web services
23	VSObjService	proxy classes for redirecting Web services calls to the access layer
24	TestClient	a Web services based test client
25	Build-xml	a script to compile and deploy the generated implementation

a UML tool to the NSUML [16] in-memory UML repository. Before invoking the template engine, the model is analyzed in this repository to instantiate the prepared classes and fill the instances with model information. Afterwards, the instances are put in the Velocity context.

As an example, Fig. 7 illustrates a part of the template *VSObjAccBean* that has been used to generate the implementation of the *createSuccessor_Local* method from Fig. 6. Velocity statements begin with the # character. The $ character is used to retrieve a value from the context. The reference *class* (see, for example, lines 1 and 8) represents an instance of a prepared class that aggregates information from the UML Metamodel classes *Class, Generalization, Stereotype, TagDefinition*, and *TaggedValue*. Since the multiplicity of the relationship end *teaser* that belongs to the relationship *R3* in Fig. 5 is *many*, the statements in lines 23–34 are used in the generated example from Fig. 6.

4   Evaluation

It is difficult to come up with a realistic estimate of how large individual features of versioning systems are just by examining the feature models and the UML profile from Sect. 2. For this purpose, in Sect. 4.1, we first examine the properties of the example versioning system generated for the information model from Fig. 5. Note that this examination does not apply to how the system is generated, although we used the generator to gradually add new features and examine the differences in the generated code. The results give an orientation of how labor-intensive a manual implementation of the

```
1:    public ${class.name}Local createSuccessor_Local(${class.name}Local object, HashMap recursionMap)
2:    throws Exception {
3:        if (!object.getFrozen()) { // ... Exception throwing code }
4:    #if ( $package.getIntegerTaggedValue("maxSuccessors", -1) > 0 )
5:        if (getSuccessors_Local(object).size() >=
6:            ${package.getIntTaggedVal("maxSuccessors", -1)}) { // ... Exception throwing code }
7:    #end
8:        ${class.name}Local newCopy = null;
9:        newCopy = mHomeInterface.create(object.getObjectId());
10:       object.getSuccessors().add(newCopy);
11:   #foreach( $attribute in $class.attributes )
12:       newCopy.set${attribute.nameUpperCase}(object.get${attribute.nameUpperCase}());
13:   #end
14:       recursionMap.put(object.getGlobalId(), newCopy);
15:   #foreach( $associationEnd in $class.associationEnds )
16:   #if ( $associationEnd.association.hasStereotype("RelationshipType") &&
17:        ($associationEnd.oppositeEnd.getTaggedVal("propCreateSuccessor") == "true") &&
18:        ($associationEnd.oppositeEnd.participant.hasStereotype("VersionedObjectType") ||
19:         $associationEnd.oppositeEnd.participant.hasStereotype("WorkspaceType") ) )
20:   ${associationEnd.oppositeEnd.participant.name}AccessLocal ${associationEnd.oppositeEnd.name}AccessBean =
21:       get${associationEnd.oppositeEnd.participant.name}AccessBean();
22:   #if ( $associationEnd.oppositeEnd.isMultiValued() )
23:       for (Iterator it=get${associationEnd.oppositeEnd.nameUpperCase}_Local(object).iterator(); it.hasNext();) {
24:           ${associationEnd.oppositeEnd.participant.name}Local linked =
25:               (${associationEnd.oppositeEnd.participant.name}Local)it.next();
26:           if (linked.getFrozen()) {
27:               ${associationEnd.oppositeEnd.participant.name}Local newLinked = null;
28:               if (!recursionMap.containsKey(linked.getGlobalId())) newLinked =
29:                   ${associationEnd.oppositeEnd.name}AccessBean.createSuccessor_Local(linked, recursionMap);
30:               else newLinked =
31:                   (${associationEnd.oppositeEnd.participant.name}Local)recursionMap.get(linked.getGlobalId());
32:               add${associationEnd.oppositeEnd.nameUpperCase}_Local(newCopy, newLinked);
33:           }
34:       }
35:   #else
36:       ${associationEnd.oppositeEnd.participant.name}Local
37:           linked${associationEnd.oppositeEnd.participant.nameUpperCase} =
38:               get${associationEnd.oppositeEnd.participant.nameUpperCase}_Local(object);
39:       if (linked${associationEnd.oppositeEnd.participant.nameUpperCase}.getFrozen()) {
40:           ${associationEnd.oppositeEnd.participant.name}Local
41:               new${associationEnd.oppositeEnd.participant.nameUpperCase} = null;
42:           if (!recursionMap.containsKey(
43:               linked${associationEnd.oppositeEnd.participant.nameUpperCase}.getGlobalId()))
44:               new${associationEnd.oppositeEnd.participant.nameUpperCase} =
45:                   ${associationEnd.oppositeEnd.name}AccessBean.createSuccessor_Local(
46:                       linked${associationEnd.oppositeEnd.participant.nameUpperCase}, recursionMap);
47:           else
48:               new${associationEnd.oppositeEnd.participant.nameUpperCase} =
49:                   (${associationEnd.oppositeEnd.participant.name}Local)recursionMap.get(
50:                       linked${associationEnd.oppositeEnd.participant.nameUpperCase}.getGlobalId());
51:           add${associationEnd.oppositeEnd.nameUpperCase}_Local(newCopy,
52:               new${associationEnd.oppositeEnd.participant.nameUpperCase});
53:       }
54:   #end ## End of #if ( $associationEnd.oppositeEnd.isMultiValued() )
55:   #end ## End of #if ($associationEnd.association.hasStereotype("RelationshipType") && ...
56:   #end ## End of #foreach( $associationEnd in $class.associationEnds )
57:       return newCopy;
58:   }
```

Fig. 7. Part of the template *VSObjAccBean* used for generating *createSuccessor_Local* method

features would be. To evaluate the generation approach itself, Sect. 4.2 examines the properties of the templates presented by Table 1.

4.1 Properties of the Example Versioning System

We analyzed the code generated with VS-Gen for the sample information model from Fig. 5 by trying to trace different code parts back to the corresponding configuration concepts from the UML profile (see Table 2). In terms of the lines-of-code (LOC) mea-

Table 2. Parts of the generated implementation

Implementation part	%LOC
Object and workspace types	**62.47%**
- Article	14.35%
- EditorialDepartment	13.30%
- Image	8.88%
- Menu	13.04%
- Teaser	12.90%
Relationship types	**21.93%**
- R1 (Menu-Menu)	6.44%
- R2 (Menu-Teaser)	7.11%
- R3 (Teaser-Article)	6.61%
- R4 (Article-Image)	1.77%

Implementation part	%LOC
Attachment rel. types	**11.40%**
- R5 (EditorialDep-Menu)	3.68%
- R6 (EditorialDep-Teaser)	3.78%
- R7 (EditorialDep-Article)	3.93%
Remaining parts	**4.21%**

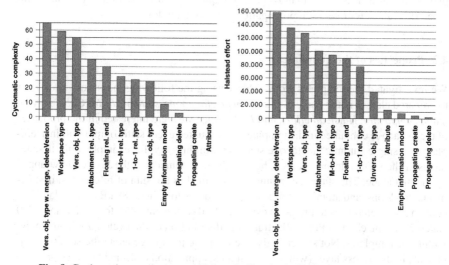

Fig. 8. Cyclomatic complexity and Halstead effort for individual concepts / features

sure, the largest part of the generated code (62.47%) belongs to the object and work-space types. As evident from Table 2, an unversioned object type (*Image*) requires sub-stantially less code than versioned types and workspaces. A unidirectional relationship type *R4* (between *Article* and *Image*) with no floating ends is far easier to support than other relationship types. Also note that the three attachment relationship types that con-nect the workspace type *EditorialDepartment* to object types *Menu*, *Teaser*, and *Article* are less demanding than regular relationships types. The remaining percentage of code (4.21%) represents the counters for managing *objectIds* and *versionIds* and can not be directly ascribed to any configuration concept.

We were also interested in the values for *McCabe's cyclomatic complexity* [13] and *Halstead effort* [8] that can be attributed to individual concepts and features. The results of this analysis are illustrated by Fig. 8. The two values (complexity and effort) for an empty information model were obtained by generating a versioning system from a mod-el with no object, relationship, and workspace types. Afterwards, we added an unversioned object type, versioned object type (separately with *merge* and *deleteVersion* operations), and a workspace type and observed the differences in comparison with the values obtained for an empty model. Starting from an object type and a workspace type, we added an attribute, an attachment relationship type, a regular one-to-one relationship type, and a regular many-to-many relationship type to the model and observed the differences. Afterwards, we made both ends of the many-to-many relationship type floating and halved the obtained complexity and effort differences to obtain the values that can be ascribed to a single floating relationship end. Finally, for an existing relationship, we additionally chose delete propagation and create propagation. As evident from Fig. 8, the largest complexity and effort values are obtained for versioned object types and workspace types (in contrast to this, an unversioned object type is less demanding than a one-to-one relationship type). A floating relationship end alone adds more complexity and a bit less effort than originally required for a many-to-many relationship type. The values for operation propagation are extremely low.

4.2 Properties of the Templates

We investigated the templates from Table 1 using the following measures: *references* to prepared classes in the context, *if-statements, for-loops, statements, McCabe's cyclomatic complexity, Halstead effort*, and *LOC*. Since we were interested in the properties of the metacode contained in the templates, we counted every static output within a template as a single "atomic" metacode statement. In this way, for example, only if-statements of the metacode are counted, but not the if-statements in the Java code wrapped by the metacode. The statement count was obtained as the sum of references, if-statements, for-loops, and atomic outputs of static code. Altogether, 288 kB of template files contain 3013 references to prepared classes, 542 if-statements, 128 for-loops, and 6670 statements. The chart in Fig. 9 illustrates the distribution of the cyclomatic complexity within the templates. Not surprisingly, the template used to generate the session components in the access layer (which contain most application code and are very prone to feature selections) proves as the most complex one.

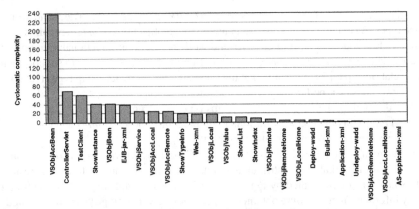

Fig. 9. Cyclomatic complexity of the templates

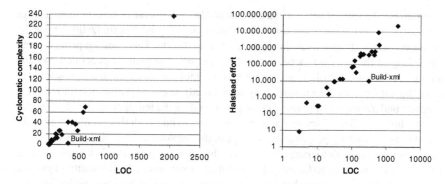

Fig. 10. Correlation between the cyclomatic complexity / Halstead effort and LOC

We were also interested whether there is a correlation between the LOC-value and the cyclomatic complexity and the Halstead effort of the metacode. As illustrated by Fig. 10, the cyclomatic complexity grows in a linear proportion to the LOC-value of a template. A steady growth trend can be observed for the Halstead effort if we use logarithmic scales for both axes. The specially marked outlier is the template *Build-xml*. This template (for generating the compile and build script for a versioning system) contains only a minor part of metacode in proportion to its static parts.

5   How Fast Are Generated Versioning Systems?

There are two ways of integrating a versioning system with clients. Development environments usually contain a set of existing clients (tools), each with a private storage manager with a logical data model not necessary corresponding to that of the versioning system. In this case, *translators* [4] (also called *data exchange switches*) that convert the data between the versioning system and the storage managers need to be developed. In the second case, the versioning system is used interactively by the tools. In this case, users will develop new tools using the generated API or wrap this API so that it can be used with the existing tools. Long-lasting accesses to the versioning system in both cases, where a large number of stored objects is traversed, are disturbing for developers. A fast versioning system assures short modification, build, and test cycles in any kind of development process that uses versioned data.

Do generated versioning systems provide better performance that generic ones? To answer this question, we developed an alternative implementation of the product line in form of a *framework*. In the framework approach, the user implements a desired versioning system by extending the framework superclasses with classes specific to the information model and providing call-back methods that will be invoked by the framework through reflection. What are the differences between the systems obtained in two different ways, i.e., generated by VS-Gen or obtained by instantiating the framework? As described in Sect. 3, template metacode assures a wide range of optimizations, e.g., materializing the pinned version in a CVC or hardwiring operation propagation settings in the implementation of the access layer. Unfortunately, these optimizations raise the complexity of the database schema and the generated code. This does not prove a problem as long as the system is accessed by the client only through the generated API and as long as no adaptation of the generated code is required. However, if a user wanted to query the database of the versioning system directly using SQL, this would require a complete understanding of optimizations performed by the template metacode (also see our conclusion in Sect. 7 for an alternative way of dealing with this problem). In addition, due to hardwiring propagation settings in the implementation of the access layer, the settings are difficult to trace down and modify. For this reason, when implementing the framework, we tried to factor out a great deal of versioning functionality to *generic parts* and implement them so that they can be used with any information model, increasing the simplicity of the obtained system (especially the database schema) without loosing too much on performance. The differences between systems generated by VS-Gen and systems developed by extending the framework are summarized in Table 3.

We took advantage of the fact that all API calls supported by a generated system are also supported by a framework-based system (in fact, a framework-based system will usually provide a somewhat more elaborate API for an information model because, for example, all object types are versioned). This means that clients that run against a generated system run with no modifications against a framework-based system. In our performance comparison, we used the information model from Fig. 5 for a generated and

Table 3. Differences between generated and framework-based versioning systems

Concept / feature	VS-Gen	Framework
Versioning information (predecessor to a given version, information whether a version is frozen)	The information is directly integrated in the entity components that represent object types.	Stored by a special table used by all object types. The versioning information is represented as an additional entity component.
Merging information (what versions have been merged with other versions)	Implemented as a separate reflexive many-to-many relationship on an entity component for a particular object type.	Implemented as a reflexive relationship on the entity component that represents versions.
Unversioned object types	Supported.	Not supported - all object types are versioned.
Non-floating relationship ends	Supported.	Not supported - all ends are floating.
Relationship types	Implemented separately for every relationship type. Represented as relationships among the entities that represent object types, allowing context-based prefetch.	All relationships are stored by a special table. A relationship is represented as an additional entity component.
Latest version of a CVC	Materialized as a separate relationship between entities and thus immediately available in filtered navigation. If the multiplicity of the floating end is one, only one join will be required.	The candidate versions, determined within the relationship table, have to be scanned to determine the latest version.
Pinned versions	Implemented separately for every floating relationship end. Represented as relationships between the entities.	All pin settings are stored by a special table. A pin setting is represented as an additional entity component.
Attachment relationship types	Implemented separately for every attachment relationship type defined in the information model.	Stored by a special table. Attachments are represented as additional entity components.
Checkout locks	Available as a one-to-many relationship between the workspace type and the object type.	Stored by a special table. Checkout locks are represented as an additional entity component.
Operation propagation settings	Hardwired directly in the session components in the access layer.	Stored in a special table that can be modified for a running versioning system. The table needs to be queried for every invocation of an operation that might propagate.

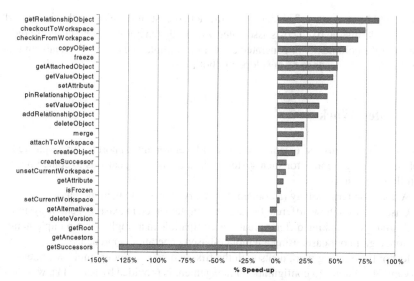

Fig. 11. Speed-up of a generated towards a framework-based versioning system

framework-based versioning system. A benchmark client that was used to simulate a typical content-management scenario for this information model carried out 192,148 operations. A detailed comparison of execution times (we subtracted the communication times between the client and server) for diverse operations is given by Fig. 11.

The speed-ups illustrated in Fig. 11 were calculated as the ratio $(t_{fw}-t_{gen})/t_{fw}$, where t_{fw} represents the time required by the framework-based implementation and t_{gen} the time required by the generated implementation. The entire run of the benchmark took 505.30 seconds for the framework-based implementation and 370.86 seconds for the generated implementation, yielding a 26.61% overall speed-up of the generated implementation. Note that execution times in Fig. 11 have been categorized, e.g., *pinRelationshipObject* represents all pinning operations carried out for objects and relationships of diverse types defined by the information model in Fig. 5. The times used for t_{fw} and t_{gen} were then obtained as median execution times within a category (median times are used instead of average times to reduce the effect of outliers.) As evident from Fig. 11, version graph navigation operations (*getAlternatives, getRoot, getAncestors,* and *getDifferences*) and the *deleteVersion* operation prove more efficient for a framework-based system due to differences in representing versioning information as described in Table 3.

Is improved performance the only reason for implementing a generator? Our experience shows that instantiating the framework by writing derived classes is a very labor-intensive task. It requires the developer to get familiar with the framework and is also very error-prone, e.g., due to naming conventions the call-back methods need to follow. For the information model from Fig. 5, 45 derived classes with a total 3822 LOC and a Halstead effort of 12,490 were required. So even for the framework-based approach used in a commercial setting, we claim that a simple generator for framework instantiation would be necessary. This increases the actual cost of developing the framework when considering the fixed costs associated with both generators. These costs are independent of the complexity of generated code. For example, the facility for analyzing information models needs to be developed in both cases.

6   Related Work

A good analysis of diverse existing systems with versioning support is a prerequisite for implementing a generator for such systems. As a result, our goal was to come up with the following results.

- A common terminology (a domain dictionary) for our domain model.
- Case studies of how different features are implemented in existing generic systems.
- A strategy to making different features compatible in a single domain implementation, e.g., in our case, using a template-based generation approach.

Most of the existing work deals with the first two points. For example, an extensive overview of version and configuration management is provided by Katz [11], who proposes a *unified framework for version modeling* in engineering databases. The author analyzes a variety of existing terminologies and mechanisms for representing versioned data. A lot of recent applications to versioning are used for versioning hypermedia content. Whitehead [22] analyzes this domain and gives an overview of existing systems.

Some examples of versioning systems include CVS/RCS [7], Microsoft Meta Data Services [15], Unisys UREP [21], IBM Rational ClearCase [10], and IBM XML Registry [9]. While early systems like CVS/RCS use a file system for storage, most recent systems, like VS-Gen, rely on a database to allow the structuring of information models either as relational or OODBMS schemas, queries, and transactions. Conradi and Westfechtel [6] examine a variety of version models in both commercial and research systems and discuss fundamental concepts of the domain, such as *versions, revisions, variants, configurations*, and *changes*. Whitehead and Gordon [23] use *containment data models* (a specialized form of the ER model) to analyze 11 configuration management systems (including CVS and ClearCase). A comparison of these surveys to VS-Gen reveals that, at the moment, our domain model covers merely a portion of existing version models. Following the results from this work, we plan to gradually improve the VS-Gen's UML profile and domain implementation to support new features.

Versioning of metadata (relational and XML schemas, interface definitions for operations, etc.) has become significant for data and application integration approaches. In this cases, metadata (which is subject to change over time and thus needs to be versioned) is needed for analyzing and dealing with syntactic and semantic heterogeneity of diverse data sources that need to be integrated (see [12]). In case a versioning system supports a fine-grained navigational access among stored objects for the clients, much like the systems generated by VS-Gen, another common term for such a system is *repository* (see Bernstein [4] for the description of additional functionality that is usually provided by repositories, e.g., workflow management for tracing the lifecycle of stored objects). Although the majority of existing approaches support the generation of implementation parts that are specific for the user-defined information model, they restrain from treating versioning functionality in terms of features that could be selected by the user. This usually leads to framework-based solutions similar to the one we presented in Sect. 5, with a decreased performance and only minor possibilities to customize the versioning semantics.

In our current implementation, the merge operation merely connects two branches in the version tree, relying on the user to resolve the semantic conflicts between the versions. However, the topic of automatic merging has already been considered by some authors. For example, Melnik et al. [14] discuss the definition of a *reintegrate operator* that can be used for model merging. The operator relies on automatic discovery of structural and semantic model correspondences. We plan to explore the relevance of these results to VS-Gen in our future work.

7 Conclusion and Future Work

This paper presented VS-Gen which is our approach to template-based generation of versioning systems from information models branded with system features selected by the user. In comparison to the framework-based solution that relies on a series of generic implementation components, a generated versioning system demonstrated an improved performance of 27% measured by our benchmark. The time spent on the VS-Gen project can be summarized as follows. A development team of two with a background in version management spent four months analyzing and comparing different versioning systems to come up with the domain model. The development of the UML profile, model analysis facility, prepared classes and the templates was carried out in an iterative fashion by adding a specific feature to these parts, adjusting the implementation of existing features, and carrying out the tests. These iterations took six months, the development of the templates taking the effective portion of approx. 75% of this time. The effective time for getting familiar with different technologies we use in VS-Gen (NSUML, Velocity, and Axis) is estimated to one month. Both developers had a strong background in J2EE, UML profiles, and XMI. Due to our existing experience with the implementation of versioning systems we generate and simpler optimization requirements, the development of the framework (developed after the generator part was completed) took less than three months.

The following are the lessons we learned from VS-Gen.

- Current IDEs lack sufficient support for developing templates. The minimal requirement would include syntax highlighting to easily separate code from metacode. Velocity templates 13–16 from Table 1 were especially difficult to develop since they generate JSP pages, which themselves act as templates for HTML output. Further requirements would include a quick examination of generated code by filling in the context values directly in the IDE with no need to start the entire generation process. Adding new features to our domain often required a reimplementation of existing templates. A good IDE for template-based development should support a clear overview of what parts of a template are related to a specific feature.
- Many templates were developed by first considering examples of what needs to be generated for a selection of features and afterwards generalizing these examples to

a template. The most complex case for this were different examples for the combination of floating/non-floating relationship ends with their multiplicities. These combinations affect different parts of access components that deal with relationship traversal, creation, and deletion of a relationship. We assume that this kind of example-based development could be automated to some extent by tools that compare different examples and identify varying pieces of code.

- Templates for generating code with a great deal of application logic are especially difficult to develop and test. Using the cyclomatic complexity scale proposed by [5], the templates for generating access components, the controller servlet, and the test client would fall into the category of programs with very high risk that are practically untestable. A solution would be to break down the template into many parts that can be used in a superordinated template. In case a part is used more than once, this allows reuse of code and metacode. Velocity supports the described reuse by *include*, *parse*, and *macro* directives [1]. However, in VS-Gen, no repeating parts of metacode occur in the first place, making metacode refactoring impossible. Thus the only solution is to refactor the code that needs to be generated to many parts (classes) and implement many small templates for these parts.

Our benchmark results are to be treated with care. The overall speed-up of a generated versioning system towards a framework-based system depends on the concrete selection of features and proportions among the categories of operations carried out by the benchmark. This means that the *categories* illustrated in Fig. 11 are more relevant for discussing the benefits of generated systems than the overall speed-up of 27%. To our knowledge, no well-accepted benchmarks for versioning systems exist, probably due to a large variety of existing versioning models. As mentioned by [4], in the most simple case, OODB benchmarks can be used for measuring the performance of navigational access operations in a versioning system. However, this excludes versioning operations and the effects of operation propagation that are also interesting to us.

Our work fails to answer the most important question: *How many* versioning systems implemented manually justify the effort required for developing the templates for the generative approach? In answering this question, it proves unavoidable to come up with a measure that reasonably combines the properties of the metacode and static code in a template. Having not solved this problem, we simply state that even for the case of a small information model, such as the one in Fig. 5, the LOC-value for the generated versioning system is 2.7-times greater than the LOC-value of the templates, although this result is to be treated with utmost care. Our future work will focus on a detailed examination of template metacode to determine a set of appropriate measures that can be used for evaluating the metacode's properties.

Presenting developers with a generated middleware API for accessing the data in the versioning system is not the only possible way of tackling the problem. For this reason, in a related project, we are developing a domain-specific SQL-like language for dealing with versioned data. Data definition statements in this language, which describe the information model and the selection of features are translated to SQL-DDL statements. Query and update statements are translated to SQL-DML statements. The translation takes place in a special database driver that wraps the native driver.

Company mergers often require not only integration of enterprise data but also integration of engineering data for the products, which is usually versioned. Understanding variability in different versioning models is a key prerequisite for such integration. In our future work in this area, we want to extend VS-Gen with a support for generative development of wrappers to utilize the integration of legacy versioning systems.

References

1. The Apache Jakarta Project: Velocity, available as: http://jakarta.apache.org/velocity/
2. The Apache Web Services Project - Axis, available as: http://ws.apache.org/axis/
3. Bernstein, P.A.: Repositories and Object-Oriented Databases, in: SIGMOD Record 27:11 (1998), pp. 34-46
4. Bernstein, P.A., Dayal, U.: An Overview of Repository Technology, in: Proc. VLDB 1994, Santiago, Sept. 1994, pp. 707-713
5. Carnegie Mellon University, Software Engineering Institute: Software Technology Roadmap - Cyclomatic Complexity, available as:
    http://www.sei.cmu.edu/str/descriptions/cyclomatic_body.html
6. Conradi, R., Westfechtel, B.: Version Models of Software Configuration Management, in: ACM Computing Surveys, 30:2 (1998), pp. 232-282
7. CVS - Concurrent Versions Systems - The Open Standard for Version Control, available as: http://www.cvshome.org/
8. Halstead, M.H.: Elements of Software Science, Elsevier, 1977
9. IBM Corp., IBM alphaWorks: XML Registry, available as:
    http://www.alphaworks.ibm.com/tech/xrr
10. IBM Corp.: IBM Rational ClearCase, available as:
    http://www.ibm.com/software/awdtools/clearcase/
11. Katz, R.H.: Toward a Unified Framework for Version Modeling in Engineering Databases, in: ACM Computing Surveys 22:4 (1990), pp 375-409
12. Madhavan, J., Bernstein, P.A., Rahm, E.: Generic Schema Matching with Cupid, in: Proc. VLDB 2001, Rome, Sept. 2001, pp. 49-58
13. McCabe, T.J.: A Complexity Measure, in: IEEE Transactions on Software Engineering 2:4 (1976), pp. 308-320
14. Melnik, S., Rahm, E., Bernstein P.A.: Developing Metadata-Intensive Applications with Rondo, in: Journal of Web Semantics, 1:1 (2003)
15. Microsoft Corp., Microsoft Developer Network: Meta Data Services Architecture, available as: http://msdn.microsoft.com/
16. Novosoft Inc.: NSUML – Novosoft Metadata Framework and UML Library, available from: http://nsuml.sourceforge.net/
17. Seshadri, G.: Understanding JavaServer Pages Model 2 Architecture: Exploring the MVC Design Pattern, JavaWorld, Dec. 1999, available from: http://www.javaworld.com/
18. Sturm, T., von Voss, J., Boger, M.: Generating Code from UML with Velocity Templates, in: Proc. UML 2002, Dresden, Oct. 2002, 150-161
19. Sun Microsystems, Inc.: Enterprise JavaBeans Specification, v2.1, Nov. 2003
20. Sun Microsystems, Inc.: Java 2 Platform Enterprise Edition Specification, v1.4, Apr. 2003
21. Unisys Universal Repository: Tool Builder's Guide, Unisys Corp., 1999.
22. Whitehead, J.E.: An Analysis of the Hypertext Versioning Domain, Ph.D. dissertation, Univ. of California, Irvine, Sept. 2000
23. Whitehead, J.E., Gordon, D.: Uniform Comparison of Configuration Data Models, in: Proc. SCM-11, Portland, May 2003, pp. 70-85

A Model-Driven Approach
for Smart Card Configuration

Stéphane Bonnet[1,2], Olivier Potonniée[1],
Raphaël Marvie[2], and Jean-Marc Geib[2]

[1] Gemplus, Systems Research Labs, La Vigie, ZI Athelia, La Ciotat, France
{stephane.bonnet,olivier.potonniee}@research.gemplus.com
[2] Laboratoire d'Informatique Fondamentale de Lille, UMR CNRS 8022
Université des Sciences et Techniques de Lille, Villeneuve d'Ascq, France
{raphael.marvie,jean-marc.geib}@lifl.fr

Abstract. The configuration of smart cards is a complex multi-level process. Addressing this process efficiently is a major challenge of the smart card industry. In the context of the forthcoming evolutions of smart card systems, we are ex-perimenting new configuration methods. We propose to rely on both model-driven engineering and software product lines to formalize and automate the smart card configuration process. We are applying separation of concerns as a methodological support to implement variability management. This paper describes our approach as well as its motivations and provides a concrete example.

1 Introduction

Similar in size to plastic credit cards, smart cards embed card a silicon chip that provides both data storage and processing capabilities. Due of their reduced size enabling data portability, and thanks to their built-in hardware ensuring an advanced level of security, smart cards are used as access-control devices in miscellaneous environments, such as mobile telecommunication for example.

The nature of smart cards makes their configuration a complex multi-level process, requiring both hardware and software customization: Batch specialization is required by card issuers and personalization by individual end-users. Addressing efficiently the configuration issues is a major challenge of the smart card industry. The forthcoming evolutions of smart card systems give us the opportunity to investigate new configuration methods. In this paper, we describe an approach relying on both model-driven engineering and software product lines to formalize and automate the configuration processes.

This paper is organized as follows. Section 2 presents smart cards and their configuration process. Section 3 introduces the application of model-driven engineering to software product lines for smart card configuration. Our approach is illustrated in section 4. It details a strategy to personalize on-card applications and introduces a model-driven framework for its automation. In section 5, this framework use is depicted through a case study. Finally, section 6 discusses related works and section 7 concludes this article.

G. Karsai and E. Visser (Eds.): GPCE 2004, LNCS 3286, pp. 416–435, 2004.

2   Smart Card Configuration Process

While smart cards have been at the center of many banking[1] and mobile telecommunication infrastructures for the past 15 years, the information age is now introducing new privacy and security concerns that require advanced smart card applications. Among others, more and more governmental or healthcare-related organizations are relying on solutions based on smart cards. An efficient implementation of mass-customization is one key of smart card manufacturing processes.

A microprocessor card is similar to a miniature computer. It is embedding a chip with volatile as well as non-volatile memory and running an operating system. Thus, the architecture of a smart card consists in common hardware and basic software layer, on top of which domain specific applications are installed, with configurations that are specific to the card issuers. In addition, each card is personalized for its end-user – i.e., the card holder. This layered configuration process, illustrated by Figure 1, is an important specificity of the smart card industry.

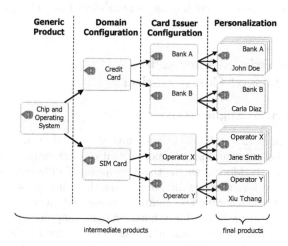

Fig. 1. The smart card layered configuration process

Both software and hardware have specific production constraints. The hardware production consists in manufacturing chips with appropriate ROM burned-in[2], assembling the chip as well as the plastic card, and writing the application and customer configuration in the card programmable memory. Depending on the context – which is often defined by security or privacy concerns – configuration of software can be done differently. While the simplest approach consists in

---

[1] Mostly in Europe and Asia.

[2] Putting software in read-only or volatile memory is a decision that is part of the configuration.

loading on the card an already-configured version of the software and its data, a more evolved one consists in performing the configuration step only on-card.

As smart card systems are getting more evolved, manufacturers are concerned by the improvement of their configuration multi-level process. They are notably facing two essential challenges.

- *Reducing the configuration-specific development to the minimum.* Intermediate products should be configurable enough to minimize the development effort required to produce a refined configuration.
- *Minimizing production delays.* To achieve this objective, hardware and software configuration should be performed in parallel: the hardware production process should be started before the software configuration is completed. This would allow hardware products to remain generic as long as possible.

In the rest of the paper, we are focusing on software configuration issues. This concern fits in the general need to produce software that meets the requirements of increasingly heterogeneous markets without harming considerably the efficiency of mass production. The next section describes how we are relying on a combination of model-driven engineering and product lines, two state-of-the-art software design approaches.

3 A Model-Driven Approach for Smart Card Configuration

3.1 Model-Driven Engineering

Model-Driven Engineering (MDE) offers a migration path from present object- and component-based solutions to a more ambitious and scalable approach for designing software [1]. Models enable the description of different views of a system, at different levels of abstraction. For a while, the primary purpose of models has been to ease understanding and communication, but their role in MDE is to enable generative approaches, using refinements and mappings [2].

As its interpretation must be unambiguous, a model must be associated with a unique meta-model that provides its semantics. A meta-model is a language to write models, and at the upper layer, a meta-meta-model is a language to write meta-models. According to the Object Management Group (OMG), the Meta Object Facility (MOF) contains all the features needed to write and manipulate meta-models, and is meant to be the unique meta-meta-model for all software-related purposes [3].

To encourage the move from contemplative to productive models, the OMG has introduced in 2001 the Model Driven Architecture (MDA), a framework for leveraging in-place modeling specifications and standardizing model-driven software development [4]. The MDA specification implements a restricted vision of the separation of concerns: It establishes the dependency regarding a specific platform as the main criterion to organize models, by introducing the notions of Platform-Independent Models (PIM) and Platform-Specific Models (PSM). An extension of this basic classification is needed to enable aspect-oriented modeling [5, 6].

MDE is meant to leverage the automation of software production. Therefore, standardized mappings and code generation techniques are necessary to make models first-class citizens of the engineering. A transformation between two models roughly consists in sets of rules that establish correspondences between elements of the source model and elements of the target model.

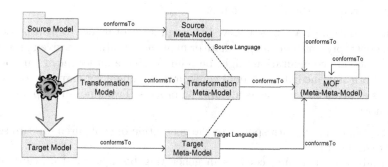

Fig. 2. General model-to-model transformation

Figure 2 presents the general scheme for reasoning in terms of models, and shows that transformations could be themselves considered as models. Then, the concepts to be used in order to define transformations must be defined using a meta-model. To that extend, the OMG has issued in 2002 a Request For Proposal (RFP), called MOF 2.0 Query/Views/Transformations, which goal is to standardize a unified transformation language [7].

3.2   A Software Product Line for Smart Card Configuration

We propose to handle smart card configuration with an approach based on Software Product Lines (SPL). A SPL is based on a set of core software assets, from which multiple products are derived [8, 9]. The core artifacts address the common requirements of a given domain, while variability points define where and when functional and technical choices have to be made. From a SPL point of view, smart card products are built on several kinds of assets, corresponding to different maturity levels. For instance, generic products are combinations of OS artifacts, while customer products reuse domain-specific assets.

Managing variability efficiently at different stages of the development is a key success factor of this approach. MDE complements SPLs in the sense that it provides means to establish a clear distinction between the models of core assets and the variability concerns, much like functional and technical concerns are kept separated in the MDA [10]. The actual product derivation is achieved through model transformations. Relying on MDE, our approach is based upon the following design principles:

- Core assets are described using models. These models are based on MOF-compliant meta-models that may be specific to their corresponding domain.
- Variability points are categorized by concerns that can either be functional or technical.
- Each set of variability points is associated with one or several meta-models that define the concepts allowing the expression of the variability requirements.
- A mark-based mechanism permits the annotation of the core asset models with variability-specific information.

The product derivation is achieved through a set of model transformations. Each model represents one intermediate or final configuration of a given product. An intermediate configuration might be refined using another set of variability points. Both intermediate and final configurations might be mapped to actual products at given steps of the configuration process. Two kinds of mappings are envisioned:

- A simple mapping corresponds to the generation of configured on-card software and data.
- An advanced mapping consists in generating both on- and off-card code dedicated to the customization of a specific product.

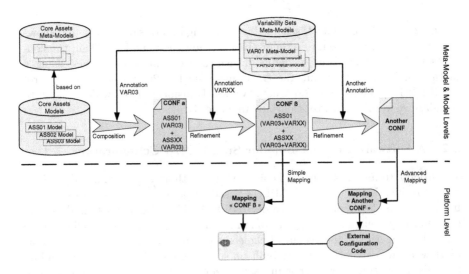

Fig. 3. Model-driven card configuration process

It is not in the scope of this paper to explicitly detail the real card production process, the different meta-models or variability sets. Figure 3 gives an overview of the configuration process. At the meta-model and model levels, each step corresponds to a composition of core assets models that are enriched with concern-specific annotations. At the platform level, the two kinds of mappings are illustrated.

Relying on MDE to implement the smart card SPL allows us to establish the separation of concerns principle as a strong methodological support to organize the configuration process. In the following section, we illustrate this approach with the final personalization of on-card software, which is one particular step of the configuration process. Personalization in that context is considered as one particular concern, and thus gathers a set of related variability points.

4   A Framework for Personalizing On-Card Software

4.1   Personalization of Smart Card Applications

Our goal is to automate as much as possible the model creations and transformations required to instantiate user-specific configurations of a given on-card application. The personalization process consists in the following steps, which are independent of the technical implementation:

- identifying which elements of the application are user-specific,
- organizing a structured management of end-user information, and
- implementing the mapping of application personalizable elements with user relevant data items.

We are investigating how the next generation of smart card applications will be personalized. We are assuming these applications are written in Java. This is already the case with the Java Card specification, which defines a limited Java runtime environment for smart card [11]. The forthcoming releases of this specification will take advantage of the evolution of hardware, which is going to offer enhanced computing power and larger memory space. As we anticipate this evolution, we deliberately omit in our development restrictions that are imposed by today's smart card execution environments. We are assuming the availability of a garbage collector, and make use of the full Java language without the Java Card version 2 restrictions. In particular, these assumptions allow us not to be concerned about the size of the generated code.

We want to automate smart card application personalization in such a way that the application developer does not have to be aware of how the personalization process is implemented. Hence we do not impose any coding requirement to the application developer: The application is written as any Java application, and the framework produces the personalization code that seamlessly interacts with the developer's code. As depicted by Figure 4, two kinds of classes are generated:

1. For each Java class that must be customized, we generate a `Personalizer` inner class, which exposes public operations to access all the identified configurable class elements, either public or private. The `Personalizer` class gives access to private members of the applicative class during the personalization process. Once personalized, access to the `Personalizer` class can be deactivated by means that are not discussed here.

2. The personalization itself, which differentiate each card from one another, is implemented in a Java method named **activator**. This method processes the card holder personalization by invoking, using user-specific values, the methods offered by the generated **Personalizer** inner classes.

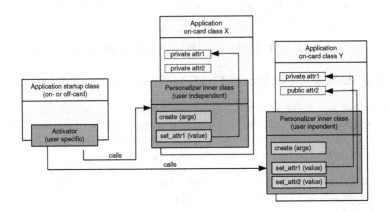

Fig. 4. Code personalization

The activation code can be inserted into the embedded code of the application, in which case it is executed on-card. For example, this allows personalization of applications when smart cards are already distributed to their final users. But when personalization only occurs during the manufacturing process, as it is mostly the case today, the **activator** can be executed off-card. For the later alternative, a remote communication is established between the on-card **Personalizer** classes and the off-card **activator** for example using Java Card RMI[3]. As future execution environments will offer other mechanisms, we do not make any assumption here on how this communication is implemented.

The separation between the inner classes and the activator optimizes the smart card configuration process, as it capitalizes on the generic code – the **Personalizer** classes are not user-dependent –, and minimizes the user-specific code – the **activator**. The following sections detail the model-driven process that leads to the generation of these pieces of code.

4.2   The Framework

Figure 5 describes the structure of the framework. This structure follows the MDA organization: The upper layer can be considered as a set of PIMs, the middle layer represents a mapping of these models to PSMs – in that case the specific platform is the Java environment. The bottom layer is a running embedded Java application.

---

[3] A limited version of Java RMI.

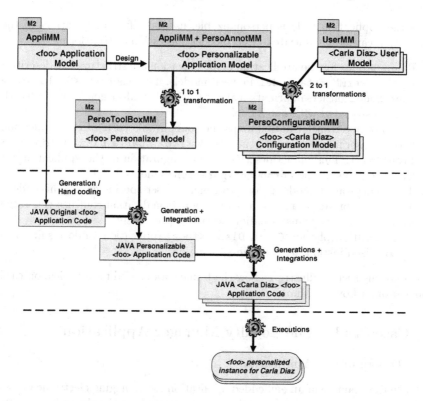

Fig. 5. The personalization framework

As explained previously, the goal of the framework is to produce two kinds of code modifications. As it is not user-specific, the transformation process that makes the application code personalizable – creation of the `Personalizer` inner classes – is performed only once for a given application. It consists in the following steps:

1. The `<foo>` application is designed with our `AppliMM` meta-model. The application designer does not need to take into account any personalization related concern.
2. The refinement of the `<foo>` application model with personalization information is done using the concepts described in the `PersoAnnotMM` meta-model. Such personalization annotations can, for example, specify whether and how a class or an attribute can be customized.
3. A one-to-one transformation takes the annotated model as an input, and produces a model of the personalization routines which must be added to the original application code. This `<foo>` `Personalizer` Model is based on the `PersoToolBoxMM` meta-model.
4. The Java inner `Personalizer` classes and methods are generated from this model and integrated to the original application code.

Once the application code is personalizable, user-specific configurations of the application can be instantiated after another succession of transformations:

1. Relevant data for the application personalization are structured as described by the `UserMM` meta-model in user models. For example, `<Carla Diaz> User Model` gathers information about Carla Diaz. More generally, each end-user is associated with one model.
2. A two-to-one transformation maps the configurable parts of the application with the user information to generate the `<foo> <Carla Diaz> Configuration Model`. This model describes the configuration of the application for Carla Diaz, using the `PersoConfigurationMM` meta-model.
3. The configuration model is used to generate user-specific code. This code is an application `activator` that calls the personalization routines generated by the one-to-one transformation described previously.
4. The execution of the `<Carla Diaz> <foo>` Application Code results in a personalized instantiation of the application.

The following section illustrates how the framework is used for a typical on-card application: a Loyalty Manager.

5   Case Study: The Loyalty Manager Application

5.1   Design of the Application

We take the example of an embedded application for managing electronic purses and loyalty accounts. This application is voluntarily kept simple, as its purpose is only to illustrate the model processing.

A card is delivered by a card issuer. Each card might host one or several electronic purses from different operators. Each purse can be used in several shops, according to the commercial agreements existing between the merchants and the purse operator. Each merchant might have a loyalty program. Card issuers can manage loyalty accounts on behalf of merchants, like they do with purses on behalf on purse operators. The relationships between purses and loyalty accounts is embedded in smart cards.

Figure 6 depicts the model of the application, which implements simple principles:

- A `LoyaltyAccount` handles `LoyaltyPoints`. Each customer is associated with one `LoyaltyAccount` per shop.
- `LoyaltyPoints` increase with expenses and decrease with time.
- According to the amount of `LoyaltyPoints`, a client is respectively considered as `BronzeClient`, `SilverClient`, and `GoldClient` for a given shop.
- A rebate percentage is associated with each `CustomerStatus`.

The application code is derived from the model of Figure 6. Each class is translated in an interface and its implementation. For example, each `Purse` model element becomes `Purse` interface and `PurseImpl` class.

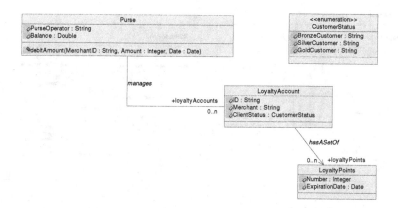

Fig. 6. The Loyalty Manager application

5.2 Annotation of the Application Model

To personalize the LoyaltyManager application at pre- or post-issuance time, the card provider must create for each end-user the list of their electronic purses, of their loyalty accounts, and of the links between them.

As explained in Sect. 4.2, the PersoAnnotMM meta-model defines the concepts needed by the personalization designer to express what in the application is dependent on the final user. Figure 7 presents a simplified version of this PersoAnnotMM meta-model, and describes how it relates to the concepts of AppliMM, the core asset meta-model. The annotation mechanism is further explained in [12]. To keep the figure readable, only a few elements of the AppliMM meta-model appear. The personalization variability set allows:

- to add information about the instantiation of certain classes, using the M2ClassPersonalizer and M2FactoryKind concepts,
- to specify whether an attribute will be given a user-specific value, using the M2AttributePersonalizer concept as well as to specify which kind of access to this attribute is required, and
- to specify whether the link defined by an association must be integrated in the personalization or not, using the M2AssociationPersonalizer concept.

Figure 8 provides an informal overview of how the original application model can be annotated. Figure 5 showed that the annotated application model is used both for making the code personalizable, and for configuring user-specific instantiations. The following sections describe these two transformation chains.

5.3 Making the Application Code Personalizable

Preparing the application code to make it personalizable is the result of a model processing involving both model transformation and code generation. First, the

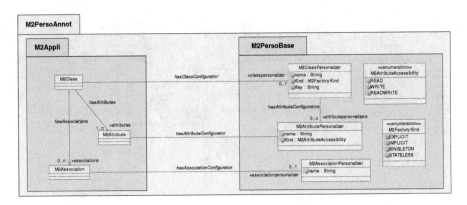

Fig. 7. Personalization variability set meta-model

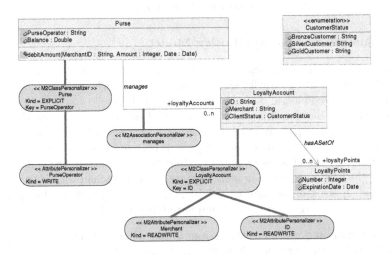

Fig. 8. Annotated Loyalty Manager application model

annotated application model is taken as an input in a one-to-one transformation mapping the concepts of the meta-models `AppliMM` & `PersoAnnotMM` with the ones of `PersoToolBoxMM`, partly described by Figure 9. This results in the creation of the `Personalizer` model, from which the code of the inner `Personalizer` classes is generated.

This transformation is reusable across different applications. It is a set of mapping rules written in Java, using JMI repositories [13]. The meta-models are written with a graphical tool and saved in a serialized form. The JMI repositories are generated using Modfact [14]. The design of the transformation has been inspired by the classification of model transformation approaches, described in [15], but its implementation is not discussed here. Among others, the transformation contains the following rules:

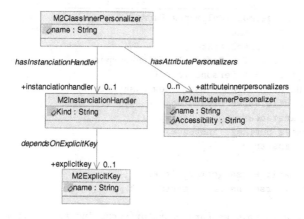

Fig. 9. `PersoToolBoxMM` meta-model

- `M2ClassPersonalizer` is mapped to `M2ClassInnerPersonalizer` and `M2InstantiationHandler`,
- the `Kind` attribute of the `M2InstantiationHandler` is given the string value of the `Kind` attribute of the `M2ClassPersonalizer`,
- if the value of the `Kind` attribute is `EXPLICIT`, then a `M2ExplicitKey` element is also created in the `Personalizer` model, and
- `M2AttributePersonalizer` is mapped to `M2AttributeInnerPersonalizer`.

Figure 10 shows a graphical representation of the obtained Personalizer Model. This model is used to obtain the final personalization code. From each `M2Class-Personalizer` element is generated an inner class `Personalizer`, with a content determined by the `InstantiationHandler` and `AttributePersonalizer` elements. The piece of code of Figure 11 shows the integration of a generated inner class for the original `PurseImpl` class.

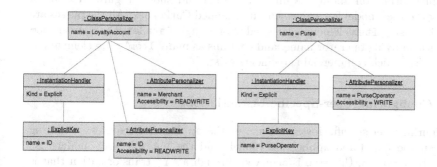

Fig. 10. The `personalizer` model for the Loyalty Manager application

```
public class PurseImpl implements Purse {
  private double Balance;
  private String PurseOperator;
  // generated code for Personalization purpose
  public static class Personalizer {
    static Hashtable instances = new Hashtable();
    public static Purse create(Object key) {
      Purse instance = new PurseImpl();
      instances.put(key, instance);
      return instance;
    }
    public static Purse get(Object key) {
      return (Purse)instances.get(key) ;
    }
    public static void setPurseOperator(Purse instance, String value){
      ((PurseImpl)inst).PurseOperator = value;
    }
    public static String getPurseOperator(Purse instance) {
      return ((PurseImpl)instance).PurseOperator;
    }
  } // End of generated code, rest of the original code not shown
```

Fig. 11. Generated Personalizer inner class

5.4   Making the Application Code Personalizable

In parallel to the design step that consists in annotating the application model, relevant user data must be collected and structured. To that extend, we provide the basic UserModelMM meta-model which allows to express user profiles that can either be specific to an application or shared among several ones. Figure 12 presents this meta-model.

In the context of the Loyalty Manager application, the User model must contain information about the different purses and shops. Figure 13 shows a part of the user model for a given end-user named Carla Diaz. All the purses are described using Item elements, gathered in one single DataSet. Each purse Item is identified by its operator name, and contains as many ItemValue elements as shops with which commercial agreements exist.

5.5   Configuring User-Specific Instantiations

Configuring user-specific instantiations of the application requires a weaving between the annotated application model, and the multiple user models. As shown by Figure 5, this step is achieved through a "Y" transformation that is applied for each card. The "Y" scheme refers to a configuration where the two upper branches of the "Y" represent two input sets of information that have to be combined in order to result in one single set. For example, the global structure of the MDA is actually a "Y" scheme where:

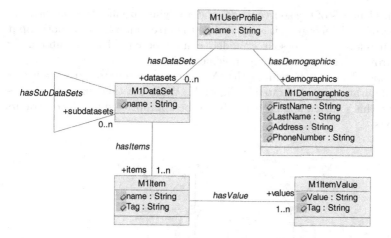

Fig. 12. UserMM meta-model

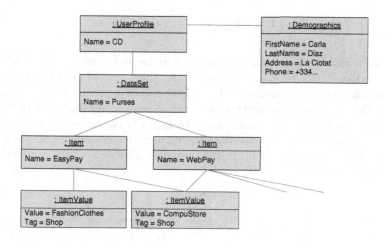

Fig. 13. User model for Carla Diaz

- the left branch of the "Y" contains successive refinements of PIMs,
- the right branch contains Platform Description Models (PDMs), and
- the bottom branch contains the successive PSMs refinements as well as the final code.

The binding step, which corresponds to the center of the "Y", remains one of the most difficult and unanswered question about the MDA [2]. In the following, we concentrate on a concrete model merging example introduced in Sect.4.2, Figure 5.

Despite using different formalisms, tools, or practices, most approaches for handling one-to-one transformations rely on a common strategy that consists in parsing the elements of the source model and applying specific rules on them. In the context of model merging, it is impossible to parse simultaneously both input models. Therefore, the two source models cannot be considered as absolutely equal regarding the transformation implementation.

Our proposal consists in refining the "Y" scheme, in order to retrieve a better known configuration, as illustrated in Figure 14. While meeting our particular requirements, this solution might obviously not be appropriated for all constraints nor contexts.

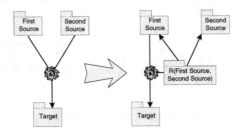

Fig. 14. Handling the "Y" transformation

As the transformation main parsing can only be performed on one of the two source models, we propose to create a third model R(FirstSource, SecondSource) that establishes relationships between elements of the two source models. The "Y" transformation then becomes a one-to-one parameterized transformation, where the actual source for parsing is FirstSource. We are providing a set of Java classes implementing the core mechanisms of the transformation [12]. However, it is still up to the designer to implement the correlations between the two source models.

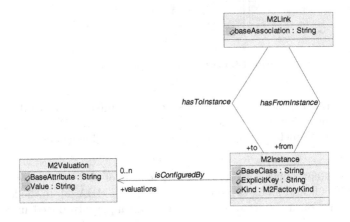

Fig. 15. PersoConfigurationMM meta-model

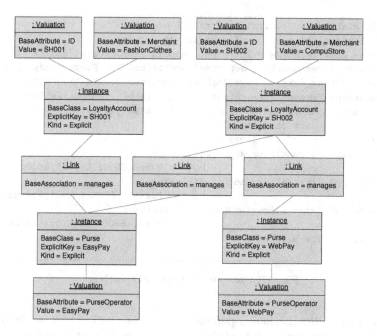

Fig. 16. Configuration model for Carla Diaz

In the context of the Loyalty Manager application, the source model is the Application Model, while the User Model plays the role of the second source. The parameterization model contains relationships which state that, for example, the DataSet user model elements named "Purses" must be related to Purse elements of the application model.

For a given user model, the result of this transformation is a user-specific Configuration Model, which describes the activator of the application. While Figure 15 illustrates the PersoConfigurationMM meta-model, Figure 16 shows the Configuration model for Carla Diaz. The activator() method described by Figure 17 is generated from this model. It is called during the application startup.

6   Related Work

The ultimate goal of software product lines is to leverage generative programming techniques to maximize the automation of software development. Our work essentially relates to architectural concerns for building software product lines, and in particular to variability management. Variability concepts and surveys of enabling mechanisms are introduced in [16] and more extensively in [17]. The explicit representation of the variability is a key aspect of the SPL approaches. This requires the modeling of both the variation points and their variable parts, as explained in [18].

```
public static void activator( String[] argv ) {
    // instantiation and configuration of purses
    Purse EasyPay_Purse = PurseImpl.Personalizer.create("EasyPay");
    PurseImpl.Personalizer.setPurseOperator(EasyPay_Purse,"EasyPay");
    Purse WebPay_Purse = PurseImpl.Personalizer.create("WebPay");
    PurseImpl.Personalizer.setPurseOperator(WebPay_Purse,"WebPay");
    // instantiation and configuration of LoyaltyAccounts
    // . . .   (not shown here) . . .
    // management of the links
    PurseImpl.Personalizer.addLoyaltyAccounts(
                            EasyPay_Purse,SH001_LoyaltyAccount);
    PurseImpl.Personalizer.addLoyaltyAccounts(
                            EasyPay_Purse, SH002_LoyaltyAccount);
    PurseImpl.Personalizer.addLoyaltyAccounts(
                            WebPay_Purse, SH002_LoyaltyAccount);
    // end of the activator
}
```

Fig. 17. Generated `activator()` method

The interest for the model paradigm has significantly increased in recent years. Both an interesting state-of-the-art and an overview of some forthcoming challenges are provided by [1]. MDE provides means to describe variability concepts at a high-level, and therefore enables an early integration of these concerns in the process of building a product line. Approaches relying on UML extensions are described in [19, 20]: profiles including stereotypes, tagged values and structural constraints are used to express variability. More generally, the relevance of MDA as a technological approach for product line engineering is generating multiple discussions about how this specification can address product line issues such as variability modeling or derivation support. In [10] for example, the authors identify two main benefits, i.e., postponing the binding time and mechanism selection for a given variation point.

While our work comes within the scope of this global research effort that tries to leverage the combination of MDE and SPL, it slightly differs from the majority of the approaches because:

- we do not want to restrict our modeling environment to UML, the profile-based solution does not fit our needs, and
- platform dependence is not our exclusive concern. We therefore need to rely on a more advanced model classification than the one proposed by MDA.

Our concern-based management of variability requires structuring our modeling environment accordingly. Therefore, we are relying on a model annotation mechanism inspired by the definition in [5] of a meta-modeling framework based on the separation of concerns principle. The adaptation of this framework to the context of smart card configuration is further detailed in [12].

Separation of concerns is actually one of the software engineering design principle that is getting a great attention from practitioners and researchers to promote design and code reuse [21]. The Software Engineering Institute's "Framework for Software Product Line Practice" discusses, in the section on the definition of software architectures, different software practices and mechanisms for building product line architectures and achieving variability [9]. It mentions aspect-orientation as a possible approach, but does not provide any guidance as to how it might be best applied. The way aspect-oriented techniques can help construct program families or product lines is discussed in [22]. A particular focus is put on explaining how concerns must be implemented to reduce unwarranted dependencies.

7   Conclusion

Configuring a smart card is a multi-level process including both hardware and software tailoring, and involving actors such as customers, marketers, or engineers. The customization level ranges from clients such as bank or telecommunication operators to individual card holders. The forthcoming evolutions of smart cards systems and applications are calling for advanced configuration solutions, and therefore provide an opportunity to enhance the in-place processes.

Model-driven engineering and software product lines are two of the emerging ways of designing information systems. Both rely on generative techniques and aim at maximizing automation. In this paper, we are experimenting how they can be combined to formalize the whole smart card configuration process, and improve product configurability.

The architecture of our model-driven software product line consists in modeling the core software artifacts that define product families, and in marking these models with variability-specific annotations. Variability points are gathered together by concerns, and each set of variability is associated with one or several dedicated meta-models.

To illustrate and experiment this approach, we focus on the personalization of card applications. The personalization of a loyalty management application, from the specification of models and annotations to the code generation is used as an example. While the first results are encouraging, especially regarding the clear expression of variability through the annotation mechanism, the design of the product line is still in its early stages. Further experimentations are required to evaluate how well it can scale up. Several issues have already been identified.

- *The problem of possible dependencies between different sets of variability points has not yet been explicitly addressed.* The way crosscutting concerns are treated by aspect-oriented programming [23] and more recently by aspect-oriented modeling [24] provide research directions to tackle this issue, and
- *The result of the QVT RFP is likely to change the implementation of our transformations.* It will be interesting to see up to what point this specification will change the current modeling landscape, and how the different approaches for transforming model, including ours, will be leveraged or called into question.

While we have so far focused on technical matters enabling the design of the product line architecture, the next big step is the design of the product line with the specification of the actual domain assets and variability sets. This phase will require the participation of the configuration process stakeholders.

References

1. Bézivin, J.: MDA: From Hype to Hope, and Reality. Invited talk. In: "UML" 2003, San Fransisco, USA (2003)
2. Bézivin, J., Gérard, S., Muller, P.A., Rioux, L.: MDA Components: Challenges and Opportunities. In: Workshop on Metamodelling for MDA, Yorg, UK (2003)
3. Meta-Object Facility (MOF): OMG Specification (2001)
4. Model Driven Architecture (MDA) Guide version 1.0.1: OMG Document (2003)
5. Marvie, R.: Separation of Concerns and Meta-Modeling applied to Software Architecture Handling. PhD thesis, Université des Sciences et Technologies de Lille, France (2002)
6. Mellor, S.J.: A Framework for Aspect-Oriented Modeling. In: 4th AOSD Modeling with UML Workshop, San Fransisco, USA (2003)
7. MOF 2.0 Query/Views/Transformations: OMG Request For Proposal (2002)
8. Bass, L., Clements, P., Kazman, R.: Software Architecture in Practice. Addison Wesley (1997)
9. P. Clements and L. Northrop: A Framework for Software Product Line Practice, Web Document, version 4.2 (2004)
10. Deelstra, S., Sinnema, M., van Gurp, J., Bosh, J.: Model Driven Architecture as Approach to Manage Variability in Software Product Families. In: Workshop on Model Driven Architecture: Foundations and Applications (MDAFA 2003), University of Twente, Enschede, The Netherlands (2003)
11. Chen, Z.: Java Card Technology for Smart Cards : Architecture and Programmer's Guide. The Java Series. Addison-Wesley (2000)
12. Bonnet, S., Marvie, R., Geib, J.M.: Putting Concern-Oriented Modeling into Practice. In: 2nd Nordic Workshop on UML, Modeling, Methods and Tools (MWUML 2004), Turku, Finland (2004)
13. Java[TM] Metadata Interface (JMI[TM]): Specification Version 1.0 (2002) http://java.sun.com/products/jmi/.
14. Modfact: Open Source Framework Providing MDA services (2002-2003) http://modfact.lip6.fr.
15. Czarnecki, K., Helsen, S.: Classification of Model Transformation Approaches. In: Workshop on Generative Techniques in the Context of MDA (OOPSLA 2003), Anaheim, USA (2003)
16. Svahnberg, M., Bosh, J.: Issues Concerning Variability in Software Product Lines. In: 3rd International Workshop on Software Architecture for Product Families. Volume 1951 of LNCS., Las Palmas de Gran Canaria, Spain, Springer-Verlag (2000) 146–157
17. van Gurp, J., Bosh, J., Svahnberg, M.: On the Notion of Variability in Software Product Lines. In: Working IEEE/IFIP Conference on Software Architecture (WISCA 2001), Amsterdam, The Netherlands, IEEE Computer Society Press (2001) 45–54
18. Jacobson, I., Griss, M., Jonsson, P.: Software Reuse: Architecture, Process and Organization for Business Success. Addison Wesley (1997)

19. Ziadi, T., Hélouët, L., Jézéquel, J.M.: Towards a UML Profile for Software Product Lines. In: 5th International Workshop on Software Product Family Engineering (PFE 2003), Siena, Italy (2003)
20. Clauß, M.: Generic Modeling using UML Extensions for Variability. In: Workshop on Domain Specific Visual Languages (OOPSLA 2001), Tampa Bay, USA (2001)
21. Lopes, C., Hursch, W.: Separation of concerns. Technical report, College of Computer Science, Northeastern University, Boston, MA, Etats-Unis (1995)
22. Coyler, A., Rashid, A., Blair, G.: On the separation of concerns in program families. Technical Report COMP-001-2004, Computing Department, Lancaster University, Lancaster, UK (2004)
23. Kiczales, G., Lamping, J., Mendhekar, A., Maeda, C., Lopes, C., Loingtier, J.M., Irwin, J.: Aspect-Oriented Programming. In: 11th European Conference on Object-Oriented Programming (ECOOP'97). Volume 1241 of LNCS., Jyväskylä, Finland, Springer-Verlag (1997) 220–242
24. Gray, J., Bapty, T., Neema, S., Schmidt, D.C., Gokhale, A., Natarajan, B.: An Approach for Supporting Aspect-Oriented Domain Modeling. In: Generative Programming and Component Engineering conference (GPCE 2003). Volume 2830 of LNCS., Erfurt, Germany, Springer-Verlag (2003) 151–168

On Designing a Target-Independent DSL for Safe OS Process-Scheduling Components

Julia L. Lawall[1], Anne-Françoise Le Meur[1,*], and Gilles Muller[2]

[1] DIKU, University of Copenhagen, 2100 Copenhagen Ø, Denmark
{julia,lemeur}@diku.dk
[2] Ecole des Mines de Nantes/INRIA, 44307 Nantes Cedex 3, France
Gilles.Muller@emn.fr

Abstract. Developing new process-scheduling components for multiple OSes is challenging because of the tight interdependence between an OS and its scheduler and because of the stringent safety requirements that OS code must satisfy. In this context, a domain-specific language (DSL), designed by a scheduling expert, can encapsulate scheduling expertise and thus facilitate scheduler programming and verification. Nevertheless, designing a DSL that is target-independent and provides safety guarantees requires expertise not only in scheduling but also in the structure of various OSes. To address these issues, we propose the introduction of an OS expert into the DSL design process and the use of a type system to enable the OS expert to express relevant OS properties.
This paper instantiates our approach in the context of the Bossa process-scheduling framework and describes how the types provided by an OS expert are used to ensure that Bossa scheduling components are safe.

1 Introduction

A domain-specific language (DSL) is a programming language dedicated to a given family of problems, known as a *domain*. Such a language provides high-level abstractions allowing the *DSL programmer* to focus on what to compute rather than on how to perform this computation [7]. Specifically, the DSL approach relieves the programmer both of constructing code appropriate for a given target and of ensuring that this code satisfies target-specific requirements. Instead, these issues are addressed by the compiler and verifier of the DSL.

Commonly, the responsibilities of designing a DSL and providing the associated compiler and verifier are delegated to a *domain expert*. Such an expert has a broad view of the algorithms relevant to the domain, and thus can select appropriate language abstractions. Nevertheless, this kind of knowledge is not sufficient to create a complete implementation of the language. Constructing a compiler and verifier requires low-level understanding of the target. When there are multiple targets, taking them all into account multiplies the expertise required and the complexity of the compiler and verifier implementations.

---

* Author's current address: Université des Sciences et Technologies de Lille, LIFL, INRIA project Jacquard, 59655 Villeneuve d'Ascq, France.

G. Karsai and E. Visser (Eds.): GPCE 2004, LNCS 3286, pp. 436–455, 2004.

In this paper, we examine these issues in the context of the DSL provided by the Bossa framework for implementing operating system (OS) process-scheduling components [14, 16]. The goal of Bossa is to facilitate the integration of new schedulers in existing OSes, both general-purpose OSes, such as Linux and Windows, and those that address special needs, such as OSes for real-time and embedded systems. In the domain of scheduling, there is a substantial gap between expertise in the domain itself and expertise in the target, *i.e.*, a given OS. Scheduling policies are typically developed and presented at a theoretical level, where the main concerns are high-level properties such as liveness and CPU utilization. Implementing a scheduling policy, on the other hand, requires a deep knowledge of the interaction between the OS and its scheduler, and this interaction differs for each OS. Few scheduling experts possess both expertises, particularly across the range of OSes targeted by Bossa.

Our Approach. To address the need for OS expertise and for OS independence in the design of a DSL for process scheduling, we propose two extensions to the DSL design process. First, we introduce an *OS expert*, *i.e.*, an expert in the target OS, who provides information about OS behavior relevant to the domain of scheduling. Second, we propose that the scheduling expert define a *type system* to be used by the OS expert to create types describing this information. The scheduling domain expert constructs a compiler and a verifier that use these types in generating code appropriate to the target OS and in checking that the behavior of a scheduling policy implementation satisfies OS requirements. This approach allows the DSL to be targeted to many OSes, without complicating its implementation, and eases subsequent evolution of the language to new OSes. In the context of process scheduling, we focus on the problems of codifying the behavior that a target OS requires from its scheduler and of checking that a given scheduler implementation satisfies these requirements, as these are the main sources of OS dependence in this domain.

The specific contributions of this paper are:

- We present a novel approach to the design of a DSL for process scheduling. This approach incorporates an OS expert and a type system to make the language implementation target-independent.
- We instantiate this approach in the context of the DSL of the Bossa process-scheduling framework. In this context, we present a type system that enables an OS expert to express OS information relevant to scheduling.
- We show how to exploit the information provided by the OS expert in the verifier, by presenting a static analysis that checks whether a Bossa scheduling policy satisfies the OS requirements specified using the type system.
- We illustrate the use of the analysis on typical Bossa code.

The rest of this paper is organized as follows. Section 2 presents an overview of our approach and instantiates this approach for the Bossa framework. Section 3 presents the type system used in Bossa and the corresponding analysis. Section 4 illustrates the various features of the analysis on a realistic example. Finally, Section 5 describes related work and Section 6 concludes.

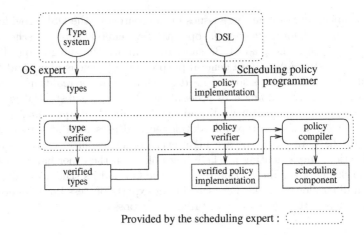

Fig. 1. Verification and compilation tools

2   DSL Design Approach

We first give an overview of our approach, and then instantiate it in the context of the Bossa framework. The languages and tools used in our approach are illustrated in Figure 1.

2.1   Methodology

Based on an analysis of the range of scheduling policies, the scheduling expert identifies the kinds of programming abstractions and properties of OS behavior that are relevant to the scheduling domain. He then designs a DSL incorporating the identified abstractions and codifies the range of properties in a type system. Having designed the language and the type system, the scheduling expert implements a verifier and compiler that are parameterized by type information. The verifier checks that the implementation of a scheduling policy satisfies the provided types, while the compiler uses type information to optimize the code generated to produce the scheduling component.

Each OS has its own properties and conventions. To make these apparent, the OS expert describes the interface that must be provided by the implementation of a scheduling policy and uses the type system to create types describing the expected behavior of each definition required by this interface. The OS expert then configures the verifier and compiler developed by the scheduling expert with this type information. The result is a verifier and compiler specific to the given OS. The types are also given as documentation to the scheduling policy programmer to guide scheduler development. Even though this approach implies that the resulting scheduling components are OS-specific, in practice there are substantial opportunities for code re-use between policy implementations for different OSes.

Because understanding OS behavior is difficult, we propose that the scheduling expert also provide the OS expert with a verifier to check basic properties of the types. Such a verifier may check, for example, that a complete set of types is provided and that the types satisfy certain properties generic to scheduling. Details of this verifier are out of the scope of this paper.

2.2 Scheduling Expertise

The design of the Bossa framework has been based on an extensive study of scheduling policies, both those found in commercial OSes and those developed for special needs, such as multimedia and real-time applications. A scheduling policy describes how to elect a new process for execution when requested to do so by the kernel. Whether a process is eligible for election depends on its current state (*i.e.*, running, ready to run, or blocked). Thus, a scheduling policy also typically specifies how to react to process state changes. Requests to elect a new process and process state changes can be viewed as *events*. The Bossa framework is organized around a set of *event notifications* that are generated by the kernel[1] and handled by a scheduling component.

In the role of the scheduling expert, we have designed the Bossa DSL and the type system for use within this framework. The Bossa DSL organizes the implementation of a scheduling policy as a collection of event handlers, of which one elects a new process and the others respond to process state changes. The types of the Bossa type system amount to pre- and post-conditions that describe the possible states of relevant processes when an event notification is generated and the allowed effects of the corresponding handler on these process states. Checking of these types ensures that each handler treats all possible input configurations and adjusts process states as required by the OS.

The Bossa DSL. The Bossa DSL provides facilities for declaring process states and associated data structures, for managing the association of processes to states, and for performing other kinds of relevant computation (*e.g.*, arithmetic). We illustrate the DSL using excerpts of a Bossa implementation of the Linux scheduling policy (Figure 2).

The process states used by the Linux policy are defined in lines 1–8 of Figure 2. Each state is associated with a *state class*, indicating the schedulability of the processes in the given state. The state class RUNNING describes the process that is currently running. The state class READY describes a process that is ready to run (runnable). The state class BLOCKED describes a process that is blocked, waiting for a resource. The state class TERMINATED describes a process that is terminating. Each state declaration also indicates whether a single variable (process) or a queue (queue) should be used to record the set of processes currently in the state. One state in the state class READY is designated as select, indicating that processes are elected for execution from this state. State classes

---

[1] A kernel must be prepared for use with Bossa by inserting these event notifications at the points of scheduling-related actions. We have addressed this issue elsewhere [1].

```
1   states = {                        10  On unblock.preemptive {
2     RUNNING running : process;       11    if (e.target in blocked) {
3     READY ready : select queue;      12      if ((!empty(running))
4     READY expired : queue;           13         && (e.target > running)) {
5     READY yield : process;           14        running => ready;
6     BLOCKED blocked : queue;         15      }
7     TERMINATED terminated;           16      e.target => ready;
8   }                                  17    }
9                                      18  }
```

Fig. 2. Extract of the Linux policy

Table 1. Code size of some Bossa schedulers

Process schedulers	Lines of code
The Linux 2.4 scheduling policy	201
Progress-based scheduling [21]	234
Lottery scheduling (one currency) [22]	128
Earliest-Deadline First	124
Rate Monotonic (RM)	134
RM + aperiodic processes (polling server)	262

describe the semantics of the declared states, and are crucial to the verification process, as described in Section 3.

The handler for the unblock.preemptive event is shown in lines 10-18 of Figure 2. This event is generated by the Bossa version of the Linux OS when a process unblocks and the scheduler is allowed to preempt the running process. Bossa event handlers are written using a syntax that amounts to a restricted version of C, but includes operators specific to the manipulation of process states. The unblock.preemptive handler first checks whether the unblocking process, referred to as the *target* process or e.target, is currently in the blocked state. If so, lines 12–15 determine whether some process is running, and if so, whether this running process should be preempted. These lines first test whether there is a process in the running state, using the Bossa primitive empty (line 12), and if so check whether the priority of the target process is greater than that of the running process (line 13). If both tests succeed, the state of the running process is changed to ready (line 14), indicating that the running process should be preempted. Finally, the state of the target process is also changed to ready (line 16), indicating that the target process is newly ready to run.

The Bossa DSL has been used to implement a variety of scheduling policies. Implementations are concise, as shown in Table 1. A grammar of the language and some example policy implementations can be found at the Bossa web site[2].

The Bossa Type System. The Bossa type system allows the OS expert to describe pre- and post-conditions on the behavior required by a particular OS, in a policy-independent way. Accordingly, types are expressed using state classes, rather

---

[2] http://www.emn.fr/x-info/bossa/

than the states defined by a specific policy implementation. In addition to the state classes used in state declarations, the state class NOWHERE is used to describe a process that is being created and thus not yet managed by the scheduler.

A type consists of a collection of rules having the form *input* → *output*, defined as follows:

Input configuration:	*input*	::=	$[in_1, \ldots, in_n]$
Input component:	*in*	::=	$[p_1,\ldots,p_n]$ in c_{in} | $[]$ = c_{in}
Input state classes	c_{in}	::=	RUNNING | READY | BLOCKED | NOWHERE
Output configuration:	*output*	::=	$[out_1, \ldots, out_n]$
Output component:	*out*	::=	$[p_1,\ldots,p_n]$ in c_{out} | $[p_1,\ldots,p_n]$ in $c_{out}!$ | $c_{out}!$
Output state classes	c_{out}	::=	RUNNING | READY | BLOCKED | TERMINATED
Process names:	*p*	::=	src | tgt | p1 | ... | pn

An input configuration describes possible process states on entering the handler and an output configuration describes process states required on exiting the handler. An input configuration can specify that specific processes are in a given state class ($[p_1,\ldots,p_n]$ in c_{in}) or that there are no processes in a given state class ($[]$ = c_{in}). Output configurations are similar, but $c_{out}!$ indicates that processes may change state within the given state class. The names src and tgt refer to the source[3] and target processes of the event, respectively. The names p1, ..., pn refer to arbitrary processes distinct from the source and target processes. State classes and process names cannot be duplicated in a configuration and only process names occurring in the input configuration can occur in the output configuration.

As an example, an OS expert might use the following type to describe the behavior of a naive unblock event handler:

```
[[tgt] in BLOCKED] -> [[tgt] in READY]
[[p] in RUNNING, [tgt] in BLOCKED] -> [[p,tgt] in READY]
```

The first rule indicates that the target process is initially blocked, and that the event handler should change the state of this process such that the policy subsequently considers the process to be runnable. No other state change is allowed. The second rule indicates that if there is currently some running process p, then the event handler can change the state of both the running process and the target process such that both processes are subsequently considered to be runnable. Again, no other state change is allowed.

The pseudo-parallelism introduced by interrupts must be accounted for when analyzing the interactions between event handlers. To describe possible run-time interactions between handlers, the type system includes automata to allow the OS expert to specify possible sequences of events. The transitions in these sequences are specified to be interruptible or uninterruptible. The type information also includes a list of the events that can occur during interrupts.

---

[3] An event has a source process if the originator of the event is a process other than the processes affected by the event (the target process). For example, the event corresponding to process creation has both a source and a target process.

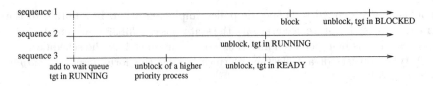

Fig. 3. Event sequences involving `unblock.preemptive`

2.3   OS Expertise

The OS expert identifies the interface and types particular to an OS that has been prepared for use with Bossa. We have created a version of Linux 2.4 for use with Bossa that uses the following 11 basic events: process creation, process termination, blocking, three variants of yielding, two variants of unblocking, clock tick, timer expiration, and process election [1]. The OS expert declares one type for each event.

In most cases, the types of the Linux events are intuitive. For example, the type of an unblocking event requires that a blocked process change from a state in the BLOCKED state class to a state in the READY state class. Nevertheless, the sequences of events that can occur due to interrupts in the Linux kernel imply that sometimes an event handler can receive processes that are not in the states expected by an intuitive description of the handler behavior. We illustrate this issue using the `unblock.preemptive` event. Some possible event sequences involving this event are shown in Figure 3. In the Linux kernel, a process blocks by first placing itself on a wait queue and then requesting to be blocked. A process can be unblocked as soon as it is on a wait queue. If the process has already blocked, as illustrated by the first sequence, then this process, *i.e.*, the target process from the point of view of the handler, is in a state in the BLOCKED state class, and the rules presented in Section 2.2 apply. If the process has not yet blocked, then it is normally in a state in the RUNNING state class, as illustrated by the second sequence, but may be in a state in the READY state class, *e.g.*, if it has been preempted by the unblocking of a higher priority process, as illustrated by the third sequence. In the latter two cases the process should remain in its current state. The complete type for `unblock.preemptive` is thus as follows:

```
[[tgt] in BLOCKED] -> [[tgt] in READY]
[[p] in RUNNING, [tgt] in BLOCKED] -> [[p,tgt] in READY]
[[tgt] in RUNNING] -> []
[[tgt] in READY] -> []
```

The Bossa type verifier (Figure 1) checks that this type is consistent with the declared event sequences.

The considerations that go into the development of the types for `unblock.-preemptive` require a deep understanding of a range of Linux mechanisms (blocking, interrupts, *etc.*). A correct policy implementation can, however, often be constructed based on only the knowledge of what cases should be treated and what transitions are allowed. This information is made available to the programmer by the inclusion of the types in the Bossa documentation. Even when more information about kernel behavior is needed to define an event handler, the types are still useful in signaling the possibility of unexpected behavior.

3   Static Analysis for Bossa

The Bossa verifier connects a policy implemented using the DSL provided by the scheduling expert to the types provided by the OS expert. Specifically, the verifier checks that the policy implementation satisfies the types, and is thus coherent with the behavior of the target OS. We first present the semantics of a core subset of the DSL and then present the type checking analysis used by the verifier. This analysis relies critically on features of the DSL that make process-state properties explicit, such as the classification of process states into state classes and the use of explicit state names in operations that test state contents and implement state changes.

3.1   Semantics of the Bossa DSL

The types provided by the OS expert describe changes in process states. We thus consider a core subset of the Bossa DSL that focuses on the operations that relate to the states of processes. The syntax of this core language is as follows:

Statements: $stmt ::= exp \Rightarrow state \mid \texttt{foreach} \ (\ x \ \texttt{in} \ state \ ) \ stmt$
                          $\mid \texttt{if} \ (\ bexp \ ) \ stmt_1 \ \texttt{else} \ stmt_2 \mid \{stmt_1 \ ; \ stmt_2\} \mid \{ \ \}$
Process expressions: $exp ::= \texttt{e.source} \mid \texttt{e.target} \mid x \mid state \mid \texttt{select()}$
Boolean expressions: $bexp ::= \texttt{empty}(state) \mid exp \ \texttt{in} \ state \mid exp_1 > exp_2$

The only constructs not previously presented are e.source, which refers to the source process, foreach, which iterates over the set of processes in a given state, and select(), which elects the highest priority process in the state designated as sorted.

The big-step operational semantics [18] of this language is given in Figure 4. The semantics is defined in terms of the following judgments:

Statements: $\phi, \sigma \vdash stmt \rightarrow \sigma'$
Process expressions: $\phi, \sigma \vdash exp \rightarrow process$
Boolean expressions: $\phi, \sigma \vdash bexp \rightarrow bool$

An auxiliary judgment $\pi, \phi, \sigma \vdash^x stmt \rightarrow \sigma$ is used to control the iteration in the semantics of foreach. These judgments refer to the following semantic objects:

Variable environment: $\phi : (var \cup \{\texttt{e.source}, \texttt{e.target}\}) \rightarrow process$
State environment: $\sigma, \sigma' : state \rightarrow \mathcal{P}(process)$
Process: $process : process\_id \times priority$

The set of processes, $process$, is finite. A state environment σ partitions the set of processes, i.e., a process cannot be in more than one state at a time. Each

Statements

$$\text{state\_info}(state) = \text{queue} \lor \sigma(state) = \emptyset$$

$$\frac{\phi, \sigma \vdash exp \to p \quad \sigma^{-1}(p) = pstate \quad \sigma' = \sigma[pstate \mapsto \sigma(pstate) - \{p\}] \quad \phi, \sigma \vdash \{\ \} \to \sigma}{\phi, \sigma \vdash exp \implies state \to \sigma'[state \mapsto \sigma'(state) \cup \{p\}]}$$

$$\frac{\sigma(state) = \pi \quad \pi, \phi, \sigma \vdash^x stmt \to \sigma'}{\phi, \sigma \vdash \texttt{foreach} \ (\ x \ \texttt{in} \ state\ )\ stmt \to \sigma'} \qquad \emptyset, \phi, \sigma \vdash^x stmt \to \sigma \qquad \frac{p \in \pi \quad \phi[x \to p], \sigma \vdash stmt \to \sigma' \quad \pi - \{p\}, \phi, \sigma' \vdash^x stmt \to \sigma''}{\pi, \phi, \sigma \vdash^x stmt \to \sigma''}$$

$$\frac{\phi, \sigma \vdash bexp \to true \quad \phi, \sigma \vdash stmt_1 \to \sigma'}{\phi, \sigma \vdash \texttt{if} \ (\ bexp\ )\ stmt_1 \ \texttt{else} \ stmt_2 \to \sigma'} \qquad \frac{\phi, \sigma \vdash bexp \to false \quad \phi, \sigma \vdash stmt_2 \to \sigma'}{\phi, \sigma \vdash \texttt{if} \ (\ bexp\ )\ stmt_1 \ \texttt{else} \ stmt_2 \to \sigma'}$$

$$\frac{\phi, \sigma \vdash stmt_1 \to \sigma_1 \quad \phi, \sigma_1 \vdash stmt_2 \to \sigma_2}{\phi, \sigma \vdash \{stmt_1 \ ; \ stmt_2\} \to \sigma_2}$$

Process expressions

$$\phi, \sigma \vdash \texttt{e.target} \to \phi(\texttt{e.target})$$
$$\phi, \sigma \vdash \texttt{e.source} \to \phi(\texttt{e.source})$$
$$\qquad \phi, \sigma \vdash x \to \phi(x) \qquad \frac{\text{state\_info}(state) = \text{process} \quad \sigma(state) = \{p\}}{\phi, \sigma \vdash state \to p}$$

$$\frac{\sigma(s) = \pi \quad prio = \max\{prio' \mid (\_, prio') \in \pi\} \quad (id, prio) \in \pi}{\phi, \sigma \vdash \texttt{select}() \to (id, prio)} \ (s \ \text{is the state designated as} \ \texttt{select})$$

Boolean expressions

$$\phi, \sigma \vdash \texttt{empty}(state)$$
$$\to \sigma(state) = \emptyset$$
$$\qquad \frac{\phi, \sigma \vdash exp \to p}{\phi, \sigma \vdash exp \ \texttt{in} \ state \to p \in \sigma(state)} \qquad \frac{\phi, \sigma \vdash exp_1 \to (id_1, prio_1) \quad \phi, \sigma \vdash exp_2 \to (id_2, prio_2)}{\phi, \sigma \vdash exp_1 > exp_2 \to prio_1 > prio_2}$$

Fig. 4. Semantics of a core subset of Bossa

process is associated with a unique identifier *process_id* and a priority drawn from some totally ordered domain. By a slight abuse of notation, we use σ^{-1} to designate a function that maps a process to its current state as defined by σ. The semantics also uses the function state_info(*state*), which returns the kind of data structure (queue or process variable) implementing *state*.

3.2   Analysis of Bossa Programs

The analysis performed by the Bossa verifier is based on a number of well-known dataflow-analysis techniques, including inferring information from conditional-test expressions, not merging the results of analyzing conditional branches, and maintaining a precise representation of the contents of data structures. In the context of Bossa, the simple program structure (*e.g.*, the absence of function calls) and the use of domain-specific constructs imply that these techniques can be used more effectively than is typically possible in a general-purpose language. The result is an analysis that is precise enough to identify policy implementations that satisfy the types provided by the OS expert, while detecting implementations that violate OS requirements.

The analysis is inter-procedural (*i.e.*, inter-handler) following a graph of possible execution paths through the policy implementation derived from the event sequences given by the OS expert. Each step in the analysis considers a pair of a handler and an abstract state environment that has not previously been explored. The analysis simulates the behavior of the handler on the state environment, producing a set of possible resulting state environments. These environments are then checked against the type of the handler. If the type is satisfied, then all possible successor handlers are paired with each of the resulting state environments, and pairs that have not been considered previously are added to the set of pairs to explore.

The analysis manipulates a set of abstract values. We first present these abstract values, then present some useful functions, and finally present the analysis rules. The analysis has been implemented in the Bossa verifier.

Abstract Values. The information contained in the abstract values is determined by the kinds of properties described by the types. Types describe the starting and ending state classes of various processes, notably the source and target processes, as well as the allowed transitions between state classes and within the states of a state class. Accordingly, the abstract values keep track of the state of the source process and the state of the target process and permit to determine both the original and current state of each process.

A *process description*, *pd*, is a pair of one of the forms (src, *state*), (tgt, *state*), (x, *state*), (x, *class*), or (x, $\top$), where src, tgt, and x are constants that represent the source, target, and any other process, respectively. Process descriptions are ordered as follows:

$$(\mathsf{src}, state), (\mathsf{tgt}, state) \sqsubseteq (\mathsf{x}, state) \sqsubseteq (\mathsf{x}, class) \sqsubseteq (\mathsf{x}, \top)$$

(x, *state*) $\sqsubseteq$ (x, *class*) only holds if *state* was declared to be in the state class *class*. If the second component is the name of a state or state class, it is the state or state class of the process at the start of the handler. If this component is $\top$, the state of the process at the start of the handler is unknown (the starting state of the source or target process is always known). A process description can either represent a specific process or one of a set of possible processes. Those of the form (src, *state*) or (tgt, *state*), or of the form (x, *state*) where *state* is represented as a process variable, can only represent a single process. Such a process description is said to be *unique*. The predicate unique(*pd*) is true only for these process descriptions.

The analysis is defined in terms of an abstract state environment that associates with each state a *contents description*, *cd* of the form [] or ⟨*must, may*⟩. The description [] indicates that it is known that there are no processes in the state. A description ⟨*must, may*⟩ describes the set of processes in a state using "must" and "may" information, analogous to that used in alias analysis [15]. Specifically, *must* is a set of process descriptions of which each element represents a distinct process that is known to be in the state, and *may* is a set of process descriptions that describes a safe approximation (superset) of all processes that may be in the state. Redundant information is not allowed in may information; for example, may information can contain only one of (tgt, *state*) and (x, *state*). For convenience, the functions must and may return the corresponding components of a contents description of the form ⟨*must, may*⟩, and return ∅ for the [] contents description. The maintaining of both must and may information often enables the analysis to return a precise result (*i.e.*, *true* or *false*) as the result of analyzing the domain-specific boolean expressions empty(*exp*) and *exp* in *state*.

The ordering on contents descriptions is defined as follows:

$$[] \sqsubseteq [] \qquad \dfrac{must_2 = \{pd'_1, \ldots, pd'_n\} \quad \exists (pd_1, \ldots, pd_n) \in \mathsf{choose}(must_1, n).\forall i.pd_i \sqsubseteq pd'_i}{\forall pd \in may_1.\exists pd' \in may_2.pd \sqsubseteq pd'}$$
$$[] \sqsubseteq \langle \emptyset, may \rangle \qquad \overline{\langle must_1, may_1 \rangle \sqsubseteq \langle must_2, may_2 \rangle}$$

The function $\mathsf{choose}(\pi, n)$ returns all possible tuples of n distinct elements of π. Descriptions lower in the ordering are more informative than those higher in the ordering. This ordering is a partial order and extends pointwise to state environments. Based on this ordering, an upper bound of two contents descriptions is computed as follows. $[\,]\sqcup[\,]=[\,]$. Otherwise $cd_1 \sqcup cd_2 = \langle \alpha \cup \beta \cup \gamma \cup \delta, \mathsf{may}(cd_1) \uplus \mathsf{may}(cd_2) \rangle$ where α, β, γ, δ, and $\uplus$ are defined as follows:

$$must_1 = \mathsf{must}(cd_1), \quad must_2 = \mathsf{must}(cd_2),$$
$$must_1' = \{(\mathsf{x}, s) \mid (p, s) \in must_1 - must_2\}, \quad must_2' = \{(\mathsf{x}, s) \mid (p, s) \in must_2 - must_1\},$$
$$must_1'' = \{(\mathsf{x}, c) \mid (\mathsf{x}, s) \in must_1' - must_2' \wedge \text{state } s \text{ in state class } c\},$$
$$must_2'' = \{(\mathsf{x}, c) \mid (\mathsf{x}, s) \in must_2' - must_1' \wedge \text{state } s \text{ in state class } c\},$$
$$\alpha = must_1 \cap must_2, \quad \beta = must_1' \cap must_2', \quad \gamma = must_1'' \cap must_2''$$
$$\delta = \{(\mathsf{x}, \top)\}, \text{ if } |\alpha \cup \beta| < \min(|\, must_1 \,|, |\, must_2 \,|). \text{ Otherwise, } \emptyset.$$
$$\pi_1 \uplus \pi_2 = \{pd \mid pd \in \pi_1 \cup \pi_2 \wedge \forall pd' \in ((\pi_1 \cup \pi_2) - \{pd\}).pd' \not\sqsupseteq pd\}$$

Some Useful Functions. The main purpose of the analysis is to track changes in process states. For this, the analysis uses two key functions, add and remove, that add a process description to the information known about a state and remove a process description from the information known about a state, respectively, in some abstract state environment Σ, mapping states to contents descriptions.

There are two cases in the definition of add, depending on whether the process description is unique:

$$\text{if } \mathsf{unique}(pd), must = \mathsf{must}(\Sigma(state)), may = \mathsf{may}(\Sigma(state)):$$
$$\mathsf{add}(pd, state, \Sigma) = \Sigma(\{state \mapsto \langle \{pd\} \cup must, \{pd\} \uplus may \rangle \}$$
$$\cup \{state' \mapsto \langle must', may' - \{pd\}\rangle \mid$$
$$state' \neq state \wedge \Sigma(state') = \langle must', may'\rangle\})$$

$$\text{if } \neg\mathsf{unique}(pd), must = \mathsf{must}(\Sigma(state)), may = \mathsf{may}(\Sigma(state)):$$
$$\mathsf{add}(pd, state, \Sigma) = \Sigma[state \mapsto \langle \{pd\} \cup must, \{pd\} \uplus may \rangle]$$

In both cases, the process description is added to the must and may information (in the latter case, the use of $\uplus$ implies that the process description is only added if it is not already described by some process description in the may information). If the process description is unique, then adding it to the must information of the current state implies that it cannot be in any other state. It is an invariant of the analysis that when add is used, if the process description is unique, it cannot be in the must information of any state. It can, however, be part of the may information, due to the use of the $\sqcup$ operation. The add operation thus removes the process description from the may information of the other states.

There are three cases in the definition of remove, depending on whether the process description is unique, and if so depending on the implementation of the state, if any, for which the process description occurs in the must information:

$$\frac{\mathsf{unique}(pd) \quad \Sigma(state) = \langle must, may \rangle \quad pd \in must \quad state\_info(state) = \mathsf{queue}}{\mathsf{remove}(pd, \Sigma) = (\{state\}, \Sigma[state \mapsto \langle must - \{pd\}, may \rangle])}$$

$$\frac{\mathsf{unique}(pd) \quad \Sigma(state) = \langle must, may \rangle \quad pd \in must \quad state\_info(state) = \mathsf{process}}{\mathsf{remove}(pd, \Sigma) = (\{state\}, \Sigma[state \mapsto [\,]])}$$

$$\frac{\begin{array}{c}\neg \mathsf{unique}(pd) \vee \forall state.pd \notin \mathsf{must}(\Sigma(state)) \\ s = \{state \mid \exists pd' \in \alpha(pd).pd' \in \mathsf{may}(\Sigma(state))\}\end{array}}{\mathsf{remove}(pd, \Sigma) = (s, \Sigma\{state \mapsto \langle \mathsf{must}(\Sigma(state)) - \alpha(pd), \mathsf{may}(\Sigma(state))\rangle \mid state \in s\})}$$

$$\alpha(pd) = \{pd' \mid pd \sqsubseteq pd' \vee pd' \sqsubseteq pd\}$$

This function returns both a set of states in which the process represented by the process description pd may occur, and a state environment in which any possible representation of this process has been removed from the must information. In the first two rules, because the process description is unique and occurs in must information, we know the state of the associated process. If this state is implemented as a queue, then the process description is simply removed from the must information in the resulting state environment. If this state is implemented as a process variable, then removing the process makes the state empty. Thus, the information associated with the state is replaced by [ ]. In the final rule, either the process description is not unique, or it does not occur in any must information. In this case, the process may occur in any state whose may information contains a process description related to the given process description, as computed using α. All elements of $\alpha(pd)$ are removed from the must information of such states. All such states are returned as the set of possible states of the process.

Analysis Rules. The analysis simulates the execution of a Bossa handler with respect to variable and state environments described in terms of process descriptions and contents descriptions, respectively. The result of the analysis is a set of state environments, which are then checked against the type of the handler to determine whether the handler satisfies OS requirements. The analysis rules are shown in Figure 5 and are defined using the following judgments:

$$\begin{array}{ll}\text{Statements:} & \Phi, \Sigma \vdash_{\mathsf{s}} stmt : S \\ \text{Process expressions:} & \Phi, \Sigma \vdash_{\mathsf{e}} exp : (pd, s, \Sigma') \\ \text{Boolean expressions:} & \Phi, \Sigma \vdash_{\mathsf{b}} bexp : bool^+\end{array}$$

The environments Φ and Σ and the results S, s, and $bool^+$ are defined as:

$$\begin{array}{lll}\Phi : (var \cup \{\mathsf{e.source, e.target}\}) \rightarrow pd & S : \mathcal{P}(state \rightarrow cd) & s : \mathcal{P}(state) \\ \Sigma, \Sigma' : state \rightarrow cd & bool^+ : bool + ((state \rightarrow cd) \times (state \rightarrow cd))\end{array}$$

The initial variable environment Φ contains information about the source and target process, derived from the initial state environment under consideration.

Analysis of a statement returns a set of state environments, representing the effect on process states of the various execution paths through the statement. To increase precision, the analysis keeps the results of analyzing individual conditional branches separate, rather than computing a single environment approximating their different effects. This degree of precision is tractable because of the simple structure of Bossa handlers. Analysis of a process expression returns a process description pd describing the value of the expression, a set s of states representing a safe approximation (superset) of the state of this process, and a state environment Σ' that is a safe approximation of the effect of removing the process from its current state. This information is used in the analysis of

Statements

$$\frac{\Phi, \Sigma \vdash_e exp : (pd, s, \Sigma') \quad state\_info(state) = queue \vee \Sigma'(state) = [] \quad pd \notin must(\Sigma'(state))}{\Phi, \Sigma \vdash_s exp \Rightarrow state : \{add(pd, state, \Sigma')\}} \quad (1)$$

$$\frac{\Phi, \Sigma \vdash_e exp : (pd, s, \Sigma') \quad state\_info(state) = queue \vee \Sigma'(state) = [] \quad pd \in must(\Sigma'(state))}{pd' = min(\{pd' \mid pd' \in (\alpha(pd)) \wedge pd' \sqsupseteq pd \wedge (pd' \notin must(\Sigma'(state)) \vee pd' = (x, \top))\})}{\Phi, \Sigma \vdash_s exp \Rightarrow state : \{\Sigma'[state \mapsto \langle\{pd'\} \cup must(\Sigma'(state)), \{pd\} \uplus may(\Sigma'(state))\rangle]\}} \quad (2)$$

$$\frac{\Phi[x \mapsto \sqcup may(\Sigma(state))], \Sigma \sqcup (\sqcup S) \vdash_s stmt : S}{\Phi, \Sigma \vdash_s \text{foreach} (x \text{ in } state) stmt : S \sqcup \{\Sigma\}} \quad (3) \qquad \Phi, \Sigma \vdash_s \{ \} : \{\Sigma\} \quad (4)$$

$$\frac{\Phi, \Sigma \vdash_b bexp : true \quad \Phi, \Sigma \vdash_s stmt_1 : S}{\Phi, \Sigma \vdash_s \text{if} (bexp) stmt_1 \text{ else } stmt_2 : S} \quad (5) \qquad \frac{\Phi, \Sigma \vdash_b bexp : false \quad \Phi, \Sigma \vdash_s stmt_2 : S}{\Phi, \Sigma \vdash_s \text{if} (bexp) stmt_1 \text{ else } stmt_2 : S} \quad (6)$$

$$\frac{\Phi, \Sigma \vdash_b bexp : \langle trueEnv, falseEnv \rangle}{\Phi, trueEnv \vdash_s stmt_1 : S_1 \quad \Phi, falseEnv \vdash_s stmt_2 : S_2}{\Phi, \Sigma \vdash_s \text{if} (bexp) stmt_1 \text{ else } stmt_2 : S_1 \sqcup S_2} \quad (7) \qquad \frac{\Phi, \Sigma \vdash_s stmt_1 : S_1}{S_2 = \bigcup\{S \mid \Sigma' \in S_1 \wedge \Phi, \Sigma' \vdash_s stmt_2 : S\}}{\Phi, \Sigma \vdash_s \{stmt_1 ; stmt_2\} : S_2} \quad (8)$$

Process expressions

$$\frac{\Phi(e.source) = pd \quad (s, \Sigma') = remove(pd, \Sigma)}{\Phi, \Sigma \vdash_e e.source : (pd, s, \Sigma')} \quad (9) \qquad \frac{\Phi(e.target) = pd \quad (s, \Sigma') = remove(pd, \Sigma)}{\Phi, \Sigma \vdash_e e.target : (pd, s, \Sigma')} \quad (10)$$

$$\frac{\Phi(x) = pd \quad (s, \Sigma') = remove(pd, \Sigma)}{\Phi, \Sigma \vdash_e x : (pd, s, \Sigma')} \quad (11) \qquad \frac{state\_info(state) = process \quad \Sigma(state) = \langle\{pd\}, may\rangle}{\Phi, \Sigma \vdash_e state : (pd, \{state\}, \Sigma[state \mapsto []])} \quad (12)$$

$$\frac{\Sigma(s) = \langle must, may \rangle \quad may \neq \emptyset \quad |must| \leq 1}{\Phi, \Sigma \vdash_e \text{select}() : (\sqcup may, \{s\}, \Sigma[s \mapsto \langle \emptyset, may \rangle])} \quad (13) \qquad \frac{\Sigma(s) = \langle must, may \rangle \quad may \neq \emptyset \quad |must| > 1}{\Phi, \Sigma \vdash_e \text{select}() : (\sqcup may, \{s\},}{\Sigma[s \mapsto \langle \emptyset, \emptyset \rangle])} \quad (14)$$

In the above two rules, s is the state designated as select   add

Boolean expressions

$$\frac{\Sigma(state) = []}{\Phi, \Sigma \vdash_b \text{empty}(state) : true} \quad (15) \qquad \frac{\Sigma(state) = \langle\{pd_1, \dots, pd_n\}, may\rangle \quad n \neq 0}{\Phi, \Sigma \vdash_b \text{empty}(state) : false} \quad (16)$$

$$\frac{\Sigma(state) = \langle \emptyset, may \rangle}{\Phi, \Sigma \vdash_b \text{empty}(state) : \langle \Sigma[state \mapsto []], add(\sqcup may, state, \Sigma) \rangle} \quad (17)$$

$$\frac{\Phi, \Sigma \vdash_e exp_1 : (pd_1, s_1, \Sigma_1)}{\Phi, \Sigma \vdash_e exp_2 : (pd_2, s_2, \Sigma_2)}{\Phi, \Sigma \vdash_b exp_1 > exp_2 : \langle \Sigma, \Sigma \rangle} \quad (18) \qquad \frac{\Phi, \Sigma \vdash_e exp : (pd, s, \Sigma')}{unique(pd)}{pd \in must(\Sigma(state))}{\Phi, \Sigma \vdash_b exp \text{ in } state : true} \quad (19) \qquad \frac{\Phi, \Sigma \vdash_e exp : (pd, s, \Sigma')}{state \notin s}{\Phi, \Sigma \vdash_b exp \text{ in } state : false} \quad (20)$$

$$\frac{\Phi, \Sigma \vdash_e exp : (pd, s, \Sigma') \quad \forall pd' \in must(\Sigma(state)).pd' \notin \alpha(pd)}{\Phi, \Sigma \vdash_b exp \text{ in } state : \langle add(pd, state, \Sigma), \Sigma \rangle} \quad (21) \qquad \frac{\Phi, \Sigma \vdash_e exp : (pd, s, \Sigma')}{\Phi, \Sigma \vdash_b exp \text{ in } state : \langle \Sigma, \Sigma \rangle} \quad (22)$$

Rules (21) and (22) only apply if no preceding rule applies.

Auxiliary functions: unique, must, may, $\uplus$, α, add, and remove are defined in Section 3.2.

Fig. 5. Analysis rules for a core subset of Bossa

an **in** expression and in the analysis of a state-change statement. Analysis of a boolean expression returns either a boolean value or a pair of state environments. In the latter case, the pair components represent the current state environment enhanced with information derived from the assumption that the boolean expression is true or false, respectively. The domain-specific boolean expressions empty(*state*) and *exp* **in** *state* often enable useful information to be incorporated into these environments, which are used in the analysis of a conditional statement. The relationship between the analysis and the semantics is formalized in the appendix.

4   Analysis Example

The analysis must be precise enough to be able to both accept correct handlers and give useful feedback for incorrect handlers. To illustrate the behavior of the Bossa analysis, we consider the following example:

```
1   On unblock.preemptive {
2     if (empty(running)) { }
3     else running => ready;
4     e.target => ready;
5   }
```

This handler is typical in its size, structure, and use of domain-specific constructs. Nevertheless, it is incorrect for the Linux OS because it does not take into account the possibility that the target process might not be blocked.

We consider the analysis of this handler with respect to a state environment in which the target process is initially in the **ready** state and no information is known about the set of processes in the other states. For conciseness, we only include the **running**, **ready**, and **blocked** states, as only these states are relevant to the handler. The initial state environment is thus represented as follows:

$$\{\texttt{running} \mapsto \langle \emptyset, \{(\mathsf{x}, \texttt{running})\}\rangle, \texttt{ready} \mapsto \langle \{(\texttt{tgt}, \texttt{ready})\}, \{(\mathsf{x}, \texttt{ready})\}\rangle,$$
$$\texttt{blocked} \mapsto \langle \emptyset, \{(\mathsf{x}, \texttt{blocked})\}\rangle\}$$

In this state environment, the must information $\{(\texttt{tgt}, \texttt{ready})\}$ for **ready** indicates that the target process is initially in this state, and the must information $\emptyset$ for the other states indicates that nothing is known about their contents. In each case, the may information indicates that some process x may be in the given state and that any such process is initially in the given state itself. Figure 6 illustrates the steps in the analysis of the handler with respect to this state environment.

The analysis begins by analyzing the test expression, empty(running) (line 2), of the initial conditional. At this point the contents description associated with **running** is $\langle \emptyset, \{(\mathsf{x}, \texttt{running})\}\rangle$, implying that this state is neither known to be empty, nor known to be non-empty. Rule (7) is used, which creates refined state environments, B and C in Figure 6, describing the cases where the state is empty and non-empty. These environments will be used in the analysis of the then and else branches of the conditional, respectively.

The analysis of the then branch, {} (line 2), is trivial, and simply returns the current state environment B. The analysis of the else branch, running => ready (line 3), uses the first state-transition rule, rule (1). This rule first analyzes the expression **running**, obtaining as the first component of the result the process description pd associated with the process in this state, and as the third component of the result a state environment Σ' describing the effect of removing this process from its current state. The result of analyzing the entire statement is then the state environment C obtained by adding the representation pd of the process to its new state **ready** in the state environment Σ'.

Because the value of the test expression empty(running) could not be determined, the result of analyzing the conditional (lines 2-3) is the union of the sets of the state environments resulting from the analysis of the branches, according to rule (7). The rule for sequence statements, rule (8), implies that the next statement of the handler, e.target => ready (line 4) is analyzed with respect to each of these environments, D and E, individually. The analysis proceeds similarly to that of running => ready, and produces the two state environments, F and G, shown at the bottom of Figure 6.

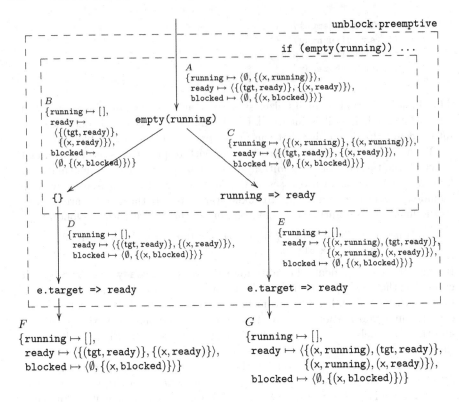

Fig. 6. Steps in the analysis of the `unblock.preemptive` handler

The final step is to compare the two resulting state environments to the type of the event. As described in Section 2.3, the type of `unblock.preemptive` for Linux 2.4 is:

```
[[tgt] in BLOCKED] -> [[tgt] in READY]
[[p] in RUNNING, [tgt] in BLOCKED] -> [[p,tgt] in READY]
[[tgt] in RUNNING] -> []
[[tgt] in READY] -> []
```

We first consider the output state environment F:

$$\{\text{running} \mapsto [], \text{ready} \mapsto \langle\{(\text{tgt}, \text{ready})\}, \{(\text{x}, \text{ready})\}\rangle,$$
$$\text{blocked} \mapsto \langle\emptyset, \{(\text{x}, \text{blocked})\}\rangle\}$$

To match this state environment against the type rules, the verifier must determine the starting and ending state of each process. The starting state of a process is stored in the second component of the associated process description. Thus, in environment F, the starting state of the target process is **ready**. The ending state of a process is indicated by the state that is mapped to the contents description containing the given process. Thus, in environment F, the target process ends up in the **ready** state. Other state changes are indicated by the must and may information associated with each state. In environment F, the may information associated with each state contains only process descriptions originating in the state itself. Thus, we conclude that the handler does not change the state of any process. The state environment is thus compatible with the type rule [tgt in READY] -> [].

We next consider the output state environment G:

$$\{\text{running} \mapsto [\,], \text{ready} \mapsto \langle\{(\text{x}, \text{running}), (\text{tgt}, \text{ready})\}, \{(\text{x}, \text{running}), (\text{x}, \text{ready})\}\rangle,$$
$$\text{blocked} \mapsto \langle\emptyset, \{(\text{x}, \text{blocked})\}\rangle\}$$

This environment indicates that both the process initially in the **running** state and the process initially in the **ready** state end up in the **ready** state. This behavior is not described by any of the type rules, which require that if the running process is preempted, then the target process is initially in a state of the **BLOCKED** state class. The policy is thus rejected by the Bossa verifier.

The problem with the given handler implementation is that it preempts the running process regardless of the state of the target process, whereas the type only allows preemption when the target process is initially in a state of the **BLOCKED** state class. Indeed, a programmer might write such a handler on the assumption that the target process is always initially blocked, which, in the absence of detailed information about the kernel, is a natural assumption. The type of the event, however, clearly shows that the **RUNNING** and **READY** state classes must be taken into account. A correct version of the handler is:

```
On unblock.preemptive {
    if (tgt in blocked) {
        if (empty(running)) { }
        else running => ready;
        e.target => ready;
    }
}
```

Analysis of this handler yields state environments that satisfy the type of **unblock.preemptive**.

5   Related Work

Recently, there has been increasing interest in compile-time error detection in the context of OS code. CCured [17], Cyclone [12] and Splint [10] check C programs for common programming errors, such as invalid pointer references, relying to a varying degree on user annotations. These approaches provide little or no support for checking domain-specific properties. Meta-level Compilation [9] checks properties that can be described using an extended automata language, and has been used to find many bugs in OS code. Nevertheless, this approach provides only bug finding; it does not guarantee satisfaction of the checked property. The SLAM model checker has been used to verify properties of device driver code [2].

The effectiveness of all of these strategies depends on the will of the programmer to follow anticipated (or inferred, in the case of Meta-level Compilation [8]) coding conventions. A DSL, on the other hand, restricts the programmer to a limited set of abstractions, thus making feasible more precise verifications.

The SPIN extensible operating system [4] addresses the need to check the safety of OS extensions by requiring that extensions be implemented using a variant of Modula-3, which is a type safe language. Nevertheless, this approach only suffices for properties that can be encoded using the general-purpose Modula-3 types. In particular, there is no framework for declaring and checking high-level domain-specific properties, as we have proposed here.

Numerous DSLs exploit the use of high-level domain-specific constructs to provide verification of domain-specific properties. We present a few examples. Devil is a language for implementing the hardware interaction code in a device driver. The Devil compiler verifies properties of the internal consistency of the Devil code; these checks have been shown to drastically reduce the chance of runtime errors [19]. Nevertheless, there is no verification of the relationship between a Devil specification and the target OS. Several approaches, including Teapot [6], Promela++ [3], and ESP [13], have combined DSLs with model checking to check algorithmic properties, such as liveness. Our focus is on easing the integration of DSL program with a target system rather than on algorithmic properties of the DSL program itself. The design of the Apostle language for parallel discrete event simulation recognizes the importance of connecting DSL constructs to specific type and effect information [5]. Again this information is used to check algorithmic properties.

The Bossa DSL is a stand-alone language, with its own syntax, semantics, parser, verifier, and compiler. An *embedded DSL*, on the other hand, is a controlled extension of an existing language, allowing reuse of host-language processing tools and enabling the mixing of the DSL with host language features [11]. Traditionally, an embedded DSL is simply a library, where constraints of the host language, such as type constraints, ensure that library constructs are used in a consistent, language-like manner. In this variant, the only verification that is possible is verification of properties that can be encoded in a way that they are checked by the host language. It seems awkward, if not impossible, to express high-level domain-specific properties in this setting. In another variant, an embedded DSL is implemented via macros that translate DSL constructs into the host language [20]. These macros can allow host language constructs to appear at specific places in a DSL program giving a controlled combination of the host language and the DSL. Our approach is directly applicable to this setting, as the macro expander can perform verification as well as translation. Nevertheless, if host language constructs are allowed, parts of the DSL program cannot be verified, which is not desirable in a domain such as process scheduling that has stringent safety requirements.

6   Conclusion

Extending an existing OS with new scheduling strategies is a difficult task, but one that is essential to providing good performance to many emerging applications. In this paper, we have presented the design of a DSL for scheduling and a type-based approach to expressing and checking OS requirements on a scheduling component. By making OS conventions explicit to both the verifier and the scheduling policy programmer, this approach reduces the expertise needed to extend an OS with new scheduling components, enabling programmers to address the needs of applications with specific scheduling requirements.

In future work, we plan to extend this approach to other OS services individually and in combination. An approach that includes multiple OS services could be useful in the context of embedded systems, where for example energy constraints require specific management strategies for multiple resources. Such cooperating extensions must take into account more complex interactions than extensions of a single functionality, making an approach for describing OS requirements even more important.

Acknowledgments. We thank Mads Sig Ager, Olivier Danvy and Henning Korsholm Rohde for comments on this paper. This work was supported in part by a Microsoft Embedded research grant and by ACI CORSS. Anne-Françoise Le Meur was supported by a postdoc fellowship from the Danish Research Agency.

Availability. A grammar of the complete Bossa language, the Bossa compiler and verifier, a run-time system for Linux, and numerous Bossa scheduling policy implementations are available at `http://www.emn.fr/x-info/bossa`.

References

1. R. A. Åberg, J. L. Lawall, M. Südholt, G. Muller, and A.-F. Le Meur. On the automatic evolution of an os kernel using temporal logic and aop. In *Proceedings of the 18th IEEE International Conference on Automated Software Engineering (ASE 2003)*, pages 196–204, Montreal, Canada, Oct. 2003. IEEE Computer Society Press.
2. T. Ball and S. K. Rajamani. Automatically validating temporal safety properties of interfaces. In *Model Checking Software, 8th International SPIN Workshop*, volume 2057 of *Lecture Notes in Computer Science*, pages 103–122, Toronto, Canada, May 2001.
3. A. Basu, M. Hayden, G. Morrisett, and T. von Eicken. A language-based approach to protocol construction. In *Proceedings of the ACM SIGPLAN Workshop on Domain Specific Languages*, Paris, France, Jan. 1997.
4. B. Bershad, S. Savage, P. Pardyak, E. Gün Sirer, M. Fiuczynski, D. Becker, C. Chambers, and S. Eggers. Extensibility, safety and performance in the SPIN operating system. In *Proceedings of the 15th ACM Symposium on Operating Systems Principles*, pages 267–283, Copper Mountain Resort, CO, USA, Dec. 1995. ACM Operating Systems Reviews, 29(5), ACM Press.
5. D. Bruce. What makes a good domain-specific language? APOSTLE, and its approach to parallel discrete event simulation. In *Proceedings of the ACM SIGPLAN Workshop on Domain Specific Languages*, pages 17–35, Paris, France, Jan. 1997.

6. S. Chandra, B. Richards, and J. Larus. Teapot: Language support for writing memory coherence protocols. In *Proceedings of the ACM SIGPLAN'96 Conference on Programming Language Design and Implementation*, pages 237–248, 1996.

7. C. Consel and R. Marlet. Architecturing software using a methodology for language development. In C. Palamidessi, H. Glaser, and K. Meinke, editors, *Proceedings of the 10th International Symposium on Programming Language Implementation and Logic Programming*, volume 1490 of *Lecture Notes in Computer Science*, pages 170–194, Pisa, Italy, Sept. 1998.

8. A. Engler, D. Yu, S. Hallem, A. Chou, and B. Chelf. Bugs as deviant behavior: A general approach to inferring errors in systems code. In *Proceedings of the 18th ACM Symposium on Operating Systems Principles*, Banff, Canada, Oct. 2001.

9. D. Engler, B. Chelf, A. Chou, and S. Hallem. Checking system rules using system-specific, programmer-written compiler extensions. In *Proceedings of the Fourth Symposium on Operating Systems Design and Implementation*, pages 1–16, San Diego, California, Oct. 2000.

10. D. Evans and D. Larochelle. Improving security using extensible lightweight static analysis. *IEEE Software*, 19(1):42–51, January/February 2002.

11. P. Hudak. Modular domain specific languages and tools. In *Proceedings of Fifth International Conference on Software Reuse*, pages 134–142, Victoria, Canada, June 1998.

12. T. Jim, G. Morrisett, D. Grossman, M. Hicks, J. Cheney, and Y. Wang. Cyclone: A safe dialect of C. In *USENIX Annual Technical Conference*, Monterey, CA, June 2002.

13. S. Kumar, Y. Mandelbaum, X. Yu, and K. Li. ESP: a language for programmable devices. In *Proceedings of the ACM SIGPLAN'01 Conference on Programming Language Design and Implementation*, pages 309–320, Snowbird, UT, USA, June 2001.

14. J. L. Lawall, G. Muller, and L. P. Barreto. Capturing OS expertise in a modular type system: the Bossa experience. In *Proceedings of the ACM SIGOPS European Workshop 2002 (EW2002)*, pages 54–62, Saint-Emilion, France, Sept. 2002.

15. S. Muchnick. *Advanced Compiler Design and Implementation*. Morgan Kaufmann, 1997.

16. G. Muller, J. L. Lawall, L. P. Barreto, and J.-F. Susini. A framework for simplifying the development of kernel schedulers: Design and performance evaluation. Technical report 03/2/INFO, Ecole des Mines de Nantes, 2003.

17. G. Necula, S. McPeak, and W. Weimer. CCured: type-safe retrofitting of legacy code. In *Conference Record of POPL 2002: The 29th SIGPLAN-SIGACT Symposium on Principles of Programming Languages*, pages 128–139, Portland, OR, Jan. 2002.

18. G. D. Plotkin. A structural approach to operational semantics. Technical Report FN-19, DAIMI, Department of Computer Science, University of Aarhus, Aarhus, Denmark, Sept. 1981.

19. L. Réveillère and G. Muller. Improving driver robustness: an evaluation of the Devil approach. In *The International Conference on Dependable Systems and Networks*, pages 131–140, Göteborg, Sweden, July 2001. IEEE Computer Society.

20. O. Shivers. A universal scripting framework, or Lambda: the ultimate "little language.". In J. Jaffar and R. H. C. Yap, editors, *Concurrency and Parallelism, Programming, Networking, and Security (ASIAN'96)*, volume 1179 of *Lecture Notes in Computer Science*, pages 254–265, Singapore, Dec. 1996.

21. D. Steere, A. Goel, J. Gruenberg, D. McNamee, C. Pu, and J. Walpole. A feedback-driven proportion allocator for real-rate scheduling. In *Proceedings of the Third USENIX Symposium on Operating Systems Design and Implementation (OSDI)*, pages 145–158, New Orleans, LA, Feb. 1999.

22. C. A. Waldspurger and W. E. Weihl. Lottery scheduling: Flexible proportional-share resource management. In *Proceedings of the 1st USENIX Symposium on Operating Systems Design and Implementation (OSDI'94)*, pages 1–11, Monterey, CA, USA, Nov. 1994.

Appendix

Definition 1 (Relation on process descriptions). *For any processes src and tgt, and any initial state environment σ_0, a process p is related to an abstract process description pd, iff $src, tgt, \sigma_0 \models_p p : pd$, which is defined as follows:*

$$src, tgt, \sigma_0 \models_p src : (\mathsf{src}, \sigma_0^{-1}(src)) \qquad src, tgt, \sigma_0 \models_p p : (\mathsf{x}, \sigma_0^{-1}(p))$$
$$src, tgt, \sigma_0 \models_p tgt : (\mathsf{tgt}, \sigma_0^{-1}(tgt)) \qquad src, tgt, \sigma_0 \models_p p : (\mathsf{x}, \top)$$
$$src, tgt, \sigma_0 \models_p p : (\mathsf{x}, class), \text{if } \sigma_0^{-1}(p) \text{ is in state class } class$$

This relation extends pointwise to variable environments, as $src, tgt, \sigma_0 \models_v \phi : \Phi$.

Definition 2 (Relation on contents descriptions). *For any processes src and tgt, and any initial state environment σ_0, a set of processes π is related to an abstract contents description cd, iff $src, tgt, \sigma_0 \models_c \pi : cd$, defined as follows:*

$$src, tgt, \sigma_0 \models_c \emptyset : [] \qquad \frac{\exists (p_1, \ldots, p_n) \in \mathsf{choose}(\pi, n). \forall i. src, tgt, \sigma_0 \models_p p_i : pd_i}{\forall p \in \pi. \exists pd \in may. src, tgt, \sigma_0 \models_p p : pd}$$
$$\frac{}{src, tgt, \sigma_0 \models_c \pi : \langle \{pd_1, \ldots, pd_n\}, may\rangle}$$

This relation extends pointwise to state environments, as $src, tgt, \sigma_0 \models_s \sigma : \Sigma$.

The analysis and the semantics are then related as follows, proved by induction on the structure of the derivation:

Lemma 1 (Process expression). *If $\Phi, \Sigma \vdash_e exp : (pd, s, \Sigma')$ and $src, tgt, \sigma_0 \models_v \phi : \Phi$ and $src, tgt, \sigma_0 \models_s \sigma : \Sigma$ and $\phi, \sigma \vdash exp \to p$, then $src, tgt, \sigma_0 \models_p p : pd$, $\sigma^{-1}(p) \in s$, and $src, tgt, \sigma_0 \models_s \sigma[\sigma^{-1}(p) \mapsto \sigma(\sigma^{-1}(p)) - \{p\}] : \Sigma'$.*

Lemma 2 (Boolean expression with a known value). *If $\Phi, \Sigma \vdash_b bexp : b$ and $b \in \{true, false\}$ and $src, tgt, \sigma_0 \models_v \phi : \Phi$ and $src, tgt, \sigma_0 \models_s \sigma : \Sigma$ and $\phi, \sigma \vdash bexp \to v$, then $b = v$.*

Lemma 3 (Boolean expression with an unknown value). *If $\Phi, \Sigma \vdash_b bexp : \langle \Sigma_t, \Sigma_f \rangle$ and $src, tgt, \sigma_0 \models_v \phi : \Phi$ and $src, tgt, \sigma_0 \models_s \sigma : \Sigma$ and $\phi, \sigma \vdash bexp \to b$, then if $b = true$ then $src, tgt, \sigma_0 \models_s \sigma : \Sigma_t$ and if $b = false$ then $src, tgt, \sigma_0 \models_s \sigma : \Sigma_f$.*

Theorem 1 (Soundness). *If $\Phi, \Sigma \vdash_s stmt : S$ and $src, tgt, \sigma \models_v \phi : \Phi$ and $src, tgt, \sigma \models_s \sigma : \Sigma$ and $\phi, \sigma \vdash stmt \to \sigma'$, then for some $\Sigma' \in S$, $src, tgt, \sigma \models_s \sigma' : \Sigma'$.*

A Generative Framework for Managed Services

Liam Peyton and Arif Rajwani

School of Information Technology and Engineering, University of Ottawa
800 King Edward, Ottawa, ON, Canada, K1N 6N5
{lpeyton,arajwani}@site.uottawa.ca

Abstract. We identify a special category of applications that manage delivery of services by reporting and configuring services based on data collected in the delivery of services. Managed delivery has typically been an aspect of software systems entangled in domain specific application logic. Generative approaches, and in particular domain specific languages, have attempted to release application logic from such aspects. We demonstrate that such aspects can be considered applications in their own right. For managed delivery of services, key elements of a generative approach are the domain specialist, reports, metrics, data model, configuration parameters, rules, and template-based generation.

Keywords: generative programming, templates, rules, data model, metrics, managed services.

1 Introduction

There is an increasing interest on the part of organizations to measure and manage the quality and effectiveness of their business processes and the services they deliver. Organizations collect data and establish metrics to measure and report on how well they are meeting objectives. A business uses metrics like average profit margin across product lines, or average customer satisfaction rating by sales region, or employee turn over rate in order to quantify how well they are doing as an organization as well as to detect and address potential problem areas. Kaplan and Norton [6] established a systematic approach to managing an organization in this fashion with their work on balanced scorecards. Metrics are also an important tool for managing software engineering processes with metrics for things like developer productivity, system complexity, and defect rate. [2]

Increasingly, as business processes move online, there is a requirement to integrate such data collection and reporting into application software. This is especially true for electronic commerce systems. Application software in these situations also introduces new elements and new opportunities for data collection and reporting which are important for managing service delivery. Security, scalability [1], database access [16], and personalization [9, 11] are examples of areas where organizations are using metrics to manage and troubleshoot their on-line business processes. Typically, electronic commerce systems need to be available 24x7. As a result, it is desirable if these areas can be changed and improved while the system is still running.

Each of these example areas is an aspect of the application software that can become tangled with the core business logic during implementation. In a traditional

G. Karsai and E. Visser (Eds.): GPCE 2004, LNCS 3286, pp. 456–468, 2004.

generative programming approach one can create a domain specific language for the application independent of these other aspects. Developers can use an aspect oriented programming language like AspectJ [8] to code these other aspects and integrate them during generation of the application software. However, these "aspects" are domains in their own right with domain experts who specialize in managing such aspects and who want to control the manner in which data is collected and reported. More than a tangling of "aspects" with business logic, there is a tangling of different applications and managed services. Each such managed service will benefit from its own domain specific language and generative approach to create an application that domain experts can use to manage, report, and troubleshoot that aspect of an electronic commerce system. Generation of the managed service must be done in such a manner to ensure seamless integration with all the other managed services and applications that make up an electronic commerce system.

In this paper, we present a generative framework for the development of managed services and their integration with application software in the context of electronic commerce systems. In doing so, we define and categorize managed services in terms of the data that is collected for reporting and the manner in which that data can be used to configure and improve the service – in most cases while the application and service is still running. The essential elements in generating a managed service are identified as the domain specialist, reports, metrics, data model, configuration parameters, rules and template-based generation.

The approach is illustrated with two managed services: one to manage personalization in an application, and the other to manage scalability and reliability of the application. Our analysis draws from our experiences as part of a product team, which created a personalization engine for electronic commerce web sites, ADAPTe, that is effective and highly scalable, while remaining easy to implement and use with a minimum of technical support [12, 17]. ADAPTe is now owned by Digital Connexxions, who has been awarded United States Patent and Trademark Office, Patent Number 6,466,975 [4].

2 Background and Related Work

An essential element of our framework is recognizing that an electronic commerce system can be viewed from many different perspectives, and that potentially each such perspective may represent a managed service for which there is a domain expert and associated application. The importance of targeting generative approaches to domain experts, as opposed to professional software engineers is well established in [15] as well as the advantages of end user programming environments that accurately reflect the lexicon of the domain expert. Our work on managed services is also related to the concept of acceptability oriented computing articulated in [13] which introduced layers around programming code that can observe and modify the behavior of the code in order to ensure better reliability. In our case, we focus on a statistical approach using metrics to quantify results as the mechanism for observation and a generative approach using configuration parameters, rules and templates to modify behavior. The use of rules in our framework is similar to policy based approaches for self-managing behaviors [3] in autonomic systems. Our emphasis is less on software that is self-managing, and more on integrating collection and reporting aspects into software to allow organizational validation of the policies that are implemented.

Architectural considerations are also fundamental to the generative framework we have created. Separation of concerns (aspects), integration of services and applications, and configurable, dynamic document generation are all fundamental aspects of electronic commerce systems [14]. A good discussion of domain driven development in such a context is presented in [7]. A thorough analysis is presented in [10] of the tradeoffs for addressing separation of concerns using a language tool like AspectJ, an application framework for aspects, or a purely architectural approach. Our approach is architectural since our framework is used to generate an entire managed service application integrated with other applications in an electronic commerce system in order to address a single aspect.

3 A Generative Framework for Managed Services

The motivation for this research comes from our experiences on the ADAPTe project in developing a personalization server for electronic commerce web sites. The initial focus of the project was to implement an API that developers could call from within an electronic commerce system to personalize the content display using facts known about a person. For example, women's ice skates are shown if the person is female, while men's ice skates are shown if the person is male.

However, it quickly became apparent that web site developers would NOT be the focus of ADAPTe. Rather, the main users of the server are marketing specialist who want to configure the content displayed by an electronic commerce system, completely independently of any developers, in order to manage personalization. The most important requirement for the personalization is that it collect and report metrics on customer behavior in order to manage the effectiveness of the content being displayed and troubleshoot potential problem areas in the system.

It also became clear that system administrators are another important user of the system. Many electronic commerce sites have massive requirements in terms of both scalability and reliability. The extra processing associated with personalization has the potential to impact both [1]. System administrators need the server to allow them to collect detailed statistics of system performance in order to measure the impact of personalization and scalability, and the server needs to allow them to adjust the configuration of the system in order to optimize the performance of the system as load and usage varies. As with the marketing specialist, this needs to be done independent of any interaction with developers and changes need to be handled dynamically while the system was running.

While the target users for the two situations are quite different, the same general framework is used. Figure 1, below depicts the key elements of that framework. The components of the existing electronic commerce system, including the developer and user of the electronic commerce system are shown in plain face, while the components of an integrated managed service and the specialist who is the main user responsible for the service are shown in bold face.

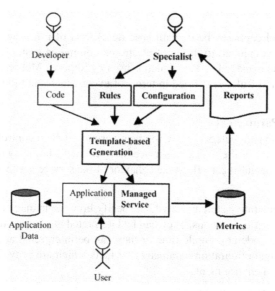

Fig. 1. A Generative Framework for Managed Services

The application and the managed service are linked at run-time via an API, but the essential element of the framework is the template-based generation that allows the developer and specialist to work independently, but have the results of their work integrated dynamically at predefined join pints while the electronic commerce system is running.

We briefly define the key elements of the generative framework and then illustrate how they can be applied drawing from our experiences with the ADAPTe project with respect to a managed service for personalization and a managed service for scalability and reliability.

Domain Specialist

The domain specialist is the central person or actor for the managed service. It is their domain expertise and objectives that drives the requirements for the managed service. A successful generative framework is dependent on their input to define the domain specific aspects of the framework (Reports, Metrics, Configuration Parameters, and Rules).

Reports

Reports are documents or interfaces specific to the domain that allow the domain specialist to visualize and communicate the status of the managed service as well as troubleshoot potential problem areas. They are based on the statistics collected by the managed service while it is running.

Metrics

Metrics quantify the behavior of the managed service using statistics collected by the managed service. The measurements and statistics are based on facts associated with events specific to the domain that occur during the running of the managed service.

Data Model

A data model captures the domain specific aspects of a managed service so it can easily be deployed to different electronic commerce systems. The essential lexicon of the managed service which is used by Reports, Metrics, Configuration Parameters and Rules is defined in terms of events, facts, and their possible values.

Configuration Parameters

Configuration parameters are environment variables which control or parameterize the behavior of the managed service in a generic fashion. By changing these, the domain specialist can adjust the behavior of the service while it is running.

Rules

Rules are declarative statements which specify how the managed service should behave in specific situations. They can be interpreted at compile time to generate and integrate code at compile time or they can be interpreted at run time. They can reference configuration parameters, or facts which are provided through the API or system environment.

Template-Based Generation

For integration with existing applications and managed services it is essential that templates be defined that clearly indicate join points for integration so that applications and managed services can be successfully weaved into a single electronic commerce system as they are generated. This integration may happen at run time or at compile time. If it happens at compile time, then the rules can be applied to control the source code that is generated and compiled. In that case, the only run-time control that a domain specialist will have, will be in the setting of configuration parameters.

4 Managed Service for Personalization

The key elements of the framework are recognized and established by a careful analysis of the reports the marketing specialist uses to quantify results and troubleshoot potential trouble spots. The report in figure 2 below is fictional but based on trials of the ADAPTe server for a customer in their on-line store for selling baby-related merchandise [17].

Last Month: Total Click Thru 4%
This Month: Total Click Thru 8%

Location	Category	Content	Click Thru
BabyLink	MidWest, Male	Winnie	12%
BabyLink	MidWest, Female	Winnie	4%
BabyLink	East, Male	Mickey	12%
BabyLink	East, Female	Mickey	4%
BabyLink	Total	All	8%

Fig. 2. Report on Personalization

The marketing specialist is trying to promote the new baby section of the store by designing a graphic associated with a link to the store that will be attractive to customers. Last month, only 4% of visitors actually clicked on the link to visit the store. This month, the marketing specialist had heard that Winnie the Pooh was more popular in the Midwest, while Mickey Mouse are more popular in the East. The web site is modified so that the graphic associated with the link to the baby section features a crib with Winnie the Pooh bedding for the Midwest, and Mickey Mouse bedding for the East. The personalization is a success since the overall click through rate jumped from 4% to 8%. However, the report shows that the success is due to the impact on male shoppers with no impact on female shoppers.

To develop a generative framework for managing personalization we analyze the report the marketing specialist is using and determine:

1. The metrics being used to measure the service
   - click through rate
2. The structure of the data that must be collected to generate the report
   - locations
   - content
   - number of times shown
   - number of times successful (associated link clicked on)
   - customer categorization (based on facts known about them).
3. The parameters that the specialist can vary to affect performance
   - content shown at a location
   - categorization (facts) used to select content
4. The join points for integration when generating the managed service
   - a reference to the content is generated in HTML at specific locations
   - the managed service is notified when the link for the content is clicked

Based on this analysis:

1) A template is defined for generating and integrating the code into the on-line store to select content and track success events (click through)
2) A simple rule language is designed for selecting content
3) A domain lexicon is defined so the framework will work for any on-line store by specifying the locations, content, and customer facts for the new store.

4.1 Template-Based Generation

In electronic commerce systems, it is a common practice to generate the HTML of a web site using templates [7, 14]. The structure and static content of a web site are defined in HTML templates. The spots where the dynamic aspects of the web site must be filled in are identified by custom tags. This allows an HTML specialist to design the look of the web site, while the developers can code the business logic that generates dynamic content.

This same mechanism is used to integrate the managed service for personalization. In figure 3, on the next page, is a diagram of an HTML template that has been divided into sub parts using custom tags. Each of the custom tags (banner, footer, navigational menu, body, and promotion) identifies content that is dynamically generated by the electronic commerce system. Most of the tags are linked to code written by the application developers for the system. In our case, the promotion tag is linked to the managed service for personalization that dynamically generates the HTML and scripting code at run-time to display content according to the rules defined by the marketing specialist and collect data to track the success of the content (by counting click through events).

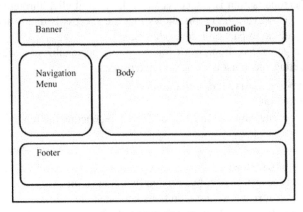

Fig. 3. HTML Template

4.2   Rules and Domain Lexicon

The rules and lexicon for the managed service are defined by the marketing specialist in an interface that is natural for their domain. It is similar to the type of interface that might be used to collect facts about a customer. Below is a rule that indicates that Males, 18-55, from the East should be shown a MickeyMouseCrib graphic for the link to the Baby Section of the on-line store.

```
Location: BabyLink
   RULE1:
        Content:  MickeyMouseCrib
        Category:
           REGION
                    ___ South
                    ___North
                    ___West
                    ___Midwest
                    X East
           GENDER
                    X Male
                    ___Female
           AGE
                    X 18 to 30
                    X 30 to 55
                    ___ over 55
```

The marketing specialist defines the possible locations, and content. They also define the facts and possible values for facts that will be available in creating rules. In this manner, the marketing specialist can specify their domain completely and have the behavior of the managed service be fully specified by the rules they create.

This initial framework can also be extended to provide more sophistication in the managed service. In most cases, the marketing specialists want to predefine certain standard customer categories that they are targeting. Rather than checking off the same facts every time when creating a rule, one can define a customer category "MaleEasterner" as in the rule above and then rewrite the rule as follows:

Location: BabyLink
RULE1:
      Content: MickeyMouseCrib
      Category: MaleEasterner

Another improvement is to link the statistics gathering of the managed service to the selection of content. Marketing Specialists will often experiment with content. In the rule below, three different pieced of content are listed. The managed service will rotate through the content for 20% of the shoppers on an ongoing basis collecting statistics, but then it will show the one with the highest click through rate to the other 80%.

Location: BabyLink
RULE1:
      Content: MickeyMouseCrib, MinnieMouseCrib, WinnieThePoohCrib
      Category: FemaleEasterner
      Rotate: 20%

4.3 Architecture

The architecture for the generative framework is shown in Figure 4. The interface to the managed service is a database application that allows the marketing specialist to specify the domain and the rules and to see reports of the statistics collected in the database. The managed service is a dedicated server. The custom tags from the HTML templates link to the managed service via an API that communicates with the server. Within the personalization server, a rule engine applies rules to select content based on the facts contained in the profile for the customer. Profiles are managed by the profile manager which retrieves them from a profiles database and caches them in memory. A database manager loads the rules from the database and writes statistics.

The creation of a separate server for a managed service is not unusual for an electronic commerce system. A separate server provides more flexibility in order to support scalability and reliability requirements (discussed in the next section). In particular, the personalization server could be deployed as a server cluster (sharing the same database) to ensure scalability and fail over reliability.

5 Managed Service for Scalability and Reliability

As with personalization, the key elements of a generative framework are recognized and established by a careful analysis of the reports the domain specialist uses to quantify results and troubleshoot potential trouble spots. In this case, the specialist is a system administrator who is responsible for ensuring the scalability and reliability of the personalization server particularly as it might affect the overall electronic commerce system.

Figure 5, shows an example of a fictional report based on trials performed by system administrators using ADAPTe. The facts about a customer are cached in memory as profiles for the duration of a session in order to improve the response time as

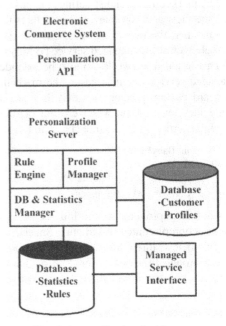

Fig. 4. Personalization Architecture

many personalization requests would be made for the same profile over the duration of a session. Under extreme load, though, the number of profiles in memory could get quite large and start to affect performance. The report below shows how the server is performing under simulated load. The server does quite well with up to 10,000 profiles. In particular we are measuring two critical actions that are performed by components of the server. The rule engine is able to select content almost instantaneously, and there is only modest overhead for the profile manager to clean the cache of stale profiles (which happens in the background once every 5 minutes). Measurements are also made at the server level in terms of how much load is on the server, how much memory is being used, how many requests per second it can process and how long on average each request is taking.

At 100,000 profiles, the overhead in memory and time taken to clean the cache is becoming significant but performance is still strong. At 1 million profiles the performance of the server is clearly starting to degrade.

Impact of Session Profiles Cache (Average Individual Profile Size: 200 Bytes)

Profiles	1,000	10,000	100,000	1,000,000
Server Load	18 %	18 %	18 %	28 %
Server Memory	17 MB	17 MB	55 MB	226 MB
Select Content	5 ms	5 ms	5 ms	50 ms
Throughput	770 req/s	790 req/s	750 req/s	230 req/s
Clean Cache	100 ms	200 ms	500 ms	65000 ms

Fig. 5. Scalability Report

To develop a generative framework for managing scalability and reliability we analyze this report and others to determine:

1. The metrics being used to measure the service
   - average load
   - average memory usage
   - average response time (select content, clean cache ...) per request
   - average throughput
2. The structure of the data that must be collected to generate the report
   - requests (to personalization server)
   - actions (by personalization server)
   - time
   - facts known by the system (load, memory,...).
3. The parameters that the specialist can vary to affect performance
   - cache size (and other attributes of personalization server)
   - generic system attributes (e.g. that affect memory usage)
4. The join points for integration when generating the managed service
   - measure personalization server requests and actions (start, end)

Based on this analysis:

1) A template is defined for generating and integrating code to measure and configure performance into the personalization server
2) A domain lexicon is defined based on generic system elements (load, memory usage) and application specific elements (including actions or events like Clean Cache, Select Content)
3) Rules and policies are articulated for optimizing performance and explaining the relationship between things like Profile Cache Size, Clean Cache Frequency and performance.

5.1 Template-Based Generation

Logging of debug or performance information is a classic application area for aspect-oriented programming in a language like AspectJ in conjunction with a logging tool like Log4J [5, 8]. Join points are defined (typically at the start or end of methods), where debugging code will be automatically inserted as the system is compiled. Most literature in this area, though, focuses on enabling developers to test, study and debug their systems while keeping the logging code separate from their application code.

We use the same approach, but the focus is on creating a managed service for performance that a system administrator can use while the system is running in production without interacting with developers. As such, our coding in AspectJ is a predefined configuration that can take any service and instrument it.

The following is captured in generic templates:

- Match any top level server request as a join point for request level logging
- Match any top level call to a component in the server as action level logging
- Standardize a set of generally available environment facts that can be logged

- Identify a configurable set of parameters read from the server's configuration
- Complete parameterization to turn on and off what logging is done where
- Conditional logic to prevent any computation when logging is turned off.

The result is that at compile time, AspectJ generates and compiles code into the application which makes calls to a managed service logging API built on top of Log4J. Log4J is configured to send those requests on to a performance server that processes them and saves them into a performance database from which the system administrator can receive reports.

5.2 Configuration Parameters and Domain Lexicon

In addition to logged data for reports, the performance database contains the complete domain lexicon and configuration parameters as defined and set by the system administrator. The system administrator has an interface that allows them to:

- Define and set configuration parameters for the personalizatin server.
- Set configuration parameters to control what and how much is logged
- Coordinate an entire server cluster in this manner, including a status window and trace window.

The last item is important since it allows the personalization server to scale by running several servers at the same time on separate machines.

5.3 Architecture

The architecture for the managed service is shown in Figure 6. The interface is a database application to specify and set configuration parameters and see reports of the statistics collected in the database. AspectJ generates and integrates code into the personalization servers that call the logging API to communicate with the server. The policies or rules about how to configure the server for various situations have not been captured formally as they were more complex and not as well understood as the rules for the personalization managed service.

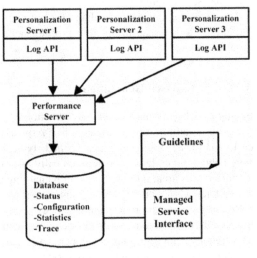

Fig. 6. Server Cluster Architecture

Instead, a document was written that captured informally some basic guidelines to follow in configuring the server.

The performance server also facilitates management and deployment of a server cluster configuration for the personalization server. One of the ways in which the system administrator can adjust the performance of the electronic commerce system is by varying how many personalization servers are deployed on what machines.

6 Conclusions

In electronic commerce systems, there are many aspects which may be orthogonal to the core business logic, but which are of critical importance nonetheless. Many of these aspects will correspond to a category of applications which we have defined as managed services. Managed services are usually characterized by domain specialists and extensive requirements for data collection and reporting in order to manage the service. A generative framework for creating domain specific managed services has been introduced and illustrated with examples drawn from industry experiences with the framework.

Acknowledgements

Gustavo Denicolay, Olivier Dupuy and Darren Nelson and many others participated in the development of ADAPTe. The concept of ADAPTe came from Deborah Sterling. Jim Scott, Bruce Casey, John Ching, and Dev Sainani contributed ideas as ADAPTe evolved. This research has been supported by funds from S.I.T.E, the Faculty of Engineering and the University of Ottawa.

References

1. M. Arlitt, D. Krishnamurthy, J. Rolia, Characterizing the Scalability of a Large Web Based Shopping System, *ACM Transactions on Internet Technology*, Vol. 1, No. 1, August 2001, Pages 44–69.
2. K. Bassin, S. Biyani, and P. Santhanam, Metrics to evaluate vendor-developed software based on test case execution results, IBM Systems Journal, Software Testing and Verification, Volume 41, Number 1, 2002. http://www.research.ibm.com/journal/sj/411/bassin.html
3. Hoi Chan, Bill Arnold, A Policy Based System to Incorporate Self-Managing Behaviors in Applications, Proceedings of OOPSLA'03, October 2003.
4. Digital Connexxions, U.S. Patent & Trademark Office Patent Number 6,466,975, February 18, 2003. http://www.dconx.com/11.html
5. J. Davies, N. Huismans, R. Slaney, S. Whiting, M. Webster , and R. Berry, An Aspect Oriented Performance Analysis Environment, International Conference on Aspect Oriented Software Development, 2003. http://aosd.net/archive/2003/program/davies.pdf
6. R. S. Kaplan, D. P. Norton. The Balanced Scorecard, Harvard Business School Press, 1996.
7. Sergei Kojarski David H. Lorenz, Domain Driven Web Development With WebJinn, Proceedings of OOPSLA'03, October 2003.
8. R. Laddad, Simplify your logging with AspectJ, excerpt from AspectJ in Action: Practical Aspect-Oriented Programming, Manning Publications, ISBN 1930110936, July 2003. http://www.developer.com/java/other/article.php/10936_3109831_1

9. B. Mobasher, R. Cooley, and J. Srivastava, Automatic Personalization Based on Web Usage Mining. Communications of the ACM, vol. 43 num. 8, 142-151, 2000.
10. J. Pace and M. Campo, Analyzing the role of aspects in software design, Vol. 44, No. 10 Communications of the ACM, October 2001
11. L. Paganelli & F. Paternò. Intelligent Analysis of User Interactions with web applications. Proceedings of the ACM Intelligent User Interfaces Conference (IUI), Jan. 2002.
12. L. Peyton, Measuring and Managing the Effectiveness of Personalization, Proceedings of the International Conference on Electronic Commerce, October 2003.
13. M. Rinard, Acceptability Oriented Computing, Proceedings of OOPSLA'03, October 2003.
14. L. Singh, B. Stearns, M. Johnson, and Enterprise Team, Designing Enterprise Applications with the J2EE Platform, 2nd Edition, Addison-Wesley, 20002. ISBN: 0201787903
15. D. Thomas and B. Barry, Model Driven Development – The case for domain oriented programming, Proceedings of OOPSLA'03, October 2003.
16. Varlamis, I., & Vazirgiannis M., Bridging XML Schema and relational databases. ACM Symposium on Document Engineering, pp. 105-114. 2001.
17. C. Waltner, CRM Makes Online Shopping Personal, in InformationWeek.com, page 3, January 29, 2001. http://www.site.uottawa.ca/~lpeyton/adapte_informationweek.htm

A Generative Approach
to the Implementation of Language Bindings
for the Document Object Model*

Luca Padovani, Claudio Sacerdoti Coen, and Stefano Zacchiroli

Department of Computer Science, University of Bologna
Mura Anteo Zamboni, 7 – 40127 Bologna, IT
{lpadovan,sacerdot,zacchiro}@cs.unibo.it

Abstract. The availability of a C implementation of the Document
Object Model (DOM) offers the interesting opportunity of generating
bindings for different programming languages automatically. Because of
the DOM bias towards Java-like languages, a C implementation that
fakes objects, inheritance, polymorphism, exceptions and uses reference-
counting introduces a gap between the API specification and its actual
implementation that the bindings should try to close. In this paper we
overview the generative approach in this particular context and apply it
for the generation of C++ and OCaml bindings.

1 Introduction

The widespread use of XML imposes every mainstream programming language
to be equipped with an implementation of the main W3C technologies, among
which is the Document Object Model (DOM) [7,8]. Quite often these standard
technologies require substantial development efforts that small communities cannot always afford. One way to address this problem is the introduction of a common platform, like the recent .NET, that enables direct library sharing among
different languages. The alternative, traditional solution is to implement a given
API in a low-level programming language (typically C) and to write *bindings*
to this implementation for all the other programming languages. This approach
has the advantage of requiring no modification to the language implementation.
On the other hand the low-level implementation introduces a gap between the
original high-level specification of the API and the low-level provided interface.
The gap must be closed in the binding process by providing a high-level API
that is as close as possible to the original specification. In this paper we overview
a framework for the generation of bindings for a C DOM implementation[1].

---

* This work was partly supported by the European Project IST-2001-33562 MoWGLI.
Luca Padovani received partial support from the Ontario Research Centre for Computer Algebra.

[1] We take Gdome [1,5], the GNOME DOM Engine, as our representative DOM implementation. See http://gdome2.cs.unibo.it.

The DOM API, as well as several other W3C technologies, is blatantly biased towards an object-oriented programming language with support for inheritance, polymorphism, exceptions and garbage collection, like Java. This bias is perfectly acceptable in the bleak world of mainstream programming languages where even sensibly different languages tend to converge towards a common, limited set of syntactical and semantical aspects. In other communities this tendency turns out to be too constraining. In particular, the larger the gap between the binding target language and Java, the greater the efforts for implementing smoothly the aforementioned APIs.

In order to get a clearer idea of the problems, let us have a look at some code that uses the Gdome C DOM implementation. The following code fragment is meant to perform an apparently trivial task: iterate over the child elements of a given element el, and perform some unspecified action on each of them:

```
GdomeException exc;
GdomeNode *p = gdome_el_firstChild (el, &exc);
while (p != NULL) {
  GdomeNode *next = gdome_n_nextSibling (p, &exc);
  if (gdome_n_nodeType (p, &exc) == GDOME_ELEMENT_NODE) {
    GdomeElement *pel = gdome_el_cast (p);
    /* do something with the element */
  }
  gdome_n_unref (p, &exc);
  p = next;
}
```

Note how: (1) each method invocation carries an extra argument exc for detecting exceptions and that, for brevity, we do not perform error checking; (2) safe downcasting is done via explicit macros, but there is always the dangerous temptation of using C casting because, all considered, "it works"; (3) reference-counted objects requires lots of careful coding to avoid memory leaks. Besides, Gdome uses its own UTF-8 strings meaning that, prior to calling any method accepting a string as a parameter, the programmer has to allocate a GdomeDOMString object, initialize it, and free it after the call. These details, which are not visible at the DOM specification level, sensibly increase the programmer's discomfort and annoyance.

Since DOM provides a set of standard interfaces with good uniformity of names and types, there is the interesting opportunity of generating language bindings automatically, instead of hand-coding them. The advantages of this approach include reduced development time, increased maintainability and modularity of the bindings. Besides, an XML specification of the DOM interfaces is already available within the DOM recommendation itself. Although its main use is for generating documentation and test cases, it happens to have most of the information needed for the generation of a language binding once the appropriate design choices have been made.

The architecture we propose for the automatic generation of DOM bindings is shown in Figure 1. On the left hand side we have the XML specification of the DOM interfaces. Most of the specification is the actual W3C XML specifi-

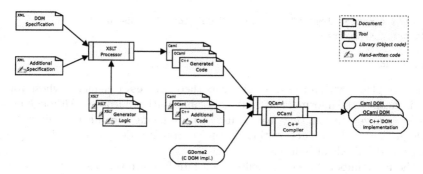

Fig. 1. Architecture of the generator for DOM bindings.

cation, but, as we will see in Section 2, we need additional information that is contained in a separate document. Being the specification encoded in XML, we have implemented the generator as the combination of an XSLT engine along with a set of XSLT stylesheets [6]. The code of different bindings based on different binding logics is generated by different XSLT stylesheets. The generated code is then combined with hand-written code which cannot be generated automatically (it amounts to a handful of lines) and linked against the Gdome DOM implementation in order to produce the final binding library.

The outline of the paper is as follows: in Section 2 we overview the format of the high-level DOM specification, what kind of information is available and how it is organized. Sections 3 and 4 cover the main design choices for the bindings currently implemented: C++ and OCaml [12]. In particular, we emphasize those aspects of the DOM API for which C++ and OCaml provide more natural implementations than C does. In Section 5 we show three templates for the three bindings highlighting similarities and differences among them. These also show what kind of XSLT code is required to be written when following our approach. We conclude the paper in Section 6 trying to quantify the effectiveness of the whole approach. The source code of the framework is freely available at the address http://gmetadom.sourceforge.net. In the rest of the paper some knowledge of the Document Object Model is assumed.

2   DOM Interface Specification

In this section we briefly overview the XML description of the DOM interfaces as it is provided by the W3C [2]. Each DOM interface is described by an `interface` element characterized by a name and possibly the base interface this interface derives from. In the following example we see the `Element` interface extending the `Node` interface:

---

[2] This description is not directly advertised by the W3C, it can be found as part of the source XML files of the DOM recommendation,
http://www.w3.org/TR/2000/REC-DOM-Level-2-Core-20001113/DOM2-Core.zip.

```
<interface name="Element" inherits="Node" id="ID-745549614">
 <descr>...</descr>
 ...
</interface>
```

In several places within the XML elements there are descr elements whose content is meant to be informal and used for documentation purposes. Although useless for code generation, they may be used for producing documenting comments aside method and class declarations in the generated code, possibly adhering to some standardized conventions[3].

The most important components of an interface are the descriptions of attributes and methods. Each attribute is specified in terms of a name, a type, and a readonly flag. Here is the declaration for the nextSibling attribute in the Node interface:

```
<attribute readonly="yes" type="Node" name="nextSibling"
           id="ID-6AC54C2F">
 <descr>
  <p>The node immediately following this node.
   If there is no such node, this returns
   <code>null</code>.</p>
 </descr>
</attribute>
```

Methods are characterized by a name, a list of parameters, the type of the returned object, and an optional raises section which lists the exceptions that can be raised by the method. Each parameter comes with a name, a type, and passing style which, in the case of DOM interfaces, is always in (that is, input parameters). Here is the declaration for the replaceChild method in the Element interface:

```
<method name="replaceChild" id="ID-785887307">
 <descr>...</descr>
 <parameters>
  <param name="newChild" type="Node" attr="in">
   <descr>...</descr>
  </param>
  <param name="oldChild" type="Node" attr="in">
   <descr>...</descr>
  </param>
 </parameters>
 <returns type="Node">
  <descr>...</descr>
 </returns>
 <raises>
  <exception name="DOMException">
   <descr>
    <p>HIERARCHY_REQUEST_ERR: ...</p>
```

---

[3] These are typically simplified forms of literal programming.

```
  <p>WRONG_DOCUMENT_ERR: ...</p>
    ...
   </descr>
  </exception>
 </raises>
</method>
```

There is only one DOM exception (at least within the Core DOM module), which is parameterized by an exception code (whose symbolic names can be seen in the description within the **exception** element).

Occasionally an interface also defines a list of constants within a **group** element. Each constant has a symbolic name, a type, and a value. The most important constants are those determining the type of a DOM node and can be found inside the **Node** interface:

```
<group id="ID-1841493061" name="NodeType">
 <descr>
  <p>An integer indicating which type of node this is.</p>
  ...
 </descr>
 <constant name="ELEMENT_NODE" type="unsigned short" value="1">
  <descr>...</descr>
 </constant>
 <constant name="ATTRIBUTE_NODE" type="unsigned short" value="2">
  <descr>...</descr>
 </constant>
 <constant name="TEXT_NODE" type="unsigned short" value="3">
  <descr>...</descr>
 </constant>
  ...
</group>
```

There is one piece of information that is missing from the XML description of the DOM interfaces and that is important during the code generation phase: no indication is given as to whether an attribute, a parameter or the value returned by a method can be *null*[4]. This detail has no practical consequences in Java simply because in this language **null** is a special, distinguished value that any pointer can take. But this is not the case in general: for example, a C++ reference cannot be null; hence C++ references cannot be used for representing types of nullable entities. Even more delicate are functional languages, where there is usually no notion of "null object", or at least this notion has to be used in a type-safe manner: there can be an empty list or an empty tree, but the general approach for representing nullable or optional values is to use the α **option** type (in Objective Caml and SML) which permits the construction of "an object x" as **Some** x and the construction of "no object" as **None**. Symmetrically, optional

---

[4] In some cases this can be heuristically inferred by the description of the entity (see the **nextSibling** attribute shown previously). What we mean is that there is no systematic, exploitable information about this fact.

values must be properly deconstructed using pattern matching. Clearly this may become annoying and exceedingly verbose, especially in those cases when a parameter is *required to be non-null* or a returned value *cannot be null*. What is missing is a `nullable` attribute in the XML specification of DOM attributes, methods and parameters indicating whether that particular entity admits `null` among the possible values. This way, during the code generation phase, we are able to generate the most appropriate type. In particular, when generating code for a functional language we are forced to use optional values only where strictly needed. As a side effect, the API produced is also lighter and more usable.

Instead of modifying the original XML specifications, we have preferred to store this information in a parallel set of complementary XML resources, called annotations. A fragment of these annotations relative to the `Node` interface is shown below:

```
<Annotations>
  ...
  <Attribute name="parentNode" nullable="yes"/>
  <Attribute name="childNodes" nullable="no"/>
  ...
  <Method name="insertBefore" nullable="no">
   <Param name="newChild" nullable="no"/>
   <Param name="refChild" nullable="yes"/>
  </Method>
  ...
</Annotations>
```

3   C++ Binding

We have decided to keep the C++ binding as much lightweight as possible, considering the overhead that is intrinsic in the layered architecture of the DOM implementation[5]. The C++ binding consists of a set of classes, one for each DOM interface, which act like wrappers for the corresponding, lower-level C structures. Wrappers provide one method for each method in the DOM interface, and getter/setter methods for attributes (the setter method is only generated if the attribute is writable). The classes are declared in the `GdomeSmartDOM` namespace, which is typically abbreviated in the application source code with an alias directive

```
namespace DOM = GdomeSmartDOM;
```

Basically the wrapping classes are *smart pointers* [9–11] that relieve the programmer from worrying about memory management. The only unusual feature is that the counter is already present at the `Gdome` level, so the wrappers only automate the increment and decrement operations. Each wrapper class has two constructors:

---

[5] The `Gdome` DOM implementation is itself a wrapper for a non-conformant, DOM-like library.

```
class Node
{
public:
  explicit Node(GdomeNode* = 0);
protected:
  explicit Node(GdomeNode* obj, bool) : gdome_obj(obj) { }
  ...
};
```

The public constructor behaves normally from the developer's viewpoint, it increments the reference counter of the Gdome object whenever this is non-null. The protected constructor, distinguished because of an unused boolean argument, is used internally in the generated code for initializing a wrapper with an object returned by a Gdome method: Gdome already increments the counter of any returned object, hence it would be an error to increment it twice (or we would have to decrement it explicitly at some extra cost). The following code fragment shows the generated implementation of the **setAttributeNode** method in the Element interface:

```
Attr
Element::setAttributeNode(const Attr& newAttr) const
{
  GdomeException exc_ = 0;
  GdomeAttr* res_ =
    gdome_el_setAttributeNode(
      (GdomeElement*) gdome_obj,      // self
      (GdomeAttr*) newAttr.gdome_obj, // projection Attr -> GdomeAttr*
      &exc_);
  if (exc_ != 0)
    throw DOMException(exc_, "Element::setAttributeNode");
  return Attr(res_, true); // promotion GdomeAttr* -> Attr
}
```

As inheritance and polymorphism are handled at the Gdome level, the only support that we have automated has been the provision for casting. This is possible because the XML description of the DOM interfaces includes information about the relationship between interfaces. Upcasting is implemented by deriving wrapping classes for extended interfaces from wrapping classes for the base interface:

```
class Element : public Node { ... };
```

Safe downcasting is implemented by generating, in each wrapping class for a derived interface, a set of constructors taking as a parameter a wrapper class for an ancestor interface:

```
class Text : public CharacterData
{
  // ...
  Text(const Text&);
  Text(const CharacterData&);
  Text(const Node&);
};
```

If the cast fails the wrapper object is initialized with a NULL pointer (this is the same behavior of the dynamic_cast operator on plain C++ pointers). Casts like Element to Text, which are statically known to be unsafe, are prevented simply because no suitable copy-constructor that applies is generated. Finally, appropriate cast constructors are also generated whenever a DOM object is meant to implement multiple DOM interfaces (this is the case of Node and EventTarget, which belong to different, orthogonal DOM modules).

String management had to be coded manually, but since it is completely unrelated to all the other design choices related to the C++ binding it has been separated from the rest of the code so that it is reusable from alternative C++ bindings that we might want to experiment with in the future. Gdome has its own (reference counted) structures for representing strings encoded in UTF-8, whereas C++ comes with an extremely general string implementation in the STL library, but such implementation does not take into account encoding issues directly. We wanted to provide easy conversions from Gdome's internal encoding (which, in principle, the programmer should not be concerned about), to a limited set of generally useful encodings (UTF-16 and UCS4) without introducing at the same time gratuitous inefficiencies. Hence we have structured string management on two levels. At the bottom level is the DOM::GdomeString class which is just a wrapper to Gdome's GdomeDOMString type and provides only basic operations like comparison and initialization from plain C++ strings. At a higher level are DOM::UTF8String, DOM::UTF16String, DOM::UCS4String, which are typedefs for instantiations of std::basic_string with appropriate char types chosen to match the required number of bits but also the standard C++ char types. On most architectures, DOM::UTF8String and DOM::UCS4String are just aliases for std::string and std::wstring respectively.

Appropriate operators and constructors are provided for transparent encoding translation passing through the DOM::GdomeString type. It is thus possible to write

```
DOM::UTF16String s = n.get_nodeName();
// ...do something with s...
n.set_nodeValue(s);
```

without worrying about the fact that those methods return and accept DOM::GdomeString parameters. Note however that a string returned by a DOM method and passed unchanged to another DOM method need not go through any conversion.

Once all the pieces are put together, the conceptually simple but obfuscated example shown in Section 1 can be recast to the following crystal clear piece of C++ code:

```
for (DOM::Node p = el.get_firstChild(); p; p = p.get_nextSibling())
  if (DOM::Element pel = p) {
    // do something with the element
  }
```

4   OCaml Binding

Objective Caml (OCaml) is a class-based, object-oriented extension of Caml, a multi-paradigm language of the ML family whose main characteristics are the strongly-typed functional core augmented with imperative constructs, memory management delegated to a garbage collector, a type-inference based type system that relieves the programmer from having to explicitly declare the type of each function, and an expressive module system that can effectively replace objects and classes whenever late binding is not necessary. Higher-order functions and parametric polymorphism yield a very expressive type system where casts are not necessary at all, and are left out of the language.

The object-oriented capabilities of OCaml differ from traditional object-oriented languages like Java or C++ in that in OCaml subtyping is not related to inheritance. OCaml inheritance is just syntactic sugar to avoid code duplication, and subtyping and interfaces are not necessary: the type of a function or a method can be a generic object type τ that is the type of all the objects that expose *at least* the methods listed in τ. For instance, every object that has a `as_xml` method that returns an XML representation of the object itself matches the generic object type $\tau = <$ `method as_xml: xml` ; ... $>$, which can be used to type the argument of a method. Despite these differences, a Java class hierarchy can be faithfully mapped using the OCaml class system, so we are able, at least in principle, to provide a DOM binding which can be used in a way that is syntactically similar to more conventional object-oriented languages.

Unfortunately, in OCaml it is not possible to bind directly external functions to object methods. Thus, to provide an object-oriented DOM binding we are forced to adopt a layered approach: the lower level is a binding for the functional core of the language; the upper level builds an object-oriented abstraction on top of the lower level. An user can choose, according to her preferences and programming style, the functional interface of the lower level, or the object-oriented interface. In the latter case the lower level can remain completely hidden.

Assuming the existence of the lower level, the second layer is not complex. A DOM object of type T is implemented as a value of type T' at the lower level and as an object of an OCaml class T'' at the higher level. At the lower level a DOM method is implemented as a pre-method, a function whose first argument is the *self* parameter of type T'. As the C DOM implementation is also based on pre-methods, the OCaml function is easily bound to its native counterpart.

At the higher level the OCaml class has one field of type T' representing *self* at the lower level. This field is hidden to the user, but it is available within the OCaml class via a `as_`T' method. All the requests sent to an object are delegated to the lower level. Any parameter of type T'' which is pertinent to the higher level is converted to the corresponding type T' at the lower level by means of the `as_`T' projection. Conversely, any value of type T' returned by the pre-method is wrapped by a new object instance of type T''. The following example, which shows a fragment of the generated implementation of the OCaml `element` class, should clarify the basic mechanisms:

```
class element (self : TElement.t) =     (* TElement.t lower-level type *)
 object
  inherit (node (self :> TNode.t))      (* TElement.t subtype of TNode.t *)
   method as_Element = self             (* projection method *)
   method setAttributeNode ~newAttr =
    let res =
     IElement.setAttributeNode          (* pre-method call *)
      ~this:self
      ~newAttr:
        ((newAttr : attr)#as_Attr)      (* projection attr -> TAttr.t *)
    in
      new attr res                      (* promotion TAttr.t -> attr *)
 end
```

The similarity of the OCaml higher-level binding with the C++ binding should be evident. In both cases, the code builds an object-oriented abstraction on top of a pre-method system. The same similarity is also found between the two binding logics, described in the XSLT stylesheets, and provides further evidence in favor of the generative approach. String management, that was a major design decision for the C++ binding, has also been solved in a similar way for the OCaml binding. Thus the only major difference between the two bindings is the handling of NULL values, which was discussed in Section 2.

The low-level OCaml binding presents all the difficulties already faced in the C++ binding and a few new challenges, such as the interaction of the Gdome reference counting machinery with the OCaml garbage collector. In particular, the DOM Events Module API requires callback functions for event listeners, thus Gdome must register OCaml callback functions. Since OCaml functions are represented at run-time as closures that are managed by the garbage collector, their memory location can change at each collection. As a consequence the generated code is quite involved, and the most part of the bugs found in the development phase were related to memory management.

Notwithstanding the previous considerations, the greatest challenge in the design of the low-level OCaml binding has been related to typing issues. In particular, the problem consists in defining a collection of OCaml types T for which the subtyping relation is in accordance with the inheritance relation between DOM interfaces. For instance, for the previous example to be statically well-typed, we have to define two types TElement.t, TNode.t $\in T$ such that TElement.t is a subtype of TNode.t.

The simplest solution is declaring a different abstract data type for each Gdome class. The type must be abstract since the OCaml compiler has no direct way of manipulating external C values, which are wrapped in garbage collected memory references and which can be manipulated only by external C functions. Since up-casts from a subtype S to a supertype T are always safe C casts in the Gdome implementation, we can make functions of the C casts and bound them to OCaml external functions of type $S \to T$. One major drawback of this solution is that the obtained code is quite inefficient, since the frequently called casting functions, which are nothing more than identity functions, cannot be optimized neither by the C compiler, nor by the OCaml compiler. Moreover, up-casting a value to one of its ancestor classes would require a number of applications of externally defined casting functions equal to the length of the path from the sub-class to the super-class in the inheritance graph or, alternatively, the definition of one distinct casting function between each pair of classes in the inheritance relation.

Due to the previous issues, an alternative, more complex solution has been preferred to the simpler one. The alternative solution is based on a combination of the *phantom types* technique [2, 3] with *polymorphic variants* [4], which are an extension of the type system of OCaml that introduce subtyping in the core language without resorting to the object-oriented extension. As the following explanation should make clear, the combination of the two techniques is cumbersome and definitely not suitable for manual application in large contexts, as a language binding is. Moreover, a local change in the DOM class hierarchy, like those introduced when a new DOM module is implemented, implies global changes in the binding code that are annoying and error prone. Meta-programming solves the problem in an elegant and effective way.

The basic idea is to declare just one abstract phantom data type $\alpha\ \tau$, contravariant in the type parameter α. An instance of $\alpha\ \tau$ is bound to each foreign C type that corresponds to a DOM class. The type $\alpha\ \tau$ is called a *phantom type* since it is parameterized over a type variable α that is not used in the definition of the phantom type and that has no influence on the run-time representation of values. In other words, two values of distinct types $\sigma_1\ \tau$ and $\sigma_2\ \tau$ have the same memory representation and could be casted – if casts were part of the language – to any other type instance $\sigma\ \tau$. The latter propriety is interesting in our context since we want to simulate in the OCaml type system the subsumption rule of the DOM type system, that is casting a value of type $\sigma_1\ \tau$ bound to a DOM class c_1 to the type $\sigma_2\ \tau$ bound to a DOM class c_2 when c_2 is a supertype of c_1. At the same time, we want to statically rule out every pre-method application that is ill-typed at the DOM level. Since OCaml does not have casts nor an implicit subsumption rule, we must simulate both features using parametric polymorphism only.

Our solution consists in declaring any foreign function whose input is a DOM class c_1 and whose output is a DOM class c_2 as having type $[c_1]_i\ \tau \to [c_2]_o\ \tau$ where $[\_]_i$ and $[\_]_o$ are two encodings from DOM classes to OCaml types such that for each pair of DOM classes c_1' and c_2', if c_1' is a subtype of c_2' in the DOM type system, then a value of type $[c_1']_o\ \tau$ is a valid input for a function of type $[c_2]_i\ \tau \to \sigma$ in the OCaml type system. Notice that the latter property is the counterpart for parametric polymorphism of asking $[c_1']_o\ \tau$ to be a subtype of $[c_2']_i\ \tau$ for subtype polymorphism. Polymorphic variants [4] can be used to declare two meta-level functions $[\_]_i$ and $[\_]_o$ that satisfy the required constraints.

Intuitively, a polymorphic variant value is a tag associated with an optional value (its content). Since we are not interested in the content, we simplify the picture saying that a polymorphic variant is simply a tag. For instance, `'Node` and `'Element` are two values whose tags are respectively `Node` and `Element`.

Table 1. Example of corresponding types in the DOM specification and in the low-level OCaml binding.

	DOM	OCaml
Supertype	`Node`	`['Node]` τ
Subtype	`Element`	`['Node	'Element]` τ
Relation	`Element <: Node` because `Element extends Node`	`['Node	'Element]` $\tau$ `<:` `['Node]` $\tau$ because $\alpha$ is contravariant in $\alpha$ $\tau$ and `['Node] <: ['Node	'Element]` since $\{$`'Node`$\} \subset \{$`'Node`,`'Element`$\}$
Method	`m : Node` $\rightarrow T$	`m : [> 'Node	..]` $\tau \rightarrow [T]_o$
Object	`e : Element`	`e : ['Node	'Element]` τ
Application	`m(e)` well typed because `e : Element` $\Rightarrow$ `e : Node` by subsumption	`m(e)` well typed because `['Node	'Element]` $\tau$ matches `[> 'Node	..]` τ

A *close polymorphic variant type* lists several distinct tags. For instance, $\sigma_1 =$ `['EventTarget | 'Node]` is the type of all the values that are either a `'Node` or an `'EventTarget`. The subtyping relation between close polymorphic variant types is in accordance with the subset relation between the sets of tags, hence for example `['Node]` is a subtype of `['EventTarget | 'Node]`. A *parametric polymorphic variant type* has an unnamed parameter representing an unspecified tag set. For instance, $\sigma_2 =$ `[> 'EventTarget | ..]` is the parametric type of all the values that are either an `'EventTarget` or belong to the unnamed tag set parameter indicated by the ellipsis. Moreover, the type σ_1 τ matches σ_2 τ (by instantiating the unnamed parameter `..` with the singleton set $\{$`'Node`$\}$), hence the application of a function of type σ_2 $\tau \rightarrow \sigma$ to a value of type σ_1 τ is well-typed. On the contrary, the application of the same function to a value of type `['NodeList]` τ is not well-typed.

We can interpret the list of tags in a closed contravariant phantom type instance as a list of *provided* capabilities of an object (e.g. providing both the `EventTarget` and `Node` interfaces in σ_1 τ) and the list of tags in a parametric contravariant phantom type instance as a list of *required* capabilities (e.g. requiring at least the `EventTarget` interface in σ_2). The contravariance requirement must be understood in terms of this interpretation: σ_1 τ is a subtype of σ_2 τ when σ_1 has more capabilities than σ_2, i.e. when σ_2 is a subtype of σ_1. Table 1 summarizes the type relationships in the specific case of the `Element` interface.

According to the previous observations, we can implement in XSLT the two meta-level functions $[\_]_i$ and $[\_]_o$ in the following way: let c_n be a DOM class that recursively inherits from $c_1, \ldots, c_{n-1}$ by means of either single or multiple inheritance; we define $[c_n]_i$ as the polymorphic variant type $[> 'C_1 | \ldots | 'C_n]$ and $[c_n]_o$ as the polymorphic variant type $['C_1 | \ldots | 'C_n]$ where C_i is a tag obtained by mangling the name of the class c_i. For instance, `TElement.t` is defined as $[$`Element`$]_o = [$`'EventTarget | 'Node | 'Element`$]$ since a DOM

Element inherits from a DOM Node (see the DOM Core Specification [7]) and it is also an EventTarget (as described in the DOM Events Specification [8]).

The following example shows the generated code for the low-level OCaml binding of the setAttributeNode method:

```
module GdomeT = struct
  type -'a t  (* abstract phantom type, contravariant in 'a *)
  end

module TElement = struct
  type t = ['EventTarget | 'Node | 'Element] GdomeT.t
  end

module TAttr = struct
  type t = ['EventTarget | 'Node | 'Attr] GdomeT.t
  end

external setAttributeNode :
 this:[> 'Element] GdomeT.t ->
 newAttr:[> 'Attr] GdomeT.t ->
   TAttr.t
= "ml_gdome_el_setAttributeNode"
```

The C function ml_gdome_el_setAttributeNode, which is also automatically generated as part of the low-level binding, is defined as follows:

```
value
ml_gdome_el_setAttributeNode(value self, value p_newAttr)
{
  CAMLparam2(self, p_newAttr); /* Directive to the garbage collector */
  GdomeException exc_;
  GdomeAttr* res_;
  res_ = gdome_el_setAttributeNode(Element_val(self),
                 Attr_val(p_newAttr), &exc_);
  if (exc_ != 0)
    /* Raises an Ocaml exception */
    throw_exception(exc_, "Element.setAttributeNode");
  g_assert(res_ != NULL);
  CAMLreturn(Val_Attr(res_)); /* Directive to the garbage collector */
}
```

Once all the pieces are put together, the conceptually simple but obfuscated example shown in Section 1 can be recast to the following pieces of OCaml code:

```
(* Object-oriented *)                (* Purely functional *)
let rec iter =                       let rec iter =
 function                             function
   None -> ()                           None -> ()
 | Some p when p#get_nodeType =       | Some p when INode.get_nodeType p =
   GdomeNodeTypeT.ELEMENT_NODE          GdomeNodeTypeT.ELEMENT_NODE
   ->                                   ->
```

```
    let p' =                          let p' =
      Gdome.element_of_node p in        IElement.of_Node p in
      (* do something with p' *)        (* do something with p' *)
      iter p#get_nextSibling           iter (INode.get_nextSibling ~this:p)
  | Some p ->                        | Some p ->
      iter p#get_nextSibling           iter (INode.get_nextSibling ~this:p)
  in                                 in
    iter el#get_firstChild             iter (INode.get_firstChild ~this:el)
```

The code is slightly more verbose than the C++ equivalent. This is mainly a consequence of the bias of the DOM API towards an imperative, first order approach. Note also that, whereas in the object-oriented API inheritance relieves the user from remembering in which class a method is defined, in the purely functional approach each pre-method is qualified with the name of the module it is defined in. For instance, we have to remember that the `get_nextSibling` is a pre-method of the DOM `Node` class.

5   Generator Logic

In this section we look at significant fragments of the XSLT stylesheets that implement the generator logic for the various bindings. We classify the generated code according to the following tasks:

1. *prepare* the pre-method arguments: objects are projected, primitive values are converted if needed;
2. *invoke* the pre-method (high-level OCaml binding) or the `Gdome` method (C++ and low-level OCaml binding);
3. *check* if the pre-method has raised a DOM exception, and, if so, propagate the exception at the target language level. This is only done for the C++ and low-level OCaml bindings only since the high-level OCaml binding uses the same exceptions as the low-level one;
4. *return* the method result by promotion or conversion as necessary.

In addition, each template may also perform a few operations that are specific to the target language.

Here is the template for the C++ binding:

```
1   <xsl:template match="method">
2     <xsl:param name="interface" select="''"/>
3     <xsl:param name="prefix" select="''"/>
4     <xsl:call-template name="returnTypeOfType">
5       <xsl:with-param name="type" select="returns/@type"/>
6     </xsl:call-template>
7     <xsl:text> </xsl:text>
8     <xsl:value-of select="$interface"/>
9     <xsl:text>::</xsl:text>
10    <xsl:value-of select="@name"/>
11      (<xsl:apply-templates select="parameters"/>) const
```

```
12     {
13       GdomeException exc_ = 0;
14       <xsl:apply-templates select="parameters" mode="convert"/>
15       <xsl:call-template name="gdome-result">
16         <xsl:with-param name="type" select="returns/@type"/>
17         <xsl:with-param name="init">
18           <xsl:text>gdome_</xsl:text>
19           <xsl:value-of select="$prefix"/>
20           <xsl:text>_</xsl:text>
21           <xsl:value-of select="@name"/>
22           ((Gdome<xsl:value-of select="$interface"/>*) gdome_obj,
23             <xsl:apply-templates select="parameters" mode="pass"/>
24             &exc_)
25         </xsl:with-param>
26       </xsl:call-template>;
27       <xsl:apply-templates select="parameters" mode="free"/>
28       if (exc_ != 0)
29         throw DOMException(exc_,
30         "<xsl:value-of select="$interface"/>
31         <xsl:text>::</xsl:text>
32         <xsl:value-of select="@name"/>");
33       <xsl:call-template name="return-result">
34         <xsl:with-param name="type" select="returns/@type"/>
35       </xsl:call-template>
36     }
37  </xsl:template>
```

The template invocation on line 23 generates the projection code while lines 17–25 generate the Gdome method call. The generated code is passed as a parameter to the template gdome-result (lines 15–26), which is responsible for adding the promotion code if required. Lines 28–32 produce the code that checks the result of the function, possibly raising a C++ exception. All the residual lines handle the language specific issues (e.g. allocating and releasing temporary variables).

Here is the template for the high-level OCaml binding:

```
1   <xsl:template match="method">
2     <xsl:param name="interface" select="''"/>
3     <xsl:param name="prefix" select="''"/>
4     <xsl:variable name="name" select="@name"/>
5     <xsl:text>  method </xsl:text>
6     <xsl:value-of select="@name"/>
7     <xsl:apply-templates mode="left" select="parameters">
8       <xsl:with-param name="@name"/>
9     </xsl:apply-templates>
10    <xsl:text> = </xsl:text>
11    <xsl:call-template name="call_pre_method">
12      <xsl:with-param name="type" select="returns/@type"/>
13      <xsl:with-param name="isNullable"
14        select="document($annotations)/Annotations/Method
```

```
15            [@name=$name]/@nullable='yes'"/>
16       <xsl:with-param name="action">
17        <xsl:text>I</xsl:text>
18        <xsl:value-of select="$interface"/>.
19        <xsl:value-of select="@name"/>
20        <xsl:text> ~this:obj </xsl:text>
21        <xsl:apply-templates mode="right" select="parameters">
22         <xsl:with-param name="name" select="@name"/>
23        </xsl:apply-templates>
24       </xsl:with-param>
25      </xsl:call-template>
26   </xsl:template>
```

The template invocation on lines 21–23 generates the projection code and lines 16–24 generate the pre-method call. The generated code is passed as a parameter to the template call_pre_method, which is responsible for adding the promotion code if required. Lines 13–15 retrieve the annotation for the method which contains information about which arguments of the method are nullable.

Finally, here is the template for the low-level OCaml binding:

```
1   <xsl:template match="method">
2     <xsl:param name="interface" select="''"/>
3     <xsl:param name="prefix" select="''"/>
4   value
5     <xsl:text>ml_gdome_</xsl:text><xsl:value-of select="$prefix"/>
6     <xsl:text>_</xsl:text><xsl:value-of select="@name"/>
7     <xsl:text>(value self</xsl:text>
8     <xsl:apply-templates select="parameters"/>)
9   {
10    <xsl:apply-templates select="parameters" mode="declare"/>
11    GdomeException exc_ = 0;
12    <xsl:if test="returns/@type != 'void'">
13      <xsl:call-template name="gdomeTypeOfType">
14        <xsl:with-param name="type" select="returns/@type"/>
15      </xsl:call-template> res_;
16    </xsl:if>
17    <xsl:apply-templates select="parameters" mode="convert">
18      <xsl:with-param name="methodName" select="@name"/>
19    </xsl:apply-templates>
20    <xsl:if test="returns/@type = 'DOMString'">  value res__;</xsl:if>
21    <xsl:if test="returns/@type != 'void'">res_ = </xsl:if>
22    <xsl:text>gdome_</xsl:text>
23    <xsl:value-of select="$prefix"/>_<xsl:value-of select="@name"/>
24    <xsl:text>(</xsl:text>
25    <xsl:value-of select="$interface"/>_val(self),
26    <xsl:apply-templates select="parameters" mode="pass">
27      <xsl:with-param name="methodName" select="@name"/>
28    </xsl:apply-templates>&amp;exc_);
29    <xsl:apply-templates select="parameters" mode="free">
30      <xsl:with-param name="methodName" select="@name"/>
```

Table 2. Differences in binding logic sizes in number of lines.

	DOM Core module			+ DOM Events module		
	Binding logic (XSLT)	Hand written code (target language)	Generated code (target language)	Binding logic (XSLT)	Hand written code (target language)	Generated code (target language)
C++	768	1405	4289	+40	+74	+915
+ Caml	+1514	+1305	4557	+15	+176	+807
+ OCaml	+640	+291	+2407	+4	+44	+284

```
31    </xsl:apply-templates>
32    <xsl:text>if (exc_ != 0) throw_exception(exc_, "</xsl:text>
33    <xsl:value-of select="$interface"/>.<xsl:value-of select="@name"/>");
34    <xsl:call-template name="methodReturn">
35      <xsl:with-param name="name" select="@name"/>
36      <xsl:with-param name="type" select="returns/@type"/>
37    </xsl:call-template>
38    }
39  </xsl:template>
```

Lines 26–28 generate the projection code. Lines 21–28 generate the call to the Gdome method and store the result in the local variable res_, which is implicitly used later in the methodReturn template for the generation of the promotion code (lines 34–37). Lines 32–33 produce the code that checks the result of the function, possibly raising an OCaml exception using the throw_exception function.

6   Concluding Remarks

Automatic generation of stubs and bindings is a well-established technique with clear and well-known advantages of increased code correctness and maintenance. Thus the benefits of its application to bindings of W3C APIs – DOM in primis – are not under discussion. In this paper we stress the idea a bit further by developing a framework for the generation of DOM bindings. The main idea of the framework is to exploit the already existent XML specification that, although meant to be just a source for automatic documentation generation, is rich enough for automatic code generation. The missing information that is not available in the XML specification is manually provided and stored in additional XML documents. The binding logic for each target programming language is described in an XSLT stylesheet. Any off-the-shelf XSLT engine can be used as a meta-generator that must be applied to both the binding logic and the XML specification.

To test our framework, we applied it to the generation of a C++ binding for the DOM Core module. Later on we also developed two layered OCaml bindings, one that exposes a functional interface based on pre-methods and another one that exposes an object-oriented interface that is much closer to the DOM API specification. A few months later an implementation of the DOM Events module was also released, and the three binding logics have been updated to cover the new module as well. We are now able to estimate the amount of code that must be provided to add new DOM modules and new binding logics. Table 2 shows the number of lines of code required for the original C++ binding of the DOM Core module, and the number of lines of additional code written to enable the two OCaml bindings and the DOM Events module. In particular, the numbers in the column "+ DOM Events module" show the additional lines related to the Events module with respect to the Core module (i.e. each cell in the right column shows the increment with respect to the corresponding cell in the left column, on the same row). In the first column, the "+ Caml" line shows the increment with respect to the C++ binding, and the "+ OCaml" line shows the increment with respect to the Caml binding (i.e. the object-oriented layer vs the purely functional layer).

The data shown in the table deserve an explanation. First of all, let us consider the case of the addition of a new DOM module to the binding. In any one of the three cases (C++, Caml, OCaml), the number of hand-written lines of code necessary for the new module is very limited, and much smaller than the number of lines necessary for the generation of the first module considered. The number of lines of binding logic that are necessary for the new module is also very small (e.g. 40 lines vs 768 lines for the C++ binding). Nevertheless, the reader could have expected this number to be 0. The reason for having to extend the binding logic can easily be explained: whereas in the DOM Core module there is just one class hierarchy based on single inheritance, the DOM Events module introduces new interfaces that must be implemented by the objects described in the DOM Core module. Thus, to deal with the new module, we had to add multiple inheritance to the binding logic. From the previous observations we can conclude that our framework behaves as expected for vertical extension, that is the application of the framework to new XML specifications.

Let us consider now the extension to a new target language. Comparing the cells of the first column, we note that the effort required for the Caml binding is similar to the effort spent for the C++ binding. On the contrary, the addition of the OCaml binding on top of the previous two bindings was less expensive. These results can be easily explained. Every code generator is made of a frontend, which interprets the specification, and a backend for the generation of code. The C++ binding and the Caml binding share the frontend, but not the backend. On the contrary, the two OCaml bindings can also share part of the backend, since they have in common several utility functions used by the binding logic, such as name mangling functions or the generator of phantom type instances. One important datum that is not shown in the table is the real amount of code reuse between the C++ binding and the Caml binding, i.e. the number of lines of code that form the frontend. Thanks to the adoption of XML technologies in our framework, this number is basically 0. Indeed, being the specification written in XML, the meta-generator – an XSLT processor – works directly on the parsed XML document, reducing the backend to a very few auxiliary functions and a small set of XSLT template guards. From the previous observations we can conclude that our framework also behaves positively for horizontal extension, that is the application of the framework to new target languages.

Our approach was made practical largely because of the availability of the DOM specification in XML format. Thus we expect that it should be possible to apply our framework without any major modifications to other W3C standards as well, provided that a compliant low-level C implementation exists. Indeed, it is a real pity for the XML specification to be undocumented and almost neglected by the W3C itself. Surprisingly, we have been able to exploit the specification for code generation, but we have faced serious problems when trying to automatically document the generated code. The prose in the XML specification contains pieces of code that are marked to be rendered in a particular way. Nevertheless, the markup elements do not convey enough information to understand the nature of the values in the code. Thus it is often impossible to convert them to the sensible values in the target language. For instance, it is not possible to know whether a value v is of a nullable type, to show it in the OCaml examples as (Some v).

References

1. Paolo Casarini, Luca Padovani, "The Gnome DOM Engine", in Markup Languages: Theory & Practice, Vol. 3, Issue 2, pp. 173–190, ISSN 1099-6621, MIT Press, April 2002.
2. M. Fluet, R. Pucella, "Phantom Types and Subtyping". Proceedings of the 2nd IFIP International Conference on Theoretical Computer Science (TCS 2002), pp. 448-460, August 2002.
3. Sigbjorn Finne, Daan Leijen, Erik Meijer and Simon L. Peyton Jones, "Calling Hell From Heaven and Heaven From Hell", in Proceedings of the International Conference on Functional Programming, 114-125, 1999.
4. Jacques Garrigue, "Programming with polymorphic variants". In ML Workshop, September 1998.
   http://wwwfun.kurims.kyoto-u.ac.jp/~garrigue/papers/variants.ps.gz
5. Raph Levien, "Design considerations for a Gnome DOM", informal note, 28 March 1999, http://www.levien.com/gnome/dom-design.html
6. James Clark (Eds), "XML Transformations (XSLT) Version 1.0", W3C Recommendation (1999), http://www.w3.org/TR/1999/REC-xslt-19991116
7. Arnaud Le Hors and Philippe Le Hégaret and Gavin Nicol and Jonathan Robie and Mike Champion et al. (Eds), "Document Object Model (DOM) Level 2 Core Specification", Version 1.0, W3C Recommendation, November 2000, http://www.w3.org/TR/DOM-Level-2-Core/
8. Tom Pixley, "Document Object Model (DOM) Level 2 Events Specification", Version 1.0, W3C Recommendation, November 2000,
   http://www.w3.org/TR/DOM-Level-2-Events
9. Daniel R. Edelson, "Smart Pointers: They're Smart, But They're Not Pointers", Proceedings of the C++ Conference, pp. 1–19, 1992.
10. D.Vandevoorde, N. M. Josuttis, "C++ Templates: The Complete Guide", Addison-Wesley, 2002.
11. Bjarne Stroustrup, "The C++ Programming Language", Third Edition, Addison-Wesley, 1997.
12. Xavier Leroy and Damien Doligez and Jacques Garrigue and Didier Rémy and Jérôme Vouillon, "The Objective Caml system release 3.07 Documentation and user's manual", http://caml.inria.fr/ocaml/htmlman/

Software Factories:
Assembling Applications
with Patterns, Models, Frameworks and Tools

Jack Greenfield

Visual Studio Team System, Microsoft
jackgr@microsoft.com
http://www.softwarefactories.com

Increasingly complex and rapidly changing requirements and technologies are making application development increasingly difficult. This talk examines this phenomenon, and presents a simple pattern for building languages, patterns, frameworks and tools for specific domains, such as user interface construction or database design. Software Factories integrate critical innovations in adaptive assembly, software product lines, and model driven development to reduce the cost of implementing this pattern, making it cost effective for narrower and more specialized domains, such as B2B commerce and employee self service portals.

In a nutshell, a software factory is a development environment configured to support the rapid development of a specific type of application. At the heart of the methodology is the software factory schema, a network of viewpoints describing the artifacts that comprise the members of a family of software products, and the languages, patterns, frameworks and tools used to build them. Mappings between the viewpoints support traceability, validation, assisted development and complete or partial transformation. They also support a style of agile development called constraint based scheduling, which scales up to large, geographically distributed and long running projects.

While Software Factories are really just the logical next step in the continuing evolution of software development methods and practices, building on lessons learned about patterns and frameworks, and extending the kinds of automation already provided by Rapid Application Development (RAD) environments, they promise to change the character of the software industry by introducing patterns of industrialization. By automating many development tasks, and creating contracts that support separations of concerns, Software Factories promote outsourcing and the formation of software supply chains, paving the way for mass customization.

G. Karsai and E. Visser (Eds.): GPCE 2004, LNCS 3286, p. 488, 2004.

Modular Language Descriptions

Peter D. Mosses

BRICS* & Department of Computer Science
University of Aarhus, Denmark
pdmosses@brics.dk
http://www.brics.dk/~pdm

Formal semantic descriptions of full-scale programming languages can be notoriously difficult to write, as well as to read. Writing a description of a language usually starts from scratch: reuse from previous language descriptions requires first locating a relevant one, then manually copying bits of it – perhaps with extensive reformulation. Semantic descriptions are often intricate and intimidating documents to read, requiring a good grasp of the formalism used, as well an understanding of the interplay between the parts of the description concerned with different language constructs. Evolution of semantic descriptions, to cope with small changes or extensions to the described language, may require global reformulation.

In other words: however elegant the theoretical foundations of semantic descriptions may be, their pragmatic aspects are often reminiscent of programming large systems before modern software engineering techniques were introduced. A good dose of *semantics engineering* is needed: analogous partly to component engineering (raising the level of modularization and analysis in semantic descriptions), partly to the use of domain-specific formalisms (elevating semantic descriptions to compact domain-specific notations that are easier to read, write and maintain).

The most extreme modularization imaginable in semantic descriptions is when each individual programming construct is described as a separate and independent component. For instance, consider a particular kind of conditional statement: its description is to be independent of whether evaluating the condition might have side-effects, throw exceptions, etc. Such modules could be made available in a repository; a description of a complete language would then merely refer to the required modules, which must not need any adaptation when combined. Reuse would be encouraged, and made explicit. The designer of a new language would be free to focus on the description of novel constructs.

Unfortunately, some well-known semantic frameworks (e.g., conventional Structural Operational Semantics [14] and Denotational Semantics [6]) do not allow such extreme modularization as envisaged above: the description of each language construct inherently depends on which other (kinds of) constructs are included in the language being described. Other frameworks go quite a long way towards it (e.g., Monadic Denotational Semantics [5], and the Montages vari-

* Basic Research in Computer Science (www.brics.dk), funded by the Danish National Research Foundation.

G. Karsai and E. Visser (Eds.): GPCE 2004, LNCS 3286, pp. 489–490, 2004.
© Springer-Verlag Berlin Heidelberg 2004

ant of Abstract State Machines [4]). The following two lesser-known frameworks have recently been adapted specifically to support extreme modularization:

- *Action Semantics* – a hybrid of operational and denotational semantics, developed since the end of the 80's [3, 7, 8, 13, 15] (not to be confused with the action semantics of UML); and
- *Modular SOS* (MSOS) – a variant of Structural Operational Semantics where labels on transitions are fully exploited [9–12].

Action Semantics appears to be an appropriate basis for generation of prototype compilers, and some tool support for developing and validating semantic descriptions has been implemented [1, 2]. MSOS has so far been used in earnest only for defining the Action Notation used in Action Semantics, and for teaching semantics. Both frameworks are quite unbiased towards description of particular kinds of programming languages, and their support for extreme modularization should make them especially attractive for describing domain-specific languages.

References

1. M. G. J. van den Brand, J. Iversen, and P. D. Mosses. An action environment. In *LDTA 2004*, ENTCS, 2004. To appear.
2. M. G. J. van den Brand, J. Iversen, and P. D. Mosses. An action environment (tool demonstration). In *LDTA 2004*, ENTCS, 2004. To appear.
3. K.-G. Doh and P. D. Mosses. Composing programming languages by combining action-semantics modules. *Sci. Comput. Programming*, 47(1):3–36, 2003.
4. P. Kutter and A. Pierantonio. Montages: Specifications of realistic programming languages. *JUCS* , 3(5):416–442, 1997.
5. E. Moggi. Notions of computation and monads. *Inf. and Comp.*, 93:55–92, 1991.
6. P. D. Mosses. Denotational semantics. In J. van Leeuwen, editor, *Handbook of Theoretical Computer Science*, volume B, chapter 11, pages 575–631. Elsevier Science Publishers, Amsterdam; and MIT Press, 1990.
7. P. D. Mosses. *Action Semantics*. Cambridge Tracts in Theoretical Computer Science 26. Cambridge University Press, 1992.
8. P. D. Mosses. Theory and practice of Action Semantics. In *MFCS '96*, LNCS 1113, pages 37–61. Springer, 1996.
9. P. D. Mosses. Foundations of modular SOS. BRICS RS-99-54, Dept. of Computer Science, Univ. of Aarhus, 1999.
10. P. D. Mosses. Pragmatics of modular SOS. In *AMAST'02*, LNCS 2422, pages 21–40. Springer, 2002.
11. P. D. Mosses. Exploiting labels in structural operational semantics. *Fundamenata Informaticae*, 60:17–31, 2004.
12. P. D. Mosses. Modular structural operational semantics. *J. Logic and Algebraic Programming*, 60–61:195–228, 2004. Special issue on SOS.
13. P. D. Mosses and D. A. Watt. The use of action semantics. In *Formal Description of Programming Concepts III, IFIP TC2 Working Conf., Gl. Avernæ 1986, Proceedings*, pages 135–166. North-Holland, 1987.
14. G. D. Plotkin. A structural approach to operational semantics. *J. Logic and Algebraic Programming*, 60–61:17–139, 2004. Special issue on SOS. Originally published as DAIMI FN-19, Dept. of Computer Science, Univ. of Aarhus, 1981.
15. D. A. Watt. *Programming Language Syntax and Semantics*. Prentice-Hall, 1991.

Author Index

Lecture Notes in Computer Science

For information about Vols. 1–3181

please contact your bookseller or Springer